FOR REFERENCE

Do Not Take From This Room

MILESTONE DOCUMENTS IN WORLD HISTORY

Exploring the Primary Sources
That Shaped the World

MILESTONE DOCUMENTS IN WORLD HISTORY

Exploring the Primary Sources
That Shaped the World

Volume 1
2350 BCE – 1058 CE

Brian Bonhomme
Editor in Chief

Cathleen Boivin
Consulting Editor

Schlager Group
Dallas, Texas

Milestone Documents in World History
Copyright © 2010 by Schlager Group Inc.

All rights reserved. No part of this book may be reproduced or utilized in any form or by any means, electronic or mechanical, including photocopying, recording, or by any information storage or retrieval systems, without permission in writing from the publisher. For information, contact:

Schlager Group Inc.
2501 Oak Lawn Avenue, Suite 440
Dallas, Tex. 75219
USA

You can find Schlager Group on the World Wide Web at
http://www.schlagergroup.com
Text and cover design by Patricia Moritz

Printed in the United States of America

10 9 8 7 6 5 4 3 2 1

ISBN: 978-0-9797758-6-4

This book is printed on acid-free paper.

CONTENTS

VOLUME 2: 1082–1833

Welcome to *Milestone Documents in World History*, the third installment in our Milestone Documents series of reference books and the first to take us outside the realm of American history. Librarians and readers who are familiar with our previous sets, *Milestone Documents in American History* and *Milestone Documents of American Leaders*, will immediately recognize our award-winning methodology in this set. We combine famous historical documents with in-depth analysis by historians, in the process helping students and teachers explore and understand the past in new, rewarding ways.

As readers will expect, this set posed a host of challenges that were not present in our American history publications. Covering three centuries of American history is, it's true, easier than gathering and writing about documents from two millennia and from every society and culture around the globe. Our project editor, Marcia Merryman-Means, worked tirelessly alongside our advisory board of historians and our roster of scholarly contributors to find suitable sources for the documents, translate them into English when necessary, abridge when essential, and convert to electronic form.

Through conversations with librarians and history educators in the past two years, I've heard again and again about how much more difficult it is to teach world history than U.S. history and how much harder it is to find suitable primary source documents to use in the classroom. Even when documents exist, students—and very often teachers as well—struggle with the unfamiliar wording and arcane references that are found in the texts.

Our task here was to address those challenges and make the broad sweep of world history more accessible to educators and students alike. We think we've done that, from our clear and straightforward explanations of each document text to the discussion of historical context surrounding each source to the glossaries defining strange words and terms. In addition, with our Teachers' Activity Guides (found in the set's front matter) and the "Questions for Further Study" (found in every entry), we've given educators and students many different ways to engage with these historical documents and to better understand the civilizations and individuals that produced them.

Librarians are reminded that, as with all of our sets, the entire contents are available for free in electronic form to all institutions that have purchased the print set. That electronic resource is Salem History (http://history.salempress.com/), via our distributor, Salem Press. Instructions for accessing the data can be found in the insert included in Volume 1 of the set.

Thank you for your time and attention, and I hope you find the articles in this set to be useful and illuminating.

NEIL SCHLAGER
Founder and President, Schlager Group
neil@schlagergroup.com

Other Titles in the Milestone Documents Series

• *Milestone Documents in American History* (2008, ISBN 978-0-9797758-0-2, *Choice* Outstanding Academic Title, *Booklist* Editor's Choice award)

• *Milestone Documents of American Leaders* (2009, ISBN 978-0-9797758-5-7, *Choice* Outstanding Academic Title, *Booklist* Editor's Choice award)

• *Milestone Documents in African American History* (June 2010, ISBN 978-1-935306-05-4)

• *Milestone Documents of World Religions* (November 2010, ISBN 978-0-9797758-8-8)

Editor in Chief

BRIAN BONHOMME
Associate Professor of History, Youngstown State University

Consulting Editor

CATHLEEN BOIVIN
History Teacher, West Springfield High School (Springfield, Virginia)

Advisory Board

CHRISTOPHER BLACKWELL
Furman University

FRANK L. CHANCE
University of Pennsylvania

ELEANOR CONGDON
Youngstown State University

R. HUNT DAVIS
University of Florida

AINSLEE EMBREE
Columbia University

RONALD LEPROHON
University of Toronto

THOMAS METCALF
University of California, Berkeley

PAUL R. GOLDIN
University of Pennsylvania

JAMES A. REILLY
University of Toronto

LAWRENCE WALDRON
St. John's University

Contributors

FATMA ACUN
University of Hacettepe, Turkey

STEPHEN E. BALZARINI
Gonzaga University

THOMAS W. BARKER
University of Kansas

MARTIN BERGER
Youngstown State University (emeritus)

BRIAN BONHOMME
Youngstown State University

PETER J. BRAND
University of Memphis

MARTIN BUNTON
University of Victoria

LEE BUTLER
Independent Scholar, Cleveland, Ohio

M. CALLAHAN
Independent Scholar, London, England

SCOTT CASHION
University of Arkansas

BODHISATTVA CHATTOPADHYAY
University of Oslo, Norway

MARK W. CHAVALAS
University of Wisconsin–La Crosse

SAMANTHA CHRISTIANSEN
Northeastern University

ELISABETTA COLLA
Macau Scientific and Cultural Centre, Portugal

ELEANOR CONGDON
Youngstown State University

DAVID COMMINS
Dickinson College

ERIC CUNNINGHAM
Gonzaga University

JOHN S. EDER
Fayetteville State University

PAUL M. EDWARDS
Center for the Study of the Korean War

JAMES ELLISON
Dickinson College

TODD W. EWING
Williams Baptist College

HARVEY M. FEINBERG
Connecticut State University

MATTHEW FIORILLO
Independent Scholar, New York City

ROB FOSTER
Berea College

BEN C. FULWIDER
Austin Peay State University

JAMES L. GELVIN
University of California, Los Angeles

THOMAS GOBBITT
Institute for Medieval Studies, University of Leeds, U.K.

JAMES L. HUFFMAN
Wittenberg University

SADAN JHA
Centre for Social Studies, Surat, India

DAVID CONRAD JOHNSON
Elmhurst College

KEITH N. KNAPP
The Citadel, The Military College of South Carolina

PATRICK G. LAKE
The Hill School

STEPHANIE M. LANGIN-HOOPER
University of California, Berkeley

MARISA LERER
The Graduate Center, CUNY

MICHAEL LOWER
University of Minnesota

TEREASA MAILLIE
University of Alberta

ERIC L. MAY
Independent Scholar, Chicago, Illinois

TIMOTHY MAY
North Georgia College & State University

PATIT PABAN MISHRA
Sambalpur University, Orissa, India

LAUREN MOREAU
University of Leeds, U.K.

IAN MORLEY
Chinese University of Hong Kong

T. MUSACCHIO
John Jay College/CUNY

OLIVER NICHOLSON
University of Minnesota

CHRISTOPHER OHAN
American University of Kuwait

MICHAEL J. O'NEAL
Independent Scholar, Moscow, Idaho

JACQUELINE PAK
Cornell University

FRANKLIN RAUSCH
University of British Columbia

TOBIAS RETTIG
Singapore Management University

PETER ROBINSON
University of Tokyo, Japan

CHRIS SAUNDERS
University of Cape Town, South Africa

ZACHARY A. SCARLETT
Northeastern University

SARAH M. SCHELLINGER
University of Toronto

CAROLE SCHROEDER
Boise State University

ALLISON SELLERS
Independent Scholar, Columbus, Georgia

DAVID SIMONELLI
Youngstown State University

BRADLEY A. SKEEN
Independent Scholar, St. Louis, Missouri

TAMARA SHIRCLIFF SPIKE
North Georgia College & State University

ROBERT N. STACY
Independent Scholar, Leominster, Massachusetts

DAN TAMIR
University of Zürich, Switzerland

TERRI TANAKA
University of California, Berkeley

JOEL E. TISHKEN
Washington State University

LISA TRAN
California State University, Fullerton

THOMAS TURNER
Independent Scholar, Manassas, Virginia

PATRICIA VAN DER SPUY
Castleton State College

MELINDA VARNER
University of Kansas

EZEKIEL A. WALKER
University of Central Florida

Q. Edward Wang
Rowan University

Andrew J. Waskey
Dalton State College

Torsten Weber
Leiden University, The Netherlands

J. Tia Wheeler
University of St. Andrews, U.K.

Dianne White Oyler
Fayetteville State University

Anne York
Youngstown State University

Schlager Group would like to thank the following organizations for granting permission to reprint primary source documents:

Reform Edict of Urukagina: from Douglas Frayne, *Royal Inscriptions of Mesopotamia, Early Periods*, vol. 1: *Pre-Sargonic Period (to 2334 B.C.)*. University of Toronto Press, 2004. Reprinted by permission of the publisher.

Victory Stela of Piankhi: from William Kelly Simpson, ed., *The Literature of Ancient Egypt*, 3rd edition, Yale University Press, 2003.

Theodosian Code: from Pharr, Clyde, *The Theodosian Code and Novels and the Sermondian Constitutions*. Copyright © 1952 in the name of the author, 1980 renewed in the name of Roy Pharr, executor. All material from p. 3, 11–35 copyright © 1944 by Theresa Sherrer Davidson. Reprinted by permission of Princeton University Press.

Han Yu's "Memorial on the Buddha's Bones": from Victor Mair, Nancy Steinhardt, and Paul Goldin, eds., *Hawaii Reader in Traditional Chinese Culture*, University of Hawaii Press, 2004. Reprinted by permission of the publisher.

II Aethelstan, or the Grately Code: from Dorothy Whitelock, *English Historical Documents, Volume 1 (500–1042)*, copyright © 1996, Routledge, pp. 381–386. Reprinted by permission of Taylor & Francis Books UK.

Al-Māwardī's "On Qāḍīs": from Bernard Lewis, *Islam: From the Prophet Muhammad to the Capture of Constantinople*, Volume 2: *Religion and Society*, 1987, pp. 40–42. Reprinted by permission of Oxford University Press Inc.

Niẓām al-Mulk's *Book of Government; or, Rules for Kings*: from Hubert Darke, *The Book of Government or Rules for Kings*, copyright © 2001, Routledge. Reprinted by permission of Taylor & Francis Books UK.

Usamah ibn Munqidh's "A Muslim View of the Crusades": from Paul M. Cobb, trans., *The Book of Contemplation: Islam and the Crusades* by Usama Ibn Munqidh, Penguin Books, 2008. Copyright © Paul M. Cobb, 2008. Reprinted by permission of Penguin Books Ltd.

Popol Vuh: Reprinted with the permission of Simon & Schuster, Inc., from *Popol Vuh* by Dennis Tedlock. Copyright © 1985, 1996 by Dennis Tedlock. All Rights Reserved.

Ulozhenie, or Great Muscovite Law Code: from Richard Hellie, trans., *The Muscovite Law Code (Ulozhenie) of 1649*, Charles Schlacks, Publisher, 1988. Reprinted by permission.

Diplomatic Correspondence between Muhammad al-Kānamī and Muhammad Bello: from Thomas Hodgkin, *Nigerian Perspectives*, 2nd edition, pp. 198–205. Reprinted by permission of Oxford University Press Inc.

Lin Zexu's "Moral Advice to Queen Victoria": reprinted by permission of the publisher from *China's Response to the West: A Documentary Survey, 1839–1923*, by Ssu-yü Têng and John King Fairbank, pp. 24–27, Cambridge, Mass.: Harvard University Press, copyright © 1954, 1979 by the President and Fellows of Harvard College, copyright renewed 1982 by Ssu-yü Têng and John King Fairbank.

Theodor Herzl's "A Solution to the Jewish Question": From James L. Gelvin, *The Modern Middle East: A History*, 2nd edition, 2005, pp. 217–218. Reprinted by permission of Oxford University Press Inc.

Emiliano Zapata's Plan of Ayala: from Timothy J. Henderson and Gilbert M. Joseph, eds., *The Mexico Reader*, pp. 339–343. Copyright © 2002, Duke University Press. All rights reserved. Reprinted by permission of the publisher.

Jawaharlal Nehru's Speeches on the Granting of Indian Independence: from *Jawaharlal Nehru's Speeches*, 1983. Courtesy of the Publications Division, Government of India. Reprinted by permission.

Patrice Lumumba's Speech at the Proclamation of Congolese Independence: from *Lumumba Speaks* by Patrice Lumumba. Copyright © 1963 by Editions Presence Africaine; copyright © 1972 by Little, Brown and Company, Inc. (Translation). Reprinted by permission of Little, Brown and Company.

"Mao Tse-tung's Thought Is the Telescope and Microscope of Our Revolutionary Cause": From *Peking Review* 24, June 10, 1966, pp. 6–7, found online at http://www.morningsun.org/red/telescope_6101966.html.

Osama bin Laden's Declaration of Jihad against Americans: From Osama bin Laden, *Messages to the World*, Verso, pp. 23–30. Reprinted by permission of the publisher.

Overview

Milestone Documents in World History represents a unique and innovative approach to history reference. Combining full-text primary sources with in-depth expert analysis, the 125 entries in the set cover important and influential primary source documents from the third millennium BCE to the twenty-first century and include documents that range from laws and legal codes to letters, from treaties to constitutions, from royal edicts to political speeches.

Organization

The set is organized chronologically in four volumes:

- Volume 1: 2350 BCE–1058 CE
- Volume 2: 1082–1833
- Volume 3: 1839–1941
- Volume 4: 1942–2000

Within each volume, entries likewise are arranged chronologically by year.

Entry Format

Each entry in *Milestone Documents in World History* follows the same structure using the same standardized headings. The entries are divided into two main sections: analysis and document text. Following is the full list of entry headings:

- **Overview** gives a brief summary of the primary source document and its importance in history.
- **Context** places the document in its historical framework.
- **Time Line** chronicles key events surrounding the writing of the document.
- **About the Author** presents a brief biographical profile of the person or persons who wrote the document.
- **Explanation and Analysis of the Document** consists of a detailed examination of the document text, generally in section-by-section or paragraph-by-paragraph format.
- **Audience** discusses the intended audience of the document's author.
- **Impact** examines the historical influence of the document.

- **Questions for Further Study** proposes study questions for students.
- **Essential Quotes** offers a selection of key quotes from the document and, in some cases, about the document.
- **Further Reading** lists articles, books, and Web sites for further research.
- **Document Text** gives the actual text of the primary document.
- **Glossary** defines important, difficult, or unusual terms in the document text.

Each entry features the byline of the scholar who wrote the analysis. Readers should note that in most entries the Document Text section includes the full text of the primary source document. However, in the case of lengthy documents, key portions have been excerpted for analysis.

Features

In addition to the text of the 125 entries, the set includes nearly 250 photographs and illustrations. The front matter of Volume 1 has a sections of interest to educators: "Teachers' Activity Guides." The latter comprises ten distinct guides, all of which are tied to the National History Standards and which make use of the documents covered in this set. These ten sections were written by Consulting Editor Cathleen Boivin. Rounding out the front matter are an "Introduction" to the set, written by Editor in Chief Brian Bonhomme; a section of "Advisers and Contributors"; a "Publisher's Note"; "Editorial and Production Staff"; and "Acknowledgments." At the end of Volume 4, readers will find an "Index of Documents by Category," an "Index of Documents by Region," and a cumulative "Subject Index."

Questions

We welcome questions and comments about the set. Readers may address all such comments to the following address:

The Editor
MILESTONE DOCUMENTS IN WORLD HISTORY
Schlager Group Inc.
2501 Oak Lawn Avenue, Suite 440
Dallas, Texas 75219

Many years ago, as an undergraduate student, I struck up a conversation with a classmate about our plans for the summer, which was then fast approaching. He told me about a science project he intended to work on with his chemistry professor. I, in turn, shared my plans for a weeklong trip to an out-of-state history conference, at which I expected to hear various individuals and panels discuss their current research. What my classmate said next has stuck in my mind ever since. He asked me if this would not be a rather boring affair—after all, history is not like science, where there are always new things to be discovered and shared. History, he said, is already well known; and so the work of uncovering it and writing about it is essentially "finished." This being so, what could the researchers I had mentioned be working on? Surely they could only restate what others had already said?

This turns out to be a very common misperception. Although we do indeed know quite a bit about the past, there is much that remains unclear, controversial, or even unknown. This is especially so when we move beyond the well-worn narratives and facts (the treaties, battles, great leaders, and so on) and toward engagement with the more interesting questions of intention, interpretation, experience, and memory. In many ways, the field of history is more dynamic and eventful now than at any time in the past—characterized by lively debates and disagreements, reinterpretations of old ideas, many new questions, the constant production of new knowledge, and, yes, even discoveries. There are several reasons this is so, not all of which can be discussed here. The most important ones, however, concern the role played by primary source materials in the writing of history—and by extension, the very nature of history itself.

Despite what many people think, history is not simply a record of the past, accepted and agreed upon by all and never to be altered. Our knowledge of previous times is instead an ongoing work of *construction*—something put together (and occasionally taken apart) painstakingly and bit by bit over a long period of time by a large and multi-generational pool of scholars and researchers. Most of these people work on small and specific questions, although they are always mindful of larger contexts. Usually, they present their findings first to colleagues at symposia and conferences and then to wider audiences through refereed journals, books, Web sites, and so on. Eventually their research, if successful, may become part of the general historical pictures presented in textbooks and curricula and in the popular media.

If history is constructed, then an important question arises: What is it constructed from? The main answer is *primary source materials*—including exactly the kinds of origi-

nal historical texts presented in this collection. These are the raw materials, if you like, from which historians craft their narratives and analyses, which we call *secondary sources*. This being so, the purpose of an education in history should not be simply to memorize facts about the past (though this is certainly important) but also to engage frequently and meaningfully with primary sources. This engagement includes learning what they are (both their advantages and limitations), how to select ones suitable to a given study, and, above all, how to use them skillfully and appropriately in order to create viable new knowledge about the past. Let us look a little more closely at these questions.

What is a primary source? The simple answer is that a primary source is a piece of evidence that is from the place and time under study. It could be a written document (as in this collection), an artifact such as a picture or piece of clothing, or something else entirely. Types of written documents include items ranging from laws and legal codes to letters, from royal proclamations to treaties. The single subject of trade with Asia can be elucidated using such a variety of primary sources, including Lin Zexu's letter "Moral Advice to Queen Victoria," asking the monarch for a peaceful resolution to the problem of the opium trade; the Treaty of Nanjing, ending the Opium War; and Queen Victoria's Proclamation concerning India, assuming control of Britain's Indian colonies and removing them from the administration of the British East India Company. The legal structure of medieval times across the globe is revealed through such sources as II Aethelstan, or the Grately Code; Al-Māwardī's treatise "On Qāḍīs"; and the Russkaia Pravda, or Justice of the Rus.

Another basic definition is that a primary source is not a secondary source. Secondary sources are works that result from the use of primary sources. A secondary source would be, for example, a book about the rise and spread of Communism written by a historian living and writing today. That historian might base his book on such diverse primary sources as political treatises (Karl Marx and Friedrich Engel's *Communist Manifesto* or Vladimir Lenin's *What Is to Be Done?*), the speeches of politicians (Winston Churchill's "The Sinews of Peace"), and even newspaper articles and editorials ("Mao Tse-tung's Thought Is the Telescope and Microscope of Our Revolutionary Cause"). Secondary sources do not come directly from the events described but from consideration and interpretation of them afterward. This leads us to an alternative, and slightly more sophisticated, definition of a primary source—namely, that it is a piece of evidence that has not yet been interpreted by a historian. It is still in its raw state, waiting for someone to make it speak. Precisely for this reason, primary sources allow a unique and particularly authentic glimpse into the past. They provide an unequalled opportunity to really "get inside" historical events and to directly encounter other times, places, and persons. The work and the challenge of the historian are then to question, interpret, and communicate those experiences.

How does one find and select primary sources? One of the first issues to consider is the relationship between the sources to be used and the question to be asked. For example, can the chosen sources actually answer the intended question? What other questions might they answer? The constitutions of Sparta and Athens tell us about the ways in which these city-states of ancient Greece were organized. At the same time, they allow us a glimpse into the everyday lives of the people of the time. Often a skilled historian or an imaginative student can use sources in more creative ways. The same constitutions, for example, provide the basics for a discussion of the evolution of democracy from ancient Greece to the modern world.

When beginning a research project, the question of where to start usually arises. Does one start with the research question or with the sources? Each has it advantages and disadvantages. Historians often like to begin with a particular question—perhaps because this is what fascinates them or perhaps because the question is fundamentally important and needs answering. However, beginning with the question can often make the search for sources more arduous and fraught. What kind of sources might be needed? Do they exist? If so, where are they? In what language are they? How accessible are they? Might expensive travel, transcription, or copying services be necessary? Students may sometimes prefer to work the other way around, starting with quality source materials and then choosing a question that the materials can be made to answer. Either route can produce excellent results. A typical study may well involve both methods.

There are numerous places to find primary sources. Many are published in readers or sourcebooks that can be found with relative ease in libraries or online. Often, however, these references present very short excerpts rather than the fuller selections offered here. Further materials may be found in newspapers, magazines, and periodicals from the time and place in question; these, too, are usually accessible in libraries or online. As the historian delves ever more deeply into a topic, however, he or she will likely need to make use of *unpublished* sources, typically stored in archives. Archives range from the small and informal, such as a box of unsorted items in a family home, to the very large and well-funded, such as a country's national archives. Depending on the historian's interests, the search for primary sources may lead well beyond these places. I recently encountered a colleague who, in his search for information about public health in early-modern Europe

had been excavating and testing samples from five-hundred-year-old latrines!

How are primary sources used? This is the most important part of the process. Once sources have been chosen, the historian must interrogate them and probe them for meaning and answers. In a few cases, depending on the question to be asked, this may be relatively straightforward. Someone reading a medieval law code, for example, may simply wish to know what it said on a given subject. The more interesting questions, however, usually require greater effort and skill. What might the same law code tell us about medieval views on childrearing or family life? What does it suggest about attitudes toward foreigners or toward the poor? What does it say about religion? Here, one will have to read between the lines, teasing out clues and making reasonable inferences. It will be necessary also to consult other primary sources and to compare them, to consult secondary sources on the same or a related topic, and then to make judgments about the applicability or validity of others' findings. In this manner, the historian's endeavor becomes a sort of detective work, involving and requiring skills of analysis, interpretation, and critical thinking. This is what makes historical writing a creative act rather than just one involving memorization and communication. It is also what makes history an endlessly fascinating and busy field of study, one in which there are many opportunities to ask and to say something new.

All this, of course, places upon the historian a substantial burden of responsibility—one that must be properly shouldered. Like any type of raw material, primary historical sources can be made into different things to serve different purposes, depending on the will and skill of the historian wielding them. In order to be history, rather than fantasy or mere polemics, historical accounts must remain grounded in the evidence contained in the primary sources. They must not ignore or suppress evidence or select or twist it to fit preconceived notions or agendas. In many cases, this may mean abandoning a cherished theory or assumption that the primary sources do not support. Or it may mean reworking the original question, if the sources do not provide real answers. Sometimes the study of history will challenge previously held notions and foster new thoughts and questions. Indeed, this is one of the most important functions of the study of history, at any level.

The historian must also apply the same critical thinking standards to the primary sources themselves and to their authors. Just because someone was an eyewitness to or a participant in a historical event does not mean that his or her account is objectively true or that it is the only possible interpretation. To one degree or another, all primary sources reflect the biases, assumptions, perspectives, and circumstances of their authors and of their time and place of origin. The modern historian, working with this in mind, will always want to begin by asking preliminary questions of every primary source, including these: Who wrote this? For what purpose? From what perspective? With the answers to these questions established, the process of engagement with the primary source—of constructing and writing history—can begin in earnest.

Far from being essentially complete and finished, then, history remains more than ever an active field of important research—one where the thrill of discovery awaits. And it is not always a question of finding obscure new primary sources. Many historians have done their most interesting and important work instead by returning to key, well-known sources and rereading them in novel ways, asking fresh questions, and bringing new methods and perspectives to bear. In this spirit, the present collection offers two things: a guided selection of some of the most important documents in world history and an opportunity for engagement and discovery relating to some of the most critical events and turning points in the human story so far. Happy reading!

Brian Bonhomme
Associate Professor of History
Youngstown State University

The following activity guides correspond to the National History Standards for World History as published by the National Center for History in the Schools. The documents in *Milestone Documents in World History* relate to most, though not all, of the world history eras and standards found in the National History Standards. The documents listed in **bold** type are covered in this set.

Era 1: The Beginnings of Human Society

Standard 1: The biological and cultural processes that gave rise to the earliest human communities

Standard 1B: The student understands how human communities populated the major regions of the world and adapted to a variety of environments.

Focus Question: How did various cultures explain the peopling of the earth?

- Review with students the different theories about the populating of the earth and evidence of migration patterns.

- Have students examine the creation myths according to the Epic of Gilgamesh and **Popol Vuh** (ca. 1544) from the Americas. How are these myths similar or different?

- Have students research, online or in their libraries, other creation myths, such as those of Oceania or Africa. Do these myths have elements in common with the Epic of Gilgamesh and the Popol Vuh? How are they characteristic of the societies that produced them? Discuss with students why the various cultures endeavored to explain their beliefs and customs in this way. How were these myths preserved or recorded?

Era 2: Early Civilizations and the Emergence of Pastoral Peoples, 4000–1000 BCE

Standard 1: The major characteristics of civilization and how civilizations emerged in Mesopotamia, Egypt, and the Indus valley

Standard 1A: The student understands how Mesopotamia, Egypt, and the Indus valley became centers of dense population, urbanization, and cultural innovation in the fourth and third millennia BCE.

Standard 3: The political, social, and cultural consequences of population movements and militarization in Eurasia in the second millennium BCE

Standard 3B: The student understands the social and cultural effects that militarization and the emergence of new kingdoms had on peoples of Southwest Asia and Egypt in the second millennium BCE.

Focus Question: Why did early civilizations develop a written code of legal ethics?

- Initiate a class discussion on what makes a civilization. What are the characteristics common to civilizations?

- Divide students into four groups and have each group read and summarize one of the following documents: the **Reform Edict of Urukagina** (ca. 2350 BCE), the **Code of Hammurabi** (ca. 1752 BCE), the **Hittite Laws** (ca. 1650–1400 BCE), or the **Middle Assyrian Laws** (ca. 1115–1077 BCE). Students should focus on how each set of codes shaped society and culture in Sumeria, Babylonia, Central Anatolia, and Mesopotamia. Why did these early societies feel the need to articulate and define a code of laws? Did these laws apply equally to all members of the society? Who was a citizen? What were women's roles and rights? How were slaves and servants represented? Discuss with students the ways in which laws and legal requirements shape our society in the twenty-first century.

Focus Question: How did competing empires develop in Anatolia and in Egypt in this period?

- Have students research the locations and political boundaries of both the Hittite and the Egyptian kingdoms prior to 1280 BCE. Discuss how these kingdoms came into direct conflict with each other during periods of expansion.

- Ask the students to conduct research on the Battle of Kadesh. Why is this battle historically significant? How did chariot technology affect the outcome? Note: Both the Hittites under and the Egyptians claimed victory. Egyptian versions of the conflict can be found at http://www.reshafim.org.il/ad/egypt/kadeshaccounts.htm.

- Ask students to read both the Egyptian and the Hittite version of the **Egyptian-Hittite Peace Treaty** of 1259 BCE, one of the earliest recorded peace treaties, and view the following replica of the treaty between the Egyptian pharaoh Ramses II and Emperor Hattusilis III of the Hittites: http://www.unmultimedia.org/photo/detail/111/0111527.html. As a class, discuss the elements of a good peace treaty. Have the students name other famous peace treaties. Were they successful at maintaining the peace? What modern organization is often involved in the resolution of hostilities and peace treaties?

Standard 3: The political, social, and cultural consequences of population movements and militarization in Eurasia in the second millennium BCE

Standard 3B: The student understands the social and cultural effects that militarization and the emergence of new kingdoms had on peoples of Southwest Asia and Egypt in the second millennium BCE.

Focus Question: How can we interpret artifacts and often scarce written evidence to determine how early urban societies functioned?

- Ask students to take on the role of archeologists. What do archeologists do? What types of evidence (artifacts) are available to shed light on cultures such as that of the Hittites? How can this evidence be used to inform us about the development of Hittite culture and religious practices? Have students read the **Hittite Laws** and the **Code of Hammurabi** and, using these documents and the artifact evidence they can find through online research, generate a chart comparing these early societies in terms of their cultural development. Which civilization has the most evidence? Which one has the least?

Focus Question: How did the Hittites and Egyptians defend their legitimacy as governments?

- In the classroom, discuss the processes by which leaders come into power today. How do these systems work for the citizens of a nation? What happens when a leader dies, ends his or her term of office, or fails to adequately lead the people? What systems generally ensure a peaceful transition of power?

- Why did the Hittite civilization come to an end? Who replaced them? How did both the Hittites and Egyptians claim legal power? Ask students to read the **Hittite Laws** and the **Divine Birth and Coronation Inscriptions of Hatshepsut** (ca. 1473 BCE) for insights into these questions.

Standard 4: Major trends in Eurasia and Africa from 4000 to 1000 BCE

Standard 4A: The student understands major trends in Eurasia and Africa from 4000 to 1000 BCE.

Focus Question: How did the status of women evolve in patriarchal societies?

- Discuss with students what is meant by a "patriarchal society." Have students research the various gender roles practiced in very early agricultural societies. How did the status of women change when larger urban areas developed? Was this status different for aristocratic compared with peasant women? Ask students to research the reign of Queen Hatshepsut of Egypt and to read the **Divine Birth and Coronation Inscriptions of Hatshepsut** and then read "The Queen Who Would Be King" by Elizabeth B. Wilson (*Smithsonian Magazine*, September 2006; http://www.smithsonianmag .com/history-archaeology/The-Queen-Who-Would-Be-King.html). How has recent scholarship changed our understanding of Hatshepsut's reign? Ask students how Wilson used historical excavations and new evidence to outline the differing views that have been taken about Hatshepsut and her reign. Have them review documents such as the **Middle Assyrian Laws**, the **Code of Hammurabi**, and other early law codes to discuss the ways in which laws differentiated between rights for men and women.

Era 3: Classical Traditions, Major Religions, and Giant Empires, 1000 BCE–300 CE

Standard 1: Innovation and change from 1000 to 600 BCE: horses, ships, iron, and monotheistic faith

Standard 1C: The student understands how states developed in the upper Nile valley and Red Sea region and how iron technology contributed to the expansion of agricultural societies in sub-Saharan Africa.

Focus Question: How did ancient Egypt interact with other states in North Africa during this period?

- In class, review with the students a map of Egypt of the eighth century BCE. Have them identify Egypt and surrounding states and important cities in this period. Then ask them to research the patterns of trade and cultural interaction between Egypt and its African neighbors.

- Ask the students to examine the **Victory Stele of Piankhi** (ca. 725 BCE) and to look at a photograph of the stele at http://wysinger.homestead.com/selaofpiye.html. Have the students explore the language of the stele. What style of written language was used on the monument? After ancient Egypt declined, the ability to translate this script was lost. Using online and library resources, ask students to research what discovery allowed later scholars to break the code. How? What does the text on the stele tell us about political life and expansion in Egypt during this period?

Standard 2: The emergence of Aegean civilization and how interrelations developed among peoples of the eastern Mediterranean and Southwest Asia, 600–200 BCE

Standard 2A: The student understands the achievements and limitations of the democratic institutions that developed in Athens and other Aegean city-states.

Standard 2B: The student understands the major cultural achievements of Greek civilization.

Focus Question: How did patterns of government in the Greek city-states contribute to the development of political and cultural thought in the West?

- Divide the class into two groups. One group is to research Athens, and the other will research Sparta. Ask each group to work together to write a play based on the government and culture of their assigned city-state. Students should include important people and highlight the social structure, citizenship and political organization, religious practices, and culture in their script. They will then perform their short play.

- While watching the play, other students should take notes on the main points brought out during the performance. Class discussion will then center on the similarities and differences between the two city-states. Ask the students to read excerpts from the *Athenian Constitution* (ca. 328 BCE) and the **Spartan Constitution** (ca. 650 BCE), as interpreted by Aristotle. How did these differences lead to conflict? How did the Peloponnesian League (led by Sparta) unite to defeat Athens? Which city-state emerged from the conflict in a dominant position? What important leader is most closely associated with the golden age of Athens?

- Ask students to locate information on Pericles, Socrates, Plato, Aristotle, Archimedes, Hippocrates, Pythagoras, and Homer. Have students explain the contributions of each to the development of Greek culture.

- Ask students to read the **Funeral Oration of Pericles** (431 BCE) and **Plato's "Allegory of the Cave"** (ca. 380 BCE) and explain their relevance to democratic thought. How do these documents compare to each other? What is the significance of the Funeral Oration? Why does Plato use an allegory to explain his political philosophy? Which document has the most impact on modern readers and their understanding of the world? Why?

Standard 3: How major religions and large-scale empires arose in the Mediterranean basin, China, and India, 500 BCE–300 CE

Standard 3A: The student understands the causes and consequences of the unification of the Mediterranean basin under Roman rule.

Focus Question: Why did the early Roman Republic develop a code of laws to maintain the structure of its society, and how were these laws successfully applied to Rome's Empire?

- Have the students read the **Twelve Tables of Roman Law** (451 BCE) and compare them to the first codified law code—the **Code of Hammurabi**. Ask the students to describe the ways in which these laws are characteristic of the societies that applied them. How did they serve to hold their societies together? How did they each guarantee specific rights? Did they apply to each class equally? Did they protect or discriminate against women?

- Ask the students to research the concept of Roman citizenship. As Roman territory expanded, how were these laws of the Twelve Tables amended and interpreted to suit the needs of other more complex societies? Have the students find examples of modern laws that originated in the Roman Republic under the Twelve Tables.

- Have the students read the **Law of Caesar on Municipalities** (ca. 44 BCE). Ask them to explain how these laws expanded on the Twelve Tables. Have them give examples of similarities and differences in the ways in which similar laws are applied to the cities and towns in which we live today. Why did the Romans felt the need to articulate these rules? How did they benefit society as a whole?

Standard 3C: The student understands how China became unified under the early Imperial dynasties.

Focus Question: How did Confucian philosophy aid in the spread of Chinese ethics and ideals into East Asia and along the Silk Road?

- Instruct the students to research the philosophy of Confucius and the ways in which it related to ideas of government. Ask them to read the **Canon of Filial Piety** (ca. 300–239 BCE) and the excerpts from the Analects at Washington State University at http://wsu.edu/~wldciv/world_civ_reader/world_civ_reader_1/confucius.html. Why are these documents studied today?

- Have students explain why Confucianism is a philosophy and not a religion. What is the difference between the two? Ask students to research Hinduism, a religion that began in India and spread east to China in this period. How did it spread? What Chinese innovations and developments in Han China (206 BCE to approximately 220 CE) spread to other regions? Have students draw a map of Han China and surrounding regions and indicate the paths along which goods and ideas and philosophies such as Confucianism spread.

Standard 3D: The student understands religious and cultural developments in India in the era of the Gangetic states and the Mauryan Empire.

Focus Question: How was the Emperor Aśoka instrumental in the expansion of Buddhism in India?

- Ask students to explain how Hinduism is both a religion and a social system. Ask them to read chapter 1 of the *Laws of Manu*, found at http://www.sacred-texts.com/hin/manu/manu01.htm. In class discussion, have students elucidate the concept of the caste system, citing examples from the reading. Who might have expressed dissatisfaction with the caste system and the limitations on social mobility?

- Ask students to research the basic tenets of Buddhism and to explain how it differs from Hinduism. Have them examine which segments of the population Buddhism appealed to most and why. Have the students read the **Rock and Pillar Edicts of Aśoka** (257–240 BCE) and study a map of the Mauryan Empire. Ask them to summarize what happened in the life of Aśoka that influenced him to convert to Buddhism. Have them investigate the rapid spread of Buddhism in Asia and compare it with the rise of Hinduism in India.

Era 4: Expanding Zones of Exchange and Encounter, 300–1000 CE

Standard 1: Imperial crises and their aftermath, 300–700 CE

Standard 1A: The student understands the decline of the Roman and Han Empires.

Focus Question: How did the Byzantine Empire develop very differently than its Western counterpart, and how did it create a new Christian culture?

- Instruct the students to research the decline of the Roman Empire and prepare a flowchart depicting the major events in the Western and Eastern Roman Empire from 284 to 476. Ask students to explain how they chose the events that were the most significant or pivotal. Next, have them compare the Western and Eastern portions of the Roman Empire. What were the events that weakened the Western Roman Empire?

- Ask the students to read **Laws Ending Persecution of Christians in the Roman Empire** (311 and 313) and to summarize how these documents were pivotal to the development of Western civilization. How did they serve to unify parts of the Roman Empire? What religion did both sections of the Roman Empire have in common? How did the branches of the religion develop differently? What practices or beliefs divided the two branches of Christianity? What light do these laws shed on the relationship between Western and Eastern Christians?

- Discuss the development of Roman law from the **Twelve Tables** through the **Theodosian Code** (438) and the **Code of Justinian** (534). How were the two Byzantine codes similar to or different from the ancient Roman laws? How did the later law codes serve to perpetuate Roman laws? Did they equally affect the West?

Standard 3: Major developments in East Asia and Southeast Asia in the era of the Tang dynasty, 600–900 CE

Standard 3B: The student understands developments in Japan, Korea, and Southeast Asia in an era of Chinese ascendancy.

Focus Question: How did Japan borrow and adapt Chinese culture in the sixth and seventh centuries?

- Have the students study a map showing the movement of Chinese culture and Buddhism into Japan. Instruct the students to read **Prince Shōtoku's Seventeen-Article Constitution** (604) and the **New Year's Day Taika Reform Edict** (646) to explore the impact of Chinese culture in Japan. Discuss with them the idea of cultural diffusion. Ask them to suggest ways in which the Japanese adaptation of certain Chinese cultural values and Buddhism a good example of such diffusion.

Standard 4: The search for political, social, and cultural redefinition in Europe, 500–1000 CE

Standard 4A: The student understands the foundations of a new empire in Western Christendom in the five hundred years following the breakup of the Western Roman Empire.

Focus Question: What was the impact of the Carolingian Dynasty on the development of the feudal state and the growth of papal power in Europe?

- Ask students to read the **Capitulary of Charlemagne** (802) and to summarize the key concepts. How did this document promote order? How was the Catholic Church a factor in the government? How did Charlemagne define the system?

- Ask students to explain the concept of feudalism. What were the roles of the king, lords, vassals (knights), and serfs (villeins)? Divide the class by roles and ask the students to use online resources or the library to research the rights of their class and the duties owed to their superiors or underlings. Ask each group to write and perform a short skit on the interaction of their group with the others. Then discuss with them the benefits and drawbacks of the feudal system.

Era 5: Intensified Hemispheric Interactions, 1000–1500 CE

Standard 2: The redefining of European society and culture, 1000–1300 CE

Standard 2A: The student understands feudalism and the growth of centralized monarchies and city-states in Europe.

Focus Question: How did English legal practices lead to the development of modern democracies?

- Review with the students the concepts of the feudal state and how groups developed as a means of counteracting the power of monarchies. Research the institutions of Parlement and the Estates-General in France and Parliament in England. How did they grow out of the structures of early medieval councils?

- Discuss the concepts of early Anglo-Saxon law as defined in **II Aethelstan, or the Grately Code** (924–939). Ask students to explain this document in terms of the civil law and taxation.

- One of the most important dates in English history is 1066, the year of the Norman Conquest. Have the students review the events of the conquest and trace the events leading up to it as well as the invasion itself through the images of the Bayeux Tapestry.

- Have students read the selection of the ***Domesday Book*** (1084) and discuss why the Normans ordered this property survey. How and why is it useful to historians? How was it related to taxation?

- Have students read and summarize the main points of one of the following English documents: the Charter of Liberties of King Henry I, also called the Coronation Charter (1100) (http://www.nhinet.org/ccs/docs/char-lib.htm); Henry II's **Constitutions of Clarendon** (1164); and the **Magna Carta** (1215). Ask students how these documents helped define or curtail the power of the king and enhance the power of the Catholic Church and the development of representative government.

Standard 2B: The student understands the expansion of Christian Europe after 1000.

Focus Question: What conditions in Europe provided the impetus for the Crusades and what were the consequences of these hostile encounters between the Christian invaders and the Muslim inhabitants of Syria and Palestine?

- Divide students into two groups. Using online resources and the library, have them research the causes and consequences of the Crusades. Both groups will then prepare a PowerPoint or Photo Story presentation from either the Christian or the Muslim viewpoint. Suggested documents are **Urban II's Call to the Crusade** (1095) and **Usama ibn Munqidh's "A Muslim View of the Crusaders"** (ca. 1185). Students should endeavor to present a fair and impartial explanation of these events.

- Ask students to listen to both presentations and then locate current newspaper articles that address the ongoing conflict today between Islam on the one hand and Judaism and the Christian West on the other. Why do these disputes still exist today? Who should have access to the disputed areas in the Middle East that are sacred to Islam, Judaism, and Christianity?

Standard 3: The rise of the Mongol empire and its consequences for Eurasian peoples, 1200–1350 CE

Standard 3A: The student understands the world-historical significance of the Mongol empire.

Focus Question: What was the impact of Mongol law on conquered territories?

- Ask students to read the **Great Yasa of Chinggis Khan** (thirteenth through fifteenth centuries) and be prepared to discuss the impact of nomadism on cultures such as that of the Mongols during this era.

Focus Question: How did Mongol rule affect the economy, society, and culture of China and Korea?

- What contemporary evidence exists concerning Mongol rule in China? Have the students read **Marco Polo's Description of Hangzhou** (ca. 1298) and examine his description of a Chinese city in the context of the *Secret History of the Mongols*. A translated excerpt is available at http://www.macalester.edu/~cuffel/mongols.htm. What do the two documents tell modern readers about the structure and belief system of the Mongols? Why did many Europeans doubt Marco Polo's story? How did Europe benefit from this contact with Yuan China?

Era 6: The Emergence of the First Global Age, 1450–1770

Standard 1: How the transoceanic interlinking of all major regions of the world from 1450 to 1600 led to global transformations

Focus Question: What were the contributing factors and effects of European exploration and interaction with other continents and cultures?

- Have the students examine various maps of the known world during this time period. Students can start with an earlier map, such as the thirteenth-century Psalter Map, as a point of comparison: http://iws.ccccd.edu/Andrade/World Lit2332/Psalter.html. Then they can examine the sixteenth-century Waldseemüller Map (http://www.loc.gov/loc/lcib /0706/map.html and the Cantino Map (http://www.historicalatlas.ca/website/hacolp/national_perspectives/exploration/ UNIT_05/U05_staticmap_cantino_1502.htm). What changes are apparent from the thirteenth to the sixteenth centuries? What landforms are recognizable? How did the science of cartography change as exploration accelerated?

- Using the school library or online resources, have students research the trade routes that connected Europe with the Americas during this era. What commodities were traded? Ask students to trace the history of these important trade goods. Why were they so necessary to the Europeans? Explore the lines of communication between these groups. Have students read **Christopher Columbus's Letter to Raphael Sanxis on the Discovery of America** (1493). Discuss the social, economic, and cultural significance of the exchange of commodities, ideas, and beliefs.

- Review the concepts of creating WebQuests at http://www.education-world.com/a_tech/tech/tech011.shtml or http://www.webquest.org/index-create.php. Ask students to work in groups to create a WebQuest on the motives, technological advances, and consequences of the Age of Discovery. Students should include primary sources and prepare an introduction, task, process, resources, evaluation, and conclusion.

Standard 2: How European society experienced political, economic, and cultural transformations in an age of global intercommunication, 1450–1750

Focus Question: How did the values of the Renaissance lead to religious disunity in Europe?

- Discuss with the students the power of the Catholic Church in Renaissance Europe. How is this power evident in the arts and literature? How did the Catholic Church control the lives of European people? What pivotal event disrupted this focus? Documents that might shed light on these questions include the **Requerimiento** (1513), **Martin Luther's Ninety-five Theses** (1517), and **Niccolò Machiavelli's The Prince** (1513).

- Have students prepare a Virtual Museum of paintings, sculpture, architecture, and decorative arts representing the Renaissance. How and why are the images and perspectives different?

- Ask students to read Niccolò Machiavelli's *The Prince*. How does this work reflect secular instead of religious values? Discuss with students the moral and ethical values we expect in our twenty-first-century political leaders. Ask them if we can apply Machiavellian principles to any current world leaders?

- Ask students to use online sources or their school library to research the lives, works, and influence of Ulrich Zwingli, Desiderius Erasmus, Martin Luther, John Calvin, John Knox, and King Henry VIII. What practices of the Catholic Church led to reform movements in the sixteenth century? Ask the students to read **Martin Luther's Ninety-five Theses**. What corruptions in the Catholic Church did Luther object to? Why did he choose this method of protest and why was it markedly successful?

- Ask students to draw a flowchart showing the progress of the Protestant Movement in Europe. Then have them draw a map of Europe showing the areas occupied by the various new Protestant denominations and predominantly Catholic areas. How have these areas changed or remained the same?

- Lead a class discussion on the goals of the Catholic Counter-Reformation at the Council of Trent. What major reforms in the Catholic Church occurred as a result of these meetings? Why was the Inquisition reinstituted? Students can gain insight by reading the **Dutch Declaration of Independence** (1581). What was the Society of Jesus and how did it become globally significant?

- Have the students examine the period of religious wars in sixteenth- and seventeenth-century Europe. Divide students into four groups. Each group will research the causes and consequences of religious wars and conflict in one of the following places: England, France, the German states, and Spain. Ask students to generate a lesson plan for their region, including visuals (paintings and political cartoons, for example), leaders, maps, political objectives, and primary sources.

- Ask the students to sum up the results of religious disunity in Europe. Focus on the shift in the political balance of power following the Thirty Years' War. Ask the students to read the **Treaty of Westphalia** (1648) and discuss the terms. How did this document affect the Holy Roman Empire and the legitimization of Protestant Europe?

Standard 2C: The student understands the rising military and bureaucratic power of European states between the sixteenth and eighteenth centuries.

Focus Question: How did Enlightenment ideas contribute to the emergence of the preeminence of representative governments?

- Discuss with the students the concept of absolute monarchy. What was the divine right of kings? Ask them to read about the English Civil War. Which groups were involved? How did religion enter into the conflict? Who won? What happened to the king? Ask the students to sum up conditions in England during the interregnum or Commonwealth period. What was the Restoration? What was the Glorious Revolution of 1688? Ask students to read and analyze the **Habeas Corpus Act of the Restoration** (1679), **John Locke's *Second Treatise on Civil Government*** (1690), and the **English Bill of Rights** (1689.) How did these documents affect the subsequent American Revolution? Distribute copies of the Declaration of Independence and the U.S. Constitution and its first ten amendments (known as the Bill of Rights), all of which are available online at http://www.MilestoneDocuments.com. Discuss the progression of government from absolute monarchies to representative governments. How did this progress protect the individual rights of the people and guarantee legal protection and democratic practices?

Standard 5: Transformations in Asian societies in the era of European expansion

Focus Question: How did the feudal rulers of Tokugawa Japan centralize their power and limit Japanese interaction with the West?

- Ask students to compare European feudalism to that of seventeenth-century Japan. Have students read **Laws Governing Military Households** (1615) and explain how this document centralized power and reordered roles in society. Instruct the students to write an essay using examples from the reading, highlighting how these laws contributed to the unification of Japan and consolidated authority.

- Have the students read **Japan's Closed Country Edict** (1635). Why did Japan limit its contact with the West in this era? How long did this period of relative isolation last?

Era 7: An Age of Revolutions, 1750–1914

Standard 1: The causes and consequences of political revolutions in the late eighteenth and early nineteenth centuries

Standard 1A: The student understands how the French Revolution contributed to transformations in Europe and the world.

Focus Question: How did the Enlightenment philosophes influence political revolutions in the Americas and Europe in the nineteenth century?

- Pass out copies of the Declaration of Independence, the Constitution of the United States and the Bill of Rights (all available at http://www.MilestoneDocuments.com). Have students identify specific examples of Enlightenment thought represented in these documents and the person who is most closely identified with these specific ideas. How do these documents represent a reaction against British policies in their colonies? Why was the Bill of Rights added to the U.S. Constitution? What group or groups might have been omitted from these documents and why? Have students compare the ideas presented in these documents with those presented in such documents as **John Locke's *Second Treatise on Civil Government***, the **Declaration of the Rights of Man and of the Citizen** (1789) and **Declaration of the Rights of Woman and of the Female Citizen** (1791), and the **Constitution of Haiti** (1801).

- Lead a class discussion on the political, social, and economic causes of the French Revolution. Then ask students to work in groups to produce statements that revolutionary groups might have drafted to address these issues. Ask the class to compile a list of these suggestions and compare them against the Declaration of the Rights of Man and of the Citizen.

- Analyze a copy of the Declaration of the Rights of Woman and of the Female Citizen, by Olympe de Gouges. Why did de Gouges write this document? Did either the Declaration of the Rights of Man or the Declaration of the Rights of Woman address the issues of gender inequality and rights in France during this period?

- Discuss the Constitution of Haiti. What issues did it address that made it more far reaching than any constitution up to that time? What influence did the French Revolution have on the development of the Constitution of Haiti?

- Have the students read excerpts of the Code Napoléon (found at http://www.historyguide.org/intellect/code_nap.html) and discuss why Napoléon Bonaparte found it necessary to issue the code in 1804. Ask students to research ways in which this document affected subsequent political revolutions in the Americas. Have students research which state in the United States has laws based on the Code Napoléon and not traditional Anglo-Saxon law. Discuss the differences. Have the students write a paper on the progression of ideas from the French Revolution to the Napoleonic Wars to the emergence of democratic institutions in Europe and the Americas.

- Lead a class discussion of the power of ideas and the ways in which political change became a global phenomenon. Ask students to write an essay analyzing the origins of human rights legislation and constitutionalism and how they understand it to be interpreted in the world today.

Standard 1B: The student understands how Latin American countries achieved independence in the early nineteenth century.

- Discuss with students the French failure to subjugate Spain in the Peninsular War of 1807–1814 and the ascendency of British power in the Atlantic basin. How did these events in Europe affect the movements toward independence in South America in the late nineteenth century? Students can read the **Constitution of Haiti** and **Simón Bolívar's Cartagena Manifesto** (1812) for insights into these issues. Ask students to prepare group oral reports on these independence movements, analyzing the political and ideological motivations between 1808 and 1830, including leaders and their social backgrounds, support groups, objectives, and goals. Were their objectives met? Who benefited? Who lost out? Which groups maintained and strengthened their control over these areas? What, if any, was the role of the Catholic Church?

- Have students read and summarize the main points of the **Treaty of Córdoba** (1821) and explain its relevance to other documents expressing the same sentiments.

Standard 2: The causes and consequences of the agricultural and industrial revolutions, 1700–1850

Focus Question: How did the development of the Industrial Revolution influence reform movements in Europe and other parts of the globe?

- Divide the class into two groups. Have them read Andrew Ure's *Philosophy of Manufactures* (1835) and Edwin Chadwick's *Sanitary Condition of the Labouring Population* (1842) and then prepare a debate on the pros and cons of industrialization. Did the benefits outweigh the drawbacks? Why or why not?

- Ask students to read Friedrich Engels's *The Condition of the Working Class in England in 1844* and selections from the **Communist Manifesto** (1848) by Karl Marx and Friedrich Engels. Have students write a short reaction paper on the capitalist system versus the theories of scientific Socialists such as Marx and Engels.

- Ask students to research depictions of slavery and slave conditions in the early nineteenth century and the biographies of William Wilberforce and Olaudah Equiano as well as members of the Anti-Slavery Society (founded in England in 1823). Have them read the **Act for the Abolition of Slavery throughout the British Colonies** (1833). Distribute a world map and ask students to shade the areas of the world that were affected by this legislation.

Standard 3: The transformation of Eurasian societies in an era of global trade and rising European power, 1750–1870

Standard 3C: The student understands the consequences of political and military encounters between Europeans and peoples of South and Southeast Asia.

Focus Question: How did the breakdown of political authority in China lead to a large European sphere of influence and the resulting European domination of Chinese markets?

- Ask students to write a narrative of Chinese history from 1773 to 1912 from the point of view of either a British trader or a Chinese government official. For information, students can read **Qianlong's Letter to George III** (1793), **Lin Zexu's "Moral Advice to Queen Victoria"** (1839), and the **Treaty of Nanjing** (1842).

- Have students review Chinese trade practices with the West until the 1830s and write a brief report on why China maintained these practices. Ask students to read Qianlong's Letter to George III. What policies did the Chinese Qing Empire practice? How was trade limited? To where? Why? What concession did the British demand? What was the Chinese emperor's response? What trade good from India had been introduced to China in 1773?

- Ask students to read Lin Zexu's "Moral Advice to Queen Victoria" and explain the causes and progress of the Opium War. What position did Lin Zexu take? Why? How does Lin Zexu's letter reflect cultural differences between China and the West?

- Have students prepare contrasting lists of how China and Great Britain each benefited from the Treaty of Nanjing, which ended the Opium War. What was the result of this treaty?

- Explain to the students the establishment of various European spheres of influence in China and other portions of Asia (Hong Kong, Kowloon, Indochina, Manchuria, Korea, and others) during this period. Refer to http://hoover.archives .gov/exhibits/China/Political%20Evolution/19thc/index.html. Students can use the political cartoon at this site under the heading "Spheres of Influence" to assist them. Ask students to explain the point of view of the Chinese versus the Europeans and why the United States did not take part in the colonization of Asia.

- Have students read the **Emperor Guangxu's Abolition of the Examination System** (1898). How was this document tied to the Hundred Days' Reform? What did the Chinese hope to gain? Was the reform movement successful?

- Have students read **Articles Providing for the Favorable Treatment of the Great Ching Emperor after His Abdication** (1912) and, using this document, to prepare a time line for the key events before and after the Boxer Rebellion. Then, using this document in connection with **Sun Yat-sen's "The Three Principles of the People"** (1921), discuss with students the form of government that was established in China in 1911 and why that change in government was important.

Era 8: A Half Century of Crisis and Achievement, 1900–1945

Standard 1: Reform, revolution, and social change in the world economy of the early century

Focus Question: What role did social class play in the Russian and Mexican rebellions at the beginning of the twentieth century?

- Have students research the ideas of capitalism, Socialism, liberalism, and conservatism and identify the social groups that tended to support each one in Russia, Mexico, China, and other countries.

- Ask students to read **Emiliano Zapata's Plan of Ayala** (1911), **Vladimir Lenin's *What Is to Be Done?*** (1902), and **Mao Zedong's "Report on an Investigation of the Peasant Movement in Hunan"** (1927). Have them examine these documents and explain the role of peasants in rebellions, focusing on the ownership of land and control of resources. When were serfs freed in Russia? When did much of Latin America achieve independence from European countries? How did Zapata and Lenin propose to correct the injustices they saw? What did Mao Zedong propose doing with "counterrevolutionaries"?

Standard 3: The search for peace and stability in the 1920s and 1930s

Focus Question: How did the settlements at the end of World War I lead to conditions that set up the next global conflict?

- Discuss with the students the main long-term causes of World War I, including nationalism, militarization, the alliance system, and major-power competition. What was the immediate cause of the war? What part did Germany play in the escalation of the conflict?

- Have students read the **Treaty of Versailles** (1919). Then ask students to read Woodrow Wilson's "Fourteen Points" (available at http://www.MilestoneDocuments.com). What part of the proposal was implemented in the Treaty of Versailles? Have students prepare a report card on the provisions of the treaty. Lead a class discussion on the question of whether a less punitive peace treaty would have prevented another global war.

- Have students read the **Treaty of Lausanne** (1923). What empire was dissolved by this treaty? Why was the dissolution of this empire of long-term importance? Ask students to compare and contrast the very different consequences of the Treaty of Versailles and the Treaty of Lausanne.

- Have students read the **Covenant of the League of Nations** (1919). Ask students to explore other postwar peace initiatives, such as the Kellogg-Briand Pact. Why were these attempts failures? Which countries never joined the League of Nations? Why?

Standard 4: The causes and global consequences of World War II

Focus Question: How were the governments of Germany and Italy able to further their economic and political platforms in the interwar period?

- Have students research the Great Depression. What were the causes? How did it affect economic conditions in Russia, Germany, and Italy after World War I?

- Divide students into three groups and ask each group to select and prepare a presentation on one of the following ideologies: Communism, Nazism, or Fascism. Have them explain the political, social, and economic platforms of each. Ask students to respond to the following questions: Which leaders were involved? What policies did they formulate to turn the economic crisis around? What were their attitudes toward opponents? Did they suppress individual rights? What symbols did they employ? How did these groups use propaganda? Have each group of students complete a comparison chart on the three totalitarian dictators.

- Ask students to read **Benito Mussolini's "The Doctrine of Facism"** (1932), **Adolf Hitler's Proclamation to the German People** (1933), and Joseph Stalin's "Industrialization of the Country and the Right Deviation." Hold a class discussion on how these documents influenced public opinion. Discuss the idea of persuasive political speeches and propaganda. How did they glorify their own agenda and demonize or blame opponents?

Focus Question: What political and economic factors led to the Japanese attack on Pearl Harbor in December 1941?

- Distribute a blank map of Asia to the students. Ask them to locate and label the areas of Japanese expansion into China, Indochina, and other areas in the Pacific in the 1930s. How does this expansion explain Japanese policies in the inter-war period? What was the Tripartite Pact? Why did the United States freeze Japanese assets in the United States and impose sanctions on Japan? How did these actions lead to Japanese aggression against the United States? Ask students to read **Japan's Fourteen-part Message** (1941) and to explain the controversy surrounding the timing of the Japanese declaration of war on the United States.

Era 9: The Twentieth Century since 1945: Promises and Paradoxes

Standard 1: How post–World War II reconstruction occurred, new international power relations took shape, and colonial empires broke up

Standard 1A: The student understands major political and economic changes that accompanied postwar recovery.

Focus Question: How was the United States instrumental in providing the mechanism for the political and economic stabilization of Western Europe and Japan?

- Have students research the Marshall Plan. Why was this plan so significant? Which countries received U.S. aid? Why did the Soviet Union decline it?

- Ask students to explain the U.S. occupation of Japan after World War II. How was Japan's government changed? What was the role of the emperor? Have students read the **Japanese Constitution** (1947) and compare the occupation of Japan with the postwar occupation of Germany. How were they similar and how different?

Standard 1B: The student understands why global power shifts took place and the cold war broke out in the aftermath of World War II.

Focus Question: How did the USSR gain control of Eastern Europe and what were the consequences for the West?

- Ask students to read **Winston Churchill's "The Sinews of Peace"** (1946) and explain the impact of Soviet domination of Eastern Europe for East-West relations.

Focus Question: What factors caused the demise of the Guomindang (the National People's Party) and the rise of the Chinese Communist Party from 1936 to 1949?

- Ask students to read "China's Christian Warrior" (http://www.time.com/time/asia/asia/magazine/1999/990823/cks.html) and "Flawed Icon of China's Resurgence" (http://www.cnn.com/SPECIALS/1999/china.50/inside.china/profiles/mao.tse tung/). Ask students to prepare contrasting biographies of Chiang Kai-shek and Mao Zedong and explain why the two men had differing visions for China.

- Who assumed control of the Chinese Communist Party in the 1940s? What was the Long March? What group was most significant in Mao's rise to power? Discuss the concepts forwarded by Chairman Mao in the Great Leap Forward and the Cultural Revolution. Ask the students to read **"Mao Tse-tung's Thought Is the Telescope and Microscope of Our Revolutionary Cause"** (1966) and explain what Mao's "revolutionary cause" was and how he proposed to implement that cause.

- Where did the Guomindang and their supporters go after being forced out of mainland China? What is the relationship between the two groups today? Ask students to read **Gamal Abdel Nasser on the Nationalization of the Suez Canal** (1956) and explain how the dispute between the "two Chinas" has had an impact on geopolitical events in other parts of the world.

Standard 1C: The student understands how African, Asian, and Caribbean peoples achieved independence from European colonial rule.

Focus Question: How did India achieve independence from Great Britain after centuries of British control?

- Ask students to work in groups to create a commemorative newspaper examining the interaction between the British and the Indians from the time of the Seven Years' War to independence in 1948. How did the British attempt to subjugate the people of the Indian Subcontinent? In what ways did the Indians try to resist? Students should present several points of view, "interviews" with famous people involved in the process, editorials, and so on. Ask students to use the **British Regulating Act** (1773), the **Government of India Act** (1919), **Mahatma Gandhi's Speech to the All Indian Congress Committee** (1942), and **Jawaharlal Nehru's Speeches on the Granting of Indian Independence** (1947) to guide their research. How did all of these historical developments culminate in Indian independence, the formation of Pakistan, and the **Indian Constitution** (1949)? Classroom discussion should follow on the ideas of imperialism, cultural diffusion, and nationalism. What ideas presented in the "newspaper" represent each?

Focus Question: Why did the Indian Subcontinent become fragmented along religious lines?

- Ask students to read the **Lahore Resolution** (1940) and the Indian Constitution. Conduct a class discussion on the formation of the Indian National Congress and the Muslim League. Was partition inevitable?

Focus Question: Why was the process toward independence in India markedly different from that in much of Africa?

- Have students examine the map at http://exploringafrica.matrix.msu.edu/students/curriculum/m9/activity4.php and the map chart explaining the resources that European powers gained from Africa. Ask them how colonization and exploitation of Africa aided the process of industrialization in Europe. What were the benefits and drawbacks for Africa?

- Examine the map showing the areas and dates of African independence at http://www.empathosnationenterprises.com/Consulate/EN-Library/Black-Studies/afindep.html. Which areas used armed conflict or revolts in their struggle for independence? Which countries achieved independence first? Ask students to choose a country and research its path to independence. Then have them report out on what they discovered.

- Have students read excerpts from the following documents and compare the differences between British- and French-controlled countries: **Proclamation of the Algerian National Liberation Front** (1954), **Patrice Lumumba's Speech at the Proclamation of Congolese Independence** (1960), the **Arusha Declaration** (1967) and **Nelson Mandela's Inaugural Address** (1994). Then ask them to write a comparison paper analyzing the question and covering causes and effects.

Focus Question: How did the idea of Zionism lead to the emergence of the state of Israel after World War II, and why is there still armed conflict there today?

- Have students read these documents: **Theodor Herzl's "A Solution to the Jewish Question"** (1896), the **Balfour Declaration** (1917), and the **Nuremberg Laws** (1935). Ask them to prepare a one-paragraph summary of each. Then ask them to read the **Declaration of the Establishment of the State of Israel** (1948), **UN Security Council Resolution 242** (1967), and the **Palestinian National Charter** (1968) and explain how the three later documents were culminations of developments reflected in the three earlier documents.

- Ask students to construct a K-W-L chart (What I Know, What I Want to Know, What I Learned). A template is available at http://www.eduplace.com/graphicorganizer/pdf/kwl.pdf . Have the students to use their summaries and explanations of the documents, along with classroom brainstorming, to complete each column in the chart. Provide various newspaper and magazine articles on the Arab-Israeli conflict and debate whether a peace settlement can hold in that region.

Standard 2: The search for community, stability, and peace in an interdependent world

Standard 2B: The student understands how increasing economic interdependence has transformed human society.

Focus Question: What is the purpose of the European Union (EU) and how has it changed European economic and political connectivity?

- Ask the students to define these terms: Common Market, European Economic Community, and European Union.

- Have the students read the **Treaty on European Union** (1992). Hold a classroom discussion on the points addressed in the reading. How has this document shaped Europe today? Ask students if they have been to Europe. What currency did they use? How did this facilitate their travel? Discuss the idea of open borders. How does a common currency benefit Europe's economic activities and trade? What impact does political interconnectivity have on nationalism? Why has Britain maintained its own currency? What countries want to join the EU? Why?

Standard 2C: The student understands how liberal democracy, market economies, and human rights movements have reshaped political and social life.

Focus Question: Why did the events of the early twentieth century necessitate the issuing of a Universal Declaration of Human Rights and what was its impact on individual rights in the late twentieth and early twenty-first centuries?

- Give students background information on the formation of the United Nations in 1945. Have students read the **Universal Declaration of Human Rights** (1948). Why was this document issued? How was the United Nations different from the League of Nations?

- Read **A. B. Xuma's "Bridging the Gap between White and Black in South Africa"** (1930) and **Nelson Mandela's Inaugural Address** (1992). What progress was made regarding human rights in South Africa in the years between 1930 and 1992?

- Ask students to give other examples of human rights violations since 1948. What actions were taken by the United Nations to guarantee these rights? How has the Universal Declaration of Human Rights prevented abuses?

Standard 2D: The student understands major sources of tension and conflict in the contemporary world and efforts that have been made to address them.

Standard 2F: The student understands worldwide cultural trends of the second half of the twentieth century.

Focus Question: Why have terrorist organizations risen in the contemporary world and how do they affect global relationships?

- Give students a blank world map and ask them to circle areas that have been affected by terrorist actions in the twentieth and twenty-first centuries. Then ask them to use another color to circle the areas believed to harbor terrorist groups. Have them explain their choices. Discuss the issues involved in the terrorist activities. Are they the same everywhere?

- Have students read the **Proclamation of the Provisional Government of the Irish Republic** (1916) and the **Northern Ireland Peace Agreement** (1998). Ask them whether they circled Ireland on their maps. Have them explain the evolution of the issue of Ireland's relationship with Great Britain.

- Have the students read **Ayatollah Khomeini's** *Islamic Government: Governance of the Jurist* (1970) and **Osama bin Laden's Declaration of Jihad against Americans** (1996). Ask them to explain what these documents have in common with the previous two. Additionally, ask them to explain the role that religious beliefs and practices play in ongoing conflict between the West and some Islamic countries and groups.

- As students to read the United Nations Security Council Resolution 1373, available at http://daccess-dds-ny.un.org/doc/UNDOC/GEN/N01/557/43/PDF/N0155743.pdf?OpenElement. What methods are being used to combat terrorist groups? What impact have these groups had on the world's trade, economy, politics, and cultural norms?

Era 10: World History across the Eras Overview

Standard 1: Long-term changes and recurring patterns in world history

Focus Question: Have the revolutionary movements and conflicts of the past three centuries been successes or failures?

• Ask students to take a pro or con position on the question posed and then to select documents that would provide evidence to support their thesis.

Focus on a discussion of the **Agreement on Reconciliation between South and North Korea** (1992) and **African Union Constitutive Act** (2000). Have students locate a newspaper article that ties into one of these and trace the content of the article back to the onset of the conflict. Have the issues that confronted these areas been resolved? Ask students what movement towards peace they see. Have them defend their answer.

MILESTONE DOCUMENTS
IN WORLD HISTORY

Exploring the Primary Sources
That Shaped the World

Reform Edict of Urukagina

"URU-KA-gina ... would never subjugate the orphan [or] widow to the powerful."

Overview

The societal reforms of Urukagina (ca. 2350 BCE), Sumerian king of Lagash, were preserved over the millennia on six inscriptions found on five ceremonial clay nails and an oval clay plaque. (The Sumerians often wrote their documents on all types of objects, including ceremonial maces and statues and other items not normally considered media for writing.) The reforms were written in Sumerian, the world's earliest written language. There are at least three versions of the Reform Edict, which constituted a covenant between the monarch and Ningirsu, the patron deity of the Sumerian kingdom of Lagash-Girsu, ensuring that the socially disenfranchised (such as widows and orphans) would not be abused by those in power. The composite reform texts begin with a description of building activities and canal excavations performed by the crown. It appears that each edition of the Reform Edict was written for a slightly different occasion—the renaming of a canal, the liberation of the people of Lagash, or the cataloging of various abuses. Overall, however, the reforms have been exceedingly difficult to translate and thus to interpret.

Context

Although developments in Mesopotamian history and political institutions in the third millennium BCE are imperfectly understood, because of fortunate circumstances numerous royal inscriptions from the vicinity of Lagash, in the south of modern-day Iraq, have shed light on a portion of this period (ca. 2500–2340 BCE). The late-nineteenth-century French excavations at Tello (ancient Girsu) and American work in the 1970s at al-Hiba (ancient Lagash) unearthed thousands of cuneiform texts written in Sumerian. Included among these texts are over one hundred royal inscriptions and fragments in multiple copies that delineate a 150-year period during which the kingdom of Lagash, comprising the cities of Lagash, Girsu, and Nina, played a significant role in the region. Mentioned in the inscriptions are nine kings of Lagash, the last of which is Urukagina.

The Lagash kings describe many building (and rebuilding) projects for a multiplicity of deities, the most important being Ningirsu, the aforementioned city god of Lagash. Significant texts from Girsu concern a boundary dispute with a neighboring kingdom, Umma. The earliest king of Lagash known to have left inscriptions was Urnanshe (ca. 2500 BCE), who fought against an alliance of Umma and another Sumerian city-kingdom, Ur. A historical, if perhaps propagandistic, perspective on the border conflict was recorded during the reign of the third known king of Lagash, Eanatum (ca. 2450 BCE), in his so-called Stele of the Vultures. Here, the Lagash king wrote a history of the conflict tracing the issue back to Urnanshe, his grandfather. He argued that Umma had violated an agreement over the use of an agricultural area between the two territories called Gu'edena (a term etymologically related to the Hebrew "Eden"), which belonged to the kingdom of Lagash (in the name of the god Ningirsu). During the reign of Eanatum, the Lagashite king forced the Ummaite monarch to swear an oath that he was to use Gu'edena as an interest-bearing loan. The conflict was reignited during the reigns of the next kings, Enanatum I and Enmetena, both of whom claimed victories over their Ummaite enemies.

Few royal inscriptions from the next Lagash kings have been unearthed, but there are over sixty surviving texts from the last monarch, Urukagina, who was defeated in about his seventh year by Lugalzaggisi, king of the neighboring city of Umma. Apparently, the Lagash king, though defeated, was able to claim the title "king of Girsu," perhaps implying rule over a smaller territory. In addition to the royal inscriptions, more than seventeen hundred administrative texts have been dated to the last three Lagash monarchs (Enentarzi, Lugalanda, and Urukagina), most of which are concerned with the Emi, the bureaucratic structure organized by the wife of the *ensi* (a major Lagashite official). The wife of Urukagina, Sa-Sa, is mentioned several times in these texts.

Although the date of its composition is uncertain, the earliest version of the Urukagina Reform Edict was most certainly written before Urukagina's defeat by Lugalzaggisi, the king of Umma and of the city of Uruk. Later versions describe Urukagina as the king of Girsu, and thus they were probably promulgated after his defeat by the

CA. 2500—
2360 BCE

- A border conflict takes place between Lagash and Umma, lasting from the reign of Urnanshe to the reign of Urukagina.

CA. 2450 BCE

- In the Stele of the Vultures, Eanatum, the third known king of Lagash, writes a history of the border conflict, tracing the issue back to Urnanshe, his grandfather.

CA. 2360 BCE

- Urukagina's reforms are instituted in the midst of the Lagash-Umma border war, early in his reign.

CA. 2350 BCE

- Lugalzaggisi of Umma defeats Urukagina, ending his reign of Lagash; he remains king of Girsu.

in a period of political unification that lasted for over a century (ca. 2340 BCE). Urukagina was first mentioned as a high official during the reign of the previous king, Lugalanda. In fact, he did not take the title of "king" until the second year of his reign. His relationship to the previous monarch, as well as to the entire Lagashite dynasty before him, is unknown; Urukagina never mentions his father in any of the extant inscriptions. Some modern scholars speculate that Urukagina was a usurper, but no concrete evidence supports this. He must have had some affinity (or at least some connection) to the previous administration, as deliveries of supplies for various temples in the Lagash vicinity were still being made in the name of Bara-Namtara, the wife of Lugalanda, during the first year of Urukagina's reign. This may imply that he considered himself a legitimate successor to the previous king.

In Urukagina's third year, he began making offerings to the gods of Umma and Nippur (the holy city of the Sumerians), perhaps in a diplomatic effort to assuage the imperialistic designs of the Ummaite king, Lugalzaggisi. However, within a few years, perhaps during the seventh year of Urukagina's reign, the Ummaite king attacked and burned many of the Lagash temples. In a later version of the reforms, Urukagina calls himself "king of Girsu," perhaps implying that he had lost the territory of Lagash to the Ummaite conqueror. Indeed, in later inscriptions, Urukagina's records indicate that he then restricted his building to the area and towns surrounding Girsu. The destruction of Lagash by Lugalzaggisi is known by a unique document from Lagash, in which Urukagina complains about the Ummaite king's plundering of Lagashite temples, the destruction of Lagashite barley fields, and the sacking of the city of Lagash itself. Urukagina considered these acts to be sins against the city deity of Lagash, Ningirsu, and even against Nisaba, the god of Lugalzaggisi. Urukagina makes clear in this text that he was not at fault for the invasion. Interestingly, many of the areas taken by Lugalzaggisi were perhaps restored to Lagash and Urukagina during the reign of Sargon of Akkad (as described in a text of Manishtushu, one of the royal sons of Sargon).

Explanation and Analysis of the Document

By abolishing former abusive customs and replacing them with new precepts through the Reform Edict, Urukagina evidently proclaimed a general amnesty in Lagash (written "Lagaš" in the text) concerning the old precepts. He furthermore established divine ownership over estates that had been administered by members of the royal family. He also claimed to have changed the taxes collected on special occasions, such as weddings, divorces, and funerals.

The text of the first and most complete version of the reforms appears to consist of four parts. The first section is the introduction and dedication to Urukagina's god, Ningirsu (written "Ninĝirsu"), with a brief note about building projects and dedications. Second, Urukagina outlines vari-

Ummaite. The Reform Edict begins with a description of a number of building projects completed by the monarch for a plurality of gods. The Lagashite king then delineates a series of abuses by previous Lagashite monarchs (to whom he was evidently not related). These abuses included grain taxes on priests, excessive fees imposed upon mourners, the exploitation of the poor by the rich, and the exploitation of the property of the masses by the crown. To atone for these abuses, Urukagina pledged to fix certain prices, to cancel certain debts, and to protect widows and orphans.

About the Author

Urukagina was the last king of the Sumerian kingdom of Lagash before the era of Sargon, an Akkadian king who conquered Mesopotamia and neighboring areas, ushering

ous abuses committed by previous monarchs (primarily concerning the appropriation of temple property). He next describes his own elevation to kingship and the new practices that were then introduced. He concludes with a contract between himself and Ningirsu. In the third version of the text, a key passage concerns the position of women.

◆ Column i

The text begins with a prologue concerning the city god of the Lagash region, Ningirsu (apparently the Lagashite form of Ninurta, a major Sumerian deity), celebrating the building and dedication of various structures. This god was the son of Enlil, the active head of the Sumerian pantheon. Ningirsu combined both military and agricultural attributes. To begin, he was a mighty warrior god who destroyed the mountain enemies of Sumer as well as the Anzu, a mythical birdlike creature who had threatened the god's authority over humankind. Moreover, Ningirsu gave humans advice on farming, as evidenced in the Sumerian text "Farmer's Instructions." In one myth, this god defeated the demon Asag and proceeded to organize the world by making the Tigris and Euphrates rivers usable for irrigation and agriculture.

Both Tirash ("Tiraš") and Antasur, attested to as early as the Lagashite king Urnanshe, were either geographic regions or structures (either temples or palaces) dedicated to Ningirsu. Baba, the divine consort of Ningirsu, is also found in the earliest inscriptions from the vicinity of Lagash. It is not certain what type of structure Baba's "pantry" was. The literal meaning of the term is "stone bowl," and some scholars have surmised that the building in question was a storehouse where stone bowls were kept to be used for temple provisions. Some Lagash archival texts mention a building with a similar description at Girsu ("G̃irsu") that provided emmer, a breed of wheat, for the monthly provisions of the god Ningirsu. Thus, the Urukagina text may be referring to a like structure.

◆ Column ii

One of the other major goddesses of the region, Nanshe ("Nanše"), had her seat of residence at Nina, the least known of the three major cities of the region of Lagash. In Sumerian mythology, she was the daughter of Enki, the god of wisdom, and Ninhursag. In the myth concerning Enki and the world order, Nanshe was given the Persian Gulf by her father as her dominion. By the time of Gudea, a king of Lagash (ca. 2130 BCE), Nanshe was considered the goddess of social justice, defending the rights of orphans, widows, debtors, and refugees. She was also described as the "Lady of the Storerooms."

The "sheep-plucking shed," mentioned in various texts from Girsu, stored emmer for the monthly provisions of the god Ningirsu, perhaps being similar to the "pantry" mentioned in column i. The "Nimin-DU canal" evidently went out of the area of Lagash to the south and east, heading toward the Persian Gulf. The "wall of G̃irsu" was presumably a portion of the city wall of Girsu, dedicated to Ningirsu himself. The second edition of the reforms includes

Ceremonial stone mace head from the kingdom of Lagash, deposited at a temple (© The Trustees of the British Museum)

mention of more deities to whom Urukagina dedicated canals and temples.

◆ Column iii

After the dedicatory prologue, the main body of the text is first concerned with abuses of previous royal administrations, which had been perpetuated "since time immemorial." Although Urukagina does not mention any monarch by name, it is implicitly understood that the previous Lagashite kings are held guilty of taking advantage of many in society. It is not clear what these officials (head boatmen, livestock officials, and so on) were doing improperly. Perhaps they had usurped the prerogatives of the temple administrators, a situation that Urukagina planned to reform.

The identity of the town of Ambar is uncertain, as is its location. It may have been either a town near the province of Lagash or a town near the northern city of Kish, the titular head of the Sumerian city-states. The lustration (purification) priests were evidently involved in farming land that was subject to a grain tax. It is not clear, however, why the demand of this tax at the city of Ambar was considered abusive. The fragmented third edition of the Reform Edict adds that the priests were required to build grain storehouses at Ambar. These priests were also mentioned in earlier administrative texts from Shuruppak, a Sumerian city to the northwest.

◆ Column iv

Once again, it appears that the different administrators (surveyor, brewer, and others) were improperly collecting taxes. Historians do not know why the garlic and cucumber plots of the rulers are singled out in this section. However, it is clear that, according to Urukagina, they should have belonged to the divine estates. White sheep were brought to the palace by state administrators and were sheared to be used as offerings. The third edition of the Reform Edict elucidates that the shepherds had been required to pay a five-shekel silver tax in addition to the tax of wool, demands that must have been considered abusive by Urukagina

◆ Column v

Evidently, the temple administrators were also guilty of abuse and took improper items as payments. The various lists of items in this column most certainly refer to funerary goods. Similar lists are found in a great variety of literary documents, including the version of the Epic of Gilgamesh recorded by the Akkadians (another people group living in southern Mesopotamia), which describes items used in the funeral for Enkidu. Enkidu is described in Sumerian and Akkadian literature as the semidivine friend of Gilgamesh, the fifth king of Uruk. Similar items are mentioned in a text describing the death of Ur-Nammu, a Sumerian king of Ur. Many of these items may have been of a ceremonial nature. The "Ear of the Mongoose" may have been a sort of earmuff dedicated to the deity Ninkilim (symbolized by the mongoose). The meaning of "ŠU.GABA.UR" is uncertain, but it appears to have something to do with a cloth that holds the hand to the chest. A similar item (a chest covering) is found among a list of funerary goods for the deity Bilala. Similarly, the "outer woolen garment" and "linen draping" of the reforms can also be compared to like items found in archival texts from Girsu dating to the reign of Urukagina. The term *throw-stick/bow* is derived from earlier Sumerian sources, but the precise nature of the item in question is uncertain; in mythological contexts it is referred to as a magic staff connected to the underworld. Archival texts from Girsu describe fishermen along with assorted birds, including, as here, "yellow ravens"; perhaps the inhabitants of the underworld were decked out in these birds' feathers.

◆ Column vi

The temple administrators also abused the poor, as is seen in this column. The translation "undertaker" (that is, priest performing funeral rites) is not certain, but it fits the context here. The "reeds of Enki" perhaps signal a healing or burial ceremony. A Lagash incantation text from the time of Urnanshe connects the use of the reed in magic to Enki, who was the god of the subterranean freshwater ocean and was associated with the arts (especially magic). He was often depicted wearing a sorcerer's hat. His primary cult center was at the southern city of Eridu, recognized by the Sumerians as the first city. Although the meaning is uncertain, given the context, the *shu-ila* ("*šuila*") rites must have also been funerary in nature. Bread is also connected to *shu-ila* rites mentioned in the Epic of Gilgamesh.

◆ Column vii

The "safe passage toll" perhaps refers to the passage of the dead to the netherworld, as similar to Greek mythology. The "great gate" is probably the gate through which individuals had to pass in order to reach their final resting places. A probable iconographic depiction of this gate comes from a seal impression from this period that features a boat approaching a winged gate, presumably the gate of the netherworld.

The lady and children described here appear to be the ruler's family. Once again, it is not clear what abuse is being referred to. The ruler's family and their property had either grown to a level that prohibited more expansion or were administered together. In any event, the reform concerning this issue describes a separation of the royal family properties that were assigned to different temple organizations.

The boundary of the god Ningirsu signified the area of the kingdom of Lagash, bordering Umma to the north and west and the marshland to the south and east (as far as the Persian Gulf). The "subordinate to the king" seems to have been a collective term for chain gangs, perhaps in relation to agricultural and even military work. The term *blind workers* probably refers to a lower class of unfree workers rather than to those who were legally blind. Alternatively, in some periods of Mesopotamian history (especially in the Neo-Assyrian period, ca. 900–612 BCE), prisoners of war were blinded to inhibit their mobility. The column concludes with a summary statement about all of the abuses outlined in the previous sections.

◆ Column viii

As with most kings in the ancient Near East, Urukagina claimed that his authority to rule came from a divine source—in this case, from Ningirsu, the city god of Lagash. However, he did not claim authority also for hereditary reasons but instead only because the god chose him from among the "myriad people." He thus proved his legitimacy by reversing the abuses of former times, stopping the royal administrators from continuing their improper tax collections, and restoring the social order to its proper state.

◆ Column ix

In this section Urukagina outlines the installation of the temple administration over many of the estates that had been under the control of the crown. Shulshagana ("Šulšagana") was the offspring of Ningirsu and Baba. It seems likely that the royal family's property was divided into three organizations, all technically under the ownership of the divine family of Ningirsu. Interestingly, Shulshagana is not mentioned in the later editions of the reforms.

◆ Column x

The actual gender of the personnel described here is unclear; some commentators argue that "old men" are also listed, in addition to the "wailing women." In any event, these individuals were probably connected with lamentation rites and thus were associated with the lamentation singers. Perhaps this section is describing a tax on a particular mourning ceremony, different from the "reed of Enki" tax in column vi and in the opening of this column. The "*lu-ziga* attendants" were probably lamentation singers connected to burials. The *mud* and *sadug* were liquid or dry measures, probably fabricated to a standard size.

◆ Column xi

The different times of day mentioned here are likely referring to the hours when religious ceremonies were to be performed. The *sagbur* ("*saḡbur*") were perhaps associated with the lamentation singers, but their particular function is not clear. The *sagbur* were perhaps responsible for removing the clothes of the deceased before they were wrapped for burial.

◆ Column xii

The practice of indenturing family members to secure loans is well known from other texts in this period. Moreover, many documents from the Ur III dynasty (ca. 2112–2006 BCE) describe whole families that were forced into servitude because of debt or other criminal activities. The earliest attestation of the cancellation of debts comes from a few generations before Urukagina, during the reign of the Lagash king Entemena, who claimed to have cancelled debts for Lagash. Interestingly, the Sumerian term for cancellation of debts, *ama.ar.gi*, literally means "return to the mother," signifying a release from either public obligations (taxation and conscription) or private debts.

◆ Version 3: Column iii

The words "exceeding her rank" (sometimes translated as "transgressing moral limits") probably refer to a woman's attempting to transcend her social status, although it is unclear what that would have entailed. Sumerian contracts from this period occasionally contain a clause about a wooden stake driven into the mouth of the accused. Whether this is to be taken literally or figuratively is not known. Interestingly, section 22 of the legal Ur-Nammu Code reads, "If someone's slave woman, presuming her to be the equal of her mistress, has sworn at her, she shall scour out her mouth with one quart of salt" (Roth, p. 19) The references in Job 29:17 and Psalms 3:7 to the breaking of the teeth or jaws of the wicked occur in legal contexts and perhaps indicate a related custom.

Much has been said about this section and its meaning. Although the phrasing is clear—in former times, a man could marry two women—its cultural meaning is not. Instead of polyandry or polygamy, neither of which are confirmed anywhere in Sumerian sources, the phrase is probably referring to women who were married more than once. However, an alternative view is that men could "take" (perhaps not legally) two wives, with the second serving as a sort of insurance policy for debt release. In other words, if a man was released from his debts, he would no longer need to take a second wife.

Audience

As with many documents from ancient Mesopotamia, the Urukagina reform texts do not reveal much, if anything, about their intended audience. A significant percentage of the Sumerian texts from Girsu were uncovered by French archaeologists in the late nineteenth century, when excavations were relatively primitive, at least by modern standards. As such, many of the original spatial contexts of the artifacts were not recorded. In fact, historians are not even certain as to which excavation site some of the documents came from. In turn, some of the texts that were uncovered by the American team at Lagash in the 1970s had evidently been reused by succeeding monarchs as fill material for construction projects.

In general, many Mesopotamian public inscriptions were intended for display on monuments, delineating the accomplishments of the ruler in power. However, only scribes were literate; the masses and even the ruling aristocracy for the most part were not trained to read. One can thus surmise that the contents of such displayed texts (for example, the Code of Hammurabi) were read by a public herald. Yet there were still other members of society, so to speak, who could read—the gods. Thus, monuments on public display were perhaps intended for a divine audience, as sort of a résumé of the monarch making the gods aware of his accomplishments on earth. This theory is enhanced by the fact that many documents were specifically dedicated to deities. In some cases, royal documents were deposited in building foundations or built into the structures themselves, to be read by the gods or by future monarchs who would expose them during reconstruction projects. Other inscriptions, however, were dedicatory and were meant only for divine inspection.

The original context and function of Urukagina's reform texts are not known. They were not excavated but acquired by purchase, and thus they have no precise context (though it is most reasonable to assume that they were from Girsu). Thus, it is impossible to discern the immediate audience for the texts. The issue is made more complex by the fact that each edition of the Reform Edict seems to have been written for a different purpose.

Impact

Although previous Lagashite kings (such as Entemena) refer to edicts against social inequality and governmental abuse, the reforms of Urukagina represent the earliest known systematic treatment of legal and social reform in world history. Although they do not employ the "if … , then …" clauses of later monumental inscriptions, the reform texts are clearly antecedents to later Mesopotamian and other ancient Near Eastern legal texts, including the Ur-Nammu Code (ca. 2110 BCE), the Code of Hammurabi (ca. 1792 BCE), and the Middle Assyrian Laws (ca. 1100 BCE). Moreover, many royal hymns of Ur-Nammu, Shulgi (ca. 2095–2047 BCE), and Hammurabi, as well as later royal inscriptions of the Assyrian kings Sargon II (ca. 721–705 BCE) and Ashurbanipal (ca. 668–627 BCE) and the Persian Darius I (ca. 521–486 BCE) reflect a concern for social and legal reform. In addition, the Mosaic laws (ca. 1300 BCE), especially in Exodus 22:20–36,

"Now, since time immemorial, since the seed [of life] came forth—In those days [before me], the head boatman appropriated boats, the livestock official appropriated asses, the livestock manager appropriated sheep, the fisheries inspector appropriated taxes, and the lustration priests measured out grain taxes [as payment] at [the town of] AMBAR."

(Column iii)

"When the god Ninğirsu, warrior of the god Enlil, granted the kingship of Lagaš to URU-KA-gina, selecting him from among the myriad people, he restored the customs of former times, carrying out the command that the god Ninğirsu, his master, had given him."

(Columns vii–viii)

"URU-KA-gina made a binding oral agreement with the god Ninğirsu that he would never subjugate the orphan [or] widow to the powerful."

(Column xii)

"As for women of former times—a man [could] take two of them; but for women of today—indemnity payments [for debts?] have been removed [and the practice has been abolished]."

(Version 3, Column iii)

exhibit a similar concern for social reforms, with additional inclusions concerning the "stranger," or non-Israelite.

A major theme in Urukagina's Reform Edict is that of general amnesty. In fact, the amnesty promulgations listed in the reforms are the earliest on record in history. In particular, pardons were given to a variety of criminals, debtors, thieves, and murderers. Even if Urukagina was simply providing legal and social rhetoric, the possibility of amnesty for criminals is unprecedented in Mesopotamian legal texts. At any rate, the Urukagina reforms, contrary to the view of some scholars, are surely not evidence of a dramatic "democratic" revolution but were instead well-placed promulgations that allowed the crown to have greater control over its populace. Toward this end, somewhat ironically, the reforms clearly gave the temple administrators significant power that had been in the hands of the state. This particular issue clouds historians' understanding of Urukagina's true motives for his Reform Edict. He was perhaps

more connected to the religious establishment than to the previous monarchy, but this is speculation.

Further Reading

■ **Articles**

Foster, Benjamin. "A New Look at the Sumerian Temple Estate." *Journal of the Economic and Social History of the Orient* 24 (1981): 225–241.

■ **Books**

Cooper, Jerrold, S. *Reconstructing History from Ancient Inscriptions: The Lagash-Umma Border Conflict.* Malibu, Calif.: Undena, 1983.

———. *Sumerian and Akkadian Royal Inscriptions.* Vol. 1: *Presargonic Inscriptions.* New Haven, Conn.: American Oriental Society, 1986.

Frayne, Douglas R. *The Royal Inscriptions of Mesopotamia.* Vol. 1: *Presargonic Period, 2700–2350 BC.* Toronto: University of Toronto Press, 2008.

Kramer, Samuel N. *The Sumerians: Their History, Culture, and Character.* Chicago: University of Chicago Press, 1963.

Kuhrt, Amélie. *The Ancient Near East.* 2 vols. London: Routledge, 1995.

Magid, Glenn. "Sumerian Early Dynastic Royal Inscriptions." In *The Ancient Near East: Historical Sources in Translation,* ed. Mark W. Chavalas. Oxford, U.K.: Blackwell, 2006.

Oppenheim, A. Leo. *Ancient Mesopotamia: Portrait of a Dead Civilization.* 2nd ed. Chicago: University of Chicago Press, 1977.

Roth, Martha. *Law Collections from Mesopotamia and Asia Minor.* 2nd ed. Atlanta: Scholars Press, 1997.

Van de Mieroop, Marc. *A History of the Ancient Near East, ca. 3000–323 b.c.* 2nd ed. Oxford, U.K.: Blackwell, 2006.

———. "Women in the Economy of Sumer." In *Women's Earliest Records: From Ancient Egypt and Western Asia,* ed. Barbara S. Lesko. Atlanta: Scholars Press, 1989.

Wilcke, Claus. "Early Dynastic and Sargonic Periods." In *A History of Ancient Near Eastern Law,* vol. 1, ed. Raymond Westbrook. Leiden, Netherlands: Brill, 2003.

—Mark Chavalas

Questions for Further Study

1. The texts discovered in the vicinity of Lagash seem to place emphasis on buildings that were constructed in the name of deities. Why do you think concern with buildings and architecture was so pronounced at this time and in this place?

2. What role did religious belief appear to play in the political and economic affairs of Lagash?

3. Compare the Reform Edict of Urukagina with the New Year's Day Taika Reform Edict in seventh-century Japan. Do you see any similarities or pronounced differences between the nature of the reforms enacted and the reasons for enacting them? Explain.

4. Compare the Reform Edict of Urukagina with the medieval English Domesday Book. To what extent were governmental concerns the same or different in medieval England and ancient Mesopotamia?

5. To what extent can the Reform Edict of Urukagina be regarded as a "milestone" document? Why is it important? What place does it occupy in the development of social institutions in the ancient world?

REFORM EDICT OF URUKAGINA

1

i 1–2) For the god Ninĝirsu, warrior of the god Enlil,

i 3–5) URU-KA-gina, king of Lagaš,

i 6–7) built the "palace" of [the city of] Tiraš,

i 8–9) built the Antasur ["Northern(?) Boundary"],

i 10–ii 3) built the temple of the goddess Baba and built a pantry[?] for her, her building of regular provisions,

ii 4–6) and built her sheep-plucking shed in the holy precinct for her.

ii 7–13) For the goddess Nanše, he dug the Nimin-DU canal, her beloved canal, and extended its outlet to the sea.

ii 14–iii 1) He built the wall of Ĝirsu for him [the god Ninĝirsu].

iii 2–3) Now, since time immemorial, since the seed [of life] came forth—

iii 4–6) In those days [before me], the head boatman appropriated boats,

iii 7–8) the livestock official appropriated asses,

iii 9–10) the livestock manager appropriated sheep,

iii 11–13) the fisheries inspector appropriated taxes,

iii 14–17) and the lustration priests measured out grain taxes [as payment] at [the town of] AMBAR.

iii 18–iv 1) The shepherds of wool-bearing sheep paid [a tax] in silver instead of [the correct practice of giving] a white sheep,

iv 2–8) and the surveyor, chief lamentation singer, supervisor, brewer, and foremen paid [a tax] in silver instead of [the correct practice of giving] and offering lamb.

iv 9–18) The oxen of the gods [i.e., of the temples] ploughed the garlic plot of the ruler, and the best fields of the gods [i.e., of the temples] became the garlic and cucumber plots of the ruler.

iv 19–22) Teamed asses and unblemished oxen were yoked for the temple administrators,

v 1–3) and the grain of the temple administrators was divided up by the [work/military] crews of the ruler.

v 4–21) The temple administrators took [the following items as payments] instead of corvée duty:

[woolen garments of the type] "Ear of the Mongoose," U.AŠ, and ŠU.GABA.UR, an outer woolen garment, a … linen draping, naked flax, flax tied in bundles, a bronze helmet, a bronze arrow[?], a bronze throw-stick/bow[?], burnished leather, wing[-feathers] of a yellow raven, shoots [for] … and a goat with its full fleece.

v 22–vi 3) The … temple administrators ripped out the orchards of the poor and tied up [the fruit] in bundles.

vi 4–12) When a corpse was brought to the grave, the undertaker took his seven jugs of beer, his 420 loaves of bread, 2 *gur* of *hazi*-grain, one woolen garment, one lead goat, and one bed.

vi 13–14) The wailing women took one *ul* of barley.

vi 15–16) When a man was brought [for burial] at the "reeds of Enki,"

vi 17–24) the undertaker took his seven jugs of beer, his 420 loaves of bread, 2 *ul* of barley, one woolen garment, one bed, and one chair.

vi 25–27) The old wailing women took one *gur* of barley.

vi 28–vii l) The craftsmen [took] the bread for the *šuila* rite,

vii 2–4) and the two "young men" received the safe passage toll for the "great gate" [to the world beyond].

vii 5–11) The estate and fields of the ruler, the estate and fields of the "Lady" [the "Woman," i.e., the ruler's wife] and the estate and fields of the "Organization of the Children" [i.e., the ruler's children] were consolidated[?].

vii 12–16) Bailiffs [of the court] held jurisdiction from the boundary of the god Ninĝirsu to the sea.

vii 17–19) When a subordinate to the king would build a well on the narrow edge of his field.

vii 20–21) the blind workers were appropriated [for the work],

vii 22–25) and the blind workers were also appropriated for [work on] the irrigation canals which were in the field.

vii 26–28) These were the proprietary rights of former days.

vii 29–30) When the god Ninĝirsu, warrior of the god Enlil,

viii 1–4) granted the kingship of Lagaš to URU-KA-gina,

viii 5–6) selecting him from among the myriad people,

viii 7–13) he restored the customs of former times, carrying out the command that the god Ninĝirsu, his master, had given him.

viii 14–16) He removed the head boatman from [control over] the boats,

viii 17–20) he removed the livestock official from [control over] asses and sheep,

viii 21–23) he removed the fisheries inspector from [control over] taxes,

viii 24–27) he removed the silo supervisor from [control over] the grain taxes of the lustration priests,

viii 28–ix 1) he removed the [court bailiff responsible] for the paying [of duties] in silver instead of white sheep and young lambs,

ix 2–6) and he removed the [responsibility] for the delivery of duties by the temple administrators to the palace.

ix 7–11) He installed Ninĝirsu as proprietor over the ruler's estate and the king's fields;

ix 12–16) he installed Baba as proprietor of the estate of the women's organization and the fields of the women's establishment;

ix 17–21) and he installed Šulšagana as proprietor of the children's estate.

ix 22–25) From the boundary of the god Ninĝirsu to the sea bailiffs ceased operations.

ix 26–32) When a corpse is brought for burial, the undertaker takes his 3 jugs of beer, his 80 loaves of bread, one bed, and one "leading goat,"

ix 33–34) and the wailing women takes 3 *ban* of barley.

ix 35–x 1) When a man is brought for the "reed of Enki,"

x 2–6) then the undertaker takes his 4 jugs of beer, his 420 loaves of bread, and one *gur* of barley;

x 7–9) the wailing women take 3 *ban* of barley,

x 10–13) and the *ereš-diĝir*-priestess takes one lady's cloth headdress, and one *sila* of aromatic oil.

x 14–15) 420 loaves of dry bread are the bread duty,

x 16–17) 40 loaves of hot bread are for the meal,

x 18–19) and 10 loaves of hot bread are for the table bread;

x 20) 5 loaves of bread are for the *lu-ziga* attendants,

x 21–23) 2 *mud* vessels and 1 *sadug* vessel of beer are for the lamentation singers of Ĝirsu;

x 24–27) 490 loaves of bread, 2 *mud* vessels, and one *sadug* vessel of beer are for the lamentation singers of Lagaš;

x 28–30) 406 loaves of bread, one *mud* vessel, and one *sadug* vessel of beer are for the [other] lamentation singers;

x 31–33) 250 loaves of bread and one *mud* vessel of beer are for the old wailing women;

x 34–37) 180 loaves of bread and one *mud* vessel of beer are for the old women of Niĝin.

x 38–xi 6) For the blind ones who wait anxiously—one loaf is their evening bread, five loaves are their bread for the middle of the night, one loaf is their bread for dawn, and six loaves are their bread for mid-day.

xi 7–10) 60 loaves, one *mud* vessel of beer, and 3 *bar* of barley are for those who perform the role of *saĝbur*.

xi 11–13) He removed the safe passage toll of the great gate for the pair or workers,

xi 14–16) and lifted the [payment] of *šuila* bread for the craftsmen.

xi 17–19) The administrators no longer plunder the orchards of the poor.

xi 20–24) When a fine ass is born to a *šub-lugal*, and his foreman says to him, "I want to buy [it] from you";

xi 25–28) whether he lets him buy it from him and says to him, "Pay me the price I want!"

xi 29–31) or whether he does not let him buy [it] from him, the foreman must not strike at him in anger.

xi 32–34) When the house of a *šub-lugal* adjoins the house of a *šub-lugal*,

xi 35–37) and this … says to him, "I want to buy it from you,"

xi 38–xii 6) whether he lets him buy it from him, having said to him, "Pay me the price I want! My house is a large chest—fill it with barley for me!"

xii 7) Whether he does not let him buy it from him,

xii 8–11) that … must not strike the *šub-lugal* in anger.

xii 12) [These things] he proclaimed.

xii 13–22) As for the citizens of Lagaš—the one living in debt, the one who had set up [a false] *gur* measure, the one who had [fraudulently] filled up the [legal] *gur* measure with barley, the thief, the murderer—he swept the prison clear [of them] and established their freedom.

xii 23–28) URU-KA-gina made a binding oral agreement with the god Ninĝirsu that he would never subjugate the orphan [or] widow to the powerful.

xii 29–38) In that year URU-KA-gina dug for the god Ninğirsu the "Little Canal which belongs to Ğirsu," and restored its former name, calling it "The God Ninğirsu Received [His] Authority from Nippur."

xii 39–44) He extended it to the Nimin-DU, a canal. The canal is pure, its flood is bright—may it [ever] bring flowing water to the goddess Nanše!...

3 _____

... iii 14–19) If a female speaks to a male [in a way] exceeding her rank [or position in society] one covers the mouth of that women with a baked clay "brick"[?], and that baked brick is hung [in display] at the city gate.

iii 20'–24') As for women of former times—a man [could] take two of them; but for women of today—indemnity payments [for debts?] have been removed [and the practice has been abolished].

Glossary

ban	a measure of capacity or volume
corvée	unpaid labor exacted by the government or a lord
ereš-dī̃gir-priestess	a type of priestess probably connected to the royal family
gur	a large unit of dry measure
hazi-grain	an unknown, unspecified type of grain
lustration	purification
lu-ziga attendants	lamentation singers connected to burials
mud vessel	vessel that holds liquid of an unknown amount
sadug vessel	vessel that holds liquid of an unknown amount
sila	a unit of dry measure
šuila rite	thought to have been a funerary rite
sağbur	a role associated with the lamentation singers, but the particular function is not known
šub-lugal	subordinates to the king, a lower class than the aristocrats but higher than slaves and debtors
ul	a measure of capacity

CODE OF HAMMURABI

" Let any wronged man who has a lawsuit

come before the statue of me, the king of justice. "

Overview

The Code of Hammurabi was written around 1752 BCE in Babylonia—modern-day Iraq—by King Hammurabi of the First Dynasty of Babylon and was carved into a monumental stone stela. At that point in time, Hammurabi had just finished conquering several powerful states to establish his own kingdom as the preeminent power in the ancient Near East. Hammurabi was in the process of solidifying his kingdom, a course of action that depended on his fulfilling the role of a good Mesopotamian king by worshipping the gods, providing for his people, and creating a peaceful, just society in all of his cities.

Hammurabi wrote his law code in order to achieve these goals. The monumental stela bears an image and three sections of text: prologue, laws, and epilogue. In the image, prologue, and epilogue, the primary focus is on establishing Hammurabi as a good, just, and divinely sanctioned king. In the law section, Hammurabi demonstrates his judicial wisdom, given by the sun god Shamash, through 282 prescriptive legal scenarios. These laws combine traditional Babylonian laws of monetary compensation with Amorite tribal *talion* law—which is based on retribution, as in the maxim "an eye for an eye"—and a strong concern for the rights of the oppressed and marginalized. It is the longest, most organized, and most famous law code of the ancient Near East.

Context

Prior to Hammurabi's reign, Babylonia—then known as "Sumer and Akkad"—was in prolonged political turmoil. Many city-states were ruled by kings of Amorite descent (their origins being land west of Sumer and Akkad) who had seized power from native Sumerians and Akkadians during the political upheaval. Isin and Larsa were two of the most powerful cities. Each was able to build a small kingdom, yet neither ever controlled all the cities of Sumer and Akkad. Babylon, which before this period had been an unimportant town, was one of the cities that proved able to

maintain its autonomy. The First Dynasty of Babylon began in 1894 BCE (dated according to the Middle Chronology used by most historians studying ancient Babylonia) with the reign of its first king, an Amorite named Sumu-abum. By the time Larsa conquered Isin one hundred years later, the kingdom of Babylon controlled much of northern Babylonia—including the cities of Sippar, Kish, and Borsippa—and rivaled Larsa in size.

Hammurabi succeeded his father, Sinmuballit, to the throne of Babylon in 1792 BCE, becoming the sixth king of the First Dynasty of Babylon. After inheriting this small but powerful kingdom, Hammurabi began the work of fortifying his territory and establishing his kingship. He fulfilled the roles required of a good king in Mesopotamian tradition by providing for the gods and temples in all of the cities he controlled. Additionally, he fulfilled the royal role of good "shepherd" for his people by fortifying city walls to protect the inhabitants and building new irrigation canals, which were needed for productive farming across his kingdom.

Hammurabi also sought to expand his territory by conquest. However, in doing so, he quickly came into disputes with powerful states outside Babylonia: the kingdoms of Upper Mesopotamia (with major cities at Shubat-Enlil and Mari) and Elam (in Iran). Instead of fighting these kingdoms, Hammurabi opted for a diplomatic strategy, contracting an alliance with King Shamshi-Adad of the Upper Mesopotamian kingdom in 1783 BCE. Similar alliances were forged with Elam, but these proved short-lived, as the Elamite king became interested in adding Babylon to his own territory. In 1765 BCE, Elam attacked a town on the border of the kingdom of Babylon. Hammurabi, with the help of Zimri-Lim, the new king of a now-independent kingdom of Mari, fought and defeated Elam the next year, in 1764 BCE. This major victory effectively forced Elam to withdraw from Babylonia. While Hammurabi did not win any territory in these battles, the battles ensured that the kingdom of Babylon was to be taken seriously as a dominant political power in the region.

In the wake of this success, Hammurabi began to expand his kingdom on an unprecedented scale. A year later, in 1763 BCE, Hammurabi, with the aid of the kingdoms of Eshnunna and Mari, invaded and conquered the southern Babylonian city-state of Larsa and all of its large

1894 BCE
- Sumu-abum, the first king of the First Dynasty of Babylon, begins his reign.

1792 BCE
- Hammurabi succeeds his father, Sinmuballit, to the throne as the sixth king of the First Dynasty of Babylon, marking the beginning of what scholars consider the Old Babylonian period.

1764 BCE
- Hammurabi, with the aid of the kingdom of Mari, defeats Elam and expels Elamite control and influence from the region.

1763 BCE
- With the aid of Mari and Eshnunna, Hammurabi conquers the southern Babylonian city-state of Larsa.

1762 BCE
- Hammurabi conquers Eshnunna.

1761 BCE
- Hammurabi conquers Mari, and the kingdom of Babylon becomes the greatest political entity in the ancient Near East.

territory. After this conquest, Babylon controlled a unified southern Babylonia. Hammurabi then turned his attention to the north of Babylonia, where his former allies in the two large kingdoms of Eshnunna and Mari were beginning to grow wary of his increasing power. Hammurabi first battled against Eshnunna, the nearer of these two kingdoms, inflicting defeat in 1762 BCE. He continued this campaign up into northern Mesopotamia and captured the minor kingdoms of Subartu, whose kings were then forced to submit to his rule. This action left the kingdom of Mari as Hammurabi's only major rival for control and power over Mesopotamia. Hammurabi turned immediately to a campaign against Mari, and he defeated King Zimri-Lim in 1761 BCE. With this conquest complete, Hammurabi now controlled all of Babylonia, as well as much of the territory around it and upriver on the Euphrates. He had built the kingdom of Babylon into the largest and most powerful political entity of its time.

With this enormous series of military campaigns behind him, Hammurabi turned his attention back to the duties of being a good Mesopotamian king, which had occupied him throughout the beginning years of his reign. However, now that he was in control of a vast and, as yet, divided kingdom, Hammurabi needed to be a good king in the eyes of disparate groups of people who were not necessarily inclined to be peaceful and obedient toward him. Hammurabi thus devoted himself carefully to fulfilling his kingly roles—maintaining the temples, furnishing the gods with offerings, and shepherding his people by providing for their sustenance and security—in the cities across his large kingdom. Hammurabi was an able administrator who usually attended to small details himself, and his meticulous attention to his kingdom's cities, temples, and people helped improve his popularity and more firmly established his right to rule. As a major part of this project to create a stable, peaceable kingdom out of the many distinct regions he had conquered, Hammurabi commissioned the carving of a monumental stela bearing his law code. It is likely that many such stelae were carved in similar or identical form and set up in the cities around Babylonia between 1752 and 1750 BCE, at the end of Hammurabi's reign. The Code of Hammurabi known to modern historians comes from a stela presumed to have been erected in the city of Sippar—the only one of these stelae that has survived intact.

About the Author

Very few details about Hammurabi's early life are known to historians, owing to the lack of interest in this kind of record keeping on the part of ancient scribes. Since Hammurabi enjoyed a reign of forty-three years, it is likely that he came to the throne as a young man, but not so young as to require a regent to rule in his place. If we suggest that he came to the throne at the approximate age of twenty, Hammurabi would have been born in about 1812 BCE. He was almost certainly born in Babylon, the city his father ruled, although this information is also not recorded. No details about Hammurabi's life are known for certain until his accession to kingship over Babylon in 1792 BCE. Hammurabi composed his law code and commissioned the carving of the stela that bore the inscription around 1752–1750 BCE, late in his reign. Just a few years later, Hammurabi became so seriously ill that his son, Samsuiluna, was forced to take over his father's royal duties. The people of Babylonia reacted by dedicating prayers and offerings in the temples for Hammurabi's recovery, but these measures failed. Hammurabi died in 1750 BCE.

In both ancient and modern times, King Hammurabi of Babylon is credited with the writing of his own law code. He certainly commissioned the monument, and it was erected on his authority. In the text, Hammurabi "speaks" directly to his audience through the use of first-person statements. However, the Mesopotamian idea of authorship was different from modern notions: The important person who spoke the words of a document—or even just gave the order for it to be written—was considered the text's author, not the scribe who wrote the text. Thus, historians have no way of knowing whether Hammurabi actually composed the words of his text, though the final words used would have been subject to his royal approval.

Explanation and Analysis of the Document

The Code of Hammurabi is inscribed on a diorite stela seven and a half feet tall. Diorite is a very hard, lustrous black stone that was a highly desirable material for the production of permanent, unalterable, and impressive royal monuments in ancient Mesopotamia. This diorite stela was left in an irregular, natural shape, with a flat front, uneven top profile, and rounded back. Both sides were carved, with image and text, almost in their entirety.

The text on the monument was written in Akkadian, a Babylonian-based Semitic language that was commonly spoken throughout Mesopotamia in the Old Babylonian period. Cuneiform ("wedge-shaped") script was used to write Akkadian. On this stela, the cuneiform text was carved in a vertical orientation, as had been used to write Sumerian and early Akkadian documents. The vertical script orientation seems to have been going out of use in the Old Babylonian period, in favor of the horizontal orientation that became ubiquitous in the later Kassite period. But during the Old Babylonian period, the vertical script was retained for writing monumental texts, probably in order to create a visual connection with earlier Babylonian stelae and statues still on public display. By combining this archaic script orientation and the classic literary-prose style of the prologue and epilogue text with the contemporary style used to write the laws themselves, Hammurabi conveyed the historical legitimacy of his document while preserving the accessibility of its meaning.

◆ **Image**

At the top of the monument on the front side, an engraved relief covers almost one-third of the stela's face.

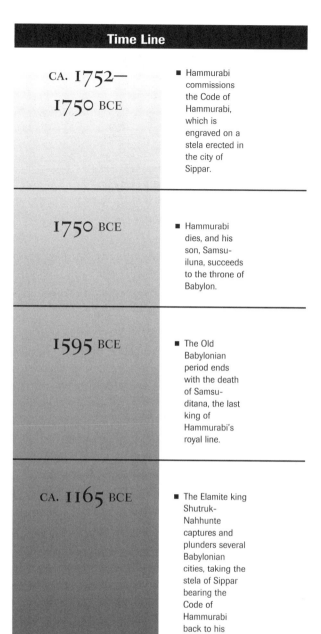

Time Line

CA. **1752–1750** BCE	■ Hammurabi commissions the Code of Hammurabi, which is engraved on a stela erected in the city of Sippar.
1750 BCE	■ Hammurabi dies, and his son, Samsu-iluna, succeeds to the throne of Babylon.
1595 BCE	■ The Old Babylonian period ends with the death of Samsu-ditana, the last king of Hammurabi's royal line.
CA. **1165** BCE	■ The Elamite king Shutruk-Nahhunte captures and plunders several Babylonian cities, taking the stela of Sippar bearing the Code of Hammurabi back to his capital at Susa.

This engraved image shows Hammurabi standing before the god Shamash, who is seated on his throne, wearing the divine horned headdress, with the rays of the sun rising from his shoulders. Shamash was the god of justice and of the sun. In his hand, Shamash holds the "rod and ring"—traditional symbols of Mesopotamian kingship—which he offers to Hammurabi. The king holds his right hand in front of his mouth, which was a gesture of respect traditionally offered before a god. Hammurabi wears the thickly banded headdress typical of Mesopotamian rulers during the period of 2100–1700 BCE. Neither of the two figures is labeled, so it is based upon their visual attributes and the context of the text inscription that their identities are understood.

In this image Shamash is acting as a representative of all the gods, on whose behalf he bestows kingship upon

Code of laws of the Babylonian king, Hammurabi
(© Bettmann/CORBIS)

Hammurabi. While Hammurabi was already well established as king of Babylon by the time this monument was carved, the image of divinely given kingship was important in justifying his rule over all his vast and diverse territory. The choice of Shamash as the gods' representative also would have provided religious legitimacy and a sense of justice to the royal authority Hammurabi used to proclaim and enforce his laws. These themes of divine legitimacy, for both Hammurabi's kingship and his lawmaking abilities, are continued and reinforced in the text of the prologue.

◆ **Prologue**

The prologue of the Code of Hammurabi does not function, in the modern sense, as an introduction to or explanation of the laws. Rather, the text of the prologue is designed to glorify Hammurabi, giving importance and authority to his laws. This praise takes three forms, all of which were common on Mesopotamian royal monuments: explaining how the gods chose Hammurabi to rule, describing his admirable personal qualities, and demonstrating how he completely fulfilled his role as an ideal Mesopotamian king. This latter point is illustrated through the use of detailed examples, in which Hammurabi is described as piously restoring specific temples, venerating all the gods of the Mesopotamian pantheon individually, and providing

for various named cities. All the cities and temples mentioned in this long list were under Hammurabi's territorial control. Included with each mention of a city or temple is a corresponding description of the king's relationship with the individual city god—relationships described in such terms as the god's hearing Hammurabi's prayers, the god's considering him "beloved" or "favored," or the god's finding his offerings to be "bountiful" or "pleasing." As with the stela's image, the overall effect of this list is to give the impression that harmonious and beneficial relationships existed between the king and all of the gods. Such relationships gave Hammurabi divine legitimacy for his kingship, for his power over vast territories, and for his law code.

Hammurabi makes this divine sanction for his law code more explicit when he emphasizes his special connection with the god Shamash. In the prologue, he compares himself and his role to that of Shamash: He is "to rise like the sun-god Shamash over all humankind, to illuminate the land." In the epilogue, in turn, Hammurabi claims that Shamash has given him judicial wisdom: "I am Hammurabi, king of justice, to whom the god Shamash has granted (insight into) the truth." All of these concepts were interrelated in the Babylonian idea of justice, whereby it was believed that if all facts could be brought into the light of the sun and fully seen, then the truth of a case would become obvious, and justice could be done. By saying that Shamash has given him the vision and light required to see that justice is served, Hammurabi provides the ultimate divine authority for his law code.

◆ **Laws**

The Code of Hammurabi consists of 282 known laws. Because of gaps in the text caused by later damage to the stela done by the Elamite king Shutruk-Nahhunte, it is unclear how many laws the stela originally included; there may have been as many as three hundred. On the stela, the laws are organized roughly into thematic groups, but the themes are not marked or formally divided, nor are the laws numbered. The laws are also not comprehensive: Many possible crimes (and even categories of crimes or disputes) are left undiscussed, even though very specific and elaborate descriptions of other crime scenarios are included.

This apparent disorganization exists because Hammurabi's laws do not operate as generalizable rules of behavior, in which statements such as "you will not do this" or "this is illegal" are used. Rather, Hammurabi's laws are prescriptive, with statements formulated as: "If a person does X, then Y will result." In prescriptive law statements, the results of specific cases do not determine or extrapolate to more general rules. Thus, Hammurabi's laws were never meant to cover every eventuality. Historians cannot, therefore, assume that just because certain actions are not discussed, they were legal; indeed, records of actual law cases from the era show evidence that other laws or legal precedents were used. It is possible that the particular laws listed in the Code of Hammurabi were only the laws that the king wanted to make a particular point of decreeing with his royal authority equally across the whole kingdom. It is also possible that this law code was simply an impressive collection or sample of difficult cases that Hammurabi had personally judged, which he then selected to validate his claim, before both the gods and his subjects, that he was a king of justice.

Crimes in the Code of Hammurabi were generally punished according to a form of law known as *talion* law. *Talion* law, also known as the judicial system of retaliation ("an eye for an eye"), operates on the principle that a punishment or penalty should be in similar kind and equal severity to the original crime. This type of law was generally applied in the seminomadic and pastoral societies that lived west of Babylonia and was probably included in the Code of Hammurabi because of the king's Amorite heritage. In the code, offenses among individuals of the same social class—*awīlum* (free people, including most craftsmen and laborers), *mushkenum* (commoners or dependents), and *wardum* (slaves)—were generally governed by talion laws. However, throughout his laws, Hammurabi emphasizes the state's right—and not the right of the victim or the victim's family—to judge the case and inflict the required punishment. Thus the government, under the rule of the king, claimed control and authority over all forms of justice, even those that had previously been the domain of the family.

The Code of Hammurabi prescribes *talion* punishments only to a certain extent. Punishments stronger than those usually used in talion law were also given out, particularly for liars and thieves, as well as for any low-status person who committed a crime against a person of higher rank. Liars were probably singled out for harsh punishment (usually death) owing to their active role in obscuring facts, which hindered the divinely mandated practice of seeking justice through the illumination of truth and subverted Hammurabi's royal power to oversee his kingdom. The Code of Hammurabi was also influenced by the earlier laws of Babylonian society, in which payments to the victim or victim's family were standard punishments. These types of monetary punishments were preserved in Hammurabi's law code, particularly for offenses perpetrated by high-status individuals against persons of lesser rank.

In addition to setting forth laws concerning violent criminal cases, theft, and lying, Hammurabi's code also deals in great detail with issues of land use, inheritance, adoption, slave ownership, merchant and contractor liabilities, establishing prices, loans and debts, divorce, and property disputes. These civil laws are not divided out from the criminal laws in the Code of Hammurabi, and many such civil cases have punishments equal to those stipulated for crimes where loss of person, property, or health resulted. The severe punishments meted out in some of these cases—particularly for fraud or misuse of property—supported Hammurabi's stated goals of protecting the weak from the powerful. While adult male property holders of the *awīlu* class clearly had greater rights than others, their rights were not unlimited, and persons of lesser status could have recourse against their actions. This is particularly well illustrated in some of the laws concerning women and children: Divorced or sick wives could not be abandoned without monetary compensation, adulterous hus-

Terra-cotta plaque (of the Old Babylonian period) of a bull-man, an attendant of the sun god Shamash (© The Trustees of the British Museum)

bands were held to account, and children could not be disinherited without good cause.

Hammurabi's lengthy focus on the issues of land, economy, and contracts also demonstrates that he was fulfilling the traditional Mesopotamian royal role of being a good shepherd to his people. As a shepherd of humankind, Hammurabi's duty before the gods was to establish peace throughout the land. Peaceful communities depend not only on the absence of violent crime but also on a stable, reliable economic structure; trust in contractual relationships; and defined methods of conflict resolution—all of which Hammurabi provided through his law code. In his role as good shepherd, he was also expected to provide the necessities of life for his people. This explains the importance of land, farm animals, and mercantile activity in the laws. By legislating the fair and continuous use of resources, Hammurabi was taking an active hand in ensuring that produce yields would be high and prosperity would ensue.

◆ **Epilogue**

In the epilogue, Hammurabi describes the purpose and function of his monument: It was set up "in order to render the judgments of the land, to give the verdicts of the land,

and to provide just ways for the wronged." This is the first indication in the entire text of how the monument should be used, which is further elucidated a few lines later, when Hammurabi encourages "any wronged man who has a lawsuit [to] come before the statue of me, the king of justice, and let him have my inscribed stela read aloud to him, thus may he hear my precious pronouncements and let my stela reveal the lawsuit for him." This passage is remarkable not only because it is one of the very rare instances in which a Mesopotamian monument describes its own social function, but also because of its focus on helping the weak, oppressed, or wronged man. It was a traditional duty of Mesopotamian kings to provide justice, but this focus on justice specifically for the oppressed is undocumented in earlier Babylonian history. By virtue of Hammurabi's precedent, providing justice for the oppressed became a feature in later ancient Near Eastern law codes as well.

The majority of the epilogue is concerned with future rulers who would see the monument. Hammurabi sets himself up as an example for these future kings, who he believes should recognize and praise his wisdom. However, Hammurabi realized that future rulers were likely to destroy or remove his monument (as the Elamite king Shutruk-Nahhunte eventually did), and so he spends the rest of the epilogue exhorting elaborate curses from the gods on anyone who would alter, displace, or destroy his stela. The use of such curses was common practice on Mesopotamian monuments as a way for kings to ensure the permanence of their stelae, the perpetual fame of their names, and the immortality of their accomplishments.

Audience

The primary audience for the Code of Hammurabi would have been the gods and the local elite people of the city in which the stela bearing the code was erected. Although historians do not know for certain the original location of the law code stela, it was intended for display and would have been erected in a prominent place; the most likely such place was in front of the Ebabbar Temple of Shamash in Sippar. Thus, the primary audience would have been the priests and elites of the city of Sippar (all of whom had full access to the temple and could read the text written on the stela) as well as the Babylonian gods (who were thought of as omnipresent in their temples). For this audience, the stela would have functioned to display Hammurabi's judicial wisdom, confirm his close personal relationship with the local patron god, and demonstrate that he was a pious and faithful king.

Nonelite people would have also been a major audience for the Code of Hammurabi. The text itself declares that its purpose was to be read aloud to the people, particularly the unfortunate people who were downtrodden and in need of justice. In making his text accessible to the common people, most of whom were illiterate, Hammurabi attempted to legitimize himself in their eyes and gain their support. In so doing, he also took some political power away from the temples and local rulers who had previously provided law and order in their cities. By destabilizing the popular support for these local power structures, Hammurabi could more effectively establish and govern his central royal administration.

Hammurabi explicitly mentions a third major audience—future kings—in the epilogue, where he expresses his desire that later rulers will read his laws and emulate his judicial wisdom in creating their own law codes. Hammurabi probably intended that this future royal audience would foremost comprise his dynastic successors to the throne of Babylon, who continued to rule his kingdom for centuries and who probably did read his law code. The future royal audience for the Code of Hammurabi also included the many additional Babylonian kings who reigned after the end of Hammurabi's dynasty, as well as the Elamite king Shutruk-Nahhunte, who captured the Code of Hammurabi in 1165 BCE.

Impact

The Code of Hammurabi had its intended impact: The kingdom was consolidated and secured, Hammurabi's rule was seen as legitimate, and his royal line was able to rule successfully over most of his kingdom for a further 155 years. The lawmaking impact of the code, however, was not so straightforward. Most actual recorded legal cases from the Old Babylonian period do not follow Hammurabi's system of justice and punishments, and the prices set for goods in his laws were never instituted. Scholars still debate why such discrepancies existed between the Code of Hammurabi and actual Old Babylonian legal practice.

Hammurabi's laws did, however, influence Babylonian legal scholarship. The laws were distributed throughout the kingdom on clay tablets, dozens of which have been recovered from excavations around Babylonia. Extracts and commentaries on the laws have also been found, some of which are roughly contemporary with the erection of the stela, and some of which date to much later periods. The existence of these secondary, analytical documents indicates that the Code of Hammurabi, for all its propagandistic functions, made a considerable and long-lasting impact on legal and scholarly thinking across Babylonia. This influence can be seen in Mesopotamian history, as later kings utilized the Code of Hammurabi as the foundational document of their own law codes.

The effect of the Code of Hammurabi on greater civilization has been substantial. Ever since the monument was unearthed during the French excavations of Susa in 1901–1902 and deciphered by Assyriologists, the code has held a prominent place in both the scholarly conception and popular imagination of ancient Babylon. It is now known that Hammurabi's was not the first law code to be established; the oldest surviving law code is that of King Shulgi of the Third Dynasty of Ur (ca. 2074 BCE), and even that law code was preceded by judicial proclamations and records of

"*The gods Anu and Enlil ... named me by my name: Hammurabi, the pious prince, who venerates the gods, to make justice prevail in the land, to abolish the wicked and the evil, to prevent the strong from oppressing the weak, to rise like the sun-god Shamash over all humankind, to illuminate the land.*"

(Prologue)

"*If a man accuses another man and charges him with homicide but cannot bring proof against him, his accuser shall be killed.*"

(Law 1)

"*If the owner of the lost property could not produce witnesses who can identify his lost property, he is a liar, he has indeed spread malicious charges, he shall be killed.*"

(Law 11)

"*If an awīlu should blind the eye of another awīlu, they shall blind his eye. If he should break the bone of another awīlu they shall break his bone. If he should blind the eye ... or break the bone of a commoner, he shall weigh and deliver 60 shekels of silver. If he should blind the eye ... or break the bone of an awīlu's slave, he shall weigh and deliver one-half of his value.*"

(Laws 196–199)

"*Let any wronged man who has a lawsuit come before the statue of me, the king of justice, and let him have my inscribed stela read aloud to him, thus may he hear my precious pronouncements and let my stela reveal the lawsuit for him.*"

(Epilogue)

court proceedings from earlier periods of Mesopotamian history. Scholars also no longer think that Hammurabi's laws were strictly meant to be followed but rather were intended to demonstrate his power, divine sanction, and role as king of justice. However, none of these subsequent finds have lessened the Code of Hammurabi's impact over the centuries. Hammurabi is still the author of the longest and most organized of the law codes from the ancient Near East, in which he created order for a vast society and, perhaps most significantly, provided help and justice for the oppressed, the lower classes, women, and children. Because of his groundbreaking law code, Hammurabi's fame continued throughout Mesopotamian history. Now, as a result of its rediscovery, he is famous in modern culture as well.

Further Reading

■ Articles

Leemans, W. F. "Hammurabi's Babylon, Centre of Trade, Administration and Justice." *Sumer* 41, nos. 1–2 (1985): 91–96.

Roth, Martha T. "Mesopotamian Legal Traditions and the Laws of Hammurabi." *Chicago-Kent Law Review* 71, no. 1 (1995): 13–39.

Veenhof, K. R. "The Relation between Royal Decrees and 'Law Codes' of the Old Babylonian Period." *Jaarbericht Ex Oriente Lux* 35/36 (1997–2000): 49–83.

■ Books

Roth, Martha T. *Law Collections from Mesopotamia and Asia Minor*. Atlanta, Ga.: Scholars Press, 1997.

Schmandt-Besserat, Denise. *When Writing Met Art: From Symbol to Story*. Austin: University of Texas Press, 2007.

Van de Mieroop, Marc. *King Hammurabi of Babylon: A Biography*. Malden, Mass.: Blackwell Publishing, 2005.

■ Web Sites

"Babylonia: Country, Language, Religion, Culture." Livius "Articles on Ancient History" Web site.
  http://www.livius.org/ba-bd/babylon/babylonia.html.

—Stephanie M. Langin-Hooper

Questions for Further Study

1. If you are familiar with the Old Testament of the Bible, particularly what Jews refer to as the Torah, or the first five books of the Old Testament (sometimes called the Pentateuch), compare and contrast it with the Code of Hammurabi.

2. How does the Code of Hammurabi suggest an evolution from a pastoral, nomadic, and tribal community to a more settled, organized, agrarian community?

3. Compare and contrast Hammurabi's laws with some of the laws in effect in modern societies today. Are there any similarities, in, for example, laws governing inheritances or crime?

4. Why is the Code of Hammurabi considered a "milestone" document in the history of law and, indeed, of civilization itself? What, if anything, is unique about it?

5. Historians note that documents such as this often have the purpose of legitimizing a reign. In this regard, compare the Code of Hammurabi with another document, such as "Mandate of Heaven: The Numerous Officers" from China or Deeds of the Divine Augustus from ancient Rome. How do the two documents set about establishing the authority and legitimacy of the rulers?

CODE OF HAMMURABI

Prologue

... The gods Anu and Enlil ... named me by my name: Hammurabi, the pious prince, who venerates the gods, to make justice prevail in the land, to abolish the wicked and the evil, to prevent the strong from oppressing the weak, to rise like the sun-god Shamash over all humankind, to illuminate the land.

I am Hammurabi, the shepherd...

discerning king, obedient to the god Shamash, the mighty one, who establishes the foundations of the city of Sippar, who ... made famous the temple of Ebabbar which is akin to the abode of heaven;

the warrior, who shows mercy to the city of Larsa, who renews the Ebabbar temple for the god Shamash his ally;

the lord who revitalizes the city of Uruk, who provides abundant waters for its people, who raises high the summit of the Eanna temple, who heaps up bountiful produce for the gods Anu and Ishtar;

the protecting canopy of the land, who gathers together the scattered peoples of the city of Isin ...

the judicious one, the noble one, who allots pasturage and watering place for the cities of Lagash and Girsu, who provides plentiful food offerings for the Eninnu temple;

who seizes the enemies, beloved of (the goddess Ishtar) the able one ... who gladdens the heart of the goddess Ishtar;

the pure prince, whose prayers the god Adad acknowledges ...

wise one, the organizer, he who has mastered all wisdom, who shelters the people of the city of Malgium in the face of annihilation, who founds their settlements in abundance ...

leader of kings, who subdues the settlements along the Euphrates River by the oracular command of the god Dagan, his creator, who showed mercy to the people of the cities of Mari and Tuttul;

the pious prince ... who sustains his people in crisis, who secures their foundations in peace in the midst of the city of Babylon;

shepherd of the people, whose deeds are pleasing to the goddess Ishtar ...

who proclaims truth, who guides the population properly ...

who quells the rebellious ...

the pious one, who prays ceaselessly for the great gods ... mighty heir of Sin-muballit, eternal seed of royalty mighty king, solar disk of the city of Babylon, who spreads light over the lands of Sumer and Akkad, king who makes the four regions [north, south, east, west] obedient, favored of the goddess Ishtar, am I.

When the god Marduk commanded me to provide just ways for the people of the land (in order to attain) appropriate behavior, I established truth and justice as the declaration of the land, I enhanced the well-being of the people.

At that time:

Laws

1. If a man accuses another man and charges him with homicide but cannot bring proof against him, his accuser shall be killed....

3. If a man comes forward to give false testimony in a case but cannot bring evidence for his accusation, if that case involves a capital offense, that man shall be killed.

4. If he comes forward to give (false) testimony for (a case whose penalty is) grain or silver, he shall be assessed the penalty for that case.

5. If a judge renders a judgment, gives a verdict, or deposits a sealed opinion, after which he reverses his judgment ... they shall unseat him from his judgeship in the assembly, and he shall never again sit in judgment with the judges.

6. If a man steals valuables belonging to the god or to the palace, that man shall be killed, and also he who received the stolen goods from him shall he killed.

7. If a man should purchase silver, gold, a slave, a slave woman, an ox, a sheep, a donkey, or anything else whatsoever, from a son of a man or from a slave of a man without witnesses or a contract—or if he accepts the goods for safekeeping—that man is a thief, he shall be killed.

8. If a man steals an ox, a sheep, a donkey, a pig, or a boat—if it belongs either to the god or to the palace, he shall give thirtyfold: if it belongs to a commoner, he shall replace it tenfold; if the thief does not have anything to give, he shall be killed.

9. If a man who claims to have lost property then discovers his lost property in another man's possession … the judges shall examine their cases, and the witnesses in whose presence the purchase was made and the witnesses who can identify the lost property shall state the facts known to them before the god, then, it is the seller who is the thief, he shall be killed.…

11. If the owner of the lost property could not produce witnesses who can identify his lost property, he is a liar, he has indeed spread malicious charges, he shall be killed.…

14. If a man should kidnap the young child of another man, he shall be killed.

15. If a man should enable a palace slave, a palace slave woman, a commoner's slave, or a commoner's slave woman to leave through the main city-gate, he shall be killed.

16. If a man should harbor a fugitive slave or slave woman of either the palace or of a commoner in his house and not bring him out at the herald's public proclamation, that householder shall be killed.

17. If a man seizes a fugitive slave or slave woman in the open country and leads him back to his owner, the slave owner shall give him 2 shekels of silver.…

19. If he should detain that slave in his own house and afterward the slave is discovered in his possession, that man shall be killed.…

21. If a man breaks into a house, they shall kill him and hang him in front of that very breach.

22. If a man commits a robbery and is then seized, that man shall be killed.…

24. If a life (is lost during the robbery), the city and the governor shall weigh and deliver to his kinsmen 60 shekels of silver.

25. If a fire breaks out in a man's house, and a man who came to help put it out covets the household furnishings belonging to the householder, and takes household furnishings belonging to the householder, that man shall be cast into that very fire.

26. If either a soldier or a fisherman who is ordered to go on a royal campaign does not go, or hires and sends a hireling as his substitute, that soldier or fisherman shall be killed: the one who informs against him shall take full legal possession of his estate.…

28. If there is either a soldier or a fisherman who is taken captive while serving in a royal fortress, and his son is able to perform the service obligation, the field and orchard shall be given to him and he shall perform his father's service obligation.…

30. If either a soldier or a fisherman abandons his field, orchard, or house because of·the service obli-

gation and then absents himself … if he then returns and claims his field, orchard, or house, it will not be given to him: he who has taken possession of it and has performed his service obligation shall be the one to continue to perform the obligation.…

34. If either a captain or a sergeant should take a soldier's household furnishings, oppress a soldier, hire out a soldier, deliver a soldier into the power of an influential person in a law case, or take a gift that the king gave to a soldier, that captain or sergeant shall be killed.…

37. If a man should purchase a field, orchard, or house of a soldier, fisherman, or a state tenant, his deed shall be invalidated and he shall forfeit his silver; the field, orchard, or house shall revert to its owner.

38. (Furthermore), a soldier, fisherman, or a state tenant will not assign in writing to his wife or daughter any part of a field, orchard, or house attached to his service obligation, nor will he give it to meet any outstanding obligation.…

42. If a man rents a field in tenancy but does not plant any grain, they shall charge and convict him of not performing the required work in the field, and he shall give to the owner of the field grain in accordance with his neighbor's yield.…

44. If a man rents a previously uncultivated field for a three-year term with the intention of opening it for cultivation but he is negligent and does not open the field, in the fourth year he shall plow, hoe, and harrow the field and return it to the owner of the field; and in addition he shall measure and deliver 3,000 silas of grain per 18 ikus (of field) .…

48. If a man has a debt lodged against him, and the storm-god Adad devastates his field or a flood sweeps away the crops, or there is no grain grown in the field due to insufficient water—in that year he will not repay grain to his creditor; he shall suspend performance of his contract and he will not give interest payments for that year.…

53. If a man neglects to reinforce the embankment of (the irrigation canal of) his field and does not reinforce its embankment, and then a breach opens in its embankment and allows the water to carry away the common irrigated area, the man in whose embankment the breach opened shall replace the grain whose loss he caused.

54. If he cannot replace the grain, they shall sell him and his property, and the residents of the common irrigated area whose grain crops the water carried away shall divide (the proceeds).

55. If a man opens his branch of the canal for irrigation and negligently allows the water to carry away

his neighbor's field, he shall measure and deliver grain in accordance with his neighbor's yield....

57. If a shepherd does not make an agreement with the owner of the field to graze sheep and goats ... the owner of the field shall harvest his field and the shepherd who grazed sheep and goats on the field without the permission of the owner of the field shall give in addition 6,000 silas of grain per 18 ikus (of field) to the owner of the field....

60. If a man gives a field to a gardener to plant as a date orchard and the gardener plants the orchard, he shall cultivate the orchard for four years; in the fifth year, the owner of the orchard and the gardener shall divide the yield in equal shares; the owner of the orchard shall select and take his share first....

62. If he does not plant as a date orchard the field which was given to him—if it is arable land, the gardener shall measure and deliver to the owner of the field the estimated yield of the field for the years it is left fallow in accordance with his neighbor's yield; furthermore he shall perform the required work on the field and return it to the owner of the field....

64. If a man gives his orchard to a gardener to pollinate (the date palms), as long as the gardener is in possession of the orchard, he shall give to the owner of the orchard two thirds of the yield of the orchard, and he himself shall take one third.

65. If the gardener does not pollinate the (date palms in the) orchard and thus diminishes the yield, the gardener [shall measure and deliver] a yield for the orchard to (the owner of the orchard in accordance with) his neighbor's yields....

[gap]t If a merchant gives grain or silver as an interest-bearing loan, he shall take 100 silas of grain per kur as interest (= 33%); if he gives silver as an interest-bearing loan, he shall take 36 barleycorns per shekel of silver as interest (= 20%).

[gap]u If a man who has an interest-bearing loan does not have silver with which to repay it, he (the merchant) shall take grain and silver in accordance with the royal edict and the interest on it at the annual rate of 60 silas per 1 kur (= 20%)....

[gap]x If a merchant gives grain or silver as an interest-bearing loan and when he gives it as an interest-bearing loan he gives the silver according to the small weight or the grain according to the small seah-measure but when he receives payment he receives the silver according to the large weight or the grain according to the large seah-measure, [that merchant] shall forfeit [anything that he gave] ....

102. If a merchant should give silver to a trading agent for an investment venture, and he incurs a loss

on his journeys, he shall return silver to the merchant in the amount of the capital sum.

103. If enemy forces should make him abandon whatever goods he is transporting while on his business trip, the trading agent shall swear an oath by the god and shall be released....

112. If a man is engaged in a trading expedition and gives silver, gold, precious stones, or any other goods to another under consignment for transportation, and the latter man ... appropriates it, the owner of the consigned property shall charge and convict that man of whatever ... he failed to deliver, and that man shall give to the owner ... fivefold the property that had been given to him....

117. If an obligation is outstanding against a man and he sells or gives into debt service his wife, his son, or his daughter, they shall perform service in the house of their buyer or of the one who holds them in debt service for three years; their release shall be secured in the fourth year.

118. If he should give a male or female slave into debt service, the merchant may extend the term (beyond the three years), he may sell him; there are no grounds for a claim....

120. If a man stores his grain in another man's house, and a loss occurs in the storage bin or the householder opens the granary and takes the grain or he completely denies receiving the grain that was stored in his house—the owner of the grain shall establish his grain before the god, and the householder shall give to the owner of the grain twofold the grain that he took (in storage)....

122. If a man intends to give silver, gold, or anything else to another man for safekeeping, he shall exhibit before witnesses anything which he intends to give, he shall draw up a written contract, and (in this manner) he shall give goods for safekeeping.

123. If he gives goods for safekeeping without witnesses or a written contract, and they deny that he gave anything, that case has no basis for a claim....

127. If a man causes a finger to be pointed in accusation against ... a man's wife but cannot bring proof, they shall flog that man before the judges and they shall shave off half of his hair.

128. If a man marries a wife but does not draw up a formal contract for her, that woman is not a wife.

129. If a man's wife should be seized lying with another male, they shall bind them and cast them into the water; if the wife's master allows his wife to live, then the king shall allow his subject (i.e., the other male) to live.

130. If a man pins down another man's virgin wife who is still residing in her father's house, and they seize him lying with her, that man shall be killed; that woman shall be released.

131. If her husband accuses his own wife (of adultery), although she has not been seized lying with another male, she shall swear (to her innocence by) an oath by the god, and return to her house.

132. If a man's wife should have a finger pointed against her in accusation involving another male, although she has not been seized lying with another male, she shall submit to the divine River Ordeal....

134. If a man should be captured and there are not sufficient provisions in his house, his wife may enter another's house; that woman will not be subject to any penalty....

138. If a man intends to divorce his first-ranking wife who did not bear him children, he shall give her silver as much as was her bridewealth and restore to her the dowry that she brought from her father's house, and he shall divorce her.

139. If there is no bridewealth, he shall give her 60 shekels of silver as a divorce settlement.

140. If he is a commoner, he shall give her 20 shekels of silver.

141. If the wife of a man who is residing in the man's house should decide to leave, and she appropriates goods, squanders her household possessions, or disparages her husband, they shall charge and convict her; and if her husband should declare his intention to divorce her, then he shall divorce her; neither her travel expenses, nor her divorce settlement, nor anything else shall be given to her. If her husband should declare his intention to not divorce her, then her husband may marry another woman and that (first) woman shall reside in her husband's house as a slave woman.

142. If a woman repudiates her husband, and declares, "You will not have marital relations with me"—her circumstances shall be investigated by the authorities of her city quarter, and if she is circumspect and without fault, but her husband is wayward and disparages her greatly that woman will not be subject to any penalty; she shall take her dowry and she shall depart for her father's house.

143. If she is not circumspect but is wayward, squanders her household possessions, and disparages her husband, they shall cast that woman into the water....

148. It a man marries a woman, and later *la'bum*-disease seizes her and he decides to marry another woman, he may marry, he will not divorce his wife whom *la'bum*-disease seized; she shall reside in quarters he constructs and he shall continue to support her as long as she lives....

150. If a man awards to his wife a field, orchard, house, or movable property, and makes out a sealed document for her, after her husband's death her children will not bring claim against her; the mother shall give her estate to whichever of her children she loves, but she will not give it to an outsider....

153 If a man's wife has her husband killed on account of (her relationship with) another male, they shall impale that woman.

154. If a man should carnally know his daughter, they shall banish that man from the city....

156. If a man selects a bride for his son and his son does not yet carnally know her, and he himself then lies with her, he shall weigh and deliver to her 30 shekels of silver; moreover, he shall restore to her whatever she brought from her father's house, and a husband of her choice shall marry her.

157. If a man, after his father's death, should lie with his mother, they shall burn them both.

158. If a man, after his father's death, should be discovered in the lap of his (the father's) principal wife who had borne children, that man shall be disinherited from the paternal estate.

159. If a man who has the ceremonial marriage presentation brought to the house of his father-in-law, and who gives the bridewealth, should have his attention diverted to another woman and declare to his father-in-law, "I will not marry your daughter," the father of the daughter shall take full legal possession of whatever had been brought to him....

162. If a man marries a wife, she bears him children, and that woman then goes to her fate, her father shall have no claim to her dowry; her dowry belongs only to her children....

166. If a man provides wives for his eligible sons but does not provide a wife for his youngest son, when the brothers divide the estate after the father goes to his fate, they shall establish the silver value of the bridewealth for their young unmarried brother from the property of the paternal estate, in addition to his inheritance share, and thereby enable him to obtain a wife....

168. If a man should decide to disinherit his son and declares to the judges, "I will disinherit my son," the judges shall investigate his case and if the son is not guilty of a grave offense deserving the penalty of disinheritance, the father may not disinherit his son.

169. If he should be guilty of a grave offense deserving the penalty of disinheritance by his father, they shall pardon him for his first one; if he should

commit a grave offense a second time, the father may disinherit his son....

175. If a slave of the palace or a slave of a commoner marries a woman of the *awīlu*-class and she then bears children, the owner of the slave will have no claims of slavery against the children of the woman of the *awīlu*-class....

177. If a widow whose children are still young should decide to enter another's house, she will not enter without (the prior approval of) the judges. When she enters another's house, the judges shall investigate the estate of her former husband, and they shall entrust the estate of her former husband to her later husband and to that woman, and they shall have them record a tablet (inventorying the estate). They shall safeguard the estate and they shall raise the young children; they will not sell the household goods. Any buyer who buys the household goods of the children of a widow shall forfeit his silver; the property shall revert to its owner....

180. If a father does not award a dowry to his daughter who is a cloistered *nadītu* or a *sekretu*, after the father goes to his fate, she shall have a share of the property of the paternal estate comparable in value to that of one heir; as long as she lives she shall enjoy its use; her estate belongs only to her brothers....

185. If a man takes in adoption a young child at birth and then rears him, that rearling will not be reclaimed....

188. If a craftsman takes a young child to rear and then teaches him his craft, he will not be reclaimed....

190. If a man should not reckon the young child whom he took and raised in adoption as equal with his children, that rearling shall return to his father's house....

192. If the child of (i.e., reared by) a courtier or the child of (i.e., reared by) a *sekretu* should say to the father who raised him or to the mother who raised him, "You are not my father," or "You are not my mother," they shall cut out his tongue.

193. If the child of (i.e., reared by) a courtier or the child of (i.e., reared by) a *sekretu* identifies with his father's house and repudiates the father who raised him or the mother who raised him and departs for his father's house, they shall pluck out his eye.

194. If a man gives his son to a wet nurse and that child then dies while in the care of the wet nurse, and the wet nurse then contracts for another child without the knowledge of his father and mother, they shall charge and convict her, and, because she con-

tracted for another child without the consent of his father and mother, they shall cut off her breast.

195. If a child should strike his father, they shall cut off his hand.

196. If an *awīlu* should blind the eye of another *awīlu*, they shall blind his eye.

197. If he should break the bone of another *awīlu*, they shall break his bone.

198. If he should blind the eye of a commoner or break the bone of a commoner, he shall weigh and deliver 60 shekels of silver.

199. If he should blind the eye of an *awīlu's* slave or break the bone of an *awīlu's* slave, he shall weigh and deliver one-half of his value (in silver).

200. If an *awīlu* should knock out the tooth of another *awīlu* of his own rank, they shall knock out his tooth.

201. If he should knock out the tooth of a commoner, he shall weigh and deliver 20 shekels of silver.

202. If an *awīlu* should strike the cheek of an *awīlu* who is of status higher than his own, he shall be flogged in the public assembly with 60 stripes of an ox whip.

203. If a member of the *awīlu*-class should strike the cheek of another member of the *awīlu*-class who is his equal, he shall weigh and deliver 60 shekels of silver.

204. If a commoner should strike the cheek of another commoner, he shall weigh and deliver 10 shekels of silver.

205. If an *awīlu's* slave should strike the cheek of a member of the *awīlu*-class, they shall cut off his ear....

209. If an *awīlu* strikes a woman of the *awīlu*-class and thereby causes her to miscarry her fetus, he shall weigh and deliver 10 shekels of silver for her fetus.

210. If that woman should die, they shall kill his daughter.

211. If he should cause a woman of the commoner-class to miscarry her fetus by the beating, he shall weigh and deliver 5 shekels of silver.

212. If that woman should die, he shall weigh and deliver 30 shekels of silver.

213. If he strikes an *awīlu's* slave woman and thereby causes her to miscarry her fetus, he shall weigh and deliver 2 shekels of silver.

214. If that slave woman should die, he shall weigh and deliver 20 shekels of silver.

215. If a physician performs major surgery with a bronze lancet upon an *awīlu* and thus heals the *awīlu*, or opens an *awīlu's* temple with a bronze

lancet and thus heals the *awīlu's* eye, he shall take 10 shekels of silver (as his fee).

216. If he (the patient) is a member of the commoner-class, he shall take 5 shekels of silver (as his fee).

217. If he (the patient) is an *awīlu's* slave, the slave's master shall give to the physician 2 shekels of silver.

218. If a physician performs major surgery with a bronze lancet upon an *awīlu* and thus causes the *awīlu's* death, or opens an *awīlu's* temple with a bronze lancet and thus blinds the *awīlu's* eye, they shall cut off his hand.

219. If a physician performs major surgery with a bronze lancet upon a slave of a commoner and thus causes the slave's death, he shall replace the slave with a slave of comparable value.

220. If he opens his (the commoner's slave's) temple with a bronze lancet and thus blinds his eye, he shall weigh and deliver silver equal to half his value....

226. If a barber shaves off the slave-hairlock of a slave not belonging to him without the consent of the slave's owner, they shall cut off that barber's hand.

227. If a man misinforms a barber so that he then shaves off the slave-hairlock of a slave not belonging to him, they shall kill that man and hang him in his own doorway; the barber shall swear, "I did not knowingly shave it off," and he shall be released.

228. If a builder constructs a house for a man to his satisfaction, he shall give him 2 shekels of silver for each sar of house as his compensation.

229. If a builder constructs a house for a man but does not make his work sound, and the house that he constructs collapses and causes the death of the householder, that builder shall be killed.

230. If it should cause the death of a son of the householder, they shall kill a son of that builder.

231. If it should cause the death of a slave of the householder, he shall give to the householder a slave of comparable value for the slave.

232. If it should cause the loss of property, he shall replace anything that is lost; moreover, because he did not make sound the house which he constructed and it collapsed, he shall construct (anew) the house which collapsed at his own expense....

234. If a boatman caulks a boat of 60-kur capacity for a man, he shall give him 2 shekels of silver as his compensation....

236. If a man gives his boat to a boatman for hire, and the boatman is negligent and causes the boat to

sink or to become lost, the boatman shall replace the boat for the owner of the boat....

239. If a man hires a boatman, he shall give him 1,800 silas of grain per year....

241. If a man should distrain an ox, he shall weigh and deliver 20 shekels of silver.

242/243. If a man rents it for one year, he shall give to its owner 1,200 silas of grain as the hire of an ox for the rear (of the team), and 900 silas of grain as the hire of an ox for the middle (of the team).

244. If a man rents an ox or a donkey and a lion kills it in the open country, it is the owner's loss.

245. If a man rents an ox and causes its death either by negligence or by physical abuse, he shall replace the ox with an ox of comparable value for the owner of the ox....

249. If a man rents an ox, and a god strikes it down dead, the man who rented the ox shall swear an oath by the god and he shall be released.

250. If an ox gores to death a man while it is passing through the streets, that case has no basis for a claim.

251. If a man's ox is a known gorer, and the authorities of his city quarter notify him that it is a known gorer, but he does not blunt(?) its horns or control his ox, and that ox gores to death a member of the *awīlu*-class, he (the owner) shall give 30 shekels of silver.

252. If it is a man's slave (who is fatally gored), he shall give 20 shekels of silver.

253. If a man hires another man to care for his field, that is, he entrusts to him the stored grain, hands over to him care of the cattle, and contracts with him for the cultivation of the field—if that man steals the seed or fodder and it is then discovered in his possession, they shall cut off his hand....

257. If a man hires an agricultural laborer, he shall give him 2,400 silas of grain per year.

258. If a man hires an ox driver, he shall give him 1,800 silas of grain per year....

261. If a man hires a herdsman to herd the cattle or the sheep and goats, he shall give him 2,400 silas of grain per year....

264. If a shepherd, to whom cattle or sheep and goats were given for shepherding, is in receipt of his complete hire to his satisfaction, then allows the number of cattle to decrease, or the number of sheep and goats to decrease, or the number of offspring to diminish, he shall give for the (loss of) offspring and by-products in accordance with the terms of his contract....

266. If, in the [protective] enclosure, an epidemic should break out or a lion make a kill, the shep-

herd shall clear himself before the god, and the owner of the enclosure shall accept responsibility for him for the loss sustained in the enclosure....

268. If a man rents an ox for threshing, 20 silas of grain is its hire.

269. If he rents a donkey for threshing, 10 silas of grain is its hire.

270. If he rents a goat for threshing, 1 sila of grain is its hire.

271. If a man rents cattle, a wagon, and its driver, he shall give 180 silas of grain per day.

272. If a man rents only the wagon, he shall give 40 silas of grain per day.

273. If a man hires a hireling, he shall give 6 barleycorns of silver per day from the beginning of the year until (the end of) the fifth month and 5 barleycorns of silver per day from the sixth month until the end of the year....

276. If a man rents a boat for traveling upstream, he shall give 2½ barleycorns of silver as its hire per day....

282. If a slave should declare to his master. "You are not my master," he (the master) shall bring charge and proof against him that he is indeed his slave, and his master shall cut off his ear.

Epilogue

These are the just decisions which Hammurabi, the able king, has established and thereby has directed the land along the course of truth and the correct way of life.

I am Hammurabi, noble king. I have not been careless or negligent toward humankind, granted to my care by the god Enlil, and with whose shepherding the god Marduk charged me. I have sought for them peaceful places, I removed serious difficulties, I spread light over them. With the mighty weapon which the gods Zababa and Ishtar bestowed upon me, with the wisdom which the god Ea allotted to me, with the ability which the god Marduk gave me, I annihilated enemies everywhere, I put an end to wars, I enhanced the well-being of the land, I made the people of all settlements lie in safe pastures, I did not tolerate anyone intimidating them. The great gods having chosen me, I am indeed the shepherd who brings peace, whose scepter is just. My benevolent shade is spread over my city. I held the people of the lands of Sumer and Akkad safely on my lap. They prospered under my protective spirit, I maintained them in peace, with my skillful wisdom I sheltered them.

In order that the mighty not wrong the weak, to provide just ways for the waif and the widow, I have inscribed my precious pronouncements upon my stela and set it up before the statue of me, the king of justice, in the city of Babylon, the city which the gods Anu and Enlil have elevated, within the Esagil, the temple whose foundations are fixed as are heaven and earth, in order to render the judgments of the land, to give the verdicts of the land, and to provide just ways for the wronged.

I am the king preeminent among kings. My pronouncements are choice, my ability is unrivaled. By the command of the god Shamash, the great judge of heaven and earth, may my justice prevail in the land. By the order of the god Marduk, my lord, may my engraved image not be confronted by someone who would remove it. May my name always be remembered favorably in the Esagil temple which I love.

Let any wronged man who has a lawsuit come before the statue of me, the king of justice, and let him have my inscribed stela read aloud to him, thus may he hear my precious pronouncements and let my stela reveal the lawsuit for him; may he examine his case, may he calm his (troubled) heart, (and may he praise me), saying:

"Hammurabi, the lord, who is like a father and begetter to his people, submitted himself to the command of the god Marduk, his lord, and achieved victory for the god Marduk everywhere. He gladdened the heart of the god Marduk, his lord and he secured the eternal well-being of the people and provided just ways for the land." ...

May any king who will appear in the land in the future, at any time, observe the pronouncements of justice that I inscribed upon my stela. May he not alter the judgments that I rendered and the verdicts that I gave, not remove my engraved image. If that man has discernment, and is capable of providing just ways for his land, may he heed the pronouncements I have inscribed upon my stela, may that stela reveal for him the traditions, the proper conduct, the judgments of the land that I rendered, the verdicts of the land that I gave and may he, too, provide just ways for all humankind in his care....

I am Hammurabi, king of justice, to whom the god Shamash has granted (insight into) the truth. My pronouncements are choice and my achievements are unrivalled.... If that man (a future ruler) heeds my pronouncements ... and does not reject my judgments ... then may the god Shamash lengthen his reign, just as (he has done) for me, the king of justice, and so may he shepherd his people with justice.

(But) should that man not heed my pronouncements, which I have inscribed upon my stela, and should he slight my curses and not fear the curses of the gods, and thus overturn the judgments that I rendered, change my pronouncements, alter my engraved image, erase my inscribed name and inscribe his own name (in its place)—or should he, because of fear of these curses, have someone else do so—that man, whether he is a king, a lord, or a governor, or any person at all, may the great god Anu, father of the gods, who has proclaimed my reign, deprive him of the sheen of royalty, smash his scepter, and curse his destiny.

May the god Enlil, the lord, who determines destinies, whose utterance cannot be countermanded, who magnifies my kingship, incite against him even in his own residence disorder that cannot be quelled and a rebellion that will result in his obliteration; may he cast as his fate a reign of groaning, of few days, of years of famine, of darkness without illumination, and of sudden death; may he declare with his venerable speech the obliteration of his city, the dispersion of his people, the supplanting of his dynasty, and the blotting out of his name and his memory from the land.

May the goddess Ninlil, the great mother … may she induce the divine king Enlil to pronounce the destruction of his land, the obliteration of his people, and the spilling of his life force like water.

May the god Ea … the sage among the gods, all-knowing … may he dam up his rivers at the source; may he not allow any life-sustaining grain in his land.

May the god Shamash, the great judge of heaven and earth, who provides just ways for all living creatures … may he not render his judgments, may he confuse his path … may he uproot him from among the living above and make his ghost thirst for water below in the nether world.

May the god Sin … impose upon him an onerous punishment, a great penalty for him, which will not depart from his body; … may he unveil before him a contender for the kingship; may he decree for him a life that is no better than death.

May the god Adad, lord of abundance, the canal-inspector of heaven and earth … deprive him of the benefits of rain from heaven and flood from the

Glossary

awīlu	a free person of the upper class
barleycorn	a unit of currency, often silver, the size of a grain of barley
bridewealth	amount paid to the parents of a bride by the groom or his family
iku, kur, sar, seah-measure, sila	ancient measurements of area, weight, or volume for which there are no precise equivalents today
la'bum **disease**	a malarial-type fever or a skin disease
nadītu	a priestess who was forbidden to have children
River Ordeal	truth verification process where a witness, accuser, or potential criminal was required to submit to a trial of integrity. The person in question was made to dive into the river and swim a certain distance underwater before coming back to the surface. If the person succeeded, he was thought to have told the truth and was free from further obligations or suspicion. If the person either came up too soon or drowned, he was considered to have lied and (if he survived) was subject to penalties or even death.
sekretu	woman isolated in a harem or a temple
shekel	a weight measure used for silver and unrelated to modern Israeli currency
Sin-Muballit	father of Hammurabi
virgin wife	fiancée

springs, and may he obliterate his land through destitution and famine....

May the god Zababa, the great warrior, ... who travels at my right side, smash his weapon upon the field of battle; may he turn day into night for him, and make his enemy triumph over him.

May the goddess Ishtar, mistress of battle and warfare, who bares my weapon, ... who loves my reign, curse his kingship with her angry heart and great fury ... strike down his warriors, drench the earth with their blood, make a heap of the corpses of his soldiers upon the plain, and may she show his soldiers no mercy; as for him, may she deliver him into the hand of his enemies....

May the goddess Nintu, august mistress of the lands, the mother, my creator, deprive him of an heir and give him no offspring; may she not allow a human child to be born among his people....

May the great gods of heaven and earth, ... the protective spirit of the temple, the very brickwork of the Ebabbar temple, curse that one his seed, his land, his troops, his people, and his army with a terrible curse.

May the god Enlil, whose command cannot be countermanded, curse him with these curses and may they swiftly overtake him.

HITTITE LAWS

"If anyone breaks the horn or leg of an ox, he shall take that ox for himself and give an ox in good condition to the owner of the injured ox."

Overview

The Hittite Laws comprise an anonymously authored collection of two hundred laws from Central Anatolia (modern-day Turkey) dating to the second millennium BCE. The laws are written on clay tablets in cuneiform script. Cuneiform, from the Latin meaning "wedge-shaped," is one of the earliest known writing systems and is composed of signs, both logographic (representing a word) and syllabic (representing a unit of sound). Scribes, who were specially trained to compose and copy documents, wrote cuneiform by pressing a stylus, usually made of reed, into the damp clay of the tablet.

The Hittites divided the collection of laws into two series that they named after the first few words of the texts, "If a man" and "If a vine." The laws cover a wide range of topics, from personal injury to marriage to prices of various items, including livestock and food. The first series, "If a man," begins with cases of manslaughter, while the second series, "If a vine," starts with instances of the theft of plants. Many legal scholars consider the term *code*, or comprehensive body of law, to be inaccurate for ancient law collections such as this one because this legal collection is not exhaustive. For example, the collection lacks mention of an ordinary case of premeditated murder. Because of its similarity in form and content to the law collections from Mesopotamia and ancient Israel, and because of the importance of the Hittites in the late Bronze Age (fourteenth to twelfth centuries BCE), modern scholars continue to study this text with great interest.

Context

The kingdom of the Hittites, Hatti, was located in Central Anatolia (roughly modern-day Turkey). At the height of their power, during the fourteenth and thirteenth centuries BCE, the Hittites ruled an extensive network of vassal states, stretching from the Aegean Sea in the west (the western coast of modern-day Turkey) to the Euphrates River in the east (present-day Iraq). Hatti, Egypt, Babylonia, and Mitanni were the major powers during this time.

The kings wrote to each other in Akkadian, the language of Babylonia, which was the lingua franca—or language of international communication—in the ancient Near East.

This law collection exists in several manuscripts, which were copied over a period of time. As is the case with many ancient texts, both the author of the law collection and the events leading up to the writing of the text are unknown. Although the earliest copies date to the time of the Hittite Old Kingdom period (ca. 1650–1400 BCE), Hittite scribes continued to make copies of the text through the Hittite New Kingdom period (ca. 1400–1180 BCE). These cuneiform tablets were excavated from various sites at the capital city of Hattushash (modern-day Bogazköy), including the temple and the plateau of Büyükkale (meaning "Great Fortress" in Turkish), which contained the palace and several other important buildings. Because the Hittites normally wrote on clay tablets, which are fragile, no complete or even almost-complete copy of the laws exists. Modern-day scholars have painstakingly pieced together the text from fragments of several copies of the document.

About the Author

Although many of the Hittite texts can be identified with specific kings, the author of the Hittite Laws is unknown. A king often plays an important role in a text, such as initiating and setting out the terms of a treaty or recording his deeds in his annals. Sometimes on cuneiform tablets the name of the king is mentioned in a section at the end of the tablet (called a colophon), which gives such details as the name of the author or the copyist or the title of the text. This is not the case with the Hittite Laws. The surviving colophons on the different copies identify only the title of the composition—"If a man" or "If a vine"—or the name of the scribe who copied the tablet. However, in the colophon of one tablet belonging to the first series, the enigmatic statement "Of the father of His Majesty" appears. In addition, an unnamed "father of the king" is mentioned in law 55. These references provide hints, but not conclusive evidence, about the authorship.

Scholars have speculated about the identity of this "father of the king." Alfonso Archi suggests that the "father" is Hat-

CA. 1650 BCE

- Hattusilis I, possibly the "father of the king" mentioned in the law collection, begins his approximately thirty-year reign.

CA. 1650– 1400 BCE

- The oldest copies of the Hittite Laws date from this period, which is called the Old Kingdom.

CA. 1620 BCE

- Mursilis I, possibly the king mentioned in the law collection, begins his approximately thirty-year reign.

CA. 1525 BCE

- Telipinus, also possibly a king mentioned in the law collection, begins his approximately twenty-five-year reign.

CA. 1400– 1180 BCE

- Late copies of the laws date from this period, which is known as the New Kingdom.

CA. 1200– 1180 BCE

- The city of Hattushah is destroyed, and the Hittite Empire collapses.

tusilis I, the earliest clearly verifiable ruler of Hatti, who reigned from approximately 1650 to 1620 BCE. This suggestion is attractive because of Hattusilis I's importance in Hittite history. Hattusilis I not only moved the capital to Hattushah but also portrayed himself as a model king, known for both his military prowess and his mercy. This would mean that the king in question is Mursilis I (ca. 1620–1590 BCE), who was Hattusilis I's grandson, adopted son, and chosen successor. Mursilis I was known for his military exploits, including the destruction of Babylon in about 1595 BCE. This identification cannot be proved conclusively, however.

Other scholars propose that these laws could be attributed to Telipinus (ca. 1525–1500 BCE), because he issued a proclamation that deals with a case of ordinary premeditated murder, a crime not mentioned in the Hittite Laws. The existence of Telipinus's proclamation about premeditated murder, as noted by Harry Hoffner, could explain its omission from the law collection. This is a theory that also cannot be proved irrefutably. (Telipinus was the first known Hittite king to make a treaty of alliance, setting a policy that would be continued by later kings.)

Explanation and Analysis of the Document

For several reasons, the Hittite Laws do not comprise a document, in the sense of an original and unchanging written record of events or information in a particular form. First, there is no original version, only several copies spanning the entire period for which written evidence exists. The earliest copy of the Hittite Laws comes from the Old Kingdom period, but internal evidence from the text suggests that the text was revised from an earlier version. Unfortunately, no copies of this earlier form have been found to date. An example of the internal evidence can be seen in the construction "Formerly ... but now ..." (in the Hittite language, *karu ... kinuna ...*), which is used to reduce the fine or soften the penalty for violating a law, suggesting the existence of an earlier law and penalty. For example, law 7 states, "If anyone blinds a free person or knocks out his tooth, they used to pay 40 shekels of silver. But now he shall pay 20 shekels of silver." (One shekel of silver was the wage for one month of work for an ordinary laborer.) In law 92, which deals with the case of the theft of two or three beehives, the offender formerly would have been exposed to stinging bees, but the penalty is now monetary (6 shekels of silver). Further, errors that could be made only in the copying process exist in all the texts, indicating that these are scribal copies, not originals.

Second, the Hittite Laws cannot be considered a document because no complete version of the text exists. What we know as the Hittite Laws is actually a composite text reconstructed by modern-day scholars from fragments of various copies, with some of the laws yet unaccounted for.

Third, although several copies of certain sections of the text exist, variations among the copies indicate that scribes had some freedom in choosing how to write the text. For example, for the word *person*, one version may use the logographic writing, where a symbol represents the entire word, while another version may write out the word *antuhšan* using the syllabic signs *an-tu-uh-ša-an*.

Fourth, the later versions differ from the earlier versions of the laws in both spelling and grammar. Although an Old Kingdom scribe might write "he abducts" as *ta-a-i-ez-zi*, a New Kingdom scribe would most likely use *da-a-i-ez-zi*. Clearly, the Hittite scribes did not hesitate to modernize the spelling and the grammar when making copies. Finally, one late copy revises some of the laws. As an example, compare the following: The Old Kingdom version of law 7, as quoted earlier and reproduced in the accompanying document, says, "If anyone blinds a free person or knocks out his tooth, they used to pay 40 shekels of silver. But now he shall pay 20 shekels of silver. He shall look to his house for it." The New Kingdom version says, "If anyone blinds a free man in a quarrel, he shall pay 40 shekels of silver. If it is an accident, he shall pay 20 shekels of silver" (qtd. in Hoffner, 1997, p. 21).

Even if the Hittite Laws do not constitute a document, as that term is ordinarily understood, modern scholars have a fairly good idea of the content of the laws. As already noted, there are two hundred extant laws, divided into two sections labeled, respectively, "If a man" and "If a vine," after the first words of each section. Although modern-day scholars cannot always discern the Hittites' reasoning behind the organization of the laws, the laws within each section can be divided roughly into thematic groups for the purpose of discussion. On occasion, laws appear that do not seem to fit into a thematic group. Most of the laws are casuistic—that is, written in the form of a case—and use the format: "If such-and-such happens, then so-and-so is the penalty." An interesting feature of the laws is the differences in the penalty, depending on the social status of the offender or the victim—whether the person is free or a slave. If the victim is a free person, the penalty is often twice as much as if the victim is a slave. For example, the penalty for blinding a free person is 20 shekels of silver (law 7), while the penalty for blinding a slave is only 10 shekels of silver (law 8). The relationship between gender and compensation, however, is not as clear. The wages for a male harvester, for instance, are more than twice the wages for a female harvester (law 158), but the laws seem to be indifferent to the gender of a slave in assigning penalties for his or her injury or accidental death. The penalty for blinding a slave is 10 shekels (law 8), whether the slave is male or female. The selections from the abridged document reproduced here are representative of the full text of the two hundred laws.

◆ "If a man"

In this first section, the laws can be divided into a number of thematic groups, covering crimes from homicide to abduction to arson and social arrangements such as marriage.

HOMICIDE (LAWS 1–6; 37; 38; 42–44A) This section begins with penalties for manslaughter (the accidental or unintentional killing) of both free persons and slaves (laws 1–4). Law 5 deals with the special case of the premeditated murder of a merchant. The penalty is extraordinarily high (100 minas, or 4,000 shekels of silver), which sug-

Time Line	
1894 CE	■ The French archaeologist Ernest Chantre discovers the first tablets at Bogazköy, which was the ancient city of Hattushash.
1906	■ A German expedition finds the archives of the Hittite kings at the Hittite capital, Hattushash (modern-day Bogazköy).
1915	■ Bedřich (Friedrich) Hrozný, a Czech scholar, proves that the Hittite language belongs to the Indo-European language family, which allows the tablets to be deciphered.
1922	■ Hrozný publishes the first modern edition of the Hittite Laws (in French) and is the first to number the sections 1–200.

gests that merchants enjoyed either a high or a protected status. Given that financial gain could provide a greater motivation for murdering a merchant, it is not surprising that the exceptionally high penalty might be imposed as a deterrent, in the same way that killing a police officer or judge carries a stricter penalty in the United States. Law 6 deals with compensation for the heir of a person who is killed while away from home. Laws 37 and 38 and 42–44a deal with very specific cases of homicide. The reason for singling out these cases and separating them from the other homicide laws is unknown.

PERSONAL INJURY (LAWS 7–12; 17; 18) A diverse but not exhaustive list of personal injury cases appears in this section. The cases include blinding someone or knocking out someone's tooth (laws 7–8), injuring a person's head (law 9), temporarily incapacitating a person (law 10), breaking a person's arm or leg (laws 11–12), and causing a woman to miscarry (laws 17–18).

ABDUCTION (LAWS 19 AND 22) This section begins with the abduction of free persons (law19). Law 22 deals with the return of and the compensation for runaway slaves.

PURITY (LAWS 25 AND 44B) Scholars are unsure how a person can be "impure in a vessel or a vat" (law 25). Calvert Watkins suggests that it is a euphemism for "urinates," but this explanation is not certain. Law 44b concerns the proper disposal of the remnants of a purification ritual. The concern here is about contamination, which is one aspect of sorcery. Sorcery is such a serious issue that it is one of the few that the king himself must decide. (Law 111 also deals with sorcery and refers it to the king.) These laws underscore the Hittites' concern for purity.

MARRIAGE (LAWS 26–36) This section contains various laws dealing with marriage, including divorce and the subsequent division of property and custody of the children, the breaking of a betrothal, and the social status of a person who marries someone of a different social status.

LAND TENURE (LAWS 40; 48; 49; 55) These sections deal with the obligations and services rendered for holding a piece of land from the king. Although the specifics of the "TUKUL-obligations" and "šahhan-services" are unknown, the consequences for failure to keep the obligation or render the service are clearly spelled out.

IMPLEMENTS (LAW 45) This law deals with the case of someone who finds implements belonging to another person. If the person returns the implements, the owner must give a reward; if the person keeps the implements, it is considered to be theft.

THEFT OF ANIMALS (LAWS 57; 60–63; 66; 70; 71) The Hittites were greatly concerned with the theft of animals, as is demonstrated by both the sheer number of cases and the penalties. The theft of each type of animal—cattle, horses, and sheep—is described in a separate law. The penalties are quite severe: In addition to returning the animal, the thief must pay restitution from two to fifteen times the number of animals. The strict penalties are most likely meant as a deterrent to theft, given the obvious importance of these animals for human survival in an agrarian society.

ACCIDENTAL DEATH OF OR INJURY TO ANIMALS (LAWS 72; 74–80) This section provides for restitution in the case of the accidental death of an animal or penalties for injuring an animal. A contemporary reader may find some of the cases baffling. For example, in law 74, the same penalty applies for breaking the horn or the leg of an ox. Since modern oxen are often dehorned, the concern over a broken horn might seem puzzling. Certain yokes, however, require that oxen have horns. A head yoke, for instance, is attached to the horns of the ox. Although it is not known what type of yokes the Hittites used, it is possible that concern over yoking an ox was behind this penalty.

THEFT, ACCIDENTAL DEATH, OR INJURY OF OTHER ANIMALS (LAWS 81; 87; 91; 92) This section gives further details about theft, accidental death, or injury of animals. Here the animals concerned are pigs, dogs, and bees. The thief must pay a financial penalty rather than providing a larger number of the animal stolen, as is the case for the theft of cattle, horses, or sheep. Since it is not known how the Hittites classified animals, it is unclear whether these laws are separated from the other laws because these animals were considered to belong to a different class or whether these animals were of lesser economic importance.

UNLAWFUL ENTRY (LAWS 93–97) Different types of unlawful entry are covered in this section. Here there are differences in the penalties based on the status of the offender. A free person who commits one of these crimes is fined twice as much as a slave for the same offense.

ARSON (LAWS 98–100) In this section, the perpetrator must pay compensation equal to the goods lost in the fire. If a slave is the perpetrator of arson, the owner of the slave must either pay compensation (with the slave being disfigured) or forfeit the slave.

◆ "If a vine"

In this second section, the laws can be arranged into thematic groups largely (but not exclusively) related to property and the land—covering its cultivation and care, along with animals kept and laborers hired to work it.

THEFT OF OR DAMAGE TO PLANTS (LAWS 101; 104–109; 113) The penalties for the theft of or damage to various types of plants, such as vines or trees, are given here. Different penalties are cited, depending on the type of plant or the type of damage done.

CLAY (LAWS 110 AND 111) Law 110 deals with the theft of clay from a pit. Although scholars are unsure why this law is inserted at this point, the theme of "clay" connects it to the next law, the use of clay for sorcery. Sorcery is a serious offense that requires that the king himself deal with it.

LAND TENURE (LAW 112) This law returns to the issue of land tenure. Why this law is separated from similar laws in the first section is not known.

THEFT OF OR DAMAGE TO IMPLEMENTS OR OTHER OBJECTS (LAWS 121; 122; 124–129; 131; 132; 143; 144) Fines are imposed for the theft of or damage to implements or other objects. These objects include everything from plows to doors to bricks to copper shears. Hoffner suggests that the stealing of a door would leave the owner of the house and his possessions vulnerable, explaining why the thief would be responsible for losses suffered by the owner.

WAGES, HIRE, SALES (LAWS 145; 149–152; 157; 159; 160; 161; 176B; 177) This section sets standards for the wages of different types of workers, including harvesters and smiths. Fees for renting various animals or implements are also given. Law 149 and laws 176b and 177 deal with the sale of slaves, both skilled and unskilled.

OBSTRUCTION OF A SALE (LAWS 146–148) The regulations regarding the obstruction of a sale appear here. The thematic link between law 148 and law 149 appears to be the idea of "sale."

MISCELLANEOUS LAWS (LAWS 162 AND 163) There does not appear to be any theme linking these laws. Law 162a deals with irrigation, while law 163 deals with the disposal of the elements of a purification ritual for animals.

SACRED OFFENSES (LAWS 164–169) Although on the surface these laws seem diverse, they are linked, according to Hoffner, by the use of the verb "to make sacred or holy again; reconsecrate." These laws are concerned with correcting damage to both the secular and the sacred sphere of houses, fields, and boundaries.

SNAKES (LAW 170) As Hoffner argues, the issue here is analogic magic, which is the performance of an action in one set of circumstances in order to cause a similar effect or outcome in a different set of circumstances. Thus, by killing a snake and speaking the name of another person, the intention is to cause the death of that other person.

MORE MISCELLANEOUS LAWS (LAWS 171–176A) This section covers topics as diverse as disinheritance (law 171), rejecting the king's judgment (law 173a), and keeping a bull outside of a corral (law 176a). Many of these laws are poorly understood. For example, scholars do not agree on what it means for a slave to "go into a clay jar" (law 173b). The scholar Richard Haase sees it as a type of discipline to cure the slave's rebellious attitude: Imagine a slave sitting in a large jar, being forced to reflect on his sins. The majority of scholars take it to be a euphemism for the death penalty, although they differ in their interpretation of the form this penalty would have taken. Part of the difficulty is that, as Hoffner points out, the verb that is translated as "rebels" (*arawezzi*) in older versions of the text becomes a different verb that implies rebellion with physical assault or even attempted murder (*araizzi*) in later versions of the text. It is possible, then, that later scribes reinterpreted this law and its punishment.

PRICES (LAW 178) This law gives the standard prices for various bovines and equines. Setting prices was evidently a royal duty in the ancient Near East, as lists of prices also appear in both law collections and royal edicts from Mesopotamia. Many scholars regard these as reflecting actual prices.

SEXUAL RELATIONS (LAWS 187–200A) Permitted and unpermitted sexual pairings are the focus of this section. The laws describe which pairings the Hittites considered intrinsically inappropriate. For example, a man is permitted to have sexual relations with his stepmother, but only if his father is already dead (law 190). Hittite law also regulated bestiality, forbidding sexual relations between humans and cattle, sheep, pigs, and dogs. Although sexual relations with horses and mules were not penalized, such relations permanently defiled a person, making the person ineligible to go before the king or become a priest.

APPRENTICESHIP (LAW 200B) The final law deals with the appropriate fees due to a master for training a person as a carpenter, smith, weaver, leather worker, or fuller.

Audience

Both the author and the circumstances surrounding the writing of the Hittite Laws are unknown. This makes it difficult to determine what audience was intended. Per-

A sculpted figure still stands in the ruins of the ancient Hattushash city gate. (© Richard T. Nowitz/CORBIS)

haps it is more accurate to think of "audiences" than of a single "audience," since the law collection exists in several versions that were copied over time. Unlike other law collections from the ancient Near East, there is no prologue or epilogue—or at least none preserved—for the Hittite Laws, which might give hints about the intended audience. It is improbable that average citizens would have been able to read the law collection, given the specialized training needed to read and write cuneiform. Nevertheless, three different, but not mutually exclusive, audiences should be considered.

The first possible audience would be rulers. It is clear that kings considered this law collection to be important, since most of the copies of the Hittite Laws come from the royal archives. Given that justice was an important aspect of kingship in the ancient Near East, it is not surprising that this collection continued to be copied over several hundred years.

The second audience would be scribes. One colophon of a tablet records the name of the scribe who copied the law collection. Although little is known about Hittite scribal training, it is known that Mesopotamian scribes were trained by copying excerpts from texts. Given the large numbers of copies, it is possible that some copies were scribal exercises.

"*[If] anyone kills [a man] or a woman in a [quarr]el, he shall [bring him] for burial and shall give 4 persons, male or female respectively. He shall look [to his house for it.]*"

(Law 1)

"*When [a delegation of] Hittites, men owing šahhan-services, came, they did reverence to the father of the king, and said: 'No one pays us a wage. They say to us: "You are men required to perform your jobs as a šahhan-service!"' The father of the king stepped into the assembly and declared under his seal: 'You must continue to perform šahhan-services just like your colleagues.'*"

(Law 55)

"*If anyone breaks the horn or leg of an ox, he shall take that ox for himself and give an ox in good condition to the owner of the injured ox. If the owner of the ox says: 'I will take my own ox,' he shall take his ox, and the offender shall pay 2 shekels of silver.*"

(Law 74)

"*If anyone steals a vine, a vine branch, a … , or an onion/garlic, formerly [they paid] one shekel of silver for one vine and one shekel of silver for a vine branch…. But now if he is a free man, he shall pay 6 shekels [of silver].*"

(Law 101)

The third audience would be legal officials. Most scholars agree that the Hittite Laws reflect actual legal practice. If this is the situation, then legal officials would have needed to consult the laws in deciding court cases that would have affected even ordinary citizens.

Impact

Given the uncertainty about the authorship, context, and audience of the Hittite Laws, its impact in its own day cannot be estimated. Because no record of the law collection exists, from the time of the fall of the Hittite Empire in the twelfth century BCE to the time of its rediscovery in the early twentieth century, it is unlikely to have had any significant impact during the interim period. Since the first modern edition of the Hittite Laws appeared in 1922,

however, scholars have been interested in four aspects of the law collection: orthography (the way the cuneiform signs are written), language, comparative law, and society and its values.

Because the Hittite Laws exist in several manuscripts, copied over many years, scholars can look at developments in orthography over time. Orthography is important in helping to date texts. Scholars can compare the orthography of an undated text to the orthography from known time periods to estimate when a text may have been written.

Then, too, by looking at the differences in the various copies of the Hittite Laws, scholars are able to study the development of the Hittite language itself—in terms of grammar, spelling, and vocabulary. Because Hittite is one of the oldest known members of the Indo-European family of languages, the laws provide one source of data for looking at the development of this language family.

The Hittite Laws can be directly compared with Mesopotamian legal collections, but they are of particular interest to scholars of biblical law. Of all the ancient Near Eastern legal collections, for example, only the Hittite and the biblical law collections are concerned with regulating sexual pairings that are innately unacceptable in these two cultures. This is not surprising, given that both cultures seemed to regard sexual relations in general as somehow defiling a person. Further, these two law collections are the only ones that regulate bestiality; while it is unacceptable in all forms under biblical law, Hittite law forbids only sexual relationships with cattle, sheep, pigs, or dogs.

Scholars have used the Hittite Laws in conjunction with other texts to attempt to discern aspects of Hittite society and values. The law collection in conjunction with various known rituals shows that the Hittites valued purity. And, on the basis of the reduction in fines or lessening of the severity of the penalties, Alfonso Archi argues that the Hittites were more humane than their neighbors.

Further Reading

■ Articles

Archi, Alfonso. "Sulla formazione del testo delle leggi ittite." *SMEA* 7 (1968): 54–89.

Haase, Richard. "Überlegungen zu §173 (*58) der hethitischen Gesetze." *Anatolica* 20 (1994): 221–225.

Watkins, Calvert. "Hittite and Indo-European Studies: The Denominative Statives in -e-." *TPS* (1973): 51–93.

■ Books

Archi, Alfonso. "L'humanité des Hittites." In *Florilegium anatolicum: Mélanges offerts à Emmanuel Laroche*, ed. E. Masson. Paris: Éditions E. de Boccard, 1979.

Bryce, Trevor. *Life and Society in the Hittite World*. New York: Oxford University Press, 2002.

———. *The Kingdom of the Hittites*, rev. ed. New York: Oxford University Press, 2005.

Hoffner, Harry A., Jr. *The Laws of the Hittites: A Critical Edition*. Leiden, Netherlands: Brill, 1997.

———. "Legal and Social Institutions of Hittite Anatolia." In *Civilizations of the Ancient Near East*, vol. 1, ed. Jack M. Sasson. Peabody, Mass: Hendrickson, 2000.

Roth, Martha. *Law Collections from Mesopotamia and Asia Minor*, 2nd ed. Atlanta, Ga.: Scholars Press, 1997.

■ Web Sites

"Hittite Home Page."
    http://www.mesas.emory.edu/hittitehome/

—Terri Tanaka

Questions for Further Study

1. Numerous "milestone" documents from the ancient and medieval worlds have to do with the establishment of law codes. Why was the development of a legal code a primary concern of these empires and nations and their rulers? How did differing historical circumstances lead to fundamentally different law codes—and, conversely, how did similar historical circumstances lead to fundamentally similar law codes?

2. What picture of ancient Hittite society emerges from the laws? What were the society's values and concerns? Was it a civil, just society? A violent, arbitrary society? Was it governed by reason, or by superstition? Explain your response.

3. Documents such as this one illuminate the procedures and questions of archeologists, historians, and others who are interested in the ancient world. What does your reading of this document and its discussion teach you about how archeologists and others go about their work?

4. Select one of the Hittite laws and compare it with what you might know about a corresponding law in modern society. Do any of the Hittite laws strike you as peculiarly "modern"? Explain.

5. To what extent did social status affect the penalties imposed on wrongdoers in ancient Hittite society? Do you believe that social class continues to affect sentencing for crimes in modern America, despite laws intended to prevent such disparities?

HITTITE LAWS

1 [If] anyone kills [a man] or a woman in a [quarr]el, he shall [bring him] for burial and shall give 4 persons, male or female respectively. He shall look [to his house for it.]

2 [If] anyone kills [a male] or female slave in a quarrel, he shall bring him for burial [and] shall give [2] persons, male or female respectively. He shall look to his house for it.

3 [If] anyone strikes a free [man] or woman so that he dies, but it is an accident, he shall bring him for burial and shall give 2 persons. He shall look to his house for it.

4 If anyone strikes a male or female slave so that he dies, but it is an accident, he shall bring him for burial and shall give one person. He shall look to his house for it.

5 If anyone kills a merchant (in a foreign land), he shall pay 4,000 shekels of silver. He shall look to his house for it. If it is in the lands of Luwiya or Pala, he shall pay the 4,000 shekels of silver and also replace his goods. If it is in the land of Hatti, he shall also bring the merchant himself for burial.

6 If a person, man or woman, is killed in another city, the victim's heir shall deduct 12,000 square meters from the land of the person on whose property the person was killed and shall take it for himself.

7 If anyone blinds a free person or knocks out his tooth, they used to pay 40 shekels of silver. But now he shall pay 20 shekels of silver. He shall look to his house for it.

8 If anyone blinds a male or female slave or knocks out his tooth, he shall pay 10 shekels of silver. He shall look to his house for it.

9 If anyone injures a person's head, they used to pay 6 shekels of silver: the injured party took 3 shekels of silver, and they used to take 3 shekels of silver for the palace. But now the king has waived the palace share, so that only the injured party takes 3 shekels of silver.

10 If anyone injures a person and temporarily incapacitates him, he shall provide medical care for him. In his place he shall provide a person to work on his estate until he recovers. When he recovers, his assailant shall pay him 6 shekels of silver and shall pay the physician's fee as well.

11 If anyone breaks a free person's arm or leg, he shall pay him 20 shekels of silver. He shall look to his house for it.

12 If anyone breaks a male or female slave's arm or leg, he shall pay 10 shekels of silver. He shall look to his house for it....

17 If anyone causes a free woman to miscarry, [if] it is her tenth month, he shall pay 10 shekels of silver, if it is her fifth month, he shall pay 5 shekels of silver. He shall look to his house for it.

18 If anyone causes a female slave to miscarry, [if] it is her tenth month, he shall pay 5 shekels of silver.

19a If a Luwian abducts a free person, man or woman, from the land of Hatti, and leads him away to the land of Luwiya/Arzawa, and subsequently the abducted person's owner recognizes him, the abductor shall bring (i.e., forfeit) his entire house.

19b If a Hittite abducts a Luwian man in the land of Hatti itself, and leads him away to the land of Luwiya, formerly they gave 12 persons, but now he shall give 6 persons. He shall look to his house for it....

22a If a male slave runs away, and someone brings him back, if he seizes him nearby, his owner shall give shoes to the finder.

22b If he seizes him on the near side of the river, he shall pay 2 shekels of silver. If on the far side of the river, he shall pay him 3 shekels of silver....

25a [If] a person is impure in a vessel or a vat, they used to pay 6 shekels of silver: the one who is impure pays 3 shekels of silver, and they used to take 3 shekels for the [king]'s house.

25b But now the king has [waived] the palace's share. The one who is impure only pays 3 shekels of silver. The claimant shall look to his/her house for it.

26a If a woman re[fuses] a man, [the man] shall give [her ...], and [the woman shall take] a wage for her seed. But the man [shall take the land] and the children. [...]

26b But if a man divor[ces] a woman, [and she ... s, he shall] s[ell her.] Whoever buys her *[shall] pa[y him] 12 shekels of silver.*

27 If a man takes his wife and leads [her] away to his house, he shall carry her dowry to his house. If the woman [dies] th[ere], they shall burn her personal possessions, and the man shall take her dowry. If

she dies in her father's house, and there [are] children, the man shall not [take] her dowry.

28a If a daughter has been promised to a man, but another man runs off with her, he who runs off with her shall give to the first man whatever he paid and shall compensate him. The father and mother (of the woman) shall not make compensation.

28b If her father and mother give her to another man, the father and mother shall make compensation (to the first man).

28c If the father and mother refuse to do so, they shall separate her from him.

29 If a daughter has been betrothed to a man, and he pays a brideprice for her, but afterwards the father and mother contest the agreement, they shall separate her from the man, but they shall restore the brideprice double.

30 But if before a man has taken the daughter in marriage he refuses her, he shall forfeit the brideprice which he has paid.

31 If a free man and a female slave are lovers and live together, and he takes her as his wife, and they make a house and children, but afterwards either they become estranged or they each find a new marriage partner, they shall divide the house equally, and the man shall take the children, with the woman taking one child.

32 If a male slave [takes] a [free] woman in marriage, [and they make a home and children, when they divide their house], they shall divide their possessions [equally, and the free woman shall take] most of [the children,] with [the male slave taking] one child.

33 If a male slave takes a female slave in marriage, [and they have children,] when they divide their house, they shall divide their possessions equally. [The slave woman shall take] mos[t of the children,] with the male slave [taking] one child.

34 If a male slave pays a brideprice for a woman and takes her as his wife, no one shall free her from slavery.

35 If a herdsman [takes] a free woman [in marriage], she will become a slave for (only) 3 years.

36 If a slave pays a brideprice for a free young man and acquires him as a son-in-law, no one shall free him from slavery.

37 If anyone elopes with a woman, and a group of supporters goes after them, if 3 or 2 men are killed, there shall be no compensation: "You (singular) have become a wolf."

38 If persons are engaged in a lawsuit, and some supporter goes to them, if a litigant becomes furious and strikes the supporter, so that he dies, there shall be no compensation....

40 If a man who has a TUKUL-obligation defaults, and a man owing *šahhan*-services has taken his place, the man owing *šahhan*-services shall say: "This is my TUKUL-obligation, and this other is my obligation for *šahhan*-services." He shall secure for himself a sealed deed concerning the land of the man having the TUKUL-obligation, he shall hold the TUKUL-obligation and perform the *šahhan*-services. But if he refuses the TUKUL-obligation, they will declare the land to be that of a man having a TUKUL-obligation who has defaulted, and the men of the village will work it. If the king gives an *arnuwalaš*-man, they will give him the land, and he will become a TUKUL-(man)....

42 If anyone hires a person, and that person goes on a military campaign and is killed, if the hire has been paid, there shall be no compensation. But if the hire has not been paid, the hirer shall give one slave.

43 If a man is crossing a river with his ox, and another man pushes him off (the ox's tail), seizes the tail of the ox, and crosses the river, but the river carries off the owner of the ox, the dead man's heirs shall take that man who pushes him off.

44a If anyone makes a man fall into a fire, so that he dies, he shall give a son in return.

44b If anyone performs a purification ritual on a person, he shall dispose of the remnants (of the ritual) in the incineration dumps. But if he disposes of them in someone's house, it is sorcery and a case for the king.

45 If anyone finds implements, [he shall bring] them back to their owner. He (the owner) will reward him. But if the finder does not give them (back), he shall be considered a thief....

48 A *hipparaš*-man renders the *luzzi*-services. Let no one transact business with a *hipparaš*-man. Let no one buy his child, his land, or his vineyard(s). Whoever transacts business with a *hipparaš*-man shall forfeit his purchase price, and the *hipparaš*-man shall take back whatever he sold.

49 [If] a *hipparaš*-man steals, there will be no compensation. But [if] ... , only his ... shall give compensation. If they (i.e., the *hipparaš*-man) [were] to have to give (compensation for) theft, they would all have been dishonest, or would have become thieves. This one would have seized that one, and that one this one. [They] would have overturned the king's authority(?)....

55 When [a delegation of] Hittites, men owing *šahhan*-services, came, they did reverence to the father of the king, and said: "No one pays us a wage. They say to us: 'You are men required to perform your jobs as a *šahhan* service!'" The father of the king

stepped into the assembly and declared under his seal: "You must continue to perform *šahhan*-services just like your colleagues."…

57 If anyone steals a bull—if it is a weanling calf, it is not a "bull"; if it is a yearling calf, it is not a "bull"; if it is a 2-year-old bovine, that is a "bull." Formerly they gave 30 cattle. But now he shall give 15 cattle: 5 two-year-olds, 5 yearlings, and 5 weanlings. He shall look to his house for it.…

60 If anyone finds a bull and castrates it, when its owner claims it, the finder shall give 7 cattle: 2 two-year-olds, 3 yearlings, and 2 weanlings. He shall look to his house for it.

61 If anyone finds a stallion and castrates it, when its owner claims it, the finder shall give 7 horses: 2 two-year-olds, 3 yearlings, and 2 weanlings. He shall look to his house for it.

62 If anyone finds a ram and castrates it, when its owner claims it, the finder shall give 7 sheep: 2 ewes, 3 wethers, and 2 sexually immature sheep. He shall look to his house for it.

63 If anyone steals a plow ox, formerly they gave 15 cattle, but now he shall give 10 cattle: 3 two-year-olds, 3 yearlings, and 4 weanlings. He shall look to his house for it.…

66 If a plow ox, a draft horse, a cow, or a mare strays into another corral, if a trained he-goat, a ewe, or a wether strays into another pen, and its owner finds it, he shall take it back in full. He shall not have the pen's owner arrested as a thief.…

70 If anyone steals an ox, a horse, a mule, or an ass, when its owner claims it, [he shall take] it in full. In addition the thief shall give to him double. He shall look to his house for it.

71 If anyone finds an ox, a horse, or a mule, he shall drive it to the king's gate. If he finds it in the country, they shall present it to the elders. The finder shall harness it (i.e., use it while it is in his custody). When its owner finds it, he shall take it in full but he shall not have the finder arrested as a thief. But if the finder does not present it to the elders, he shall be considered a thief.

72 If an ox is found dead on someone's property, the property-owner shall give 2 oxen. He shall look to his house for it.…

74 If anyone breaks the horn or leg of an ox, he shall take that ox for himself and give an ox in good condition to the owner of the injured ox. If the owner of the ox says: "I will take my own ox," he shall take his ox, and the offender shall pay 2 shekels of silver.

75 If anyone hitches up an ox, a horse, a mule or an ass, and it dies, [or] a wolf devours [it], or it gets lost, he shall give it in full. But if he says: "It died by the hand of a god," he shall take an oath to that effect.

76 If anyone impresses an ox, a horse, a mule or an ass, and it dies at his place, he shall bring it and shall pay its rent also.

77a If anyone strikes a pregnant cow, so that it miscarries, he shall pay 2 shekels of silver. If anyone strikes a pregnant horse, so that it miscarries, he shall pay 3 shekels of silver.

77b If anyone blinds the eye of an ox or an ass, he shall pay 6 shekels of silver. He shall look to his house for it.

78 If anyone rents an ox and then puts on it a leather … or a leather … , and its owner finds it he shall give 50 liters of barley.

79 If oxen enter another man's field, and the field's owner finds them, he may hitch them up for one day until the stars come out Then he shall drive them back to their owner.

80 If any shepherd throws a sheep to a wolf, its owner shall take the meat, but the shepherd shall take the sheepskin.

81 If anyone steals a fattened pig, they used to pay 40 shekels of silver. But now he shall pay 12 shekels of silver. He shall look to his house for it.…

87 If anyone strikes the dog of a herdsman a lethal blow, he shall pay 20 shekels of silver. He shall look to his house for it.…

91 [If] anyone [steals bees] in a swarm, [formerly] they paid [… shekels of silver], but now he shall pay 5 shekels of silver. He shall look to his house for it.

92 [If] anyone steals [2] or 3 bee hives, formerly the offender would have been exposed to bee-sting. But now he shall pay 6 shekels of silver. If anyone steals a bee-hive, if there are no bees in the hive, he shall pay 3 shekels of silver.

93 If they seize a free man at the outset, before he enters the house, he shall pay 12 shekels of silver. If they seize a slave at the outset, before he enters the house, he shall pay 6 shekels of silver.

94 If a free man burglarizes a house, he shall pay in full. Formerly they paid 40 shekels of silver as fine for the theft, but now [he shall pay] 12 shekels of silver. If he steals much, they will impose much upon him. If he steals little, they shall impose little upon him. He shall look to his house for it.

95 If a slave burglarizes a house, he shall pay in full. He shall pay 6 shekels of silver for the theft. He shall disfigure the nose and ears of the slave and they will give him back to his owner. If he steals much,

they will impose much upon him; if he steals little, they will impose little upon him. [If] his owner says: "I will make compensation for him," then he shall make it. But [if] he refuses, he shall lose that slave.

96 If a free man breaks into a grain storage pit, and finds grain in the storage pit, he shall fill the storage pit with grain and pay 12 shekels of silver. He shall look to his house for it.

97 If a slave breaks into a grain storage pit, and finds grain in the storage pit, he shall fill the storage pit with grain and pay 6 shekels of silver. He shall look to his house for it.

98 If a free man sets fire to a house, he shall rebuild [the house]. And whatever perished in the house—whether it is persons, [cattle, or sheep], it is damage(?). He shall make compensation for it.

99 If a slave sets fire to a house, his owner shall make compensation for him, and they shall disfigure the slave's nose and ears and return him to his owner. But if the owner will not make compensation, he shall forfeit that slave.

100 If anyone sets fire to a shed, he shall feed his (the owner's) cattle and bring them through to the following spring. He shall give back the shed. If there was no straw in it, he shall (simply) rebuild the shed.

101 If anyone steals a vine, a vine branch, a ... , or an onion/garlic, formerly [they paid] one shekel of silver for one vine and one shekel of silver for a vine branch, one shekel of silver [for one *karpina*, one] shekel of silver for one clove of garlic. And they shall strike a spear on his [...] [Formerly] they proceeded so. But now if he is a free man, he shall pay 6 shekels [of silver]. But if he is a slave, he shall pay 3 shekels of silver....

104 [If] anyone cuts down a pear(?) tree or plum(?) tree, he shall pay [... shekels] of silver. He shall look to his house for it.

105 [If] anyone sets [fire] to a field, and the fire catches a vineyard with fruit on its vines, if a vine, an apple tree, a pear(?) tree or a plum tree burns, he shall pay 6 shekels of silver for each tree. He shall replant [the planting]. And he shall look to his house for it. If it is a slave, he shall pay 3 shekels of silver for each tree.

106 If anyone carries embers into his field, catches(??) it while in fruit, and ignites the field, he who sets the fire shall himself take the burnt-over field. He shall give a good field to the owner of the burnt-over field, and he will reap it.

107 If a person lets his sheep into a productive vineyard, and ruins it, if it has fruit on the vines, he shall pay 10 shekels of silver for each 3,600 square meters. But if it is bare, he shall pay 3 shekels of silver.

108 If anyone steals vine branches from a fenced-in vineyard, if he steals 100 vines, he shall pay 6 shekels of silver. He shall look to his house for it. But if the vineyard is not fenced in, and he steals vine branches, he shall pay 3 shekels of silver.

109 If anyone cuts off fruit trees from their irrigation ditch, if there are 100 trees, he shall pay 6 shekels of silver.

110 If anyone steals clay from a pit, [however much] he steals, he shall give the same amount in addition.

111 [If] anyone forms clay for [an image] (for magical purposes), it is sorcery and a case for the king's court.

112 [If] they give [to an *arnuwalaš*-man] the land of a man having a TUKUL-obligation who has disappeared, [for 3 years] they shall perform no [*šahhan*-services], but in the fourth year he shall begin to perform *šahhan*-services and join the men having TUKUL-obligations.

113 [If] anyone cuts down a vine, he shall take the cut-down [vine] for himself and give to the owner of the vine the use of a good vine. The original owner of the cut-down vine shall gather fruit from the new vine [until] his own vine recovers....

121 If some free man steals a plow, and its owner finds it, he shall put [(the offender's) neck] upon the ... , and [he shall be put to death] by the oxen. So they proceeded formerly. But now he shall pay 6 shekels of silver. He shall look to his house for it. If it is a slave, [he shall pay] 3 shekels of silver.

122 If anyone steals a wagon with all its accessories, initially they paid one shekel of silver, [but now] he shall pay [... shekels of silver]. He shall look [to his] house [for it]....

124 If anyone steals a ... tree, he shall pay 3 shekels of silver. He shall look to his house for it. If anyone loads a wagon, [leaves] it in his field, and someone steals it, he shall pay 3 shekels of silver. He shall look to his house for it.

125 If anyone steals a wooden water trough, he shall pay [...] + one shekel of silver. If anyone steals a leather ... or a leather ... , he shall pay one shekel of silver.

126 If anyone steals a wooden ... in the gate of the palace, he shall pay 6 shekels of silver. If anyone steals a bronze spear in the gate of the palace, he shall be put to death. If anyone steals a copper pin, he shall give 25 liters of barley. If anyone steals the threads (or strands of wool) of one bolt of cloth, he shall give one bolt of woolen cloth.

127 If anyone steals a door in a quarrel, he shall replace everything that may get lost in the house, and he shall pay 40 shekels of silver. He shall look to his house for it.

128 If anyone steals bricks, however many he steals, he shall give the same number a second time over. If [anyone] steals stones from a foundation, for 2 stones he shall give 10 stones. If anyone steals a stela or a ... stone, he shall pay 2 shekels of silver.

129 If anyone steals a leather ... , a leather ... , a [...], or a bronze bell(?) <of> a horse or a mule, formerly they paid 40 shekels of silver, but now [he shall pay] 12 shekels of silver. He shall look to his house for it....

131 If [anyone steals] a leather harness(?), he shall pay 6 shekels of silver. [He shall look to his house for it.]

132 If a free man [steals ... , he shall pay] 6 shekels of silver. [He shall look to his house for it.] If he is a slave, [he shall pay 3 shekels of silver.] ...

143 If a free man [steals] copper shears(?) [or] a copper nail file(?), he shall pay 6 shekels of silver. [He shall look to] his house [for it]. If it is a slave, he shall pay 3 shekels of silver.

144 If a barber gives copper [... s] to his associate, and the latter ruins them, he shall replace [them] in full If anyone cuts fine cloth with a ... , he shall pay 10 shekels of silver. If anyone cuts [...], he shall pay 5 shekels of silver.

145 If anyone builds an ox barn, his employer shall pay him 6 shekels of silver. [If] he leaves out [...], he shall forfeit his wage.

146a If anyone offers a house, a village, a garden or a pasture for sale, and another goes and obstructs(?) the sale, and makes a sale of his own instead, as a fine for his offense he shall pay 40 shekels of silver, and buy [the ...] at the original prices.

146b [If] anyone offers a [...] person for sale, and another person obstructs(?) the sale, for his offense he shall pay 10 shekels of silver. He shall buy the person at the original prices.

147 [If] anyone offers an unskilled person for sale, and another person obstructs(?) the sale, as the fine for his offense he shall pay 5 shekels of silver.

148 [If] anyone [offers] an ox, a horse, a mule, or an ass [for sale], and another person preempts(?), as the fine for his offense he shall pay ... shekels of silver.

149 If anyone sells a trained person, and (afterwards, before delivery) says: "He has died," but his (new) owner tracks him down, he shall take him for himself, and in addition the seller shall give 2 persons to him. He shall look to his house for it.

150 If a man hires himself out for wages, his employer [shall pay ... shekels of silver] for [one month. If a woman] hires herself out for wages, her employer [shall pay ... shekels] for one month.

151 If anyone rents a plow ox, [he shall pay] one shekel [of silver] for one month. [If] anyone rents a [..., he shall pay] a half shekel of silver for one month.

152 If anyone rents a horse, a mule, or an ass, he shall pay one shekel of silver [for one month].

157 If a bronze axe weighs 1.54 kg, its rent shall be one shekel of silver for one month. If a copper axe weighs 0.77 kg, its rent shall be ½ shekel of silver for one month. If a bronze ...-tool weighs 0.5 kg, its rent shall be ½ shekel of silver for one month.

158a If a free man hires himself out for wages, to bind sheaves, load them on wagons, deposit them in barns, and clear the threshing floors, his wages for 3 months shall be 1,500 liters of barley.

158b If a woman hires herself out for wages in the harvest season, her wages shall be 600 liters of barley for 3 months' work.

159 If anyone hitches up a team of oxen for one day, its rent shall be 25 liters of barley.

160a If a smith makes a copper box weighing 1½ minas, his wages shall be 5,000 liters of barley.

160b If he makes a bronze axe weighing 2 minas, his wages shall be 50 liters of wheat.

161 If he makes a copper axe weighing one mina, his wages shall be 50 liters of barley.

162a If anyone diverts an irrigation ditch, he shall pay one shekel of silver. If anyone stealthily takes water from an irrigation ditch, he/it is ...ed. If he takes water at a point below the other's branch, it is his to use.

162b [If] anyone takes [...], whosoever [...] he prepares, [...]. [If] anyone [...s] sheep from a pasture, [... will be] the compensation, and he shall give its hide and meat.

163 If anyone's animals go crazy(?), and he performs a purification ritual upon them, and drives them back home, and he puts the mud(?) (used in the ritual) on the mud pile(?), but doesn't tell his colleague, so that the colleague doesn't know, and drives his own animals there, and they die, there will be compensation.

164 If anyone goes to someone's house to impress something, starts a quarrel, and breaks either the sacrificial bread or the libation vessel.

165 he shall give one sheep, 10 loaves of bread, and one jug of ... beer, and reconsecrate his house. Until [a year's] time has passed he shall keep away from his house.

166 If anyone sows his own seed on top of another man's seed, his neck shall be placed upon a plow. They shall hitch up 2 teams of oxen: they shall turn the faces of one team one way and the other team the other. Both the offender and the oxen will be put to death, and the party who first sowed the field shall reap it for himself. This is the way they used to proceed.

167 But now they shall substitute one sheep for the man and 2 sheep for the oxen. He shall give 30 loaves of bread and 3 jugs of … beer, and reconsecrate (the land?). And he who sowed the field first shall reap it.

168 If anyone violates the boundary of a field and takes one furrow off the neighbor's field, the owner of the violated field shall cut off a strip of his neighbor's land 0.25 meter deep along their common boundary and take it for himself. He who violated the boundary shall give one sheep, 10 loaves, and one jug of … beer and reconsecrate the field.

169 If anyone buys a field and violates the boundary, he shall take a thick loaf and break it to the Sungod [and] say: "You …ed my scales into the ground" And he shall speak thus: "O Sungod, O Stormgod. No quarrel (was intended)."

170 If a free man kills a snake, and speaks another's name, he shall pay 40 shekels of silver. If it is a slave, he alone shall be put to death.

171 If a mother removes her son's garment she is disinheriting her sons. If her son comes back into her house (i.e., is reinstated), he/she takes her door and removes it, he/she takes her … and her … and removes them, in this way she takes them (i.e., the sons) back; she makes her son her son again.

172 If anyone preserves a free man's life in a year of famine, the saved man shall give a substitute for himself. If it is a slave, he shall pay 10 shekels of silver.

173a If anyone rejects a judgment of the king, his house will become a heap of ruins. If anyone rejects a judgment of a magistrate, they shall cut off his head.

173b If a slave rebels against his owner, he shall go into a clay jar.

174 If men are hitting each other, and one of them dies, the other shall give one slave.

175 If either a shepherd or a foreman takes a free woman in marriage, she will become a slave after either two or four years. They shall … her children, but no one shall seize their belts.

176a If anyone keeps a bull outside a corral, it shall be a case for the king's court They shall sell the

bull. A bull is an animal that is capable of breeding in its third year. A plow ox, a ram, and a he-goat are animals that are capable of breeding in their third year.

176b If anyone buys a trained artisan: either a potter, a smith, a carpenter, a leather-worker, a fuller, a weaver, or a maker of leggings, he shall pay 10 shekels of silver.

177 If anyone buys a man trained as an augur(?), he shall pay 25 shekels of silver. If anyone buys an unskilled man or woman, he shall pay 20 shekels of silver.

178 The price of a plow ox is 12 shekels of silver. The price of a bull is 10 shekels of silver. The price of a full-grown cow is 7 shekels of silver. The price of a yearling plow ox or cow is 5 shekels of silver. The price of a weaned calf is 4 shekels of silver. If the cow is pregnant with a calf, the price is 8 shekels of silver. The price of one calf is 2 (variant: 3) shekels of silver. The price of one stallion, one mare, one male donkey, and one female donkey are the same….

187 If a man has sexual relations with a cow, it is an unpermitted sexual pairing: he will be put to death. They shall conduct him to the king's court. Whether the king orders him killed or spares his life, he shall not appear before the king (lest he defile the royal person).

188 If a man has sexual relations with a sheep, it is an unpermitted sexual pairing: he will be put to death. They will conduct him [to the] king's [court]. The king may have him executed, or may spare his life. But he shall not appear before the king.

189 If a man has sexual relations with his own mother, it is an unpermitted sexual pairing. If a man has sexual relations with his daughter, it is an unpermitted sexual pairing. If a man has sexual relations with his son, it is an unpermitted sexual pairing.

190 If they … with the dead—man, woman—it is not an offense. If a man has sexual relations with his stepmother, it is not an offense. But if his father is still living, it is an unpermitted sexual pairing.

191 If a free man sleeps with free sisters who have the same mother and with their mother—one in one country and the other in another, it is not an offense. But if it happens in the same location, and he knows the women are related, it is an unpermitted sexual pairing.

192 If a man's wife dies, [he may take her] sister [as his wife.] It is not an offense.

193 If a man has a wife, and the man dies, his brother shall take his widow as wife. (If the brother dies,) his father shall take her. When afterwards his

father dies, his (i.e., the father's) brother shall take the woman whom he had.

194 If a free man sleeps with slave women who have the same mother and with their mother, it is not an offense. If brothers sleep with a free woman, it is not an offense. If father and son sleep with the same female slave or prostitute, it is not an offense.

195a If a man sleeps with his brother's wife, while his brother is alive, it is an unpermitted sexual pairing.

195b If a free man has a free woman in marriage and approaches her daughter sexually, it is an unpermitted sexual pairing.

195c If he has the daughter in marriage and approaches her mother or her sister sexually, it is an unpermitted sexual pairing.

196 If anyone's male and female slaves enter into unpermitted sexual pairings, they shall move them elsewhere: they shall settle one in one city and one in another. A sheep shall be offered in place of one and a sheep in place of the other.

197 If a man seizes a woman in the mountains (and rapes her), it is the man's offense, but if he seizes her in her house, it is the woman's offense: the woman shall die. If the woman's husband discovers them in the act, he may kill them without committing a crime.

198 If he brings them to the palace gate (i.e., the royal court) and says: "My wife shall not die," he can spare his wife's life, but he must also spare the lover and 'clothe his head.' If he says, "Both of them shall die," they shall 'roll the wheel.' The king may have them killed or he may spare them.

199 If anyone has sexual relations with a pig or a dog, he shall die. He shall bring him to the palace gate (i.e., the royal court). The king may have them (i.e., the human and the animal) killed or he may spare them, but the human shall not approach the king. If an ox leaps on a man (in sexual excitement), the ox shall die; the man shall not die. They shall substitute one sheep for the man and put it to death. If a pig leaps on a man (in sexual excitement), it is not an offense.

200a If a man has sexual relations with either a horse or a mule, it is not an offense, but he shall not approach the king, nor shall he become a priest. If anyone sleeps with an *arnuwalaš*-woman, and also sleeps with her mother, it is not an offense.

200b If anyone gives his son for training either as a carpenter or a smith, a weaver or a leatherworker or a fuller, he shall pay 6 shekels of silver as the fee for the training. If the teacher makes him an expert, the student shall give to his teacher one person.

Glossary

***arnuwalaš*-man/ woman**	a person captured in battle
***šahhan*-services**	a type of service for the state
he shall give 4 persons	This and other stipulations like it ("2 persons" and so on) refer to the turning over of people to the family of the victim or the owner of the slave who was killed; it is unknown who was to be turned over.
He shall look [to his house for it.]	A greatly debated phrase in Hittite law that is thought to indicate that an injured party or his or her family has the right to receive compensation / damages from the estate of the perpetrator of the crime.
hipparaš	captive; prisoner of war
karpina	a type of tree
they shall roll the wheel	Although some scholars see this as a type of punishment or even execution (the exact nature of which is unknown), this interpretation is not certain.
TUKUL-obligation	a type of service for the state

DIVINE BIRTH AND CORONATION INSCRIPTIONS OF HATSHEPSUT

"[Amon] found her as she slept in the beauty of her palace. She waked at the fragrance of the god."

Overview

In ca.1473 BCE, a woman named Hatshepsut was crowned the pharaoh of Egypt. Queens—typically mothers or wives of the king—were common in ancient Egypt, and there is strong evidence to suggest that women had ruled as sole pharaoh earlier in Egyptian history. Unlike previous female pharaohs, however, Hatshepsut was an effective king who ruled over Egypt for more than twenty years. She ruled powerfully during a time when the country was strong, and her actions, including international trade and military campaigns, strengthened Egypt's place as an international power. She was unique, however, in that she was depicted not as a queen but as a king; she used male titles, and images of her show a male ruler, despite the use of female pronouns in her texts.

Hatshepsut was not the true heir to the throne. Her father was King Thutmose I, and she married her half-brother, Thutmose II; however, her nephew/stepson, Thutmose III, was the next in line for the kingship after Hatshepsut's husband died. Thutmose III was quite young when his father died, so Hatshepsut began to reign as his regent in about 1479 BCE. The two shared the throne until Hatshepsut's death. In order to justify her rulership, Hatshepsut commissioned an inscription detailing her divine birth and her coronation. In the history she wrote for herself, her mother was visited in the night by Amon, one of the chief gods in the Egyptian pantheon, and she was the result of that union. Thus, in her retelling, Hatshepsut's coronation made perfect sense; she went from possibly being seen as a usurper to being the legitimate heir to the throne. In later years, after Hatshepsut's death, Thutmose III and his successors went to great lengths to downplay her rule and erase the record of her name. Far from erasing her memory, the obscuring of her records has only highlighted the power that Hatshepsut wielded as a female pharaoh.

Context

Hatshepsut took the throne as the fifth pharaoh of the Eighteenth Dynasty during the epoch in Egyptian history known as the New Kingdom. The New Kingdom (the third major period in Egyptian history, following the Old and Middle Kingdoms) was inaugurated when Pharaoh Ahmose I and his brother, Kamose, defeated the Hyksos, who were a group of foreign rulers who had slowly begun to amass power and threaten native Egyptian rule. As a result of the threat of foreign rule, pharaohs of the New Kingdom turned more toward foreign expansion as well as political and military domination of the surrounding areas than their predecessors had.

The New Kingdom was a time of great imperial expansion, when Egypt saw its power spread outward from the banks of the Nile north along the Mediterranean coast into the Levant and south throughout Nubia (ancient Sudan). The Eighteenth Dynasty was the height of this growth. Egypt battled enemies in the north, extending its borders and controlling territory to the north as far as the Euphrates River, and it sponsored expeditions via the Red Sea south into Punt, a land far south of Egypt along the eastern African coast.

The Eighteenth Dynasty was also a time of religious upheaval. The most significant religious changes occurred after Hatshepsut's reign, when Pharaoh Amenhotep IV changed his name to Akhenaton and instituted a religion based on worship of a previously minor god, Aton. However, even at the beginning of the Eighteenth Dynasty, records reflect the growing power of the god Amon-Re, a syncretized version of the creator god Amon with the sun god Re. Hatshepsut claimed to have been divinely born, with Amon-Re as her father. Because Hatshepsut was not the direct heir to the throne, the crucial link with Amon-Re that her divine birth gave her was an essential precursor to her coronation, showing clearly that she was deserving of the throne.

About the Author

Hatshepsut was royal by birth, the daughter of King Thutmose I and his principal wife, Ahmose. Typically, in ancient Egypt the throne would pass to the eldest son of the pharaoh and his principal wife. In this case, Thutmose and Ahmose had no sons who survived childhood. The crown prince was Thutmose II (the son of Thutmose I and a lesser wife, Mutnofret). Marriages between half siblings

CA. **1550** BCE

- The Eighteenth Dynasty (and with it the New Kingdom) begins with the reign of Ahmose I, who comes to power after having expelled the Hyksos, foreign rulers who had grown powerful after settling in the northern part of Egypt.

CA. **1504** BCE

- Hatshepsut's father, Thutmose I, takes the throne and rules for twelve years before he dies, appointing his son, Thutmose II, as his successor.

CA. **1492** BCE

- Hatshepsut's husband and stepbrother, Thutmose II, takes the throne and rules for thirteen years before his death.

CA. **1479** BCE

- After the death of Thutmose II, his son (by a lesser wife), Thutmose III, takes the throne. Because Thutmose III is still young, Hatshepsut acts as regent.

CA. **1473** BCE

- By the seventh year of Thutmose III's reign, Hatshepsut has been crowned king. Now that she is officially the king—and not the king's mother—she does not lose the throne when Thutmose III comes of age.

were common amongst members of the royal family as a way of preserving the bloodline; therefore, Thutmose II and Hatshepsut were married. They had one child together, a daughter named Neferure. As they had no sons, at Thutmose II's death the throne passed to Thutmose III, who was the son of Thutmose II and a lesser wife, Isis. Because Thutmose III was quite young at the time of his father's death, Hatshepsut served as regent prior to her coronation around 1473 BCE. Hatshepsut never remarried, although evidence of a close relationship with one of her officials, Senenmut, has led some scholars to speculate that theirs may have been an intimate relationship. Senenmut served as the royal tutor for Neferure, and several statues depict him holding Neferure.

Although women in Egypt, especially in the royal family, could hold prestigious titles and important positions, the pharaoh was male, and the power of royal women was officially limited. Prior to her coronation, Hatshepsut had held the important titles of Great King's Wife and God's Wife of Amon. But after the death of her husband, Hatshepsut's power increased. Given that she was, in effect, ruling and the underage Thutmose III was probably not heavily involved, it makes sense that Hatshepsut would have wanted the title of pharaoh to go along with the responsibility of rulership. She was an effective ruler and led several military campaigns, in at least one of which, in Nubia, she may have fought. She also had commissioned a trade expedition to Punt, and it was commemorated on the walls of her mortuary temple at Deir el-Bahri. Her divine birth, also depicted at Deir el-Bahri along with her coronation, confirmed that she had been ordained as royalty by the gods even before her birth.

Conceptually, however, Hatshepsut's reign posed a problem for Egyptian society. The office of pharaoh was a male position, and the royal insignia that marked the pharaoh included a beard. Hatshepsut solved this by having herself depicted as a male, with a beard and royal (male) dress. Her inscriptions continued to refer to her as female, but the depictions of her while she was a pharaoh showed a male.

After Hatshepsut's death, an effort was undertaken by Thutmose III to efface her name from many of her monuments. The female pronouns used to refer to her were scratched out, and her images were chipped or hacked out. In some instances, her representations were replaced with other representations; for instance, her cartouche (an oval or oblong figure surrounding a monarch's name) was often replaced with that of her husband, Thutmose II. While some scholars have referred to this as a *damnatio memoriae*, or an attempt to erase Hatshepsut's memory and therefore her existence, Thutmose III's erasure of Hatshepsut was inconsistent. Additionally, the effacing of the monuments was not done immediately after her death. In fact, it may have occurred as many as twenty years later, suggesting that it was not an immediate reaction to invalidate her reign.

Controversy surrounding Hatshepsut was once more reawakened in 2007, when Zahi Hawass, the secretary general of Egypt's Supreme Council of Antiquities announced that the body of Hatshepsut, whose whereabouts for centuries had been unknown, was placed in storage in the Cairo Museum after its removal from a sealed tomb in the Valley of the Kings. Many royal mummies of the New Kingdom had been moved from their original tombs by Egyptian priests toward the end of the New Kingdom for protection against tomb robberies, and several bodies had been frequently misplaced and mislabeled. A box, known to be from Hatshepsut's tomb and labeled with her name, contained a tooth that matched a gap in the jaw of the mummy now suspected by Hawass and others to be the body of Hatshepsut.

Explanation and Analysis of the Document

The text of Hatshepsut's divine birth opens with her conception. In this first scene, the narrative describes Hatshepsut's mother, Ahmose, receiving a nocturnal visit from Amon-Re, who has taken the form of her husband in order to impregnate her. She awakes and immediately recognizes the deity, however, based on his scent; he smells sweet, like perfume from Punt. The Latin phrase *coivit cum ea*, literally meaning "he joined with her," indicates that Ahmose and the god had intercourse. Amon-Re then reveals his divine majesty to Ahmose, which impresses her sufficiently for her to allow the god to be able to do "all that he desired with her." After their union is complete, Amon-Re tells Ahmose that she will shortly give birth to a daughter who will become king. In one iconographic vignette, Ahmose is depicted as visibly pregnant before Hatshepsut is born.

The idea of divine birth had precedents in Egyptian literature. A tale recorded on the Westcar Papyrus, set during the Old Kingdom but probably dating to the Middle Kingdom, tells a similar story. In the Westcar Papyrus tale, a bored King Khufu of the Fourth Dynasty is being entertained by stories from his sons. When one of his sons introduces a magician, Khufu begs the magician to reveal his secrets. The magician holds off, telling Khufu that the secrets would be revealed to Khufu by the sons of a woman named Rededet. Rededet, the wife of the chief priest of Re (this story had happened before Amon and Re were syncretized), was impregnated in a fashion nearly identical to that of Ahmose and Amon-Re. The god, smelling of perfume, approached Rededet in the night under the guise of her husband. Hatshepsut's divine birth was also picked up by later pharaohs such as Amenhotep III, who used narratives of divine birth to assert their divinity.

In the next scene from the text, Amon calls forward the god Khnum to "make her, together with her *ka*, from these limbs which are in me." He reasserts that the child Hatshepsut is his own and asks Khnum, a ram-headed potter god, to "fashion her better than all gods." True to his profession as a potter, Khnum was often shown with a potter's wheel. In Egyptian mythology, he was said to literally create man on his wheel and place the created child into the womb of the mother.

According to the narrative, Khnum is thus responsible for the creation of Hatshepsut's *ka*. The Egyptians divided spiritual personhood into several distinct parts. Each per-

Time Line

CA. 1458 BCE
- Upon the death of Hatshepsut, Thutmose III takes the throne as sole king.

CA. 1437– 1427 BCE
- Thutmose III has Hatshepsut's name erased from many of her monuments.

CA. 1427 BCE
- Thutmose III dies after having ruled or coruled Egypt for more than fifty years.

son possessed a *ka*, a *ba*, and an *akh*. The *ba* and *akh* became most important at death and were each depicted as birds, with the *akh* being the spirit that is released at death and the *ba* being a human-headed bird that could travel back and forth between the body in the physical living world and the afterlife. The *ka*, on the other hand, was essentially the body's spiritual double. It could move around independently of the body and was the recipient of food offerings. The *ka* also played an essential role after death: The *ka* was the deceased's living memory. Obliterating someone's name or monuments, as Thutmose III may have tried with Hatshepsut, amounted to obliterating their *ka* and taking away their afterlife.

In the text, Khnum agrees to fashion the child, named Maatkare Hatshepsut (called Makere in the document). Once again this story is apocryphal: Hatshepsut adopted the name Maatkare later in life and was not given it at birth. Literally, Maatkare translates as "Maat is the *ka* of Re," which also indicates that the *ka* of the god Re was *maat*, an Egyptian concept that translates as "truth, justice, and order in the world." By associating herself with both Re and *maat* in her name, Hatshepsut furthers the idea that her reign is legitimate.

The baby Hatshepsut, the child Khnum fashions, and its double were all depicted as male in images that accompanied the text. However, the text itself uses feminine grammatical forms, with Khnum referring to Hatshepsut as a female as he addresses the child directly to tell her that he has fulfilled Amon-Re's wishes in making her glorious. Amon-Re, responding, is pleased with Khnum's work and with his daughter.

The next section, the coronation, continues immediately from the divine birth, suggesting that Hatshepsut saw her coronation as a necessary outgrowth of her divine birth; her right to rule was ordained since Amon-Re

The mummy of Queen Hatshepsut (AP/Wide World Photos)

approached her mother in the night. The carved images that accompanied the text depicted scenes of the coronation. In the inscription, Amon-Re expresses his satisfaction with Hatshepsut and asserts her fitness to rule. He echoes the language and the phraseology used in the birth scene, such as repeatedly stressing her dominion over the entire land, and this textual similarity promotes continuity between the two inscriptions.

A trip that Hatshepsut is alleged to have taken is narrated in the next section of the text. As the daughter of a pharaoh, this trip is one that likely would have been taken by a woman of her status. However, it is unknown whether this is a true narration of actual events or a continuation of the mythology surrounding her birth and coronation. The purpose of its inclusion in this text, however, is to suggest that her right to rule had been acknowledged and accepted even during her childhood, which again promotes the idea that she is a fit ruler and a worthy heir to the throne.

Throughout the text, Hatshepsut's divinity is stressed. In ancient Egypt, the office of the kingship was divine. This meant that the pharaoh, while recognized to be mortal, accepted a position that bestowed upon him quasi-divinity. He was thus both man and god, and after his death he would become wholly divine and take his place in the pantheon of Egyptian deities. By describing this trip in terms that continually reference the ways in which Hatshepsut is like a god,

the text is suggesting that at every point throughout her life Hatshepsut has been recognized as a pharaoh-to-be.

The trip also has special geographic significance. Although Eighteenth Dynasty pharaohs lived in and ruled from Thebes, in the southern part of Egypt, the traditional capital of Egypt was in the north, at Memphis. Ancient Egypt was divided into two major regions, Upper Egypt (in the south, reversed from our expectations because of the flow of the Nile from south to north) and Lower Egypt (in the north). The country had not always been united, and keeping the two halves of the country united was a major role of the pharaoh. Even in times of peace, the duality between Upper and Lower Egypt was an important part of the pharaonic iconography. The pharaoh wore a dual crown that combined the individual crowns of Upper and Lower Egypt. He often sat on a throne that depicted Seth (called "Set" in the document) and Horus, the emblematic gods of Upper and Lower Egypt, respectively, as they tied papyrus and lotus plants representing the two kingdoms around the hieroglyph for the verb meaning "uniting."

As the parade of gods, including Hathor, Amon, Atum, Khnum, and "all the gods that are in Thebes" welcome Hatshepsut during her travels, they are accepting her into their ranks—a status uniquely accorded to the pharaoh. The gods speak to her, ostensibly still a child, telling her in the future tense what she will do during her reign: "set [the land] in order," defeat Egypt's traditional enemies (the Tehenu, the Troglodytes/East Africans, and the chiefs of Retenu), and give offerings in Thebes with Amon-Re.

The acts of the coronation itself are recorded in the next chapter. The crowns are placed upon her head, first the red crown of Lower Egypt and then the white crown of Upper Egypt, creating the "double crown" of both lands. Each of three important gods is present to witness and confirm her coronation: Amon-Re, her father and the head of the pantheon; Atum, the creator god; and Thoth, the god of wisdom and of writing, who records the scene. The iconography is not fully preserved here, and it is likely that other gods would have been depicted as present as well.

The coronation is said by the text to have taken place on New Year's Day in order to bring the best fortune upon the event and Hatshepsut's reign. Her father is said to have chosen this day; again, this is apocryphal. Although Thutmose I supported the advancement of Hatshepsut's career, at least through an advantageous marriage that set her up as the king's wife upon his death, there is no evidence to suggest that Thutmose I recognized Hatshepsut as his successor.

In the next paragraph, Hatshepsut's father, Thutmose I, gives her the double crown with an invocation of his pride and her worthiness, proclaiming (again in the future tense) his expectations of her reign: that she will "be powerful in the Two Lands," fight against Egypt's enemies, and wear the crown. In other words, she will remain pharaoh and have a successful reign. He calls forth his courtiers to make the coronation official in front of an audience, and stresses that she is his chosen successor. Thus, according to the inscription, not only is Hatshepsut divinely born, an indication of her fitness as pharaoh, but she has also been selected by a previous pharaoh. His address to his court is as much of an endorsement of Hatshepsut's reign as it is an exhortation to his court to accept her reign. In response, his court acknowledges that they accept her as pharaoh.

To conclude the coronation, Thutmose I leads Hatshepsut in a ceremony. Running the circuit was a common Egyptian ceremony intended to show the strength and power (usually, the virility) of the king. Thutmose I also proclaims the names that Hatshepsut is now given to celebrate her accession to the throne, which is complete at this point. In the concluding remarks, the newly crowned Hatshepsut is led away by the gods to complete the ceremonies. Hatshepsut is purified, and her newly established reign is inaugurated with a blessing from Horus.

Audience

Both Hatshepsut's coronation and her divine birth were inscribed into the walls of her mortuary temple at Deir el-Bahri, near Luxor, Egypt. The pharaohs of the New Kingdom tended to have a tomb (typically subterranean) and a mortuary temple, which were usually separated. Hatshepsut's mortuary temple, named Djeser-Djeseru, or "holy of holies," is still largely intact and a phenomenal piece of architecture, with columned courts spanning three levels.

Granite statue of Senenmut holding Princess Neferure
(© The Trustees of the British Museum)

It remains a standing monument to the magnificence of Hatshepsut, both visually striking and laden with inscriptions attesting to her divinity and majesty. In ancient times, her mortuary temple was an integral part of an annual procession in which a representation of the god Amon-Re would travel from his major temple across the river to Hatshepsut's temple with great fanfare. This procession furthered her association with Amon-Re.

Who exactly would have seen—and understood—the inscriptions in Hatshepsut's mortuary temple is open for debate. While almost any Egyptian living in or near Thebes (ancient Luxor) would have seen the monument and likely would have known that it was Hatshepsut's, only high-ranking Egyptian elites probably visited the temple itself. Furthermore, few Egyptians would have been able to read the inscriptions, as literacy rates in ancient Egypt were low. According to even liberal estimates, it is likely that less than 10 percent of the population was able to read. The divine birth and coronation inscriptions are lavishly illustrated and located on the middle terrace of the temple. Other inscriptions on this same level are dedicated to the goddess Hathor and the jackal-headed god Anubis and again stress Hatshepsut's divinity as pharaoh.

Temple of Deir el-Bahri, built in the reign of Hatshepsut (Library of Congress)

Impact

The evidence from Hatshepsut's reign, such as the massive monuments she was able to build and the expeditions she is known to have undertaken, suggests that she ruled peacefully as king for at least fifteen years. Her reign, however, did not pave the way for a succession of female rulers. Instead, the attempts by Thutmose III to obliterate many of her records may have been partly in reaction to the idea of a female pharaoh. Women, especially royal women, were accorded high status in Egyptian society, but this was in positions like those held by Hatshepsut prior to her coronation, such as god's wife or king's mother—important positions, but not pharaoh. The king of Egypt was a male, and after Hatshepsut's death it may have been easier to erase her legacy rather than to rewrite Egyptian royal ideology around a female ruler who had been essentially an anomaly.

"[Amon] found her as she slept in the beauty of her palace. She waked at the fragrance of the god…. He went to her immediately, coivit cum ea, he imposed his desire upon her, he caused that she should see him in his form of a god…. She rejoiced at the sight of his beauty, his love passed into her limbs, which the fragrance of the god flooded; all his odors were from Punt."

(Birth of Queen Hatshepsut)

"They [the gods] said, 'Welcome, daughter of Amon-Re; thou hast seen thy administration in the land, thou shall set in order, thou shalt restore that which has gone to its ruin, thou shalt make thy monuments in this house, thou shalt victual the offering-tables of him who begat thee, thou shalt pass through the land and thou shalt embrace many countries.'"

(Coronation of Queen Hatshepsut)

"They [the gods] shall set thy boundary as far as the breadth of heaven, as far as the limits of the twelfth hour of the night; the Two Lands shall be filled with children—, thy numerous children are [as] the number of thy grain."

(Coronation of Queen Hatshepsut)

"Said his majesty [Thutmose I] to her: 'Come, glorious one; I have placed (thee) before me; that thou mayest see thy administration in the palace, and the excellent deeds of thy ka's that thou mayest assume thy royal dignity, glorious in thy magic, mighty in thy strength. Thou shalt be powerful in the Two Lands; thou shalt seize the rebellious; thou shalt appear in the palace, thy forehead shall be adorned with the double diadem'."

(Coronation of Queen Hatshepsut)

"As for any man who shall love her in his heart, and shall do her homage every day, he shall shine, and he shall flourish exceedingly; [but] as for any man who shall speak against the name of her majesty, the god shall determine his death immediately, even by the gods who exercise protection behind her every day."

(Coronation of Queen Hatshepsut)

Years later, during the Nineteenth Dynasty, many of Hatshepsut's monuments were restored. She does appear in the history of Egypt written by the priest Manetho in the third century BCE, although no other classical sources make mention of her. With the dawn of modern Egyptology and the decipherment of hieroglyphs in the early nineteenth century, scholars were left with puzzling clues about this enigmatic woman who was often depicted as a man. Her divine birth and coronation came off in early scholarly interpretations as desperate attempts to justify a succession that was likely fraught with intrigue and controversy.

Modern historians are still left with as many questions as answers about the person of Hatshepsut, her divine birth, and her coronation. While some see her as a feminist icon to be heralded, others view her as an exception. Current scholarship has tended to focus less on the significance of her gender and more on the innovative ways in which she adapted iconography and ideology to accommodate her reign. Whether her coronation indicates that the Egyptians were more progressive toward gender relations than many ancient societies or whether her proscription indicates that she was an aberration, Hatshepsut's divine birth and coronation gave her a lasting place in the Egyptian canon of kings—and beyond.

Further Reading

■ Articles

Brown, Chip. "The King Herself." *National Geographic* (April 2009): 88–111. Available online. National Geographic Web site. http://ngm.nationalgeographic.com/2009/04/hatshepsut/brown-text.html.

Forbes, Dennis. "Power behind the Throne: Senenmut." *KMT* 1, no. 1 (Spring 1990): 14–19.

————. "Maatkare Hatshepset: The Female Pharaoh." *KMT* 16, no. 3 (Fall 2005): 26–42.

Roehrig, Catharine. "Hatshepsut and the Metropolitan." *KMT* 1, no. 1 (Spring 1990): 28–33.

Teeter, Emily. "Wearer of the Royal Uraeus: Hathsepsut." *KMT* 1, no. 1 (Spring 1990): 4–13.

■ Books

Roehrig, Catharine, et al., eds. *Hatshepsut: From Queen to Pharaoh.* New York: Metropolitan Museum of Art Publications, 2005.

Tyldesley, Joyce. *Hatchepsut: The Female Pharaoh.* New York: Penguin Books, 1998.

Winlock, H. E. *In Search of the Woman Pharaoh Hatshepsut. Excavations at Deir el-Bahri 1911–1931.* London: Kegan Paul International, 2001.

■ Web Sites

Hawass, Zahi. "The Search for Hatshepsut and the Discovery of Her Mummy." Zahi Hawass Web site. http://www.guardians.net/hawass/hatshepsut/search_for_hatshepsut.htm.

—T. Musacchio

Questions for Further Study

1. Why would it have been necessary at the time for Hatshepsut to establish divine origins?

2. Traditionally, female monarchs have faced difficulties their male counterparts have not had to face. Locate information about another female monarch or regent—one possibility is Empress Dowager Longyu, discussed in "Articles Providing for the Favorable Treatment of the Great Ching Emperor after His Abdication"—and discuss how female monarchs have dealt with such difficulties, including questions about their legitimacy.

3. Compare and contrast this document with "Mandate of Heaven: The Numerous Officers." What similarities and differences do you see in efforts of early monarchs to legitimate their rule?

4. What role did Hatshepsut play in the expansion of the Egyptian empire? Why did the Egyptians at that time feel the need to expand that empire?

5. The question is often debated as to whether Hatshepsut was a feminist icon or an aberration in the history of Egyptian pharaohs. Which do you think she was? What evidence supports your view?

Divine Birth and Coronation Inscriptions of Hatshepsut

Milestone Documents

Birth of Queen Hatshepsut

Utterance of Amon-Re, lord of Thebes, presider over Karnak. He made his form like the majesty of this husband, the King Okheperkere (Thutmose I). He found her as she slept in the beauty of her palace. She waked at the fragrance of the god, which she smelled in the presence of his majesty. He went to her immediately, coivit cum ea, he imposed his desire upon her, he caused that she should see him in his form of a god. When he came before her, she rejoiced at the sight of his beauty, his love passed into her limbs, which the fragrance of the god flooded; all his odors were from Punt.

Utterance by the king's-wife and king's-mother Ahmose, in the presence of the majesty of this august god, Amon, Lord of Thebes: "How great is thy fame. It is splendid to see thy front; thou hast united my majesty with thy favors, thy dew is in all my limbs." After this, the majesty of this god did all that he desired with her.

Utterance of Amon, Lord of the Two Lands, before her: "Khnemet-Amon-Hatshepsut shall be the name of this my daughter, whom I have placed in thy body, this saying which comes out of thy mouth. She shall exercise the excellent kingship in this whole land. My soul is hers, my [bounty] is hers, my crown [is hers,] that she may rule the Two Lands, that she may lead all the living———."

Utterance of Amon, presider over Karnak: "Go, to make her, together with her ka, from these limbs which are in me; go, to fashion her better than all gods; [shape for me,] this my daughter, whom I have begotten. I have given to her all life and satisfaction, all stability, all joy of heart from me, all offerings, and all bread, like Re, forever."

[Reply of Khnum:]

"I will form this [thy] daughter [Makere] (Hatshepsut), for life, prosperity and health; for offerings———for love of the beautiful mistress. Her form shall be more exalted than the gods, in her great dignity of King of Upper and Lower Egypt."

Utterance of Khnum, the *potter*, lord of Hirur (*Hr-wr*): "I have formed thee of these limbs of Amon, presider over Karnak. I have come to thee to fashion thee better than all gods. I have given to thee all life

and satisfaction, all stability, all joy of heart with me; I have given to thee all health, all lands; I have given to thee all countries, all people; I have given to thee all offerings, all food; I have given to thee to appear upon the throne of Horus like Re, forever; I have given to thee to be before the ka's of all the living, while thou shinest as King of Upper and Lower Egypt, of South and North, according as thy father who loves thee has commanded." ...

Utterance of [Amon] ... ———to see his daughter, his beloved, the king, Makere (Hatshepsut), living, after she was born, while his heart was exceedingly happy.

Utterance of [Amon to] his bodily daughter [Hatshepsut]: "Glorious part which has come forth from me; king, taking the Two Lands, upon the Horus-throne forever." ...

Coronation of Queen Hatshepsut

Utterance of Amon-Re, lord of [heaven to] the gods: "Behold ye, my daughter [Hatshepsut] living; be ye loving toward her, and be ye satisfied with her."

He shows her to all the gods of South and North, who come to look upon her, [doing obeisance before her].

Utterance of all the gods, [to] Amon-[Re]: "This thy daughter [Hatshepsut], who liveth, we are satisfied with her in life and peace. She is now thy daughter of thy form, whom thou hast begotten, prepared. Thou hast given to her thy soul, thy [—], thy [bounty], the magic powers of the diadem. While she was in the body of her that bare her, the lands were hers, the countries were hers; all that the heavens cover, all that the sea encircles. Thou hast now done this with her, for thou knowest the two aeons. Thou hast given to her the share of Horus in life, the years of Set in satisfaction. We have given to her...."

Her majesty saw all this thing herself, which she told to the people, who heard, falling down for terror among them. Her majesty grew beyond everything; to look upon her was more beautiful than anything; her [—] was like a god, her form was like a god, she did everything as a god, her splendor was like a god; her majesty was a maiden, beautiful, blooming, Buto in her time. She made her divine form to flourish, a [favor of] him that fashioned her.

Her majesty journeyed to the North country after her father, the King of Upper and Lower Egypt, Okheperkere, who liveth forever. There came her mother, Hathor, patroness of Thebes; Buto, mistress of Dep; Amon, lord of Thebes; Atum, lord of Heliopolis; Montu, lord of Thebes; Khnum, lord of the Cataract; all the gods that are in Thebes, all the gods of the South and North, and approached her. They traversed for her, pleasant ways, (they) came, and they brought all life and satisfaction with them, they exerted their protection behind her; one proceeded after another of them, they passed on behind her every day.

They said, "Welcome, daughter of Amon-Re; thou hast seen thy administration in the land, thou shall set in order, thou shalt restore that which has gone to its ruin, thou shalt make thy monuments in this house, thou shalt victual the offering-tables of him who begat thee, thou shalt pass through the land and thou shalt embrace many countries. Thou shalt strike among the Tehenu, thou shalt smite with the mace the Troglodytes; thou shalt cut off the beads of the soldiers, thou shalt seize the chiefs of Retenu, bearing the sword, the survivals of thy father. Thy tribute is myriads of men, the captives of thy valor; thy [reward] is thousands of men for the temples of the [Two Lands]. Thou givest offerings in Thebes, the steps of the king, Amon-Re, lord of Thebes. The gods have [endowed] thee with years, they [present] thee with life and satisfaction, they praise thee, for their heart hath given understanding to the egg which [they] have fashioned. They shall set thy boundary as far as the breadth of heaven, as far as the limits of the twelfth hour of the night; the Two Lands shall be filled with children—, thy numerous children are (as) the number of thy grain, [which] thou [—] in the hearts of thy people; it is the daughter of the bull of his mother—beloved." ...

[Inscriptions:] Presented to thee is this red crown, which is upon the head of Re; thou shalt wear the double crown, and thou shalt take the Two Lands by this its name.

Presented to thee is this white crown, mighty upon thy head; thou shalt take the lands by its diadem, by this its name....

[Inscriptions (Words of Thoth):] *"Thou hast set these thy diadems [upon thy head]."* ...

[Inscriptions:]

There saw her the majesty of her father, this Horus; how divine is her great fashioner. Her heart is glad, (for) great is her crown; she advocates her cause [in] truth, [exalter] of her royal dignity, and of that which her ka does. The living were set before her in his palace of [—]. Said his majesty to her: "Come, glorious one; I have placed (thee) before me; that thou mayest see thy administration in the palace, and the excellent deeds of thy ka's that thou mayest assume thy royal dignity, glorious in thy magic, mighty in thy strength. Thou shalt be powerful in the Two Lands; thou shalt seize the rebellious; thou shall appear in the palace, thy forehead shall be adorned with the double diadem, resting upon the head of the heiress of Horus, whom I begat, daughter of the white crown, beloved of Buto. The diadems are given to thee by him who presides over the thrones of the gods."

My majesty caused that there be brought to him the dignitaries of the king, the nobles, the companions, the officers of the court, and the chief of the people, that they may do homage, to set the majesty of the daughter of this Horus before him in his palace of [—]. There was a sitting of the king himself, in the audience-hall of the right of the [court], while these people prostrated themselves in the court.

Said his majesty before them: "This my daughter, Khnemet-Amon, Hatshepsut, who liveth, I have appointed [her]—; she is my successor upon my throne, she it assuredly is who shall sit upon my wonderful seat. She shall command the people in every place of the palace; she it is who shall lead you; ye shall proclaim her word, ye shall be united at her command. He who shall do her homage shall live, be who shall speak evil in blasphemy of her majesty shall die. Whosoever proclaims with unanimity the name of her majesty, shall enter immediately into the royal chamber, just as it was done by the name of this Horus.... For thou art divine, O daughter of a god, for whom even the gods fight; behind whom they exert their protection every day according to the command of her father, the lord of the gods."

The dignitaries of the king, the nobles and the chief of the people hear this command for the advancement of the dignity of his daughter, the king of Upper and Lower Egypt, Makere ... living forever. They kissed the earth at his feet, when the royal word fell among them; they praised all the gods for the King of Upper and Lower Egypt, Okheperkere ... , living forever. They went forth, their mouths rejoiced, they published his proclamation [to] them. All the people of all the dwellings of the court heard; they came, their mouths rejoicing, they proclaimed (it) beyond everything, dwelling on dwelling therein was announcing (it) in his name; soldiers on soldiers [—], they leaped and they danced for the double joy of their hearts. They [proclaimed], they [proclaimed] the name of her majesty as king; while her majesty was a youth, while the great god was [turning] their hearts to his daughter, Makere …, living forever, when they recognized that it was the fa[ther] of the divine daughter, and thus they were excellent in her great soul beyond everything. As for any man who shall love her in his heart, and shall do her homage every day, he shall shine, and he shall flourish exceedingly; [but] as for any man who shall speak against the name of her majesty, the god shall determine his death immediately, even by the gods who exercise protection behind her every day. The majesty of this her father hath published this, all the people have united upon the name of this his daughter for king. While her majesty was a youth, the heart of his majesty inclined to [her] exceedingly.

His majesty commanded that the ritual priests be brought to [proclaim] her great names that belonged to the assumption of the dignities of Her royal crown and for insertion in (every) work and every seal of the Favorite of the Two Goddesses, who makes the circuit north of the wall, who clothes all the gods of the Favorite of the Two Goddesses. He has recognized the auspiciousness of the coronation on New Year's Day as the beginning of the peaceful years and of the spending of myriads (of years) of very many jubilees. They proclaimed her royal names, for the god caused that it should be in their hearts to make her names according to the form with which he had made them before:

Her great name, Horus: [Woaretkew], forever;

Her great name, Favorite of the Two Goddesses: "Fresh in Years," good goddess, mistress of offering;

Her great name, Golden Horus: "Divine of diadems";

Her great name of King of Upper and Lower Egypt: "Makere, who liveth forever."

It is her real name which the god made beforehand.

[Horus says:] *"Thou hast established thy dignity as king, and appeared upon the Horus-throne."*

Glossary

Buto	cobra goddess, patron of Lower Egypt and joint protector of all Egypt
coivit cum ea	literally, "he joined with her," or had intercourse
ka	the spiritual double of the physical body of a person
Okheperkere	Thutmose I
Montu	falcon god of war

Egyptian-Hittite Peace Treaty

"He is [my] brother, and I am his brother."

Overview

In 1259 BCE the Egyptian pharaoh Ramses II and Emperor Hattusilis III (also called Hattusili) of Hatti concluded a treaty of peace and alliance, ending some eighty years of warfare between the two ancient superpowers. Although this was not the first peace treaty in history, it is the oldest known accord between independent states of equal status and power. A bronze replica prominently displayed in the United Nations building in New York reflects its status as a milestone document in diplomatic history.

Among the treaty's main provisions are a peace and nonaggression pact, a mutual defense alliance, and an extradition agreement for the return of fugitives. Most of the clauses are bilateral, meaning that each side had the same rights and responsibilities under the treaty. The one unilateral clause requires the pharaoh to come to the aid of the Hittite king or his rightful heirs if his Hittite subjects should ever attempt to overthrow him. As a legal document, the treaty takes the form of a religious oath sworn personally by the two kings to a thousand gods of Hatti and a thousand gods of Egypt.

The Egyptians and Hittites each drafted very similar, but not identical, treaty documents. They were written in the cuneiform script of the Akkadian dialect of Babylonia, the common diplomatic language of the second millennium BCE, and inscribed on silver tablets, which the kingdoms exchanged. Only copies of these tablets have survived. In the ruins of the state archives of the ancient Hittite capital of Hattushash (modern-day Bogazköy in central Turkey), archaeologists discovered clay-tablet "file copies" of the silver tablet sent by the pharaoh. In Egypt, Ramses II ordered the silver tablet sent by the Hittites to be translated into the Egyptian language and inscribed in hieroglyphs on the walls of two temples in the ancient city of Thebes (present-day Luxor in southern Egypt).

Context

The Egyptian-Hittite treaty dates to the closing centuries of the Late Bronze Age (ca. 1600–1100 BCE), when a few great empires dominated the ancient Near East (the modern-day Middle East). These empires controlled many smaller kingdoms called vassal states. Between 1550 and 1100 BCE the Egyptian empire had dominion over the eastern coast of the Mediterranean, including present-day Israel, Lebanon, and parts of western Syria. Hatti was located in the center of Turkey, with its empire extending into western Turkey. At some unknown point before 1353 BCE, Egypt and Hatti made a treaty of peace and friendship. Since they did not share a common border at this time, relations were good. But around 1340 BCE, during the reign of the Egyptian pharaoh Akhenaton, the Hittite emperor Suppiluliumas (or Suppiluliuma) I conquered much of Syria, including Amurru and Kadesh, two of Egypt's vassal provinces. This was not a clear case of Hittite aggression; the vassal king of Amurru voluntarily switched to the Hittite side, and Suppiluliumas claimed that the king of Kadesh had attacked him first. Yet Egypt refused to accept the loss of its northern border territories. Over a number of decades, between 1340 and 1269 BCE, pharaohs tried to recover these provinces by force. Military campaigns against Kadesh by the last pharaohs of the Eighteenth Dynasty (ca. 1550–1292 BCE)—Akhenaton, Tutankhamen, and possibly Horemheb—all failed.

When Tutankhamen died, his widowed queen attempted to negotiate an end to the war by marrying a Hittite prince and making him pharaoh. Historical records of the Hittite emperor Suppiluliumas I report that when the Egyptian ambassadors brought the queen's proposal, he showed them the old treaty tablet between Egypt and Hatti. The emperor was reminding the Egyptian ambassadors that the two countries had peaceful relations and a treaty in the past before the recent war. A Hittite prince was sent to Egypt after further negotiations, but he died mysteriously on the journey. Despite Egyptian denials, a furious Suppiluliumas accused them of murder. He retaliated by attacking Egyptian territory in Lebanon, and the war continued.

In the early Nineteenth Dynasty, around 1285 BCE, Pharaoh Seti I reconquered Kadesh and Amurru, but they soon returned to Hittite control. Some scholars believe that the Hittite emperor Muwatallis II negotiated a new treaty with a pharaoh at about this time, either with Horemheb or Seti I. If so, the Egyptians quickly broke it by assaulting

BEFORE 1353 BCE
- At some unknown point before the reign of Pharaoh Akhenaton, and prior to the two kingdoms' sharing a common border in Syria, Egypt and Hatti conclude a treaty of friendship.

CA. 1340 BCE
- The Hittite emperor Suppiluliumas I conquers much of Syria during the reign of Akhenaton, including the Egyptian border provinces of Amurru and Kadesh.

1324 BCE
- At the end of Tutankhamen's reign, a second Egyptian military expedition against Kadesh fails.

CA. 1295 BCE
- Egyptian and Hittite forces clash in Syria during the reigns of the last pharaoh of the Eighteenth Dynasty, Horemheb, and the Hittite emperor Mursilis (also called Mursili) II.

CA. 1285 BCE
- Seti I, the second pharaoh of the Nineteenth Dynasty, recaptures Kadesh and Amurru but is unable to hold on to them.

Kadesh again. Other scholars contend that there was no new treaty yet.

◆ The Battle of Kadesh

The Egyptian-Hittite war was not a continuous conflict but a series of battles over many years separated by periods without fighting. In 1274 BCE, the fifth year of Ramses II's sixty-seven-year reign, the largest clash took place, the famous Battle of Kadesh. This was the last of four or five Egyptian offensives against Kadesh. Never before had such huge armies met on the battlefield. The Hittites managed to ambush Egyptian forces, and historians often present the battle as a crushing defeat for Ramses II despite his personal bravery. The result was more of a draw, with no clear victor. Kadesh remained in Hittite control, and no pharaoh would ever lay siege to it again. At home, Ramses II actually immortalized the battle as a personal victory with triumphal war scenes and poetic accounts of his heroism emblazoned on the walls of great temples throughout Egypt. This huge propaganda campaign was an ancient version of mass media. The pharaoh never claimed that he captured Kadesh but instead "spun" events to highlight his own courage under fire.

After Kadesh the war continued. Ramses II twice led his armies back into Syria, bypassing Kadesh to strike deep inside Hittite territory. He captured several enemy towns, but the two empires were deadlocked in a classic military stalemate. The pharaoh could not hold on to territory captured in Syria, but the Hittites could not stop him from trying.

◆ The Egyptian-Hittite Peace Process

In 1259 BCE, fifteen years after the Battle of Kadesh and more than eighty years after the Egyptian-Hittite war began, Ramses II concluded a peace treaty with the Hittite emperor Hattusilis III. One possible impetus for peace at this point in the long, bitter conflict was that Hatti feared a new threat on its eastern border. The Assyrian Empire (in the north of modern-day Iraq) was expanding westward into Syria, where it absorbed a Hittite vassal state. Faced with a two-front war, some scholars argue, the Hittites opted for a deal with their old enemy, Egypt. Yet the Hittites were often surrounded by enemies throughout their history, making fear a dubious motive for the treaty with Egypt. A political crisis in Hatti may be a better explanation for Hattusilis III's peace offer. Several years after the Battle of Kadesh, Hattusilis III became emperor by overthrowing his nephew Urhi-Teshub in a coup d'état. Urhi-Teshub fled to Egypt, where Ramses II gave him refuge. Hattusilis III was considered an illegitimate usurper by many of his own subjects and by the other "Great Kings" of the era, and his attempts to establish friendly diplomatic relations with Assyria and Babylonia failed.

Thus, for Hattusilis III, a peace deal with the pharaoh could solve various political difficulties by giving him diplomatic recognition as a legal ruler and by neutralizing the threat from his deposed nephew, Urhi-Teshub, who remained in Egypt. As for Ramses II, he had fought the Hittites in Syria for two decades, and his kingdom had been at war for eighty years. The pharaoh had won some battles but lost others, such that Egypt's empire was no larger than when the war began; territorial gains were almost nil. Kadesh and Amurru remained in the Hittite camp. But Ramses could not go meekly to the Hittites asking for a truce. In Egyptian ideology, the pharaoh was all conquering, and he ruled the entire world. Peace was acceptable only if a defeated enemy came in submission to beg for the "breath of life." This supremacist worldview was so deeply rooted in the Egyptian psyche that the pharaoh would have found it hard to accept the reality of military failure.

Since there could be no peace without honor, Ramses had to wait for the Hittites to come to him. Even then, he probably rejected several peace offers before agreeing. One inscription of Ramses II claims that the Hittite emperor sent messages, year after year, to make peace, but the pharaoh refused. While the two sides were political equals in the treaty that was ultimately forged, Ramses presented it to his Egyptian subjects as a Hittite surrender. In reality, Ramses II made a serious and bitter concession, giving up all claims to Amurru and Kadesh. Surprisingly, however, the treaty between Ramses II and Hattusilis III never mentions borders or territory. The two sides chose to neglect the issue in the document, allowing the pharaoh to save face.

About the Author

The parallel treaty documents were composed by unnamed court scribes in Egypt and Hatti, but credit is given only to their royal masters, Ramses II and Hattusilis III. The scribes, who were trained in the Akkadian language and cuneiform script, the language of diplomacy at that time, were probably also the diplomats who negotiated the deal. The three Egyptian and four Hittite diplomats who delivered the Hittite silver tablet to Ramses II are named in the introduction to the hieroglyphic version, though the names of the second and third Egyptian ambassadors have been destroyed. The first was "the royal messenger and chariot officer Netcherwymes," whose tomb has been discovered at Saqqara, near modern-day Cairo. A "royal messenger" was a kind of Egyptian diplomat. The Hittite ambassadors are identified as Nerkil, Tili-Teshub, Yapusili, and a man labeled the "the second-ranked messenger of Hatti Ramose." While the other three names are Hittite, Ramose is an Egyptian name, and he must have been an Egyptian expatriate. Why he served the Hittite emperor is unknown. Perhaps he was a former prisoner of war who had gained his freedom through service to the Hittites in diplomatic relations with his homeland. His colleague Tili-Teshub is known from Hittite diplomatic archives.

Ramses II was the third king of Egypt's Nineteenth Dynasty and one of the greatest pharaohs. He ruled for sixty-seven years and left grand monuments throughout the Egyptian Empire. Ramses fought several military campaigns in Syria-Palestine during the first two decades of his reign, chiefly against Hittite territory in Syria.

Hattusilis III was the brother of the Hittite emperor Muwatallis II. Muwatallis was succeeded by his son Urhi-

Time Line	
1274 BCE	■ In his fifth year as pharaoh, Ramses II fights a huge battle against the Hittite emperor Muwatallis II at Kadesh but is unable to prevail.
1271 BCE	■ Ramses II begins to fight a number of wars in Hittite-controlled Syria but cannot retain the towns he captures, as the long military stalemate continues.
CA. **1270** BCE	■ The Assyrian Empire conquers a Hittite vassal kingdom in eastern Syria.
1267 BCE	■ There is political unrest in Hatti when Urhi-Teshub is overthrown by his uncle Hattusilis III, who fails to establish good relations with the Assyrian and Babylonian empires.
CA. **1260** BCE	■ Hattusilis III begins peace negotiations with Ramses II.
1259 BCE	■ In the twenty-first year of Ramses' reign, the Egyptian-Hittite peace treaty is concluded with the exchange of silver tablets inscribed with each kingdom's version of the treaty.

1245 BCE	■ Ramses marries a first daughter of Hattusilis III.
1207 BCE	■ With Egypt and Hatti remaining on peaceful terms after the deaths of Ramses II and Hattusilis III, Pharaoh Merenptah sends famine relief to the Hittites.
CA. **1180** BCE	■ The Hittite Empire is destroyed by famine, civil unrest, and foreign invasion. With the disappearance of Hatti, the treaty with Egypt is void.

Teshub, whom Hattusilis overthrew in a coup d'état several years later. As emperor, Hattusilis III's domestic and foreign policy concentrated on his gaining political acceptance. The treaty with Ramses gave him a degree of diplomatic recognition.

Explanation and Analysis of the Document

The treaty consists of two separate but broadly similar documents, one from Egypt and the other from Hatti. Both were drafted in Akkadian cuneiform, the common diplomatic language of the second millennium BCE. Each kingdom engraved the text on a silver tablet, and they exchanged the tablets with grand ceremony. Only copies survive, as the silver originals were melted down for their precious metal long ago. The Hittite version—referred to as the Akkadian version—was discovered in the ruins of the ancient Hittite capital city of Hattushash and is a "file copy" on clay tablets of the text Ramses II sent to the Hittites. It is written in Akkadian cuneiform. The Egyptian version is a public memorial of the Akkadian document that Hattusilis III sent to the pharaoh, translated into the ancient Egyptian language and hieroglyphic script and carved onto the walls of at least two temples, Karnak and the Ramesseum (in modern-day Luxor in southern Egypt).

Because these documents are thirty-three hundred years old, they both suffer from damaged passages throughout. Some lost passages can be restored because they use formulaic set phrases and have parallels elsewhere in the text. In the Hittite version, angle brackets enclose words that were omitted by the scribe, and square brackets indicate where text was damaged. In both cases, the correct wording has been confidently deduced.

The treaty as a type of legal document originated in Mesopotamia several centuries before the accord between Ramses II and Hattusilis III. Hatti often used treaties in its foreign relations. Since the Egyptians had rarely made treaties before, they followed the Hittite format. Most Hittite treaties, however, were one-sided agreements imposed on vassal kingdoms conquered by the Hittite Empire. With these treaties, Hittite emperors imposed tribute payments and other strict obligations on their vassals.

The Egyptian-Hittite compact is a parity treaty, meaning that the two kingdoms are considered equal in rank and political independence. Egypt and Hatti belonged to an elite circle of "Great Kings"; their numerous vassals were "Little Kings." As equals, Great Kings referred to each other as "brothers." This conflicted with Egyptian ideology, which claimed that the pharaoh was ruler of the entire world. In diplomacy, the pharaoh was the peer of his great "brothers," but at home he claimed superiority.

All Hittite treaties share the same basic pattern. The treaties are agreements between kings, not between their respective countries. A historical prologue, or introduction, describes the conflict that led to the treaty, while specific articles deal with the legal obligations of each side. The kings swear religious oaths to uphold every article of the treaty before a list of gods who act as witnesses. The document refers to curses in the form of divine punishment on any person who violates the treaty and to blessings on those who obey it.

The Hittite terms for *treaty* mean "binding agreement" and "oath," as treaties were religious oaths that two kings swore by the gods. The Egyptian language did not have a native word for "treaty." The Egyptian term *neta*, used for "treaty" in the hieroglyphic version, actually means "regulations" or "stipulations." A previous agreement between them is called *neta-mety*, for "normal relations" or "normal arrangement." Neither Egyptian term actually means "oath."

Most of the treaty stipulations, such as the extradition and mutual defense clauses, apply equally to both sides, as honor demanded. The historical prologue is toned down compared with Hittite vassal treaties, in which the prologue usually blames the vassal kingdom for the conflict. So that the pharaoh could avoid embarrassment, the prologue of Hattusilis III's text sent to Egypt says only that the two sides had fought in the past, without giving causes, pronouncing victors, or laying blame. The document sent by Ramses II to Hatti has no prologue. Both versions of the Egyptian-Hittite treaty ignore the territorial dispute over Amurru and Kadesh; Egypt must have renounced its claim on them, but this is never stated. Perhaps this was likewise a kind of unstated gentlemen's agreement allowing the pharaoh to save face by ignoring the issue. Among the many divine witnesses, the Egyptian sun god Ra (also spelled Re) and the Hittite storm god stand out. In the hieroglyphic version of the treaty, the Hittite storm god is identified with the Egyptian storm god Seth.

◆ **Introduction and Historical Prologue**

A ceremonial introduction to the hieroglyphic version of the treaty not found in the document Hatti sent to the pharaoh was inserted by the Egyptians. It begins with the date and Ramses II's elaborate royal titles and then reports the delivery of the Hittite silver tablet to the pharaoh in his capital city of Piramses by Egyptian and Hittite envoys. The hieroglyphic translation of the treaty is called a "copy of the silver tablet which the Great Chief of Hatti, Hattusilis III sent to Pharaoh." There is no such introduction in the document Ramses sent to the Hittite capital of Hattushash.

In the Akkadian texts of both versions, Egyptian and Hittite rulers are called "Great Kings." But because the Egyptians considered the pharaoh to be the only true "king," Hattusilis III is called "the Great Chief of Hatti" in the hieroglyphic version, while Ramses himself is "the Great Ruler of Egypt." The Egyptian translation sometimes inserts the pharaoh's elaborate titles to flatter his political vanity. Both texts mention the fathers and grandfathers of the two kings to prove their royal heritage. A passage in the Hittite prologue of the hieroglyphic version also names Hattusilis III's brother and former emperor Muwatallis II, who had fought against a pharaoh whose name is now too damaged to be read. If this opponent was Ramses II, the reference could be to the Battle of Kadesh.

◆ **Reestablishment of Peace**

The Egyptian document announces that Egypt and Hatti have established an eternal treaty of "perfect peace and perfect brotherhood." Relations between ancient kingdoms were described as familial, such that when two Great Kings were on friendly terms, they were "brothers." The treaty stipulates that neither side should ever make war on the other's territory to "take anything from it." This clause ended the long struggle for control of Syria, but borders and territorial disputes are otherwise ignored.

The treaty calls for the renewal of the peaceful relations that had once existed before the war. But regarding how many treaties were signed before this one, the wording of the hieroglyphic document is ambiguous. Some scholars believe there had been two earlier pacts, one made sometime before Suppiluliumas I and Pharaoh Akhenaton, another made by either Horemheb or Seti I with Muwatallis II. If there was indeed a second treaty before Ramses II's time, the Egyptians must have broken it by attacking Kadesh.

In the hieroglyphic edition, Hattusilis states,

"As for the normal relations which existed in the time of Suppiluliumas I ... and likewise, the normal relations which existed in the time of Muwatallis ... I take hold of it. See, Ramses II ... takes hold of the treaty which he made with us now, beginning from today. We both take hold of it and we shall behave according to the agreed stipulations."

This passage could mean that both Suppiluliumas I and Muwattalis had made treaties with the pharaohs of their day. But the text says only that a treaty "existed" and that Hattusilis as well as Ramses "take hold of it," not "them." It is more likely, then, that there was only one previous treaty.

◆ **Mutual Defense Alliance**

The treaty commits each side to come to the other's aid if attacked by a third party. The enemy could be another empire, rebellious subjects of vassal kingdoms controlled by either empire, or domestic political opponents inside either kingdom. The Akkadian version states that

if Hattusili ... [becomes angry] with his own [subjects], after they have offended against him, and he sends to Ramses ... on account of this, then Ramses ... must send his infantry and his chariotry, [and] they will destroy all with whom he is angry."

A parallel clause in similar language in the hieroglyphic edition obligates Hattusilis to likewise come to the pharaoh's aid.

◆ **Egyptian Support for the Hittite Succession**

The single one-sided clause in the treaty, in the Akkadian version, commits the pharaoh to aid Hattusilis III's son after the father's death if his subjects should "commit an offense against him." Since Hattusilis seized the throne by force, his heirs would be at risk of being challenged as illegitimate. There is no parallel clause in the hieroglyphic version because the Egyptians refused to believe that the pharaoh's throne could ever be in jeopardy or that foreigners could help him.

◆ **Extradition of Fugitives**

Both versions of the treaty have extradition clauses for the return of fugitives to their home country. Such defectors could include government officials, whole populations, or vassal kingdoms. The extradition clauses also stipulate that any fugitives returned were to be granted legal amnesty; neither they nor their families were to be killed or physically harmed in any way. With regard to returned fugitives, the hieroglyphic version states, "Do not let his crimes stand against him, do not let his house or his wives or his children be destroyed. Do not let him be killed, nor let his eyes, his ears, his mouth or his legs be harmed." The Egyptian scribe who translated the Akkadian text sent by Hattusilis into the hieroglyphic version actually misread the proper order of the columns of text on the silver tablet. In so doing, he placed the second half of the extradition clause after the list of divine witnesses and the curses and blessings, which should have been at the end of the treaty. In fact, one fugitive was never extradited: Hattusilis III's nephew, the deposed emperor Urhi-Teshub, remained in

Egypt after the treaty, despite repeated complaints by Hattusilis. Eventually, he agreed that Egypt was the safest place to leave his nephew.

◆ List of Divine Witnesses

The Egyptian-Hittite treaty is a religious oath sworn by both kings. The last sections of the Akkadian version are not preserved, but the hieroglyphic edition sent to Ramses by Hattusilis III mentions "1000 Gods and Goddesses of the land of Hatti and 1000 Gods and Goddesses of the land of Egypt" as witnesses. It names almost forty individual deities, most of them Hittite, beginning with the chief sun and storm gods of Hatti. Many of the other gods are local incarnations of the storm god resident in cities throughout the Hittite Empire, including the distant "Goddess of Nineveh," of a town located in Assyria. The list ends with three important Egyptian deities: the imperial god Amun (or Amon), the sun god Ra, and Seth, the hometown god of the Nineteenth Dynasty kings. Seth was also the Egyptian god of storms, foreign countries, and chaotic forces. He was identified with the Hittite storm god, and his name is written as the "translation" for the Hittite title "Storm-god" in the hieroglyphic version of the treaty.

◆ Curses and Blessings

To enforce the treaty, these two thousand gods were invoked to curse any king who violated the treaty and to bless all those who upheld it: "With regard to these terms … for anyone who shall not keep them, 1000 Gods of the land of Hatti and 1000 Gods of the land of Egypt will destroy his house, his land and his subjects." The Hittites took these oaths seriously, believing that the death of their mighty emperor Suppiluliumas I from plague was divine retribution for his violation of the first peace treaty between Hatti and Egypt.

◆ Egyptian Description of the Hittite State Seals Embossed on the Silver Tablet

Ancient treaties were not "signed"; they were "stamped." Seals inscribed with the names and titles of the owner were used to authenticate documents in antiquity. The hieroglyphic transcription of the silver tablet sent by Hattusilis III to Ramses II concludes with a precise description of the official seals of the Hittite emperor and his queen embossed on the silver treaty tablet. Both seals were round and featured the name and titles of the king and queen, respectively, and their personal deities. At the center of his seal, Hattusilis III is embraced by the Hittite storm god. On the queen's seal, she is protected by the Hittite sun goddess. The Egyptians were fascinated by these exotic foreign objects. Since the silver tablets are lost, scholars have no idea how Ramses II "signed" his own name.

Audience

The stated audience consists of the thousand Hittite deities and thousand Egyptian deities who witnessed the oaths. Knowledge of the treaty would have been widely circulated among the officials and courtiers in both kingdoms, to the numerous vassal kingdoms of each side, and to the other Great Kingdoms, such as Assyria and Babylonia. The hieroglyphic edition was part of Ramses II's effort to present the treaty to his own subjects as a diplomatic victory.

Impact

The Ramses II–Hattusilis III alliance ended eight decades of warfare between the two ancient superpowers of Egypt and Hatti. Although the treaty never mentions borders, Egypt must have conceded the loss of its former vassal kingdoms Amurru and Kadesh. The two empires never fought again and remained allies. Ramses II married two of Hattusilis III's daughters, the first fourteen years after the treaty was concluded.

The two royal families proceeded to exchange over one hundred diplomatic letters, addressing each other as "my brother" and their queens as "my sister." Each new message came with lavish gifts of gold, fine cloth, and even medical supplies. Egyptian doctors were sent to treat the Hittite royal family's illnesses. But the letters also betray friction in their relations. The pharaoh's tone is arrogant, while Hattusilis often complains. They squabble over the fate of Urhi-Teshub, who remained in Egypt despite the extradition clause in the treaty. The two kings even argue over what had really happened at the Battle of Kadesh so many years earlier. Ramses proposes a summit meeting in Egyptian territory, but Hattusilis makes excuses, fearing that he would be humiliated by Egyptian propaganda.

The peace held for several decades. Ramses II's heir, Merenptah, shipped boatloads of grain to alleviate famine in Hatti—history's first recorded example of foreign aid. But the Egyptians could not help their allies when the Hittite Empire was destroyed by famine, civil war, and foreign invasion around 1200 BCE. When Hatti fell, the treaty was null and void.

Further Reading

■ Articles

Bryce, Trevor. "The 'Eternal Treaty' from the Hittite Perspective." *British Museum Studies in Ancient Egypt and Sudan* 6 (October 2006): 1–11. Available online.

   http://www.britishmuseum.org/research/publications/bmsaes/issue_6/bryce.aspx.

Jakob, Stefan. "Pharaoh and His Brothers." *British Museum Studies in Ancient Egypt and Sudan* 6 (October 2006): 12–30. Available online. http://www.britishmuseum.org/research/publications/bmsaes/issue_6/jakob.aspx.

Schulman, Alan R. "Aspects of Ramesside Diplomacy: The Treaty of Year 21." *Journal of the Society for the Study of Egyptian Antiquity* 8 (1977–1978): 112–130.

"As far as the relations of the Great King, King of Egypt, [and] the Great King, King of Hatti, are concerned, from the beginning of time and forever [by means of a treaty] the god has not allowed the making of war between them. Ramses II ... is doing this in order to bring about the relationship which [the Sun-god] and the Storm-god established for Egypt with Hatti in accordance with their relationship from the beginning of time, so that for eternity he might [not permit] the making of war between [them]."

(Hittite Version)

"He is [my] brother, and I am his brother. [He is at peace with me], and I am at peace with him [forever. And] we will create our brotherhood and our [peace], and they will be better than the former brotherhood and peace of [Egypt with] Hatti."

(Hittite Version)

"Ramses II ... for all time shall not open hostilities against Hatti in order to take anything from it. And Hattusili III ... for all time shall not open hostilities against Egypt in order to take [anything] from it."

(Hittite Version)

"And if someone else, an enemy, comes against Hatti, and Hattusili III ... sends to me: "Come to me, to my aid against him,' then [Ramses, Beloved] ... must send his infantry and his chariotry, and they will defeat [his enemy and] take revenge for Hatti."

(Hittite Version)

"The treaty which the Great Chief of Hatti, Hattusilis III ... made on a silver tablet for Usermaatre-Setepenre, the Great Ruler of Egypt ... : A perfect treaty of peace and brotherhood which establishes [perfect] peace [and perfect brotherhood between] us for eternity."

(Egyptian Version)

"Or if one or two men, who are unknown, flee [from the land of Egypt] and come to the land of Hatti to become subjects of someone else, then they should not be allowed to stay in the land of Hatti. They should be returned to Ramses II, the Great Ruler of Egypt."

(Egyptian Version)

Sürenhagen, Dietrich. "Forerunners of the Hattusili-Ramesses Treaty." *British Museum Studies in Ancient Egypt and Sudan* 6 (October 2006): 59–67. Available online.
http://www.britishmuseum.org/research/publications/bmsaes/issue_6/s؛renhagen.aspx.

■ **Books**

Beckman, Gary. *Hittite Diplomatic Texts*. Atlanta: Society for Biblical Literature, 1996.

Brand, Peter J. "Ideological Imperatives: Irrational Factors in Egyptian-Hittite Relations under Ramesses II." in *Moving across Borders: Foreign Relations, Religion, and Cultural Interactions in the Ancient Mediterranean*, eds. P. Kousoulis and K. Magliveras. Leuven, Belgium: Peeters, 2007.

Bryce, Trevor. *The Kingdom of the Hittites*. New York: Oxford University Press, 2005.

Darnell, John Coleman, and Colleen Manassa. *Tutankhamun's Armies: Battle and Conquest during Ancient Egypt's Late Eighteenth Dynasty*. Hoboken, N.J.: John Wiley & Sons, 2007.

Goelet, Ogden, and Baruch A. Levine. "Making Peace in Heaven and on Earth: Religious and Legal Aspects of the Treaty between Ramesses II and Hattušili III." In *Boundaries of the Ancient Near Eastern World: A Tribute to Cyrus H. Gordon*, eds. Meir Lubetski, Claire Gottlieb, and Sharon Keller. Sheffield, U.K.: Sheffield Academic Press, 1998.

Kitchen, Kenneth A. *Pharaoh Triumphant: The Life and Times of Ramesses II, King of Egypt*. Warminster, U.K.: Aris & Phillips, 1983.

———. *Ramesside Inscriptions Translated and Annotated, Notes and Comments*, Vol. 2: *Ramesses II, Royal Inscriptions*. Oxford, U.K.: Blackwell, 1999.

Liverani, Mario. *International Relations in the Ancient Near East, 1600–1100 b.c.* New York: Palgrave, 2001.

Murnane, William J. *The Road to Kadesh: A Historical Interpretation of the Battle Reliefs of King Sety I at Karnak*. 2nd ed. Chicago: Oriental Institute of the University of Chicago, 1990.

Redford, Donald B. *Egypt, Canaan, and Israel in Ancient Times*. Princeton, N.J.: Princeton University Press, 1992.

—Peter J. Brand

Questions for Further Study

1. Historically, diplomatic relationships, peace treaties, and political alliances between nations have required political leaders within the nations to save face before their people and before the world community. What measures were taken to allow Ramses and Hattusilis to save face in concluding their peace treaty?

2. The religion of both the Egyptians and the Hittites was polytheistic, meaning that the people worshipped more than one god. What part did religious beliefs play in the crafting of the treaty? Why was so much emphasis placed on the role of the gods in forging and maintaining the terms of the treaty?

3. What were the motives that lay behind the war between the Egyptians and the Hittites? Why did the two nations find it necessary to end the war and sign a peace accord?

4. Modern readers of the history of Egypt and the Hittites would likely be struck by the fact that over the past three millennia little has changed in the nature of superpower relationships. In what ways were these relationships similar to those of more modern powers? You might consider the antagonisms that led to World War I, the aggression that provoked World War II, the relationship between the West and the Soviet Union (and its "vassal" states) during the cold war, or the hostilities in the Middle East that are still raging in the early twenty-first century.

5. In the ancient Near East, various powers, including the Egyptians and the Assyrians, devoted considerable resources to conquering nearby states and thus expanding their empires. What would have motivated this desire for empire three millennia ago?

EGYPTIAN-HITTITE PEACE TREATY

Hittite Version

§1. [The treaty which] Ramses, [Beloved] of Amon, Great King, King [of Egypt, Hero, concluded] on [a tablet of silver] with Hattusili, [Great King], King of Hatti, his brother, in order to establish [great] peace and great [brotherhood] between them forever.

§2. Thus says Ramses, Beloved of Amon, Great King, King of Egypt, Hero of All Lands; son of Minmuarea (Seti I), Great King, King of Egypt, Hero: grandson of Minpahtarea (Ramses I). Great King, King of Egypt, Hero: to Hattusili, Great King, King of Hatti, Hero: son of Mursili, Great King, King of Hatti, Hero: grandson of Suppiluliuma, Great King, King of Hatti, Hero:

§3. I have now established good brotherhood and good peace between us forever, in order likewise to establish good peace and good brotherhood in [the relations] of Egypt with Hatti forever. As far as the relations of the Great King, King of Egypt, [and] the Great King, King of Hatti, are concerned, from the beginning of time and forever [by means of a treaty] the god has not allowed the making of war between them. Ramses, Beloved of Amon, Great King, King of Egypt, is doing this in order to bring about the relationship which [the Sun-god] and the Storm-god established for Egypt with Hatti in accordance with their relationship from the beginning of time, so that for eternity he might [not permit] the making of war between [them].

§4. And Ramses, Beloved of Amon, Great King, King [of Egypt], has indeed created <it> (the relationship) [on] this [day] by means of a treaty upon a tablet of silver, with [Hattusili], Great King, King of Hatti, his brother, in order to establish good peace and good brotherhood [between them] forever. He is [my] brother, and I am his brother. <He is at peace with me>, and I am at peace with him [forever. And] we will create our brotherhood and our [peace], and they will be better than the former brotherhood and peace of [Egypt with] Hatti.

§5. Ramses, Great King, King of Egypt, is in good peace and good brotherhood with [Hattusili], Great King of Hatti. The sons of Ramses, Beloved of Amon, <Great King>, King of Egypt, will be at peace and [brothers with] the sons of Hattusili, Great King,

King of Hatti, forever. And they will remain as in our relationship of brotherhood [and of] peace, so that Egypt will be at peace with Hatti and they will be brothers like us forever.

§6. And Ramses, Beloved of Amon, Great King, King of Egypt, for all time shall not open hostilities against Hatti in order to take anything from it. And Hattusili, Great King, King of Hatti, for all time shall not open hostilities against Egypt in order to take [anything] from it. The eternal regulation which the Sun-god and the Storm-god made for Egypt with Hatti is intended <to provide> peace and brotherhood and to prohibit hostilities between them. And [Ramses], Beloved of Amon, Great King, King of Egypt, has taken it up in order to create peace from this day on. Egypt will be at peace and brotherly with Hatti forever.

§7. And if someone else, an enemy, comes against Hatti, and Hattusili, [Great King, King of Hatti], sends to me: "Come to me, to my aid against him," then [Ramses, Beloved] of Amon, Great King, King of Egypt, must send his infantry and his chariotry, and they will defeat [his enemy and] take revenge for Hatti.

§8. And if Hattusili, Great King, King of Hatti, [becomes angry) with his own [subjects], after they have offended against him, and he sends to Ramses, Great King, King of Egypt, on account of this, then Ramses, Beloved of Amon, must send his infantry and his chariotry, [and] they will destroy all with whom he is angry.

§9. [And if] someone else, an enemy, comes against Egypt, and Ramses, Beloved of Amon, [King] of Egypt, your brother, sends to Hattusili, King of Hatti, his brother: "Come to my aid against him," then Hattusili, [King] of Hatti, shall send his infantry and his chariotry, and they will defeat his enemy.

§10. And if Ramses, Beloved [of Amon, King] of Egypt, becomes angry with his own subjects, after they have committed an offense against [him, and he sends] to Hattusili, King of Hatti, his(!) brother, on account of this, then Hattusili, [King] of Hatti, his brother, shall send [his] infantry and his chariotry, and they will destroy all [with whom] I am angry.

§11. And the son of Hattusili, King of Hatti, shall be made King of Hatti in place of Hattusili, his father, after the many years of Hattusili, [King] of

Hatti. And if [the people] of Hatti commit an offense against him, then [Ramses]. Beloved of Amon, must send [infantry] and chariotry to his aid and take revenge for him.

§12. [If a nobleman) flees from Hatti, or if a population in the territory of the King of Hatti [comes over] to Ramses, Beloved of Amon, Great King, [King of Egypt], then I, Ramses, [Beloved of Amon, Great King, King of Egypt], must seize them and send [them into the hand of Hattusili, Great King, King of Hatti].

§13. [And if] a single man comes, or if two [obscure men come to Ramses, Beloved of Amon], in order to enter into [his] service, then [I, Ramses, Beloved of Amon, must seize them and send them to] Hattusili, King of Hatti.

§14. And if [a nobleman flees from Egypt, or] if a single population [comes to the King of Amurru, then Benteshina shall seize them] and send them to the King of Hatti, [his] lord. [And Hattusili, Great King, King of Hatti, shall send them to Ramses, Beloved] of Amon, Great King, King of Egypt.

§15. And [if a single man flees, or if two obscure men flee from the territory of the King] of Egypt, and [do not wish to continue in his service, then Hattusili, Great King, King of Hatti], shall give them into the hand of his brother and [not permit them to dwell in Hatti].

§16. [And if a dignitary flees from Hatti and comes to Egypt(?)—or if two] men—in order not [to continue in the service of Hattusili, Great King, King] of Hatti, [then Ramses, Beloved of Amon, must seize them] and send them to [Hattusili, Great King, King of Hatti], his brother.

§17. [And if] a single [dignitary] flees [from Egypt] and comes to [Hatti—or if two men—then] Hattusili, [Great] King, [King of Hatti, shall seize them and] send them(!) to [Ramses, Beloved] of Amon, [Great King, King of Egypt, his brother].

§18. [And if] a single man flees from [Hatti, or] two men, [or three men, and they come to] Ramses, Beloved [of Amon, Great King, King] of Egypt, his brother, [then Ramses], Beloved of Amon, Great King, [King of Egypt, must seize them and send them] to Hattusili, his brother [...]—for they are brothers. But [they shall not punish them for] their offenses. They shall [not] tear out [their tongues or their eyes]. And [they shall not mutilate(?)] their ears or [their] feet. [And they shall not destroy(?) their households, together with their wives] and their sons.

§19. And if [a single man flees from Egypt, or] two men, or three men, and [they come to Hattusili, Great King], King of Hatti, my brother shall seize

them and send [them to me, Ramses, Beloved of Amon, Great King, King) of Egypt—for Ramses, Great King, King [of Egypt, and Hattusili are brothers. But they shall not punish them for their offenses. They shall] not [tear out their tongues] or their eyes. And [they shall not mutilate(?) their ears or their feet. And they shall not destroy(?) their households], together with their wives and their sons.

[*From this point a connected translation is impossible. The lines immediately following §19 seem to continue the discussion of the problem of fugitives.... The final two lines ... indicate the presence on the original silver tablet sent from Egypt of two seals: "Seal [of Ramses, Beloved of Amon, ...], Seal [of the Sun-god(?)...]"*]

Egyptian Version

Year 21, first month of Peret, day 21 under the incarnation of the King of Upper and Lower Egypt, Usermaatre-Setepenre, Son of Ra, Ramses II, given life eternally and everlastingly, who is beloved of Amun, Ra-Horakhty, Ptah-South-of-his-Wall-the lord of Ankh-Tawy, Mut lady of Isheru, and Khonsu-Neferhotep. He has appeared on the throne of Horus of the living like his father Horus-of-the-Horizon, forever and eternally.

On this day His Majesty was at the city of Piramses-beloved-of-Amun doing what his fathers Amun-Ra-Horakhty-Atum, the Lord of the Two Lands, He of Heliopolis and what Amun-of-Ramses II and Ptah-of-Ramses II, and Seth-Great-of-strength, the Son of Nut (all) praise as they give to him millions of Jubilee Festivals and everlasting peaceful years. All lands and all foreign countries are prostrate under his sandals forever.

Arrival of the royal messenger and chariot officer Netcherwymes; the royal messenger ... [and the royal messenger] ... along with the messenger of the land of Hatti Nerkil; and of ... Tili-Teshub; and of the second-ranked messenger of Hatti Ramose; as well as the messenger [of the land of Carca]mish Yapusili; bearing the silver tablet which the Great Chief of Hatti, Hattusilis III sent to Pharaoh—alive, prosperous, and healthy—in order to beg for peace from the incarnation of the King of Upper and Lower Egypt, Usermaatre-Setepenre, the Son of Ra, Ramses II, who is given life eternally and everlastingly like his father Ra, every day.

Copy of the silver tablet which the Great Chief of Hatti, Hattusilis III sent to Pharaoh, L.P.H., in the hands of his messenger Tili-Teshub and his messenger Ramose in order to beg for peace before the incarnation of the King of Upper and Lower Egypt Usermaatre-Setepenre, Son Ra, Ramses II, the Bull of Rulers who makes his borders wherever he wishes in every land:

The treaty which the Great Chief of Hatti, Hattusilis III, the Hero, the son of Mursilis II, the Great Chief of Hatti, the Hero, and grandson of Suppiluliumas I, the Great Chief of Hatti, the Hero, made on a silver tablet for Usermaatre-Setepenre, the Great Ruler of Egypt, the Hero, the son of Menmaatre, the Great Ruler of Egypt, the Hero, and grandson of Menpehtyre, the Great Ruler of Egypt, the Hero: A perfect treaty of peace and brotherhood which establishes [perfect] peace [and perfect brotherhood between] us for eternity.

Now long ago, from time immemorial, with respect to the relations between the Great Ruler of Egypt with the Great Chief of Hatti, the God prevented hostilities from occurring between them by means of a treaty. But in the time of Muwatallis II, the Great Chief of Hatti my brother, he fought with … the Great Ruler of Egypt.

But from now on, beginning today, see: Hattusilis III, the Great Chief of Hatti [has made] a treaty to re-establish the relationship which Ra and the Storm God made between the land of Egypt and the land of Hatti to prevent hostilities from happening between them forevermore.

See: Hattusilis III the Great Chief of Hatti binds himself by treaty with Usermaatre-Setepenre the Great Ruler of Egypt starting today in order to create perfect peace and perfect brotherhood between us forever; he being brotherly and at peace with me and I being brotherly and at peace with him forevermore. Now after Muwatallis II, the Great Chief of Hatti, my brother went to his fate, Hattusilis III sat as the Great Chief of Hatti upon the throne of his father. See: I am with Ramses II, the Great Ruler of Egypt, and our peace and brotherhood is perfect. It is even better than the former peace and brotherhood which had existed in the land.

See: I, the Great Chief of Hatti, am with [Usermaatre-Setepenre] the Great Ruler of Egypt in perfect peace and perfect brotherhood. May the grandchildren of the Great Chief of Hatti have brotherhood and peace with the grandchildren of Ramses II, the Great Ruler of Egypt, for such is our plan for brotherhood and our plan for peace: that the land of Egypt might be with the land of Hatti in peace and brotherhood, just like we are, forever more, with no hostility between them.

The Great Chief of Hatti will never invade the land of Egypt in order to take something from it. Usermaatre-Setepenre, the Great Ruler of Egypt will never invade the land of Hatti in order to take anything from it.

As for the normal relations which existed in the time of Suppiluliumas I, the Great Chief of Hatti and likewise, the normal relations which existed in the time of Muwatallis, the Great Chief of Hatti, my father, I take hold of it. See: Ramses II, the Great Ruler of Egypt takes hold of the treaty which he made with us now, beginning from today. We both take hold of it and we shall behave according to the agreed stipulations.

If some enemy should invade the lands of Usermaatre-Setepenre, the Great Ruler of Egypt and he writes to the Great Chief of Hatti saying: "Come and ally with me against him," then the Great Chief of Hatti should act by [coming to ally with him], and the Great Chief of Hatti will kill his enemy. But if the Great Chief of Hatti does not wish to go, then he will dispatch his army and his chariots and they will kill his enemy.

Or, if Ramses II [the Great Ruler of Egypt] becomes enraged at his subjects, and they do some evil act against him and he goes to kill them; then the Great Chief of Hatti must [join with him to destroy] all those against whom he is angry.

Now [if some enemy should attack] the Great Chief [of Hatti, and he writes to] Usermaatre-Setepenre the [Great Ruler of Egypt, he should] come as an ally to kill his enemies. Now if the wish of Ramses II, the Great Ruler of Egypt is to come, he will come [and he will send back a response to the land of Hatti. But, if it is not the wish of Usermaatre-Setepenre, the Great Ruler of Egypt to come, he should dispatch his army and his] chariots as a response to the land of Hatti.

Or if subjects of the Great Chief of Hatti betray him and Ramses II, [the Great Ruler of Egypt hears about it, then Usermaatre-Setepenre, the Great Ruler of Egypt shall act to destroy all those against whom he is angry].

[See: The land] of Hatti and the [land of Egypt are at peace and in brotherhood forever according to our] sworn oath. I will go to my fate. Then Ramses II the Great Ruler of Egypt, who will live forever! will come to [the land of] Hatti [to ensure that they make my son their master and to prevent them from making someone else their master].

[Now if they should commit a crime against him] and are opposed to making him their master, then

Usermaatre-Setepenre, the Great Ruler of Egypt should not remain silent about it. He should come and destroy the land of Hatti, and he should restore the Great Chief of Hatti and likewise the land of Hatti.

[If a great man flees and comes to] the Great Chief of Hatti—or if a town [among those belonging] to the territory of Ramses II, the Great Ruler of Egypt flees—if they come to the Great Chief of Hatti, then the Great Chief of Hatti should not receive them. The Great Chief of Hatti should return them to Usermaatre-Setepenre, the Great Ruler of Egypt, their lord, L.P.H.

Or if one or two men, who are unknown, flee [from the land of Egypt] and come to the land of Hatti to become subjects of someone else, then they should not be allowed to stay in the land of Hatti. They should be returned to Ramses II, the Great Ruler of Egypt.

If a great man should flee from the land of Hatti and [come to] Usermaatre-Setepenre the [Great Ruler] of Egypt—or if a town, or a district, or [a city among] those belonging to the land of Hatti flees—if they come to Ramses II the Great Ruler of Egypt, then Usermaatre-Setepenre the Great Ruler of Egypt should not receive them. Ramses II, the Great Ruler of Egypt should return them to the Great Chief [of Hatti]. They shall not be left there.

Likewise if one or two men, who are unknown, flee and they come to the land of Egypt in order to become subjects of another, Usermaatre-Setepenre, the Great Ruler of Egypt shall not leave them there. He should return them to the Great Chief of Hatti.

As for these terms of the treaty which the Great Chief of Hatti has made with Ramses II, the Great Ruler [of Egypt which are inscribed] upon the silver tablet:

As for these terms, 1000 Gods and Goddesses of the land of Hatti and 1000 Gods and Goddesses of the land of Egypt are here with me as witnesses who have heard these terms:

The Sun God, the Lord of Heaven
The Sun God of the town of Arunna
The Storm God, the Lord of Heaven
The Storm God of Hatti
The Storm God of the town of Arinna
The Storm God of the town of Zippalanda
The Storm God of the town of Pattiariq
The Storm God of the town of Hissaspa
The Storm God of the town of Saressa
The Storm God of the town of Aleppo

The Storm God of the town of Lihzina
The Storm God of the town of …
  [the Storm God of the town of] …
  [the Storm God of the town of] …
  [the Storm God of the land of Masa
The Storm God of the town of Sahipina

Antaret of the land of Hatti
The God of Zitkharriya
The God of Karzis
The God of Halpantaliyas
The Goddess of the town of Karahna
The Goddess of the wastes
The Goddess of Nineveh
The Goddess of Zin …
The God of Nananti
The God of Kulitti
The God of Hebat

The Queen of Heaven
The Gods, the Lords of the Oath
The Goddess, the Mistresses of Existence
The Mistress of the Oath
Ishkhara, the Mistress
The Mountains and the Rivers of the land of Hatti
The Gods of the land of Qizzuwattna

Amun
Ra
Seth
The male Gods and female Goddesses
The Mountains and the Rivers of the land of Egypt
The Heavens, the Earth, the Great Sea, the Winds, and the Clouds

With regard to these terms which are on the silver tablet concerning the land of Hatti and the land of Egypt:

As for anyone who shall not keep them, 1000 Gods of the land of Hatti and 1000 Gods of the land of Egypt will destroy his house, his land and his subjects.

Now, as for anyone who shall keep these terms which are on this silver tablet, be they from Hatti or be they Egyptian, and if they do neglect them, then 1000 Gods of the land of Hatti and 1000 Gods of the land of Egypt make him flourish and alive, along with household, his land, and his subjects.

If a man flees from the land of Egypt, or two or three, and they come to the Great Chief of Hatti, then the Great Chief of Hatti shall seize them and he shall return them to Usermaatre-Setepenre, the Great Ruler of Egypt.

But with regard to a man who is brought back to Ramses II the Great Ruler of Egypt, do not let his crimes stand against him, do not let his house or his wives or his children be destroyed. Do not let him be killed, nor let his eyes, his ears, his mouth or his legs be harmed. Do not let any crime stand against him.

Likewise, if men flee from the land of Hatti— whether one, or two or three—and they come to Usermaatre the Great Ruler of Egypt, then let Ramses II the Great Ruler of Egypt seize them and let him let him return them to the Great Chief of Hatti.

But the Great Chief of Hatti shall not let their crimes stand against them. Do let not his house be destroyed or his wives or his children. Do not let him be killed, nor let his eyes, his ears, his mouth or his legs be harmed. Do not let any crime stand against him.

What is in the center of the front side of the silver tablet: A picture of the Storm God embracing the Great Chief of Hatti surrounded with a circle of words saying: "the seal of the Storm God, the Ruler of Earth and Heaven, the seal of the treaty which Hattusilis III the Great Chief of Hatti, Hero, and son of Mursilis II, the Great Chief of Hatti, the Hero, made."

What is inside the circular image: "the seal of the Storm God, the ruler of Earth and Heaven."

What is in the center of its other side: An image of the Goddess of Hatti embracing the Great Lady of Hatti surrounded with a circle of words saying: "the seal of the Sun God of the town of Arunna, the Lord of the Earth," and "the seal of Pudukhepa, the Great Lady of the land of Hatti; the daughter of the land of Qizzuwatana; the [priestess] of the Sun God of Arunna; the Mistress of the Land; and the servant of the Goddess."

What is inside the circular image: "the seal of the Sun God of Arunna, the lord of every land."

Glossary

Ankh-Tawy	name for the Egyptian city of Memphis, sacred to the god Ptah
Benteshina	King of the country of Amurra and a vassal of the Hittites
Go to his fate	Hittite expression for death
Heliopolis	Egyptian city, sacred to the sun god Ra
Horus	principal god of kingship
Khonsu-Neferhotep	son of Amun and Mut
L.P.H.	abbreviation for the phrase *life, prosperity, and health*, spoken as blessing for the pharaoh
Menmaatre	coronation name of Pharaoh Seti I
Menpehtyre	coronation name of Pharaoh Ramses I
Mut lady of Isheru	wife of the god Amun
Nut	goddess of the sky
Peret	ancient Egyptian winter season
Ptah-South-of-his-Wall-the lord	A variant of the name for the god Ptah, a creation god of Memphis
Pudukhepa	Wife of Hattusilis III and queen of the Hittites
Ra-Horakhty	Another form of the name for the sun god
Seth-Great-of-strength	Family god of Ramesside royal family and the god of storms

MIDDLE ASSYRIAN LAWS

"A man may [whip] his wife, pluck out her hair, mutilate her ears, or strike her, with impunity."

Overview

The Middle Assyrian Laws are a collection of laws composed in the cuneiform (wedge-shaped) writing system of ancient Mesopotamia (roughly modern-day Iraq). The documents were written in Akkadian (one of the earliest Semitic languages) in the Middle Assyrian dialect. The existing copies were apparently edited during the reign of the Assyrian king Tiglath-pileser I (ca. 1115–1077 BCE). The corpus was perhaps collected either for his royal library or for individual scribal libraries. The texts were found during excavations at the site of Qal'at Shergat (ancient Assur) in northern Iraq in the early twentieth century. They appear to be copies of originals that were likely composed at least three centuries earlier. The existing copies number about fifteen tablets, one of which is duplicated by a copy that dates to the Neo-Assyrian period (ca. 900–612 BCE). The relationship of the documents to each other, however, is not clear. Thus it is not certain whether we are dealing with a "code" of laws or a series of thematic texts with legal pronouncements that include provisions concerning women, blasphemy, assault, sexual offenses, homicide, inheritance, veiling, witchcraft, abortion, agriculture, irrigation, pledges, deposits, theft, maritime traffic, and false accusations. Moreover, the order and the nature of the laws defy easy categorization. Like earlier Mesopotamian law codes, the Middle Assyrian Laws were constructed with conditional clauses. Each tablet appears to have a specific theme. For example, the most complete tablet (labeled "A" by cuneiform scholars) deals with issues concerning women.

fifteenth century BCE, there was evidently an independent Assyrian state, and a series of royal inscriptions have been found concerning the Assyrian king Ashur-uballit I, who reigned in the middle of the fourteenth century BCE. This monarch corresponded with the kings of Egypt, showing that Assyria was now considered a major role player on the international scene.

By the time of Adad-nirari I in the early thirteenth century BCE, Assyria was able to expand deep into Syria to the west, conquering the old Mitanni capital of Washukanni and going as far west as Carchemish in present-day Turkey. Assyria was now a powerful state, bordering the Hittite kingdom to the west and the Kassite kingdom of Babylonia to the south. Numerous annals at Assur from the time of Shalmaneser I (1274–1245 BCE) attest to the continuation of Assyrian military expansion and cultural interaction with Babylon. Shalmaneser's son, Tukulti-Ninurta I, also continued this expansion, which is especially known from a unique historiographic and propagandistic document known as the Tukulti-Ninurta Epic, in which the monarch claims to have conquered and plundered Babylon, deporting many of the Kassite citizens to Assyria. Moreover, the Assyrian king began direct Assyrian rule in Babylon and transported the state deity of Babylon—Marduk—to Assyria, where the god remained for more than one hundred years. In addition, Tukulti-Ninurta I plundered numerous Babylonian literary texts, thereby creating a catalyst for Assyrian literary development. However, a palace revolt ended in the imprisonment and subsequent death of this Assyrian monarch, after which there was a dearth of textual and literary sources from Assyria until the reign of Tiglath-pileser I.

Context

Although there is a wealth of documentation concerning the history of Assyria during the late Bronze Age (ca. 1600–1200 BCE) and the early Iron Age (ca. 1200–900 BCE), knowledge of the period immediately after 1500 BCE is limited. The region of northern Iraq (Assyria) was under the control of the neighboring Hurrian kingdom of Mitanni, which was centered in coastal Syria. By the end of the

About the Author

Although it is not certain who the author of the Middle Assyrian Laws was, the existing editions were composed during the reign of Tiglath-pileser I, the first king since Tukulti-Ninurta I to exert sovereignty over foreign territories. Tiglath-pileser was able to reorganize the Assyrian armed forces and expand to the west and the south. He also appears to have been the first Assyrian king to record his

Time Line

CA. 1244–1208 BCE

■ According to the Tukulti-Ninurta Epic, Tukulti-Ninurta I conquers Babylon, plundering Babylonian literary texts and creating the catalyst for Assyrian literary development.

CA. 1115–1077 BCE

■ The Middle Assyrian Laws are edited during the reign of the Assyrian king Tiglath-pileser I.

■ The Middle Assyrian Palace Edicts, a list of more than twenty regulations concerning women and various officials connected to the palace of Tiglath-pileser I, are composed during the reign of this Assyrian king.

exploits as military annals, creating a context for other literary works, such as the law code.

Tiglath-pileser I's military exploits were described in great detail, although they defy a facile chronological order. He faced the threat of the Mushki, a people from the north (perhaps the ancestors of the later Phrygians), who crossed the Tigris River and threatened the city of Nineveh, one of the major urban centers in the Assyrian kingdom. Not only did Tiglath-pileser I claim to have defeated them, but he also pushed deep into Anatolia (modern-day Turkey), where small successor Hittite kingdoms existed, and created rock inscriptions near Lake Van. In another campaign he went west again and defeated the Phoenician states of Byblos (Jubayl) and Sidon on the Syrian coast, reaching the Mediterranean Sea. He also came across the Aramaean tribes, Semitic-speaking peoples who inhabited the regions in the Euphrates River region in Syria. They were not urbanites but independent, seminomadic pastoralist tribes who were able to raid the local areas, destroying agricultural production. Tiglath-pileser I claimed to have crossed the Euphrates River twenty-eight times to campaign against them, showing evidence that these tribes were a supreme

nuisance to the Assyrian monarch. Tiglath-pileser I also campaigned against Babylon, plundering Babylon and other urban centers, similar to what his predecessor Tukulti-Ninurta I had done. However, Tiglath-pileser I probably did not stay long in Babylonia, perhaps because of an Aramaean attack into Assyria, which may have helped cause a famine. The major Assyrian city of Nineveh may even have been captured by the Aramaeans. This event may have helped to end this Assyrian king's reign, as Tiglath-pileser I was probably assassinated, beginning a period of anarchy in Assyria that lasted for more than one hundred years.

Tiglath-pileser I, like Tukulti-Ninurta I before him, had many cultural interests. Numerous building projects were completed during his reign, including the construction of temples, royal monuments, parks, and gardens. In addition, a great library was built in Assur. The main portion of the Middle Assyrian Laws dates to his reign, and a complete edition of his royal annals lined the walls of his palace at Calah (modern-day Nimrud). Furthermore, nine fragmentary Court Edicts (also known as Palace Decrees or Harem Decrees), compiled or copied during Tiglath-pileser's reign, have been found. These decrees are a list of twenty-three regulations for palace personnel (women and the officials assigned to them), showing an intimate interest on the part of the crown in the running of its internal affairs. At least nine kings are mentioned in the texts (the last being Tiglath-pileser I), providing evidence that the documents were copied or edited over at least three centuries. Similar decrees from the fourteenth century BCE have been found at Nuzi, a provincial site in northern Assyria.

Explanation and Analysis of the Document

As noted earlier, there are at least fifteen texts and fragments of the laws, which scholars have labeled A through O. Although some texts duplicate laws (C and G, for example), each text for the most part deals with a series of particular topics. Nearly every law (or paragraph) begins with a conditional statement, followed by a resolution ("if …, then …"). The subjects of the laws are two distinct social classes, free males and male and female slaves. However, free women (wives, widows, and certain classes of priestesses) are often discussed in these texts. Moreover, modern scholars have numbered the laws. For example, Tablet A, which is devoted almost entirely to situations concerning women, has been labeled from 1 to 59. There are no obvious divisions in the original text, so scholars have made reasoned decisions about where to divide one law from another. In addition, the laws are not arranged in a way that necessarily appeals to a modern, Western audience. It is necessary to explain and comment on them in terms of themes.

◆ A1–10

This section deals with a variety of infractions, ranging from blasphemy and assault to theft and burglary. Assyrian criminal law contained a range of fixed penalties, including capital (death), talionic (punishment fitting the crime), corporal (mutilation or a series of lashes), and forced-labor penalties. The perpetrators were either men or women from the *a'īlu* class or male or female slaves. The *a'īlu*, at least in earlier Mesopotamian traditions, was considered an upper class. In the Middle Assyrian Laws, there is no easily recognizable middle class; individuals were from either the *a'īlu* or slave classes. The terms used for "slave" in the Assyrian law code were somewhat generic and not specific. They not only designated individuals who were controlled by others but also denoted anyone who was in some sense dependent upon another. Thus, all subjects of the king, including his high officials, were considered to a certain extent to be his slaves. There were also temple slaves, whose status was hereditary; captured prisoners of war; criminals; domestic servants; and those who were reduced to debt slavery, which was usually limited to the time it took to pay off debts. In many respects slavery was a form of personal dependence and was based upon economic necessity. The slave was comparatively deprived of a means of production that was more available to free citizens. Although slaves were often considered chattel, many slaves were allowed to remain with their families, own property, engage in economic activity, teach various trades, appear as witnesses, hire workers, and even own their own slaves.

Women in ancient Assyria were in many ways defined by their relationship to men, as is evident in the first two laws (A1–2). A woman was normally under the legal guardianship of a father, a brother, an uncle, a husband, or even a son in some cases. Women who did not have guardians (widows, orphans, prostitutes, or women who were in common-law arrangements) were considered to be outside the normal social and legal spheres, though in some cases women were able to enter into contract arrangements (such as buying and selling) in the name of an absent spouse. In the case of A2, though the woman is under the guardianship of a male, she alone is responsible for her offense; her male guardian is not liable. In the case of a woman who commits a sacrilege (described in A1), the authorities believed that only the gods by means of divination could make a determination of innocence or guilt.

Bodily mutilation is a significant theme throughout the extant sections of the Middle Assyrian Laws and the Assyrian Palace Edicts. Both slaves and free women were subject to having their ears and noses cut off for stealing (A4–5). In some cases female culprits who were accused of stealing or assaulting a man were subjected to a heavy fine and blows with rods (A7). Aggravated assault by a woman toward a man's reproductive organs was punished severely (A8). The woman had either a finger cut off or another significant body part gouged out. (The text is broken at this point.) It is not clear what type of assault against a free woman is alluded to in A9, but the attack is clearly obscene. The shekel described in this section is essentially the same term used in the Old Testament for weights. One shekel weighed approximately 8.33 grams. It is not certain whether the term *lead* refers to lead or to tin.

Kassite boundary stone written in cuneiform and marking the legal ownership of a piece of land (© The Trustees of the British Museum)

◆ **A11–20**

In general this section concerns illegal sexual activity (though A11 is too fragmented to translate). In the case of adultery (A15), catching a couple in the act did not negate the need for a trial. As with other ancient Near Eastern codes, the guilty couple received similar punishments (or mercies). However, a man who was unaware of the marital status of the woman involved was declared innocent (A14), probably because free men had a greater degree of sexual freedom than did women (as long as these men did not infringe upon the sexual rights of other men).

The divine River Ordeal mentioned in A17 (found also in A22 and A24–25) is not explained, but it is a recurring theme in ancient Near Eastern legal codes and other texts (as late as 600 BCE). The punishment was prescribed by judges primarily to deal with cases of adultery and witchcraft in which there were no witnesses or to verify a person's testimony. Perhaps the binding agreement in A17 concerns the length to be covered in the water (for example, the Euphrates River) by the accused. In many cases it appears that the judge also decided on the person who would swim; the ordeal was often performed by a substitute. A letter from Mari (ca. 1800 BCE), a city on the Euphrates River in Syria near the present-day border of Iraq, indicates that the individual had to swim a long distance underwater before emerging successful. Individuals who drowned were literally "married to the river." The river itself was considered to have the spirit of the river deity, who then determined the guilt or innocence of the accused, evidenced by the success or failure of the swimmer.

Active sodomy (A19–20) was a talionic capital crime; that is, the culprit was subjected to the same type of activity in which he participated. Although female homosexuality was hardly evidenced or mentioned, it was roundly condemned. Male homosexuality, however, was a more complicated issue. Although males were free to express themselves in nonsexual relations (equal male friendships), homoerotic (sexual) relations were more complex. Male same-sex erotic relations were viewed as a matter of power and dominance of one male over another. These acts were considered acceptable when the two parties were not of the same social status. However, in the cases of A18–20, the active participants were clearly of the same social order.

◆ A21–30

This section continues a discussion of female interactions in both the public and the private spheres. Marriage did not simply take place between a consenting man and woman but was negotiated by the heads of the two families. The father's consent for the woman was mandatory, even if she was under control of a creditor (A48). Other Middle Assyrian texts, however, show evidence that couples were able to conduct marriages if there were no guardians. Terms for the marriage arrangements varied depending upon the stage of the negotiations, which sometimes took years to conclude. The bridewealth (A38) was a gift of nonconsumable items (often precious metals) given to the father of the bride. The bridal gift (A30) was a gift of consumable items (food or animals). A contract was required for the completion of the marriage, as was a betrothal meal (A42–43). Even after the contract, gifts, and betrothal, a daughter could still live in her parents' house until the time of cohabitation with her husband (A25–27, A32–33, and A38).

◆ A31–40

If a widow had neither sons nor a son-in-law to support her, she could be declared legally independent (A33 and A46). She was free to remain independent or to remarry outside her husband's family. If the independent widow lived in another man's house for two years, she was able to take on the status of wife (A34). According to the few marriage contracts that have been uncovered from the Middle Assyrian period, it appears that men and women had an equal right to divorce a spouse. A37 makes it clear, however, that a man could divorce his wife without cause and did not have to pay her compensation. On the other hand, he could not take back the bridewealth (A38). Furthermore, a marriage could be dissolved if the husband was gone for an extended period of time (five years in the case of A36) or if the wife had no means of support. The type of priestess mentioned in A40 (qadiltu) was allowed to marry but then had an obligation to be veiled. Because the qadiltu was often mentioned in conjunction with midwives, it has been assumed that such women may have participated in washing or purification rituals concerning women and birth.

◆ A41–50

Nothing is known about how judges were trained or on what their qualifications were based. They were able to investigate the status of widows (A45), they could legislate in land ownership decisions (B6 and B17–18), and they had jurisdiction over criminal matters. Evidently, they dealt with both secular and religious matters. Polygamy was allowed under certain circumstances. A46 implies that a man was able to take a second wife, presumably to secure a male descendant. He also was required to take a second wife in the case of the death of his brother-in-law (as per A30). There is no evidence, however, of polyandry (the practice of having more than one husband). The woman of the a'īlu class mentioned in A42–43 probably refers to an unmarried girl under her father's authority or a daughter-in-law living with her husband in her father-in-law's house. Thus she does not appear to have had the same status as a wife of the head of the household.

◆ A51–59

Although a prostitute had low social standing, she was legally protected in the case of harm done to her that caused a miscarriage (A52). The custom of infant exposure in ancient Assyria is poorly documented. Children were exposed (that is, left for the gods to decide their fate) for a variety of reasons. A child might be exposed if the family was too poor to take care of the child and no relatives were able or willing to help or if the child was born with a physical abnormality, which was viewed as a bad omen for the household. It has been presumed that female infants were exposed more often than male infants, but there is no concrete evidence to support this theory. In the case of A53, a woman who aborted her fetus was guilty of a capital crime. It is presumed that her husband would determine the fate of the infant (but only after its birth). Forced abortion, even of a prostitute's fetus, was considered a capital crime (A52).

Rape of a virgin was punishable by marriage, if the father of the victim was agreeable (A55). The father received "triple" the amount of silver from the perpetrator, whether or not he was required to marry the victim. Perhaps unique among the Middle Assyrian Laws is the edict concerning a husband's right to punish his wife in a corporal manner, which included mutilation (A59). Since the previous two laws (A57–58) are heavily fragmented and deal with a similar subject, it is difficult to understand the context of law A59. From what can be understood, it appears that the husband had the right to perform only what was written on the "tablet," perhaps implying a judicial decree. One can also assume that punishment was carried out in the presence of judicial administrators.

◆ B1–10

There are numerous contracts from ancient Mesopotamia concerning inheritance issues. In the Middle Assyrian Laws, heirs were evidently ranked (sons and then brothers of the deceased, according to A25). A murderer or a traitor, however, lost his inheritance (and his life), and the victim's next of kin (in the case of murder) received his

*Terra-cotta plaque of a dragon, originally associated with the god Marduk
but brought to Assyria as a symbolic beast of the state god Ashur* (© The Trustees of the British Museum)

inheritance (B2–3). A man could also lose an inheritance if he participated in a harvest without cultivating his share of the land (B4).

◆ B11–20

Encroachment on someone else's property is a common theme in the Middle Assyrian Laws (as in B12–15). If a man planted an orchard, raised trees, dug a well, or even made bricks on the plot of land that was owned by another, he was required to compensate the owner with a like field, if the owner did not object. If the owner did object, the perpetrator was required to triple the compensation, suffer fifty blows with rods, and perform an unspecified community service (B14–15).

Audience

As with many ancient Near Eastern texts, it is exceedingly difficult to discern the intended audience of the laws.

As noted earlier, unlike some of the other ancient Near Eastern legal codes, the Middle Assyrian Laws were found on various tablets from Assur, most of which date to the reign of Tiglath-pileser I, presumably either for his royal library or perhaps for later scribes and their personal libraries. In their present state, the laws were most certainly not for public view or use.

One can speculate that, analogously to the other codes, the Middle Assyrian Laws may have been composed in other forms. For example, the most complete edition of the Code of Hammurabi was written on a nearly eight-foot-high black stone stela with an imposing iconographic depiction of Shamash, the god of justice, receiving the set of laws from the Babylonian king. Moreover, the laws are constructed with a lengthy prologue that stresses the god's appointment of Hammurabi (1792–1750 BCE) as king and a description of Hammurabi's various duties. Following the body of laws (nearly three hundred in total) is a long epilogue, emphasizing the military nature of the monarch and mentioning blessings for Hammurabi and his successors as

"If a woman should lay a hand upon a man and they prove the charges against her, she shall pay 1,800 shekels of lead; they shall strike her 20 blows with rods."

(A7)

"If a man intends to divorce his wife, if it is his wish, he shall give her something; if that is not his wish, he shall not give her anything, and she shall leave empty-handed."

(A37)

"In addition to the punishments for [a man's wife] that are [written] on the tablet, a man may [whip] his wife, pluck out her hair, mutilate her ears, or strike her, with impunity."

(A59)

"If a man, who has not yet received his inheritance share, takes a life, they shall hand him over to the next-of-kin. Should the next-of-kin so choose, he shall kill him, or, if he chooses to come to an accommodation, then he shall take his inheritance share."

(B2)

well as curses for those who transgress the laws or deface the monument itself. The Code of Hammurabi was publicly displayed to show the righteous rule of the king and to serve as an exemplar for future rulers. How this applies to the Middle Assyrian Laws is, of course, not certain. There are thousands of legal, administrative, and juridical texts from Assyria, none of which describes any public legal promulgation of laws. The question as to the audience for the Middle Assyrian Laws is left unresolved.

Impact

The Middle Assyrian Laws are set firmly in the ancient Near Eastern legal tradition that harks back at least to the earliest set of formalized legal promulgations written in Sumerian from the reigns of Ur-Nammu of Ur (ca. 2112–2095 BCE) and Lipit-Ishtar of Isin (ca. 1950 BCE). Moreover, legal codes written in Akkadian have been uncovered, including those of Dadusha of Eshnunna (ca.

1770 BCE) and Hammurabi of Babylon, as well as Hittite laws from Anatolia (ca. 1400–1200 BCE). There are also late-period Babylonian laws from centuries after the Middle Assyrian texts, dating to around 700 BCE. Furthermore, there are fragments of other legal codes with dates ranging from 2100 to 700 BCE. These codes suggest an overall ancient Near Eastern legal tradition that spanned different linguistic groups, geographic regions, and time periods. These legal documents have a number of things in common. Virtually all of them use the same conditional format. Moreover, the laws clearly are not comprehensive but rather deal with specific incidental situations. Many of the laws (and themes) from the early codes are duplicated and edited in later texts.

The ancient law of the Hebrew peoples, attributed to Moses and found in the books of Exodus, Leviticus, Numbers, and Deuteronomy in the Old Testament, shows evidence that it also rests firmly in the legal tradition of the ancient Near East. It is no surprise that the Middle Assyrian Laws have a special affinity to the so-called Mosaic

Laws, in terms of both themes and formalistic structure. For example, Middle Assyrian Laws concerning assault resulting in miscarriage (A21 and A50–52) are similar to those in Exodus 21:22–25. Similarly, the Middle Assyrian Laws concerning seduction and rape (A55–56) are like those in Exodus 22:15–16. Moreover, Middle Assyrian Laws about slander (A18) correspond to Deuteronomy 22:13–22. Like the Mosaic Laws, the Middle Assyrian Laws obliquely belong to an ancient legal tradition from which much of the core legal values of Western civilization stem.

Further Reading

■ Articles

Brinkman, John. "A Note on the Middle Assyrian Laws." *Revue d'Assyriologie et d'Archeologie Orientale* 79 (1985) 88–89.

Hall, M. "A Middle Assyrian Legal Summons." *Zeitschrift für die Assyriologie und Assyriologie* 73 (1981): 75–81.

Postgate, J. N. "Land Tenure in the Middle Assyrian Period: A Reconstruction." *Bulletin of the School of Oriental and African Studies* 34 (1971) 496–520.

■ Books

Driver, Godfrey R., and John C. Miles. *The Assyrian Laws*, 2nd ed. Darmstadt, Germany: Scientia Verlag Aalen, 1975.

Lafont, Sophie. "Middle Assyrian Period." In *A History of Ancient Near Eastern Law*, vol. 1, ed. Raymond Westbrook. Boston: Brill, 2003.

Meek, Theophile. "The Middle Assyrian Laws." In *Ancient Near Eastern Texts Relating to the Old Testament*, 3rd ed., ed. James B. Pritchard. Princeton, N.J.: Princeton University Press, 1969.

Paul, Shalom. "Biblical Analogues to Middle Assyrian Law." In *Religion and Law: Biblical-Judaic and Islamic Perspectives*, eds. Edwin B. Firmege et al. Winona Lake, Ind.: Eisenbrauns, 1990.

Roth, Martha T., et al. *Law Collections from Mesopotamia and Asia Minor*, 2nd ed. Atlanta: Scholars Press, 1997.

———. "The Middle Assyrian Laws (Tablet A)." In *The Context of Scripture*. Vol. 2: *Monumental Inscriptions from the Biblical World*, eds. William W. Hallo and K. Lawson Younger, Jr. Boston: Brill, 2003.

Saggs, Henry W. F. *The Might That Was Assyria*. New York: St. Martin's Press, 1990.

—Mark Chavalas

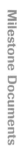

Questions for Further Study

1. List the ways in which the Middle Assyrian Laws reflect social class and the arrangement of the social order during the period in which they were written.

2. The laws make repeated references to slaves. How would slavery have been defined during this period? How did the Assyrian concept of slavery differ from the more modern understanding of slavery, such as that practiced in colonial and post-independence America?

3. The laws are rather explicit with regard to sexual behavior and are quite specific about extramarital sexual relations in various contexts, including such matters as sodomy, rape, and prostitution. Further, the laws are quite specific about charges and allegations of sexual misbehavior that might be made by a third party. Why did law writers place so much emphasis on these matters? Why would such matters have been important at this time and in this place?

4. Similarly, the laws go into considerable detail about the status of women under various circumstances, such as when a woman's husband appears to have abandoned her or what her rights were if she were left widowed. Why would such matters have been important to the Assyrians at this time?

5. Scholars study texts such as the Middle Assyrian Laws and law codes from other ancient cultures to trace the history of the development of more modern legal codes—that is, to find the ancient roots of modern legal traditions. Specify ways in which the Middle Assyrian Laws prefigure more modern law codes. For example, do you see any connection between the laws regarding evidence and hearsay (evidence based not on a witness's personal knowledge but on someone else's statement) and modern rules of courtroom evidence?

MIDDLE ASSYRIAN LAWS

Tablet A

A1. If a woman, either a man's wife or a man's daughter, should enter into a temple and steal something from the sanctuary in the temple and either it is discovered in her possession or they prove the charges against her and find her guilty, [they shall perform(?)] a divination[?], they shall inquire of the deity; they shall treat her as the deity instructs them.

A2. If a woman, either a man's wife or a man's daughter, should speak something disgraceful or utter a blasphemy, that woman alone bears responsibility for her offense; they shall have no claim against her husband, her sons, or her daughters.

A3. If a man is either ill or dead, and his wife should steal something from his house and give it either to a man, or to a woman, or to anyone else, they shall kill the man's wife as well as the receivers [of the stolen goods]. And if a man's wife, whose husband is healthy, should steal from her husband's house and give it either to a man, or to a woman, or to anyone else, the man shall prove the charges against his wife and shall impose a punishment; the receiver who received [the stolen goods] from the man's wife shall hand over the stolen goods, and they shall impose a punishment on the receiver identical to that which the man imposed on his wife.

A4. If either a slave or a slave woman should receive something from a man's wife, they shall cut off the slave's or slave woman's nose and ears; they shall restore the stolen goods; the man shall cut off his own wife's ears. But if he releases his wife and does not cut off her ears, they shall not cut off [the nose and ears] of the slave or slave woman, and they shall not restore the stolen goods.

A5. If a man's wife should steal something with a value greater than 300 shekels of lead from the house of another man, the owner of the stolen goods shall take an oath, saying, "I did not incite her, saying, 'Commit a theft in my house.'" If her husband is in agreement, he [her husband] shall hand over the stolen goods and he shall ransom her; he shall cut off her ears. If her husband does not agree to her ransom, the owner of the stolen goods shall take her and he shall cut off her nose.

A6. If a man's wife should place goods for safekeeping outside of the family, the receiver of the goods shall bear liability for stolen property.

A7. If a woman should lay a hand upon a man and they prove the charges against her, she shall pay 1,800 shekels of lead; they shall strike her 20 blows with rods.

A8. If a woman should crush a man's testicle during a quarrel, they shall cut off one of her fingers. And even if the physician should bandage it, but the second testicle then becomes infected[?] along with it and becomes ..., or if she should crush the second testicle during the quarrel—they shall gouge out both her [...]

A9. If a man lays a hand upon a woman, attacking her like a rutting bull[?], and they prove the charges against him and find him guilty, they shall cut off one of his fingers. If he should kiss her, they shall draw his lower lip across the blade[?] of an ax and cut it off.

A10. [If either] a man or a woman enters [another man's] house and kills [either a man] or a woman, [they shall hand over] the manslayers [to the head of the household]; if he so chooses, he shall kill them, or if he chooses to come to an accommodation, he shall take [their property]; and if there is [nothing of value to give from the house] of the manslayers, either a son [or a daughter ...]. ...

A12. If a wife of a man should walk along the main thoroughfare and should a man seize her and say to her, "I want to have sex with you!"—she shall not consent but she shall protect herself; should he seize her by force and fornicate with her—whether they discover him upon the woman or witnesses later prove the charges against him that he fornicated with the woman—they shall kill the man; there is no punishment for the woman.

A13. If the wife of a man should go out of her own house, and go to another man where he resides, and should he fornicate with her knowing that she is the wife of a man, they shall kill the man and the wife.

A14. If a man should fornicate with another man's wife either in an inn or in the main thoroughfare, knowing that she is the wife of a man, they shall treat the fornicator as the man declares he wishes his wife to be treated. If he should fornicate with her without knowing that she is the wife of a man, the fornicator is clear; the man shall prove the charges against his wife and he shall treat her as he wishes.

A15. If a man should seize another man upon his wife and they prove the charges against him and find him guilty, they shall kill both of them; there is no liability for him [i.e., the husband]. If he should seize him and bring him either before the king or the judges, and they prove the charges against him and find him guilty—if the woman's husband kills his wife, then he shall also kill the man; if he cuts off his wife's nose, he shall turn the man into a eunuch and they shall lacerate his entire face; but if [he wishes to release] his wife, he shall [release] the man.

A16. If a man [should fornicate] with the wife of a man [... by] her invitation, there is no punishment for the man; the man [i.e., husband] shall impose whatever punishment he chooses upon his wife. If he should fornicate with her by force and they prove the charges against him and find him guilty, his punishment shall be identical to that of the wife of the man.

A17. If a man should say to another man, "Everyone has sex with your wife," but there are no witnesses, they shall draw up a binding agreement, they shall undergo the divine River Ordeal.

A18. If a man says to his comrade, either in private or in a public quarrel, "Everyone has sex with your wife," and further, "I can prove the charges," but he is unable to prove the charges and does not prove the charges, they shall strike that man 40 blows with rods; he shall perform the king's service for one full month; they shall cut off his hair; moreover, he shall pay 3,600 shekels of lead.

A19. If a man furtively spreads rumors about his comrade, saying, "Everyone sodomizes him," or in a quarrel in public says to him, "Everyone sodomizes you," and further, "I can prove the charges against you," but he is unable to prove the charges and does not prove the charges, they shall strike that man 50 blows with rods; he shall perform the king's service for one full month; they shall cut off his hair; moreover, he shall pay 3,600 shekels of lead.

A20. If a man sodomizes his comrade and they prove the charges against him and find him guilty, they shall sodomize him and they shall turn him into a eunuch.

A21. If a man strikes a woman of the *a'īlu*-class thereby causing her to abort her fetus, and they prove the charges against him and find him guilty—he shall pay 9,000 shekels of lead; they shall strike him 50 blows with rods; he shall perform the king's service for one full month.

A22. If an unrelated man—neither her father, nor her brother, nor her son—should arrange to have a man's wife travel with him, then he shall swear an oath to the effect that he did not know that she is the wife of a man and he shall pay 7,200 shekels of lead to the woman's husband. If [he knows that she is the wife of a man], he shall pay damages and he shall swear, saying, "I did not fornicate with her." But if the man's wife should declare, "He did fornicate with me," since the man has already paid damages to the man [i.e., husband], he shall undergo the divine River Ordeal; there is no binding agreement. If he should refuse to undergo the divine River Ordeal, they shall treat him as the woman's husband treats his wife.

A23. If a man's wife should take another man's wife into her house and give her to a man for purposes of fornication, and the man knows that she is the wife of a man, they shall treat him as one who has fornicated with the wife of another man; and they treat the female procurer just as the woman's husband treats his fornicating wife. And if the woman's husband intends to do nothing to his fornicating wife, they shall do nothing to the fornicator or to the female procurer; they shall release them. But if the man's wife does not know [what was intended], and the woman who takes her into her house brings the man in to her by deceit[?], and he then fornicates with her—if, as soon as she leaves the house, she should declare that she has been the victim of fornication, they shall release the woman, she is clear; they shall kill the fornicator and the female procurer. But if the woman should not so declare, the man shall impose whatever punishment on his wife he wishes; they shall kill the fornicator and the female procurer.

A24. If a man's wife should withdraw herself from her husband and enter into the house of [another] Assyrian, either in that city or in any of the nearby towns, to a house which he assigns to her, residing with the mistress of the household, staying overnight three or four nights, and the householder is not aware that it is the wife of a man who is residing in his house, and later that woman is seized, the householder whose wife withdrew herself from him shall [mutilate] his wife and [not] take her back. As for the man's wife with whom his wife resided, they shall cut off her ears; if he pleases, her husband shall give 12,600 shekels of lead as her value, and, if he pleases, he shall take back his wife. However, if the householder knows that it is a man's wife who is residing in his house with his wife, he shall give "triple." And if he should deny [that he knew of her status], he shall declare, "I did not know," they shall undergo the divine River Ordeal. And if the man in whose house the wife of a man resided should refuse to undergo the divine River Ordeal, he shall give "triple"; if it is the man whose wife withdrew herself from him who should refuse to undergo the divine River Ordeal, he [in whose house she resided] is clear; he shall bear the expenses of the divine River Ordeal. However, if the man whose wife withdrew herself from him does not mutilate his wife, he shall take back his wife; no sanctions are imposed.

A25. If a woman is residing in her own father's house and her husband is dead, her husband's brothers have not yet divided their inheritance, and she has no son—her husband's brothers who have not yet received their inheritance shares shall take whatever valuables her husband bestowed upon her that are not missing. As for the rest [of the property], they shall resort to a verdict by the gods, they shall provide proof, and they shall take the property; they shall not be seized for [the settlement of any dispute by] the divine River Ordeal or the oath.

A26. If a woman is residing in her own father's house and her husband is dead, if there are sons of her husband, it is they who shall take whatever valuables her husband bestowed upon her; if there are no sons of her husband, she herself shall take the valuables.

A27. If a woman is residing in her own father's house and her husband visits her regularly, he himself shall take back any marriage settlement which he, her husband, gave to her; he shall have no claim to anything belonging to her father's house.

A28. If a widow should enter a man's house and she is carrying her dead husband's surviving son with her [in her womb], he grows up in the house of the man who married her but no tablet of his adoption is written, he will not take an inheritance share from the estate of the one who raised him, and he will not be responsible for its debts; he shall take an inheritance share from the estate of his begetter in accordance with his portion.

A29. If a woman should enter her husband's house, her dowry and whatever she brings with her from her father's house, and also whatever her father-in-law gave her upon her entering, are clear for her sons; her father-in-law's sons shall have no valid claim. But if her husband intends to take control of her, he shall give it to whichever of his sons he wishes.

A30. If a father should bring the ceremonial marriage prestation and present [the bridal gift] to the house of his son's father-in-law, and the woman is not yet given to his son, and another son of his, whose wife is residing in her own father's house, is dead, he

shall give the wife of his deceased son into the protection of the household of his second son to whose father-in-law's house he has presented [the ceremonial marriage prestation]. If the master of the daughter who is receiving the bridal gift decides not to agree to give his daughter [in these altered circumstances], if the father who presented the bridal gift so pleases, he shall take his daughter-in-law [i.e., the wife of his deceased son] and give her in marriage to his [second] son. And if he so pleases, as much as he presented—lead, silver, gold, and anything not edible—he shall take back in the quantities originally given; he shall have no claim to anything edible.

A31. If a man presents the bridal gift to his father-in-law's house, and although his wife is dead there are other daughters of his father-in-law, if he so pleases, he shall marry a daughter of his father-in-law in lieu of his deceased wife. Or, if he so pleases, he shall take back the silver that he gave; they shall not give back to him grain, sheep, or anything edible; he shall receive only the silver.

A32. If a woman is residing in her own father's house and her […] is given, whether or not she has been taken into her father-in-law's house, she shall be responsible for her husband's debts, transgression, or punishment.

A33. If a woman is residing in her own father's house, her husband is dead, and she has sons […], or [if he so pleases], he shall give her into the protection of the household of her father-in-law. If her husband and her father-in-law are both dead, and she has no son, she is indeed a widow; she shall go wherever she pleases.

A34. If a man should marry a widow without her formal binding agreement and she resides in his house for two years, she is a wife; she shall not leave.

A35. If a widow should enter into a man's house, whatever she brings with her belongs to her [new] husband; and if a man should enter into a woman's house, whatever he brings with him belongs to the woman.

A36. If a woman is residing in her father's house, or her husband settles her in a house elsewhere, and her husband then travels abroad but does not leave her any oil, wool, clothing, or provisions, or anything else, and sends her no provisions from abroad—that woman shall still remain [the exclusive object of rights] for her husband for five years, she shall not reside with another husband. If she has sons, they shall be hired out and provide for their own sustenance; the woman shall wait for her husband, she shall not reside with another husband. If she has no sons, she shall wait for her husband for five years; at the onset of [?] six years, she shall reside with the husband of her choice; her [first] husband, upon returning, shall have no valid claim to her; she is clear for her second husband. If he is delayed beyond the five years but is not detained of his own intention, whether because a ... seized him and he fled or because he was falsely arrested and therefore he was detained, upon returning he shall so prove, he shall give a woman comparable to his wife [to her second husband] and take his wife. And if the king should send him to another country and he is delayed beyond the five years, his wife shall wait for him [indefinitely]; she shall not go to reside with another husband. And furthermore, if she should reside with another husband before the five years are completed and should she bear children [to the second husband], because she did not wait in accordance with the agreement, but was taken in marriage [by another], her [first] husband, upon returning, shall take her and also her offspring.

A37. If a man intends to divorce his wife, if it is his wish, he shall give her something; if that is not his wish, he shall not give her anything, and she shall leave empty-handed.

A38. If a woman is residing in her own father's house and her husband divorces her, he shall take the valuables which he himself bestowed upon her; he shall have no claim to the bridewealth which he brought [to her father's house], it is clear for the woman.

A39. If a man should give one who is not his own daughter in marriage to a husband—if [this situation arose because] previously her father had been in debt and she had been made to reside as a pledge—and a prior creditor should come forward, he [i.e., the prior creditor] shall receive the value of the woman, in full, from the one who gives the woman in marriage; if he has nothing to give, he [i.e., the prior creditor] shall take the one who gives the woman in marriage. However, if she had been saved from a catastrophe, she is clear for the one who saved her. And if the one who marries the woman either causes a tablet to be ... for him or they have a claim in place against him, he shall […] the value of the woman, and the one who gives [the woman] […]

A40. Wives of a man, or [widows], or any [Assyrian] women who go out into the main thoroughfare [shall not have] their heads [bare]. Daughters of a man [... with] either a ... cloth or garments or […] shall be veiled, […] their heads [... (gap of ca. 6 lines) ...] When they go about […] in the main thoroughfare during the daytime, they shall be veiled. A concubine who goes about in the main thoroughfare with her mistress is to be veiled. A married *qadiltu*-woman is to be veiled [when she goes about] in the main thoroughfare, but an unmarried one is to leave her head bare in the main thoroughfare, she shall not veil herself. A prostitute shall not be veiled, her head shall be bare. Whoever sees a veiled prostitute shall seize her, secure witnesses, and bring her to the palace entrance. They shall not take away her jewelry, but he who has seized her takes her clothing; they shall strike her 50 blows with rods; they shall pour hot pitch over her head. And if a man should see a veiled prostitute and release her, and does not bring her to the palace entrance, they shall strike that man 50 blows with rods; the one who informs against him shall take his clothing; they shall pierce his ears, thread them on a cord, tie it at his back; he shall perform the king's service for one full month. Slave women shall not be veiled, and he who should see a veiled slave woman shall seize her and bring her to the palace entrance; they shall cut off her ears; he who seizes her shall take her clothing. If a man should see a veiled slave woman but release her and not seize her, and does not bring her to the palace entrance, and they then prove the charges against him and find him guilty, they shall strike him 50 blows with rods; they shall pierce his ears, thread them on a cord, tie it at his back; the one who informs against him shall take his garments; he shall perform the king's service for one full month.

A41. If a man intends to veil his concubine, he shall assemble five or six of his comrades, and he shall veil her in their presence, he shall declare, "She is my *aššutu*-wife"; she is his *aššutu*-wife. A concubine who is not veiled in the presence of people, whose husband did not declare, "She is my *aššutu*-wife," she is not an *aššutu*-wife, she is indeed a concubine. If a man is dead and there are no sons of his veiled wife, the sons of the concubines are indeed sons; they shall [each] take an inheritance share.

A42. If a man pours oil on the head of a woman of the *a'īlu*-class on the occasion of a holiday, or brings dishes on the occasion of a banquet, no return [of gifts] shall be made.

A43. If a man either pours oil on her head or brings [dishes for] the banquet, [after which] the son to whom he assigned the wife either dies or flees, he shall give her in marriage to whichever of his remaining sons he wishes, from the oldest to the youngest of at least ten years of age. If the father is dead and the son to whom he assigned the wife is also dead, a son of the deceased son who is at least ten years old shall marry her. If the sons of the [dead] son are less than ten years old, if the father of the daughter wishes, he shall give his daughter [to one of them], but if he wishes he shall make a full and equal return [of gifts given]. If there is no son, he shall return as much as he received, precious stones or anything not edible, in its full amount; but he shall not return anything edible.

A44. If there is an Assyrian man or an Assyrian woman who is residing in a man's house as a pledge for a debt, for as much as his value, and he is taken for the full value [i.e., his value as pledge does not exceed that of the debt], he [the pledge holder] shall whip [the pledge], pluck out [the pledge's] hair, [or] mutilate or pierce [the pledge's] ears.

A45. If a woman is given in marriage and the enemy then takes her husband prisoner, and she has neither father-in-law nor son [to support her], she shall remain [the exclusive object of rights] for her husband for two years. During these two years, if she has no provisions, she shall come forward and so declare. If she is a resident of the community dependent upon the palace, her [father(?)] shall provide for her and she shall do work for him. If she is a wife of a *hupšu*-soldier, [...] shall provide for her [and she shall do work for him]. But [if she is a wife of a man(?) whose] field and [house are not sufficient to support her(?)], she shall come forward and declare before the judges, "[I have nothing] to eat"; the judges shall question the mayor and the noblemen of the city to determine the current market rate[?] of a field in that city; they shall assign and give the field and house for her, for her provisioning for two years; she shall be resident [in that house], and they shall write a tablet for her [permitting her to stay for the two years]. She shall allow two full years to pass, and then she may go to reside with the husband of her own choice; they shall write a tablet for her as if for a widow. If later her lost husband should return to the country, he shall take back his wife who married outside the family; he shall have no claim to the sons she bore to her later husband, it is her later husband who shall take them. As for the field and house that she gave for full price outside the family for her provisioning, if it is not entered into the royal holdings[?], he shall give as much as was given, and he shall take it back. But if he should not return but dies in another country, the king shall give his field and house wherever he chooses to give.

A46. If a woman whose husband is dead does not move out of her house upon the death of her husband, if her husband [while alive] does not deed her anything in writing, she shall reside in the house of [one of] her own sons, wherever she chooses; her husband's sons shall provide for her, they shall draw up an agreement to supply her with provisions and drink as for an in-law whom they love. If she is a second wife and has no sons of her own, she shall reside with one [of her husband's sons] and they shall provide for her in common. If she does have sons, and the sons of a prior wife do not agree to provide for her, she shall reside in the house of [one of] her own sons, wherever she chooses; her own sons shall provide for her, and she shall do service for them. And if there is one among her husband's sons who is willing to marry her, [it is he who shall provide for her; her own sons] shall not provide for her.

A47. If either a man or a woman should be discovered practicing witchcraft, and should they prove the charges against them and find them guilty, they shall kill the practitioner of witchcraft. A man who heard from an eyewitness to the witchcraft that he witnessed the practice of the witchcraft, who said to him, "I myself saw it," that hearsay-witness shall go and inform the king. If the eye-witness should deny what he [i.e., the hearsay-witness] reports to the king, he [i.e., the hearsay-witness] shall declare before the divine Bull-the-Son-of-the-Sun-God, "He surely told me"—and thus he is clear. As for the eyewitness who spoke [of witnessing the deed to his comrade] and then denied [it to the king], the king shall interrogate him as he sees fit, in order to determine his intentions; an exorcist shall have the man make a declaration when they make a purification, and then he himself [i.e., the exorcist] shall say as follows, "No one shall release any of you from the oath you swore by the king and by his son; you are bound by oath to the stipulations of the agreement to which you swore by the king and by his son."

A48. If a man [wants to give in marriage] his debtor's daughter who is residing in his house as a pledge, he shall ask permission of her father and then he shall give her to a husband. If her father does not agree, he shall not give her. If her father is dead, he shall ask permission of one of her brothers and the latter shall consult with her [other] brothers. If one brother so desires he shall declare, "I will redeem my sister within one month"; if he should not redeem her within one month, the creditor, if he so pleases, shall clear her of encumbrances and shall give her to a husband....

A50. [If a man] strikes [another man's wife thereby causing her to abort her fetus ...] a man's wife

[...] and they shall treat him as he treated her; he shall make full payment of a life for her fetus. And if that woman dies, they shall kill that man; he shall make full payment of a life for her fetus. And if there is no son of that woman's husband, and his wife whom he struck aborted her fetus, they shall kill the assailant for her fetus. If her fetus was a female, he shall make full payment of a life only.

A51. If a man strikes another man's wife who does not raise her child, causing her to abort her fetus, it is a punishable offense; he shall give 7,200 shekels of lead.

A52. If a man strikes a prostitute causing her to abort her fetus, they shall assess him blow for blow, he shall make full payment of a life.

A53. If a woman aborts her fetus by her own action and they then prove the charges against her and find her guilty, they shall impale her, they shall not bury her. If she dies as a result of aborting her fetus, they shall impale her, they shall not bury her. If any persons should hide that woman because she aborted her fetus [...] ...

A55. If a man forcibly seizes and rapes a maiden who is residing in her father's house, [...] who is not betrothed[?], whose [womb(?)] is not opened, who is not married, and against whose father's house there is no outstanding claim—whether within the city or in the countryside, or at night whether in the main thoroughfare, or in a granary, or during the city festival—the father of the maiden shall take the wife of the fornicator of the maiden and hand her over to be raped; he shall not return her to her husband, but he shall take [and keep?] her; the father shall give his daughter who is the victim of fornication into the protection of the household of her fornicator. If he [the fornicator] has no wife, the fornicator shall give "triple" the silver as the value of the maiden to her father; her fornicator shall marry her; he shall not reject[?] her. If the father does not desire it so, he shall receive "triple" silver for the maiden, and he shall give his daughter in marriage to whomever he chooses.

A56. If a maiden should willingly give herself to a man, the man shall so swear; they shall have no claim to his wife; the fornicator shall pay "triple" the silver as the value of the maiden; the father shall treat his daughter in whatever manner he chooses....

A59. In addition to the punishments for [a man's wife] that are [written] on the tablet, a man may [whip] his wife, pluck out her hair, mutilate her ears, or strike her, with impunity.

Month II, day 2, eponymy of Sagiu.

Tablet B

B1. [If brothers divide the estate of their father], orchards [and wells] in the plot of land [...], the oldest son shall select and take a double share, and his brothers shall select and take shares one after the other; the youngest son is the one who apportions whatever *śiluhlu*-personnel there are and all the associated equipment in the field; the oldest son shall select and take one share, and for his second share he shall cast lots with his brothers.

B2. If a man, who has not yet received his inheritance share, takes a life, they shall hand him over to the next-of-kin. Should the next-of-kin so choose, he shall kill him, or, if he chooses to come to an accommodation, then he shall take his inheritance share.

B3. If a man, who has not yet received his inheritance share, speaks treason or flees, the disposition of his inheritance share shall be determined by the king.

B4. If there are brothers in possession of an undivided field, and one brother among them [...] sows seed [...] cultivates the field, [and a second brother] then comes and for a second time [takes the seed of] his brother's cultivation [...], and they prove the charges against him and find him guilty—[on the day that he himself] comes forward, [the brother] who cultivated [the field] shall take [his inheritance share]....

B6. [If ...] intends to purchase [a field or house ...]; before he purchases the field or house, he shall have the herald make a proclamation three times during the course of one full month within the City of Assur, and he shall also have him make a proclamation three times within the city of the field or house which he intends to purchase, as follows: "I intend to purchase the field or house, within the common irrigated area of this city, belonging to so-and-so, son of so-and-so. Let all who have a right to acquire [the property] or a contest [against this transfer] bring forth their tablets and present them before the officials, let them thus contest [the purchase], let them clear [the property of other claims], and let them take it. Of those who, during the course of this full month, bring their tablets without fail by the due date and present them before the officials, the man [whose claim is successful] shall take full possession of the extent of his field." When the herald makes his proclamation in the City of Assur, one of the royal court officials, the city scribe, the herald, and the royal officials are to be present; representing the city of the field or house that he intends to purchase, the mayor and three noblemen of the city are to be present; they also shall have the herald make his proclamation; they shall write their tablets and give [them to the purchaser, saying] as follows: The herald has made proclamations three times during the course of this full month. He who during the course of this full month has not brought his tablet and has not presented it before the officials forfeits [any claims to] the field or house; it is cleared for the benefit of the person who had the herald make the proclamation." Three tablets that the judges will write [attesting to the fact] of having the herald make a proclamation, one [tablet] the officials […] …

B8. If a man should incorporate a large border area of his comrade's [property into his own] and they prove the charges against him and find him guilty, he shall give a field "triple" that which he had incorporated; they shall cut off one of his fingers; they shall strike him 100 blows with rods; he shall perform the king's service for one full month.

B9. If a man transfers a small border area of the lots and they prove the charges against him and find him guilty, he shall give 3,600 shekels of lead; he shall give a field "triple" that which he had incorporated; they shall strike him 50 blows with rods; he shall perform the king's service for one full month.

B10. If a man digs a well and builds a permanent structure in a field not his own, he shall forfeit his claim to his well and his permanent structure; they shall strike him 30 blows with rods; he shall perform the king's service for 20 days. … […] … […] the permanent structure […] he shall swear, "[…]," and further, "I have indeed [dug] the well, I have [indeed built] a permanent structure."…

B12. If a man plants an orchard, digs a well, or raises trees in a field belonging to [his comrade], and the owner of the field notices it but does not [object], the orchard is clear for the benefit of the planter; he shall give another field in lieu of the field to the owner of the orchard.

B13. If a man either plants an orchard, or digs a well, or raises vegetables or trees in a plot not his own, and they prove the charges against him and find him guilty, when the owner of the field comes forward, he shall take the orchard together with its [new] installations.

B14. If a man digs[? a pit] and makes bricks in a plot not his own and they prove the charges against him and find him guilty, he shall give "triple" the plot; they shall take his bricks; they shall strike him 50[?] blows with rods; he shall perform the king's service for [x days].

B15. [If a man …] and makes bricks in a plot not his own, they shall take [his bricks; they shall] strike him [x blows with rods]; he shall perform [the king's service for x days.]…

B17. If there is sufficient water for irrigation available in the common irrigated area in the wells, the owners of the fields shall act together; each man shall perform the work in accordance with the extent of his field, and shall irrigate his field. But if there are some among them who are not amenable to an agreement, the one among them who is amenable to an agreement shall appeal to the judges; he shall obtain a tablet [with the decision] of the judges, and perform the work; he shall take those waters for him-

Glossary

a'īlu	the Assyrian term for the upper class, or free males and females
aŝŝutu-wife	a "wife of the first order," or first-class wife, compared with a concubine, who had a lower status and fewer privileges
eponymy of Sagiu	In the Middle Assyrian dating scheme, a date associated with an official, Sagiu, who was connected to the crown and served at some point during the reign of Tiglath-pileser I
hupŝu-soldier	a soldier from the lower classes who was perhaps given land in exchange for service to the state, though it is not certain
prestation	gift exchange that took place at marriage (for example, dowry and bridewealth)
qadiltu	a person or a group of lesser temple officials or dedicatees
ŝiluhlu-personnel	a dependent class of agricultural worker

self, and irrigate his own field; no one else may irrigate [with the waters].

B18. If there is sufficient rain-water for irrigation available, the owners of the fields shall act together; each man shall perform the work in accordance with the extent of his field, and shall irrigate his field. But if there are some among them who are not amenable to an agreement, then the one among them who is amenable to an agreement shall take the tablet [with the decision] of the judges before those who are not amenable to an agreement; the mayor and five noblemen [of the city shall be present … (gap) … they shall strike] him [x blows with rods]; he shall perform [the king's service for x days].

B19. If a man intends to cultivate the field of his comrade, [and …] prevented[?] him, [… he swore for] him an oath by the king and he cultivated it. [If …] he should come forth, the cultivator of the field shall harvest and thresh [the grain] at harvest time, he shall store [the grain] in the storage facility, [… and] he shall return the [straw(?)] to the barn; in accordance with the yield of a field of the city, he shall give two shares [to the owner] of the field.

B20. If a man digs […] in a field not belonging to him, surrounds it with a border, sets up a boundary stone, and says, ["…,"] and they prove the charges against him and find him guilty,[…]

VICTORY STELA OF PIANKHI

"His Majesty himself went to arrange the battle formation of the ships ....
Then Memphis was taken like a cloudburst."

Overview

The Victory Stela of Piankhi—also known as Piye, the name used on the stone slab—dates to Egypt's Twenty-fifth Dynasty (ca. 747–656 BCE), during the twenty-first year of Piankhi's reign (ca. 747–716 BCE). It was intended to justify his rulership over all of Egypt. The stela was designed to represent Piankhi, who was a Nubian, as a true Egyptian and as superior to his Libyan opponent in the Nile Delta. Nubia was located along the Nile River just south of Egypt in an area between modern-day Aswan and Meroë, Sudan. During the Twenty-fifth Dynasty, the capital of Nubia was located at Napata, from which Piankhi reigned.

The stela, made of dark-gray granite, was discovered in the temple of the god Amun (spelled "Amon" in the document) at Jebel Barkal in 1862. It measures approximately six feet in height; four feet, seven inches in width; and one foot, five inches in thickness and weighs some two and a quarter tons. The text on the stela consists of 159 lines. When discovered, the stela was almost intact, with the exception of one piece from the right-hand portion of the reverse side, which compromises parts of lines 35–50 of the text.

This was the second stela commissioned by Piankhi. The first one commemorated his initial military expedition to Egypt, a journey Piankhi made after his coronation, presumably to reaffirm oaths of allegiance made by the Egyptians to his father, Kashta. During his time in Egypt, Piankhi probably made a trip to Thebes, where he would have been crowned in the Temple of Amun, thus establishing himself as the rightful ruler of Egypt. Connections between the Piankhi stela and the stela of Thutmose III, both found at Jebel Barkal, are apparent, even though they were commissioned more than seven hundred years apart. Among differences between the texts, Piankhi's is considerably longer, as the design of the text in Thutmose III's stela was inscribed on only one side; the single-sidedness of the inscription indicates that it was intended to be placed against a wall, whereas Piankhi's stela is inscribed on all four sides and was intended to be a freestanding piece. The modifications and expansions made by Piankhi may have been done in competition with Thutmose III, a renowned ruler from the fifteenth century BCE, during the New Kingdom era. By making his stela bigger and the text longer, Piankhi was attempting to portray his accomplishments as more important than those of his predecessors, especially the Egyptian pharaohs.

Piankhi's relationship with the god Amun was probably the motivating force for creating the stela. Although the significance of Amun to the Nubians during the reign of Piankhi is unknown, Amun had been adopted as a primary deity in the Nubian pantheon after being introduced by the Egyptians. In the Egyptian pantheon, Amun had his cult center at Thebes. The importance of Amun to Piankhi might have influenced his response and subsequent military action when the Theban troop commander pleaded with Piankhi for assistance.

Context

Egypt underwent many foreign invasions following the end of the Twentieth Dynasty (ca. 1190–1069 BCE), which was marked by the death of Ramses XI. During his reign, many acts and periods of upheaval occurred, including robberies of the royal tombs, worker strikes, and the civil war of Panehsy, the "King's Son of Cush" (that is, governor of Cush, or Kush—the province of Nubia). The Twenty-first through Twenty-fifth dynasties cover a period referred to by scholars as the Third Intermediate Period, a time of civil unrest under a weak central government. The Twenty-fifth Dynasty, beginning in the eighth century BCE, was a time of foreign rule in Egypt, as the country was controlled by the Nubians, with additional foreign forces attempting to exert their authority over Egypt. Historians are uncertain as to the events leading up to the Nubian conquest of Egypt, but it is believed to have begun sometime during the reign of either Alara or Kashta, rulers who were sparsely documented. The Egyptians and Nubians had contact with each other from the earliest times, with documentation of expeditions to Nubia by Egyptian dignitaries dating to as early as the Sixth Dynasty (ca. 2345–2181 BCE). Through their contact, the Egyptians gained access to various natural Nubian resources, with the primary one being gold. The abundance of gold in Nubia may have contributed to the

CA. 760 BCE	■ Kashta ascends to the Nubian throne and leads a campaign into Egypt.
CA. 747 BCE	■ Piankhi ascends to the Nubian throne.
CA. 743 BCE	■ Piankhi embarks on his first campaign into Egypt; while there, he is crowned in the Temple of Amun and establishes his rightful rule over Egypt.
CA. 727 BCE	■ Piankhi sends his army to Egypt.
CA. 726 BCE	■ Embarking on his second campaign into Egypt, Piankhi defeats the rulers Namlot and Tefnakhte.
CA. 725 BCE	■ Piankhi has his Egyptian victory recorded on a stela.
CA. 716 BCE	■ Piankhi dies, and his brother Shabaka ascends to the Nubian throne.

the monuments of his descendants. He may not have progressed beyond the first cataract of the Nile at Aswan, where he erected a dedication stela on the island of Elephantine. Kashta's northward march marked the first attempt of Nubian expansion into Egypt after the New Kingdom.

Piankhi succeeded Kashta around 747 BCE, and he began his first campaign into Egypt shortly thereafter. This campaign, which probably took place in Piankhi's fourth regnal year, may have resulted in the extension of Piankhi's rule to Thebes and the installation of his sister Amenirdis I as "God's Wife of Amun," one of the most important positions held by women in ancient Egypt. Afterward, Piankhi returned to Nubia, where he enlarged the Temple of Amun at Jebel Barkal. In his twentieth regnal year, Piankhi invaded Egypt again. This latter campaign resulted in the defeat of Tefnakhte (or Tefnakht), ruler of Sais. After defeating Tefnakhte, Piankhi returned to his capital city of Napata, where he erected a victory stela in his twenty-first regnal year.

About the Author

The Victory Stela of Piankhi was commissioned sometime after the ruler's twenty-first year on the throne. Piankhi was the third ruler of the Twenty-fifth Dynasty and reigned from about 747 to 716 BCE from the Nubian capital at Napata. He was buried in the royal cemetery at el-Kurru, located just downriver from the capital. His greatest documented military victory was over the Libyan king Tefnakhte, who was located in the Nile Delta and attempted to conquer all of Egypt. Not much else is known about the reign of Piankhi. Although the victory stela was commissioned by Piankhi, it is unlikely that it was constructed in Nubia. The expert use of classical Middle Egyptian indicates an Egyptian author. Since Middle Egyptian had been out of use for nearly half a millennium, it is likely that the author was a member of the Theban clergy, as which he would have been well educated in the language. Another possibility is that Piankhi dictated the contents of the inscription to his royal scribe, who would have been responsible for writing down all decrees of the king.

Explanation and Analysis of the Document

The top of the stela (also known as the lunette) depicts Piankhi standing with his back toward the god Amun and the goddess Nut. Piankhi faces Namlot, the ruler of Hermopolis, who is shown bringing a horse and shaking a *sistrum*, a musical instrument of the percussion family that was popular in the cult of Hathor, the goddess of love. *Sistra* were often used during religious ceremonies and processions. On the level below Namlot are three Libyan kings, who are shown in a pose of subservience. Behind Nut stand five Libyan princes in the same pose as the Libyan kings—two on the top level and three on the bottom. Beneath the lunette is the text of the stela.

development of the name *Nubia* since the ancient Egyptian word for "gold" is *nbw*.

Takeloth III and Osorkon III were coregents ruling Egypt when the Nubians, led by Piankhi's father, Kashta, began their northward march into Egypt sometime during his reign. Kashta's name occurs only in relational mentions on

The stela text is written in flawless classical Middle Egyptian and is remarkably well preserved. This is unique, because for over four hundred years before the date of this text, there was no literary tradition in Upper Nubia. The lack of documentation is curious because it is highly unlikely that the Nubians had no written records when they modeled so much of their culture after the Egyptians, who documented everything. Although the primary portions of the text were written in classical Middle Egyptian, when Padiese and Tefnakhte address Piankhi, the language switches to contemporary grammar, which indicates that Padiese and Tefnakhte were considered to be of a lower status than Piankhi. The stela is not divided into specific sections, but an attempt has been made to create breaks in the text, for readability.

While the text of the stela may appear straightforward, it actually has various levels. Foremost, it is a simple outline of a military campaign in which the king sends his troops to stop the resistance of an opposing ruler. Through the subsequent battles, the king reclaims his rightful place as ruler of Egypt and Nubia. The beginning of the stela indicates ultimate victory for the author, since Piankhi states that he has done more than the ancestors that came before. Piankhi's journey to achieve victory is a long one, as seen through the mention of the various sites visited and the resistance experienced at each city. Eventually, all his enemies surrender and acknowledge Piankhi as the rightful ruler and maintainer of *ma'at*, the Egyptian concept of truth and justice.

◆ Paragraph 1: Opening Speech

At the beginning of the stela is the date of "regnal year 21, first month of Inundation," where inundation season was the time of year when the Nile flooded and rich soil was deposited on the surrounding farmland. Following the date, the decree of Piankhi states that he has done more than his predecessors, which was a common declaration among kings—each one always wanted to do more than his predecessors and prove that he was the rightful heir to the throne. Piankhi also states that he is the manifestation of the god Atum, the son of Ra (or Re), and is beloved of Amun ("Amon"), those names being typical elements in Egyptian pharaonic names. His affiliation with these powerful deities provided additional justification for his reign not only in Nubia but in Egypt as well.

◆ Paragraphs 2–24: Piankhi in Nubia

In paragraphs 2–4, a messenger sent to Piankhi informs him of Tefnakhte's advance southward. The information is related through mention of the various nomes, or provinces of ancient Egypt, that Tefnakhte has fought and conquered. These nomes were under the authority of various local rulers, called *nomarchs*, whose roles were indicative of the lack of a centralized government at this time. Since the country was not unified under one ruler, Tefnakhte saw the opportunity to gain more territory and therefore began his own campaign southward with the goal of expanding his sphere of influence.

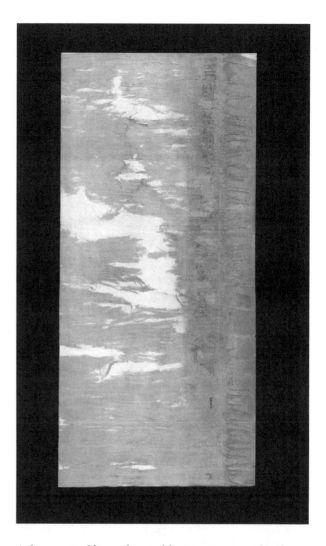

A fragment of linen donated by Piye to a temple of Amun, possibly at Karnak. A column of inscription close to the fringed edge of the cloth gives the king's titles and a year from his reign. (© The Trustees of the British Museum)

In paragraphs 8 and 11, Piankhi comments on the pleas for help, represented in paragraph 6, sent by the local rulers now under the authority of Tefnakhte. The nomarchs believed that Piankhi was taking an isolationist approach and ignoring the situation in Egypt. This rouses Piankhi to action, and as a result he orders his commanders stationed in Egypt to fight. In paragraphs 10–13, Piankhi sends his troops to Egypt and gives them orders regarding what is considered to be proper and improper conduct. He wants his troops to fight nobly; thus, he tells them to engage in battle only during daylight hours and to announce to the opponent that attack is imminent. Piankhi also tells them that before they may fight at Thebes, they need to be pure and avoid arrogance, which is the mark of a man ignorant of the power the god Amun will use to support the troops. Following his instructions, the army praises Piankhi (paragraph 15) and proceeds to Thebes. Once the order is given,

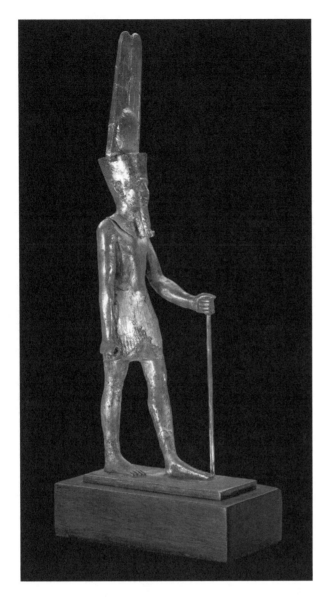

Gilded silver statuette of Amun from the Temple of Amun at Karnak, Thebes, Egypt (© The Trustees of the British Museum)

the army of Piankhi fight against and conquer the united forces of Tefnakhte at Heracleopolis (paragraph 16), forces that consist of rulers and kings from Lower Egypt. This was the final battle at which Piankhi was not in attendance.

Paragraphs 17–25 provide a list of names of the rulers of Lower Egypt and the fate they encounter when fighting Piankhi's forces. The army fights against the rulers of Lower Egypt, and those who remain, including King Namlot, flee back to their homes. After this attack, the army reports back (in paragraph 25) to Piankhi, detailing their victories in his name.

◆ Paragraph 26–33: Piankhi Goes to Egypt

After the battle at Heracleopolis, King Namlot retreats to Hermopolis to warn the people of the impending bat-

tle. Upon hearing of the escape of the enemies, Piankhi is said to have "raged because of it like a panther" and resolved to go to Egypt himself. Piankhi also states that the driving motivations for his travel to Egypt were to reaffirm the oaths made by previous local rulers to his father and to participate in the celebrations of New Year's and Opet. The New Year's festival was seasonal and was intended to bring prosperity to the coming year. The Opet festival was classified as a divine festival because it involved the procession of the Theban triad of gods—Amun, Mut, and Khonsu—from Thebes to Luxor Temple and back again.

◆ Paragraphs 34–37: The Battle at Hermopolis

From a military point of view, the text of the stela has two primary episodes: the victory at Hermopolis and, later, the victory at Memphis (described in paragraphs 55–66). In this first episode, Piankhi joins his forces at Hermopolis, telling his army, "It is the year for finalizing a conclusion, for placing fear of me in Lower Egypt, and for inflicting upon them a severe and painful defeat by striking." After days of battle, "Hermopolis threw itself upon its belly," in submission "before the King of Lower Egypt."

◆ Paragraphs 38–46: Namlot Surrenders

Piankhi also had two primary victories against his enemies, namely, the surrender of Namlot and the later submission of Tefnakhte. At the time of Namlot's surrender, Namlot enlists the assistance of his wife, who seeks support from the women in Piankhi's company. Because the role of women was typically a secondary one in ancient Egypt, for Namlot to ask the help of his wife indicated that he held her in high regard. When the two rulers meet, Piankhi opts to take pity on Namlot because he has classified Namlot's actions as being a result of insanity. The strangest part of this meeting is that Namlot, as part of his tribute, leads a horse by his right hand and holds a *sistrum* in his left. There is no logical explanation for this gesture, and it was odd enough even to Piankhi that he had it depicted on the lunette of the stela.

◆ Paragraph 47 and 48: Piankhi Tours Namlot's Residence

While exploring Namlot's residence, Piankhi goes into the stables and discovers the horses in a state of starvation. This angers him because horses were an important element of Nubian culture. Piankhi had horses depicted at the top of this stela as well as on the walls of the temple of Amun at Jebel Barkal. He also began the practice of entombing horses in a cemetery near the royal burial site of el-Kurru, located just east of the Nile's fourth cataract. Three of his successors also had horse burials. Although Piankhi attempted to identify with his Egyptian predecessors and emulated them, he built the first true pyramid in Nubia, and the anger he experienced when faced with the conditions under which the horses were kept demonstrated that he maintained his Nubian values.

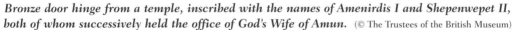

Bronze door hinge from a temple, inscribed with the names of Amenirdis I and Shepenwepet II, both of whom successively held the office of God's Wife of Amun. (© The Trustees of the British Museum)

◆ **Paragraphs 49–54: Additional Rulers Surrender**

Following Namlot, the ruler of Heracleopolis as well as rulers from additional towns announce their surrender and bring tribute to Piankhi. The presentation of tribute and their throwing themselves upon their bellies were customary practices of the defeated. Piankhi was slowly regaining control over Egypt.

◆ **Paragraphs 55–66: The Capture of Memphis**

The second major military episode was Piankhi's surprise attack and victory at Memphis. Even though the army did not experience great victories until Piankhi joined them in Egypt, they were respectably victorious, and therefore Piankhi's constant raging "like a panther" was unwarranted. Mention of this might have been included to justify Piankhi's decision to join his forces and personally fight his enemies.

Piankhi details that the Memphite contingency consisted of eight thousand troops. This is a direct parallel with Thutmose III's mention that at the Battle of Megiddo his army faced forces totaling one thousand settlements and all the chiefs of the northern countries. Although the numbers are clearly exaggerated, they are inflated to emphasize the victories of the kings.

◆ **Paragraphs 67 and 68: The Surrender of Three Additional Rulers**

Following the capture of Memphis, "every nome" in the region hears the news, "opening their fortifications and fleeing in flight." King Iuput, ruler of Leontopolis in the delta region of Lower Egypt, along with the ruler Akanosh and the prince Padiese, surrendered and brought tribute to present to Piankhi.

◆ **Paragraphs 69–71: Piankhi Visits Heliopolis**

The day after King Iuput, Akanosh, and Padiese surrender, Piankhi travels east to Heliopolis, giving offerings along the way to the god Atum and to the "Ennead," a group of nine gods, including Ra (spelled "Re" in the document), his children Shu and Tefnut, and their descendants Geb, Isis, Nephthys, Nut, Osiris, and Se. This he does to ensure that he would live a life of prosperity and health.

◆ **Paragraphs 72–80: Padiese and Other Northern Rulers Surrender**

In paragraphs 72–77 the prince Padiese surrenders directly to Piankhi and invites him to visit his palace at Athribis in Lower Egypt. Piankhi goes to the palace and receives tribute in the form of gold, gemstones, jewelry, and royal linen. Padiese also offers any of his horses to Piankhi, an offer that have appealed to a Nubian in his love of horses. Paragraph 78 lists northern rulers, all of whom were defeated and bring tribute offerings to Piankhi. The last two paragraphs, with breaks in the text, seem to describe an episode of resistance on the part of Padiese's troops. Piankhi's forces quell it, killing everyone.

◆ **Paragraphs 81–85: Tefnakhte's Submission**

Piankhi's second personal victory was the submission of Tefnakhte, who never participated in battle against

"Have you been silent so as to ignore Upper Egypt and the nomes of the Residence, while Tefnakht seizes what is before him, having found no resistance? Namlot … has gone to be a subordinate at his (Tefnakht's) heels, having shrugged off allegiance to His Majesty."

(Paragraph 6)

"He [Piankhi] made for himself a camp at the southwest of Hermopolis, keeping a stranglehold on it daily…. Days passed, and Hermopolis became foul to the nose, deprived of its ability to breathe. Then Hermopolis threw itself upon its belly, pleading before the King of Lower Egypt, while messengers came and went bearing everything beautiful to behold."

(Paragraph 36)

"His Majesty then proceeded to the stable of the horses and the quarters of the foals. When he saw [that] / they were starved, he said: 'As I live, as Re loves me, as my nose is rejuvenated with life, how much more painful it is in my heart that my horses have been starved than any other crime that you have committed at your discretion."

(Paragraph 47)

"Then he sent his ships and his troops to assault the harbor of Memphis. … [There was not] a common solider who wept among the entire army of His Majesty. His Majesty himself went to arrange the battle formation of the ships …. Then Memphis was taken like a cloudburst, with numerous people slain within it, in addition to those brought as prisoners to the place where His Majesty was."

(Paragraphs 63–65)

"These two rulers of Upper Egypt and two rulers of Lower Egypt, those entitled to royal uraei, came to kiss the ground because of the wrathful power of His Majesty. Now, however, … their legs / were like the legs of women. They could not enter into the palace since they were uncircumcised and eaters of fish—such is an abomination of the palace."

(Paragraph 87)

Piankhi. After Piankhi returned to Nubia, Tefnakhte might have regained some of his power but no longer attempted to rule all of Egypt. In submitting, he suggests that the two rulers come to an agreement that would prevent Piankhi from having to fight beyond the Egyptian borders. The oath of Tefnakhte is taken at Thebes in the presence of witnesses. The location used, the temple of Neith at Sais, was probably chosen because Tefnakhte would give his oath before the city's patron deity. The witnesses, representatives of Theban religious and military factions, were there presumably because they were the ones who originally had pleaded for Piankhi's aid and they would be responsible for ensuring that Tefnakhte followed through with his oath after Piankhi returned to Nubia.

◆ **Paragraphs 86–89: Piankhi Returns to Nubia**

In these final paragraphs, the remaining rebels surrender to Piankhi and his forces. Piankhi has achieved total victory, as he is told that "there is no nome sealed against His Majesty among the nomes of the South and North, while the West, the East and the islands in between are upon their bellies through fear of him." At dawn, the rulers bowed in subservience to him. After the display of submission, Piankhi's loot was loaded onto boats and the king returned to Nubia as his subjects recited a chant of jubilation to him, ending with the words "You are eternal, your victory enduring, / O ruler beloved of Thebes!"

Audience

Throughout the text of the stela there are various speakers and addressees. The speakers include Piankhi, messengers, inhabitants of the various cities visited by Piankhi,

Namlot and his wives, Tefnakhte, generals, priests, rulers who were conquered by Piankhi, and the people praising Piankhi at the end. The various addressees include general readers, Piankhi, the armies, Namlot, inhabitants of the cities, and priests.

The variety of speakers and addressees indicates that this stela had a specialized intended audience. Since most of the general population was illiterate, the stela was not meant for them. Additionally, the stela was located in a portion of the temple not readily accessible to the public, which would have limited the viewing audience to the temple priests and the king. Thus, considering the placement of the stela as well as the repetition throughout the text that Piankhi is beloved of Amun, it is possible that the actual intended audience was the god himself. If Amun was the intended audience, it would have indicated a continued allegiance to the deity and reaffirmed Amun's importance to the Nubians of the Twenty-fifth Dynasty.

Impact

The campaign detailed on the Victory Stela of Piankhi was a major milestone in the fight for Nubian control over Egypt, and the stela itself is one of the most extensive military documents dating to this time period. Before the Twenty-fifth Dynasty, the Nubians were generally under Egyptian control, as is evident in Middle Kingdom Egyptian forts in the region as well as a statement placed on the boundary stela of Sesostris III, of the nineteenth century BCE. These forts were intended to house branches of the Egyptian military, which was in Nubia to maintain control over the country. The boundary stela states that no one—that is, no Nubian—is permitted to cross the border without permis-

Questions for Further Study

1. The rulers of ancient dynasties often believed that they had to justify their rulership. Select another document—possibilities include "Mandate of Heaven: The Numerous Officers" and Divine Birth and Coronation Inscriptions of Hatshepsut—and compare and contrast the nature of the justifications they used.

2. Historians, particularly Egyptologists (those who study ancient Egypt), often have to rely on incomplete information or on such documents as the Victory Stela of Piankhi. What are some of the possible difficulties that historians face in reconstructing the history of any ancient culture on the basis of these kinds of records?

3. What can modern readers learn about the religious beliefs of ancient Egyptians by reading the Victory Stela of Piankhi?

4. What conditions in ancient Egypt enabled the Nubians under Piankhi to take control of Egypt?

5. Why were the Nubians bent on conquering Egypt? What material or political advantages did they gain by doing so?

sion. However, at the onset of the Twenty-fifth Dynasty, the Nubians took advantage of unstable political conditions in Egypt and moved to conquer the land to the north. Following his victory, Piankhi returned to Nubia and began a large building program at Jebel Barkal, expanding the temple of Amun and making additional documentation of his victory in Egypt. It is thought that he never returned to Egypt, even though he was recognized as its ruler until his death.

Piankhi's precedent provided the incentive for his successors to embark on their own Egyptian campaigns. In his second regnal year, 715 BCE, Shabaka began a drive into Egypt and eventually conquered Memphis. Because the Nubians were already very familiar with many aspects of Egyptian culture, including key concepts of Egyptian religion and kingship, they were able to portray themselves as rightful pharaohs rather than as foreigners. The Victory Stela of Piankhi thus marked the beginning of a long Nubian occupation of Egypt. Piankhi and his successors were able to maintain their control over Egypt until 656 BCE, when Tanwetamani was expelled by the Assyrian army. After their expulsion from Egypt, the Nubians continued to rule in Nubia until the end of the Meroitic period (350 CE). The Nubian empire proved a noteworthy civilization in eastern Africa that prospered for twelve hundred years.

Owing to the abundance of contact between the Egyptians and Nubians, aspects of Egyptian culture became evident in Nubian society. This tendency is referred to as "archaism" and can be seen in both monumental and non-monumental remains. The Nubians adopted a connection with the Theban god Amun, which can be seen through their construction of a temple to Amun at Napata. The Nubian rulers likewise utilized Egyptian royal titles as well as Egyptian royal regalia. They built Egyptian-inspired pyramids and placed Egyptian-style grave goods within them. The Nubians also modified traditional Egyptian elements, making them uniquely Nubian. Headdresses were fashioned with double uraei (figures of sacred serpents) rather than a single uraeus, and there was the development of a new headdress known as the "Kushite cap." Their Egyptian-style tendencies may have reflected a desire to legitimize the reigns of the various kings in both Egypt and Nubia in order to declare themselves restorers of *ma'at*—or the Nubian rulers might have simply been emulating aspects of a culture they appreciated and respected.

Further Reading

■ Articles

Depuydt, Leo. "The Date of Piye's Egyptian Campaign and the Chronology of the Twenty-fifth Dynasty." *Journal of Egyptian Archaeology* 79 (1993): 269–274.

Gardiner, Alan. "Piankhi's Instructions to His Army." *Journal of Egyptian Archaeology* 21, no. 2 (December 1935): 219–223.

■ Books

Aubin, Henry T. *The Rescue of Jerusalem: The Alliance between Hebrews and Africans in 701 BC*. New York: Soho Press, 2002.

Haynes, Joyce L. *Nubia: Ancient Kingdoms of Africa*. Boston: Museum of Fine Arts, 1992.

Kendall, Timothy. *Kush: Lost Kingdom of the Nile*. Brockton, Mass.: Brockton Art Museum/Fuller Memorial, 1982.

Kitchen, Kenneth A. *The Third Intermediate Period in Egypt, 1100–650 bc*. 2nd ed. Oxford, U.K.: Aris Phillips, 2004.

Lichtheim, Miriam. *Ancient Egyptian Literature*. Vol. 3: *The Late Period*. Berkeley: University of California Press, 1980.

Morkot, Robert G. *The Black Pharaohs: Egypt's Nubian Rulers*. London: Rubicon Press, 2000.

Redford, Donald B. *From Slave to Pharaoh: The Black Experience of Ancient Egypt*. Baltimore, Md.: Johns Hopkins University Press, 2004.

Ritner, Robert K. "The Victory Stela of Piye." In *The Literature of Ancient Egypt: An Anthology of Stories, Instructions, Stelae, Autobiographies, and Poetry*, ed. William Kelly Simpson. 3rd ed. New Haven, Conn.: Yale University Press, 2003.

—Sarah M. Schellinger

VICTORY STELA OF PIANKHI

Regnal year 21, first month of Inundation, under the Majesty of the King of Upper and Lower Egypt, Piye, beloved of Amon, living forever. The decree which My Majesty has spoken:

"Hear what I have done in exceeding the
   ancestors.
I am the king, the representation of god,
the living image of Atum,
who issued from the womb marked as ruler,
who is feared by those greater than he,
[whose father] knew and whose mother perceived
even in the egg that he would be ruler,
the good god, beloved of the gods,
the Son of Re, who acts with his two arms,
Piye, beloved of Amon."

One came to say to His Majesty: "The Chief of the West, the count and chief in Behbeit el-Hagar, Tefnakht, is in the (Harpoon) nome, in the nome of Xois, in Hapi, in [...], in the marshy region of Kom el-Hisn, in Per-noub and in the nome of Memphis. He has seized the West even in its entirety, from the northern coastal marshes to Lisht, sailing southward with a sizable army, while the Two Lands are united behind him, and the counts and rulers of estates are as dogs at his heels.

No stronghold has closed [its doors in] the nomes of Upper Egypt: Meidum, the Fort of Osorkon I, Crocodilopolis (Medinet el-Faiyum), Oxyrhynchus (el-Bahnasa), and Takinash. Every city of the West has opened doors just through fear of him. When he turned about to the nomes of the East, then they opened to him likewise: The Mansion of the Phoenix, El-Hibeh, the Mansion of the King, and Aphroditopolis (Atfih).

Behold, [he is] / beleaguering Heracleopolis (Ihnasya el-Medina), and he has made himself an enclosing uroborous, not allowing goers to go nor allowing entrants to enter, while fighting every day. In its full circuit he has measured it, with every count knowing his (assigned) wall, while he stations every man among the counts and rulers of estates to besiege his section." Then [His Majesty] heard [this] defiantly, laughing and amused.

But these chiefs, counts and generals who were in their cities were sending word to His Majesty daily saying:

"Have you been silent so as to ignore Upper Egypt and the nomes of the Residence, while Tefnakht seizes what is before him, having found no resistance? Namlot, [ruler of Hermopolis], count of Hutweret, has thrown down the wall of Nefrusy. He has demolished his own city through fear of the one who would seize it for himself in order to beleaguer another city. Behold, he has gone to be a subordinate at his (Tefnakht's) heels, having shrugged off allegiance to His Majesty. He stands with him just like one of [his followers] in the nome of Oxyrhynchus, while he (Tefnakht) gives to him rewards as his desire dictates from among everything that he has found."

Then His Majesty sent word to the counts and generals who were in Egypt, the commander Pawerem, and the commander Lamersekny, and every commander of His Majesty who was in Egypt:

"Proceed in battle formation, engage in combat, encircle and beleaguer it! Capture its people, its herds, its ships upon the river! Do not allow the cultivators to go forth to the fields! Do not allow the plowmen to plow! Beleaguer the frontier of the Hare nome; fight against it every day!"

Then they did likewise.

Then His Majesty sent an army to Egypt, charging them forcefully:

"Do not attack at / night in the manner of a game. You should fight when there is sight. Announce battle to him from afar! If he should say: 'Wait for the troops and cavalry of another city,' then may you sit until his army comes. Fight when he says. If, further, his supporters are in another city, let one wait for them. The counts, these whom he has brought to support him, and the trusted Libyan troops, let one announce battle to them in advance, saying:

'O you whom we do not know how to address in mustering the troops! Yoke the best steeds of your stable! Line up in battle formation! Be informed that Amon is the god who sent us!'

When you arrive within Thebes before Karnak, you should enter into the water. Purify yourselves in the river! Clothe yourselves in the best linen! Lay down the bow, withdraw the arrow! Do not boast of greatness as a possessor of strength! The mighty has no strength in ignorance of him (Amon), for he makes the broken-armed strong-armed. (Thus) do multitudes turn tail to the few; one seizes a thousand men. Sprinkle yourselves with the water of his altars. You should kiss the ground before him and you should say to him: 'Give us passage, that we might fight in the shadow of your strong arm! The corps of recruits whom you have sent, let its onslaught occur while multitudes tremble before it.'"

Then they placed (themselves) on their bellies before His Majesty, (saying):

"It is your name that will serve as our strong arm,
your counsel that brings your army to port,
with your bread in our bellies on every passage,
and your beer / quenching our thirst.
It is your valor that provides our strong arm,
so that one is terrified at the mention of your name.
No army profits whose commander is a coward.
Who is your equal there?
You are a mighty king, who acts with his two arms,
the master of the art of war."

They then went sailing northward and they arrived at Thebes; they did exactly as His Majesty had said. They then went sailing northward on the river, finding that numerous ships had come southward with soldiers, sailors, and troops of every valiant warrior of Lower Egypt equipped with weapons of warfare to fight against the army of His Majesty.

Then a great slaughter was made among them, in incalculable numbers. Their army and their ships were captured and brought away as captives to the place where His Majesty was. They then advanced to the frontier of Heracleopolis, announcing battle.

List of the counts and kings of Lower Egypt:

King Namlot and King Iuput,
Chief of the Ma, Sheshonq, of Busiris,
Great Chief of the Ma, Djedamoniuefankh, of Mendes,
and his eldest son, who was the general of Hermopolis Parva,
the army of Hereditary Prince Bakennefi
and his eldest son, the Chief of the Ma, Nesnaiu, in Hesebu,

every plume-wearing chief who was in Lower Egypt,
and King Osorkon (IV) who was in Bubastis and the district of Ranefer,
with every count and ruler of estates in the West, in the East, and the islands in between being united in a single alliance as subordinates at the heels of the Great Chief of the West, the ruler of estates of Lower Egypt, the prophet of Neith, Lady of Sais,
the *setem*-priest of Ptah, Tefhakht.

They then went forth against them. Then they made a great slaughter among them, greater than anything, and their ships on the river were captured. The remnant then crossed over, landing on the West in the vicinity of Perpega.

As the land lightened and the morning dawned, the army of His Majesty crossed over against them, so that army joined battle with army.

Then they slew numerous men among them together with horses in incalculable numbers, with trembling occurring in the remnant so that they fled to Lower Egypt from a beating more severe and painful than anything.

List of the slaughter which was made among them.

Men: (hellip;) persons. (Horses: …)

King Namlot fled upstream to the South when he was told: "Hermopolis is faced with enemies from the troops of His Majesty, with its people and its herds captured."

Then he entered into Hermopolis while the troops of His Majesty were on the river and the bank of the Hare nome.

Then they heard it and surrounded the Hare nome on its four sides, without letting those who would go out go out nor letting those who would enter enter. They sent word explicitly to report to the Majesty of the King of Upper and Lower Egypt, Piye, beloved of Amon, given life, detailing every attack which they had made, detailing every victory of His Majesty.

Then His Majesty raged because of it like a panther: "Have they allowed a remnant to remain among the troops of Lower Egypt so as to let go an escapee among them to relate his campaign, not killing them to exterminate the last of them? As I live, as Re loves me, as my father Amon favors me, I shall go northward myself, that I might overturn / what he has done, that I might cause that he retreat from fighting for the course of eternity! After the rites of the New Year are performed, when I offer to my father Amon in his beautiful festival, when he makes his beautiful appearance of the New Year, let him send me in peace to behold Amon in the beautiful festival of the Opet feast, that I might convey his image in procession to Luxor temple in his beautiful festival of "The Night Feast of Opet" and the festival of "Abiding in Thebes" which Re devised for him in the primordial time, that I might convey him in procession to his house in order to rest on his throne on the day of ushering in the god in the third month of Inundation season, day 2, and that I might make Lower Egypt taste the taste of my fingers."

Then the troops who were there in Egypt heard the raging that His Majesty had made against them.

Then they fought against Oxyrhynchus of the Oxyrhynchite nome, taking it like a burst of water and sending word before His Majesty, but his heart was not appeased because of it.

Then they fought against "The Peak, Great of Victories," finding it filled with troops comprising every valiant warrior of Lower Egypt.

Then a battering ram was employed against it, so that its walls were demolished and a great slaughter made among them in incalculable numbers, including the son of the Chief of the Ma, Tefnakht.

Then they sent word to His Majesty because of it, but his heart was not appeased regarding it.

Then they fought against Hutbenu, so that its interior was opened and the troops of His Majesty entered into it.

Then they sent word to His Majesty, but his heart was not appeased regarding it.

First month of Inundation season, day 9. His Majesty then came sailing northward to Thebes. At the feast of Opet, he celebrated the festival of Amon. His Majesty then went / sailing northward to the quay of the Hare nome. His Majesty came out of the cabin of the barge, the horses were yoked, the chariots were mounted, so that the grandeur of His Majesty extended to the hinterlands of the Asiatics, and every heart was quaking before him.

Then His Majesty burst forth to revile his army, raging at it like a panther: "Do they endure while your combat is such that my business is delayed? It is the year for finalizing a conclusion, for placing fear of me in Lower Egypt, and for inflicting upon them a severe and painful defeat by striking."

He made for himself a camp at the southwest of Hermopolis, keeping a stranglehold on it daily. A talus was made to clothe the wall, and a platform was erected to elevate the archers when shooting and the slingers when slinging stones, slaying the people among them daily. Days passed, and Hermopolis became foul to the nose, deprived of its ability to breathe.

Then Hermopolis threw itself upon its belly, pleading before the King of Lower Egypt, while messengers came and went bearing everything beautiful to behold: gold, every sort of precious gemstone, clothing by the chest, and the diadem which had been on his brow, the uraeus which had inspired respect of him, without ceasing for numerous days, imploring his crown.

Then One (King Namlot) sent his wife, the royal wife and royal daughter, Nestanetmehu, to implore the royal wives, the royal concubines, the royal daughters, and the royal sisters, and she threw herself upon her belly in the women's house before the royal women:

"Come to me, royal wives, royal daughters and royal sisters! May you appease Horus, Lord of the palace, whose wrath is great, whose vindication is grand! Cause / that he [...] me. Behold, he [...] [...] him. Behold, [...] ... [Speak (?)] to him, so that [he] might then turn about to the one who praises him. [...]"

[...] provision [...] [...] of life in [...] / [...] [...] they filled(?) with what was efficacious [...] praise him [...] the royal wives, the royal sisters [... They threw] themselves upon their bellies [before His Majesty ...] the royal wives [... Namlot,] ruler of Hutweret. [...] for his city (?), the ruler / [...] [...] as ruler [...] in the city (?) [...] [...] through lack of [...] / [...] to the place where [His] Majesty was. [His] Majesty spoke (?) to him [...]:

"Who [...] your mother? Who has guided you? Who has guided you? Who, then, has guided you? Who has guided you [so that you have abandoned] the path of life? Has heaven then rained with arrows? I was [content] when Southerners bowed down and Northerners (said): 'Place us within your shade!' Was it bad that the King (?) [of Hermopolis came (?)] bearing his offerings? The heart is a rudder, which capsizes its owner by what issues from the wrath of god, when he has seen flame in the cool waters in (?) the heart. [...] / There is no adult who is seen with his father, for your nomes are filled (only) with children."

Then he threw himself on his belly in the presence of His Majesty: "[Peace be with you,] Horus, Lord of the palace! It is your wrath which has done this against me. I am one of the King's servants who pays taxes to the treasury as daily offerings. Make a reckoning of their taxes. I have provided for you far more than they."

Then he presented silver, gold, lapis lazuli, turquoise, copper, and every sort of gemstone in great quantity.

Then the treasury was filled with this tribute, and he brought a horse with his right hand and a sistrum in his left—a sistrum of gold and lapis lazuli.

Then His Majesty appeared in splendor from his palace, proceeding to the temple of Thoth, Lord of Hermopolis, and he sacrificed long-horned cattle, short-horned cattle, and fowl for his father Thoth, Lord of Hermopolis, and the Ogdoad in the temple of the / Ogdoad.

The troops of the Hare nome proceeded to shout and sing, saying:

"How beautiful is Horus, appeased in his city,
The Son of Re, Piye!
May you celebrate for us a jubilee,
As you protect the Hare nome!"

His Majesty then proceeded to the house of King Namlot, and he went into every chamber of the palace, his treasury and his storehouses. He caused that there be presented to him the royal wives and the royal daughters. They proceeded to hail His Majesty with feminine wiles, but His Majesty did not pay attention to them. His Majesty then proceeded to the stable of the horses and the quarters of the foals. When he saw [that] / they were starved, he said: "As I live, as Re loves me, as my nose is rejuvenated with life, how much more painful it is in my heart that my horses have been starved than any other crime that you have committed at your discretion. Your neighbor's fear of you is testimony for me. Are you unaware that the shadow of god is over me, and that my deeds have not failed because of him? If only another had done it to me, whom I did not know, whom I had not rebuked because of it! I am one fashioned in the womb and created in the egg of god, with the seed of god within me! As his *ka*-spirit endures, I have not acted in ignorance of him! He is the one who commanded me to act!"

Then his property was assigned to the treasury / and his granary to the endowment of Amon in Karnak.

The ruler of Heracleopolis, Peftchauauibast, then came bearing tribute to Pharaoh: gold, silver, every sort of gemstone, and the pick of the horses of the stable. He threw himself upon his belly in the presence of His Majesty, saying:

"Hail to you, Horus, mighty King, bull who attacks bulls!

The netherworld has seized me, and I am deep in darkness!
O you who give me the enlightenment of your face,
I cannot find a friend on a day of distress,
who will stand up on a day of fighting,'
except for you, O mighty King!
From me you have stripped away the darkness
I shall be a servant together with my property, while
Heracleopolis is levied with taxes / for your domain.
You are indeed Horachty, chief of the imperishable stars!
As he exists, so do you exist as king.
He will not perish, nor will you perish,
O King of Upper and Lower Egypt, Piye, living forever!"

His Majesty then sailed northward to the opening of the canal beside Illahun, and he found Per-Sekhemkhepere with its ramparts heightened, its fortress closed, and filled with every valiant warrior of Lower Egypt. Then His Majesty sent word to them saying:

"O living dead! O living dead!
O miserable wretches! O living dead!
If the moment passes without opening to me,
behold, you belong to the tally of the fallen!
Such is the one subjected to royal punishment.
Do not bar the gates of your life so as to confront the
slaughter block of this day!
Do not desire death so as to hate life!
[Choose (?)] life in the presence of the entire land!"
Then they sent word to His Majesty, saying:
"Behold, the shadow of god is upon you.
The son of Nut, may he give to you his arm's,
then your wish will come to pass directly
like what issues from the mouth of the god
Behold, you are born of god,
because we see (it) by the actions of your arms.
Behold, as for your city and its fortifications,
/ [do what pleases] you with them.
May entrants enter and goers go;
may His Majesty do what he will."

Then they came out with a son of the Chief of the Ma, Tefhakht. The troops of His Majesty then entered into it, without his slaying anyone among all the people whom he found [there....] men and treasurers to seal his possessions, while his treasuries were assigned to the treasury, and his granaries to the endowment of his father Amon-Re, Lord of the Thrones of the Two Lands. His Majesty then went sailing northward and he found that in Meidum, the House of Sokar, Lord of Illumination, had been closed, not having been attacked, and had intent to fight. [...] seized them; fear [over-powered (?)] them; awe sealed their mouths.

Then His Majesty sent word to them, saying:
"Behold, two ways are before you; choose as you wish.
Open, you will live; close, you will die.
My Majesty will not pass by a closed city!"

Then they opened to him directly, and His Majesty entered within this city and he presented a [great] offering [to] Imenhy, foremost of Illumination. Its treasury and granaries were assigned to the endowment of Amon in Karnak. His Majesty then sailed north to Lisht, and he found the stronghold closed and the walls filled with valiant troops of Lower Egypt.

Then they opened the fortifications and they threw themselves on their bellies in the presence of [His Majesty, and they said to] His Majesty:

"Your father has entrusted to you his legacy.
Yours are the Two Lands, and yours those in them.
You are the Lord of what is upon earth."

His Majesty then proceeded to have a great offering presented to the gods who are in this city, consisting of long-horned cattle, short-horned cattle, fowl, and everything good and pure.

Then its treasury was assigned to the treasury and its granaries to the endowment of / his father Amon-[Re, Lord of the Thrones of the Two Lands. His Majesty then sailed northward to] Memphis.

Then he sent word to them, saying: "Do not close; do not fight, O residence of Shu from the primordial time! The entrant—let him enter; the goer—let him go! No traveler will be hindered, I shall offer an oblation to Ptah and the gods who are in the Memphite nome; I shall make offering to Sokar in his sanctuary; I shall behold (Ptah) South-of-His-Wall; and I shall sail northward in peace, [while the people] of Memphis are safe and sound, and children are not

mourned. Look, then, to the nomes of the South. None among them has been slain except for the rebels who blasphemed god, so that a slaughter was made among the traitors."

Then they closed their fortification and they sent out troops against some of the troops of His Majesty, who were but craftsmen, architects and sailors who had come [... to] the harbor of Memphis. Now that Chief of Sais arrived in Memphis at night, ordering his soldiers, his sailors, all the elite of his army, a total of 8,000 men, ordering them firmly:

"Behold, Memphis is filled with troops comprising all the elite of Lower Egypt, with barley, emmer, every sort of grain, with the granaries overflowing, and with every sort of weapon [of war. It is protected(?) by a] stronghold; a great battlement has been built as a work of skillful craftsmanship; the river encircles its East, and fighting will not be found there. The stables here are filled with oxen, the treasuries supplied with everything: silver, gold, copper, clothing, incense, honey, and oil. I shall go that I might give things to the Chiefs of Lower Egypt, that I might open for them their nomes, and that I might become [...] days until I return."

He then mounted upon his horse, as he did not trust his chariot. He then went northward in fear of His Majesty. As the land lightened and the morning dawned, His Majesty arrived at Memphis. When he moored on its north, he found the water risen to the ramparts, with ships moored at / [the houses of] Memphis.

Then His Majesty saw that it was strong, the enclosure walls high with new construction, and the battlements supplied in strength. No way of attacking it was found. Every man proceeded to state his opinion among the troops of His Majesty, entailing every tactic of fighting, with every man saying: "Let us lay siege [to Memphis.] Behold, its army is numerous," while others were saying: "Make a ramp against it so that we elevate the ground to its ramparts. Let us put together a, (siege) platform, erecting masts and using sails as walls for it. Let us divide it by this means on every side of it, with talus and [...] on its north, to elevate the ground to its rampart so that we might find a path for our feet."

Then His Majesty raged against it like a panther, saying:

"As I live, as Re loves me, as my father Amon favors me, I have discovered that this has happened for it by the command of Amon, This is what [all] men [of Lower Egypt] and the nomes of the South say: 'Let them open to him from afar! They do not place Amon in their hearts, nor do they know what he has commanded. He has done it expressly to give evidence of his wrath and to cause that his grandeur be seen.' I shall seize it like a cloudburst; [my father Amon] has commanded me."

Then he sent his ships and his troops to assault the harbor of Memphis, and they brought away for him every boat, every ferry, every pleasure boat, as many ships as were moored at the harbor of Memphis with prow rope fastened among its houses. / [There was not] a common soldier who wept among the entire army of His Majesty. His Majesty himself went to arrange the battle formation of the ships, as many as they were. His Majesty commanded his army:

"Forward against it! Mount the ramparts! Enter the houses atop the river! If one among you enters over the rampart, no one will stand in his way, […] no troops will repel you. It would be vile, then, that we should seal Upper Egypt, moor at Lower Egypt, and yet sit in siege at "The Balance of the Two Lands.""

Then Memphis was taken like a cloudburst, with numerous people slain within it, in addition to those brought as prisoners to the place where His Majesty was. Now [after the land] lightened and a second day occurred, His Majesty sent men into it, protecting the temples of the god for him, consecrating the shrines of the gods, offering cool water to the divine tribunal of Hikuptah, purifying Memphis with natron and incense, and putting priests in their assigned places. His Majesty proceeded to the estate of [Ptah], his purification was performed in the robing room, and there was performed for him every ritual which is performed for a king. He entered into the temple. A great offering was made to his father Ptah, South-of-His-Wall, consisting of long-horned cattle, short-horned cattle, fowl and everything good. His Majesty then returned to his house.

Then every nome that was in the region of Memphis heard (it): Heripademi, Peninaiua, The Fort of Biu, and The Oasis of Bit, opening their fortifications and fleeing in flight, and no one knew where they went.

King Iuput then came together with the Chief of the Ma, Akanosh, and the Hereditary Prince, Padiese, / and all the counts of Lower Egypt, bearing their tribute in order to behold the beauty of His Majesty.

Then the treasuries and granaries of Memphis were assigned, made over to the endowments of Amon, of Ptah and of the Ennead which is in Hikuptah.

As the land lightened and the morning dawned, His Majesty proceeded to the East. An offering to Atum was made in Babylon (Old Cairo), to the Ennead in the Estate of the Ennead, and to the cavern and the gods within it, consisting of long-horned cattle, short-horned cattle, and fowl, so that they might give life, prosperity, and health to the King of Upper and Lower Egypt, Piye, living forever.

His Majesty proceeded to Heliopolis over that mountain of Babylon on the road of the god Sepa to Babylon. His Majesty proceeded to the camp which is on the west of Ity, his purification was performed, he was purified in the midst of the Lake of Cool Water, and his face was washed in the river of Nun where Re washed his face.

Proceeding to the High Sand in Heliopolis. Making a great offering on the High Sand in Heliopolis in the sight of Re at his rising, consisting of white oxen, milk, myrrh, incense, and every sort of sweet-smelling perfume pellets. Coming in procession to the Estate of Re. Entering into the temple in great acclamation, with lector priests adoring god and ritually repelling enemies from the king. Performing the rites of the robing room. Tying on the *sedeb*-garment. Purifying him with incense and cool water. Presenting to him bouquets of the Mansion of the *Benben*-mound. Bringing to him amulets of life. Mounting the stairway to the great window to behold Re in the Mansion of the *Benben*-mound, while the king himself stood alone. Breaking the seals of the doorbolts. Opening the doors. Seeing his father Re in the Mansion of the *Benben*-mound, Consecrating the morning-bark for Re and the evening-bark for Atum. Bringing the doors back into position. Applying the clay. Sealing / with the king's own seal. Giving orders to the priests: "I myself have inspected the seal. No other can enter into it, among all the kings who may arise." Before His Majesty they placed themselves on their bellies, saying: "(It is) to be established and enduring without fail, O Horus, beloved of Heliopolis!" Coming and entering the Estate of Atum. Presenting myrrh to the image of his father Atum-Khepri, the great one of Heliopolis. King Osorkon (IV) came expressly to behold the beauty of His Majesty.

As the land lightened and the morning dawned, His Majesty proceeded to the harbor at the head of his ships and crossed over to the harbor of the nome of Athribis, and the camp of His Majesty was made on the south of Kaheny, on the east of the nome of Athribis. Then there came these kings and counts of Lower Egypt, all the plume-wearing chiefs, all viziers, all chiefs, all royal confidants, from the West, from the East, and from the islands in between, to behold the beauty of His Majesty. Then the Hereditary Prince Padiese threw himself upon his belly in the presence of His Majesty, saying:

"Come to Athribis, that you might behold the god Khentykhety that the goddess Khuyt might protect you, that you might present an offering to Horus in his temple, consisting of long-horned cattle, short-horned cattle, and fowl. May you enter into my house, for my treasury is open to you. I shall gratify you with my ancestral property, and I shall give you gold to the limits of your desire, turquoise heaped up before you, and many horses from the best of the stable, the foremost of the stall."

His Majesty then proceeded to the Estate of Horus Khentykhety to have long-horned cattle, short-horned cattle, and fowl presented to his father Horus Khentykhety, Lord of Athribis. His Majesty proceeded to the house of Hereditary Prince Padiese, who presented him with silver, gold, / lapis lazuli, turquoise, a great heap of everything, clothing of royal linen of every thread count, couches spread with fine linen, myrrh, unguent in jars, and horses both male and female, being all the foremost of his stable. He purified himself by a divine oath even in the sight of these kings and great chiefs of Lower Egypt:

"Any one here who conceals his horses or who hides for himself his worth, he shall die the death of his father! I have said this just so that you might testify for me, your humble servant, in all that you know that I possess. You should say whether I have hidden from His Majesty anything of my father's house: gold ingots, gemstones, every sort of vase, armlets, gold bracelets, necklaces, collars inlaid with gemstones, amulets of every limb, garland crowns for the head, rings for the ears, every royal adornment, all the vessels of the king's purification in gold and every sort of gemstone. All of these I have presented in the royal presence, and clothing of royal linen by the thousands, being all the best of my weaving workshop.

I know that you will be satisfied with it. Proceed to the stall, choose what you wish among all the horses that you desire."

Then His Majesty did likewise. These kings and counts said before His Majesty: "Send us to our towns that we might open out treasuries, that we might choose in accordance with what your heart desires, and that we might bring to you the best of our stalls, the foremost of our horses." Then His Majesty did likewise.

The list of them:

King Osorkon (IV) in Bubastis and the district of Ranefer,

King Iuput (II) in Leontopolis (Tell Moqdam) and Taan,

Count Djedamoniuefankh / in Mendes and The Granary of Re,

His eldest son, the general in Hermopolis Parva, Ankhhor,

Count Akanosh in Sebennytos, in Iseopolis (Behbeit el-Hagar), and Diospolis Inferior,

Count and Chief of the Ma, Patchenefy in Saft el-Henneh and in the Granary of Memphis,

Count and Chief of the Ma, Pamai in Busiris,

Count and Chief of the Ma, Nesnaiu in Hesebu,

Count and Chief of the Ma, Nakhthornashenu in Pergerer,

Chief of the Ma, Pentaweret,

Chief of the Ma, Pentabekhnet,

Prophet of Horus, Lord of Letopolis (Ausim), Padihorsomtus,

Count Horbes in the Estate of Sakhmet, Lady of Eset, and the Estate of Sakhmet, Lady of Rahesu,

Count Djedkhiu in Khentnefer,

Count Pabasa in Babylon (Old Cairo) and in Atar el-Nabi, bearing all their good tribute […] of gold, silver, […] couches spread [with fine] linen, myrrh in jars, […] of good value, horses / [both male and female, being all the foremost of his stable …]

[Now after]wards, one came to say to [His] Majesty […] army(?) […] him [his] walls [through fear (?)] of you, while he has set fire to his treasury [and to his ships on] the river. He has reinforced Mosdai with soldiers even while he […].

Then His Majesty sent his army to see what had happened there among the troops of the Hereditary Prince Padiese. They returned to report / to His Majesty, saying: "We slew every man whom we found there." Then His Majesty gave it as a gift to the Hereditary Prince Padiese.

Then the Chief of the Ma Tefnakht heard it and sent a messenger in fawning supplication to the place where His Majesty was, saying:

"Peace be with you! I cannot look upon your face in days of shame. I cannot stand before your fiery blast, for I am terrified of your grandeur. Indeed, you are the Ombite (Seth), Lord of Upper Egypt, Montu, the strong-armed bull! To whatever city you might turn your attention, you cannot not find me, your humble servant, until I have reached the islands of the sea, / for I am fearful of your wrath, saying: 'His flame is hostile to me.' Is not the heart of Your Majesty cooled by these things that you have done to me? I am indeed one justly reproached, but you did not smite me commensurably with my crime. Weigh with the balance, ascertain with the weights! May you multiply them for me in triplicate, (but) leave the seed that you may harvest it in season. Do not tear out the grove to its roots! As your *ka*-spirit endures, terror of you is in my body, fear of you is within my bones! I cannot sit in the beer hall, nor has the harp been played for me. For I have eaten bread in hunger, I have drunk water in / thirst, since that day when you heard my name! Bitterness is in my bones, my head is balding, my clothing rags, until Neith is appeased toward me! Long is the course that you have brought upon me, and your face is against me yet. It is a year for purging my soul. Cleanse the servant of his fault! Let my property be received into the treasury: gold and every sort of gemstone, even the foremost of the horses, repayments in every kind. Send to me a messenger in haste, that he might dispel fear from my heart! Then I shall go to the temple in his sight to cleanse myself by a divine / oath.

When His Majesty sent the chief lector priest Padiamon(neb)nesuttawy and the general Pawerem, he (Tefnakht) presented him with silver, gold, clothing, and every sort of precious gemstone. When he went into the temple, he praised god and cleansed himself by a divine oath, saying:

"I shall not transgress the royal command. I shall not thrust aside that which His Majesty says, I shall not do wrong to a count without your knowledge. I shall act in accordance with what the king has said. I shall not transgress what he has commanded."

Then His Majesty was satisfied concerning it.

One came to say / to His Majesty: "Crocodilopolis has opened its fortress and Aphroditopolis is placed upon its belly. There is no nome sealed against His Majesty among the nomes of the South and North, while the West, the East and the islands in between are upon their bellies through fear of him, having their property sent to the place where His Majesty is, like servants of the palace."

As the land lightened and the morning dawned, these two rulers of Upper Egypt and two rulers of Lower Egypt, those entitled to royal uraei, came to kiss the ground because of the wrathful power of His Majesty. Now, however, these kings and counts of Lower Egypt who came to behold the beauty of His Majesty, their legs / were like the legs of women. They could not enter into the palace since they were uncircumcised and eaters of fish—such is an abomination of the palace. However, king Namlot entered into the palace since he was pure and did not eat fish. Three stood in their positions while one entered the palace.

Then the ships were loaded with silver, gold, copper, clothing, and everything of Lower Egypt, every product of Syria, every incense pellet of god's land. / His Majesty then sailed southward with his heart gladdened and all those on both sides of him shouting. The West and East took up the announcement, shouting round about His Majesty.

The chant of jubilation which they said:

Glossary

High Sand	a flood barrier
***ka*-spirit**	in the religion of ancient Egypt, the vital force or spiritual twin
morning-bark … evening-bark	in Egyptian mythology, the boats on which the sun traveled
nome	a province in ancient Egypt
***setem*-priest**	embalmer who produced mummies and said the appropriate prayers during the process
talus	a mound of rock debris piled in a slope against a wall
uraeus	the emblem of Lower Egypt, a rearing cobra, worn as part of a ruler's headdress
uroborous	a symbol that shows a snake eating its tail, used in reference to the king's completely surrounding the city

"O mighty ruler, O mighty ruler! Piye, O
   mighty ruler!
You return having conquered Lower Egypt;
making bulls into women!
Happy is the heart of the mother who bore
   you,
and of the male whose seed is within you!
Those in the Nile valley praise her,
the cow who gave birth to a bull!
You are eternal, your victory enduring,
O ruler beloved of Thebes!"

"MANDATE OF HEAVEN: THE NUMEROUS OFFICERS"

"If you can reverently obey, Heaven will favour and compassionate you."

Overview

The Mandate of Heaven is a key concept of Chinese political culture. Thought to have been formulated during the Western Zhou Dynasty, the notion of *tianming* ("heavenly will" or "heavenly mandate") has been used across the centuries to legitimate power, whether in imperial, republican, or Communist China, from 221 BCE to the present day. According to Chinese tradition, the concept of the Mandate of Heaven was laid out for the first time in the Shang shu (traditionally dated between 1766 and 1122 BCE). This text, whose title rendered into English is "Venerated Documents" (or "Ancient Documents"), is one of the earliest Chinese collections of historical fragments—writings spanning seven centuries but with considerable lapses in the chronology. The work is also known as Shu jing (Classic of Documents), commonly rendered in English as the "Book of History" or "Classic of History." It is recognized as perhaps the most important extant work for the study of ancient Chinese political thought—thought that still has wide influence on contemporary political structure in China.

The first use of the Mandate of Heaven to justify the takeover of a government is traditionally attributed to Zhou Gong, the duke of Zhou. After his brother King Wu died, the duke reigned on behalf of his young nephew, King Cheng. King Wu and his Zhou warriors had defeated the forces of the reigning Shang Dynasty (ca. 1600–ca. 1100 BCE) at the Battle of Muye in about 1046 or 1045 BCE. On taking over the government for his nephew, the duke of Zhou put forward the idea that the takeover was possible and legitimate because he had received his mandate from heaven itself. Confusion reigned, however, between the duke of Zhou and his half brother, the duke of Shao. The duke of Shao quarreled with the duke of Zhou because he wanted power and argued that both were endowed from birth with unique virtues. The duke of Zhou, though, believed that men held their own fate in their hands. The debate was ended by the duke of Zhou, who referred to the Mandate of Heaven, which he claimed he had received. This debate between Zhou and Shao has been revived throughout Chinese history, and the duke of Zhou emerges as a model of the virtuous minister.

The Classic of History, a collection of sayings of the rulers of the Shang and Zhou dynasties, exists in two versions, one in modern script and another in ancient script. The ancient version is considered to be the orthodox one. According to tradition, most copies of this text were destroyed during the Qin Dynasty book burning (213 BCE), when Qin Shi Huangdi, known as "First Emperor" of a unified China, ordered the destruction of classical books that were considered useless. The scholar Fu Sheng hid the Classic of History in a wall of his house, saving it from the flames. The Classic of History is a political work, focusing on the practices of government. It is an anthology of quotations that give a sense of the moral attitudes of the time, while also containing speeches addressed mainly to members of the royal family and to ancestors.

Context

The Zhou Dynasty (ca. 1045–256 BCE) is divided in two periods: the Western Zhou (ca. 1045–771 BCE), the era in which the concept of the Mandate of Heaven was formulated, and the Eastern Zhou (770–256 BCE). The historian and scribe Sima Qian (ca. 145–87 BCE) wrote in his classic history the Shi ji (Records of the Grand Historian) that the Zhou Dynasty came to free the suffering people from Shang tyrants. King Zhou (also known as King Wen) was a model of virtue. He provoked the envy of the last Shang ruler, who imprisoned him. When King Wen died in prison, his son King Wu attacked the Shang and defeated them in the Battle of Muye (ca. 1046/1045 BCE).

The transfer of leadership from the Shang Dynasty to the Zhou Dynasty marked a change not only in government but also in concepts of the divine. The Shang worshipped the Shang Di (supreme emperor), from whom they believed themselves to descend. The Zhou Dynasty continued to worship the same divine being but introduced a new understanding of *tian* (heaven) and *de* (moral virtue). Since the founders of the Zhou Dynasty were confronted with the problem of installing a lasting government, they tried to find an argument that would make them acceptable as the new rulers. The Battle of Muye marked a turning point in the theory of the Mandate of Heaven. Tradition held that

CA. 1766–1122 BCE

- The concept of the Mandate of Heaven is laid out for the first time in the Classic of History, a fragmented collection of historical writings.

CA. 1046/1045 BCE

- King Wu attacks the Shang and defeats them in the Battle of Muye, marking a turning point in the Mandate of Heaven.

CA. 1043

- King Wu dies, leaving the kingdom to his son, King Cheng. Cheng's uncle, the duke of Zhou, becomes regent, using the Mandate of Heaven as his justification.

the winner in battle received the Mandate of Heaven; virtuous rulers would be given a prize for their good conduct. The fall of the Shang Dynasty and the rise of the Zhou Dynasty, as noted, were explained by the duke of Zhou as happening because the Mandate of Heaven was transferred from the Shang to the Zhou, who had won the battle. The new Zhou Dynasty was considered legitimate to rule as the result of meritocracy, with governance in the hands of those who were able to rule thanks to their impeccable moral conduct and not just because of their military skills.

Modern scholars theorize that the Classic of History, in which the "Mandate of Heaven: The Numerous Officers" appears, covers a historical span from 2500 to 500 BCE, offering a compilation of documents from the ancestral past up to the Confucian era. The Classic of History consists of the consultations of rulers or ministers, pieces of ministerial advice, battlefield proclamations, and royal announcements and decrees. This text is considered a very important source for the early Western Zhou conception of government, mainly based on the concept of virtue (de). De is a symbol of power and communication between heaven and the ruler and then through the ruler to the people.

Chinese philosophers believed that there were close connections between heaven and earth. Parallels and correlations existed everywhere between the macrocosm and the microcosm: Heaven was round (symbolizing the head), and earth was square (symbolizing the feet); humankind was placed between the two, and everything was interconnected. This kind of correlative thinking was also applied to dynastic power and the process of its cyclical succession.

The relation of the ruler to tian, or heaven, was conceived in this cosmological context. There were at least five different meanings of tian: a material or physical sky, in opposition to the earth; an anthropomorphic and ruling Tian, linked to the figure of Shang Di (or supreme emperor), the venerated figure of the Shang Dynasty; a fatalistic tian, which includes the meaning of fate (ming); a naturalistic tian, rendered in English as "nature"; and, finally, an ethical tian, considered the highest and primordial moral principle of the universe.

Society was based on strict ritual and on codes of conduct as well as norms that were accepted and based (at least theoretically) on human virtues and linked to the divine world. According to the Western Zhou, rulers were to follow an ethical code of conduct. Moral behavior was a fundamental prerequisite to ruling the country. According to Confucian theory, everyone has a specific role to play in life. Respecting one's social position meant that one was maintaining the social, economic, and political order in China; such respect was necessary for keeping public order. The communication between heaven, the ruler, and the ruled aimed to ensure social harmony. If harmony shifted to discord, something in this three-part communication was considered to be missing, or lacking.

Since the Shang Dynasty there had been strict ritual observances ruled by heavenly omens. The observation of heavenly events marked the activities of human beings, who performed a set of rituals aimed at maintaining the harmony between human conduct and natural events. Since humankind played an important role in the cosmic process, this idea of mutual influence was especially applicable to the relationship between the ruler and heaven. The ruler was a moral person whose activities were to be focused on specific ritual activities. As a result, bad government was seen as potentially producing natural catastrophes.

The practice of legitimizing imperial power through the Mandate of Heaven, as noted, was introduced by the Zhou rulers. Heaven had the power to legitimate a ruler: If the ruler was benevolent toward his subjects, he kept the Mandate of Heaven. If he lacked virtue, he lost the Mandate of Heaven. In this model of imperial rule, a tight relationship between heaven and humankind is evident. This concept was a milestone in Chinese history, remaining a pivotal concept in theory and in practice.

Heaven's will was made explicit by various means: through messengers, objects, and texts. According to a standard formula, tian was linked to the dao (the way, or the path to be followed in order to reach and maintain virtue). Theoretically, the Mandate of Heaven had no effect without the support of the ruled, who played a key role in

King Wen of Zhou (© British Library Board. All Rights Reserved 071088)

authenticating rulership. Meanwhile, a set of precious objects, known as imperial treasures, consisting of ritual tripod vessels, seals, incense burners, swords, and special texts, reflected both the political and religious power of the ruler. Natural phenomena, such as famines, comets, and earthquakes, were considered signs from heaven that were connected to legitimizing the power of a ruler.

In theory, the Mandate of Heaven transmitted royal power to the firstborn male descendant. At least since the Shang Dynasty, imperial families have been believed to be the heirs of a divine figure and in contact with the supernatural world. In this sense, the Mandate of Heaven stood in contrast to the imperial monopoly of power: The ruler who received the Mandate of Heaven was following the "way" on behalf of heaven and had, in theory, the moral obligation to keep the "all under Heaven" peaceful, in a state of well-being, and satisfied. The ruled looked upon the king as a deity. This is a perception that still endures in the twenty-first century, as authority continues to be perceived, in symbolic terms, as being bestowed through the Mandate of Heaven and therefore the ruler as being under a moral obligation to serve the people.

About the Author

The author of the Classic of History is unknown. Most probably it was the work of different teams of authors who added layer after layer over the course of centuries. It is one of the Wu jing, the so-called Five Classics of Confucianism, together with the Yi jing (better known in the West as I Ching, or Classic of Changes), the Shi jing (Classic of Poetry, or Book of Odes), the Li ji (Classic of Rites), and the Chun qiu (Spring and Autumn Annals). A sixth classic—Yue jing (Classic of Music)—is also considered part of the canon but was lost by the time of the Han Dynasty (206 BCE–220 CE). These Chinese classics were connected to the four main disciplines (poetry, history, rites, and music), which, from 136 BCE to 1905 CE, constituted the basic curriculum for any learned Chinese who wanted to join the imperial bureaucracy. The texts were traditionally attributed to Confucius and were collected under Han Dynasty patronage. No one prior to 100 BCE identifies Confucius as the author, editor, or compiler of this collection, but he is considered to have compiled and edited the work. Written on bound bamboo strips, the Five Classics represent the ground for the Confucian thought expressed in the Analects (a set of dialogues that Master Kong, known to us today as Confucius, had with his disciples).

Explanation and Analysis of the Document

During the first phase of the reign of King Cheng (ca. 1043–1021 BCE), a set of gao (announcements) was put forth about the role of heaven in political affairs, the principle of succession, the function of divination, the relationship between king and ministries, and the establishment of a capital. *Duo shi* is the name in Chinese of the chapter concerning the Mandate of Heaven. The "numerous officers" referred to are the officers of the Shang Dynasty who had been removed, along with the people, to the new city of Luo (spelled "Lǒ" in the document) when the city of Chengzhou (Ching-chow, the eastern capital) was established by the Zhou.

At the time when King Cheng was the nominal ruler, while the duke of Zhou (called the "duke of Chow" in the document) was the effective ruler, the announcement by the duke of Zhou, which is the content of "Mandate of Heaven: The Numerous Officers," aimed to reconcile the minds of the people of Yin (an alternate name for the Shang Dynasty), especially the higher classes, to the rule of Zhou. The duke of Zhou treated the Yin people generously and kindly, and therefore the Yin were obligated to remain loyal to their new rulers.

◆ Part I

The larger text is preceded by an introduction divided into three parts. The first part explicitly states that the rulership of the duke of Zhou is legal, noting that this announcement was made to the officers of the Shang Dynasty in the third month of the new dynasty. The announcement was made in the city of Luo. The pronouncement asserts that "great ruin came down on Yin from the want of pity in compassionate Heaven, and we, the princes of Chow, received its favouring decree." It goes on to say that heaven's "bright terrors" caused the new dynasty to inflict punishment on the Yin. The new dynasty did not seek power, but heaven "was not with" the Yin and would not strengthen its misrule. Heaven helped the Zhou to overcome the Yin government, which was ruling in a devious manner.

◆ Part II

Part II explains the cause for the defeat of the Yin (Shang) Dynasty with reference to the overthrow by the Yin of the Hea Dynasty (called Xia Dynasty today). When the founder of the Shang Dynasty, Tang (here termed "T'ang"), successfully set the Xia aside, he sought to make his virtue illustrious by means of able men to rule the empire and by duly attending to sacrifices. The document makes reference to the emperor "Këē," or Kieh kwei (1818–1767 BCE), who was regarded as vicious and immoral. Thus, "Heaven no longer regarded nor heard him," allowing the Shang to come to power. The document then acknowledges that earlier Shang rulers had ruled virtuously. They were "humbly careful not to lose the favour of God." More recent Shang rulers, though, failed to follow this example. They showed themselves "greatly ignorant of *the ways of* Heaven," and, "abandoned to dissolute idleness," and the recent Shang ruler "paid no regard to the bright principles of Heaven, nor the awfulness of the people." The result of this failure to heed the "earnest labours of his fathers for the country" was that he was punished, in the same way that all states, large and small, are punished for similar failings. The document then states that the Zhou sovereigns are "charged with the work of God" and that the officers of the Yin must submit to them.

Shang Dynasty oracle bone used for divination

◆ Part III

The document then demonstrates that the king had found it necessary to remove the people of Luo and explains that the city "in the west" was built with good purpose and intention. Heaven intervened for the sake of the Yin because the situation in the city of Luo was not right; the Yin had obliged the king to remove them from Luo. He treated them kindly and was prepared to give more to them, but they continued to exhibit lawlessness and disaffection. The king reiterates his position in declaring that this action was dictated by heaven and that therefore the people should not offer any resistance, just as the Xia had been overthrown by the Shang when that dynasty acquired the Mandate of Heaven. The king then makes a declaration of pity toward the Yin people and the clear pronouncement that the situation was simply determined by the decree of heaven.

Part III also aimed to show how disaffection had brought only misery and ruin to the Yin people, while virtuous conduct under the Mandate of Heaven could generate only prosperity and comfort in the city of Luo. The king follows this argument by saying that when he had come from Yan (Yen), he had tried to mitigate punishment and had spared the lives of people within the four states. Moreover, he had built the city of Luo because there was no other place to receive guests from the four quarters. He goes on to say that the Shang officers, with "zealous activity," could "perform the part of ministers to us with much obedience." He reassures his audience that "you have still here I may

say your grounds, and here you may still rest in your duties and dwellings." He stresses again the key role played by heaven, which would have favored and have been compassionate to the Yin people if they obeyed God.

Audience

The Mandate of Heaven was invoked by Chinese emperors from the beginning of the Zhou Dynasty. Depending on the kind of statement or announcement, the audience was composed of a very small group of literati and of the army. Nevertheless, the process of legitimizing imperial power was naturally promulgated widely and known by all the population. The Mandate of Heaven remained a key concept of power legitimation both for scholars and for ordinary people.

Impact

The concept of the Mandate of Heaven was apparently successful. The Zhou gained control, appointing their officials to government positions; those Shang Dynasty holdovers who retained their positions were required to comply with Zhou regulations. In the years that followed, the Zhou empire expanded, as marriages cemented relationships with allies. The Zhou were backed by a strong

"*The king speaks to this effect:—'Ye numerous officers who remain from the dynasty of Yin, great ruin came down on Yin from the want of pity in compassionate Heaven, and we, the princes of Chow, received its favouring decree.'*"

(Part I)

"*Hereupon it charged your founder, T'ang [Tang] the Successful, to set Hea [Xia] aside, and by means of able men to rule the empire.... Greatly abandoned to dissolute idleness, he paid no regard to the bright principles of Heaven, nor the awfulness of the people. On this account God no longer protected him.... Heaven was not with him because he did not seek to illustrate his virtue.*"

(Part II)

"*The king says, 'Ho! I declare to you, ye numerous officers, it is simply on account of these things that I have removed and settled you in the west; it was not that I, the one man, considered it a part of my virtue to make you untranquil. The thing was from the decree of Heaven; do not resist me; I dare not have any further* change *for you.*"

(Part III)

"*If you can reverently obey, Heaven will favour and compassionate you. If you cannot reverently obey, you will not only not have your lands, but I will also carry the utmost Heaven's inflictions on your persona.*"

(Part III)

military and technological achievements that enabled them to dominate the regions they annexed. They also created a formidable navy because of their shipbuilding and navigational skills. Additionally, the Zhou Dynasty was stable enough to allow widespread accomplishments in literature and philosophy, with Confucianism becoming the dominant philosophical underpinning of the government.

As the dynasty grew, however, it became increasingly difficult to rule it centrally. For this reason, the government became decentralized, with administrators overseeing the activities of districts while still nominally required to submit to the central authority of the dynasty. Inevitably, how-

ever, a kind of centrifugal force pushed these districts out of the ambit of the central government, and the government was therefore weakened. The result was often war between the districts, giving rise to what came to be called the Warring States Period. In the estimation of the Qin Dynasty that followed, the Zhou had lost the Mandate of Heaven and were unfit to rule. Just as the Shang had overthrown the Xia and the Zhou had overthrown the Shang, so too the Mandate of Heaven dictated that the Qin relieve the Zhou of power, beginning the process anew.

There are always echoes of the past in the present, and this is evident in the political rhetoric of contemporary

China. More significantly, the theory of *tianming* was undoubtedly a milestone in the history of Chinese politics, for potentially, through the Mandate of Heaven, only a virtuous monarch could govern China. Further, the people had the right to overthrow a government that had lost the Mandate of Heaven. Chinese political leaders recognized this ingrained view in Chinese society and used it to their advantage. Mao Zedong, the leader of the Communist revolution in China in the 1940s, exploited the concept through the cult of his personality.

Revolution, or *geming* in Chinese, means literally "to change the mandate." As long as a ruler could maintain a stable, productive society, he had legitimacy to govern. The term *geming* implies the traditional idea of overthrowing a dynasty that had lost its mandate. In modern terms, it means that a political system is to be replaced when it is no longer viable, by force if necessary. This idea was further elaborated by Mencius, a Confucian philosopher during the Zhou Dynasty who idealized the concept of the Mandate of Heaven and articulated the virtues and self-development effective rulers needed. Thus, revolution in China has long been linked to the idea of a violent but righteous heaven, which has the right to grant or withdraw the mandate to rule. In the modern Communist era, the Chinese use the term *reform* (*gaige*), which has the slight flavor of premodern dynastic renewal.

The sacred rituals of political sucession, which implied that each governing dynasty coming to power as the result of the heaven's favor, has thus been invoked by contemporary "emperors" such as Mao Zedong and Deng Xiaoping. Chinese political culture is so imbued with the role played by the will of heaven, the notion of wise rule, and the performance of ritual duties that when these duties are not performed on behalf of the nation, the formula "the Heaven has withdrawn its mandate" is still used today to justify a change in the political regime. The old imperial tradition is somehow present in post-1949 China. Traditional concepts such as loyalty to the ruler strengthened the cult of personality of Mao and Deng. The metaphor is used to describe both court intrigues of the past and present situation in a context of Chinese imperial autocracy.

Further Reading

■ Articles

Loewe, Michael. "The Cosmological Context of Sovereignty in Han Times." *Bulletin of the School of Oriental and African Studies, University of London* 65, no. 2 (2002): 342–349.

T'ang, Chün-i. "The T'ien Ming [Heavenly Ordinance] in Pre-Chin China." *Philosophy East and West* 11, no. 4 (1962): 195–218.

Wang, Gungwu. "To Reform a Revolution: Under the Righteous Mandate." *Daedalus* 122 (Spring 1993): 71–94.

■ Books

Chan, Alan Kam-leung, and Sor-hoon Tan. *Filial Piety in Chinese Thought and History*. New York: RoutledgeCurzon, 2004.

Feng, Youlang, and Derk Bodde. *A History of Chinese Philosophy*. Princeton, N.J.: Princeton University Press, 1983.

Questions for Further Study

1. Compare and contrast "Mandate of Heaven" with the Canon of Filial Piety. To what extent do the two documents present similar and differing visions of leadership and rule?

2. Compare and contrast "Mandate of Heaven" with a Western document such as Charlemagne's Capitulary of 802. How do the documents represent similar and differing visions of rule? Specifically, how did the authors of the two documents envision the moral and ethical requirements of leaders?

3. Why would an early Chinese emperor have had to claim divine origins for his rule? What advantage did he gain by doing so?

4. Throughout the history of the world, people have often risen up against governments that they perceived to be unjust. "Mandate of Heaven" provides an intellectual foundation for doing so in ancient China. How did John Locke, in *Second Treatise of Civil Government*, examine this same issue? How did the authors of Freedom Charter of South Africa examine the issue?

5. When modern politicians win an election, they often claim to have a mandate from the voters to enact their agendas. How does the modern concept of "mandate" differ from that of ancient China?

Henderson, John. *Scripture, Canon, and Commentary: A Comparison of Confucian and Western Exegesis*. Princeton, N.J.: Princeton University Press, 1991.

Loewe, Michael, and Edward L. Shaughnessy. *The Cambridge History of Ancient China: From the Origins of Civilization to 221 b.c.* New York: Cambridge University Press, 1999.

Nylan, Michael. *The Five "Confucian" Classics*. New Haven, Conn.: Yale University Press, 2001.

Salisbury, Harrison E. *The New Emperors: Mao and Deng: A Dual Biography*. New York: HarperCollins, 1993.

Schwartz, Benjamin I. *The World of Thought in Ancient China*. Cambridge, Mass: Belknap Press of Harvard University Press, 1985.

—Elisabetta Colla and Mike O'Neal

"MANDATE OF HEAVEN: THE NUMEROUS OFFICERS"

I. In the third month, at the commencement of *the government of* the duke of Chow in the new city of Lŏ, he announced *the royal will* to the officers of the Shang dynasty, *saying,* "The king speaks to this effect:—'Ye numerous officers who remain from the dynasty of Yin, great ruin came down on Yin from the want of pity in compassionate Heaven, and we, the princes of Chow, received its favouring decree. We accordingly felt charged with its bright terrors; carried out the punishments which kings inflict; rightly disposed of the appointment of Yin; and finished *the work* of God. Now, ye numerous officers, it was not that our small country dared to aim at the appointment of Yin. But Heaven was not with *Yin,* for indeed it would not strengthen its misrule. It *therefore* helped us;—did we dare to seek the throne of ourselves? God was not for *Yin,* as appeared from the conduct of our inferior people, in which there is the brilliant dreadfulness of Heaven.

II. 'I have heard the saying—God leads men to tranquil security; but the sovereign of Hea would not move to such security, whereupon God sent down *corrections,* indicating His mind to him. *Kĕē,* however, would not be warned by God, but proceeded to greater dissoluteness and sloth and excuses for himself. Then Heaven no longer regarded nor heard him, but disallowed his great appointment, and inflicted extreme punishment. Hereupon it charged your founder, T'ang [Tang] the Successful, to set Hea [Xia] aside, and by means of able men to rule the empire. From T'ang the Successful down to the emperor Yih, every sovereign sought to make his virtue illustrious, and duly attended to the sacrifices. And thus it was that while Heaven exerted a great establishing influence, preserving and regulating the house of Yin, its sovereigns on their part were humbly careful not to lose the favour of God, and strove to manifest a good doing corresponding to that of Heaven. But in these times, their successor showed himself greatly ignorant of *the ways of* Heaven, and much less could it be expected of him that he would be regardful of the earnest labours of his fathers for the country. Greatly abandoned to dissolute idleness, he paid no regard to the bright principles of Heaven, nor the awfulness of the people. On this account God no longer protected him, but

sent down the great ruin which we have witnessed. Heaven was not with him because he did not seek to illustrate his virtue. *Indeed,* with regard to the overthrow of all States, great and small, throughout the four quarters of the empire, in every case there are reasons to be alleged for their punishment.'"

"The king speaks to this effect:—'Ye numerous officers of Yin, the case now is this, that the sovereigns of our Chow, from their great goodness were charged with the work of God. There was the charge to them, Cut off Yin. *They proceeded to perform it,* and announced the correcting work to God. In our affairs we have followed no double aims:—ye of the royal house *of Yin* must follow us.

III. 'May I not say that you were very lawless? I did not *want to* remove you. The thing came from your own city. When I consider also how Heaven has drawn near to Yin with *so* great tribulations, it must be that there was *there* what was not right.'"

"The king says, 'Ho! I declare to you, ye numerous officers, it is simply on account of these things that I have removed and settled you in the west;—it was not that I, the one man, considered it a part of my virtue to make you untranquil. The thing was from the decree of Heaven; do not resist me; I dare not have any further *change for you.* Do not murmur against me. Ye know that your fathers of the Yin dynasty had their archives and narratives *showing* how Yin superseded the appointment of Hea. Ye now indeed say further, "*The officers of* Hea were chosen and promoted to the imperial court, or had their places among the mass of officers." I, the one man, listen only to the virtuous and employ them; and it was with this view that I presumed to seek you out in *your* heavenly city of Shang. I thereby follow the ancient *example,* and have pity on you. *Your present non-employment* is no fault of mine; it is by the decree of Heaven.'"

"The king says, 'Ye numerous officers, formerly, when I came from Yen, I greatly mitigated the penalty in favour of the lives of the people of your four countries. At the same time I made evident the punishment appointed by Heaven, and removed you to this distant abode, that you might be near the ministers who had served in our honoured *capital,* and *learn* their much obedience.'"

"The king says, 'I declare to you, ye numerous officers of Yin,—now I have not put you to death, and therefore I repeat to you my charge again. I have built this great city here in Lŏ, considering that there was no other place in which to receive my guests from the four quarters, and also that you, ye numerous officers, might here with zealous activity, perform the part of ministers to us with much obedience. You have still here I may say your grounds, and here you may still rest in your duties and dwellings.

If you can reverently obey, Heaven will favour and compassionate you. If you cannot reverently obey, you will not only not have your lands, but I will also carry to the utmost Heaven's inflictions on your persona. Now you may here dwell in your villages, and perpetuate your families; you may pursue your occupations and enjoy your years in this Lŏ; your children also will prosper:—*all* from your being removed here.'"

"The king says,—; and again he says, 'Whatsoever I have spoken, is all on account of *my anxiety about your residence here.*'"

decree of Heaven	the Mandate of Heaven of which this document was a part
great ruin	the Warring States Period
its bright terrors	the harsh penalties mandated by Heaven for the misbehaviors of the Yin

TWELVE TABLES OF ROMAN LAW

"Affairs of great importance shall
not be transacted without the vote of the people."

Overview

In 451–450 BCE, Roman politicians appointed a committee of ten legislators to control the government and to compile an outline of the private and public laws of the Roman Republic. Through their efforts twelve tablets containing information on specific points of law were posted in the main Forum of Rome for public approval. Previously known only to the elite patrician classes, these descriptions and definitions of procedures, parental rights, remedies, and rights and responsibilities of creditors and debtors would be instrumental in helping ease the social stresses that threatened to overturn the newly created republic. After a great deal of deliberation, an attempted coup by members of this committee, and their subsequent removal from power, the Laws of the Twelve Tables were finalized and submitted for approval. After much pressure from the plebeians (commoners), the Senate formally promulgated the laws in 449 BCE, and they became the centerpieces of the burgeoning Roman legal system. Six decades later, however, in 390 BCE, the Gauls, a neighboring people originating in what is now southern France, sacked Rome and burned it, destroying the tablets forever. No full record of them survives, and what little information has been passed down about them has been reconstructed from quotations in the works of ancient authors and from legal texts.

By enumerating the legal rights of the citizenry, the committee called the decemvirate (a group of ten men) removed a shroud of mystery from Roman legal proceedings and opened up for the public the laws' interpretation and analysis. This move greatly influenced the power structure of the Roman world, untangling the reins of legislative power from the upper patrician class and allowing greater political and legal freedom and influence for the lower plebeian class. This development in turn was pivotal in the eventual resolution of the period known as the Conflict of the Orders. The Twelve Tables would become the basis of further Roman legal codification, which would serve as the origin for nearly all of the legal systems of modern Europe. The Twelve Tables marked the only attempt at a compilation of Roman law until the emperor

Theodosius I's codex was published in 438 CE, nearly a thousand years later.

Context

Republican Rome during the period called the Conflict of the Orders (494–287 BCE) was rife with social unrest. The constant struggle between the interests of two groups, the patricians and the plebeians, was the primary impetus behind many of the events during this period. Like many elements of very early Roman history, the origins of this class hierarchy are uncertain. According to tradition, the founder of Rome, Romulus, created the first Roman Senate, and from the descendents of those original hundred men, termed *patres* (fathers), the patrician class came into being. Modern historians are skeptical of that explanation and believe that the patrician class may have come about during the rule of the monarchy and included aristocratic clans from peoples that migrated into or joined with Rome during the regnal period—the time under which Rome was ruled by a series of kings, from the date of the mythical founding of Rome in 753 BCE by Romulus to the overthrow of Tarquin the Proud in 509 BCE.

Regardless of their origin, the patricians monopolized power in the early Roman Republic because of their wealth and influence. In contrast, the plebeian order constituted the remainder of the Roman citizenry, consigned to subordinate positions as the supporters and clients of the patrician class. This distinction was particularly onerous to the plebeians. Although many of them came from families of distinction and privilege, without patrician heritage they were denied the highest offices, particularly those involving membership in the College of Pontiffs—high religious posts that held enormous sway over the maintenance of the Roman state.

Roman religion was highly public and civic in orientation. Its main focus was on the observance of protocol and ritual. The priestly classes were thus nominated from the patrician order. These religious offices were beneficial for a variety of reasons in terms of possible economic benefit and prestige; however, these officials also served as the sole caretakers and interpreters of the law, which at this point

753 BCE
- According to legend, Rome is founded by Romulus.

509 BCE
- The Etruscan kings are overthrown and the monarchy destroyed, leading to the establishment of the Roman Republic.

494 BCE
- The plebs secede in Rome.

471 BCE
- The office of tribune of the plebs (two of whom are elected annually) and the Concilium Plebis are created.

462 BCE
- A tribune of the plebs, Gaius Terentilius Harsa, calls for the establishment of a committee to write down the laws of Rome.

451 BCE
- The decemvirate (council of ten men) is established, replacing the consuls, and the council is charged with writing down previously unpublished Roman laws.
- The Laws of the Twelve Tables are published by the decemvirate and are posted in the Roman Forum for public approval.

consisted primarily of an unorganized mixture of written precedents and a loose system of orally transmitted laws. The plebeians were thus left without any real knowledge of what the law was or what recourse they had if they felt that their rights had been violated.

Prior to the drafting of the Twelve Tables, the rights of the plebeians had been asserted by their repeated withdrawal from public life, termed *secessio* (secessions), until their demands were met. In 494 BCE the plebeians had reacted against what they saw as the biased and unjust enforcement of laws, especially those regarding debt, and they seceded from the government, encamping on the nearby Aventine Hill until their demands were met. This first secession led to the creation of a new legal post, the tribune of the plebs, designed to safeguard their rights; the pressure generated by it also allowed for the formation of the Concilium Plebis (Plebeian Council) in 471 BCE, a separate legislative assembly with the purpose of allowing the plebeians to elect their own officials and hold trials for noncapital offenses.

The prevailing scholarly view is that though the patricians wished to maintain their hold on political hegemony, they were forced to cede these rights to the plebeians out of necessity: Rome during the first half of the fifth century BCE was constantly warring with neighboring peoples, specifically the Volsci and the Aequi, and plebeian participation in the military was needed for adequate defense of the city. Some theories even suggest that it was this constant warfare that drove the plebeians' desire for a greater understanding of their legal rights—the warfare along Rome's borders hit small plebeian freeholders the hardest. In the aftermath of an enemy excursion, these farmers often found themselves deprived of both their crops and their livestock. To maintain themselves, they resorted to mortgage of their land to patrician lenders in return for resupply, sinking deeper into debt.

According to ancient sources, in 462 BCE a tribune of the plebs, Gaius Terentilius Harsa, first put forth the idea that a committee should be formed to establish the laws publicly, a concept that would not be taken up again until the military and social atmosphere worsened a decade later. With the pressures of war mounting, the plebeian tribunes continued their push for a codification of the existing laws and possibly even pressured the Senate into sending a delegation to Athens to study the laws of Solon, an earlier attempt by the neighboring Greeks to codify their own laws. When the delegation returned, it was decided that in 451 BCE a council of ten men, made up primarily of patricians, would take control of all executive power in Rome and assume the tasks of compiling the existing laws and managing the government.

The efforts of the decemvirs were appreciated by the people, and at the end of the term the council had drawn up ten tables of law. There was a suggestion that another committee of ten men should again be nominated because of the decemvirs' seemingly fair rule and because some felt that the ten tables were insufficient or incomplete. The precise details of the events that surrounded these efforts are inconsistent. The prevailing view of the ensuing events is that Appius Claudius, elected president of the first committee, was seen as a natural fit to lead the second. He utilized his influence among the senators and other patricians to have his supporters nominated as well, turning the body into his personal coterie and, in effect, transforming the Roman government into a dictatorship. Although this ruling body did put forth an additional two tables supplementing the original ten, the once-benign administration quickly devolved. Appius's increasingly arrogant and autocratic behavior gave many in the Roman government pause, though; because the normal apparatuses of government, including all magistracies and the office of the tribune of the plebs, were in hiatus, there was nothing legally to be done. The historians Livy and Dionysius of Halicarnassus both wrote on this period, recounting legendary exploits of Appius's cruelty and even charging him with the attempted abduction of a young woman named Verginia, daughter of a respected centurion. Contemporary historians regard all references to this act as mythic, yet what can be determined is that the tone of these reports indicate that Appius had a reputation for abusing the power entrusted to him and the decemvirs.

None of these events can be verified by contemporaries, but the tale of what happened next is generally accepted: Because of eventual administrative mismanagement, the decemvirate was abolished, and the government was reinstated. The plebeians, an integral part of this restoration of normalcy, were concerned that a return to the previous form of government would leave them with little or no voice in government; for this reason they seceded for a third time, demanding that the Twelve Tables be ratified officially. Powerless against the demands of so many and still embroiled in border wars, the patricians acquiesced, and the laws were formally promulgated in 449 BCE.

About the Author

According to the two primary ancient historians who discussed this period, the decemvirs nominated in 451 BCE were Appius (elected president of the body), Titus Genucius, Publius Sestius, Titus Veturius, Gaius Julius, Aulus Manlius, Servius Sulpicius, Publius Curiatius, Titus Romilius, and Spurius Postumius. Surprisingly little is known about each of these legislators, though the actions and the character of Appius, the most prominently mentioned and the leader of the dictatorial regime that developed from the decemvirate, are described. What is known about all of the men is that they were wealthy and powerful; nearly all were members of the patrician class (though that fact has been questioned by some modern historians), and many either had been previously elected consul or, like Appius and Titus Genucius, were nominated the year that the decemvirate was established. As such, each of these men had a vested interest in maintaining the influence and power of their order. The patricians held an enormous amount of power in the Roman Republic and had no desire, other than the maintenance of the public order and the continuing cooperation of the plebeians in military and economic affairs, to change the status quo.

Milestone Documents

Time Line

449 BCE
- In response to the abuses of the decemvirs, the plebeians again secede, withdrawing to reinstate the consulate and have the Twelve Tables approved formally. The Senate and Comitia Centuriata (Assembly of the Centuries) officially promulgate the laws.

287 BCE
- The plebs secede for the final time. As a result, the Lex Hortensia is passed, giving plebiscites (popular votes taken by the Concilium Plebis) the power of law for the entire Roman people and effectively granting full equality between patricians and plebeians.

Appius, nominated again as the leader of the second set of decemvirs the following year, is characterized in the writings of Livy and Dionysius as villainous in his attempts to maintain his power over the Roman people, personifying the cruelties that led in 449 BCE to the second secession of the plebs, which ended the reign of the decemvirate.

Explanation and Analysis of the Document

The Law of the Twelve Tables is separated into twelve separate sections, each referring to one or more public or private legal concepts in detail. Although the originals were destroyed in 390 BCE, references to them from ancient sources have allowed for their re-creation.

◆ Table I
The ten laws of Table I deal with procedural elements of summonses to court and of the trial itself. They cover the

responsibilities of both plaintiffs and defendants in response to a summons, stipulating that if a defendant does not appear, the plaintiff could "seize his reluctant adversary" (Law II); if a defendant was ill or infirm of body, the plaintiff was required to supply "an animal, as a means of transport" (Law IV). However, the plaintiff was not responsible for supplying an expensive litter, or covered chair designed to be carried by attendants.

Furthermore, Law VI expands upon who could act as a "surety" or "defender" of someone in court, whether the plaintiff and defendant could settle the issue themselves, and what their recourse would be if a compromise could not be made. Although it is often referred to as a military rank, the "Praetor" (Law VII) was an official charged with the responsibility of deciding disputes between citizens. A combination of both judge and counselor, the praetor was considered a colleague of the "consul," or supreme elected leader during the Roman Republic, and charged with being part of the system of courts as well as presiding over the senate and other legislative bodies.

◆ Table II

The eleven laws in this table have to do with the expectations of the plaintiff and the defendant in reference to judgment. Additionally, this table includes specific laws regarding theft and the appropriate actions that could be taken if someone was caught in the act of stealing.

In Law I, rules regarding the postponement of a trial or obtaining a witness are laid out, including allowances for "discharge" of vows to the gods or to "meet an alien." Vows to the gods were an integral part of Roman religion. The formula followed was that the supplicant asked the gods for their favor in a particular act, good health, safe return from a journey, success in business dealings, and so on; in return, the supplicant would perform certain duties or give offerings to them. Because of the highly formalistic nature of Roman religion, the execution of these vows was considered legally binding. The reference to an "alien" here simply refers to a foreigner or even someone who is not considered to be from the same locality. This is most likely a reference to business dealings made with those from afar and considered important enough to justify a delay in a legal proceeding.

Table II goes on to discuss theft and the laws surrounding it. Particularly noteworthy is the mention in Law VII of detecting theft by means of "dish and girdle." One of the rights granted by traditional Roman law at the time was that an individual who suspected his neighbor of theft might be allowed to search the neighbor's premises to confirm the theft. The only stipulation was that the accuser would do so wearing solely a "girdle"—a belt or, more specifically, a loincloth or other small piece of clothing. This requirement was meant to prevent theft on the part of the accuser once inside the neighbor's home. The only other item allowed to be brought into the suspect's home was a dish or platter, the explanation of which is uncertain. Some historians believe that it served as a ritualistic method to convey the stolen property out of the home, if it

was discovered. Others postulate that it may have served as a screen to hide the accuser's face while inside.

The remainder of the table discusses the potential punishments for various infractions, separating the judgments according to the social status of the perpetrator; the result was that punishment was worse for slaves than for freeman and worse for adults than for minors.

◆ Table III

The third table, made up of ten laws, discusses a topic of intense interest to the Roman citizen, both plebeian and patrician—laws regarding property and debt. The first three laws, which restrict financial transactions, begin the table. In Law III the exacting use of the term *usucaption* is noteworthy. In Roman law it refers to the process by which someone may acquire rights to the use and ownership of another's property through unrestricted use of it for a predetermined length of time—typically a year or two. However, this extension of "squatter's rights" does not extend to "aliens," or foreigners. Laws IV–X outline penalties for nonpayment of debt, leading the unfortunate debtor, if he remains unable to pay, reduced to slavery, either to the creditor or "beyond the Tiber," meaning in a locality beyond the city of Rome's borders.

The severity of the debt laws described here no doubt shocked the plebeians, and it is unsurprising that upon publication of the laws and after their political agitation to have them written in the first place, the plebeians were only more incensed at their lack of political clout. There is no mention specifically of class within their text, yet the consensus of historical opinion is that the laws were drafted with the aim of aiding the recovery of patrician debts to the detriment of plebeian debtors and served to solidify the inequitable status quo.

◆ Table IV

The four laws of Table IV address fatherhood and marriage. Specifically, they outline the extent to which an adult Roman male could exercise his *patria potestas* (power of fatherhood) over his family. In Roman society the oldest adult male of a family had literal power of life and death over the entire household, including his children, wife, and slaves.

The first law dictates a father's rights regarding his son, stipulating that if the father "sold [him] three times," his son would be freed from those rights. The law was intended to act as a bulwark against unscrupulous fathers who sold their children repeatedly into slavery. It was also used by men who wished their sons to be free to start their own families and thus possess their own *patria potestas*. Fathers could thus find friendly buyers to purchase and then sell back their sons until the sons were deemed "free" and able to establish their own families with their own "potestas."

◆ Table V

Issues pertaining to wills, trusts, and inheritance are discussed in the seven laws of Table V. Law I is unequivocal in stating that heads of households could dispose of their goods in any way they saw fit and their decisions

Palatine Hill overlooking the Roman Forum (AP/Wide World Photos)

"shall have the force of law"—a stipulation firmly reinforcing an individual's property rights against claims by both family and state.

Additionally, the use of the term *agnate* in Law II has a specific legal meaning in Roman law, as it still does in legal systems today. In Roman law "agnati" were considered to be only male relations in the father's bloodline (as opposed to "cognate," which referred to all family relations). The orderly succession of property would then be passed along patrilineal lines; only if there was no living male on the father's side would inheritance pass to the mother's side and then only to the male relatives.

◆ Table VI

The ten laws of Table VI deal primarily with ownership and property and mention both women and slaves in regard to their legal status as possessions under Roman law. Although the category is termed "immovable property," the reference in Law IV is to land. Land that is unused by its owner can be claimed by usucaption.

Law V states that women were deemed to be under the *potestas* (power) of any man with whom they cohabited for an entire year. However, if they spent three nights or more per month beyond the confines of their home, it was possible to circumvent the law. This loophole, termed *trinoctium* (the three-night interval), allowed many Roman women to keep a relative degree of independence, even in a society as patriarchal as that of ancient Rome's.

◆ Table VII

Damages and remedies with respect to crimes are the focus of Table VII, consisting of seventeen laws. Although they are clearly fragmentary, the seemingly random mixture of laws—ranging from issues regarding the responsibilities of an owner if an animal causes damage to punishment for anyone who "by means of incantations and magic arts" prevented another's crops from growing—showcases the

"exceptional" nature of the laws. Rather than list clearly the punishments for particular crimes, this table explains the issues for situations that may not have been immediately intuited from oral common law.

There are also penalties for particularly harsh crimes, including the murder of relatives. The mention of the killing of an "ascendant" in Law XV refers to murder of an older relative, either male or female, from whom a person is directly descended—typically, a mother or father. Since the murder of a near relative was considered especially heinous, the perpetrator's placement in a sack was traditionally accompanied by the addition of a dog, cock, viper, or ape before the sack was sewn up and hurled into the water—though the additions are not mentioned in the extant text of this table.

Deterrence by means of brutality was not uncommon in Roman legal formulas, which is further evinced by Laws XII and XVII. The former mentions that anyone giving "false testimony," that is, lying or acting as a false witness, would be punished by being hurled from the Tarpeian Rock—a steep cliff situated near the southern part of the Capitoline Hill in Rome. This punishment carried with it not only the terror of a death sentence but also the stigma of shame, since it was reserved for those who were deemed to have committed a traitorous act.

XVII mentions that any patron defrauding his client should be "dedicated to the infernal gods," a statement that utilizes the same phrasing as religious descriptions of human sacrifice. The "infernal gods" were those deities who resided in the underworld, Roman mythology's representation of the afterlife. To be "dedicated" to them meant to be given as sacrificial offering. Although human sacrifice would eventually fall out of favor in Roman religion, it was not officially outlawed until 97 BCE. Thus, in the time surrounding the drafting of the Twelve Tables, it was considered a conceivable remedy for an infraction of what was a highly important aspect of Roman society—the patron/client relationship. The mention

Cast bronze figure of Romulus and Remus with the she-wolf who is said to have nutured them
(© The Trustees of the British Museum)

of patrons and clients describes a specialized system of social relations whereupon a free person could bind himself to a "patron," usually a very wealthy, well-connected citizen, in exchange for favors or legal protection, the client, in turn, acting as a political supporter or part of the patron's bodyguard.

◆ Table VIII

Table VIII, made up of nine laws, discusses property and, in particular, how boundaries were established. Rules relating to tree removal and disputes over boundaries between fields and questions of whether someone was permitted to "drive an animal over the land" of those who lived adjacent to the highway point to the highly agrarian nature of Roman society during this period.

◆ Table IX

Table IX is one of the few tables that refer to a broad set of laws with guidelines similar to a bill of rights. Law IV of these seven laws explains that no "decision with reference to the life or liberty of a Roman citizen" should be given except by a greater legislative body, such as the Comitia Centuriata. The implication was that no Roman citizen could be put to death without serious deliberation by "the

people," and the table outlines the rights that would eventually become foundational Western legal concepts.

◆ Table X

The eighteen laws in Table X refer entirely to religious practices and center mostly on the restrictions and procedures regarding burial. The intense focus on burial rules was a by-product of the ever-present desire in Roman society to showcase social status. This desire had progressed to the degree that the compilers of the Twelve Tables thought it necessary to limit the extravagance of funerals, since they had become so overwrought that they impinged on the day-to-day functioning of the city.

◆ Table XI

Added by the second decemvirate in 450 BCE, Table XI contains the contentious clause that no one who was part of the "Senatorial Order," meaning the patricians, was to "contract marriage with plebeians." This example of government bias against the plebeians helped spark the demand for secession in 449 BCE, an event that ended the decemvirate and returned the Roman Republic to the governance of the consuls.

"When anyone summons another before the tribunal of a judge, the latter must, without hesitation, immediately appear."

(Table I, Law I)

"Where anyone, having acknowledged a debt, has a judgment rendered against him requiring payment, thirty days shall be given to him in which to pay the money and satisfy the judgment."

(Table III, Law IV)

"A father shall have the right of life and death over his son born in lawful marriage, and shall also have the power to render him independent, after he has been sold three times."

(Table IV, Law I)

"No privileges, or statutes, shall be enacted in favor of private persons, to the injury of others contrary to the law common to all citizens, and which individuals, no matter of what rank, have a right to make use of."

(Table IX, Law I)

"Affairs of great importance shall not be transacted without the vote of the people, with whom rests the power to appoint magistrates, to condemn citizens, and to enact laws. Laws subsequently passed always take preference over former ones."

(Table XI, Law I)

"Those who belong to the Senatorial Order and are styled Fathers, shall not contract marriage with plebeians."

(Table XI, Law II)

♦ **Table XII**

A miscellany of supplementary laws, Table XII outlines the responsibilities of slave owners for damages caused by their slaves, procedures regarding legal appeals, and a ruling as to whether one could purchase an item considered "sacred" or usable in a religious rite if there was currently a charge against him for nonpayment of a debt or default on a loan.

Audience

The laws of the Twelve Tables were aimed at the entirety of the Roman population in an attempt to clarify the content of the law for all. Their posting in the Roman Forum, a central meeting area and marketplace, ensured that anyone who wished to consult the laws would be able to do so. This availability was especially helpful for plebeians suffering under the debt laws, which, though not ameliorated by the Twelve Tables, were clearly spelled out for both creditor and debtor. It is said that the first ten tables were displayed for public perusal to showcase what the decemvirs had planned and to allow for any possible amendments that the people might want. Once the laws had been posted for an undisclosed amount of time, they were taken back, finalized, and put forth to the Roman government.

In order for the laws to become official, they needed to be examined and approved, not just by the public but also by the legislative bodies of the Roman Republic, including both the Senate and the Comitia Centuriata, an advisory body made up of members of the Roman military. The Senate consisted mostly of patricians, though some plebeians were members. Highly aristocratic, the Senate was made up of the highest element of Roman society.

Once the laws passed through the Senate without censure, they were put to the Comitia Centuriata to be voted on by members of the Roman military. The divisions between the voting blocks, "centuries," in the assembly were determined by wealth and were devised so that the most wealthy, though they were the least numerous, were most influential. Because the majority of the assembly consisted of plebeians, some of whom were *proletarii* (members of one of the poorest social classes), it was the patricians and the wealthiest members of the plebeian families who again held most of the power.

Impact

The impact of the Twelve Tables was felt immediately in the context of the Conflict of the Orders as the laws showcased the legal bias of the government toward the patrician faction. The promulgation of the laws also precipitated yet another plebeian secession that would lead to more political rights for plebeians in the form of increasing powers for the tribune of the plebs and would end the decemvirate permanently. In the long term, the Twelve Tables served as the basis for the Roman legal code until it was replaced by the far more systematic Theodosian Code of the fifth century CE. The Theodosian Code would provide the basis for all other legal systems that later evolved in Western Europe, serving as the bedrock of what is now known as the civil law.

The exact reaction from the Roman people upon receiving the Twelve Tables is not clear from ancient sources. It is known, however, that along with the laws' promulgation, another by-product of the secession of 449 BCE was the passing of the Leges Valeria Horatiae, or Valerian and Horatian Laws. These laws immediately expanded the rights of the plebeians by increasing the powers of the tribune of the plebs, increasing the tribune's ability to intercede on the behalf of the plebeians in the patrician-controlled Senate. Furthermore, four years later the Lex Canuleia was passed, overturning the stipulation in Table XI that no patrician was permitted to marry a plebeian and allowing for the eventual merging of the two orders.

Questions for Further Study

1. What impact did the Twelve Tables of Roman Law have on the development of Western legal systems? Why is the document important?

2. What impact did class structure have on the development of Roman law in general and on the Twelve Tables of Roman Law in particular?

3. Compare the Twelve Tables of Roman Law and Aristotle's summary of the Athenian Constitution. Both Rome and Greece had significant impact on the development of Western democracy. How do the two documents reflect similar conditions and legal concerns? In particular, how does each deal with the issue of debt?

4. Numerous "milestone" documents have to do with the establishment of laws and legal codes. Select one such document to compare with the Twelve Tables—possibilities include the Athenian Constitution; the Russkaia Pravda, or Justice of the Rus; Middle Assyrian Laws; the Constitutions of Clarendon; and the Magna Carta—and explicate how each of the two documents arose from political, economic, and social conditions.

5. The Twelve Tables of Roman Law attempted to end, at least in part, the conflict between patricians and plebeians. Did it succeed in this goal? From a human standpoint, why is it so difficult for societies to achieve social equality between and among social classes? How did conditions in the Roman Republic illustrate this difficulty?

These laws did not solve the conflict between the orders, nor did they usher in a new era of democratic rule. However, taken as part of the greater evolution of the relationship between the patricians and the plebs, the passage of the Twelve Tables can be seen as a pivotal moment in Roman history. The next 180 years of the Roman Republic witnessed the slow but inevitable growth of patrician and plebeian equality, culminating in the passage of the decisive Lex Hortensia in 287 BCE. This law granted the decisions of the Concilium Plebis the power of law over the entirety of the Roman population, essentially ending any legal difference between patrician and plebeian.

The influence of the Twelve Tables as a legal document gradually faded within the tradition of the Roman legal system. Because the Twelve Tables had been destroyed in 390 BCE, they were referenced by legal theorists and scholars as a precedent, though they were eventually supplanted by more contemporaneous interpretations of legal practice and procedure. Nevertheless, they remained the only attempted written organization of Roman law until the emperor Theodosius commissioned the Theodosian Code in 429 CE. Its publication nine years later set the stage for the final codification of Roman law, the Corpus Juris Civilis (Body of Civil Law) of the emperor Justinian, completed in 534 CE. Both of these codifications drew directly on the Twelve Tables, as the earliest extant record of Roman law, and inspired the civil law—the predominant legal system in Europe and South America, taking a great deal of its structure and content from Roman sources.

Further Reading

■ Articles

Pharr, Clyde. "Roman Legal Education." Classical Journal 34, no. 5 (1939): 257–270.

Steinberg, Michael. "The Twelve Tables and Their Origins: An Eighteenth-Century Debate." Journal of the History of Ideas 43, no. 3 (1982): 379–396.

■ Books

Dionysius of Halicarnassus. *Roman Antiquities*, vol. 3. Cambridge, Mass.: Harvard University Press, 1940.

Grant, Michael. *History of Rome*. New York: Scribners, 1978.

Livy. *A History of Rome: Selections*, trans. Moses Hadas. New York: Modern Library, 1962.

Taylor, T. M. *A Constitutional and Political History of Rome: From the Earliest Times to the Reign of Domitian*. 1899. Reprint. Holmes Beach, Fla.: Gaunt, 1997.

Warmington, E. H, ed. and trans. *Remains of Old Latin*, vol. 3. Cambridge, Mass.: Harvard University Press, 1938.

Watson, Alan. *Rome of the XII Tables*. Princeton, N.J.: Princeton University Press, 1975.

———. *The State, Law, and Religion: Pagan Rome*. Athens: University of Georgia Press, 1992.

—Eric May

TWELVE TABLES OF ROMAN LAW

Table I.

Concerning the summons to court.

◆ **Law I.**

When anyone summons another before the tribunal of a judge, the latter must, without hesitation, immediately appear.

◆ **Law II.**

If, after having been summoned, he does not appear, or refuses to come before the tribunal of the judge, let the party who summoned him call upon any citizens who are present to bear witness. Then let him seize his reluctant adversary; so that he may be brought into court, as a captive, by apparent force.

◆ **Law III.**

When anyone who has been summoned to court is guilty of evasion, or attempts to flee, let him be arrested by the plaintiff.

◆ **Law IV.**

If bodily infirmity or advanced age should prevent the party summoned to court from appearing, let him who summoned him furnish him with an animal, as a means of transport. If he is unwilling to accept it, the plaintiff cannot legally be compelled to provide the defendant with a vehicle constructed of boards, or a covered litter.

◆ **Law V.**

If he who is summoned has either a sponsor or a defender, let him be dismissed, and his representative can take his place in court.

◆ **Law VI.**

The defender, or the surety of a wealthy man, must himself be rich; but anyone who desires to do so can come to the assistance of a person who is poor, and occupy his place.

◆ **Law VII.**

When litigants wish to settle their dispute among themselves, even while they are on their way to appear before the Praetor, they shall have the right to make peace; and whatever agreement they enter into, it shall be considered just, and shall be confirmed.

◆ **Law VIII.**

If the plaintiff and defendant do not settle their dispute, as above mentioned, let them state their cases either in the *Comitium* or the Forum, by making a brief statement in the presence of the judge, between the rising of the sun and noon; and, both of them being present, let them speak so that each party may hear.

◆ **Law IX.**

In the afternoon, let the judge grant the right to bring the action, and render his decision in the presence of the plaintiff and the defendant.

◆ **Law X.**

The setting of the sun shall be the extreme limit of time within which a judge must render his decision.

Table II.

Concerning judgments and thefts.

◆ **Law I.**

When issue has been joined in the presence of the judge, sureties and their substitutes for appearance at the trial must be furnished on both sides. The parties shall appear in person, unless prevented by disease of a serious character; or where vows which they have taken must be discharged to the Gods; or where the proceedings are interrupted through their absence on business for the State; or where a day has been appointed by them to meet an alien.

◆ **Law II.**

If any of the above mentioned occurrences takes place, that is, if one of the parties is seriously ill, or a vow has to be performed, or one of them is absent on business for the State, or a day has been appointed for an interview with an alien, so that the judge, the arbiter, or the defendant is prevented from being present, and the furnishing of security is postponed on this account, the hearing of the case shall be deferred.

◆ **Law III.**

Where anyone is deprived of the evidence of a witness let him call him with a loud voice in front of his house, on three market-days.

◆ **Law IV.**

Where anyone commits a theft by night, and having been caught in the act is killed, he is legally killed.

◆ **Law V.**

If anyone commits a theft during the day, and is caught in the act, he shall be scourged, and given up as a slave to the person against whom the theft was committed. If he who perpetrated the theft is a slave, he shall be beaten with rods and hurled from the Tarpeian Rock. If he is under the age of puberty, the Prætor shall decide whether he shall be scourged, and surrendered by way of reparation for the injury.

◆ **Law VI.**

When any persons commit a theft during the day and in the light, whether they be freemen or slaves, of full age or minors, and attempt to defend themselves with weapons, or with any kind of implements; and the party against whom the violence is committed raises the cry of thief, and calls upon other persons, if any are present, to come to his assistance; and this is done, and the thieves are killed by him in the defence of his person and property, it is legal, and no liability attaches to the homicide.

◆ **Law VII.**

If a theft be detected by means of a dish and a girdle, it is the same as manifest theft, and shall be punished as such.

◆ **Law VIII.**

When anyone accuses and convicts another of theft which is not manifest, and no stolen property is found, judgment shall be rendered to compel the thief to pay double the value of what was stolen.

◆ **Law IX.**

Where anyone secretly cuts down trees belonging to another, he shall pay twenty-five *asses* for each tree cut down.

◆ **Law X.**

Where anyone, in order to favor a thief, makes a compromise for the loss sustained, he cannot afterwards prosecute him for theft.

◆ **Law XI.**

Stolen property shall always be his to whom it formerly belonged; nor can the lawful owner ever be deprived of it by long possession, without regard to its duration; nor can it ever be acquired by another, no matter in what way this may take place.

Table III.

Concerning property which is lent.

◆ **Law I.**

When anyone, with fraudulent intent, appropriates property deposited with him for safe keeping, he shall be condemned to pay double its value.

◆ **Law II.**

When anyone collects interest on money loaned at a higher rate per annum than that of the *unciæ*, he shall pay quadruple the amount by way of penalty.

◆ **Law III.**

An alien cannot acquire the property of another by usucaption; but a Roman citizen, who is the lawful owner of the property, shall always have the right to demand it from him.

◆ **Law IV.**

Where anyone, having acknowledged a debt, has a judgment rendered against him requiring payment, thirty days shall be given to him in which to pay the money and satisfy the judgment.

◆ **Law V.**

After the term of thirty days granted by the law to debtors who have had judgment rendered against them has expired, and in the meantime, they have not satisfied the judgment, their creditors shall be permitted to forcibly seize them and bring them again into court.

◆ **Law VI.**

When a defendant, after thirty days have elapsed, is brought into court a second time by the plaintiff, and does not satisfy the judgment; or, in the meantime, another party, or his surety does not pay it out of his own money, the creditor, or the plaintiff, after the debtor has been delivered up to him, can take the latter with him and bind him or place him in fetters; provided his chains are not of more than fifteen pounds weight; he can, however, place him in others which are lighter, if he desires to do so.

◆ Law VII.

If, after a debtor has been delivered up to his creditor, or has been placed in chains, he desires to obtain food and has the means, he shall be permitted to support himself out of his own property. But if he has nothing on which to live, his creditor, who holds him in chains, shall give him a pound of grain every day, or he can give him more than a pound, if he wishes to do so.

◆ Law VIII.

In the meantime, the party who has been delivered up to his creditor can make terms with him. If he does not, he shall be kept in chains for sixty days; and for three consecutive market-days he shall be brought before the Prætor in the place of assembly in the Forum, and the amount of the judgment against him shall be publicly proclaimed.

◆ Law IX.

After he has been kept in chains for sixty days, and the sum for which he is liable has been three times publicly proclaimed in the Forum, he shall be condemned to be reduced to slavery by him to whom he was delivered up; or, if the latter prefers, he can be sold beyond the Tiber.

◆ Law X.

Where a party is delivered up to several persons, on account of a debt, after he has been exposed in the Forum on three market days, they shall be permitted to divide their debtor into different parts, if they desire to do so; and if anyone of them should, by the division, obtain more or less than he is entitled to, he shall not be responsible.

Table IV.

Cconcerning the rights of a father, and of marriage.

◆ Law I.

A father shall have the right of life and death over his son born in lawful marriage, and shall also have the power to render him independent, after he has been sold three times.

◆ Law II.

If a father sells his son three times, the latter shall be free from paternal authority.

◆ Law III.

A father shall immediately put to death a son recently born, who is a monster, or has a form different from that of members of the human race.

◆ Law IV.

When a woman brings forth a son within the next ten months after the death of her husband, he shall be born in lawful marriage, and shall be the legal heir of his estate.

Table V.

Concerning estates and guardianships.

◆ Law I.

No matter in what way the head of a household may dispose of his estate, and appoint heirs to the same, or guardians; it shall have the force and effect of law.

◆ Law II.

Where a father dies intestate, without leaving any proper heir, his nearest agnate, or, if there is none, the next of kin among his family, shall be his heir.

◆ Law III.

When a freedman dies intestate, and does not leave any proper heir, but his patron, or the children of the latter survive him; the inheritance of the estate of the freedman shall be adjudged to the next of kin of the patron.

◆ Law IV.

When a creditor or a debtor dies, his heirs can only sue, or be sued, in proportion to their shares in the estate; and any claims, or remaining property, shall be divided among them in the same proportion.

◆ Law V.

Where co-heirs desire to obtain their shares of the property of an estate, which has not yet been divided, it shall be divided. In order that this may be properly done and no loss be sustained by the litigants, the Prætor shall appoint three arbiters, who can give to each one that to which he is entitled in accordance with law and equity.

◆ Law VI.

When the head of a family dies intestate, and leaves a proper heir who has not reached the age of puberty, his nearest agnate shall obtain the guardianship.

◆ **Law VII.**

When no guardian has been appointed for an insane person, or a spendthrift, his nearest agnates, or if there are none, his other relatives, must take charge of his property.

Table VI.

Concerning ownership and possession.

◆ **Law I.**

When anyone contracts a legal obligation with reference to his property, or sells it, by making a verbal statement or agreement concerning the same, this shall have the force and effect of law. If the party should afterwards deny his statements, and legal proceedings are instituted, he shall, by way of penalty, pay double the value of the property in question.

◆ **Law II.**

Where a slave is ordered to be free by a will, upon his compliance with a certain condition, and he complies with the condition; or if, after having paid his price to the purchaser, he claims his liberty, he shall be free.

◆ **Law III.**

Where property has been sold, even though it may have been delivered, it shall by no means be acquired by the purchaser until the price has been paid, or a surety or a pledge has been given, and the vendor satisfied in this manner.

◆ **Law IV.**

Immovable property shall be acquired by usucaption after the lapse of two years; other property after the lapse of one year.

◆ **Law V.**

Where a woman, who has not been united to a man in marriage, lives with him for an entire year without the usucaption of her being interrupted for three nights, she shall pass into his power as his legal wife.

◆ **Law VI.**

Where parties have a dispute with reference to property before the tribunal of the Praetor, both of them shall be permitted to state their claims in the presence of witnesses.

◆ **Law VII.**

Where anyone demands freedom for another against the claim of servitude, the Praetor shall render judgment in favor of liberty.

◆ **Law VIII.**

No material forming part of either a building or a vineyard shall be removed therefrom. Any one who, without the knowledge or consent of the owner, attaches a beam or anything else to his house or vineyard, shall be condemned to pay double its value.

◆ **Law IX.**

Timbers which have been dressed and prepared for building purposes, but which have not yet been attached to a building or a vineyard can legally be recovered by the owner, if they are stolen from him.

◆ **Law X.**

If a husband desires to divorce his wife, and dissolve his marriage, he must give a reason for doing so.

Table VII.

Concerning crimes.

◆ **Law I.**

If a quadruped causes injury to anyone, let the owner tender him the estimated amount of the damage; and if he is unwilling to accept it, the owner shall, by way of reparation, surrender the animal that caused the injury.

◆ **Law II.**

If you cause any unlawful damage ... accidentally and unintentionally, you must make good the loss, either by tendering what has caused it, or by payment.

◆ **Law III.**

Anyone who, by means of incantations and magic arts, prevents grain or crops of any kind belonging to another from growing, shall be sacrificed to Ceres.

◆ **Law IV.**

If anyone who has arrived at puberty, secretly, and by night, destroys or cuts and appropriates to his own use, the crop of another, which the owner of the land has laboriously obtained by plowing and the cultivation of the soil, he shall be sacrificed to Ceres, and hung.

If he is under the age of puberty, and not yet old enough to be accountable, he shall be scourged, in the discretion of the Praetor, and shall make good the loss by paying double its amount.

◆ **Law V.**

Anyone who turns cattle on the land of another, for the purpose of pasture, shall surrender the cattle, by way of reparation.

◆ **Law VI.**

Anyone who, knowingly and maliciously, burns a building, or a heap of grain left near a building, after having been placed in chains and scourged, shall be put to death by fire. If, however, he caused the damage by accident, and without malice, he shall make it good; or, if he has not the means to do so, he shall receive a lighter punishment.

◆ **Law VII.**

When a person, in any way, causes an injury to another which is not serious, he shall be punished with a fine of twenty *asses*.

◆ **Law VIII.**

When anyone publicly abuses another in a loud voice, or writes a poem for the purpose of insulting him, or rendering him infamous, he shall be beaten with a rod until he dies.

◆ **Law IX.**

When anyone breaks a member of another, and is unwilling to come to make a settlement with him, he shall be punished by the law of retaliation.

◆ **Law X.**

When anyone knocks a tooth out of the gum of a freeman, he shall be fined three hundred *asses*; if he knocks one out of the gum of a slave, he shall be fined a hundred and fifty *asses*.

◆ **Law XI.**

If anyone, after having been asked, appears either as a witness or a balance-holder, at a sale, or the execution of a will, and refuses to testify when this is required to prove the genuineness of the transaction, he shall become infamous, and cannot afterwards give evidence.

◆ **Law XII.**

Anyone who gives false testimony shall be hurled from the Tarpeian Rock.

◆ **Law XIII.**

If anyone knowingly and maliciously kills a freeman, he shall be guilty of a capital crime. If he kills him by accident, without malice and unintentionally, let him substitute a ram to be sacrificed publicly by way of expiation for the homicide of the deceased, and for the purpose of appeasing the children of the latter.

◆ **Law XIV.**

Anyone who annoys another by means of magic incantations or diabolical arts, and renders him inactive, or ill; or who prepares or administers poison to him, is guilty of a capital crime, and shall be punished with death.

◆ **Law XV.**

Anyone who kills an ascendant, shall have his head wrapped in a cloth, and after having been sewed up in a sack, shall be thrown into the water.

◆ **Law XVI.**

Where anyone is guilty of fraud in the administration of a guardianship, he shall be considered infamous; and, even after the guardianship has been terminated, if any theft is proved to have been committed, he shall, by the payment of double damages, be compelled to make good the loss which he caused.

◆ **Law XVII.**

When a patron defrauds his client, he shall be dedicated to the infernal gods.

Table VIII.

Concerning the laws of real property.

◆ **Law I.**

A space of two feet and a half must be left between neighboring buildings.

◆ **Law II.**

Societies and associations which have the right to assemble, can make, promulgate, and confirm for themselves such contracts and rules as they may desire; provided nothing is done by them contrary to public enactments, or which does not violate the common law.

◆ **Law III.**

The space of five feet shall be left between adjoining fields, by means of which the owners can visit their property, or drive and plow around it. No one shall ever have the right to acquire this space by usucaption.

◆ **Law IV.**

If any persons are in possession of adjoining fields, and a dispute arises with reference to the boundaries of the same, the Prætor shall appoint three arbiters, who shall take cognizance of the case, and, after the boundaries have been established, he shall assign to each party that to which he is entitled.

◆ **Law V.**

When a tree overhangs the land of a neighbor, so as to cause injury by its branches and its shade, it shall be cut off fifteen feet from the ground.

◆ **Law VI.**

When the fruit of a tree falls upon the premises of a neighbor, the owner of the tree shall have a right to gather and remove it.

◆ **Law VII.**

When rain falls upon the land of one person in such a quantity as to cause water to rise and injure the property of another, the Prætor shall appoint three arbiters for the purpose of confining the water, and providing against damage to the other party.

◆ **Law VIII.**

Where a road runs in a straight line, it shall be eight feet, and where it curves, it shall be sixteen feet in width.

◆ **Law IX.**

When a man's land lies adjacent to the highway, he can enclose it in any way that he chooses; but if he neglects to do so, any other person can drive an animal over the land wherever he pleases.

Table IX.

Concerning public law.

◆ **Law I.**

No privileges, or statutes, shall be enacted in favor of private persons, to the injury of others contrary to the law common to all citizens, and which individuals, no matter of what rank, have a right to make use of.

◆ **Law II.**

The same rights shall be conferred upon, and the same laws shall be considered to have been enacted for all the people residing in and beyond Latium, that have been enacted for good and steadfast Roman citizens.

◆ **Law III.**

When a judge, or an arbiter appointed to hear a case, accepts money, or other gifts, for the purpose of influencing his decision, he shall suffer the penalty of death.

◆ **Law IV.**

No decision with reference to the life or liberty of a Roman citizen shall be rendered except by the vote of the Greater *Comitia*.

◆ **Law V.**

Public accusers in capital cases shall be appointed by the people.

◆ **Law VI.**

If anyone should cause nocturnal assemblies in the City, he shall be put to death.

◆ **Law VII.**

If anyone should stir up war against his country, or delivers a Roman citizen into the hands of the enemy, he shall be punished with death.

Table X.

Concerning religious law.

◆ **Law I.**

An oath shall have the greatest force and effect, for the purpose of compelling good faith.

◆ **Law II.**

Where a family adopts private religious rites every member of it can, afterwards, always make use of them.

◆ **Law III.**

No burial or cremation of a corpse shall take place in a city.

◆ **Law IV.**

No greater expenses or mourning than is proper shall be permitted in funeral ceremonies.

◆ **Law V.**

No one shall, hereafter, exceed the limit established by these laws for the celebration of funeral rites.

◆ **Law VI.**

Wood employed for the purpose of constructing a funeral pyre shall not be hewn, but shall be rough and unpolished.

◆ **Law VII.**

When a corpse is prepared for burial at home, not more than three women with their heads covered with mourning veils shall be permitted to perform this service. The body may be enveloped in purple robes, and when borne outside, ten flute players, at the most, shall accompany the funeral procession.

◆ **Law VIII.**

Women shall not during a funeral lacerate their faces, or tear their cheeks with their nails; nor shall they utter loud cries bewailing the dead.

◆ **Law IX.**

No bones shall be taken from the body of a person who is dead, or from his ashes after cremation, in order that funeral ceremonies may again be held elsewhere. When, however, anyone dies in a foreign country, or is killed in war, a part of his remains may be transferred to the burial place of his ancestors.

◆ **Law X.**

The body of no dead slave shall be anointed; nor shall any drinking take place at his funeral, nor a banquet of any kind be instituted in his honor.

◆ **Law XI.**

No wine flavored with myrrh, or any other precious beverage, shall be poured upon a corpse while it is burning; nor shall the funeral pile be sprinkled with wine.

◆ **Law XII.**

Large wreaths shall not be borne at a funeral; nor shall perfumes be burned on the altars.

◆ **Law XIII.**

Anyone who has rendered himself deserving of a wreath, as the reward of bravery in war, or through his having been the victor in public contests or games, whether he has obtained it through his own exertions or by means of others in his own name, and by his own money, through his horses, or his slaves, shall have a right to have the said wreath placed upon his dead body, or upon that of any of his ascendants, as long as the corpse is at his home, as well as when it is borne away; so that, during his obsequies,

he may enjoy the honor which in his lifetime he acquired by his bravery or his good fortune.

◆ **Law XIV.**

Only one funeral of an individual can take place; and it shall not be permitted to prepare several biers.

◆ **Law XV.**

Gold, no matter in what form it may be present, shall, by all means, be removed from the corpse at the time of the funeral; but if anyone's teeth should be fastened with gold, it shall be lawful either to burn, or to bury it with the body.

◆ **Law XVI.**

No one, without the knowledge or consent of the owner, shall erect a funeral pyre, or a tomb, nearer than sixty feet to the building of another.

◆ **Law XVII.**

No one can acquire by usucaption either the vestibule or approach to a tomb, or the tomb itself.

◆ **Law XVIII.**

No assembly of the people shall take place during the obsequies of any man distinguished in the State.

Table XI.

Supplement to the five preceding ones.

◆ **Law I.**

Affairs of great importance shall not be transacted without the vote of the people, with whom rests the power to appoint magistrates, to condemn citizens, and to enact laws. Laws subsequently passed always take preference over former ones.

◆ **Law II.**

Those who belong to the Senatorial Order and are styled Fathers, shall not contract marriage with plebeians.

Table XII.

Supplement to the five preceding ones.

◆ **Law I.**

No one shall render sacred any property with reference to which there is a controversy in court, where issue has already been joined; and if anyone does render such property sacred, he shall pay double its value as a penalty.

◆ **Law II.**

If the claim of anyone in whose favor judgment was rendered after the property had been illegally seized, or after possession of the same had been delivered, is found to be false, the Prætor shall appoint three arbiters, by whose award double the

amount of the profits shall be restored by him in whose favor the judgment was rendered.

◆ **Law III.**

If a slave, with the knowledge of his master, should commit a theft, or cause damage to anyone, his master shall be given up to the other party by way of reparation for the theft, injury, or damage committed by the slave.

Glossary

asses	bronze, silver, and gold coins minted by the Romans; singular form: *as*
balance-holder	a person designated to hold a brass balance, or scale, in certain ceremonies of Roman law
Ceres	in Roman mythology, the goddess of grain
Comitium	in the days of the Roman Republic, the meeting place for the senate (in Rome itself) and for popular, elective, and judicial assemblies in all Roman cities
Latium	the area centering on the coastal plain from the mouth of the Tiber; often called the cradle of Rome (both the city and the Roman Empire)
unciae	bronze coins minted by the Romans; an *uncia* was a fraction of an as.

FUNERAL ORATION OF PERICLES

"Heroes have the whole earth for their tomb."

Overview

The Funeral Oration delivered by Pericles of Athens is considered one of the most famous speeches of antiquity. The speech concluded a ritualized ceremony to honor the city's soldiers who had fallen in the first year of the Peloponnesian War. Despite the fact that Athens had secured a strong defensive position that year (431 BCE), very little had been accomplished in reducing Sparta's ability to wage war. Moreover, hostilities between Athens and Sparta had not been the result of a unanimous policy. Given that the two cities had been allies in the Persian Wars (490–479 BCE), many people objected to a course that caused a disruption of those relations. Pro-Spartan elements existed, albeit in the minority, but their presence was enough to cause tensions.

Furthermore, not all Athenians agreed with the development of democracy, which allowed nonaristocratic elements to control policy. A work known as the Constitution of Athens, assigned to Xenophon (ca. 431–352 BCE), suggested a contempt for commoners in charge, indicating the fiction of the unity presented by Pericles. In addition, the defensive strategy withdrew the citizenship behind the city's walls with the intention of relying upon maritime trade for foodstuffs to outlast Sparta's armies in the field. Unfortunately for many displaced aristocratic farmers, this policy allowed the destruction of their family holdings and livelihood.

Thus Pericles' speech did not merely praise the noble dead but also served to contrast the political and social systems of Athens and Sparta. Pericles seized the opportunity to promote the benefits of democracy and to extol its virtues in the face of the aristocratic forces that idolized the Spartan system. The oration idealized Athens and its status in order to justify the sacrifice not only of the soldiers who gave their lives but also of the citizens who faced continued hardships.

Context

The Great Peloponnesian War erupted in 431 BCE as a result of the growing rivalry between the Athenian Empire and the Peloponnesian League. Originally, Athens and Spar-

ta had been allies in the Persian Wars that culminated in the Battle of Plataea in 479 BCE. The Greek offensive turned into an effort to liberate the Greek cities of Asia Minor (modern-day Turkey) from Persian rule. Sparta's abusive leadership under Pausanius, regent to the king, created friction with the freed city-states and eventually caused his recall. The Athenian high command received an invitation to assume leadership. At the island of Delos, the various city-states and Athens forged an alliance that granted the latter prominence because of its substantial fleet. Smaller cities provided financial contributions in lieu of actual forces. Later, when Naxos, one of the island members, attempted to leave the league, Athens destroyed the city and enforced the alliance. Eventually the members of the Delian League found themselves tied to Athens by threat of force.

Tensions with Sparta began because of the construction of a series of defensive walls around Athens and its port, Piraeus; the enclosure also included the land between the two. In 465 BCE Sparta faced a helot (slave) rebellion, and Athenian forces arrived to assist. Fear of democratic influence, however, caused the Spartans to request that the Athenians return home. The Athenian general Cimon had been a strong supporter of good relations between Athens and Sparta, and this rebuff undermined his credibility. Ephialtes, an Athenian aristocrat, used the reverse to have Cimon exiled, paving the way for a series of reforms that limited the older, aristocratic Council of the Areopagus and transferred many of its powers to the assembly of the people. The new political emphasis in Athens steered away from relations with Sparta and from efforts to strengthen imperial designs. The road to war became a convoluted course in 460 BCE, when Athens involved itself in a dispute between Megara and Corinth, both Spartan allies. The conflict of interests in the region initiated what is known as the First Peloponnesian War. By 445 BCE, however, the opponents had signed the Thirty Years' Peace, and Sparta forced Athens to cede territories gained in the fifteen-year war.

Subsequent incidents, such as a revolt in Miletus that threatened to bring Persian forces back into the Aegean, strained the treaty. The Peloponnesian League debated intervention against Athens to prevent a new Persian war. Archidamas II, king of Sparta, refused, however, and even in later events continued to seek the path of arbitration.

550 BCE

- Sparta emerges as the dominant military force and creates the Peloponnesian League.

507 BCE

- Cleisthenes, a prominent Athenian aristocrat, proposes and helps institute political reforms that create the basis for democracy in Athens.

490 BCE

- The Persian Wars start after Greek city-states in Asia Minor rebel against the Persian Empire.

477 BCE

- The Delian League is formed as a means to marshal resources to fight the Persians. At this meeting the Greek city-states invite Athens to assume leadership, allowing it, because of its large navy, to become the prominent and most powerful contingent in the Aegean, thus creating a rival to Sparta.

461 BCE

- Ephialtes institutes changes in Athens, but opponents have him assassinated.

Nevertheless, when Athens and Corinth conflicted over the latter's right to interfere in the affairs of its rebellious colony Corcyra (now Corfu), voices in the Peloponnesus began to clamor for war. Corinthian pressure on Sparta increased when its colony Potidaea, under Athenian control as part of the Delian League, received an ultimatum to destroy its walls and expel Corinthian magistrates. Sparta acquiesced in summoning the league after Athens issued the Megarian Decree, which created an embargo on goods from Megara. Despite Archidamas's resistance to conflict, Athenian emissaries brashly declared that any aggression against them would be ineffective, provoking the Peloponnesians to vote for war.

In a defensive move to protect the approaches to their territory, the forces of Thebes, an ally of Sparta, advanced against the city of Plataea, an ally of Athens. The Peloponnesian forces expected Athens to attack and therefore prepared to blunt the offensive. Archidamas's strategy assumed that a decisive defeat of Athenian armies would force their surrender. If the Athenians hid behind their large wall system, the Spartans would ravage the countryside and destroy the farms and the ripening fields. If Athens persisted in a defensive war, continual loss of their crops and property would demoralize the population and, likewise, force a capitulation. The Spartan leadership, however, did not anticipate Pericles' determination to utilize a large treasury and mercantile connections to furnish the city with foodstuffs. In short, he planned to allow the Spartans to ravage the countryside, even if it took three or four years; Athens could afford the loss. Simultaneously he planned to use the large naval advantage of more than three hundred ships to ravage the Peloponnesian peninsula and demoralize the enemy. Pericles intended to make the point that Athens could not be humbled, and thus the Spartans would weary in their yearly campaign of fruitless endeavors and seek arbitration to end hostilities.

During the first year of the conflict, both sides carried out their strategies. After the Theban maneuver, Archidamas mobilized his forces and slowly advanced into Attica, the territory of Athens. He hoped that rumors of his large army would force talks so that large-scale fighting would prove unnecessary and relations could be healed. However, his slow siege of border forts caused his troops to grumble at the delay, so he proceeded with the destruction of the countryside around Athens. According to the fifth-century historian Thucydides, the population of Attica, forced to retreat into Athens to protect its cattle and moveable wealth, expressed discontent and frustration. Many found themselves obliged to live as squatters in the streets or within space between the walls that connected the city with its port.

As Sparta ravaged the countryside, the Athenian fleet also engaged in raiding operations along the Peloponnesian coast, advancing into Corinthian territory on the western coasts. Other forces seized islands and forts in Euboea, the island to the east, to prevent them from falling into enemy hands. After the Spartans ran out of supplies and retreated, Athenian troops retaliated against Megara in the fall of 431 BCE, devastating various villages. That winter, as troops returned from the campaign season, Pericles delivered his speech. Although his political connections and the naval successes helped him maintain a position of prominence and popularity among the majority of the citizens, voices of discontent criticized his strategy and policies, and even the system of government that allowed him to attain the authority which had brought Athens to its present situation.

About the Author

Pericles of Athens, born in about 495 BCE, served as a prominent *strategos*, or general, within the assembly of the city. He served with nine other generals, but with his popularity and reputation he quickly gained a significant influence in the affairs of the government. In 462 BCE he emerged into public prominence as an associate of Ephialtes, who had pioneered democratic reforms that gave more authority to the people. After his mentor's assassination, Pericles became the mouthpiece for more democratic reforms and efforts to strengthen the city, both militarily and culturally. This period is referred to as the Age of Periclean Athens because of the artists, writers, and philosophers who flourished under his patronage, creating a cultural heritage for Western civilization. Pericles' efforts to broaden Athens's authority and power in the Aegean allowed the city to dominate the Delian League and emerge as a major rival to Sparta.

With the outbreak of the Peloponnesian War, Pericles devised the defensive strategy that pulled the population of the region within the walls of the city. While Athenian naval forces raided the Peloponnesus, Spartan forces continued to ransack the countryside. An outbreak of a plague within the city stirred up the anger of the people, who punished Pericles with a large fine. He nevertheless won reelection as general in 429 BCE, only to succumb to disease later that year.

Pericles' Funeral Oration, given during the first year of hostilities, is related within Thucydides' account of the Peloponnesian War, which details a year-by-year history of the conflict between Athens and Sparta through 411 BCE. Very little information about the historian's life has survived from antiquity despite some biographical efforts, which tend to contradict each other or to proffer unsubstantiated reports. What can be gleaned with a certain amount of certainty are glimpses into Thucydides' life based on references to himself within the history. His father, Olorus, lived as a citizen of Athens, and Thucydides survived the devastating plague that struck the city in 429 BCE. In 424 BCE he served as a general in the defense of Amphipolis, a city on the northern coast of Greece, but his failure resulted in his exile for twenty years. Other trustworthy reports infer his age at around forty at the outbreak of the war in 432 BCE, placing his birth around 472 BCE. The date of his death is uncertain, but given statements about the eruption of Etna in 425 BCE and his lack of knowledge of a subsequent volcanic event in 396 BCE, historians assume that he died before that date. A belief that he suffered assassination persisted in antiquity,

Time Line

461 BCE
- Ephialtes' associate, Pericles, assumes leadership of like-minded companions, who use their influence and prestige to maintain a large degree of authority among the people.

460 BCE
- The emerging prominence and military power of Athens prompts a conflict that begins the First Peloponnesian War.

445 BCE
- The First Peloponnesian War ends with the Thirty Years' Peace, in which both sides agree not to initiate hostilities or engage in activities that threaten the hegemony of either side in the respective regions.

432 BCE
- The Megarian Decree imposes a series of trade embargoes against the city. The embargoes are perceived by the enemies of Athens as a violation of the Thirty Years' Peace, and proponents of war finally tip the balance in the assembly and declare war on Athens, starting the Great Peloponnesian War.

432 BCE

- **Autumn**
  After the withdrawal of the Spartan forces from Attica, Athenian troops raid the Megarid.

431 BCE

- **The Great Peloponnesian War begins.**

- **Summer**
  The Spartans invade Attica, ravaging the countryside and forcing the Athenians to retreat behind their walls; the Athenians initiate a series of naval raids on Peloponnesian coastal cities.

- **Winter**
  Pericles gives his Funeral Oration.

429 BCE

- Plague breaks out in Athens because of poor hygiene and living conditions.

- Pericles dies.

423 BCE

- The assembly exiles Thucydides after his failure to defend Amphipolis.

404 BCE

- The Great Peloponnesian War ends with the defeat of Athens and the dismantling of the Delian League.

explaining why his work abruptly breaks off and ends, but the details are not consistent; thus confirmation eludes modern historians.

Famous for his work *The History of the Peloponnesian War*, Thucydides stands along with the fifth-century BCE historian Herodotus as one of the fathers of history. Unlike his predecessor, whose work rambled and included a variety of traditions and legends, Thucydides is distinguished as being more technical. With an insistence on recording only those events that came from eyewitnesses, Thucydides established himself as a reliable source in antiquity. Despite some biases, a tendency to omit details unrelated to politics and military, and a few errors, the text survived as a trustworthy account of the events of Greece in the fifth century BCE.

Among the critiques about Thucydides is his treatment of speeches, which is germane to the contents of the Funeral Oration. Although he claimed to have begun compiling information from the beginning of the conflict, he acknowledged that he did not hear all of the speeches firsthand but received some from other sources. Indeed, he admitted that

> it was in all cases difficult to carry them word for word in one's memory, so my habit has been to make the speakers say what was in my opinion demanded of them by the various occasions, of course, adhering as closely as possible to the general sense of what they really said. (i.xxii.1)

Thus the style does belong to the author, but the essence of the oration seems to have been captured. Thucydides was probably an eyewitness of Pericles' delivery of the Funeral Oration, and given the speech's prominence within Athens, the community at large would not likely have accepted a fabrication of its contents.

Explanation and Analysis of the Document

The occasion for Pericles' speech centered on a ceremony that honored the dead over a three-day period. On the first day, the bodies were laid out on platforms where families could place personal objects to be buried with the dead. On the third day, the remains were placed in cypress coffins, one for each tribe, and carried to the cemetery in nearby Ceramicus. One coffin was left empty to signify those missing in action. Anyone could follow the processional, and after the burial a speech was given by a person of prominence selected by the people. Afterward the families collectively mourned before leaving for home. Later the names of the honored dead were engraved in stone in lists organized by tribe.

◆ Paragraph 1

Recognizing that not everyone in his audience supported him, Pericles opens his speech with rhetorical humility, commenting that the actions of the fallen speak for themselves, even if the speaker inadequately honors them. He

Fragment of a marble shield purporting to show Pericles, one foot placed on a fallen warrior and his raised arm obscuring his face (© The Trustees of the British Museum)

deflects potential criticism by saying that he cannot do justice to the soldiers because their deeds cannot be fully explained. Such an attempt would actually cheapen them, and some might perceive his efforts as exaggeration for the sake of a good speech. Nevertheless, since the speech is part of the ritual, he is compelled by law to speak.

◆ Paragraph 2

To justify the sacrifice of the fallen, Pericles had to focus on the cause for which they fought: Athens, which had been handed down to them by their ancestors. He does not attempt, however, simply to extol the city's past greatness but also to emphasize to his audience the present magnificence of their city. He sought to win the crowd to him by indicating that Athens stood in glory because of those who stood before him. He creates a unifying image by forging a link between the heroes of antiquity and those

contemporary "heroes." He indicates that the greatness in which they participated resulted from the democracy that reigned within the political system.

Behind Pericles' words one can see an effort to defend his policies by creating the idea that heroic greatness is not something past but that it exists as an ongoing process maintained by the continued involvement of the people. Involvement could be brought about only by a system that did not allow just the aristocracy to rule, as in the past, but that opened opportunities for all to speak out and let their voices be heard in the decision-making process. Pericles wanted his audience to consider themselves great and at the same time to associate their success with democracy.

◆ Paragraph 3

In the face of those who might want to criticize the democratic government, Pericles emphasizes the unique-

View of the Acropolis, rebuilt under the leadership of Pericles

(Alison Frantz Photographic Collection, American School of Classical Studies at Athens)

ness of a political system that promoted legal and social equality, in turn creating freedom. He stresses, however, that those freedoms did not encourage lawlessness, as some had suggested, but instead had created a sense of responsibility to respect others and to safeguard one's own reputation. Behind his qualifications one senses an effort to refute the charges of aristocrats who resisted the idea that an uneducated and common worker could maintain any self-control without strict laws. Athenian law had originated with Draco (seventh century BCE), an aristocrat whose strict laws kept the lower classes in line. Even when Solon the Idealist (ca. 630 BCE–ca. 560 BCE) reformed the legal code, an attitude persisted that only those of class could properly control the unruly masses. Pericles attempted to undermine that same attitude with his words.

◆ **Paragraph 4**

Pericles briefly wraps up his point by defining those freedoms, for example, not as a mindless pursuit of pleasure but as a means that brought forth more opportunities

for all. In times past only the rich enjoyed luxury goods, but the maritime trade had created circumstances to allow the influx of goods that enabled more people to enjoy the bounty of wealth.

◆ **Paragraph 5**

In the next paragraph Pericles moves from simply defending democracy to contrasting the Athenian system with the "antagonist." This reference to Sparta, left unspoken, perhaps in an effort to address pro-Spartan elements in the city, becomes more explicit. Pericles' audience would have been familiar with the Spartan custom of keeping outsiders at bay to prevent contamination of their social system. Pericles emphasizes their open society that allowed any to come and prosper (even if noncitizens could not earn political rights). Further, the Athenians would have recognized an implicit reference to Sparta's rigid hierarchy, which produced specific roles for each citizen within the state. Those who did not enjoy citizenship, such as the helots, existed as exploited slaves. This system had created a society of soldiers, renowned for their martial prowess, but in spite of their famed military, Pericles declares, Spartans needed allies to accomplish the invasion of Athenian territory. In contrast, Athens stood alone, dependent on its own resources, which as of yet had not been fully mobilized. Thus, he stresses, they had met with success in battle, and those setbacks that they faced were of little consequence.

♦ **Paragraph 6**
Against charges that Athenians were weak and soft (once again in contrast to Spartan strength), their citizenship had demonstrated instead that their wealth and educational system had created a unique strength and hardness. The industrious nature of the Athenians had resulted from their democratic system, which allowed all to labor and to benefit. (Spartans had slaves.) Furthermore, Athenians needed to be active and strong as they all made decisions in the assembly, once again in contrast to Spartans, who merely acquiesced to the decisions of their elders in council. Pericles idealizes Athenian courage and generosity toward helping other city-states find democracy and success. Ironically, on occasion Athens had imposed democratic governments on other states, and their "assistance" to the Delian League resulted in imperialism.

♦ **Paragraph 7**
Given all of these strengths, Pericles declares that Athens shined like a beacon and a model to others. Once again, in contrast with others, they had no need for a Homer (ninth–eighth century BCE) to proclaim their great deeds in epic poetry. Instead, Athens demonstrated its greatness through its acts and the fact that it had grown into a mighty power—a power that compelled the honored dead to sacrifice their lives and called for the living to continue in personal sacrifice.

♦ **Paragraph 8**
Pericles finally brings the focus of his speech to the celebrated dead. He indicates that their true monument was not the one erected in stone but the continued greatness of Athens, which had spawned great men whose merit rested on the fact that they were ready to die for the city. They had not been driven by fear or personal ambition, but they risked all to wreak vengeance on those who threatened their freedoms, a cause for which they felt honored to die. Once again the unspoken slight at Sparta, which fought simply to fight, was clear.

♦ **Paragraph 9**
Thus in Pericles' mind, if these men held a willingness to sacrifice, then the survivors should resolve also to defend Athens. They could not afford a lack of unity within the community. By contrasting words and actions, he hoped to shame his detractors by forcing them to participate, not just for patriotic reasons but also for Athens's continued greatness. To pursue other agendas would diminish those who had perished in the cause. They had built the city with their courage, duty, and honor, offering them-

selves as a sacrifice to the greater good. They would not be contained by a simple tomb but would create a reputation that would fill the earth.

♦ **Paragraph 10**
Finally, Pericles attempts to comfort the bereaved by reminding them that of the multiple dangers in life that can lead to death, dying for one's country is the best possible cause. He deems it better to have lost their loved ones for a great and noble cause than through a meaningless or random accident. Although he knew their loss would stay with them, he encourages them to start new families, who would grow to be noble Athenians. For those incapable of having more children, he assures them that they can rest in the eternal fame won by the sacrifice of their sons.

♦ **Paragraph 11**
To the sons and brothers, Pericles issues a subtle challenge not to become lost in the shadow of the greatness of their deceased relatives. By indicating that others would forever compare their actions with the deeds of those who sacrificed, he hoped to instill within them a determination to continue to serve and to fight. His comments to the widows reflected a typical Greek belief that the gods had created women to be good wives and mothers. Being, in their minds, weaker by nature, women fulfilled a role that kept them in secluded domestic situations. Thus while men had freedom to enjoy social and sexual pursuits, a good woman had to remain at home. Pericles expresses his hope that these widows would continue such lifestyles, so as not to be gossiped about in public.

♦ **Paragraph 12**
Pericles concludes the speech with a humble allusion that his words, though some might consider them inadequate, fulfilled the law. He challenges potential detractors, arguing that these men deserved the honors they had received. To encourage others not to lose heart in the struggle, he promises the ongoing reward that the children of those who lost their lives in the war would receive state support until grown. Beyond financial rewards, however, Athenians should look for the greater benefits of being honorable citizens who defend the glory of democratic Athens.

Audience

On the surface Pericles addressed his words to the families of those who had lost loved ones. However, given the direction of his speech, to defend democracy and to elevate the city itself, he also spoke to those in the audience who opposed him. The leadership of the pro-Spartan party in Athens had faced setbacks when their main voice, Cimon, was exiled after being rebuffed by the Spartans in the attempt to suppress their helot rebellion. They also complained about the loss of their property because of a policy that they felt had recklessly pushed Athens into a needless war with the Peloponnesians. The existence of aristocrats who rejected democ-

> *"Our constitution does not copy the laws of neighboring states; we are rather a pattern to others than imitators ourselves. Its administration favors the many instead of the few; this is why it is called a democracy."*
>
> (Paragraph 3)

> *"We throw open our city to the world, and never by alien acts exclude foreigners from any opportunity of learning or observing."*
>
> (Paragraph 5)

> *"Again, in our enterprises we present the singular spectacle of daring and deliberation, each carried to its highest point, and both united in the same persons; although with the rest of mankind decision is the fruit of ignorance, hesitation of reflection."*
>
> (Paragraph 7)

> *"Far from needing a Homer for our eulogist, or other of his craft whose verses might charm for the moment only for the impression which they gave to melt at the touch of fact, we have forced every sea and land to be the highway of our daring, and everywhere, whether for evil or for good, have left imperishable monuments behind us."*
>
> (Paragraph 8)

> *"For heroes have the whole earth for their tomb."*
>
> (Paragraph 10)

racy also threatened Pericles' position. Criticism of democracy is expressed even among the philosophical writings that emerged after the war, such as those of Plato and Aristotle, both of whom were writing in the fourth century BCE. In fact, in the immediate aftermath, Sparta helped to install an aristocratic government that sought to purge democratic ideas. Known as the Thirty Tyrants, they quickly alienated the population and in turn were overthrown themselves.

Impact

Plutarch, in his biography *Pericles*, written in about 75 CE, indicates that when Pericles concluded the speech, the women sought to touch his hands and to give him crowns of leaves to honor him, in the same way that they would have rewarded a victorious Olympic athlete. For the most part, Pericles maintained his position, and the Athenians continued with the war. His opponents waited in the wings, however. On the day of the speech, some mocked his successes against Athenian allies (Sparta) instead of Persians, whom many considered the true enemy of Greece.

The Funeral Oration of Pericles took on a greater role in modern times. As an idealized paean to democracy, it was used by nineteenth-century Europeans as a fitting defense of growing liberal democracy. The discovery of Greek and Roman antiquities encouraged scholars to go in search of historical roots to explain why industrial Europe had emerged as a dominant global force. Finding a kindred spirit in Athenian democracy, British and American political philosophers elevated Pericles' speech to a defense of their own system. Just as Pericles glorified democracy, so also did his modern counterparts utilize the Funeral Oration to remind citizens that freedom and equality are still privileges worth any sacrifice, including death.

Further Reading

■ Books

Kagan, Donald. *Pericles of Athens and the Birth of Democracy*. New York: Free Press, 1991.

———. *The Archidamian War*. Ithaca, N.Y.: Cornell University Press, 1996.

Meier, Christian. *Athens: A Portrait of the City in Its Golden Age*. New York: Metropolitan Books, 1998.

Ober, Josiah. *Political Dissent in Democratic Athens*. Princeton, N.J.: Princeton University Press, 1998.

Plutarch. *Pericles*. In *Plutarch's Lives: Pericles and Fabius Maximus; Nicias and Crassus*, trans. Bernadotte Perrin. Cambridge, Mass.: Harvard University Press, 1916.

Thucydides. *History of the Peloponnesian War*, trans. C. F. Smith. Cambridge, Mass.: Harvard University Press, 1921.

Xenophon. *Constitution of Athens*. In *Xenophon: Scripta Minora*, trans. E. C. Marchant and G. W. Bowersock. Cambridge, Mass.: Harvard University Press, 1925.

—Todd W. Ewing

Questions for Further Study

1. The Great Peloponnesian War, which erupted in the same year Pericles gave his funeral oration, was a war that probably need not have occurred, given that Athens and Sparta had earlier been allies. What circumstances led to war between the two city-states? In particular, what role did *defensive* (as opposed to offensive) maneuvering by these city-states precipitate warfare?

2. Imagine a debate that examines the following statement: Pericles' funeral oration was a work of propaganda. What would be the pros and cons in such a debate?

3. Pericles places considerable emphasis on the development of democratic institutions and practices in Athens and on this basis draws contrasts between Athens and the more authoritarian, militaristic city-state of Sparta. To what extent does the view that democracy should be spread prefigure motivations for warfare in the twentieth and twenty-first centuries?

4. Describe the role that domestic politics played in the structure and content of Pericles' oration.

5. What comfort does Pericles offer to the families of those slain in battle? To what extent do modern politicians offer similar comfort to the families and loved ones of those who fall in war?

FUNERAL ORATION OF PERICLES

Most of my predecessors in this place have commended him who made this speech part of the law, telling us that it is well that it should be delivered at the burial of those who fall in battle. For myself, I should have thought that the worth which had displayed itself in deeds would be sufficiently rewarded by honors also shown by deeds; such as you now see in this funeral prepared at the people's cost. And I could have wished that the reputations of many brave men were not to be imperiled in the mouth of a single individual, to stand or fall according as he spoke well or ill. For it is hard to speak properly upon a subject where it is even difficult to convince your hearers that you are speaking the truth. On the one hand, the friend who is familiar with every fact of the story may think that some point has not been set forth with that fullness which he wishes and knows it to deserve; on the other, he who is a stranger to the matter may be led by envy to suspect exaggeration if he hears anything above his own nature. For men can endure to hear others praised only so long as they can severally persuade themselves of their own ability to equal the actions recounted: when this point is passed, envy comes in and with it incredulity. However, since our ancestors have stamped this custom with their approval, it becomes my duty to obey the law and to try to satisfy your several wishes and opinions as best I may.

I shall begin with our ancestors: it is both just and proper that they should have the honor of the first mention on an occasion like the present. They dwelt in the country without break in the succession from generation to generation, and handed it down free to the present time by their valor. And if our more remote ancestors deserve praise, much more do our own fathers, who added to their inheritance the empire which we now possess, and spared no pains to be able to leave their acquisitions to us of the present generation. Lastly, there are few parts of our dominions that have not been augmented by those of us here, who are still more or less in the vigor of life; while the mother country has been furnished by us with everything that can enable her to depend on her own resources whether for war or for peace. That part of our history which tells of the military achievements which gave us our several possessions, or of the ready valor with which either we or our fathers stemmed the tide of Hellenic or foreign aggression, is a theme too familiar to my hearers for me to dwell upon, and I shall therefore pass it by. But what was the road by which we reached our position, what the form of government under which our greatness grew, what the national habits out of which it sprang; these are questions which I may try to solve before I proceed to my eulogy upon these men; since I think this to be a subject upon which on the present occasion a speaker may properly dwell, and to which the whole assemblage, whether citizens or foreigners, may listen with advantage.

Our constitution does not copy the laws of neighboring states; we are rather a pattern to others than imitators ourselves. Its administration favors the many instead of the few; this is why it is called a democracy. If we look to the laws, they afford equal justice to all in their private differences; if to social standing, advancement in public life falls to reputation for capacity, class considerations not being allowed to interfere with merit; nor again does poverty bar the way, if a man is able to serve the state, he is not hindered by the obscurity of his condition. The freedom which we enjoy in our government extends also to our ordinary life. There, far from exercising a jealous surveillance over each other, we do not feel called upon to be angry with our neighbor for doing what he likes, or even to indulge in those injurious looks which cannot fail to be offensive, although they inflict no real harm. But all this ease in our private relations does not make us lawless as citizens. Against this fear is our chief safeguard, teaching us to obey the magistrates and the laws, particularly such as regard the protection of the injured, whether they are actually on the statute book, or belong to that code which, although unwritten, yet cannot be broken without acknowledged disgrace.

Further, we provide plenty of means for the mind to refresh itself from business. We celebrate games and sacrifices all the year round, and the elegance of our private establishments forms a daily source of pleasure and helps to distract us from what causes us distress; while the magnitude of our city draws the produce of the world into our harbor, so that to the Athenian the fruits of other countries are as familiar a luxury as those of his own.

If we turn to our military policy, there also we differ from our antagonists. We throw open our city to the world, and never by alien acts exclude foreigners from any opportunity of learning or observing, although the eyes of an enemy may occasionally profit by our liberality; trusting less in system and policy than to the native spirit of our citizens; while in education, where our rivals from their very cradles by a painful discipline seek after manliness, at Athens we live exactly as we please, and yet are just as ready to encounter every legitimate danger. In proof of this it may be noticed that the Spartans do not invade our country alone, but bring with them all their confederates; while we Athenians advance unsupported into the territory of a neighbor, and fighting upon a foreign soil usually vanquish with ease men who are defending their homes. Our united force was never yet encountered by any enemy, because we have at once to attend to our marine and to dispatch our citizens by land upon a hundred different services; so that, wherever they engage with some such fraction of our strength, a success against a detachment is magnified into a victory over the nation, and a defeat into a reverse suffered at the hands of our entire people. And yet if with habits not of labor but of case, and courage not of art but of nature, we are still willing to encounter danger, we have the double advantage of not suffering hardships before we need to, and of facing them in the hour of need as fearlessly as those who are never free from them.

Nor are these the only points in which our city is worthy of admiration.

We cultivate refinement without extravagance and knowledge without effeminacy; wealth we employ more for use than for show, and place the real disgrace of poverty not in owning to the fact but in declining the struggle against it. Our public men have, besides politics, their private affairs to attend to, and our ordinary citizens, though occupied with the pursuits of industry, are still fair judges of public matters; for, unlike any other nation, we regard the citizen who takes no part in these duties not as unambitious but as useless, and we are able to judge proposals even if we cannot originate them; instead of looking on discussion as a stumbling-block in the way of action, we think it an indispensable preliminary to any wise action at all. Again, in our enterprises we present the singular spectacle of daring and deliberation, each carried to its highest point, and both united in the same persons; although with the rest of mankind decision is the fruit of ignorance, hesitation of reflection. But the prize for courage will

surely be awarded most justly to those who best know the difference between hardship and pleasure and yet are never tempted to shrink from danger. In generosity we are equally singular, acquiring our friends by conferring not by receiving favors. Yet, of course, the doer of the favor is the firmer friend of the two, in order by continued kindness to keep the recipient in his debt; while the debtor feels less keenly from the very consciousness that the return he makes will be a payment, not a free gift. And it is only the Athenians who, fearless of consequences, confer their benefits not from calculations of expediency, but in the confidence of liberality.

In short, I say that as a city we are the school of Hellas; while I doubt if the world can produce a man, who where he has only himself to depend upon, is equal to so many emergencies, and graced by so happy a versatility as the Athenian. And that this is no mere boast thrown out for the occasion, but plain matter of fact, is proved by the power of the state acquired by these habits. For Athens alone of her contemporaries is found when tested to be greater than her reputation, and alone gives no occasion to her assailants to blush at the antagonist by whom they have been worsted, or to her subjects to question her title to rule by merit. Rather, the admiration of the present and succeeding ages will be ours, since we have not left our power without witness, but have shown it by mighty proofs; and far from needing a Homer for our eulogist, or other of his craft whose verses might charm for the moment only for the impression which they gave to melt at the touch of fact, we have forced every sea and land to be the highway of our daring, and everywhere, whether for evil or for good, have left imperishable monuments behind us. Such is the Athens for which these men, in the assertion of their resolve not to lose her, nobly fought and died; and well may every one of their survivors be ready to suffer in her cause.

Indeed if I have dwelt at some length upon the character of our country, it has been to show that our stake in the struggle is not the same as theirs who have no such blessings to lose, and also that the eulogy of the men over whom I am now speaking might be by definite proofs established. That eulogy is now in a great measure complete; for the Athens that I have celebrated is only what the heroism of these and their like have made her, men whose fame, unlike that of most Hellenes, will be found to be no greater than what they deserve. And if a test of worth be wanted, it is to be found in their closing scene, and this not only in the cases in which it set the final seal upon their merit, but also in those in which it gave the first intimation of their having any. For there is justice in the claim that steadfastness in his country's battles should be as a cloak to cover a man's other imperfections; since the good action has blotted out the bad, and his merit as a citizen more than outweighed his demerits as an individual. But none of these allowed either wealth with its prospect of future enjoyment to unnerve his spirit, or poverty with its hope of a day of freedom and riches to tempt him to shrink from danger. No, holding that vengeance upon their enemies was more to be desired than any personal blessings, and reckoning this to be the most glorious of hazards, they joyfully determined to accept the risk, to make sure of their vengeance and to let their wishes wait; and while committing to hope the uncertainty of final success, in the business before them they thought fit to act boldly and trust in themselves. Thus choosing to die resisting, rather than to live submitting, they fled only from dishonor, but met danger face to face, and after one brief moment, while at the summit of their fortune, left behind them not their fear, but their glory.

So died these men as became Athenians. You, their survivors, must determine to have as unaltering a resolution in the field, though you may pray that it may have a happier outcome. And not contented with ideas derived only from words of the advantages which are bound up with the defense of your country, though these would furnish a valuable text to a speaker even before an audience so alive to them as the present, you must yourselves realize the power of Athens, and feed your eyes upon her from day to day, till love of her fills your hearts; and then when all her greatness shall break upon you, you must reflect that it was by courage, sense of duty, and a keen feeling of honor in action that men were enabled to win all this, and that no personal failure in an enterprise could make them consent to deprive their country of their valor, but they laid it at her feet as the most glorious contribution that they could offer. For this offering of their lives, made in common by them all, they each of them individually received that renown which never grows old, and for a tomb, not so much that in which their bones have been deposited, but that noblest of shrines wherein their glory is laid up to be eternally remembered upon every occasion on which deed or story shall be commemorated. For heroes have the whole earth for their tomb; and in lands far from their own, where the column with its epitaph declares it, there is enshrined in every breast a record unwritten with no monument to preserve it,

except that of the heart. These take as your model, and judging happiness to be the fruit of freedom and freedom of valor, never decline the dangers of war. For it is not the miserable that would most justly be unsparing of their lives; these have nothing to hope for: it is rather they to whom continued life may bring reverses as yet unknown, and to whom a fall, if it came, would be most tremendous in its consequences. And surely, to a man of spirit, the degradation of cowardice must be immeasurably more grievous than the unfelt death which strikes him in the midst of his strength and patriotism!

Comfort, therefore, not condolence, is what I have to offer to the parents of the dead who may be here. Numberless are the chances to which, as they know, the life of man is subject; but fortunate indeed are they who draw for their lot a death so glorious as that which has caused your mourning, and to whom life has been so exactly measured as to terminate in the happiness in which it has been passed. Still I know that this is a hard saying, especially when you will constantly be reminded by seeing in the homes of others blessings of which once you also enjoyed; for grief is felt not so much for the want of what we have never known as for the loss of that to which we have been long accustomed. Yet you who are still of an age to beget children must bear up in the hope of having others in their stead; not only will they help you to forget those whom you have lost, bur will be to the state at once a reinforcement and a security; for never can a fair or just policy be expected of the citizen who does not, like his fellows, bring to the decision the interests and apprehensions of a father. While those of you who have passed your prime must congratulate yourselves with the thought that the best part of your life was fortunate, and that the brief span that remains will be cheered by the fame of the departed. For it is only the love of honor that never grows old; and honor it is, not gain, as some would have it, that rejoices the heart of age and helplessness.

Turning to the sons or brothers of the dead, I see an arduous struggle before you. When a man is gone, all are wont to praise him, and should your merit be ever so transcendent, you will still find it difficult not merely to overtake, but even to approach their renown. The living have envy to contend with, while those who are no longer in our path arc honored with a goodwill into which rivalry does not enter. On the other hand if I must say anything on the subject of female excellence to those of you who will now be in widowhood, it will be all comprised in this brief exhortation. Great will be your glory in not falling short of your natural character; and greatest will be hers who is least talked of among the men whether for good or for bad.

My task is now finished. I have performed it to the best of my ability, and in words, at least, the requirements of the law are now satisfied. If deeds be in question, those who are here interred have received part of their honors already, and for the rest, their children will be brought up till manhood at the public expense: the state thus offers a valuable prize, as the garland of victory in this race of valor, for the reward both of those who have fallen and their survivors. And where the rewards for merit are greatest, there are found the best citizens.

And now that you have brought to a close your lamentations for your relatives, you may depart.

Glossary

effeminacy	in the context of the times, refinement to the point of triviality
jealous surveillance over each other	mean-spirited spying on one's neighbors
my predecessors in this place	men who had delivered earlier annual funeral orations in Athens

PLATO'S "ALLEGORY OF THE CAVE"

"The State in which the rulers are most reluctant to govern is always the best and most quietly governed."

Overview

The "Allegory of the Cave" is in Book VII of Plato's most famous and influential philosophical dialogue, *The Republic*. Plato was a classical Greek philosopher and a citizen of the Greek city-state of Athens in the first half of the fourth century BCE—one of the most fervently intellectually creative periods in human history. The larger purpose of *The Republic* is to define justice and to argue that justice is more beneficial for both the individual and society than its opposite, injustice. The main speaker in the dialogue is Plato's mentor, Socrates. It is Socrates who uses the allegory of the cave to describe metaphorically the process of education, likening an uneducated person to a prisoner bound in a dim, firelit cave who, by making his way out of the cave, escapes his limited perception and learns to understand the truth about reality. The allegory also comments on the nature of human perception, cognition, the ultimate structure of reality, and even the ideal ordering of society. The "Allegory of the Cave" has had a profound and lasting impact on such fields as educational theory, philosophy, and political science, to name but a few.

Context

The "Allegory of the Cave" of Plato's *Republic* was written during a dynamic and important time in Greek political and cultural history as well as in Plato's own life. Plato wrote *The Republic*, along with his other middle dialogues, sometime between 380 and 360 BCE. By this time his mentor, Socrates, had been dead for at least nineteen years, and Plato had established his own school, the Academy (383 BCE), and had traveled over a large extent of the Mediterranean world, encountering the ideas of the Pythagoreans and various other philosophical schools.

Politically and militarily, Athens for most of Plato's life was in a state of turmoil and decline. Athenians had enjoyed wealth and influence following the Greco-Persian Wars (497–479 BCE) as heads of the Delian League, which was established in about 477 BCE, a half century before Plato's

birth. By Plato's twenties, Athens was at last defeated by Sparta in the Peloponnesian War (431–404 BCE). According to the terms of the peace, the Spartans replaced Athens' democracy with a pro-Spartan, oligarchic regime that came to be known as the Thirty Tyrants. Two of Plato's relatives on his mother's side, Critias and his uncle Charmides, served on this government, with Critias as one of its leaders. The rule of the Thirty Tyrants lasted for only about eight months, but it was severe and marked by excessive violence and intimidation, including confiscation of property, forced exiles, and the executions of perhaps as many as fifteen hundred citizens. Plato is critical of the tyrants in *The Seventh Letter*; however, there can be little doubt that he would have been unpopular among those who supported democracy and opposed the tyrants given his own politically conservative leanings and familial relation to Critias and Charmides.

When democracy was restored in 403 BCE, the Athenians effected some recovery. After the Corinthian War (395–387 BCE), the Athenians reestablished their navy and retook some of their possessions in the Aegean Sea. But the Spartans remained the dominant power in Greece until the rise of Thebes and its victory over Sparta at the Battle of Leuctra in 371 BCE, a battle that is roughly contemporary to Plato's composition of the "Allegory of the Cave."

About the Author

Plato (ca. 424–347 BCE) is part of a distinguished philosophical lineage that began with Socrates (ca. 469–399 BCE), his teacher, and proceeded to Aristotle (ca. 384–322 BCE), Plato's own student. Together these men formed much of the basis of scientific and philosophic thought in the West. Very little is known for certain about Plato. Most of his biographical sources from antiquity either disagree at crucial points, such as regarding his birth date, or are otherwise highly unreliable, written as they were several hundred years after Plato's death without contemporary critical assessment of their source material. Modern historians do, however, have one important primary document pertaining to Plato's journeys to Sicily (ca. 388–361 BCE), *The Seventh Letter*, which most scholars accept as factual though perhaps not written by Plato himself.

Time Line

CA. 469 BCE	■ Socrates is born.
440 BCE	■ Athens enjoys the midst of its golden age.
431 BCE	■ The Peloponnesian War begins.
CA. 424 BCE	■ Plato is born.
405 BCE	■ With the destruction of the Athenian navy at the Battle of Aegospotami, Sparta secures victory in the Peloponnesian War and gains a position of military dominance in the Greek world.
404 BCE	■ The eight-month rule of the Thirty Tyrants, an oligarchic regime installed in Athens by Sparta, begins.
399 BCE	■ Socrates is tried and convicted on charges of impiety and corrupting the youth; he is forced to commit suicide by drinking hemlock.
399–387 BCE	■ Plato writes his early dialogues, including *The Apology* and *Crito*.

Plato was born in about 424 BCE in Athens or on the island of Aegina. He was part of an old aristocratic family. According to tradition, his father, Ariston, could trace his ancestry back to the last of Athens' kings, Codrus, who ruled from about 1089 to 1069 BCE, while Plato's mother, Perictione, could trace her ancestry back to the legendary Athenian lawgiver and lyric poet Solon (ca. 638–558 BCE). Two of Plato's older brothers were Adeimantus and Glaucon, who figure prominently as interlocutors in *The Republic*, and an elder sister was Potone, whose son, Speusippus, took over as head of Plato's Academy after his death. No records indicate that Plato ever married or had any children.

Plato's most influential teacher was Socrates, who took ancient philosophical thought in an entirely new direction by shifting the focus away from natural science toward ethics. His influence on Plato is clear in the "Allegory of the Cave." Not only does Plato cast Socrates as the main speaker, but also he has Socrates relate the allegory in his typical style of questioning. According to tradition, after Socrates' execution in 399 BCE, Plato traveled widely around the Mediterranean world. In the midst of these travels, around 388 BCE, Plato went to the court of the tyrant Dionysius I in the western Greek city of Syracuse, on the island of Sicily. Here he befriended the tyrant's brother-in-law Dion, an enthusiastic supporter of Plato's philosophic and political ideals. Plato would return to Syracuse two more times within the next twenty-five years, in about 367 BCE and 363 BCE, while Dionysius I's son Dionysius II was ruling. Plato never succeeded, however, in what was in part his aim for these visits: to put into practice in Syracuse the ideals of government as espoused in *The Republic*.

Explanation and Analysis of the Document

The allegory is reported in Plato's *Republic* as a conversation between Plato's teacher, Socrates, and Plato's elder brother, Glaucon. The conversation, however, is fictionalized. Plato's dialogues are generally more like philosophical theme plays than courtroom transcripts of actual conversations. Yet the conversations are realistic in that they are by and large faithful to what a given character would have said in a given situation. Although scholars debate the extent to which the Socrates of Plato's dialogues corresponds to the historical Socrates, in the allegory at least Socrates uses what was likely his typical real-life style of argumentation, known as the elenchus. Socrates' elenchus is a method of argumentation that progresses through questions, somewhat akin to a modern-day lawyer's cross-examination of a witness. As Socrates speaks in the allegory, it is rare that he does not conclude his remarks in the form of a question.

It is essential to understand the concepts presented in the books of *The Republic* leading up to Book VII in order to grasp completely the "Allegory of the Cave." In *The Republic*'s opening books, Socrates has formulated two definitions of justice that inform each other: one for justice as it operates in society and the other for justice as it operates in the individual. In both cases, Socrates argues that justice is a sort of threefold harmony, a mutually beneficial ordering. In society this consists of a harmony between rulers, guardians (a sort of auxiliary military class), and workers, where each class, in effect, "minds its own business," performing the task it is most naturally suited for without meddling in the affairs of the others. In the individual there is a corresponding harmony between reason, emotion, and appetite, with reason ruling over the other elements of the mind.

Just prior to the "Allegory of the Cave," Socrates is considering, in Book VI, how the rulers of the ideal city, who should be philosophers and kings alike, are to be trained. He argues that the most important part of their education is to understand the Form of the Good, that is to say, the idea of goodness as it exists purely in an abstract sense, not merely as a descriptive term or mental category. Socrates defines the Form of the Good as that which causes everything that partakes in it to be beneficial and useful; naturally, such a Form is important to consider for the ruler of a perfectly just society. What exactly Socrates means by "Form" is not entirely clear. Consider the example of the Form of Roundness. There are many things that are round: tires, pizzas, hula hoops, coins, and so on. While all these round things are distinct and numerous, there is one thing—the Form of Roundness—that unites them. Indeed, Socrates goes so far to argue that the Forms exist beyond their specific manifestations in such things as pizzas and hula hoops and, in fact, cause these things to be round in the first place. Moreover, as can be demonstrated easily, the existence of the Forms is not dependent on the individual objects that partake in them. Indeed, it is quite the opposite. A round pizza can be eaten, yet Roundness still exists in many other things. In short, then, the Forms are abstract entities, grasped only by the mind, which give rise to everything else in reality.

In order to explain more clearly the Form of the Good, Socrates discusses it by way of analogy, comparing the sun to the Good. He compares the way in which the eye perceives sensible reality—physical objects—to the way the mind perceives intelligible reality—the Forms, the very ideas of "good," "just," "round," and so on. The analogy is fourfold: First, the eye can see physical objects because of the sun's light, just as Forms can be "seen" or are intelligible to the mind because of the "light" of the Good. Second, a physical object's qualities—for example, grass being the color green—cannot be perceived in the absence of the sun's light, just as the qualities that Forms have are unintelligible without the Good. Third, the sun is visible, just as the Good is intelligible. And, fourth, the sun causes physical objects to grow but does not grow itself, just as the Good generates the Forms but is itself not generated.

To further explain his analogy, Socrates proposes setting forth visible and intelligible reality on a "Divided Line." Along the visible portion of the line are objects—things like trees and statues—as well as images, or copies of objects—things like reflections and shadows. Visible reality is illuminated by the sun and can give the observer only a limited understanding of full reality. The best that visible reality

Time Line

387–384 BCE	▪ Plato visits Syracuse, on the island of Sicily, for the first time.
383 BCE	▪ Plato founds the Academy.
380–360 BCE	▪ Plato writes his middle dialogues, including *The Symposium* and *The Republic*, in which the "Allegory of the Cave" appears.
360–347 BCE	▪ Plato writes *The Seventh Letter* and his late dialogues, including the *Sophist* and *Laws*.
CA. **347** BCE	▪ Plato dies, and his nephew Speusippus becomes head of the Academy.

can offer someone is an opinion (perhaps faulty, as derived from perception), that is, something far short of actual knowledge as Plato defines it: an understanding not only that something is so but also *why* it is so. It is easy, after all, to mistake someone's face at a distance or to be fooled by an optical illusion. On the other hand, along the intelligible portion of the line, which is illuminated by the Good, actual knowledge is possible. In the intelligible realm reside things that the mind "sees" rather than things the body senses, objects of thought rather than physical objects. Here Plato locates concepts and the Forms themselves. Plato uses "concept" in a very limited sense to mean only mathematical and logical figures and ideas—things that help us gain access to and approximate the Forms themselves. An example would be the circle a student draws freehand in geometry class. He does not draw a perfect circle, of course, but by studying this circle, giving it abstract qualities that it does not possess (like perfect roundness) the student can gain insight into the nature of circles in general, that is, the Form of Circle. In this way,

Engraving of the cave of Plato (© The Trustees of the British Museum)

then, an analogy exists between the way in which we can learn about physical objects by seeing their shadows and reflections and the manner in which we can learn about the Forms by thinking about their "shadows and reflections," or concepts.

Several important conclusions can be drawn regarding how Plato's ideas about the nature of reality and knowledge, as represented in the Divided Line, inform the "Allegory of the Cave." First, the ways people interact with the visible and intelligible worlds are analogous but essentially different. Second, people "see" with both the eyes and the mind, but the clarity of the mind's eye is far greater than that of the physical eyes; the eyes can give perceptions of things, which yield opinions, but only the mind can give knowledge, which results when opinion can be rationally defended. Third, the visible world is one of becoming, subject to generation and corruption, but Forms simply always exist: They do not change, they do not come to be, and they cannot be destroyed.

◆ The Prisoners of the Cave

To begin the "Allegory of the Cave," Socrates asks Glaucon to imagine the state of people who are not educated, describing them as if they were chained in a dim, firelit cave in such a way that their eyes would be able to look only at the caves' walls. Onto these walls are cast images of imitations of actual things—statues of men and horses and the like—that have been paraded before the fire behind them.

Socrates seems to be drawing directly from the idea of the Divided Line. These prisoners have access only to the lowest part of the Divided Line: the images of imitations of actual things. Thus, the fire acts like the sun, illuminating objects—here, the statues—such that shadows are cast on the wall as images. The implication is that uneducated people have no ability to access ultimate intelligible reality and therefore cannot attain any real knowledge. Through their perception, they gain only vague impressions of things that are, in fact, false. Thus, with no knowledge of actual reality, including the Good (the sun), they are doomed to make poor decisions and pursue things that are ultimately neither useful nor beneficial.

◆ Cave Ascent—Enlightenment

Socrates explains that since the inhabitants of the cave do not converse with one another and have such limited perception, they would naturally assume that the shadows

Death of Socrates (AP/Wide World Photos)

before them are true reality. Socrates asks Glaucon to consider, then, what would happen if one of the prisoners were released from his bonds and compelled to stand up and look behind him. Socrates says that such a man would find this movement painful and would have difficulty seeing, owing to the brightness of the firelight before him. Although he would now have access to a truer version of reality, he would cling to what was familiar and would be extremely distressed and annoyed by such repositioning.

Socrates is commenting on the nature of perception and reality and the difficulty of education. People cling to that which is familiar to them. If they think they have already reached the truth, they are naturally prejudiced against new ideas, against any alternate versions of reality. While education is a means of teaching people how to see the world more clearly, the brilliance of the truth is such that it is not easy for the mind's eye to adjust. Education is uncomfortable; it is difficult. The way out of the cave is described by Socrates as "rugged" and "steep."

Socrates next describes the prisoner as confronted with the light of the sun. Here he is blinded further and so chooses to look toward that which is familiar. For example, instead of looking at the trees themselves, he gazes at their shadows. Finally, he is able to consider the sun itself in its "own proper place" and deduce it to be the reason why he can perceive everything in the first place. Thus, in terms of the Divided Line, the former prisoner is moving from the

perceptible world to the intelligible world. The sun seen by the prisoner corresponds to the Good of the Divided Line, while the tree and its shadow correspond to the Form and concept, respectively.

◆ **Cave Descent—The Paradox of Leadership**

In his newly enlightened state, the former prisoner would consider himself happy but would feel pity for those still inhabiting the cave. He would even possess a certain contempt for them and would have no interest in participating in their false reality. Socrates introduces a paradox of leadership, claiming that although someone who is enlightened would have no interest in ruling, such a person must do so, as he is the most fit for such service. Socrates draws an implicit analogy between ascending from and descending into the cave. Just as it is difficult and unpleasant to leave the cave to be educated, it is equally difficult and unpleasant to return again as an educator or ruler. Nonetheless, the prisoner has a duty to improve himself, while the philosopher has a duty to improve others. In this section, Plato's Socrates perfectly meshes the two overriding concerns of *The Republic*, those of creating the ideally ordered—that is, wholly just—individual and society. The key is education. Education orders the mind properly, making reason the ruler of the individual; in turn, educated individuals ought to serve as rulers of society as a whole. In the analogy between the just harmony of society and the just harmony of mind, the ruler corresponds to reason, which rules the mind, while the guardian and worker correspond to emotion and appetite, respectively.

Socrates imagines what would happen to the unbound prisoner should he return to the cave. As his eyes would not be adjusted to the dim light, he would have trouble seeing the images cast on the cave wall as clearly as the current prisoners could. He would therefore become a laughing-stock; the inhabitants of the cave would ridicule him, saying that his eyes had been corrupted by leaving the cave. They would mock the very idea of leaving the cave and would even threaten violence against anyone who would compel them to leave. Socrates reiterates how appealing it would be for an enlightened human being to spend all of his time in the world above and how absurd things like common law courts would seem to such a man, as they are controlled by those who have seen only false representations of the just, never the Form of justice itself.

In having Socrates discuss how violent the unenlightened masses' reaction would be to an enlightened man, Plato is likely alluding to Socrates' trial and death in 399 BCE. In his dialogues with other Athenians, Socrates roused their anger because he revealed the full depth of their ignorance, their pretenses to actual knowledge. While the men Socrates questioned would assume they had some definite knowledge, in testing their opinions Socrates would always find them to be contradictory or in some way incomplete, certainly far short of actual knowledge of the truth. Just as with the prisoners in the "Allegory of the Cave," many Athenians were unwilling to be disturbed from their mental slumber by Socrates, the self-described gadfly of Athens, and thus reacted violently to his attempts to enlighten them.

◆ The Nature of Knowledge and Education

Socrates reminds his listeners that with respect to darkness and light there are two kinds of blindness: that of moving from dark to light, such as in coming out of a window-less room at midday, and that of moving from light to dark, such as in going into a dark closet from a well-lit room. He argues, based on the natures of blindness, that the process of education must be considered in a novel way. Education has traditionally been understood as a process of putting knowledge into someone's mind, just as if someone could put sight into blind eyes. Socrates argues instead that education ought to be understood as a sort of conversion or turning. Just as sight is restored by turning toward the light, intelligence comes about by turning the mind toward a contemplation of the Good. Sight is a power that inherently exists in the eye; it simply must be directed away from shadows and toward the physical objects that are illuminated by the sun's light. In the same way, intelligence inherently exists in the mind; it only has to be directed away from mere perception and toward that which is illuminated by the Good (the Forms). Thus, just as an eye turned away from light is equivalent to blindness, a mind turned away from the Good is equivalent to ignorance. And just as clear sight is a result of the eye's being turned toward light, knowledge is a result of the mind's being turned toward the Good.

According to the "Allegory of the Cave," knowledge is not something that is added to the mind but something that the mind turns toward. By its very nature, the mind has the potential to seek true knowledge; the mind actualizes that potential in being directed toward its proper object, the Good, the source of all that is useful and beneficial. Men are trained to have sharp perception to satisfy desires that serve the body, for example, food and sex. Socrates argues, however, that through education, ideally in earliest childhood, people can learn to direct their will toward things that satisfy the mind instead, for instance, truth and knowledge.

◆ The Duty of Philosopher-Kings

Socrates next reiterates his argument that only those who have gazed upon the truth and the Good are fit to be rulers. Being unwilling to take on this duty, however, these men must be persuaded to go down again among the prisoners of the cave to share in their labors and honors. Society, Socrates argues, does not exist to serve any one person. Ideally, society operates as a harmonious or just whole in the best interest of all its members. Once one has struck a harmonious union in his own mind, with reason as ruler over the emotions and the appetite, it is that person's duty to descend once again into the cave, as painful as that may be, in order to benefit the rest of society. Socrates imagines how he could persuade those who are enlightened to fulfill their duty as rulers. He warns of the destructive nature of politics as it is practiced now, saying that if lovers of honor continue to act as rulers, no harmony or justice is possible.

It is interesting to note that history has no record that Plato himself took an active role in Athenian politics. Naturally, one could argue that he chose to fulfill his own duty to society by writing dialogues like *The Republic*. Perhaps Plato also feared that his life would be in danger if he participated in Athenian politics, especially given the trial and death of his mentor, Socrates. At any rate, in Plato's defense it is important to recognize his attempt at educating an actual philosopher-king in the person of Dionysius II, tyrant of Syracuse. The extreme instability of the Athenian political system during Plato's lifetime, not to mention its democratic structure, likely made the hope of a similar attempt in Athens impossible and unrealistic. Plato himself discusses his disillusionment with Athenian politics in *The Seventh Letter*.

Audience

The primary audience of the "Allegory of the Cave" was probably the members of Plato's Academy and, more broadly, the educated elite of Athens and the wider Greek world. Plato's ideas on politics and education as espoused in the allegory and throughout *The Republic* represent a thorough revision, arguably even an intended replacement, of the traditional form of Greek politics and education. While it would be a mistake to abstract the author's political philosophy directly from the pages of *The Republic*—it is a literary-philosophic work and one in which Plato himself never

"*The prison-house is the world of sight, the light of the fire is the sun, and you will not misapprehend me if you interpret the journey upwards to be the ascent of the soul into the intellectual world.*"

"*Whether true or false, my opinion is that in the world of knowledge the idea of good appears last of all, and is seen only with an effort; ... this is the power upon which he who would act rationally, either in public or private life must have his eye fixed.*"

"*The truth is that the State in which the rulers are most reluctant to govern is always the best and most quietly governed, and the State in which they are most eager, the worst.*"

speaks—it is clear that at least something of Plato's own philosophy can be derived from the words he puts into the mouth of Socrates. Moreover, Plato's work with Dionysius II seems to be evidence that he was interested in putting into practice some of the political ideals of *The Republic*.

As with all of Plato's work, the intended audience included his ideological opponents. The "Allegory of the Cave" and *The Republic* as a whole serve as a defense of the philosophical way of life, even an argument for its superiority over competing schools of thought. Indeed, the allegory goes so far as to suggest that society will never achieve justice until philosophers are kings and vice versa.

Given the low literacy rates in Plato's Greece and the limited nature of libraries and the book trade in general in that era, very few of Plato's contemporaries would have had direct access to the text of the "Allegory of the Cave." Nonetheless, Plato's work would have almost certainly been disseminated orally, if not to the broader public—there is little evidence that Plato engaged in this sort of activity, though it was common among his contemporaries—then at least in the Academy itself. There, perhaps, given Plato's valuation of the practice of philosophy through dialogue, the allegory may have been read aloud as a means to spur further philosophical debate.

Impact

It is difficult to overestimate the impact Plato's thought has had on the shape of the world throughout history. From devel-

oping nearly all branches of philosophy—ethics, aesthetics, ontology, epistemology—to influencing the shape of early Christian thought, Plato's ideas have left an indelible mark on humanity. As a literary, political, and philosophical work, *The Republic* is one of the foremost classics of the Western canon.

Plato's influence has been so vast perhaps because of the form in which he chose to present his ideas: the philosophical dialogue. Rather than spelling out a rigid set of doctrines, Plato instead presented his philosophy in the form of conversation, one dominated by questions. Thus, by its very design Plato's writing has promoted further dialogue—dialogue that has spanned more than two millennia and has involved many of the greatest minds in human history in analyzing, interpreting, and sometimes misunderstanding his ideas.

The field of political science is given its very foundations in Plato's *Republic* and the "Allegory of the Cave." America's Founding Fathers, for example, were deeply influenced by Plato's allegory in their creation of America's form of representative democracy, which gives a pronounced voice, wide suffrage, and liberal freedoms to its citizens but which puts political decisions largely in the hands of those presumed to have expert knowledge and an interest in pursuing the public good before their own interests. Modern writers and historians have criticized some of Plato's political views. In the twentieth century, I. F. Stone attacked Plato's antidemocratic sentiments, while Karl Popper argued that Plato's political views contributed to the rise of totalitarianism. Other writers, however, have vehemently defended Plato's politics, such as R. B. Levinson in his *Defense of Plato*.

All thinkers since Plato who have considered the nature of reality or the possibility of certain knowledge—even outspoken critics of Plato's thought like Martin Heidegger—have been influenced by the "Allegory of the Cave." Such thinkers have included those of the ancient philosophical schools of Skepticism and Stoicism as well as more modern philosophers such as René Descartes, Edmund Husserl, and Ludwig Wittgenstein. In the field of education, such modern theorists as John Dewey and Friedrich Froebel, like Plato, have viewed education from the perspective of its effects on both the individual and greater society.

Perhaps the greatest long-term impact of the "Allegory of the Cave" has been on religion, specifically the rise of Christianity. The allegory was a crucial document in the emergence of Neoplatonism, a recasting of Plato in the third century CE by Plotinus, who infused Plato's metaphysics with oriental mysticism. According to Neoplatonic thought, at the summit of existence stands the One—a version of Plato's Good—as the source of all things. The One is the source of reason, serves as the infinite storehouse of all ideas (Forms), and is inserted into every facet of reality. Early Christian thinkers, among them Clement of Alexandria, Origen, Augustine, and Anicius Boethius, identified the One with God and the Forms with God's ideas. The human soul, then, longing to be released from its corporeal prison—not unlike the prisoner who longs to escape from Plato's cave—seeks to commune with God in an elevated, ecstatic state. The soul is like an eye that can see only when it is illuminated by the light of God, just as the mind's eye in Plato gains true vision when illuminated by the Good. In Christianity, of course, God is a vastly more

personal force than is Plato's Good, yet it is clear why many early Christian thinkers would have adopted some aspects of Neoplatonic philosophy and would have seen in Plato a sort of kindred Christian spirit. And so the basic Platonic idea that behind the world of the body and the senses lies an underlying spiritual reality, deriving its being from the Good—identifiable with God—becomes crucial in later Christian orthodoxy.

For over two millennia Plato has served as an intellectual gadfly in the world of human ideas much as his mentor Socrates was the gadfly of Athens. The intellectual tradition in the West—even when it has differed from Plato's—remains profoundly indebted to his foundational concepts. There is no telling whether humankind's dialogue with Plato will ever come to an end.

Further Reading

■ **Articles**

Andrew, Edward. "Descent to the Cave." *Review of Politics* 45, no. 4 (October 1983): 510–535.

Ferguson, John. "Sun, Line, and Cave Again." *Classical Quarterly*, n.s., 13, no. 2 (November 1963): 188–193.

Havelock, Eric. "Plato's Politics and the American Constitution." *Harvard Studies in Classical Philology* 93 (1990): 1–24.

Malcolm, John. "The Cave Revisited." *Classical Quarterly*, new series, 31, no. 1 (May 1981): 60–68.

Questions for Further Study

1. In the field of education, many teachers make use of what is called the Socratic method. Based on what you know from the entry, how would you define the Socratic method of teaching, and why would many educators regard this as an effective way to teach?

2. Compare and contrast Plato's views of government with those of his student Aristotle as found in the entry Athenian Constitution.

3. What, according to Plato, is a "philosopher-king"? Why did Plato place so much emphasis on this vision of rulers? Do you think that modern presidents, prime ministers, and leaders of nations exhibit any of the characteristics of the philosopher-king, or does the modern dominance of television require leaders to project a different image? Explain.

4. Imagine that you have been asked to summarize Plato's "Allegory of the Cave" in a single sentence. Compose the sentence.

5. What events in ancient Greece in and around the time Plato wrote contributed to his views of government and thus contributed to the content of the "Allegory of the Cave"?

Raven, J. E. "Sun, Divided Line, and Cave." *Classical Quarterly*, new series, 3, nos. 1–2 (May 1953): 22–32.

■ **Books**

Annas, Julia. *An Introduction to Plato's* Republic. Oxford, U.K.: Clarendon Press, 1981.

Griswold, Charles L., Jr., ed. *Platonic Writings/Platonic Readings*. New York: Routledge, 1988.

Guthrie, W. K. C. *A History of Greek Philosophy*, vol. 3. Cambridge, U.K.: Cambridge University Press, 1969.

Jowett, B. *The Dialogues of Plato*, 5 vols. New York: Oxford University Press, 1892.

Levinson, R. B. *In Defense of Plato*. Cambridge, U.K.: Cambridge University Press, 1953.

Popper, Karl. *The Open Society and Its Enemies*, vol. 1. London: Routledge, 1945.

Reeve, C. D. C. *Philosopher-Kings: The Argument of Plato's* Republic. Indianapolis, Ind.: Hackett Publishing Company, 2006.

Stone, I. F. *The Trial of Socrates*. New York: Anchor Books, 1989.

White, Nicholas P. *A Companion to Plato's* Republic. Indianapolis, Ind.: Hackett Publishing Company, 1979.

■ **Web Sites**

Suzanne, Bernard. "Plato and His Dialogues." Plato and His Dialogues Web site.
http://plato-dialogues.org/plato.htm.

—Patrick G. Lake

PLATO'S "ALLEGORY OF THE CAVE"

Socrates-Glaucon

And now, I said, let me show in a figure [of speech] how far our nature is enlightened or unenlightened:—Behold! Human beings living in a underground den, which has a mouth open towards the light and reaching all along the den; here they have been from their childhood, and have their legs and necks chained so that they cannot move, and can only see before them, being prevented by the chains from turning round their heads. Above and behind them a fire is blazing at a distance, and between the fire and the prisoners there is a raised way; and you will see, if you look, a low wall built along the way, like the screen which marionette players have in front of them, over which they show the puppets.

I see.

And do you see, I said, men passing along the wall carrying all sorts of vessels, and statues and figures of animals made of wood and stone and various materials, which appear over the wall? Some of them are talking, others silent.

You have shown me a strange image, and they are strange prisoners.

Like ourselves, I replied; and they see only their own shadows, or the shadows of one another, which the fire throws on the opposite wall of the cave?

True, he said; how could they see anything but the shadows if they were never allowed to move their heads?

And of the objects which are being carried in like manner they would only see the shadows?

Yes, he said.

And if they were able to converse with one another, would they not suppose that they were naming what was actually before them?

Very true.

And suppose further that the prison had an echo which came from the other side, would they not be sure to fancy when one of the passers-by spoke that the voice which they heard came from the passing shadow?

No question, he replied.

To them, I said, the truth would be literally nothing but the shadows of the images.

That is certain.

And now look again, and see what will naturally follow if the prisoners are released and disabused of their error. At first, when any of them is liberated and compelled suddenly to stand up and turn his neck round and walk and look towards the light, he will suffer sharp pains; the glare will distress him, and he will be unable to see the realities of which in his former state he had seen the shadows; and then conceive someone saying to him, that what he saw before was an illusion, but that now, when he is approaching nearer to being and his eye is turned towards more real existence, he has a clearer vision, what will be his reply? And you may further imagine that his instructor is pointing to the objects as they pass and requiring him to name them,—will he not be perplexed? Will he not fancy that the shadows which he formerly saw are truer than the objects which are now shown to him?

Far truer.

And if he is compelled to look straight at the light, will he not have a pain in his eyes which will make him turn away to take refuge in the objects of vision which he can see, and which he will conceive to be in reality clearer than the things which are now being shown to him?

True, he said.

And suppose once more, that he is reluctantly dragged up a steep and rugged ascent, and held fast until he's forced into the presence of the sun himself, is he not likely to be pained and irritated? When he approaches the light his eyes will be dazzled, and he will not be able to see anything at all of what are now called realities.

Not all in a moment, he said.

He will require to grow accustomed to the sight of the upper world. And first he will see the shadows best, next the reflections of men and other objects in the water, and then the objects themselves; then he will gaze upon the light of the moon and the stars and the spangled heaven; and he will see the sky and the stars by night better than the sun or the light of the sun by day?

Certainly.

Last of all he will be able to see the sun, and not mere reflections of him in the water, but he will see him in his own proper place, and not in another; and he will contemplate him as he is.

Certainly.

He will then proceed to argue that this is he who gives the season and the years, and is the guardian of all that is in the visible world, and in a certain way the cause of all things which he and his fellows have been accustomed to behold?

Clearly, he said, he would first see the sun and then reason about him.

And when he remembered his old habitation, and the wisdom of the den and his fellow-prisoners, do you not suppose that he would felicitate himself on the change, and pity them?

Certainly, he would.

And if they were in the habit of conferring honors among themselves on those who were quickest to observe the passing shadows and to remark which of them went before, and which followed after, and which were together; and who were therefore best able to draw conclusions as to the future, do you think that he would care for such honors and glories, or envy the possessors of them? Would he not say with Homer, "Better to be the poor servant of a poor master," and to endure anything, rather than think as they do and live after their manner?

Yes, he said, I think that he would rather suffer anything than entertain these false notions and live in this miserable manner.

Imagine once more, I said, such an one coming suddenly out of the sun to be replaced in his old situation; would he not be certain to have his eyes full of darkness?

To be sure, he said.

And if there were a contest, and he had to compete in measuring the shadows with the prisoners who had never moved out of the den, while his sight was still weak, and before his eyes had become steady (and the time which would be needed to acquire this new habit of sight might be very considerable) would he not be ridiculous? Men would say of him that up he went and down he came without his eyes; and that it was better not even to think of ascending; and if any one tried to loose another and lead him up to the light, let them only catch the offender, and they would put him to death.

No question, he said.

This entire allegory, I said, you may now append, dear Glaucon, to the previous argument; the prison-house is the world of sight, the light of the fire is the sun, and you will not misapprehend me if you interpret the journey upwards to be the ascent of the soul into the intellectual world according to my poor belief, which, at your desire, I have expressed

whether rightly or wrongly God knows. But, whether true or false, my opinion is that in the world of knowledge the idea of good appears last of all, and is seen only with an effort; and, when seen, is also inferred to be the universal author of all things beautiful and right, parent of light and of the lord of light in this visible world, and the immediate source of reason and truth in the intellectual; and that this is the power upon which he who would act rationally, either in public or private life must have his eye fixed.

I agree, he said, as far as I am able to understand you.

Moreover, I said, you must not wonder that those who attain to this beatific vision are unwilling to descend to human affairs; for their souls are ever hastening into the upper world where they desire to dwell; which desire of theirs is very natural, if our allegory may be trusted.

Yes, very natural.

And is there anything surprising in one who passes from divine contemplations to the evil state of man, misbehaving himself in a ridiculous manner; if, while his eyes are blinking and before he has become accustomed to the surrounding darkness, he is compelled to fight in courts of law, or in other places, about the images or the shadows of images of justice, and is endeavoring to meet the conceptions of those who have never yet seen absolute justice?

Anything but surprising, he replied.

Anyone who has common sense will remember that the bewilderments of the eyes are of two kinds, and arise from two causes, either from coming out of the light or from going into the light, which is true of the mind's eye, quite as much as of the bodily eye; and he who remembers this when he sees any one whose vision is perplexed and weak, will not be too ready to laugh; he will first ask whether that soul of man has come out of the brighter light, and is unable to see because unaccustomed to the dark, or having turned from darkness to the day is dazzled by excess of light. And he will count the one happy in his condition and state of being, and he will pity the other; or, if he have a mind to laugh at the soul which comes from below into the light, there will be more reason in this than in the laugh which greets him who returns from above out of the light into the den.

That, he said, is a very just distinction.

But then, if I am right, certain professors of education must be wrong when they say that they can put a knowledge into the soul which was not there before, like sight into blind eyes.

They undoubtedly say this, he replied.

Whereas, our argument shows that the power and capacity of learning exists in the soul already; and that just as the eye was unable to turn from darkness to light without the whole body, so too the instrument of knowledge can only by the movement of the whole soul be turned from the world of becoming into that of being, and learn by degrees to endure the sight of being, and of the brightest and best of being, or in other words, of the good.

Very true.

And must there not be some art which will effect conversion in the easiest and quickest manner; not implanting the faculty of sight, for that exists already, but has been turned in the wrong direction, and is looking away from the truth?

Yes, he said, such an art may be presumed.

And whereas the other so-called virtues of the soul seem to be akin to bodily qualities, for even when they are not originally innate they can be implanted later by habit and exercise, the virtue of wisdom more than anything else contains a divine element which always remains, and by this conversion is rendered useful and profitable; or, on the other hand, hurtful and useless. Did you never observe the narrow intelligence flashing from the keen eye of a clever rogue—how eager he is, how clearly his paltry soul sees the way to his end; he is the reverse of blind, but his keen eyesight is forced into the service of evil, and he is mischievous in proportion to his cleverness.

Very true, he said.

But what if there had been a circumcision of such natures in the days of their youth; and they had been severed from those sensual pleasures, such as eating and drinking, which, like leaden weights, were attached to them at their birth, and which drag them down and turn the vision of their souls upon the things that are below—if, I say, they had been released from these impediments and turned in the opposite direction, the very same faculty in them would have seen the truth as keenly as they see what their eyes are turned to now.

Very likely.

Yes, I said; and there is another thing which is likely, or rather a necessary inference from what has preceded, that neither the uneducated and uninformed of the truth, nor yet those who never make an end of their education, will be able ministers of State; not the former, because they have no single aim of duty which is the rule of all their actions, private as well as public; nor the latter, because they

will not act at all except upon compulsion, fancying that they are already dwelling apart in the islands of the blest.

Very true, he replied.

Then, I said, the business of us who are the founders of the State will be to compel the best minds to attain that knowledge which we have already shown to be the greatest of all—they must continue to ascend until they arrive at the good; but when they have ascended and seen enough we must not allow them to do as they do now.

What do you mean?

I mean that they remain in the upper world: but this must not be allowed; they must be made to descend again among the prisoners in the den, and partake of their labors and honors, whether they are worth having or not.

But is not this unjust? he said; ought we to give them a worse life, when they might have a better?

You have again forgotten, my friend, I said, the intention of the legislator, who did not aim at making any one class in the State happy above the rest; the happiness was to be in the whole State, and he held the citizens together by persuasion and necessity, making them benefactors of the State, and therefore benefactors of one another; to this end he created them, not to please themselves, but to be his instruments in binding up the State.

True, he said, I had forgotten.

Observe, Glaucon, that there will be no injustice in compelling our philosophers to have a care and providence of others; we shall explain to them that in other States, men of their class are not obliged to share in the toils of politics: and this is reasonable, for they grow up at their own sweet will, and the government would rather not have them. Being self-taught, they cannot be expected to show any gratitude for a culture which they have never received. But we have brought you into the world to be rulers of the hive, kings of yourselves and of the other citizens, and have educated you far better and more perfectly than they have been educated, and you are better able to share in the double duty. Wherefore each of you, when his turn comes, must go down to the general underground abode, and get the habit of seeing in the dark. When you have acquired the habit, you will see ten thousand times better than the inhabitants of the den, and you will know what the several images are, and what they represent, because you have seen the beautiful and just and good in their truth. And thus our State which is also yours will be a reality, and not a dream only, and will be administered in a spirit unlike that of other States, in which men fight with one another about shadows only and are distracted in the struggle for power, which in their eyes is a great good. Whereas the truth is that the State in which the rulers are most reluctant to govern is always the best and most quietly governed, and the State in which they are most eager, the worst.

Quite true, he replied.

And will our pupils, when they hear this, refuse to take their turn at the toils of State, when they are allowed to spend the greater part of their time with one another in the heavenly light?

Impossible, he answered; for they are just men, and the commands which we impose upon them are just; there can be no doubt that every one of them will take office as a stern necessity, and not after the fashion of our present rulers of State.

CONSTITUTION OF SPARTA

"The license of the Lacedaemonian women defeats the intention of the Spartan constitution, and is adverse to the happiness of the state."

Overview

The constitution of Sparta was written in the middle to late seventh century BCE. No known copy of it remains, and there is debate about whether Lycurgus, its supposed creator, actually existed. What is known about the constitution comes from Aristotle's *Politics*, written probably in the 320s BCE. Many of the laws in the constitution deal with strengthening the Spartan military, so the document is critical to the formation of the elite fighting force that put Sparta on the map in the ancient world.

The constitution of Sparta is one of the earliest documents of its kind in the ancient world. If the dates of the ancient historians are trustworthy, the Spartan constitution predates that of Athens by 150 years. While the constitution established a mixed government that was occasionally monarchical, oligarchic, and even at some times tyrannical, it did stress democracy. All male citizens were allowed to participate in the Demos, the Spartan assembly, which gave them immense power. Sparta was the earliest known democracy, and its constitution was both imitated and improved upon by many societies, ranging from those in the ancient world to various others throughout Western civilization. As a democracy it was rather conservative by modern standards, but it provided a model nonetheless.

Context

Sparta was not always the fearsome military power that it was known to be in its later history. The Spartans suffered numerous defeats at the hands of their enemies. Nevertheless, the Spartans were intent on expanding their influence in the surrounding area. They invaded and subdued neighboring Messenia. Once the Messenians were defeated, they were incorporated into Sparta as slaves known as Helots. These slaves revolted around 670 BCE, which led to the Second Messenian War and the further subjugation of the citizens of Messenia to Sparta. Sparta's biggest enemy, however, was the neighboring city-state of Argos. It was the Spartan defeat at the hands of Argos at

Hysiae in 669 BCE that started the Spartans down the path of reform. Shortly after, Lycurgus was said to have made the reforms that make up the bulk of the new constitution of Sparta, or Great Rhetra, as it is often called. After the reforms of the new constitution, Sparta was strengthened militarily enough to challenge the power of Argos.

Spartan society was radically changed after the reforms of Lycurgus. One of the most sweeping changes was the land-redistribution program. This plan called for all citizens of Sparta to have an equal amount of property. While this system did not last long, Sparta was the only city-state in ancient Greece at the time to have such a program. Another major reform helped Sparta become a great military power. This was the creation of the *agoge*, an institution by which boys were taken from their homes when they were seven years old and not returned to society until they were thirty and had undergone intensive military training. This military training turned them into the most elite fighting force in the ancient world at that time, the hoplites. The hoplites, named for the shields they carried, were feared by everyone and helped Sparta maintain control over the area for years. It was necessary to have completed training at the *agoge* to become a citizen. Once a Spartan male was a citizen, he took part in the *phiditia*, or common mess, where citizens would gather to take part in a communal meal. This system helped strengthen the Spartan army and society as a whole by creating a sense of unity and brotherhood. All these reforms occurred after the Messenian Helots revolted in 670 BCE and after Sparta lost to Argos at Hysiae in 669 BCE. Had these two events not occurred, Lycurgus might not have been as inclined to reform Spartan society so radically.

About the Author

Lycurgus is credited with the creation of the constitution of Sparta. This was the first and foremost law that he put forth, but there is no surviving copy of this document. Lycurgus did not want the Spartans to have any written history, literature, or laws. The implication is that all Sparta's laws and customs were passed down orally from generation to generation. Like the constitution itself, not much is

| CA. 1000 BCE | ■ The region of Sparta is settled by the Dorians. |

| CA. 800 BCE | ■ Sparta expands its territory to include the town of Amyclae. The area consists of four towns of the surrounding area. |

| 735 BCE | ■ The Spartans invade neighboring Messenia, leading to the First Messenian War. |

| 715 BCE | ■ The First Messenian War ends with Sparta taking control of the area and enslaving the Messenians. |

| 670 BCE | ■ The Messenian Helots revolt, leading to the Second Messenian War. |

| 669 BCE | ■ In the Battle of Hysiae, Sparta is defeated by Argos, its traditional enemy. This defeat leads the Spartans to consider strengthening the military. |

| CA. 650 BCE | ■ Lycurgus brings about his reforms, as set forth in the new constitution of Sparta. |

known about Lycurgus. It is not even certain that he was a real historical figure, though many leading historians of the ancient world considered him to be responsible for creating the military and community reforms that transformed Sparta into the society it is famed for being. Most ancient historians date the figure of Lycurgus to the first half of the seventh century BCE and the constitution to about 650 BCE. Lycurgus is said to have received divine inspiration for the constitution at the Oracle of Apollo at Delphi, one of the most important oracles in ancient Greece. Despite the debate on whether he was a true historical figure, Lycurgus has a significant reputation as one of the earliest lawgivers of democracy. He is depicted on a marble bas-relief in the chamber of the U.S. House of Representatives as well as on the frieze on the south wall of the Supreme Court building.

Since there is no record of the constitution left by Lycurgus, other ancient sources provide information about the document—most often the *Politics* of Aristotle. Aristotle was born in 384 BCE in Stagira, Macedonia, the son of the physician to the royal court. He was bright, as evidenced by the fact that he went to study at Plato's Academy early in life. Plato was the world's greatest philosopher, and Aristotle was clearly influenced very strongly by the ideas of his teacher. Many of Aristotle's own works would reflect this influence as he often modified the arguments of Plato in them. Plato died in 348 or 347 BCE, and Aristotle left the Academy shortly after and went to Asia Minor, where he became the tutor to Hermias, the king of Assos. It is also around this time that he is thought to have become the tutor of the young Alexander of Macedon, later Alexander the Great.

It is believed that Aristotle taught Alexander not only the basics of ethics and politics but also philosophy. In later years when Aristotle published these works, which were only given to the brightest of students, Alexander wrote Aristotle a letter lamenting the fact that Aristotle had taken away one of his biggest advantages against lesser men by making these private thoughts known to the public. When Alexander became king, Aristotle left his court and moved back to Athens, where he founded his own school, the Lyceum. Aristotle taught in this school until 323 BCE, the year before he died. It was during his time teaching at the Lyceum that Aristotle wrote *Politics*. Aristotle had experience with many different types and forms of government, and he used this experience in writing about the advantages and disadvantages of all forms of government.

Explanation and Analysis of the Document

Aristotle's views of the various types of government in *Politics* is one of the earliest and most thorough and balanced accounts of politics in the entire history of political thought. He discusses a range of the functions of politics, from the origin and purpose of the state to why regimes are classified in a certain way and why they ultimately fail. In doing so, Aristotle provides a model for other civilizations to live by. His critique of the Spartan constitution (a constitution that was revered in its day as one of the best) shows others how to do better by showing them what not to do.

Book 2 of Aristotle's work focuses on the various constitutions of the ancient world, citing which ones are the best and the worst. Part 9 of Book 2 is about the Spartan constitution and is mostly a critique that lays out why this constitution is not ideal. Each of the ten paragraphs deals with a specific problem in the Spartan form of government. The Spartan constitution was clearly regarded in its time as one of the first forms of democracy, but Aristotle shows its failings in the hope that other societies will not make the same mistakes. Throughout, Aristotle refers to "the legislator." His reference is to Lycurgus.

◆ **Paragraph 1**

The first paragraph deals with the management of the "subject population," or slaves. It raises two issues by comparing the governments of Lacedaemon (the term used for "Sparta" by the ancient Greeks and more commonly spelled "Lakedaimon") and Crete. The first is whether a particular law in a constitution is good or bad when compared with the perfect state and whether the constitution or law is consistent with the character of the lawgiver. The second issue illustrates this point in reference to the Helots. Nearly 80 percent of the people in Sparta at any given time were part of the Helot class. The Helots could not own property or participate in the *agoge*; thus they were not eligible to become citizens. This fed a vicious cycle in Sparta in which slaves revolted and Sparta clamped down on them with new reforms, which in turn made the slaves more likely to revolt again. Aristotle also cites the example of the Penestae in Thessaly, a region in central Greece. The position of the Penestae was almost identical to that of the Spartan Helots.

As Aristotle points out, all of Lacedaemon's neighbors were their enemies, and so they were more apt to go to war with the Lacedaemons; the Cretans, in contrast, enjoyed a more peaceful existence because Crete's neighbors warred with one another and were unable to tap into the discontent of Crete's slaves for aid. Aristotle compares the situation in Sparta to that in Thessaly, where the slaves originally revolted while the Thessalians were at war. In Sparta, it did not seem to matter whether the Helots were treated well or badly; they tended to revolt against their masters in any case. If they were not kept in check, they would become insolent and think that they were equal to their masters. If they were treated harshly, they would begin to hate their masters and plot against them in rebellion. It becomes clear that the citizens of Sparta had not found the secret to managing their slaves.

◆ **Paragraph 2**

The second paragraph deals with the role of Spartan women, which Aristotle cites as a second flaw in Spartan governance. Women were revered in Sparta for their role in creating a military society. It was their job and duty to produce sons who could participate in the *agoge* and become strong soldiers for Sparta. Spartan women were thought to be tougher than other women and were heavily influenced by the

Time Line

556 BCE
- Chilon is first mentioned, the man considered to be the first great ephor (magistrate) of Sparta. He expanded the power of the ephorate to rival that of the kings.

507 BCE
- The reforms of Cleisthenes bring democracy to Athens nearly 150 years after the reforms attributed to Lycurgus did the same for Sparta.

CA. 320s BCE
- Aristotle writes *Politics*.

militaristic atmosphere of their society. When Sparta went to war, the women famously told their sons and husbands to come home either *with* their shields or *on* them—that is, they were to return victorious or die on the field of battle.

Aristotle, however, singles out the behavior of Spartan women as undermining the Spartan constitution and therefore the state's well-being. Women made up 50 percent of the population of Sparta; thus, when they behaved badly, the whole state was weakened. Spartan women lived licentiously, says Aristotle, which went against the steadfast endurance of the regime. Women, he thinks, had too much power. They were given the right to rule in many situations, and their men were inclined to care more about wealth than the good of the regime. Women had achieved this status in Sparta because the men were frequently off fighting wars against the Argives, the Arcadians, and the Messenians; thus, women had gained more power than they had in other ancient Greek city-states. Aristotle appears to make a glancing reference to homosexuality among Greek warriors, who spend more time with men than with women. He also alludes to the Greek god Ares, the god of war and violence, and to Aphrodite, the goddess of love and beauty. Sparta was a warlike society, and the women were "utterly useless," especially during Sparta's invasion by Thebes, and caused even more confusion for the Spartan soldiers than the Theban invaders did. Aristotle notes that Lycurgus tried to bring the women under the law, but they resisted, and he gave up trying. He cites this as a problem for

Lycurgus seen consigning his laws to the Laconians before his death (© Bettmann/CORBIS)

Sparta, because the disorder of the women weakened the constitution and fostered avarice.

◆ **Paragraph 3**

This paragraph also concerns the Spartan women, but more indirectly. According to Aristotle, it was because of the inability to rein in the women that greed was prevalent and land was concentrated in the hands of a few people in Sparta. Some citizens in the city-state had small property holdings, while others had rather large estates, raising the question of inequality. The inequality was made worse by laws concerning inheritance and dowries. Nearly 40 percent of the land in Sparta, Aristotle says, was owned by women as a result of the laws governing dowries and heiresses' ownership of land. Aristotle believes that it would have been better for Sparta to give no dowries at all or at the least make permissible dowries much smaller. As larger dowries became more common, the land was concentrated in the hands of fewer people. To be considered a "citizen" at the time, a person had to own land. If fewer people owned land, then fewer people could be considered citizens. The population of citizens, says Aristotle, had dwindled to a mere one thousand.

While the hoplite population was kept large, the lack of citizens led to the city's ruin as it was beaten in a single battle by its enemies. The fault was with the property laws. Property ownership equalization would have been the solution. The Spartans, in earlier times ("the days of the ancient kings"), had alleviated the problem by bringing in people from the outside, granting the rights of citizenship to "strangers," or foreigners. Such was no longer the case. Exacerbating the problem were the laws governing procreation. In an effort to swell population numbers, fathers of three sons were exempted from military service and fathers with four or more sons from all "burdens of the state." This did not help matters, because the land laws, coupled with the fact that people were encouraged to have large families, led many in Sparta to fall into poverty. Issues involving land ownership, dowries, and family size provide Aristotle with a clear example of how poorly conceived laws can lead to the weakening of a state, for the laws had unintended consequences.

◆ **Paragraph 4**

This paragraph discusses one of the most important institutions in the Spartan regime, the ephorate (called the "Ephoralty" in the document). In Sparta, five ephors were elected annually by the people, and every month they swore to uphold the rule of the two kings of Sparta. This was in direct contrast to how many of them actually operated. While the ephors held an immense amount of power, they were each elected for only one year. At the end of their one-year term, they could never run for reelection.

Aristotle, though, finds the institution defective. The ephors were chosen from the entire population, so poor men were eligible, and poor men were open to bribes. Such was the case when the ephors were bribed by the Andrians. According to Aristotle, the Andrians—the people of the island of Andros, one of many in the Greek archipelago—were almost able to bring about the complete ruin of Sparta by bribing the ephors, but historians remain uncertain about the specific events Aristotle is referencing. Many of the ephors tended to be tyrannical, even to the point of forcing the kings to do their bidding. Their usurpation of power had undermined the constitution and turned the regime away from the aristocracy, making it resemble a democracy—a form of government that Aristotle found inferior to oligarchy and monarchy, for it was government for and by the needy. Still, the ephors managed to hold together the state, in that all segments of society had a stake in the status quo. Aristotle supports the democratic eligibility of all people for the post of ephor but calls the manner in which they were elected "childish." Then, too, as ordinary men, he says, they should judge according to the law, but many tried to make judgments on their own, without reference to laws. These men did not live up to the spirit of the constitution because they cared too much for license and avarice. This type of lifestyle was in contrast to the strict military nature of the regime.

◆ **Paragraph 5**

This paragraph provides a critique of the Senate, or council of elders, and the many problems of this governing body in Sparta. This council of elders, or *gerousia*, consisted of twenty-eight men over the age of sixty. They were elected for life and were also usually members of one of the two royal houses of Sparta. The two kings of Sparta were part of this council, making a total of thirty members. Their main job was to discuss matters of state policy and then present alternative solutions to the Demos, or general assembly, for consideration and implementation.

Aristotle starts his critique on a positive note. He sees the senators as good men who were well trained in manly virtue, an obvious advantage to the state. Their election to a life term, however, was not beneficial to the state. These men were judges of important state matters, and as they grew older, they did not always act for the good of the regime. Certain members of the council were even accused of taking bribes and showing partiality in judgments. Moreover, they were irresponsible in many affairs of state and often controlled by the ephors. Aristotle contends that those vying to be elected should not canvass for the position; instead, the most worthy person should be appointed, whether or not he wanted the position. To campaign for office, citizens must be ambitious. But ambition, combined with avarice, could be the motives for crime and thus detrimental to Spartan society. Aristotle's comments on the inherent weaknesses of Sparta's council of elders illustrates well his belief that pure democracy is problematic and that governance was best placed in the hands of the most worthy citizens, as well as in those who have the means and leisure to cultivate virtue.

◆ **Paragraph 6**

This paragraph deals with the Spartan monarchy—an unusual monarchy, for there were two monarchs, with one king from each royal house in the city-state: the Agiad and Eurypontids families, which, according to tradition, were the descendants, respectively, of Eurysthenes and Procles, who in turn were the descendants of Heracles, the supposed conqueror of Sparta after the Trojan War. Again according to tradition, the Agiad family arrived in Sparta first and claimed the best land, making it the more important of the two dynastic lines. While Aristotle usually debates whether kings are beneficial or not and says here that he will take up the matter elsewhere, he states unequivocally that the kingship is not good in Sparta because the hereditary kings are usually unworthy of the position. They should be chosen with regard to their personal life and conduct, but they are not. Lycurgus did not think he could make them into good men, and he distrusted their supposed virtues. The dual kingship was ineffective, because the two kings could never agree, and the resulting tension was harmful to the overall government.

◆ **Paragraph 7**

This short paragraph concerns itself with the common mess at Sparta. The common mess, or *phiditia*, was an important aspect of Spartan society. It was through these common meals that solidarity was created, especially among the soldiers. Only those who had completed training in the *agoge* could participate in the common mess. The institution was not very well regulated in Sparta. If a person was not able to contribute to the expenses of the common mess or was caught stealing to gather funds for his contribution, he would be expelled from the mess and shamed for the rest of his life. Those expelled also lost their citizenship and often the property associated with that right. Aristotle says that the entertainment should have been paid at public expense, as in Crete. In Sparta the problem was that some were too poor to contribute. Those who could not contribute could not take part in the *phiditia*, and those who could not take part lost their citizenship. The *phiditia* was supposed to be a popular institution, but again Aristotle cites the laws governing the institution as poorly crafted, creating consequences that undermined the intention of the laws. The laws pertaining to the *phiditia* were examples of laws that had the effect of reducing the number of citizens, weakening the state.

◆ **Paragraph 8**

This short paragraph discusses the office of admirals in Sparta, though Aristotle is slightly vague. He appears to be

Ruins of Delphi (AP/Wide World Photos)

referring to the tradition in Sparta that military commanders, whether generals or naval admirals, held the position for life. Aristotle notes that this law had often been rightly condemned, for the kings were seen as perpetual generals and the office of admiral was nothing more than a third king. Again, for Aristotle, this institution was flawed, for it left men in power who might no longer have deserved it. Further, it diffused the power of the monarchy, for it placed too much power in the hands of a military class that might often have operated independently of the government. Accordingly, laws pertaining to admirals (and generals) were examples of laws that failed to define precisely the role in government of a class and to vest power in a stable, recognized government institution.

◆ **Paragraph 9**

Aristotle starts this paragraph with a criticism from Plato about Lycurgus's narrow view of virtue. The only virtue in Sparta was that exhibited by the soldiers, and this was a problem for society as a whole. When the Spartans were at war, all was well; when they were not at war, however, they tended to become idle and fall prey to too much leisure time. The state had nearly been ruined during times of peace because the Spartans did not know anything but war. Aristotle also faults them for believing that the goods acquired by virtue rather than vice were more important

than the actual virtue through which the goods were obtained. Aristotle was a firm believer in virtue for its own sake. The purpose of virtue was not to gain worldly advantage but to a lead a good life. It was an end in itself, not a means to an end. Thus, Aristotle finds purely military virtues such as courage in battle inadequate for a well-ordered state, for the state that is not at war becomes unable to exercise virtue.

◆ **Paragraphs 10 and 11**

The tenth paragraph deals with the finances of Sparta. The revenues of the city-state were poorly managed; there was no money in the treasury. The people of Sparta wanted to continue to wage war, but they did not want to pay the taxes required to win wars. One of the problems had to do with land ownership. Typically, in a monarchy land was held either by the king or in the name of the king. The land, then, became a source of income for the king, and that income, in the case of Sparta, could be used to finance wars. In Sparta, however, large landowners held land in their own names. Their financial affairs were independent of the king, and each landowner had little interest in the financial affairs of the others. Thus, no one in Sparta was keeping an eye on the public treasury. This state of affairs fostered greed, and by leaving the public treasury bare, it also fostered poverty. Again, these weak-

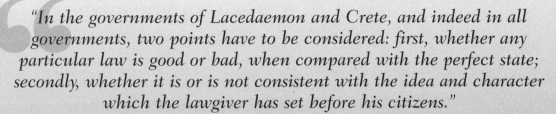

> "In the governments of Lacedaemon and Crete, and indeed in all governments, two points have to be considered: first, whether any particular law is good or bad, when compared with the perfect state; secondly, whether it is or is not consistent with the idea and character which the lawgiver has set before his citizens."

(Paragraph 1)

> "Again, the license of the Lacedaemonian women defeats the intention of the Spartan constitution, and is adverse to the happiness of the state."

(Paragraph 2)

> "The mention of avarice naturally suggests a criticism on the inequality of property. While some of the Spartan citizen[s] have quite small properties, others have very large ones; hence the land has passed into the hands of a few. And this is due also to faulty laws."

(Paragraph 3)

> "The Lacedaemonian constitution is defective in another point; I mean the Ephoralty. This magistracy has authority in the highest matters, but the Ephors are chosen from the whole people, and so the office is apt to fall into the hands of very poor men, who, being badly off, are open to bribes. There have been many examples at Sparta of this evil in former times."

(Paragraph 4)

nesses in the law and social structure undermined the state. Aristotle ends his discussion of the Spartans with one line, constituting an eleventh paragraph, saying that all he has discussed were the major defects of the Spartan constitution.

Audience

The audience of Lycurgus's reforms is the Spartan population itself. The people needed new laws, and this constitution gave it to them. It seems with a number of these reforms that Lycurgus is speaking to both the people in positions of power as well as those in the lower ranks. A number of the reforms were directed at strengthening the military and thus society as a whole in Sparta. Aristotle's

intended audience is a bit different, in that he is speaking to other societies and imploring them not to make the same mistakes as the Spartans when creating a constitution. Sparta was revered in its time as having an effective constitution, but Aristotle wants to show others that this may not have been the case in all matters.

Impact

The impact of the constitution of Sparta was felt almost immediately in the city-state. The military was significantly strengthened through the creation of the *agoge* and the common mess. The Spartan hoplites became the most elite fighting force in the ancient world. Sparta had already become the dominant power in the Peloponnesus as a result of the Second Messenian War. What followed were numerous military triumphs, the most famous of which was in the Battle of Thermopylae in 480 BCE, when a small force of Spartans made a heroic stand against a much larger Persian force. A year later Spartan military prowess was on display against the Persians in the Battle of Plataea. During the Peloponnesian Wars (431–404 BCE), Sparta developed a navy that rivaled that of its adversary, Athens. By the end of the fifth century BCE, Sparta was becoming the dominant power throughout the region, though its power began to wane later with the rise of Athens and the increasing number of Helot revolts. Under the constitution, commoners were given a large role in Sparta with the creation of the Damos (an assembly composed of free adult males, who in turn elected the council of elders) and the possibility of being elected to the ephorate. Land was redistributed so that all people, at least in theory, would have equal property rights and thus become equal citizens. This did not last long, but the idea was a radical one nevertheless. All in all, the Spartan constitution helped Sparta become the power that dominated the ancient world and the power that people still remember today.

While it was relatively conservative even by ancient standards, the Spartan constitution provided a model of democracy for others. It was considered one of the greatest forms of government of its day. The Spartan constitution was a model for Athens some 150 years later, when Cleisthenes took it upon himself to reform Athens, much as Lycurgus had done in Sparta. Athens had a council like that of Sparta's, called the boule. Cleisthenes introduced the reform of allowing the people to vote on certain issues and even vote for legislators. In other words, Sparta provided the model, which was then perfected by Athens, and it was from the Athenian constitution that modern democracies evolved.

Further Reading

▪ Articles

Dickens, Guy. "The Growth of Spartan Policy." *Journal of Hellenic Studies* 32 (1912): 1–42.

Hammond, N. G. L. "The Lycurgean Reform at Sparta." *Journal of Hellenic Studies* 70 (1950): 42–64.

Salmon, John. "Political Hoplites?" *Journal of Hellenic Studies* 97 (1977): 84–101.

Sihler, E. G. "Aristotle's Criticisms of the Spartan Government." *Classical Review* 7, no. 10 (December 1893): 439–443.

▪ Books

Cartledge, Paul. *The Spartans: The World of the Warrior-Heroes of Ancient Greece, from Utopia to Crisis and Collapse.* Woodstock, N.Y.: The Overlook Press, 2003.

Forrest, W. G. *The Emergence of Greek Democracy: The Character of Greek Politics, 800–400 B.C.* London: Weidenfeld & Nicolson, 1966.

Huxley, George Leonard. *Early Sparta.* New York: Barnes & Noble, 1970.

Powell, Anton, and Stephen Hodkinson. *The Shadow of Sparta.* London: Routledge for the Classical Press of Wales, 1994.

Questions for Further Study

1. A common theme that runs through constitutional and legal reforms in early and not-so-early societies is land reform. Select another document that deals with this issue—possibilities include Emiliano Zapata's Plan of Ayala, Mao Zedong's "Report on an Investigation of the Peasant Movement in Hunan," and the Athenian constitution—and compare the nature of land reforms (enacted or proposed) and the factors that gave rise to them.

2. Aristotle found the constitution of Sparta faulty for a number of reasons. Can you detect a common thread that runs through many or most of those reasons? What was the *fundamental* inadequacy of the Spartan constitution, according to Aristotle?

3. Warfare played a considerable role in the evolution of Spartan society. In what ways did warfare both strengthen and undermine the Spartan state?

4. To what extent was the Spartan constitution a democratic document? How did the constitution represent a step forward in the evolution of democracy?

5. What did Aristotle regard as the failings of pure democracy as a form of government?

■ **Web Sites**

"Sparta Reconsidered—Sparta the First Democracy." Elysium
Gates Web site.
    http://elysiumgates.com/~helena/Revolution.html.

"Sparta." Plato and His Dialogues Web site.
    http://plato-dialogues.org/tools/loc/sparta.htm.

    —Scott Cashion

CONSTITUTION OF SPARTA

Part IX.

In the governments of Lacedaemon and Crete, and indeed in all governments, two points have to be considered: first, whether any particular law is good or bad, when compared with the perfect state; secondly, whether it is or is not consistent with the idea and character which the lawgiver has set before his citizens. That in a well-ordered state the citizens should have leisure and not have to provide for their daily wants is generally acknowledged, but there is a difficulty in seeing how this leisure is to be attained. The Thessalian Penestae have often risen against their masters, and the Helots in like manner against the Lacedaemonians, for whose misfortunes they are always lying in wait. Nothing, however, of this kind has as yet happened to the Cretans; the reason probably is that the neighboring cities, even when at war with one another, never form an alliance with rebellious serfs, rebellions not being for their interest, since they themselves have a dependent population. Whereas all the neighbors of the Lacedaemonians, whether Argives, Messenians, or Arcadians, were their enemies. In Thessaly, again, the original revolt of the slaves occurred because the Thessalians were still at war with the neighboring Achaeans, Perrhaebians, and Magnesians. Besides, if there were no other difficulty, the treatment or management of slaves is a troublesome affair; for, if not kept in hand, they are insolent, and think that they are as good as their masters, and, if harshly treated, they hate and conspire against them. Now it is clear that when these are the results the citizens of a state have not found out the secret of managing their subject population.

Again, the license of the Lacedaemonian women defeats the intention of the Spartan constitution, and is adverse to the happiness of the state. For, a husband and wife being each a part of every family, the state may be considered as about equally divided into men and women; and, therefore, in those states in which the condition of the women is bad, half the city may be regarded as having no laws. And this is what has actually happened at Sparta; the legislator [Lycurgus] wanted to make the whole state hardy and temperate, and he has carried out his intention in the case of the men, but he has neglected the women, who live in every sort of intemperance and luxury. The consequence is that in such a state wealth is too highly valued, especially if the citizens fall under the dominion of their wives, after the manner of most warlike races, except the Celts and a few others who openly approve of male loves. The old mythologer would seem to have been right in uniting Ares and Aphrodite, for all warlike races are prone to the love either of men or of women. This was exemplified among the Spartans in the days of their greatness; many things were managed by their women. But what difference does it make whether women rule, or the rulers are ruled by women? The result is the same. Even in regard to courage, which is of no use in daily life, and is needed only in war, the influence of the Lacedaemonian women has been most mischievous. The evil showed itself in the Theban invasion, when, unlike the women other cities, they were utterly useless and caused more confusion than the enemy. This license of the Lacedaemonian women existed from the earliest times, and was only what might be expected. For, during the wars of the Lacedaemonians, first against the Argives, and afterwards against the Arcadians and Messenians, the men were long away from home, and, on the return of peace, they gave themselves into the legislator's hand, already prepared by the discipline of a soldier's life (in which there are many elements of virtue), to receive his enactments. But, when Lycurgus, as tradition says, wanted to bring the women under his laws, they resisted, and he gave up the attempt. These then are the causes of what then happened, and this defect in the constitution is clearly to be attributed to them. We are not, however, considering what is or is not to be excused, but what is right or wrong, and the disorder of the women, as I have already said, not only gives an air of indecorum to the constitution considered in itself, but tends in a measure to foster avarice.

The mention of avarice naturally suggests a criticism on the inequality of property. While some of the Spartan citizens have quite small properties, others have very large ones; hence the land has passed into the hands of a few. And this is due also to faulty laws; for, although the legislator rightly holds up to shame the sale or purchase of an inheritance, he allows anybody who likes to give or bequeath it. Yet both practices lead to the same result. And nearly two-fifths of the whole country are held by women; this is owing to the number of heiresses and to the large dowries which are customary. It would surely have been better to have given no dowries at all, or, if any, but small or moderate ones. As the law now stands, a man may bestow his heiress on any one whom he pleases, and, if he die intestate, the privilege of giving her away descends to his heir. Hence, although the country is able to maintain 1500 cavalry and 30,000 hoplites, the whole number of Spartan citizens fell below 1000. The result proves the faulty nature of their laws respecting property; for the city sank under a single defeat; the want of men was their ruin. There is a tradition that, in the days of their ancient kings, they were in the habit of giving the rights of citizenship to strangers, and therefore, in spite of their long wars, no lack of population was experienced by them; indeed, at one time Sparta is said to have numbered not less than 10,000 citizens Whether this statement is true or not, it would certainly have been better to have maintained their numbers by the equalization of property. Again, the law which relates to the procreation of children is adverse to the correction of this inequality. For the legislator, wanting to have as many Spartans as he could, encouraged the citizens to have large families; and there is a law at Sparta that the father of three sons shall be exempt from military service, and he who has four from all the burdens of the state. Yet it is obvious that, if there were many children, the land being distributed as it is, many of them must necessarily fall into poverty.

The Lacedaemonian constitution is defective in another point; I mean the Ephoralty. This magistracy has authority in the highest matters, but the Ephors are chosen from the whole people, and so the office is apt to fall into the hands of very poor men, who, being badly off, are open to bribes. There have been many examples at Sparta of this evil in former times; and quite recently, in the matter of the Andrians, certain of the Ephors who were bribed did their best to ruin the state. And so great and tyrannical is their power, that even the kings have been compelled to court them, so that, in this way as well together with the royal office, the whole constitution has deteriorated, and from being an aristocracy has turned into a democracy. The Ephoralty certainly does keep the state together; for the people are contented when they have a share in the highest office, and the result, whether due to the legislator or to chance, has been advantageous. For if a constitution is to be per-

manent, all the parts of the state must wish that it should exist and the same arrangements be maintained. This is the case at Sparta, where the kings desire its permanence because they have due honor in their own persons; the nobles because they are represented in the council of elders (for the office of elder is a reward of virtue); and the people, because all are eligible to the Ephoralty. The election of Ephors out of the whole people is perfectly right, but ought not to be carried on in the present fashion, which is too childish. Again, they have the decision of great causes, although they are quite ordinary men, and therefore they should not determine them merely on their own judgment, but according to written rules, and to the laws. Their way of life, too, is not in accordance with the spirit of the constitution— they have a deal too much license; whereas, in the case of the other citizens, the excess of strictness is so intolerable that they run away from the law into the secret indulgence of sensual pleasures.

Again, the council of elders is not free from defects. It may be said that the elders are good men and well trained in manly virtue; and that, therefore, there is an advantage to the state in having them. But that judges of important causes should hold office for life is a disputable thing, for the mind grows old as well as the body. And when men have been educated in such a manner that even the legislator himself cannot trust them, there is real danger. Many of the elders are well known to have taken bribes and to have been guilty of partiality in public affairs. And therefore they ought not to be irresponsible; yet at Sparta they are so. But (it may be replied), 'All magistracies are accountable to the Ephors.' Yes, but this prerogative is too great for them, and we maintain that the control should be exercised in some other manner. Further, the mode in which the Spartans elect their elders is childish; and it is improper that the person to be elected should canvass for the office; the worthiest should be appointed, whether he chooses or not. And here the legislator clearly indicates the same intention which appears in other parts of his constitution; he would have his citizens ambitious, and he has reckoned upon this quality in the election of the elders; for no one would ask to be elected if he were not. Yet ambition and avarice, almost more than any other passions, are the motives of crime.

Whether kings are or are not an advantage to states, I will consider at another time; they should at any rate be chosen, not as they are now, but with regard to their personal life and conduct. The legislator himself obviously did not suppose that he could make them really good men; at least he shows a great distrust of their virtue. For this reason the Spartans used to join enemies with them in the same embassy, and the quarrels between the kings were held to be conservative of the state.

Neither did the first introducer of the common meals, called 'phiditia,' regulate them well. The entertainment ought to have been provided at the public cost, as in Crete; but among the Lacedaemonians every one is expected to contribute, and some of them are too poor to afford the expense; thus the intention of the legislator is frustrated. The common meals were meant to be a popular institution, but the existing manner of regulating them is the reverse of popular. For the very poor can scarcely take part in them; and, according to ancient custom, those who cannot contribute are not allowed to retain their rights of citizenship.

The law about the Spartan admirals has often been censured, and with justice; it is a source of dissension, for the kings are perpetual generals, and this office of admiral is but the setting up of another king.

The charge which Plato brings, in the Laws, against the intention of the legislator, is likewise justified; the whole constitution has regard to one part of virtue only—the virtue of the soldier, which gives victory in war. So long as they were at war, therefore, their power was preserved, but when they had attained empire they fell for of the arts of peace they knew nothing, and had never engaged in any employment higher than war. There is another error, equally great, into which they have fallen. Although they truly think that the goods for which men contend are to be acquired by virtue rather than by vice, they err in supposing that these goods are to be preferred to the virtue which gains them.

Once more: the revenues of the state are ill-managed; there is no money in the treasury, although they are obliged to carry on great wars, and they are unwilling to pay taxes. The greater part of the land being in the hands of the Spartans, they do not look closely into one another's contributions. The result which the legislator has produced is the reverse of beneficial; for he has made his city poor, and his citizens greedy.

Enough respecting the Spartan constitution, of which these are the principal defects.

Glossary

license of the Lacedaemonian women	participation in government and other civic activities by Spartan women, contrary to Old World norms
old mythologer	unknown, but perhaps Homer

Ruins of Carthage (AP/Wide World Photos)

CONSTITUTION OF CARTHAGE

"The superiority of their constitution is proved by the fact that, although containing an element of democracy, it has been lasting."

Overview

At the beginning of the Middle Ages, North Africa was conquered by the Arabs and Western Europe went through a dark age that largely cut it off from contact with the wider world. Thus, North Africa and Europe became parts of two different cultures, two distinct worlds separated by the Mediterranean. But in antiquity, the Mediterranean unified the two continents rather than separating them. North Africa was the home of the civilization of Carthage, which the philosopher Aristotle considered the best-governed nation in the world. Carthage, a Phoenician colony whose true name was Qart Hadasht, or "New Town" (*Carthage* is as close as Latin could come to pronouncing it), ruled over modern-day Tunisia and northeastern Algeria, a land far more fertile in antiquity than now, and also controlled Sardinia and Corsica and eventually Spain.

Carthage produced no literary tradition of its own, so its history is known through Greek and Latin authors such as Aristotle, Polybius, Livy, Diodorus Siculus, and Justin, and especially through archaeology. For much of its existence Carthage was fighting for control of the central and western Mediterranean, first against the Greek colonial cities on Sicily and eventually against Rome. The ancient Greek historian Polybius, who was well aware of Aristotle's work, judged that Rome finally defeated Carthage because of the superiority of its constitution, a better mixture of the very characteristics Aristotle praised in Carthage's. As a province of the Roman Empire, North Africa was joined to Mediterranean and European civilization until the Middle Ages.

Context

The chief document that deals with the constitution of Carthage is the eleventh chapter of the second book of Aristotle's *Politics*. This work is a response to the political philosophy of his teacher, Plato, and furthers the attempt to describe an ideal organization for a national government. Unexpectedly, in view of the well-known prejudice of Greeks and of Aristotle, in particular, against non-Greeks,

or barbarians, he settles on Carthage as the closest approximation to his ideal. Partly this was because of the relatively imperfect information about Carthage available to the Greek world, allowing Aristotle to interpret the history of the city in the best light for his purposes.

About the historical development of the Carthaginian constitution we are completely in the dark. Aristotle occasionally talks about a "legislator," but that is just a manner of speech to refer to whatever process brought the constitution about. It undoubtedly developed and changed in response to crises and political necessity as the city grew and its government became more complex. For instance, it is commonly believed by historians that the Council of the One Hundred and Four was a late addition introduced as a check on the *suffetes* (co-chief executives of the Carthaginian state) once Carthage's almost constant involvement in warfare in Sicily made their role as military leaders more powerful and possibly threatening to the political order.

Carthage, in the modern-day North African country of Tunisia, was a Phoenician city, a colony of Tyre. Phoenicia covered today's territories of Lebanon and the northern part of the state of Israel. The Phoenicians were a Semitic people, closely related in language and religion to Jews and Arabs. As seafarers living in coastal towns, they dominated the trade of the Mediterranean for many centuries, beginning in about 1200 BCE. They founded colonies all around the Mediterranean basin as far as Tarshish on the Strait of Gibraltar (known as the Pillars of Hercules in antiquity). Phoenician colonies were more in the nature of trading posts than settlements. Carthage was one of them, founded according to tradition, in 814 BCE. But in 671 BCE, Carthage's home city of Tyre was conquered by the Assyrians, and many of its people came to Carthage, making it independent and the chief Phoenician city in the western Mediterranean.

The city was dominated by great families and was ruled from the late sixth to the fourth centuries by Mago and his descendants, most prominently the fifth-century navigator Hanno, who led the drive both to conquer the North African hinterland and to explore the Atlantic. Early in the fourth century, the aristocratic form of government at Carthage described by Aristotle became established with the creation of the Council of the One Hundred and Four.

CONSTITUTION OF CARTHAGE **181**

Time Line

CA. 814 BCE

- Carthage is founded as a colony of the Phoenician city of Tyre.

671 BCE

- Assyrians lay siege to Tyre and conquer it, making Carthage independent and the chief Phoenician city in the western Mediterranean.

CA. 480–460 BCE

- The Carthaginian statesman and navigator Hanno conquers the hinterland and conducts a voyage of exploration along the Atlantic coast of Africa.

CA. 397 BCE

- Lilybaeum, the principal Carthaginian colony on Sicily, is founded.

384 BCE

- Aristotle is born.

CA. 320S BCE

- Aristotle composes the *Politics*, part of which describes the government of the Carthaginians.

308 BCE

- The Carthaginian commander Bomilcar attempts to seize the government in a failed coup; the incident steers Carthage toward democracy.

In 308 BCE, the attempt of Bomilcar to make himself tyrant of the city steered Carthage in a new political direction, toward increasing democracy. Throughout this period Carthage's main overseas enterprise was the effort to conquer the Greek cities on the island of Sicily, chief among them being the great city of Syracuse. Carthage fought these wars entirely with mercenary armies, using only native Carthaginians as higher officers. Carthaginian power on Sicily waxed and waned, occasionally occupying the whole island and besieging Syracuse and at other times being reduced to control of only a few fortresses, such as Lilybaeum (present-day Marsala) on the western tip of Sicily. In 310 BCE, Agathocles of Syracuse actually invaded North Africa and won a number of victories, but he could not accomplish much, since he lacked the strategic resources necessary to lay siege to a large city like Carthage.

By the beginning of the third century, Carthage had gained the upper hand in Sicily and seemed to be in permanent control of about two-thirds of the island. However, in 264 BCE a trivial diplomatic incident sparked war with Rome, which had just solidified its control of the entire Italian peninsula. From 264 to 241 BCE, Rome and Carthage fought the First Punic War, mostly on Sicily but including an invasion of North Africa by a Roman army under the consul Regulus that was fought off by the Carthaginians in 255 BCE. Rome was ultimately successful and forced Carthage to abandon Sicily. The defeated officer Hamilcar Barca nevertheless became the leading figure in Carthaginian politics and directed the conquest of a new Carthaginian empire in Spain, where rich silver deposits were available. His son-in-law Hasdrubal and then his son Hannibal also became the leading figures in Carthage. In 218 BCE, Hannibal began a new war with Rome (known as the Second Punic War), lasting until 201 BCE. Hannibal led an army from Spain to Italy over the Alps, winning devastating victories over the Romans at present-day Lake Trasimeno in 217 BCE and Cannae in 216 BCE that are still studied as among the most perfect examples of the art of war in all history. The scope of the war was so great that for the first time Carthaginians themselves were compelled to serve in the army instead of hiring mercenaries. Nevertheless, the Romans were ultimately victorious after a successful invasion of Africa. Victory in the war established Rome as the dominant military power in the Western world, laying the foundations of the Roman Empire. Despite Hannibal's final defeat, he retained his leading position in the state and tried to gain greater power for himself against the oligarchy in alliance with the people. However, pressure from the Romans drove him into exile.

Although Carthage continued to exist as an independent state, it was completely subject to Rome, to the degree that it could not even defend itself against military attack by North African Numidian tribesmen without Rome's express approval. By 149 BCE, Rome, having conquered or reduced to client status the Greek kingdoms of Alexander the Great's successors in the eastern Mediterranean, decided that Carthage must be destroyed. Rome launched the

Third Punic War, which resulted in the destruction of the city. In 146 BCE the city was captured after a siege, its population enslaved, and every building leveled. Salt was sown into the earth to symbolically make it sterile. No ancient civilization was ever so thoroughly obliterated.

About the Author

The Greek philosopher Aristotle was the chief student of Plato and the tutor of Alexander the Great. His own school was located in the neighborhood called the Lyceum, and his philosophy is often called peripatetic (meaning "to walk up and down"), after the enclosed walkway at the front of his school. He is one of the most influential founding figures of the Western intellectual tradition. His achievements range from creating the forerunner of the modern university curriculum to devising formal logic. Aristotle was born in 384 BCE in the village of Stagira in Macedonia. His father, Nicomachus, was the court physician to Amyntas II of Macedonia. Aristotle studied with Plato; when he did not become his successor as head of the academy, he moved on to teach philosophy in various Greek cities. One of his most important positions at this time was tutoring the future Alexander the Great. He also lectured for a time in Lesbos, where he performed most of the biological experiments (including dissections of animals) that he later incorporated into his books on biology. He returned to Athens in 355 BCE but was forced to flee by anti-Macedonian agitation in 323 BCE and died a year later in Euripus (modern-day Khalkís). Aristotle's surviving works can best be described as the first attempt at an encyclopedia, since they cover every field of knowledge known in antiquity. He organized human knowledge into a systematic arrangement where all of the physical and social sciences were subordinated to philosophy.

Explanation and Analysis of the Document

Aristotle's treatise *Politics*, which contains his remarks on the constitution of Carthage, was composed in response to the *Republic* and *Laws* of his teacher, Plato. All three works aimed toward a philosophical description of the ideal form of government. For the Greeks that meant the ideal city-state, since the only other forms of government with which they were familiar were those of various tribal peoples who lived on the fringes of the Mediterranean civilization and the Persian Empire, stretching from the Mediterranean to India and deep into central Asia, which symbolized despotism, oppression, and the foreign—everything the Greeks did not want in government. The Greeks conceived that there were three possible forms of government. The first was monarchy, in which a single man held all the political power. A second was aristocracy, in which power was exercised by a council of leading citizens. The third was democracy, in which all power was exercised by the citizen body as a whole. Aristotle envisioned that a mixed con-

stitution, which had a role for all three types of governance, was best. Before turning to his ideal conceptions, he chose to discuss the actual constitutions of three states, as those best exemplifying his philosophy of government: Sparta, Crete, and Carthage. Of these three, Aristotle felt that the constitution of Carthage most nearly approached his ideal.

Aristotle believed that slavery was necessary for any successful society, since only that institution could give the governing class sufficient time necessary to their duties. As morally objectionable as this view is (and it was attacked on moral grounds even in antiquity), by and large slavery was simply accepted as a fact of life in antiquity, which speaks to the relatively undeveloped economic conditions of the ancient world. Aristotle begins the *Politics* with a famous defense of slavery, but he seems to have been unaware of the sophisticated and lucrative form of plantation slavery invented at Carthage. This points out a major flaw in Aristotle's work—that he had far less information about Carthage available to him than he did in the case of his Greek examples. Probably this was because he had to rely on intelligence from a few Greek traders who had visited

Time Line

322 BCE	■ Aristotle dies.
237 BCE	■ Hamilcar Barca and his son-in-law Hasdrubal begin to build up the Carthaginian empire in Spain.
218 BCE	■ The Carthaginian general Hannibal begins war with Rome, a conflict that lasts until 201 and ends in the defeat of Carthage and Hannibal's exile.
146 BCE	■ **Spring** At the end of the Third Punic War, the Romans capture Carthage, destroying the city and enslaving its population.

Carthage, rather than the well-known facts about Sparta and Crete that could be checked in written records.

Having discussed the constitutions of Sparta and Crete—their virtues as well as their defects—Aristotle turns to Carthage. He begins by stating that the constitution of Carthage is of the same general type as Sparta's and Crete's but is superior because it has endured through time and its democratic element has never produced a demagogic tyrant. Aristotle lists several similarities with Sparta's constitution. All Spartan citizens dined together in the same mess hall (which Aristotle considered a good means of encouraging civic equality), since they formed a permanent standing army. He attributes the same practice to Carthage. But this is a point on which Aristotle is confused. Citizenship in Carthage was conferred by belonging to one of several religious brotherhoods traditional in the city. These brotherhoods celebrated an annual religious feast similar to Easter or Passover, which is hardly comparable to the daily Spartan custom.

Aristotle next compares the kings of Carthage to those of Sparta. Many historians have made the mistake of taking Aristotle too literally here and transferring all the associations of Greek kings to the officials he talks about in Carthage. This parallel is extremely unlikely, given what else is known about Carthaginian history. The point of the comparison is more probably that just as Sparta had two kings ruling at the same time, Carthage had two chief magistrates who shared power in a joint term of office. Aristotle describes the Carthaginian kings as being "not always of the same family" and as being "selected" and "not appointed by seniority." It is clear, therefore, that he is not talking about a royal dynasty at all, but about elected officials. Indeed, Carthage was ruled by two chief executive officers who were elected annually. They were not called kings, but *suffetes*. This is the same Semitic word translated as "judge" in the Hebrew Bible, meaning an official who is not a king but who is chosen to lead a state for a specific period of time. In practice, the office of *suffete* was limited to the most powerful families in Carthage, and it often happened that a *suffete* would be elected to the same office that had been held by his father, uncle, or grandfather (not continuously but only for a few years each, with other families intervening). The same phenomenon has occurred among American presidents, but that hardly means that a royal dynasty has been established.

Aristotle also talks about the "gerusia, or council of elders." In fact, Carthage seems to have had two such councils. The Council of Thirty was composed of the leading aristocrats in the city and ruled almost in conjunction with the *suffetes*, who would have been first among equals in this council. The second council, which Aristotle appears to have in mind, was the Council of the One Hundred and Four, whose members were selected by holding certain magistracies other than the *suffetes*. This council's members exercised the judicial functions Aristotle talks about. In particular, they judged each *suffete* at the end of his administration; if they found any financial irregularities, they could, and often did, condemn him to be crucified. Aristotle's "magistracies of five" are harder to understand in

the light of other sources about Carthage. They may have been special committees of the Council of Thirty given tasks such as negotiating treaties or settling land disputes.

Aristotle gives more information about the popular assembly of all Carthaginian citizens than does any other historical source. Modern-day historians generally accept that if either of the *suffetes* wished to pursue a policy that the Council of Thirty did not approve, he could bring it before the assembly as an alternative source of validation. Note that while this assembly might have included all citizens, it was far from democratic in any modern sense, since it would have excluded women and slaves (much more than half of the population) and might have required a minimal property qualification for voting rights.

Aristotle finally turns to the defects that prevent the constitution of Carthage from creating a perfect state. Carthage, through chance, has avoided the tendency of monarchy to become tyranny and of democratic government to give rise to a demagogue and so again producing tyranny. But Aristotle thinks that the aristocracy in Carthage was devolving into oligarchy. For Aristotle, aristocracy was the ideal principle of government, the rule of the best men—that is, the wisest and most just. There is a tendency for such a government to change into an oligarchy, in which power is put into the hands of a few men chosen for their wealth and status within society rather than for their virtue. Carthage avoids this tendency entirely, in Aristotle's view, since its people voted for those who were best and wealthiest.

Aristotle's discussion of the corrupting influence of money in oligarchic politics is not hypothetical. We know from the ancient Greek historian Polybius that it was a general practice, and a perfectly legal one, for candidates for office in Carthage simply to buy the votes of citizens for cash payments from their own private wealth. Similarly, the main reason the One Hundred and Four existed was to curb officials' enriching themselves from their offices. Such a measure would hardly have been necessary had it not been all too common a practice. Once Hannibal was elected *suffete* at the end of the Second Punic War, he announced, after examining government records kept during the war, that the huge indemnity Carthage was forced to pay to Rome did not need to be raised through a new tax, as others proposed; it could be recovered from the public officials who had stolen even more than that amount from defense expenditures voted during the war. This is one reason the Carthaginian oligarchs were happy to cooperate with the Romans in driving Hannibal into exile.

Aristotle settled on Carthage as having an ideal constitution in part because it was one of his own making. His relative ignorance of conditions in Carthage allowed him to interpret the little information he had in light of current ideas of good government. As a result, what Aristotle says must always be checked against the little other information we have about Carthage. Despite its importance in the history of the ancient world, Carthage is virtually in a black hole as far as literary sources go. Thus, Aristotle's disquisition on the city constitution is all the more important. As political philosophy, Aristotle's work looks backward to the

> *"The superiority of their constitution is proved by the fact that, although containing an element of democracy, it has been lasting; the Carthaginians have never had any rebellion worth speaking of, and have never been under the rule of a tyrant."*
>
> (Paragraph 1)

> *"For the Carthaginians choose their magistrates, and particularly the highest of them—their kings and generals—with an eye both to merit and to wealth."*
>
> (Paragraph 3)

> *"Nothing is more absolutely necessary than to provide that the highest class, not only when in office, but when out of office, should have leisure and not demean themselves in any way."*
>
> (Paragraph 4)

> *"It would seem also to be a bad principle that the same person should hold many offices,... for one business is better done by one man. The legislator should see to this and not appoint the same person to be a flute-player and a shoemaker."*
>
> (Paragraph 5)

> *"Accident favours them, but the legislator should be able to provide against revolution without trusting to accidents."*
>
> (Paragraph 6)

organization of the city-state, even though he was writing at a time when the Mediterranean world was on the verge of organizing itself into governments on a national level.

Audience

The actual constitution of Carthage was almost certainly not a specific document such as the modern constitutions of the United States or France, for example. It existed as the accumulation of tradition, more like the modern British constitution, with some parts spelled out in specific laws and others simply understood as the way things were to be done in the city because they always had been done that way. The audience for such a constitution would have been the thirty or so families that held the bulk of the wealth and political power in the city and who would have been keen to exploit it to their own advantage in political struggles for power and prominence within the city. The constitution would have concerned as well the larger body of enfranchised citizens, who most likely formed an elite consisting of propertied free adult males, surely a minority in the city consisting of perhaps a quarter or a fifth of the population as a whole.

Aristotle's *Politics*, though widely read today, was originally intended as an internal document within his school, to be studied by his students; it was not circulated to a wide audience. Like all of Aristotle's extant works, it was a set of lecture notes or part of an encyclopedia kept as a reference for his students. Aristotle's attempt to find ideal political arrangements did not seem to make a very marked impression on his students who actually pursued political careers. Two of his students actually rose to high political office. At the end of his life, Alexander the Great began to finalize the political arrangements of his empire, but he moved the poorly balanced (in Aristotle's terms) constitution of Macedonia in the direction of absolute monarchy and away from the aristocratic balance favored by his teacher. Aristotle's student Demetrius Phalereus succeeded his teacher as head of the Lyceum and was eventually made governor of Athens once the city was conquered by the Hellenistic Ptolemaic dynasty of Egypt. He ruled the city as an absolute tyrant and, according to historical tradition, as a particularly cruel one, ignoring the lessons of the *Politics*.

Impact

The impact of the city of Carthage is often underestimated because Carthaginian civilization was destroyed by defeat in the Punic Wars. Although Carthaginian culture survived in North Africa and influenced the life of the city of Carthage that Julius Caesar refounded as a Roman colony in 46 BCE, it was obliterated as a living tradition by later Vandal and Arab invasions of North Africa at the end of antiquity. Most of what is known about Carthage through archaeology has been discovered by French scholars, since Tunisia and Algeria were part of the French colonial empire and their work has not been extensively translated into English. Because Carthage produced no literary tradition of its own (at least none that survives) modern histories of Carthage concentrate to a great extent on the archaeological remains of physical culture.

Aristotle gives a snapshot of the Carthaginian constitution in the mid-fourth century. We do not have such a detailed treatment for any earlier or later period. The only impetus to change the constitution seems to have come from military disasters. In 360 and 308 BCE the *suffetes* Hanno and Bomilcar both tried to become tyrant (dictator) of Carthage during military crises, but both attempts failed because they lacked popular support. After the Second Punic War, Hannibal tried to move in this direction, too, and passed a great deal of democratic reform legislation by taking it to the people rather than the Council of Thirty. One of his changes was to have the assembly directly elect the Council of the One Hundred and Four and change the

Questions for Further Study

1. For what reasons did Aristotle regard the constitution of Carthage as embodying an ideal form of government—or a least close to an ideal?

2. In ancient times, the Mediterranean Sea was literally the center ("medi") of the world ("terra"). Why did the many cultures that lived in the region regard it in this way?

3. Trade was an important component of life in Carthage and throughout the Mediterranean region in antiquity. What role did trade play in economic, social, and political development in Carthage? Why was slavery an important institution?

4. The other major nations in and around the Mediterranean region—Rome, Greece, Egypt, Persia, and others—continue to exist in some form in the twenty-first century, though their claims to empire are largely nonexistent. The Carthaginian Empire, in contrast, entirely disappeared. Why? Did the nature of Carthaginian government, as embodied in its constitutional traditions and laws, contribute to its disappearance? Or did Carthage disappear despite its form of government?

5. The government of Carthage, like that of other governments in the Mediterranean region, revolved around councils and groups of men who belonged to the aristocracy. Democratic governments in the twentieth and twenty-first centuries have tended to severely limit the influence of aristocracies in favor of extending political power to ordinary people. Why do you think a relatively small aristocracy wielded so much power and influence in ancient Carthage? Why would this form of government have been considered the most workable?

term of membership from life to one year. If his popularity gave him control of the assembly, as seems to have been the case, this would effectively have given Hannibal complete power in the state at the expense of the wealthy oligarchic faction. This led to Hannibal's exile, and his constitutional reforms probably were quickly overturned.

Polybius is the only other author who treats the Carthaginian constitution with anything approaching the detailed discussion Aristotle gives it. Polybius wished to contrast it to the Roman constitution, as part of his explanation to his Greek readers of Rome's rise to imperial power over the Greek world. He believed, as many ancient theorists did, that a constitution had a natural life span, like a human being—with a prime of life, a decline into old age, and an eventual death. He felt that Carthage's constitution had been at its prime when Aristotle described it, two hundred years before his own writing, but had since gone through a natural decline. It was Carthage's misfortune to find itself opposed to Rome, whose constitution Polybius judged the most perfect in the world and just at its prime during the Punic Wars. Ultimately, Polybius attributed Carthage's defeat to the differences between the two constitutions.

The principal impact Carthage had on history was in its economic organization, rather than its political system. Traditionally, Phoenicians had founded their colonies on isolated promontories and peninsulas to serve as trading posts, safe from any military attack from local peoples. They had little interest in control of native populations or large areas of land. But by the early fifth century, perhaps as a result of reverses in its wars with the Greeks in Sicily, Carthage turned toward the subjugation of the interior of modern-day Tunisia and northeastern Algeria. The land and slaves gained in this enterprise were not given in small parcels to individual Carthaginian farmers, since, indeed, Punic culture had little tradition of yeoman farmers. Instead, vast tracts of land were given to Carthaginian aristocrats. This rich agricultural land was turned into plantations, which gangs of slaves farmed to produce cash crops for export and trade, rather than subsistence. The plantation system was eagerly taken up by the Romans after their conquest of Carthage and was used throughout the Roman Empire. Since Carthage disappeared from world history

owing to its conquest by Rome, it was not often later cited as an ideal state, despite Aristotle's enthusiasm for it. If Carthage is remembered at all in popular culture, it is for its defiance of the hegemonic power of Rome and because of Hannibal's victories.

Further Reading

■ Articles

Sanders, Lionel J. "Punic Politics in the Fifth Century b.c." *Historia* 37 (1988): 72–89.

Scullard, H. H. "Carthage." *Greece & Rome* 2 (1955): 98–107.

Walbank, F. W. "Polybius on the Roman Constitution." *Classical Quarterly* 37 (1943): 73–89.

■ Books

Lancel, Serge. *Carthage: A History*, trans. Antonia Nevill. Oxford: Blackwell, 1995.

Picard, Gilbert Charles, and Colette Picard. *The Life and Death of Carthage: A Survey of Punic History and Culture from Its Birth to Its Final Tragedy*, trans. Dominique Collon. New York: Taplinger, 1969.

Polybius. *The Histories*, vol. 3, trans. W. R. Paton. Cambridge, Mass.: Harvard University Press, 1923.

Simpson, Peter L. *A Philosophical Commentary on the Politics of Aristotle*. Chapel Hill: University of North Carolina Press, 1998.

Warmington, B. H. *Carthage*. 2nd ed. New York: Praeger, 1969.

■ Web Sites

"Aristotle's Political Theory." Stanford Encyclopedia of Philosophy Web site.
    http://plato.stanford.edu/entries/aristole-politics.

"Carthage." Livius.org Web site.
    http://www.livius.org/cao-caz/carthage/carthage.html.

—Bradley A. Skeen

CONSTITUTION OF CARTHAGE

The Carthaginians are also considered to have an excellent form of government, which differs from that of any other state in several respects, though it is in some very like the Lacedaemonian. Indeed, all three states—the Lacedaemonian, the Cretan, and the Carthaginian—nearly resemble one another, and are very different from any others. Many of the Carthaginian institutions are excellent. The superiority of their constitution is proved by the fact that, although containing an element of democracy, it has been lasting; the Carthaginians have never had any rebellion worth speaking of, and have never been under the rule of a tyrant.

Among the points in which the Carthaginian constitution resembles the Lacedaemonian are the following:—The common tables of the clubs answer to the Spartan phiditia, and their magistracy of the 104 to the Ephors; but, whereas the Ephors are any chance persons, the magistrates of the Carthaginians are elected according to merit—this is an improvement. They have also their kings and their gerusia, or council of elders, who correspond to the kings and elders of Sparta. Their kings, unlike the Spartan, are not always of the same family, and this an ordinary one, but if there is some distinguished family they are selected out of it and not appointed by seniority—this is far better. Such officers have great power, and therefore, if they are persons of little worth, do a great deal of harm, and they have already done harm at Lacedaemon.

Most of the defects or deviations from the perfect state, for which the Carthaginian constitution would be censured, apply equally to all the forms of government which we have mentioned. But of the deflections from aristocracy and constitutional government, some incline more to democracy and some to oligarchy. The kings and elders, if unanimous, may determine whether they will or will not bring a matter before the people, but when they are not unanimous, the people may decide whether or not the matter shall be brought forward. And whatever the kings and elders bring before the people is not only heard but also determined by them, and any one who likes may oppose it; now this is not permitted in Sparta and Crete. That the magistracies of five who have under them many important matters should be co-opted, that they should choose the supreme council of 100,

and should hold office longer than other magistrates (for they are virtually rulers both before and after they hold office)—these are oligarchical features; their being without salary and not elected by lot, and any similar points, such as the practice of having all suits tried by the magistrates, and not some by one class of judges or jurors and some by another, as at Lacedaemon, are characteristic of aristocracy. The Carthaginian constitution deviates from aristocracy and inclines to oligarchy, chiefly on a point where popular opinion is on their side. For men in general think that magistrates should be chosen not only for their merit, but for their wealth: a man, they say, who is poor cannot rule well—he has not the leisure. If, then, election of magistrates for their wealth be characteristic of oligarchy, and election for merit of aristocracy, there will be a third form under which the constitution of Carthage is comprehended; for the Carthaginians choose their magistrates, and particularly the highest of them—their kings and generals—with an eye both to merit and to wealth.

But we must acknowledge that, in thus deviating from aristocracy, the legislator has committed an error. Nothing is more absolutely necessary than to provide that the highest class, not only when in office, but when out of office, should have leisure and not demean themselves in any way; and to this his attention should be first directed. Even if you must have regard to wealth, in order to secure leisure, yet it is surely a bad thing that the greatest offices, such as those of kings and generals, should be bought. The law which allows this abuse makes wealth of more account than virtue, and the whole state becomes avaricious. For, whenever the chiefs of the state deem anything honourable, the other citizens are sure to follow their example; and, where virtue has not the first place, there aristocracy cannot be firmly established. Those who have been at the expense of purchasing their places will be in the habit of repaying themselves; and it is absurd to suppose that a poor and honest man will be wanting to make gains, and that a lower stamp of man who has incurred a great expense will not. Wherefore they should rule who are able to rule best. And even if the legislator does not care to protect the good from poverty, he should at any rate secure leisure for those in office.

It would seem also to be a bad principle that the same person should hold many offices, which is a favourite practice among the Carthaginians, for one business is better done by one man. The legislator should see to this and should not appoint the same person to be a flute-player and a shoemaker. Hence, where the state is large, it is more in accordance both with constitutional and with democratic principles that the offices of state should be distributed among many persons. For, as I was saying, this arrangement is more popular, and any action familiarized by repetition is better and sooner performed. We have a proof in military and naval matters; the duties of command and of obedience in both these services extend to all.

The government of the Carthaginians is oligarchical, but they successfully escape the evils of oligarchy by their wealth, which enables them from time to time to send out some portion of the people to their colonies. This is their panacea and the means by which they give stability to the state. Accident favours them, but the legislator should be able to provide against revolution without trusting to accidents. As things are, if any misfortune occurred, and the people revolted from their rulers, there would be no way of restoring peace by legal methods.

Glossary

aristocracy	government by those believed to be best qualified, in the ancient world almost always those who had inherited wealth and privilege
chance persons	in this context, persons from the entire adult population of Sparta, compared with the circumstances among the Carthaginians, who imposed qualifications on candidates for the magistracy
Ephors	the five annually elected Spartan magistrates who had power over the king
Lacedaemonian	from the Spartan city-state of Lacedaemonia
phiditia	a communal arrangement comprising the mess hall and barracks for twenty to thirty Spartan infantrymen

ATHENIAN CONSTITUTION

"When the democracy is master of the voting-power, it is master of the constitution."

Overview

The *Athenian Constitution*, attributed to Aristotle, is a commentary on the development of constitutional democracy in ancient Greece. The transliterated Greek title is *Athenaion Politeia*, so Greek scholars often refer to the text informally as the *Ath. Pol.* or the *A.P.* Essentially, the text, portions of which have not survived, is a history of ancient Greece from a political, constitutional perspective. Thus it traces the progression of Greek rulers and the constitutional reforms they initiated—or in some cases their suppression of constitutional rights and privileges—up to the year 403 BCE. This historical survey comprises parts 1 through 42, each part essentially a brief chapter. Following this survey is an account of the Athenian constitution in Aristotle's own day, encompassing parts 42 to 69. Aristotle's text is not to be confused with a text by the ancient Greek historian Xenophon with the same title.

Some scholars argue that the document was not written by Aristotle. Aristotle conducted research on the development of constitutional democracy for his book *Politics*. Some 170 commentaries on the politics of the various city-states of ancient Greece were written over his name, but scholars generally agree that many of them were probably written by his students under his supervision. However, because Athens was Greece's most important city-state and the one where Aristotle lived at the time, it is possible, if not likely, that the philosopher himself undertook the composition of this text, perhaps writing it as a model for others written by his students. Despite some doubts about the text's authorship, in general it is regarded as Aristotle's. Scholars are uncertain about the date of composition, most putting it sometime in the 320s, perhaps around 328 BCE. But the dating of the text introduces another source of confusion, for *Politics* was written before this time, leading some to say that the *Athenian Constitution* could not have been part of Aristotle's research for the *Politics*. Nonetheless, it has been suggested that the materials for the *Athenian Constitution* could have been gathered prior to the composition of *Politics* and written up in more organized form later.

The *Athenian Constitution* did not survive as part of the corpus of Aristotle's works—what classicists refer to as the Corpus Aristotelicum. Its existence came to light only in 1890, when a portion of a papyrus codex containing the text was discovered in Egypt. (Papyrus is a thick, paperlike material made from the papyrus plant; *codex* refers to a booklike, handwritten manuscript, a format that replaced the scroll in late classical antiquity.) Classicists were excited by the discovery, for portions of the text contain information about ancient Greece that is found in no other surviving text.

Context

The first parts of the *Athenian Constitution* survey political and constitutional developments in what is now termed the archaic period of ancient Greek history. This period, which began in 750 BCE, followed the Greek dark ages and preceded the classical period. The term *archaic* sounds pejorative to modern ears; it seems to imply an era that was backward and primitive. In fact, the term comes from the field of art history and refers to a style of decoration on such objects as pottery. The archaic period, far from being primitive, was richly creative and was a time of numerous political, social, and artistic developments in Greek history.

In about 1100 BCE, the Mycenaean civilization, which emerged during the Bronze Age on the Balkan Peninsula, collapsed. This civilization, built by migrants to the peninsula, was the earliest Greek civilization. Following this period came the so-called Greek dark age—"dark" because it is a period from which little documentary or archaeological evidence survives. In about the eighth century BCE, though, written records began to emerge, based on a Phoenician alphabet that the Greeks adapted to create the Greek alphabet. Significant changes in the social order occurred, marking the beginning of the archaic period. It was this period that produced Homer and his epic poems about the Trojan War and its aftermath.

An important characteristic of this period in Greek history was that the country of Greece did not exist as a nation-state, as it does today. Greece consisted of a large number of small, self-governing poleis, a word generally translated as "city-states." It was inevitable that these city-

CA. 750 BCE	■ The archaic period of ancient Greek history begins, ending in about 480 BCE.
CA. 630 BCE	■ Solon is born.
621 BCE	■ Draco promulgates his law code.
594 BCE	■ Solon is appointed the lawgiver of Athens and inaugurates his legal reforms.
561 BCE	■ Pisistratus becomes tyrant of Athens.
CA. 560 BCE	■ Solon dies.
384 BCE	■ Aristotle is born in Stagira, Chalcidice.
CA. 343 BCE	■ Aristotle becomes director of an academy in Macedon, where he tutors Alexander the Great, son of Philip II of Macedon.
335 BCE	■ Aristotle returns to Athens and founds a school, the Lyceum.

states would emerge, for the area consists of large numbers of islands, valleys, and plains that isolated each city-state from its neighbors. Formerly, these communities had been ruled by traditional kings governing from citadels on the region's highest ground. This practice of locating the center of government on high ground was the source of the word *acropolis*, which means "high city," and polis survives in such modern English words as metropolis and politics, which originally meant "matters concerning the city." During the archaic period and continuing into the classical period that followed, these city-states, while still having kings, were ruled by bodies of citizens, and thus they represent one of the earliest forms of democracy.

In about the seventh century BCE, a class of merchants began to emerge; the chief evidence for this is the first use of coinage. This development was a source of conflict, for the bodies of citizens that wielded authority in the city-states tended to be aristocratic oligarchies, or small, elite class of citizens, usually the wealthy. This class resented the wealth and growing power of the merchant class. The ruling oligarchies were cast into a defensive posture, for the merchants themselves sought political power. The oligarchies lived in fear of being overthrown by tyrants, generally aristocrats who seized the opportunity to assume power by claiming to represent the will of the lower merchant class and of anyone who was not an aristocrat. This word in its modern sense implies a brutal dictator, but in ancient Greece, the word *tyrant* designated simply an illegitimate ruler who seized power and who may or may not have been brutal and tyrannical in his administration.

Greece's emergence from the dark ages was also characterized by an expanding population and thus a shortage of land. Sparta, one of the most powerful city-states, subjugated Messenia in about 720 BCE and turned the population into serfs, called Helots. This development, which provided Sparta with a reliable source of food and labor, freed Spartans from agricultural work and allowed them to enter the military, turning Sparta into a fully militarized city-state. Athens had similar problems, with conflict between the rich and poor exacerbated by a growing population and a consequent land shortage. An important Athenian lawgiver from the seventh century was Draco, who instituted legal reforms that were intended to reduce the conflict. Draco wrote the first Athenian constitution and is best known for his law code, promulgated in 621 BCE. On the one hand, the code represented a step forward in the emergence of democracy, for Draco insisted that the code had to be written, posted in public, and made known to every literate citizen; thus, the administration of the law under Draco was less arbitrary than it had been under earlier rulers. The code, though, was extremely harsh, specifying the death penalty for even minor offenses. Draco's name survives in the English word *draconian*, used to describe any harsh or extreme measure.

Draco's law code was in effect in Athens for about a century. One of Draco's successors, Solon, sometimes called Solon the Wise, introduced more moderate reforms in 594 BCE. After completing his reforms, he stepped down and left Athens. His reforms were supposed to remain operative for a period of time—ten years according to the historian Herodotus, a hundred years according to Aristotle. But after Solon had been absent for about four years, his reforms began to fall apart. The government of Athens was in disarray, and many of the social tensions that Solon tried to eliminate were reappearing. There was a severe food shortage as a result of a war with Megara, a city-state in Attica, Greece, over the territories of Eleusis and Salamis; the commander of the Athenian forces was Solon's relative Pisistratus. In the years that followed, factions competed for power in Athens, and Pisistratus, who enjoyed popularity as a result of his defeat of the Megarans, seized power in 546 BCE, declaring himself tyrant. He ruled Athens until his death about 527 BCE.

About the Author

Aristotle was born in Stagira, Chalcidice, near modern-day Thessaloníki, in 384 BCE. As a young adult, he attended the academy run by Plato in Athens, where he remained for two decades as a student and then as a teacher. After Plato's death, Aristotle traveled throughout Asia Minor (modern-day Turkey), married, and became the father of a daughter. In 343 BCE Philip II of Macedon, a kingdom in northeastern Greece, invited him to become director of an academy, where Aristotle's students included Philip's son, Alexander the Great, as well as the scientist Ptolemy. Aristotle returned to Athens in 335, where he established his own academy, the Lyceum; he founded what came to be called the Peripatetic School of philosophy, from his habit of walking about while teaching. (The word *peripatetic* means "wandering" or "traveling by foot," though it is also possible that the school derived its name from the *peripatoi*, or covered walkways, where the students met.) Although only about a third of Aristotle's written work survives, it is believed that the bulk of his works were written during this period, from 335 to 323 BCE, much as lectures for his students and not intended for publication. Late in his life, he was charged with impiety—with not holding the gods in sufficient reverence—probably because of his association with Macedon at a time when anti-Macedonian sentiment in Athens ran high. He fled to his mother's country estate, where he died in 322 BCE.

Aristotle (along with his mentor, Plato, and Plato's mentor, Socrates) holds a firm place as one of the foundational figures in Western civilization. Virtually no discipline escaped his scholarship: aesthetics, music, morality, ethics, metaphysics, logic, rhetoric, politics, physics, anatomy, biology, zoology, optics, astronomy, geography, medicine—the list could go on and on. He virtually created the study of logic. His work laid the foundation for the modern scientific method. He provided a classification of living organisms. Among his most important treatises were *Physics*, *Metaphysics*, *Nicomachean Ethics*, *Politics*, *De anima*, and *Poetics*. All this is not to say that Aristotle was not guilty of error. Modern philosophers have argued that most of the

Time Line

320S BCE — ■ Aristotle writes the *Athenian Constitution*.

322 BCE — ■ Aristotle dies.

1890 — ■ Portions of the *Athenian Constitution* are discovered in Egypt.

advances in thought in the modern world began with a refutation of Aristotle. Excessive devotion to Aristotle, particularly during the European Renaissance, tended to impede the development of scientific thought. Nevertheless, any statement to the effect that Aristotle was one of the most influential people ever to have lived would probably meet with few objections, and it is only a slight exaggeration to suggest that Aristotle was the last human to have known everything there was to know at the time he lived.

Explanation and Analysis of the Document

In parts 1 through 42, the *Athenian Constitution* traces the history of Greek rulers and their constitutional reforms up to the year 403 BCE. Parts 42 through 69 are an account of the Athenian constitution in Aristotle's own day. Only a short fragment of Part 1, beginning in midsentence, survives. Beginning with Part 2, however, the document is complete.

◆ Parts 2–4

In parts 2 through 4, Aristotle documents the political situation in Athens prior to and during the time of Draco, who instituted a law code in 621 BCE. Athens was ruled by an oligarchy, so few people participated in the political process. For farmers, the economic situation was hard. The geography of Greece made trade difficult, so even though farmers tended to be self-sufficient, their farms were usually small, and one poor harvest could cast a farmer into debt. To satisfy this debt, the farmer and his family were often reduced to the condition of slaves, or at best serfs; that is, they paid their debt through service to their creditor. The *hectemori*, a word meaning "sixth partners," were required to pay a sixth of their produce to masters; the *pelatae* were likewise subjects of their masters, and while the meaning of this term is vague, it is likely that *hectemori* were a subclass of the *pelatae*.

Aristotle goes on to describe the form of government that existed in that era. Membership in the oligarch was based on birth and wealth. In addition to the king there

Columns of Olympieum (Temple of Olympian Zeus) with Acropolis in background (Library of Congress)

were two other public positions. *Polemarch* was a senior military title, and an archon was a chief magistrate. The system evolved into one in which three men held the title of archon. The *thesmothetae*, six in number, were also magistrates who ruled as a body with the three archons making a total of nine. The nature of the power the archons wielded is uncertain and most likely changed over time, but the archons formed an aristocratic council with life tenure, so it was clearly an undemocratic institution.

Draco instituted a law code that was intended to reduce some of the conflict between the aristocracy and the lower classes. He extended voting rights to anyone who could furnish himself with military equipment. A person could become an archon if he owned property free of debt equal to ten minas. A mina was a unit of currency equal to a hundred drachmas; one drachma was roughly the amount that a skilled worker could earn in a day, so ten minas equaled something in the range of three years' wages for a skilled worker—a significant amount of property, but not the wealth that had formerly defined the aristocracy. The property qualifications for generals and cavalry commanders were higher, reflecting the greater skills these men would need. The sentence "These officers were required to hold to bail the Prytanes, the Strategi, and the Hipparchi of the preceding year

until their accounts had been audited, taking four securities of the same class as that to which the Strategi and the Hipparchi belonged" has been translated in various ways, but its meaning remains obscure. An important point about Draco's administration is that the archons were selected by lot from among those of voting age, and those who failed to attend meetings were fined according to their class: The highest class, based on wealth (the *pentacosiomedimnus*), paid more than knights or members of the *zeugite* class. Although historians debate who the *zeugites* were, it is clear they occupied a lower rung, perhaps as farmers or foot soldiers in the army. The Council of Areopagus remained "guardian of the laws," and citizens had redress for wrongs before the council.

◆ **Parts 5–10**

With Part 5, Aristotle takes up the administration of Solon, who was not only a lawgiver and reformer but also a poet, though most of his poetry—only fragments of which survive—consists of commentary on his administration. Aristotle notes that when Solon assumed office, "many were in slavery to the few" and "the people rose against the upper class." After the people put the constitution into Solon's hands, he directed his efforts to making the contending classes "come to terms and put an end to the quarrel existing between them." Solon was particularly distressed by what he saw as a moral decay, much of it because the rich and their "love of wealth and an overweening mind." The chief step that Solon took was to cancel debts: He "liberated the people once and for all, by prohibiting all loans on the security of the debtor's person," meaning that people could no longer be reduced to a condition of servitude because of debt. Additionally, "he made laws by which he cancelled all debts, public and private." Solon met with resistance from members of the upper class, some of whom accused Solon of perpetrating a fraud for his own benefit. Aristotle, though, rejects these stories as false, for Solon was "moderate and public-spirited in all his other actions," and the "desperate condition" of the country required him to take bold action without regard to what anyone thought.

Part 7 details changes Solon made to the constitution. Draco's laws, with the exception of those pertaining to murder, were rendered null. Solon retained the class structure from Draco: At the top were the *pentacosiomedimni*, who owned the most productive tracts of land. Beneath them were knights, or *hippeis*, followed by the *zeugitae* and a fourth class, the *thetes*, who were hired farmworkers and often served as foot soldiers in the military. A noteworthy reform was that Solon distributed archonships and other public offices according to a person's "rateable property," meaning that each class would have at least some representation and even the *thetes* would have some public role as members of the assembly or juries.

In Part 8, Aristotle details the structure of the government under Solon. He notes that candidates for high office, including archonships, were to be selected by lot (rather than by birth). He notes that Athens comprised four tribes, the broadest classification of Athenian society; each tribe, which was headed by a king, was made up of three villages. Each of these villages comprised thirty clans. The clans consisted of a group of households, generally subsistence farmers, their dependents, and any slaves they might have owned. To ensure that the Athenian population was broadly represented, Solon instituted the Council of the Four Hundred, with a hundred representatives from each tribe. Solon, however, retained Draco's Council of the Areopagus, which had the "duty of superintending the laws, acting as before as the guardian of the constitution in general." In Part 9, Aristotle sums up the chief democratic features of Solon's administration: "the prohibition of loans on the security of the debtor's person"; "the right of every person who so willed to claim redress on behalf of any one to whom wrong was being done"; and "the institution of the appeal to the jurycourts." Aristotle goes on to note that "it is to this last … that the masses have owed their strength most of all, since, when the democracy is master of the voting-power, it is master of the constitution." Part 10 deals with Solon's reforms in coinage and weights and measurements.

◆ **Parts 11–16**

This portion of the *Athenian Constitution* examines the aftermath of Solon's constitutional reforms. Solon "found himself beset by people coming to him and harassing him

Seal of Solon, thought to portray the goddess Diana
(© The Trustees of the British Museum)

concerning his laws." The upper classes were critical of his abolition of debts, and the lower classes expected that he would redistribute property more extensively. Accordingly, he left Athens. In Part 12, Aristotle reproduces passages of Solon's poetry in which he responded to the "grumblings" of Athens's citizens about his reforms. Thus, Solon wrote that "I gave to the mass of the people such rank as befitted their need, / I took not away their honour, and I granted naught to their greed." He defended his abolition of debt in terms such as these:

> Thus might and right were yoked in harmony,
> Since by the force of law I won my ends
> And kept my promise. Equal laws I gave
> To evil and to good, with even hand
> Drawing straight justice for the lot of each.

Solon was also highly critical in his poetry of the rich, referring to a situation "when riches too great are poured upon men of unbalanced soul."

After Solon's departure, his constitutional reforms began to collapse. The city was "torn by divisions" and had trouble electing archons. Party factionalism caused dissension in Athenian society. Aristotle goes on to detail how Pisistratus, under these circumstances, assumed power and declared himself tyrant. Pisistratus's administration, though, was marked by "vicissitudes" and he was expelled and then returned to power. Despite being a tyrant, "the majority alike of the upper class and of the people were in his favour; the former he won by his social intercourse with them, the latter by the assistance which he gave to their

"*Since such, then, was the organization of the constitution, and the many were in slavery to the few, the people rose against the upper class. The strife was keen, and for a long time the two parties were ranged in hostile camps against one another, till at last, by common consent, they appointed Solon to be mediator and Archon, and committed the whole constitution to his hands.*"

(Part 5)

"*Indeed, [Solon] constantly fastens the blame of the conflict on the rich; and accordingly at the beginning of the poem he says that he fears 'the love of wealth and an overweening mind', evidently meaning that it was through these that the quarrel arose.*"

(Part 5)

"*As soon as he was at the head of affairs, Solon liberated the people once and for all, by prohibiting all loans on the security of the debtor's person: and in addition he made laws by which he cancelled all debts, public and private.*"

(Part 6)

"*There are three points in the constitution of Solon which appear to be its most democratic features: first and most important, the prohibition of loans on the security of the debtor's person; secondly, the right of every person who so willed to claim redress on behalf of any one to whom wrong was being done; thirdly, the institution of the appeal to the jurycourts; and it is to this last, they say, that the masses have owed their strength most of all, since, when the democracy is master of the voting-power, it is master of the constitution.*"

(Part 9)

"*And so in matters in general [Pisistratus] burdened the people as little as possible with his government, but always cultivated peace and kept them in all quietness. Hence the tyranny of Pisistratus was often spoken of proverbially as 'the age of gold.' ... But most important of all in this respect was his popular and kindly disposition. In all things he was accustomed to observe the laws, without giving himself any exceptional privileges.*"

(Part 16)

private purses, and his nature fitted him to win the hearts of both." According to Aristotle, then, his administration was "more like constitutional government than a tyranny."

Audience

The *Athenian Constitution* was probably not written for publication, at least in the form that survives. Scholars who have examined the text find passages that are obscure, even muddled, suggesting that the text might have been a draft—in effect, notes and background research for Aristotle's book *Politics*. Most likely, the *Athenian Constitution*, like much of Aristotle's writing, was intended as a text for his students. The Lyceum that Aristotle directed was a school, but it was organized far more informally than a modern school is. There was no fixed curriculum, nor were there any specific course requirements. Students were not required to pay fees. Rather, the Lyceum was an informal gathering of young men who were interested in attending philosophical and scientific lectures and in conducting research on topics of interest. Very often the "classes" consisted of discussion and debate. Their efforts were often self-directed, with one student elected every ten days on a revolving basis to handle the school's administrative chores. The students were divided into two groups, junior members and senior members. The younger junior members attended lectures and often served as assistants to the senior members. The latter spent most of their time conducting research in philosophy and science and in many cases writing documents to which Aristotle's name was attached.

Impact

Aristotle's *Athenian Constitution* is a survey of the development of democratic institutions in ancient Greece. In the early sections of the work, Aristotle reaches back to earlier periods of Greek history, where the seeds of democracy were planted. In the excerpt reproduced here, he touches on three major figures: Draco, Solon, and Pisistratus, with emphasis on the reforms of Solon. Although Draco instituted some democratic reforms, it was Solon who can be thought of as the progenitor of Greek democracy.

In the years before Solon promulgated his law code, Athens was in a state of crisis. The rich and poor were pitted against each other. The poor were enslaved to the rich, often because of debt. Food was in short supply. The oligarchs who had ruled Athens were arrogant and indifferent to the plight of the lower social orders. Further, they were often incompetent and corrupt, for the aristocracy that ruled Athens was based on heredity, not competence. Solon believed that Athens was falling into moral decay. He replaced this emphasis on hereditary rule by dividing Athenian society into classes based on wealth and income. In the twenty-first century, such a legal and social system does not seem very democratic. Yet in Solon's time it was a step forward in an ongoing process of placing political power in the hands of broader classes of people. Solon's laws did more than grant rights; they imposed obligations on classes of people, including the upper classes. Additionally, Solon continued the Areopagus, the governing body of Athens. He created a court system and the boule, a council of citizens that conducted Athens's affairs. He intro-

Questions for Further Study

1. A common theme that runs throughout the early history of the world was the coalescence of small city-states and regions into larger, more unified nations. Why do you believe this happened in many places—not only in Greece but also, for example, Japan? To what extent did the reforms of early Greek leaders contribute to this development in Greece?

2. Historians and students continue to read and study ancient Greek texts to learn about the roots of modern-day democracy. In what precise ways did the rulers Aristotle discusses contribute to the emergence of democratic forms of government?

3. Trace the particular characteristics of the social class structure of ancient Greece as Aristotle describes it. How did this class structure promote or impede the development of democratic institutions in ancient Greece?

4. How did Solon's emphasis on wealth and income in governance represent a step forward from hereditary rule?

5. Why did the issue of debt play such an important role in the reforms instituted by Solon? In what way did the geography of ancient Greece intersect with the issue of debt, and how did these matters intersect with Greece's expanding population?

duced the four-hundred-member parliament, again devolving power downward to the people. He even instituted an unusual law requiring citizens to take a side in any civic dispute; the penalty for failing to do so was confiscation of the offender's goods. Solon's purpose in instituting this law was to increase the level of civic engagement in Athens.

The sections of the *Athenian Constitution* dealing with Pisistratus continue the history. Although Pisistratus did not initiate any noteworthy constitutional or democratic reforms, he tried to continue to enforce Solon's legal code, providing some element of stability in Athenian law. His rule provides a good example of a Greek tyrant who was not tyrannical as the word is understood now.

The remainder of the *Athenian Constitution* is an examination of the state of democracy and constitutional matters in Athens during Aristotle's lifetime. Solon was essential to Greek thinking about democracy and constitutional reform, for he was the first to encourage direct citizen participation in democratic institutions. Ultimately, these institutions would take hold in the Western world after knowledge of the institutions of Greece (and Rome) became widespread in the West during the Renaissance. European Enlightenment thinkers of the eighteenth century would use these models in overthrowing monarchies and creating the democracies that have dominated Europe, North America, and a large and growing number of other countries since then.

Further Reading

▪ Articles

Forrest, G. "Greece: The History of the Archaic Period." In *The Oxford History of the Classical World*, ed. John Boardman, Jasper Griffin, and Oswyn Murray. New York: Oxford University Press, New York, 1986.

Rhodes, Peter John. "The Reforms and Laws of Solon the Wise: An Optimistic View." In *Solon of Athens: New Historical and Philological Approaches*, ed. Josine Blok and André Lardinois. Leiden, Netherlands: Brill, 2006.

▪ Books

Day, James, and Mortimer Chambers. *Aristotle's History of Athenian Democracy*. Berkeley: University of California Press, 1962.

Irwin, Elizabeth. *Solon and Early Greek Poetry: The Politics of Exhortation*. New York: Cambridge University Press, 2005.

Keaney, John J. *The Composition of Aristotle's* Athenaion Politeia: *Observation and Explanation*. New York: Oxford University Press, 1992.

Moore, J. M. *Aristotle and Xenophon on Democracy and Oligarchy*. Berkeley: University of California Press, 1975.

Raaflaub, Kurt A., et al. *Origins of Democracy in Ancient Greece*. Berkeley: University of California Press, 2007.

Rhodes, Peter John. *Commentary on the Aristotelian Athenaion Politeia*. Oxford, U.K.: Clarendon Press, 1981.

Robinson, Eric W., ed. *Ancient Greek Democracy: Readings and Sources*. Oxford, U.K: Blackwell, 2003.

▪ Web Sites

"A History of Ancient Greece: Solon's Early Greek Legislation." International World History Project Web site.
  http://history-world.org/solon.htm.

—Michael J. O'Neal

ATHENIAN CONSTITUTION

Part 2

… There was contention for a long time between the upper classes and the populace. Not only was the constitution at this time oligarchical in every respect, but the poorer classes, men, women, and children, were the serfs of the rich. They were known as Pelatae and also as Hectemori, because they cultivated the lands of the rich at the rent thus indicated. The whole country was in the hands of a few persons, and if the tenants failed to pay their rent they were liable to be haled into slavery, and their children with them. All loans secured upon the debtor's person, a custom which prevailed until the time of Solon, who was the first to appear as the champion of the people. But the hardest and bitterest part of the constitution in the eyes of the masses was their state of serfdom. Not but what they were also discontented with every other feature of their lot; for, to speak generally, they had no part nor share in anything.

Part 3

Now the ancient constitution, as it existed before the time of Draco, was organized as follows. The magistrates were elected according to qualifications of birth and wealth. At first they governed for life, but subsequently for terms of ten years. The first magistrates, both in date and in importance, were the King, the Polemarch, and the Archon. The earliest of these offices was that of the King, which existed from ancestral antiquity. To this was added, secondly, the office of Polemarch, on account of some of the kings proving feeble in war; for it was on this account that Ion was invited to accept the post on an occasion of pressing need. The last of the three offices was that of the Archon, which most authorities state to have come into existence in the time of Medon. Others assign it to the time of Acastus, and adduce as proof the fact that the nine Archons swear to execute their oaths "as in the days of Acastus," which seems to suggest that it was in his time that the descendants of Codrus retired from the kingship in return for the prerogatives conferred upon the Archon. Whichever way it may be, the difference in date is small; but that it was the last of these magistracies to be created is shown by the fact that the Archon has no part in the ancestral sacrifices, as the King and the Polemarch have, but exclusively in those of later origin. So it is only at a comparatively late date that the office of Archon has become of great importance, through the dignity conferred by these later additions. The Thesmothetae were many years afterwards, when these offices had already become annual, with the object that they might publicly record all legal decisions, and act as guardians of them with a view to determining the issues between litigants. Accordingly their office, alone of those which have been mentioned, was never of more than annual duration.

Such, then, is the relative chronological precedence of these offices. At that time the nine Archons did not all live together. The King occupied the building now known as the Boculium, near the Prytaneum, as may be seen from the fact that even to the present day the marriage of the King's wife to Dionysus takes place there. The Archon lived in the Prytaneum, the Polemarch in the Epilyceum. The latter building was formerly called the Polemarcheum, but after Epilycus, during his term of office as Polemarch, had rebuilt it and fitted it up, it was called the Epilyceum. The Thesmothetae occupied the Thesmotheteum. In the time of Solon, however, they all came together into the Thesmotheteum. They had power to decide cases finally on their own authority, not, as now, merely to hold a preliminary hearing. Such then was the arrangement of the magistracies. The Council of Areopagus had as its constitutionally assigned duty the protection of the laws; but in point of fact it administered the greater and most important part of the government of the state, and inflicted personal punishments and fines summarily upon all who misbehaved themselves. This was the natural consequence of the facts that the Archons were elected under qualifications of birth and wealth, and that the Areopagus was composed of those who had served as Archons; for which latter reason the membership of the Areopagus is the only office which has continued to be a life-magistracy to the present day.

Part 4

Such was, in outline, the first constitution, but not very long after the events above recorded, in the archonship of Aristaichmus, Draco enacted his ordinances. Now his constitution had the following form. The franchise was given to all who could furnish themselves with a military equipment. The nine Archons and the Treasurers were elected by this body from persons possessing an unencumbered property of not less than ten minas, the less important officials from those who could furnish themselves with a military equipment, and the generals [Strategoi] and commanders of the cavalry [Hipparchoi] from those who could show an unencumbered property of not less than a hundred minas, and had children born in lawful wedlock over ten years of age. These officers were required to hold to bail the Prytanes, the Strategoi, and the Hipparchoi of the preceding year until their accounts had been audited, taking four securities of the same class as that to which the Strategoi and the Hipparchoi belonged. There was also to be a Council, consisting of four hundred and one members, elected by lot from among those who possessed the franchise. Both for this and for the other magistracies the lot was cast among those who were over thirty years of age; and no one might hold office twice until every one else had had his turn, after which they were to cast the lot afresh. If any member of the Council failed to attend when there was a sitting of the Council or of the Assembly, he paid a fine, to the amount of three drachmas if he was a Pentacosiomedimnus, two if he was a Knight, and One if he was a Zeugites. The Council of Areopagus was guardian of the laws, and kept watch over the magistrates to see that they executed their offices in accordance with the laws. Any person who felt himself wronged might lay an information before the Council of Areopagus, on declaring what law was broken by the wrong done to him. But, as has been said before, loans were secured upon the persons of the debtors, and the land was in the hands of a few.

Part 5

Since such, then, was the organization of the constitution, and the many were in slavery to the few, the people rose against the upper class. The strife was keen, and for a long time the two parties were ranged in hostile camps against one another, till at last, by common consent, they appointed Solon to be mediator and Archon, and committed the whole constitution to his hands. The immediate occasion of his appointment was his poem, which begins with the words:

> I behold, and within my heart deep sadness
>   has claimed its place,
> As I mark the oldest home of the ancient Ionian race
> Slain by the sword.

In this poem he fights and disputes on behalf of each party in turn against the other, and finally he advises them to come to terms and put an end to the quarrel existing between them. By birth and reputation Solon was one of the foremost men of the day, but in wealth and position he was of the middle class, as is generally agreed, and is, indeed, established by his own evidence in these poems, where he exhorts the wealthy not to be grasping.

> But ye who have store of good, who are sated
>   and overflow,
> Restrain your swelling soul, and still it and
>   keep it low:
> Let the heart that is great within you be
>   trained a lowlier way;
> Ye shall not have all at your will, and we will
>   not for ever obey.

Indeed, he constantly fastens the blame of the conflict on the rich; and accordingly at the beginning of the poem he says that he fears "the love of wealth and an overweening mind," evidently meaning that it was through these that the quarrel arose.

Part 6

As soon as he was at the head of affairs, Solon liberated the people once and for all, by prohibiting all loans on the security of the debtor's person: and in addition he made laws by which he cancelled all debts, public and private. This measure is commonly called the Seisachtheia [removal of burdens], since thereby the people had their loads removed from them. In connexion with it some persons try to traduce the character of Solon. It so happened that, when he was about to enact the Seisachtheia, he communicated his intention to some members of the upper class, whereupon, as the partisans of the popular party say, his friends stole a march on him; while those who wish to attack his character maintain that he too had a share in the fraud himself. For these persons borrowed money and bought up a large amount of land, and so when, a short time afterwards, all debts were cancelled, they became wealthy; and this, they say, was the origin of the families which were afterwards looked on as having been wealthy from primeval times. However, the story of the popular party is by far the most probable. A man who was so moderate and public-spirited in all his other actions, that when it was within his power to put his fellow-citizens beneath his feet and establish himself as tyrant, he preferred instead to incur the hostility of both parties by placing his honour and the general welfare above his personal aggrandisement, is not likely to have consented to defile his hands by such a petty and palpable fraud. That he had this absolute power is, in the first place, indicated by the desperate condition the country; moreover, he mentions it himself repeatedly in his poems, and it is universally admitted. We are therefore bound to consider this accusation to be false.

Part 7

Next Solon drew up a constitution and enacted new laws; and the ordinances of Draco ceased to be used, with the exception of those relating to murder. The laws were inscribed on the wooden stands, and set up in the King's Porch, and all swore to obey them; and the nine Archons made oath upon the stone, declaring that they would dedicate a golden statue if they should transgress any of them. This is the origin of the oath to that effect which they take to the present day. Solon ratified his laws for a hundred years; and the following was the fashion in which he organized the constitution. He divided the population according to property into four classes, just as it had been divided before, namely, Pentacosiomedimni, Knights, Zeugitae, and Thetes. The various magistracies, namely, the nine Archons, the Treasurers, the Commissioners for Public Contracts (Poletae), the Eleven, and Clerks (Colacretae), he assigned to the Pentacosiomedimni, the Knights, and the Zeugitae, giving offices to each class in proportion to the value of their rateable property. To who ranked among the Thetes he gave nothing but a place in the Assembly and in the juries. A man had to rank as a Pentacosiomedimnus if he made, from his own land, five hundred measures, whether liquid or solid. Those ranked as Knights who made three hundred measures, or, as some say, those who were able to maintain a horse. In support of the latter definition they adduce the name of the class, which may be supposed to be derived from this fact, and also some votive offerings of early times; for in the Acrop-

olis there is a votive offering, a statue of Diphilus, bearing this inscription:

The son of Diphilus, Athenion hight,
Raised from the Thetes and become a knight,
Did to the gods this sculptured charger bring,
For his promotion a thank-offering.

And a horse stands in evidence beside the man, implying that this was what was meant by belonging to the rank of Knight. At the same time it seems reasonable to suppose that this class, like the Pentacosiomedimni, was defined by the possession of an income of a certain number of measures. Those ranked as Zeugitae who made two hundred measures, liquid or solid; and the rest ranked as Thetes, and were not eligible for any office. Hence it is that even at the present day, when a candidate for any office is asked to what class he belongs, no one would think of saying that he belonged to the Thetes.

Part 8

The elections to the various offices Solon enacted should be by lot, out of candidates selected by each of the tribes. Each tribe selected ten candidates for the nine archonships, and among these the lot was cast. Hence it is still the custom for each tribe to choose ten candidates by lot, and then the lot is again cast among these. A proof that Solon regulated the elections to office according to the property classes may be found in the law still in force with regard to the Treasurers, which enacts that they shall be chosen from the Pentacosiomedimni. Such was Solon's legislation with respect to the nine Archons; whereas in early times the Council of Areopagus summoned suitable persons according to its own judgement and appointed them for the year to the several offices. There were four tribes, as before, and four tribe-kings. Each tribe was divided into three Trittyes [Thirds], with twelve Naucraries in each; and the Naucraries had officers of their own, called Naucrari, whose duty it was to superintend the current receipts and expenditure. Hence, among the laws of Solon now obsolete, it is repeatedly written that the Naucrari are to receive and to spend out of the Naucraric fund. Solon also appointed a Council of four hundred, a hundred from each tribe; but he assigned to the Council of the Areopagus the duty of superintending the laws, acting as before as the guardian of the constitution in general. It kept watch over the affairs of the state in most of the more important matters, and corrected offenders, with full powers to inflict either fines or personal punishment. The money received in fines it brought up into the Acropolis, without assigning the reason for the mulct. It also tried those who conspired for the overthrow of the state, Solon having enacted a process of impeachment to deal with such offenders. Further, since he saw the state often engaged in internal disputes, while many of the citizens from sheer indifference accepted whatever might turn up, he made a law with express reference to such persons, enacting that any one who, in a time civil factions, did not take up arms with either party, should lose his rights as a citizen and cease to have any part in the state.

Part 9

Such, then, was his legislation concerning the magistracies. There are three points in the constitution of Solon which appear to be its most democratic features: first and most important, the prohibition of loans on the security of the debtor's person; secondly, the right of every person who so willed to claim redress on behalf of any one to whom wrong was being done; thirdly, the institution of the appeal to the jurycourts; and it is to this last, they say, that the masses have owed their strength most of all, since, when the democracy is master of the voting-power, it is master of the constitution. Moreover, since the laws were not drawn up in simple and explicit terms (but like the one concerning inheritances and wards of state), disputes inevitably occurred, and the courts had to decide in every matter, whether public or private. Some persons in fact believe that Solon deliberately made the laws indefinite, in order that the final decision might be in the hands of the people. This, however, is not probable, and the reason no doubt was that it is impossible to attain ideal perfection when framing a law in general terms; for we must judge of his intentions, not from the actual results in the present day, but from the general tenor of the rest of his legislation.

Part 10

These seem to be the democratic features of his laws; but in addition, before the period of his legislation, he carried through his abolition of debts, and after it his increase in the standards of weights and

measures, and of the currency. During his administration the measures were made larger than those of Pheidon, and the mina, which previously had a standard of seventy drachmas, was raised to the full hundred. The standard coin in earlier times was the two-drachma piece. He also made weights corresponding with the coinage, sixty-three minas going to the talent; and the odd three minas were distributed among the staters and the other values.

Part 11

When he had completed his organization of the constitution in the manner that has been described, he found himself beset by people coming to him and harassing him concerning his laws, criticizing here and questioning there, till, as he wished neither to alter what he had decided on nor yet to be an object of ill will to every one by remaining in Athens, he set off on a journey to Egypt, with the combined objects of trade and travel, giving out that he should not return for ten years. He considered that there was no call for him to expound the laws personally, but that every one should obey them just as they were written. Moreover, his position at this time was unpleasant. Many members of the upper class had been estranged from him on account of his abolition of debts, and both parties were alienated through their disappointment at the condition of things which he had created. The mass of the people had expected him to make a complete redistribution of all property, and the upper class hoped he would restore everything to its former position, or, at any rate, make but a small change. Solon, however, had resisted both classes. He might have made himself a despot by attaching himself to whichever party he chose, but he preferred, though at the cost of incurring the enmity of both, to be the saviour of his country and the ideal lawgiver.

Part 12

The truth of this view of Solon's policy is established alike by common consent, and by the mention he has himself made of the matter in his poems. Thus:

I gave to the mass of the people such rank as befitted their need,
I took not away their honour, and I granted naught to their greed;

While those who were rich in power, who in
  wealth were glorious and great,
I bethought me that naught should befall them
  unworthy their splendour and state;
So I stood with my shield outstretched, and
  both were sale in its sight,
And I would not that either should triumph,
  when the triumph was not with right.

Again he declares how the mass of the people
ought to be treated: But thus will the people best the
voice of their leaders obey, When neither too slack is
the rein, nor violence holdeth the sway; For indulgence breedeth a child, the presumption that spurns
control,

When riches too great are poured upon men of
unbalanced soul.

And again elsewhere he speaks about the persons
who wished to redistribute the land: So they came in
search of plunder, and their cravings knew no hound,
Every one among them deeming endless wealth
would here be found. And that I with glozing
smoothness hid a cruel mind within. Fondly then
and vainly dreamt they; now they raise an angry din,
And they glare askance in anger, and the light within their eyes Burns with hostile flames upon me. Yet
therein no justice lies. All I promised, fully wrought
I with the gods at hand to cheer, Naught beyond in
folly ventured. Never to my soul was dear With a
tyrant's force to govern, nor to see the good and base
Side by side in equal portion share the rich home of
our race.

Once more he speaks of the abolition of debts and
of those who before were in servitude, but were
released owing to the Seisachtheia:

Of all the aims for which I summoned forth
The people, was there one I compassed not?
Thou, when slow time brings justice in its
  train,
O mighty mother of the Olympian gods,
Dark Earth, thou best canst witness, from
  whose breast
I swept the pillars broadcast planted there,
And made thee free, who hadst been slave of
  yore.
And many a man whom fraud or law had sold
For from his god-built land, an outcast slave,
I brought again to Athens; yea, and some,
Exiles from home through debt's oppressive
  load,
Speaking no more the dear Athenian tongue,

But wandering far and wide, I brought again;
And those that here in vilest slavery
Crouched 'neath a master's frown, I set them
  free.
Thus might and right were yoked in harmony,
Since by the force of law I won my ends
And kept my promise. Equal laws I gave
To evil and to good, with even hand
Drawing straight justice for the lot of each.
But had another held the goad as
One in whose heart was guile and greediness,
He had not kept the people back from strife.
For had I granted, now what pleased the one,
Then what their foes devised in counterpoise,
Of many a man this state had been bereft.
Therefore I showed my might on every side,
Turning at bay like wolf among the hounds.

And again he reviles both parties for their grumblings in the times that followed:

Nay, if one must lay blame where blame is due,
Wer't not for me, the people ne'er had set
Their eyes upon these blessings e'en in
  dreams:
While greater men, the men of wealthier life,
Should praise me and should court me as their
  friend.

For had any other man, he says, received this
exalted post,

He had not kept the people hack, nor ceased
Til he had robbed the richness of the milk.
But I stood forth a landmark in the midst,
And barred the foes from battle.

Part 13

Such then, were Solon's reasons for his departure
from the country. After his retirement the city was
still torn by divisions. For four years, indeed, they
lived in peace; but in the fifth year after Solon's government they were unable to elect an Archon on
account of their dissensions, and again four years
later they elected no Archon for the same reason.
Subsequently, after a similar period had elapsed,
Damasias was elected Archon; and he governed for
two years and two months, until he was forcibly
expelled from his office. After this, it was agreed, as a
compromise, to elect ten Archons, five from the

Eupatridae, three from the Agroeci, and two from the Demiurgi, and they ruled for the year following Damasias. It is clear from this that the Archon was at the time the magistrate who possessed the greatest power, since it is always in connexion with this office that conflicts are seen to arise. But altogether they were in a continual state of internal disorder. Some found the cause and justification of their discontent in the abolition of debts, because thereby they had been reduced to poverty; others were dissatisfied with the political constitution, because it had undergone a revolutionary change; while with others the motive was found in personal rivalries among themselves. The parties at this time were three in number. First there was the party of the Shore, led by Megacles the son of Alcmeon, which was considered to aim at a moderate form of government; then there were the men of the Plain, who desired an oligarchy and were led by Lycurgus; and thirdly there were the men of the Highlands, at the head of whom was Pisistratus, who was looked on as an extreme democrat. This latter party was reinforced by those who had been deprived of the debts due to them, from motives of poverty, and by those who were not of pure descent, from motives of personal apprehension. A proof of this is seen in the fact that after the tyranny was overthrown a revision was made of the citizen-roll, on the ground that many persons were partaking in the franchise without having a right to it. The names given to the respective parties were derived from the districts in which they held their lands.

Part 14

Pisistratus had the reputation of being an extreme democrat, and he also had distinguished himself greatly in the war with Megara. Taking advantage of this, he wounded himself, and by representing that his injuries had been inflicted on him by his political rivals, he persuaded the people, through a motion proposed by Aristion, to grant him a bodyguard. After he had got these "club-bearers," as they were called, he made an attack with them on the people and seized the Acropolis. This happened in the archonship of Comeas, thirty-one years after the legislation of Solon. It is related that, when Pisistratus asked for his bodyguard, Solon opposed the request, and declared that in so doing he proved himself wiser than half the people and braver than the rest, wiser than those who did not see that Pisistratus designed to make himself tyrant, and braver than those who

saw it and kept silence. But when all his words availed nothing he carried forth his armour and set it up in front of his house, saying that he had helped his country so far as lay in his power (he was already a very old man), and that he called on all others to do the same. Solon's exhortations, however, proved fruitless, and Pisistratus assumed the sovereignty. His administration was more like a constitutional government than the rule of a tyrant; but before his power was firmly established, the adherents of Megacles and Lycurgus made a coalition and drove him out. This took place in the archonship of Hegesias, five years after the first establishment of his rule. Eleven years later Megacles, being in difficulties in a party struggle, again opened negotiations with Pisistratus, proposing that the latter should marry his daughter; and on these terms he brought him back to Athens, by a very primitive and simple-minded device. He first spread abroad a rumour that Athena was bringing back Pisistratus, and then, having found a woman of great stature and beauty, named Phye (according to Herodotus, of the deme of Paeania, but as others say a Thracian flower-seller of the deme of Collytus), he dressed her in a garb resembling that of the goddess and brought her into the city with Pisistratus. The latter drove in on a chariot with the woman beside him, and the inhabitants of the city, struck with awe, received him with adoration.

Part 15

In this manner did his first return take place. He did not, however, hold his power long, for about six years after his return he was again expelled. He refused to treat the daughter of Megacles as his wife, and being afraid, in consequence, of a combination of the two opposing parties, he retired from the country. First he led a colony to a place called Rhaicelus, in the region of the Thermaic gulf; and thence he passed to the country in the neighbourhood of Mt. Pangaeus. Here he acquired wealth and hired mercenaries; and not till ten years had elapsed did he return to Eretria and make an attempt to recover the government by force. In this he had the assistance of many allies, notably the Thebans and Lygdamis of Naxos, and also the Knights who held the supreme power in the constitution of Eretria. After his victory in the battle at Pallene he captured Athens, and when he had disarmed the people he at last had his tyranny securely established, and was able to take Naxos and set up Lygdamis as ruler there. He effected the disarmament of the people in the following manner. He ordered a parade in full armour in the Theseum, and began to make a speech to the people. He spoke for a short time, until the people called out that they could not hear him, whereupon he bade them come up to the entrance of the Acropolis, in order that his voice might be better heard. Then, while he continued to speak to them at great length, men whom he had appointed for the purpose collected the arms and locked them up in the chambers of the Theseum hard by, and came and made a signal to him that it was done. Pisistratus accordingly, when he had finished the rest of what he had to say, told the people also what had happened to their arms; adding that they were not to be surprised or alarmed, but go home and attend to their private affairs, while he would himself for the future manage all the business of the state.

Part 16

Such was the origin and such the vicissitudes of the tyranny of Pisistratus. His administration was temperate, as has been said before, and more like constitutional government than a tyranny. Not only was he in every respect humane and mild and ready to forgive those who offended, but, in addition, he advanced money to the poorer people to help them in their labours, so that they might make their living by agriculture. In this he had two objects, first that they might not spend their time in the city but might be scattered over all the face of the country, and secondly that, being moderately well off and occupied with their own business, they might have neither the wish nor the time to attend to public affairs. At the same time his revenues were increased by the thorough cultivation of the country, since he imposed a tax of one

Glossary

Agroeci, Demiurgi, and Eupatridae	a reference to classes of people: the peasants, the artisans and tradespeople, and the nobility, respectively
ancient Ionian race	broadly speaking, the Greeks who were Aristotle's ancestors
Eritrea	country in the Horn of Africa on the Red Sea
deme	a country district or village, part of a city-state (polis)
glozing	flattering
King's Porch	the seat of the archon (king)
Ion, Medon, Acastus, and Codrus	a reference to various reputed leaders of Athens: Ion was commander in chief of the Athenian army under the archaic mythological king Erechtheus. Medon was the son of Codrus (the last of Athens's legendary kings) and the first archon of Athens. Acastus was the successor to Medon.
Lycurgus	Spartan lawgiver of the eighth century bce
marriage of the King's wife to Dionysus	a ceremony during which the king's wife was symbolically married to the god Dionysus
Naucrari	subdivisions of the population of the Athenian state
Pheidon	king of Argos in the eighth century bce who instituted a system of standard measurements
the Eleven	the panel in charge of prisoners and executions—a group with immense discretion in determining who was arrested and in ordering summary executions
Thermaic gulf	gulf in the Aegean Sea now called the Gulf of Salonika
Thesmothetae	the six junior archons

tenth on all the produce. For the same reasons he instituted the local justices, and often made expeditions in person into the country to inspect it and to settle disputes between individuals, that they might not come into the city and neglect their farms. It was in one of these progresses that, as the story goes, Pisistratus had his adventure with the man of Hymettus, who was cultivating the spot afterwards known as "Tax-free Farm." He saw a man digging and working at a very stony piece of ground, and being surprised he sent his attendant to ask what he got out of this plot of land. "Aches and pains," said the man; "and that's what Pisistratus ought to have his tenth of." The man spoke without knowing who his questioner was; but Pisistratus was so pleased with his frank speech and his industry that he granted him exemption from all taxes. And so in matters in general he burdened the people as little as possible with his government, but always cultivated peace and kept them in all quietness. Hence the tyranny of Pisistratus was often spoken of proverbially as "the age of gold"; for when his sons succeeded him the government became much harsh-

er. But most important of all in this respect was his popular and kindly disposition. In all things he was accustomed to observe the laws, without giving himself any exceptional privileges. Once he was summoned on a charge of homicide before the Areopagus, and he appeared in person to make his defence; but the prosecutor was afraid to present himself and abandoned the case. For these reasons he held power long, and whenever he was expelled he regained his position easily. The majority alike of the upper class and of the people were in his favour; the former he won by his social intercourse with them, the latter by the assistance which he gave to their private purses, and his nature fitted him to win the hearts of both. Moreover, the laws in reference to tyrants at that time in force at Athens were very mild, especially the one which applies more particularly to the establishment of a tyranny. The law ran as follows: "These are the ancestral statutes of the Athenians; if any persons shall make an attempt to establish a tyranny, or if any person shall join in setting up a tyranny, he shall lose his civic rights, both himself and his whole house."

CANON OF FILIAL PIETY

"In filial piety there is nothing greater than the reverential awe of one's father."

Overview

Even though the Canon of Filial Piety is the shortest of the Thirteen Classics of Confucianism, it has been one of the most influential Confucian works for more than two thousand years. The Thirteen Classics were writings acclaimed by the government because they embodied the words and acts of the ideal rulers of the golden past: the sage-kings Yao, Shun, and Yu. Much of the text's success may be attributed to its brevity, which has made it easy to memorize. Another reason it has been so highly regarded is that it heralds one of China's most treasured values: filial piety, or *xiao*, which means "to selflessly serve one's parents." Equally significant, this classic resolved one of Confucianism's major contradictions: How can one always show both filial piety to one's family and loyalty to the state? Because of its emphasis on applying the value of filial piety to the tenets of good government, the Canon has commanded unremitting attention and admiration from emperors, officials, and scholars throughout East Asia.

Many things about the Canon of Filial Piety have flummoxed scholars for centuries. We know neither precisely when it was written nor who wrote it. Many experts believe it was composed before 239 BCE; others maintain that it did not appear in complete form until the Western Han Dynasty (202 BCE–8 CE). Some scholars think that the text has distinct layers that were composed over a long span of time; thus, various authors could have composed different strata of the text. There has also been much contention over what is the more authentic version of the work. Since the Canon lacks both a preface and an epilogue, one cannot say with certainty why it was written. Judging by its contents, though, the Canon had been primarily directed at rulers and officials; the message was that filial piety was the key to ruling well.

Context

Although no one knows precisely when the Canon of Filial Piety was composed, many scholars think that the document, or at least its oldest layer, was written late in the Warring States Period, between 300 and 239 BCE. A dissenting group of researchers believes that it was created during the Western Han Dynasty or at least that the text's latest stratum then came into being. The Warring States Period (481–221 BCE) was a tumultuous era during which the unified government of the earlier years of the Zhou Dynasty (1049–256 BCE) had become but a distant memory. (Many Confucians viewed the early Zhou Dynasty as China's golden age.) During the Warring States Period, China was divided into seven major territorial states that often fought with one another. Rulers were hindered in centralizing their power because the relatives they invested as hereditary ministers amassed huge fortunes, controlled sizable fiefs, and surrounded themselves with large armies of retainers. Within each state, the minister's influence often rivaled that of the ruler.

To strengthen their control at home and to project power abroad, the rulers of these states implemented a number of reforms. Armies were transformed from having been composed of a small number of chariots manned by warrior aristocrats to large professionally led infantries composed of peasants. To field these massive forces, the rulers needed a bureaucracy to register, draft, and tax the rural population. To carry out these duties, rulers had increasingly relied less on ministers and more on talented men from the humbler classes. As a result, this period witnessed a tremendous surge in social mobility.

By 250 BCE the Qin had emerged as the strongest regime, and their conquest of other Chinese states was just a matter of time. The Qin had achieved this position thanks to their impregnable geographic position in the mountainous west. They also implemented reforms more systematically than any other state. The Qin established a comprehensive law code that generously rewarded farmers and soldiers and penalized merchants. Noble titles were granted on the basis of one's performance in battle, not one's bloodline. The government organized families into groups of five and ten and held them accountable for the behavior of each member of every household. Having abolished fiefs, the Qin organized their territory into districts that their own agents directly administered.

Rulers were in dire need of men who were talented strategists, administrators, and warriors. To take advantage

551 BCE	■ Confucius is born.
300 BCE	■ The *Commentary of Mr. Zuo* is completed.
CA. **300– 239** BCE	■ The Canon of Filial Piety is composed.
239 BCE	■ The *Annals of Mr. Lü* is compiled.
221 BCE	■ The state of Qin unifies all of China.
213 BCE	■ Qin Shi Huangdi, the First Emperor, orders the alleged "Burning of the Books."
207 BCE	■ Rebels seize the capital and burn the imperial library; the Canon of Filial Piety disappears.
202 BCE	■ The Han Dynasty is established.
191 BCE	■ Emperor Hui of Han rescinds the order that proscribed private books.

of these opportunities, men clamored for education and went from state to state in search of instructors. Private teachers such as Confucius (551–479 BCE) emerged as men of key importance. The master, or more often his students, perpetuated his teachings by recording them so that they could be transmitted within the "school" (a master-disciple network). It was by this means that philosophical and military works such as the Confucian Analects came about. There were so many teachings that this era came to be called the "Era of One Hundred Schools." Nevertheless, there were only two organized schools: the Confucians and the Mohists, the latter having been the followers of Mo Di or (also known as Mozi, ca. 468–376 BCE).

Confucians advocated that nothing is more important than cultivating one's own goodness by helping others. A true king is one who has morally purified himself, values the people's welfare, and leads by example. Since cultivating one's behavior starts at home, filial piety is the basis of the ability to act selflessly toward others. One of the hallmarks of Confucian thought was the requirement that a son, in order to show filial piety upon the death of either parent, should go into a three-year period of mourning. During that time, he should live in a lean-to, dress in hemp robes, and avoid meat, alcohol, music, and sex. The Mohists also emphasized the importance of acting morally and working on behalf of the people's welfare; thus, the ruler should live frugally and select officials for their ability without regard to their pedigree. However, one should display concern for everyone, not just his family.

One of the abiding criticisms of the Confucians was that they placed too much emphasis on filial piety. Mohists complained that the three years' mourning system hurt the state by reducing its population, destroying its wealth through burying it, and keeping the people from working. Other philosophers of the Warring States Period castigated the Confucians for privileging the father-son tie over that of the lord-retainer. Many of them condemned the following tale from the Analects: Once a governor boasted to Confucius that in his jurisdiction there was a man named Upright Gong, who was so honest that he turned in his father for stealing sheep. Confucius replied that a truly upright man would hide his father's crimes and an upright father would do the same for his son. For the critics of Confucianism, this story clearly indicates that practicing filial piety can encourage disloyalty.

About the Author

Modern researchers have reached no definite conclusion as to who authored the Canon of Filial Piety. For the past two thousand years, scholars have put forward many candidates. The work features Confucius addressing his disciple Zeng Shen. Before the Song Dynasty, the Chinese uniformly had believed that the work was Zeng Shen's record of Confucius's words. However, because the book states that Confucius was lecturing Zengzi, which literally means "Master Zeng," Song Dynasty scholars reasoned that Zeng

Shen would not refer to himself by the honorific name of Master Zeng. Obviously, one of his disciples must have written it, such as Yuezheng Zichun, who was noted for his filiality, or Zisi, who was noted for his loyalty and ritually correct behavior and has been credited with writing many other Confucian works. Because of the similarity of the language and content of the Canon to texts that took final shape during the Western Han Dynasty, a few scholars have concluded that the text, or at least its latest stratum, was written during the Han Dynasty (202 BCE–220 CE). The most likely explanation, however, is that either Yuezheng Zichun or Zisi, or even one of their disciples, wrote either the entire Canon of Filial Piety or its earliest layer.

Explanation and Analysis of the Document

One of the most interesting aspects of the Canon of Filial Piety is that it says little about how one actually practices filiality, so it clearly is not a guide to cultivating this virtue. Instead, it dwells on filiality's political aspects: the connection between filiality and loyalty, its ability to protect one's position and patrimony, and the ways in which it can help a ruler govern.

Most scholars now believe that Canon of Filial Piety was composed near the end of the Warring States Period. They arrive at this conclusion because a philosophical work titled *The Annals of Mr. Lü*—which was compiled on behalf of Lü Buwei, chief minister of Qin, around 239 BCE—contains two substantial quotations from the Canon, one of which even cites the text by name. Since the Canon also repeatedly quotes the *Commentary of Mr. Zuo*, which probably took its final form by 300 BCE, this indicates that the text was written sometime between 300 and 239 BCE. However, from as early as the Song Dynasty (960–1279 CE), scholars have suspected that the text has at least two layers. The great twelfth-century neo-Confucian philosopher Zhu Xi pointed out that the first seven chapters formed a unit that probably represented the text's oldest stratum. For him, this was the scripture, while the rest was an explanatory commentary. It could well be, then, that the later part of the text was not added until the Western Han Dynasty.

Further complicating its history, the Canon of Filial Piety was transmitted in two versions. In 213 BCE, after his unification of China, Qin Shi Huangdi, the First Emperor, confiscated all privately held books and stored them in the imperial library. This event has been called the "Burning of the Books." In 207 BCE, when rebels seized and burned the capital, Xianyang, the library went up in flames, as did most of China's earliest books. During the reign of Emperor Wen of Han in the mid-second century BCE, the Canon resurfaced in a version written in the then-current clerical script, which any literate person could read. Hence, it was called the New Text version, which has always been the most common and is the one on which the document here is based. When Prince Gong of Lu demolished a wall in Confucius's home to expand his palace in 135 BCE, he found a cache of texts written in an ancient script. One of

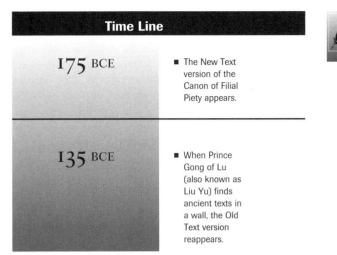

Time Line

175 BCE
- The New Text version of the Canon of Filial Piety appears.

135 BCE
- When Prince Gong of Lu (also known as Liu Yu) finds ancient texts in a wall, the Old Text version reappears.

these works was supposedly the Canon. This version became known as the Old Text. There are only two minor discrepancies between the two versions. Of the eighteen chapters of this work, ten end with quotations from the Book of Poetry, and another ends with a quotation from the Book of Documents. These are two of the most important Confucian classics because they are among the oldest (their earliest layers dating to the eleventh century BCE). The author incorporated these quotations in his text to demonstrate that his work was illustrating ideas found in these earlier classics. In other words, he was using these texts' authority to give weight to his own words.

◆ "The Scope and Meaning of the Treatise"

Confucius (called "the Master" in the document) begins by extolling the wonders of filial piety to his disciple Zengzi. By perfecting this virtue, one can unify society, eliminate discord, and bring about order. That is because filial piety is the root of all virtues. One begins the practice of filial piety with the simple task of keeping the body whole. Since the body is part of the legacy that one receives from one's parents, everything must be done to avoid injuring or mutilating it. Since earning a reputation for impeccable conduct calls attention to the quality of one's parents, accomplishing this harder task is the completion of filial piety. But what makes one's conduct impeccable? In one's youth, filial piety consists of serving one's parents well. In adulthood, it consists of serving one's lord well. One completes the task by establishing a reputation for oneself as a moral exemplar. Treating one's parents well at home is only the beginning. To truly demonstrate filial piety, one must glorify them by serving in government and earning a reputation for moral excellence. Filial piety is thus tied to behavior outside of one's home.

◆ "Filial Piety in the Son of Heaven"

This chapter sets forth the important concepts of love (*ai*) and respect (*jing*), which are the two primary components of filial piety. With reasoning reminiscent of the Mohist's idea of universal love, the author stresses that the Son of Heaven must display love and respect for everyone's parents.

Neglecting to do so will spell trouble for his parents. ("Son of Heaven" is a traditional name for the paramount ruler. Since in his person, he links heaven, earth, and the human being, he is regarded as more than an ordinary person—he is heaven's representative.) The author then presents a parallel set of behaviors: At home, the Son of Heaven must love and respect his parents; at court, he expresses his love and respect for the people. Hence, no matter whether at home or abroad, filial piety consists of both love and respect.

◆ **"Filial Piety in High Ministers and Great Officers"**

High officers preserve their patrimonies not through humility and restraint but through the Confucian virtue of *li*, which means "propriety" or "ritually appropriate behavior." Confucians believed that during the Western Zhou Dynasty the sage-kings (called "ancient kings" in the document and often referred to as "former kings" by Confucians) had ruled China perfectly by amply demonstrating their moral goodness and concern for the people. The Confucian classics preserve the former kings' words, deeds, and conduct. For great officers, then, the best means of preserving one's patrimony was to mimic the behavior of these perfect rulers by embodying the rules set forth in the Confucian classics. In doing so, high ministers and great officers could avoid public discontent and prevent rebellion.

◆ **"Filial Piety in Inferior Officers"**

This chapter underscores how love and respect link filial piety with loyalty. One loves both his mother and father; however, one does not respect one's mother because her social position is less significant than that of the father. One respects both one's father and his lord because of their authority. However, one does not love one's lord. The only person that one both loves and respects is the father. A son who practices filial piety serves his lord as he does his father; thus, his filiality becomes loyalty. He also serves his elders as he does his father; thus, his filiality becomes obedience. If one practices filial piety, he will automatically be a loyal and obedient functionary. This will guarantee that he will always enjoy his lord's favor, thereby protecting his position.

◆ **"Filial Piety in the Common People"**

Whereas all of the preceding chapters define filial piety as protecting one's patrimony, this chapter states that commoners must see that their parents' material needs are satisfied; by doing so, they practice filial piety. Filial piety thereby consists of accumulating material wealth to be used on one's parents' behalf and by curbing one's own extravagance.

The second passage sums up the previous chapters' message: No matter to which class one belongs, as long as one practices filial piety, one will safeguard himself and his patrimony from disaster. Filial piety, then, is ultimately a form of self-protection. That this passage has little to do with commoners might be why it stands alone as a separate chapter in the Old Text version. That these first six chapters form a logical unit has led a number of scholars to believe that they are the text's oldest layer.

◆ **"Filial Piety in Relation to the Three Powers"**

The next three chapters tell the reader how one uses filial piety to rule effectively. An important reason for the efficacy of filial piety is its overriding metaphysical significance. Filial piety connects people with heaven and earth and thus the universe. Upon perfecting his filial piety, a ruler becomes attuned to the principle that undergirds all things in the universe, which means that his actions can also affect them. Since he embodies the natural moral order, his laws will not have to be severe; people will want to do as he says because it is naturally right. He will merely have to nudge people in the right direction, and they will follow. More concretely, by being in tune with heaven and earth, he can transform the people merely through his example.

◆ **"Filial Piety in Government"**

Governing an empire or fief and heading a family are done in the same fashion: One never slights his subordinates. People socially below the ruler or family head deserve respect because they each fulfill an organizational role. For a leader to accomplish his goals, he needs each subordinate's help. To fulfill his duties, the leader—whether a ruler or the head of a clan—needs the cooperation of his subordinates. If he treats them with respect and solicitude, he can perfect the manifestation of filial piety and bring about peace and security. In sum, the perfection of filial piety and the creation of social order is a shared task.

◆ **"The Government of the Sages"**

Humans are the universe's highest life form, and filial piety is the loftiest form of human conduct. Nonetheless, it has gradations. Although serving one's parents well is good, it is far from being filial piety's highest form. Filial piety reaches it height when one makes one's ancestor the highest gods' sacrificial companion. Putting one's parents on the same level as heaven—making them the correlates of heaven—is thereby the greatest honor that one can give them. Nevertheless, since only the Son of Heaven can make his ancestor a sacrificial companion of the highest gods, it is an elitist definition of filial piety. Some analysts think that the Canon of Filial Piety here urges everyone to become the emperor. It is more likely that this passage betrays the tract's intended audience: the ruler himself. If one wants to be a true king, he must practice the grandest Confucian rites. One man who accomplished this task was the duke of Zhou. Confucius regarded him highly because, as regent, he safeguarded his nephew's position as Son of Heaven until he came of age.

The chapter's next section returns to the topic of how one rules with filial piety. In bringing up their children, parents become increasingly severe; by this means, they demonstrate to their children how to show respect (*jing*). At the same time, since parents also maintain intimacy with their children, they also show their children how to love (*ai*). If a ruler uses filial piety to govern his people, he shows them both love and respect. His laws do not have to be severe because the people will understand that his orders will ultimately benefit them.

Confucius and Buddha (Freer Gallery of Art, Smithsonian Institution, Washington, D.C.: Gift of Charles Lang Freer, F1916.73)

CANON OF FILIAL PIETY

213

Milestone Documents

The chapter's last part dwells on the parallelism between filial piety and loyalty. The relationship of father and son is ordained by heaven, just as is the relationship of lord and retainer. Consequently, if a man cannot love and respect his own parents, he is of no use to anyone. Since loyalty stems from filial piety, if a man cannot show the proper love and respect for his parents, how can he be expected to be loyal? In fact, he is no better than a rebel.

◆ **"An Orderly Description of the Acts of Filial Piety"**

This chapter begins with the work's most complete description of filial piety. However, the chapter's point is not merely to instruct its readers how to act toward their parents. The second section connects filial piety with the proper behavior for an official. A man who holds a high position will not be arrogant if he practices filial piety; likewise, if he practices filial piety as a subordinate, he will not rebel, and nor will he compete with his peers. Here the theme of filial piety as a form of self-preservation reemerges. If one practices it, one's behavior will not antagonize others; a person will thereby secure his position. The chapter ends by concluding that no matter how well one treats one's parents, if filiality is not reflected in one's behavior toward others, one is not truly practicing filial piety.

◆ **"Filial Piety in Relation to the Five Punishments"**

This chapter simply declares that there is no crime more heinous than the absence of filial piety; nonetheless, it goes on to describe three related acts that are equally odious. To go against one's ruler, the laws established by the sages, or one's parents are all acts that are anathema to the practice of filial piety and therefore abhorrent. Here, again, we see how one's behavior at home will have ramifications for one's behavior in the community.

◆ **"Amplification of 'the All-embracing Rule of Conduct' in Chapter I"**

This is the first of three chapters that expound upon the first chapter. It is because of these chapters that many scholars think that the Canon of Filial Piety has different layers. Once again the discussion focuses on how to rule with filial piety. However, this chapter lists four different things that must be employed to obtain good order: filial piety, brotherliness, music, and ritual propriety. It further states that ritual propriety is nothing but the concept of respect. If one displays respect toward another person, that person's relatives and subordinates will also be delighted. The ripple effects of displaying respect are so great that by revering only a few persons one may gain the respect of many.

◆ **"Amplification of 'the Perfect Virtue' in Chapter I"**

The author here further expounds upon using filial piety to transform the people's behavior. He notes that the ruler needs to display respect only to his own father; he does not need to make a show of it in many places. By respecting his father at home, he conveys the message that he respects everyone's father; by being brotherly to his brothers, he conveys that he respects everyone's brothers; by acting deferen-

tially to his lord, he conveys that he respects everyone's lord. The ruler merely has to perfect his own behavior; without even broadcasting it, his good conduct will transform others.

◆ **"Amplification of 'Making Our Name Famous' in Chapter I"**

If a ruler practices filial piety at home, his subjects will become loyal. If he is brotherly toward his elder brothers, the people will respect their elders. If he keeps his home in good order, good order will prevail in his kingdom. Hence, the ruler's reputation in later ages depends entirely on the quality of his filial piety at home.

◆ **"Filial Piety in Relation to Reproof and Remonstrance"**

The author here plainly states that filial piety cannot be equated with blind obedience. If a parent does something wrong, a son must point out his parent's mistake. If a son blindly obeys his parents, it can lead to disaster. The reason why rulers and lords do not suffer disaster even when their behavior is wrong is that they all have officials or retainers who call attention to their errors. Once again, the family parallels the state; just as a good official must point out "unrighteous conduct," so should a son.

◆ **"The Influence of Filial Piety and the Response to It"**

This chapter again discusses the significance of the ruler's filial piety and its metaphysical aspects. By demonstrating filial piety to his father, the good ruler, in effect, serves heaven; by demonstrating filial piety to his mother, the good ruler, in effect, serves earth. When heaven and earth are served through filiality, the spirits make their presence known through supernatural actions. The ruler perfects his filial piety by performing duties that stress that even he has those whom he must serve. He shows his humility by worshiping his ancestors in the temple and by deferring to older kinsmen. When a ruler humbles himself in this manner, heaven and earth respond by making their approval known.

◆ **"The Service of the Ruler"**

These two sentences describe how a retainer should serve his lord. He should demonstrate the utmost loyalty, correct the ruler's mistakes, and praise his good conduct to encourage him to do more. The result of these actions is that both the lord and his retainer are able to have fond thoughts for each other.

◆ **"Filial Piety in Mourning for Parents"**

Here the author gives the second most concrete description of filial obligations; this time he describes how one buries a parent and mourns his or her death. For the first three days after either parent's death, one does not eat. After dressing the body in grave clothes, one puts it in inner and outer coffins. After selecting a gravesite through prognostication, one buries the body and mourns it for up to three years. Upon the third year's completion, at the beginning of each season one presents

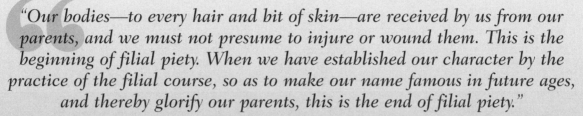

"*Our bodies—to every hair and bit of skin—are received by us from our parents, and we must not presume to injure or wound them. This is the beginning of filial piety. When we have established our character by the practice of the filial course, so as to make our name famous in future ages, and thereby glorify our parents, this is the end of filial piety.*"

("The Scope and Meaning of the Treatise")

"*Hence love is what is chiefly rendered to the mother, and reverence is what is chiefly rendered to the ruler, while both of these things are given to the father. Therefore when they serve their ruler with filial piety they are loyal; when they serve their superiors with reverence they are obedient.*"

("Filial Piety in Inferior Officers")

"*The ancient kings imitated the brilliant luminaries of Heaven and acted in accordance with the varying advantages afforded by Earth, so that they were in accord with all under Heaven, and in consequence their teachings, without being severe, were successful, and their government, without being rigorous, secured perfect order.*"

("Filial Piety in Relation to the Three Powers")

"'*Of all creatures with their different natures produced by Heaven and Earth, man is the noblest. Of all actions of man there is none greater than filial piety. In filial piety there is nothing greater than the reverential awe of one's father. In the reverential awe shown to one's father there is nothing greater than making him the correlate of Heaven.*'"

("The Government of the Sages")

sacrifices to the departed in the ancestral temple. This chapter is careful to note that one should not mourn excessively. One should not deny oneself food for more than three days; one does not grieve to the point where it threatens one's life.

Audience

Since the text mainly concerns the benefits of governing by means of filial piety, it was clearly meant for members of the ruling class. Most particularly, the author probably hoped that it would be read by rulers or their top advisers. This is especially clear in the "Government of Sages" chapter, which states that the greatest form of filial piety is to make one's father or ancestor the companion of heaven. Of course, the only person who could perform such a sacrifice was a king or the emperor. Thus, the Canon of Filial Piety is one of many documents from the Warring States Period in which the author tries to persuade a lord of the best means to rule. It was also meant, though, for any man who was a noble or served in a bureaucratic office. For instance, the chapter titled "The Service of the Ruler" is clearly addressed to someone in a subordinate position.

Impact

From the Han Dynasty to the twentieth century, educated East Asians have continuously read, published, and annotated the Canon of Filial Piety, because it offers a Confucian vision of government that emphasizes the importance of the ruler's moral virtue and the stability that practicing filial piety will bring. During the Han Dynasty, the Canon was of overwhelming importance in that the Han emperors attempted to justify their rule by means of filial piety. Hence, the word *filial* was placed before the posthumous name of each emperor. Government posts were given to men who had been recommended as "filial and incorrupt." By the Eastern Han Dynasty (25–220 CE), every government school had a lecturer on the Canon, and even imperial guardsmen had to read this scripture.

After the Han Dynasty ended, the Canon of Filial Piety still retained immense political significance. In the centuries since, a number of emperors have authored commentaries on the text. For example, in 719 CE Emperor Xuanzong ordered a court debate concerning which version, the New or Old Text, was superior. When the discussion did not yield the desired result, Xuanzong himself penned a commentary and had it engraved in stone at the entrance of the Imperial University. The scripture often attracted comment from the greatest statesmen and scholars of the day. During the Northern Song Dynasty (960–1127), the era's two greatest statesmen, Wang Anshi and Sima Guang, who were enemies, each wrote a treatise favoring a different version of the text. When northerners from the steppes conquered China, the Canon was one of the first books to be translated into their native languages. Thus, it was translated into Tabgach during the Northern Wei Dynasty (386–534), Tangut during the Western Xia Dynasty (1038–1227), Nuzhen during the Jin Dynasty (1115–1234), Mongolian during the Yuan Dynasty (1235–1368), and Manchurian during the Qing Dynasty (1644–1911). The Canon also made its way to Japan, Korea, and Vietnam, where it became essential reading for the upper class.

In addition to its political significance, the Canon of Filial Piety has remained immensely popular because of its brevity and simple language. It is only eighteen hundred Chinese characters long and uses just 388 different characters. From the Han Dynasty onward, it has often used as a primary-school primer. In premodern East Asia, any person educated in literary Chinese was familiar with this text. In medieval China it came to be seen as a text that had supernatural efficacy; it was said that by repeatedly chanting it, one could repel illnesses and bandits.

Further Reading

■ Articles

Holzman, Donald. "The Place of Filial Piety in Ancient China." *Journal of the American Oriental Society* 118, no. 2 (April–June 1998): 185–200.

■ Books

Ames, Roger T., and Henry Rosemont, Jr. *The Chinese Classic of Family Reverence: A Philosophical Translation of the Xiaojing.* Honolulu: University of Hawaii Press, 2008.

Questions for Further Study

1. Compare and contrast the vision of the king or ruler in ancient China with that outlined in Plato's "Allegory of the Cave." Was China's vision of the "sage-king" similar to Plato's version of the "philosopher-king"? What do these views tell you about the political concerns of these ancient peoples?

2. Why would the concept of filial piety have been considered so important at this time and under these historical circumstances? Why is the concept given less importance in modern life—if, in fact, you agree that it is given less importance?

3. Imagine that the author (or one of the authors) of the Canon of Filial Piety could observe contemporary American life. What do you believe this person would think about the practice of filial piety in modern-day America?

4. What impact did the philosophy of Confucius have on visions of government in early China?

5. Why do you think the Canon of Filial Piety has had such a profound impact on Chinese society? Why is it still read and studied, even by schoolchildren? To what extent do the principles of the canon still define what it is to be Chinese?

Knapp, Keith N. *Selfless Offspring: Filial Children and Social Order in Medieval China*. Honolulu: University of Hawaii Press, 2005.

Liu Ruixiang, Liu Zhihe, and Fu Genqing, trans. *The Classic of Filial Piety*. Jinan, China: Shandong Friendship Press, 1993.

Makra, Mary Lelia, trans. *The Hsiao Ching*, ed. Paul T.K. Sih. New York: St. John's University Press, 1961.

—Keith N. Knapp

Milestone Documents

CANON OF FILIAL PIETY

The Scope and Meaning of the Treatise

Once, when Zhong Ni was unoccupied, and his disciple Zeng was sitting by in attendance on him, the Master said, "The ancient kings had a perfect virtue and all-embracing rule of conduct, through which they were in accord with all under Heaven. By the practice of it the people were brought to live in peace and harmony, and there was no ill-will between superiors and inferiors. Do you know what it was?"

Zeng rose from his mat and said, "How should I, Shen, who am so devoid of intelligence, be able to know this?"

The Master said, "It was filial piety. Now filial piety is the root of all virtue, and the stem out of which grows all moral teaching. Sit down again, and I will explain the subject to you. Our bodies—to every hair and bit of skin—are received by us from our parents, and we must not presume to injure or wound them. This is the beginning of filial piety. When we have established our character by the practice of the filial course, so as to make our name famous in future ages and thereby glorify our parents, this is the end of filial piety. It commences with the service of parents; it proceeds to the service of the ruler; it is completed by the establishment of character.

It is said in the Major Odes of the Kingdom: Ever think of your ancestor, cultivating your virtue."

Filial Piety in the Son of Heaven

The Master said, "He who loves his parents will not dare to incur the risk of being hated by any man, and he who reveres his parents will not dare to incur the risk of being contemned by any man. When the love and reverence of the Son of Heaven are thus carried to the utmost in the service of his parents, the lessons of his virtue affect all the people, and he becomes a pattern to all within the four seas. This is the filial piety of the Son of Heaven.

It is said in the Marquis of Fu on Punishments: The one man will have felicity, and the millions of the people will depend on what ensures his happiness."

Filial Piety in High Ministers and Great Officers

"They do not presume to wear robes other than those appointed by the laws of the ancient kings, nor to speak words other than those sanctioned by their speech, nor to exhibit conduct other than that exemplified by their virtuous ways. Thus none of their words being contrary to those sanctions, and none of their actions contrary to the right way, from their mouths there comes no exceptionable speech, and in their conduct there are found no exceptionable actions. Their words may fill all under Heaven, and no error of speech will be found in them. Their actions may fill all under Heaven, and no dissatisfaction or dislike will be awakened by them. When these three things—their robes, their words, and their conduct—are all complete as they should be, they can then preserve their ancestral temples. This is the filial piety of high ministers and great officers.

It is said in the Book of Poetry: He is never idle, day or night, in the service of the one man."

Filial Piety in Inferior Officers

"As they serve their fathers, so they serve their mothers, and they love them equally. As they serve their fathers, so they serve their rulers, and they reverence them equally. Hence love is what is chiefly rendered to the mother, and reverence is what is chiefly rendered to the ruler, while both of these things are given to the father. Therefore when they serve their ruler with filial piety, they are loyal; when they serve their superiors with reverence, they are obedient. Not failing in this loyalty and obedience in serving those above them, they are then able to preserve their emoluments and positions, and to maintain their sacrifices. This is the filial piety of inferior officers.

It is said in the Book of Poetry: Rising early and going to sleep late, Do not disgrace those who gave you birth."

Filial Piety in the Common People

"They follow the course of Heaven in the revolving seasons; they distinguish the advantages afforded by different soils; they are careful of their conduct and economical in their expenditure—in order to nourish their parents. This is the filial piety of the common people. Therefore from the Son of Heaven down to the common people, there never has been one whose filial piety was without its beginning and end on whom calamity did not come."

Filial Piety in Relation to the Three Powers

The disciple Zeng said, "Immense indeed is the greatness of filial piety!"

The Master replied, "Yes, filial piety is the constant method of Heaven, the righteousness of Earth, and the practical duty of Man. Heaven and Earth invariably pursue the course that may be thus described, and the people take it as their pattern. The ancient kings imitated the brilliant luminaries of Heaven and acted in accordance with the varying advantages afforded by Earth, so that they were in accord with all under Heaven, and in consequence their teachings, without being severe, were successful, and their government, without being rigorous, secured perfect order.

The ancient kings, seeing how their teachings could transform the people, set before them therefore an example of the most extended love, and none of the people neglected their parents. They set forth to them the nature of virtue and righteousness, and the people roused themselves to the practice of them. They went before them with reverence and yielding courtesy, and the people had no contentions. They led them on by the rules of propriety and by music, and the people were harmonious and benignant. They showed them what they loved and what they disliked, and the people understood their prohibitions.

It is said in the Book of Poetry: Awe-inspiring are you, O Grand-Master Yin, and the people all look up to you."

Filial Piety in Government

The Master said, "Anciently, when the intelligent kings by means of filial piety ruled all under Heaven, they did not dare to receive with disrespect the ministers of small states. How much less would they do so to the dukes, marquises, counts, and barons! Thus it was that they got the princes of the myriad states with joyful hearts to assist them in the sacrificial services to their royal predecessors.

The rulers of states did not dare to slight wifeless men and widows. How much less would they slight their officers and the people! Thus it was that they got all their people with joyful hearts to assist them in serving the rulers, their predecessors.

The heads of clans did not dare to slight their servants and concubines. How much less would they slight their wives and sons! Thus it was that they got their men with joyful hearts to assist them in the service of their parents.

In such a state of things, while alive, parents reposed in the glory of their sons, and, when sacrificed to, their disembodied spirits enjoyed their offerings. Therefore for all under Heaven peace and harmony prevailed; disasters and calamities did not occur; misfortunes and rebellions did not arise.

It is said in the Book of Poetry: To an upright, virtuous conduct all in the four quarters of the state render obedient homage."

The Government of the Sages

The disciple Zeng said, "I venture to ask whether in the virtue of the sages there was not something greater than filial piety."

The Master replied, "Of all creatures with their different natures produced by Heaven and Earth, man is the noblest. Of all the actions of man there is none greater than filial piety. In filial piety there is nothing greater than the reverential awe of one's father. In the reverential awe shown to one's father there is nothing greater than the making him the correlate of Heaven. The duke of Zhou was the man who first did this.

Formerly the duke of Zhou at the border altar sacrificed to Hou Ji as the correlate of Heaven, and in the Brilliant Hall he honored king Wen and sacrificed to him as the correlate of God. The consequence was that from all the states within the four seas, every prince came in the discharge of his duty to assist in those sacrifices. In the virtue of the sages what besides was there greater than filial piety?

Now the feeling of affection grows up at the parents' knees, and as the duty of nourishing those parents is exercised, the affection daily merges in awe. The sages proceeded from the feeling of awe to teach the duties of reverence, and from that of affection to teach those of love. The teachings of the sages, without being severe, were successful, and their government, without being rigorous, was effective. What they proceeded from was the root of filial piety implanted by Heaven.

The relation and duties between father and son, thus belonging to the Heaven-conferred nature, contain in them the principle of righteousness between ruler and subject. The son derives his life from his parents, and no greater gift could possibly be transmitted. His ruler and parent in one, his father deals with him accordingly, and no generosity could be greater than this. Hence, he who does not love his parents, but loves other men, is called a rebel against virtue, and he who does not revere his parents, but reveres other men, is called a rebel against propriety. When the ruler himself thus acts contrary to the principles which should place him in accord with all men, he presents nothing for the people to imitate. He has nothing to do with what is good, but entirely and only with what is injurious to virtue. Though he may get his will, and be above others, the superior man does not give him his approval.

It is not so with the superior man. He speaks, having thought whether the words should be spoken; he acts, having thought whether his actions are sure to give pleasure. His virtue and righteousness are such as will be honored; what he initiates and does is fit to be imitated; his deportment is worthy of contemplation; his movements in advancing or retiring are all according to the proper rule. In this way does he present himself to the people, who both revere and love him, imitate and become like him. Thus he is able to make his teaching of virtue successful, and his government and orders to be carried into effect.

It is said in the Book of Poetry: The virtuous man, the princely one, Has nothing wrong in his deportment."

An Orderly Description of the Acts of Filial Piety

The Master said, "The service which a filial son does to his parents is as follows: In his general conduct to them, he manifests the utmost reverence. In his nourishing of them, his endeavor is to give them the utmost pleasure. When they are ill, he feels the greatest anxiety. In mourning for them dead, he exhibits every demonstration of grief. In sacrificing to them, he displays the utmost solemnity. When a son is complete in these five things, he may be pronounced able to serve his parents.

He who thus serves his parents, in a high situation will be free from pride, in a low situation will be free from insubordination, and among his equals will not be quarrelsome. In a high situation pride leads to ruin; in a low situation insubordination leads to pun-

ishment; among equals quarrelsomeness leads to the wielding of weapons. If those three things be not put away, though a son every day contribute beef, mutton, and pork to nourish his parents, he is not filial."

Filial Piety in Relation to the Five Punishments

The Master said, "There are three thousand offenses against which the five punishments are directed, and there is not one of them greater than being unfilial.

When constraint is put upon a ruler, that is the disowning of his superiority. When the authority of the sages is disallowed, that is the disowning of all law. When filial piety is put aside, that is the disowning of the principle of affection. These three things pave the way to anarchy."

Amplification of "the All-embracing Rule of Conduct" in Chapter I

The Master said, "For teaching the people to be affectionate and loving, there is nothing better than filial piety. For teaching them the observance of propriety and submissiveness, there is nothing better than fraternal duty. For changing their manners and altering their customs, there is nothing better than music. For securing the repose of superiors and the good order of the people, there is nothing better than the rules of propriety.

The rules of propriety are simply the development of the principle of reverence. Therefore the reverence paid to a father makes all sons pleased. The reverence paid to an elder brother makes all younger brothers pleased. The reverence paid to a ruler makes all subjects pleased. The reverence paid to the one man makes thousands and myriads of men pleased. The reverence is paid to a few, and the pleasure extends to many. This is what is meant by an "All-embracing Rule of Conduct.'"

Amplification of "the Perfect Virtue" in Chapter I

The Master said, "The teaching of filial piety by the superior man does not require that he should go to family after family and daily see the members of each. His teaching of filial piety is a tribute of reverence to all the fathers under Heaven. His teaching of fraternal submission is a tribute of reverence to all the elder brothers under Heaven. His teaching of the duty of a subject is a tribute of reverence to all the rulers under Heaven.

It is said in the Book of Poetry: The happy and courteous sovereign Is the parent of the people.

If it were not a perfect virtue, how could it be recognized as in accordance with their nature by the people so extensively as this?"

Amplification of "Making Our Name Famous" in Chapter I

The Master said, "The filial piety with which the superior man serves his parents may be transferred as loyalty to the ruler. The fraternal duty with which he serves his elder brother may be transferred as submissive deference to elders. His regulation of his family may be transferred as good government in any official position. Therefore, when his conduct is thus successful in his inner private circle, his name will be established and transmitted to future generations."

Filial Piety in Relation to Reproof and Remonstrance

The disciple Zeng said, "I have heard your instructions on the affection of love, on respect and reverence, on giving repose to the minds of our parents, and on making our names famous. I would venture to ask if simple obedience to the orders of one's father can be pronounced filial piety."

The Master replied, "What words are these! What words are these! Anciently, if the Son of Heaven had seven ministers who would remonstrate with him, although he had not right methods of government, he would not lose his possession of the kingdom. If the prince of a state had five such ministers, though his measures might be equally wrong, he would not lose his state. If a great officer had three, he would not, in a similar case, lose the headship of his clan. If an inferior officer had a friend who would remonstrate with him, a good name would not cease to be connected with his character. And the father who had a son that would remonstrate with him would not sink into the gulf of unrighteous deeds. Therefore when a case of unrighteous conduct is concerned, a son must by no means keep from remonstrating with his father, nor a minister from remonstrating with his ruler. Hence, since remonstrance is required in the case of unrighteous conduct, how

can simple obedience to the orders of a father be accounted filial piety?"

The Influence of Filial Piety and the Response to It

The Master said, "Anciently, the intelligent kings served their fathers with filial piety, and therefore they served Heaven with intelligence. They served their mothers with filial piety, and therefore they served Earth with discrimination. They pursued the right course with reference to their own seniors and juniors, and therefore they secured the regulation of the relations between superiors and inferiors throughout the kingdom. When Heaven and Earth were served with intelligence and discrimination, the spiritual intelligences displayed their retributive power. Therefore even the Son of Heaven must have some whom he honors; that is, he has his uncles of his surname. He must have some to whom he concedes the precedence; that is, he has his cousins, who bear the same surname and are older than himself. In the ancestral temple he manifests the utmost reverence, showing that he does not forget his parents. He cultivates his person and is careful of his conduct, fearing lest he should disgrace his predecessors. When in the ancestral temple he exhibits the utmost reverence, the spirits of the departed manifest themselves. Perfect filial piety and fraternal duty reach to and move the spiritual intelligences and diffuse their light on all within the four seas. They penetrate everywhere.

It is said in the Book of Poetry: From the west to the east, from the south to the north, there was not a thought but did him homage."

The Service of the Ruler

The Master said, "The superior man serves his ruler in such a way that, when at court in his presence, his thought is how to discharge his loyal duty to the utmost, and when he retires from it, his thought is how to amend his errors. He carries out with deference the measures springing from his excellent qualities and rectifies him only to save him from what are evil. Hence, as the superior and inferior, they are able to have an affection for each other.

It is said in the Book of Poetry: In my heart I love him, and why should I not say so? In the core of my heart I keep him, and never will forget him."

Filial Piety in Mourning for Parents

The Master said, "When a filial son is mourning for a parent, he wails, but not with a prolonged sobbing. In the movements of ceremony he pays no attention to his appearance. His words are without elegance of phrase. He cannot bear to wear fine clothes. When he hears music, he feels no delight. When he eats a delicacy, he is not conscious of its flavor. Such is the nature of grief and sorrow.

After three days he may partake of food, for thus the people are taught that the living should not be injured on account of the dead, and that emaciation must not be carried to the extinction of life. Such is the rule of the sages. The period of mourning does not go beyond three years, to show the people that it must have an end.

An inner and outer coffin are made; the grave-clothes also are put on, and the shroud; and the body is lifted into the coffin. The sacrificial vessels, round and square, are regularly set forth, and the sight of them fills the mourners with fresh distress. The women beat their breasts, and the men stamp with their feet, wailing and weeping, while they sorrowfully escort the coffin to the grave. They consult the tortoise-shell to determine the grave and the ground about it, and there they lay the body in peace. They prepare the ancestral temple to receive the tablet of the departed, and there they present offerings to the disembodied spirit. In spring and autumn they offer sacrifices, thinking of the deceased as the seasons come round.

The services of love and reverence to parents when alive, and those of grief and sorrow to them when dead: these completely discharge the fundamental duty of living men. The righteous claims of life and death are all satisfied, and the filial son's service of his parents is completed."

Glossary

consult the tortoise shell	practice a form of divination popular in the Shang Dynasty
correlate of Heaven … correlate of God	During the most important sacrifices to Heaven, the ruler honors his ancestor (or a former king) by sacrificing to him at the same time and with the same offerings. He is thus honoring his ancestor (or the ruler) as he does Heaven. In short, he is putting his ancestor on a par with Heaven.
five punishments	branding, cutting off the nose, cutting off the feet, castration, and beheading
Hou Ji	Chinese god thought to have been the founder of agriculture and considered the ancestor of the Zhou people
Shen	given name of the disciple Zeng
tablet of the departed	memorial plaque representing the dead person in the temple

"Here (in my domain) no living beings
are to be slaughtered or offered in sacrifice."

Overview

The Rock and Pillar edicts of the Mauryan ruler Aśoka (who reigned from 273 to 232 BCE) constitute inscriptions engraved on pillars, gigantic boulders, and caves in scattered locations across the Indian subcontinent and Afghanistan. One of the most notable rulers in world history, Aśoka — whose name with royal titles was Devanampiya ("Beloved of the Gods") Piyadasi ("Benignant, Beloved of Us") Raja ("King") Aśoka —used the form of the edicts to leave blueprints of his ideas and ideals throughout the Maurya Empire. Reflecting his benevolent attitude and activities, Aśoka issued the royal proclamations in the edicts after the fateful Kalinga War of around 261 BCE. The large-scale devastation resulting from that war greatly moved Aśoka, and he thenceforth relinquished war in favor of victory by *dhamma*, meaning "righteous path" or "piety." The concept of dharma ("religion" in Sanskrit), or *dhamma* (the Prakrit version of dharma), as used by the emperor denoted that he was advocating not religion per se but a path of self-righteousness based on moral and ethical principles. The Aśokan edicts dispersed throughout his empire thus served as heralds of *dhamma*.

These earliest records of epigraphy in India were living testimony to the greatness of Emperor Aśoka, who was very much concerned for the material and moral welfare of his subjects. He not only insisted on high ethical standards for his subjects but also set high ideals for himself. In the first Kalinga rock edict, the emperor states, "All men are my children," and, indeed, the *dhamma* of Aśoka, as based on certain moral principles and civic responsibility, became a way of life for any and all individuals. He initiated the policy of *dhamma* with the precise motive of unifying political units and people professing different faiths. This pragmatic approach resulted in his gaining support from the rising merchant class and the general masses of population, and his *dhamma* became a cementing force for the Maurya Empire. As a testament to the emperor, the modern Indian government adopted the four-lion capital crowning the Aśokan pillar at Sarnath as its national emblem when the country gained independence in 1950. The wheel of *dhamma*, in turn, was put at the center of the Indian national flag.

Context

Crowned in the year 269 BCE, Aśoka looked after the various affairs of the state while seeking to expand the territorial extent of the empire. After eight years he turned his attention toward the kingdom of Kalinga, located on the eastern coast of modern-day India (corresponding roughly to today's Orissa). The key event in the context surrounding the edicts was the Battle of Kalinga, fought in the year 261 BCE, which resulted in a victory for Aśoka's forces. Kalinga, a coastal province, was powerful as well as prosperous owing to its role in oceanic trade. Kalinga had previously been under Indian rule, but it had gained independence at the beginning of the Maurya Empire (ca. 321 BCE). The Mauryas maintained a policy of territorial expansion, so Kalingan independence was regarded as a blow and a loss of prestige. Further, the Mauryas, based in Magadha (in the area of modern-day Bihar, south of the Ganges), felt encircled. On one side lay the kingdom of Chola, and on the other side lay Kalinga. Because both were enemies of the Mauryas, the latter regarded them as natural allies. When Aśoka's father attacked Chola, it is likely that Kalinga aided Chola by attacking the Mauryas from the rear, rendering the invasion of Chola a failure. For this reason the Mauryas wished to subdue Kalinga, which Aśoka apparently vowed to do when he ascended the throne.

Additionally, the maritime activities of Kalinga were a threat to the commercial and economic interests of Magadha. The latter was not a sea power; it depended on friendly states at its borders for access to the sea and the commercial gains that would result. Fear existed that Kalinga could impose a blockade, denying Magadha access to the sea. War with Kalinga seemed inevitable.

The famous Battle of Kalinga was fought in the year 261 BCE, resulting in victory for Mauryan forces; Kalinga was then incorporated into the Maurya Empire. But the killing of about 100,000 people, the imprisonment of 150,000, the displacement of many more, and the large-scale devastation resulting from the war moved Aśoka. Although Buddhist traditions speak about the conversion of the remorseful ruler to Buddhism by the monk Upagupta after the Kalinga War, most probably Aśoka adopted the new religion gradually, after a great deal of thinking. Regardless of the pace of his

CA. 304 BCE	■ Aśoka is born.
CA. 286 BCE	■ Aśoka achieves the viceroyalty at Ujjain and marries Vidisamahadevi.
CA. 284 BCE	■ Aśoka's son, Mahendra, is born.
CA. 282 BCE	■ Aśoka's daughter, Sanghamitra, is born.
CA. 273 BCE	■ Ascending the throne of the Maurya Empire, Aśoka engages in war with his stepbrothers that lasts for several years.
CA. 269 BCE	■ Aśoka's official coronation as emperor takes place.
CA. 261 BCE	■ In his expansion of the empire, Aśoka leads his forces in the Kalinga War.
CA. 260 BCE	■ Aśoka embarks on a pious tour, probably to Bodh Gayā.
259 BCE	■ Aśoka converts to Buddhism and dispatches Buddhist missionaries.

conversion, as a patron of Buddhism, Aśoka changed the course of history not only on the Indian subcontinent but also in the Far East and Southeast Asia.

After the Kalinga War, Aśoka began to engrave his ideas on rocks and pillars as well as on the walls of caves, with the inscriptions serving as vehicles for circulating his agenda. Eschewing the earlier path of Brahmanic faith (that is, orthodox Hinduism), Aśoka envisaged a new doctrine quite different as well from the avowed principles of Buddhism—the Four Noble Truths, the Noble Eightfold Path, the transmigration of souls, and others. He propagated certain moral precepts, an approach common to all Indian religions, as inspired by Buddhism to a large extent but moving in a new direction toward lofty ideals pertaining to ethics and morality.

The edicts of Aśoka are distributed over an extensive area encompassing present-day Afghanistan, Pakistan, Nepal, and India. An examination of the locations on a map of the region shows that they are distributed roughly in a circle around India's territorial boundaries. Most (but not all) of the Pillar Edicts are located in the north, while most (but not all) of the Rock Edicts are located in the south. The edicts can all be found along trade routes, in new communities, and at religious sites; the sites were not accidental, for the intention was to bring them to the attention of as many people as possible. About forty-two sites of inscriptions on rocks, pillars, and caves are presently known, as written in three languages—Prakrit, Aramaic, and Greek. Some, in fact, are not edicts per se but instead are dedicatory inscriptions. Although the general chronology of Aśoka's era is uncertain, the inscriptions help in establishing dates, as the regnal years of the emperor are mentioned therein. The inscriptions were produced between 257 and 240 BCE.

About the Author

The author of the Rock and Pillar edicts is Aśoka, one of the greatest rulers of Indian history. He belonged to the Maurya Dynasty (322–185 BCE), which ushered in a new chapter in the political evolution of the Indian subcontinent, as a unified state came into existence encompassing present-day India, Pakistan, and Bangladesh. Aśoka was a son of Emperor Bindusāra and Subhadrangi, who exclaimed at the time of the child's birth around 304 BCE that she was *aśoka*, meaning "without sorrow," which became his name. According to Buddhist traditions, Aśoka was a cruel person in the early part of his life. A transformation took place after he embraced Buddhism; from Chandaśoka ("cruel Aśoka"), he purportedly became Dharmaśoka ("righteous Aśoka"). Most scholars regard this story as mere fiction and believe that he was attracted to Buddhism later on, after the bloodshed of the Kalinga War. In 286 BCE, Emperor Bindusāra appointed Aśoka viceroy of the province of Ujjain, and he was instrumental in suppressing a revolt in Taxila. That same year he was married to Vidisamahadevi, with whom he had two children, Mahendra and Sanghamitra. Aśoka became emperor in 273 BCE, but it took him four years to emerge victorious against his stepbrothers in the ensuing contest for the throne. Aśoka's actual coronation took place in the year 269 BCE.

Aśoka inherited from Bindusāra an extensive empire with a well-organized administrative framework. He looked after the various affairs of the state for eight years and then turned his attention toward the kingdom of Kalinga, which was a thorn in the side of the Maurya Empire, for the region had gained its independence and was a rival of the Maurya Dynasty because of its trade. The large-scale destruction and deaths of the war changed the heart of the emperor, and he was attracted to Buddhism as a result. At his behest, Buddhist missionaries were dispatched all over the subcontinent as well as abroad. The monks Sona and Uttara were sent to the region of modern-day Burma (Myanmar) and Thailand. The brother-and-sister team of Mahendra and Sanghamitra went to Ceylon (Sri Lanka). India's cultural contact with Southeast Asia thus gained pace, leading to far-reaching repercussions in the form of cultural exchanges between the two regions. Emperor Aśoka granted religious endowments, built *viharas* (monasteries), constructed eighty-four thousand stupas (reliquary mounds), and erected commemorative pillars for the propagation of Buddhism. Aśoka was one of the finest builders in ancient India; the monolithic stone columns erected in his name were architectural wonders. The Sarnath column was a marvel of the fine art of stone carving; the Sanchi stupa has remained a tourist attraction. A special class of officers called *dhammahamattas* (officers of righteousness) were appointed to propagate the *dhamma*. Aśoka also convened the Third Buddhist Council in 250 BCE to prevent potential rifts within Buddhism. The attendees at the council, held in the Pataliputra conclave, decided to compile *Saddhammasamgaha*, a text of "true Buddhist doctrine."

In ruling, Aśoka retained the general pattern of Mauryan administration but incorporated features aimed at improving the welfare of his subjects. The emperor mentions in the last of the Fourteen Rock Edicts that his dominion was *vijita*, or "vast," and, indeed, a sound and well-knit administrative system was required to keep the empire intact. The administration was centralized, with the emperor enjoying absolute power, but Aśoka's paternal despotism was benevolent. His concern for his people was evident from the fact that he undertook frequent tours to different parts of the empire. He also oversaw a massive public infrastructure program entailing the construction of canals, wells, roads, and parks. Special care was taken to protect forests from fire. The slaughter of animals was prohibited on certain days. The emperor himself stopped embarking on pleasure trips and hunting expeditions, preferring pilgrimage and tours. He breathed his last in the year 232 BCE. After this death, future emperors kept the army intact; it was neither demoralized nor reduced in number. The state was highly centralized, with the main plank of its stability being the efficiency and vision of the emperor. However, actual imperial control was not very effective in the far south. The successors were not like Emperor Aśoka, and the greatness, glory, and glamour of the Maurya Empire faded into the past after his passing.

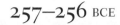
Time Line

257–256 BCE	■ The Fourteen Rock Edicts and the Kalinga Rock Edicts are inscribed, as are the Minor Rock Edicts.
CA. **251** BCE	■ Mahendra and Sanghamitra introduce Buddhism to Ceylon (now Sri Lanka).
CA. **250** BCE	■ The Third Buddhist Council is held at Pataliputra, and the Tripitaka (the canon of Buddhist scriptures) is completed.
CA. **249** BCE	■ Aśoka embarks on a pilgrimage to Lumbini along with his preceptor Upagupta.
243 BCE	■ The first six of the Seven Pillar Edicts are inscribed.
242 BCE	■ The seventh of the Seven Pillar Edicts is inscribed.
CA. **240** BCE	■ The Minor Pillar Edicts are inscribed.
232 BCE	■ Aśoka dies.

Explanation and Analysis of the Document

Aśoka emerges from the edicts as a ruler deeply concerned with the welfare of his subjects and impartial with respect to class. The inscriptions prove that Aśoka had deep commitments to health care, environmental protection, and animal welfare. Indeed, his vision was far ahead of his times. His path of *dhamma* and ahimsa (nonviolence), as enumerated and described in the edicts, is very much relevant to the contemporary world. The emphasis on state morality and the state's duty to protect its subjects also has bearing on present-day considerations of the role of government, especially in light of international terrorism. There were many monarchs in ancient and medieval Indian history, but very few were like the great Aśoka. The prescriptions, virtues, and ideals in the edicts became a frame of reference for future rulers and individuals alike.

In the Rock and Pillar edicts, the personality, perception, and philosophy of Aśoka unfold to a great extent. After the Kalinga War, the emperor set an agenda for the state, society, and individual, leaving messages in the form of inscriptions on rocks, boulders, pillars, and caves throughout the empire. The proselytizing zeal of Aśoka put Buddhism on a high pedestal not only on the Indian subcontinent but abroad as well. Some archaeological scholars initially held the view that the inscriptions were pointers of territorial extent of a pan-Indian empire, but this view has been contested. Generally, the edicts were inscribed in populated areas, demonstrating that they were intended for larger public audiences, although some edicts were inscribed in comparatively inaccessible areas.

The inscriptions fall into eight groups: the Minor Rock Edicts, the Bhābrū Edict, the Fourteen Rock Edicts, the Kalinga Rock Edicts, the Cave Inscriptions, the Tārai Pillar Inscriptions, the Seven Pillar Edicts, and the Minor Pillar Edicts. The Bhābrū Edict calls out seven passages of Buddhist scripture for special attention. The Cave Inscriptions are concise dedications of cave dwellings for the use of a particular monastic order. The very brief Tārai Pillar Inscriptions document Asoka's pilgrimage to spots sacred to Buddhism. It is the remaining edicts that merit close analysis and explication.

◆ Fourteen Rock Edicts

The edicts engraved on rocks and pillars throughout Aśoka's empire served as messages of *dhamma*, heralding a path of self-righteousness based on moral and ethical principles, as inspired by Buddhism to an extent. The emperor thus propagated certain ethical principles intended to govern the individual and his role in society. In the edicts, he lays stress on respect for father, mother, teachers, elders, Brahmans, monks, friends, the poor, and so forth. Such ideals as honesty, truthfulness, liberalism, and compassion are held to guide the life of a person. An individual is advised to abandon cruelty, anger, pride, and jealousy. In these inscriptions Aśoka advocates ahimsa, or "nonviolence," stressing sanctity of life. A spirit of religious tolerance is upheld as an important aspect of society.

Thus, in edict 1, Aśoka says that "no living beings are to be slaughtered or offered in sacrifice," and in edict 2 he prescribes medical treatment for humans and animals. Edict 3 emphasizes the need for instruction in *dhamma*, and in edict 4 he "promotes restraint in the killing and harming of living beings, proper behavior towards relatives, Brahmans [Hindus] and ascetics, and respect for mother, father and elders." Edict 4, like many of the edicts, concludes with a statement that the edict is written so that Aśoka's successors will remember it and enforce it.

With edict 5, Aśoka turns to the treatment of prisoners. He notes that he sends out his "Mahamatras," or senior officials, to instruct people in *dhamma*. Part of this instruction involves the need to treat prisoners humanely, ultimately with a view to their release. In edict 6 he turns to administration, noting that he has instructed his officials to make reports to him whenever and wherever necessary, for "there is no better work than promoting the welfare of all the people." Edict 7 takes up the issue of religion, with Aśoka insisting that "all religions should reside everywhere." He addresses religion later as well—in edict 12, where he promotes contact between religions and urges his people not to see one religion as superior to all others, concluding that "one should listen to and respect the doctrines professed by others."

Edicts 8 and 9 deal with issues surrounding entertainment and ceremony. In edict 8 Aśoka suggests that instructing people in *dhamma* is superior to hunting expeditions and pleasure tours, while in edict 9 he dismisses ceremonies, calling *dhamma* itself a ceremony, for it promotes "proper behavior towards servants and employees, respect for teachers, restraint towards living beings, and generosity towards ascetics and Brahmans." He restates this point in edict 11. In edict 10, he maintains that glory and fame are worthless without the practice of *dhamma*. Finally, in edict 13, Aśoka takes up the issue of the conquest of the Kalinga, expressing remorse for having done so at the cost of much turmoil and bloodshed. He advises future generations of rulers that if they undertake military conquests, "they be done with forbearance and light punishment, or better still, that they consider making conquest by Dhamma only."

◆ Kalinga Rock Edicts

The two Kalinga Rock edicts deal with the administration of justice. In the first, Aśoka refers to his "judicial officers" in Tosali, a city in eastern India, telling them to "act with impartiality" and to reject "envy, anger, cruelty, hate, indifference, laziness or tiredness," any of which can lead to poor judicial administration. In the second edict, Aśoka refers to Samapa, near the Kalingan border, and expresses concern for the state of mind of people in unconquered territories: "My only intention is that they live without fear of me, that they may trust me and that I may give them happiness, not sorrow." He urges his administrators in the border regions to tell the people: "The king is like a father. He feels towards us as he feels towards himself. We are to him like his own children." Of course, all this is to be achieved through the practice of *dhamma*.

Pillar edict of Emperor Aśoka (© The Trustees of the British Museum)

◆ Minor Rock Edicts

The three Minor Rock edicts are more general in nature. The first is philosophical, suggesting the need to be "zealous" in the pursuit of *dhamma* and in the desire to do good. "Even the humble," concludes Aśoka, "if they are zealous, can attain heaven." The second edict makes clear one way to achieve the good: "Father and mother should be respected and so should elders, kindness to living beings should be made strong and the truth should be spoken." In the third edict, Aśoka provides the Sangha, or members of the Buddhist community, a reading list of Buddhist texts that can instruct them in *dhamma*.

◆ Seven Pillar Edicts

The Seven Pillar edicts tend to be philosophical. They continue to emphasize *dhamma*, saying, in the first edict, that "Happiness in this world and the next is difficult to obtain without much love for the Dhamma" and noting that all of his officers, of whatever rank, practice *dhamma*. In the second pillar edict, Aśoka raises the philosophical question "What constitutes Dhamma?" and states that it includes "little evil, much good, kindness, generosity, truthfulness and purity." Edict 3 urges people to turn away from evil, along with violence, anger, cruelty, pride, and jealousy, all of which produce evil.

Edict 4 returns to the topic of the administration of justice, with officials enjoined to work for the "welfare, happiness and benefit of the people in the country." Aśoka gets specific when he calls for "uniformity in law and uniformity in sentencing." He goes on to grant an amnesty of sorts when he calls for a three-day stay for those in prison who have been tried and sentenced to death. This will allow

time for their relatives to appeal their sentences and for the condemned to prepare for the next world. Aśoka's sense of justice extends to the animal kingdom, for in edict 5 he points out that he has protected a variety of animal species.

In edicts 6 and 7, Aśoka comments on his overall intentions. In edict 6 he asks how he himself can look to the welfare of his people, noting that he has honored all religions. In edict 7 he comments specifically on the edicts. He reflects that when he asked himself how he could encourage people in the practice of *dhamma*, he came to the conclusion that the best way to do so would be through the promulgation and recording of the edicts: "It is for this purpose that proclamations on Dhamma have been announced and various instructions on Dhamma have been given and that officers who work among many promote and explain them in detail."

◆ Minor Pillar Edicts

The two Minor Pillar edicts are examples of the kinds of edicts Aśoka issued to address local affairs or local issues. The first simply records the fact that he visited the birthplace of the Buddha. The second deals with the Sangha and orders that anyone who "splits" the Sangha, or causes division among them, cannot be admitted to the Sangha and must be made to live separately.

Audience

The emperor varied the language and script of the edicts so that local people would have easy access to them. There was thus no uniformity of language and script for the

"Here (in my domain) no living beings are to be slaughtered or offered in sacrifice.... Formerly, in the kitchen of Beloved-of-the-Gods, King Piyadasi, hundreds of thousands of animals were killed every day to make curry. But now with the writing of this Dhamma edict only three creatures, two peacocks and a deer are killed, and the deer not always. And in time, not even these three creatures will be killed."

(Rock Edict 1)

"In the past, for many hundreds of years, killing or harming living beings and improper behavior towards relatives, and improper behavior towards Brahmans and ascetics has increased. But now due to Beloved-of-the-Gods, King Piyadasi's Dhamma practice, the sound of the drum has been replaced by the sound of the Dhamma."

(Rock Edict 4)

"In the past kings used to go out on pleasure tours during which there was hunting and other entertainment. But ten years after Beloved-of-the-Gods had been coronated, he went on a tour to Sambodhi and thus instituted Dhamma tours. During these tours, the following things took place: visits and gifts to Brahmans and ascetics, visits and gifts of gold to the aged, visits to people in the countryside, instructing them in Dhamma."

(Rock Edict 8)

"Even the humble, if they are zealous, can attain heaven. And this proclamation has been made with this aim. Let both humble and great be zealous, let even those on the borders know and let zeal last long. Then this zeal will increase, it will greatly increase, it will increase up to one-and-a-half times. This message has been proclaimed two hundred and fifty-six times by the king while on tour."

(Minor Rock Edict 1)

"Happiness in this world and the next is difficult to obtain without much love for the Dhamma, much self-examination, much respect, much fear (of evil), and much enthusiasm. But through my instruction this regard for Dhamma and love of Dhamma has grown day by day, and will continue to grow."

(Pillar Edict 1)

inscriptions as a collection. In Pakistan and Afghanistan, the inscriptions were in Greek and Aramaic. The majority of the inscriptions were in the Prakrit language, using the Brahmi and Kharoshthi scripts. The edicts were primarily engraved in places that were important as trade centers, sites of pilgrimage, or towns of regional significance; in other words, the edicts were situated where audiences would be larger, especially for religious or commercial purposes. However, some edicts were placed in areas that were not easily accessible, and no valid explanation for such placement has been put forth.

The edicts were meant for the people as a whole, and Aśoka's predilection for reaching out to enlighten the subjects of the empire gives something of a conversional tone to the inscriptions. In some cases, the edicts were addressed to Buddhist monks and state officials. In those addressed to monks, Buddhist practices and matters relating to monasteries were dealt with; the officials, in turn, were given various instructions for performing the tasks of *dhamma* protection and propagation. Because Buddhism was supported principally by the merchant class, trade, trade routes, and commerce-linked centers played an important role in determining the locations of the edicts. In the south, for example, where imperial control was not strong, inscriptions were nonetheless found in the gold-mining areas.

Some of the pillars stand out with respect to their locations and intended audiences. Aśoka erected a monolithic pillar in the famous Buddhist center of Sanchi, located near the notable urban center of Vidisha, which was populated by a large Buddhist trading community. In Sarnath, a revered Buddhist site and important center of trade, the emperor erected a gargantuan monolithic pillar fifty feet in height having four lions as its capital (the column's crown). The location of edicts in other important places like Allahabad, Bairat, Brahmagiri, Girnar, Kalsi, Kandhar, Mansehra, Suvarnagiri, and Taxila further supports the notion that the inscriptions were meant for public audiences.

Impact

The Aśokan inscriptions engraved on boulders, pillars, and rock walls constitute a milestone in the history of humankind. Radiating from the Indian subcontinent to reach the Middle East as well as the Far East, they had a tremendous impact in varied arenas. India's contact with Southeast Asia gained pace, leading to cultural rapprochement between the regions. The Buddhist missionary activities as enshrined in the edicts made Buddhism popular in areas that are now Burma, Thailand, Laos, Cambodia, and Vietnam. Aśoka's contact with the Hellenic world was evident from reading of the inscription. This contact was the result of the growth of the Greek empire, which had expanded to Asia Minor, central Asia, and as far east as the border with India; interaction between Buddhists and the Greeks lasted until the fifth century A.D.

Apart from constructing a chronology of events in the life of Aśoka, the edicts are important from an archaeological perspective. The monolithic stone columns of Aśoka were architectural wonders. The Sarnath column, for example, was the most exquisite among the columns, with its fine polishing, dressing, chiseling, and shaping of stone. The Pillar edicts were inscribed on chiseled and polished sandstone pillars. In contrast to the inscriptions on rock

Questions for Further Study

1. Aśoka is considered a major figure in Indian history and, in fact, in the history of the world. Why is he regarded in this light? What was his impact on history?

2. In the modern world, many Westerners have become interested in Eastern religions such as Buddhism (and Hinduism). Why do you believe this is so, and what can Westerners learn about such religious beliefs from Aśoka and his Rock and Pillar edicts?

3. What impact did the Kalinga War have on Aśoka? How did the war give rise to the beliefs he expressed in the edicts?

4. Many of the precepts expressed in the edicts would be taken for granted today. Why would Aśoka's beliefs have been considered almost revolutionary at the time? Why, for example, would his call for "uniformity in law and uniformity in sentencing" have been something innovative?

5. Some historians have argued that the Rock and Pillar edicts are the world's first document in the history of religious freedom. Why would they hold such a belief?

surfaces, the artisan needed to take great care with the medium in inscribing the script on pillar surfaces. The edicts as a collection also became important in the literary history of the Indian subcontinent, as they marked a departure from the earlier pictographic script of the Indus Valley civilization. The multilingual edicts are the earliest deciphered Indian inscriptions, throwing considerable light on contemporary state and society. The edicts have had considerable modern impact in framing a time line for ancient Indian history.

Further Reading

■ Articles

Mehta, Gita. "Ashoka, Beloved of the Gods." *Tricycle: The Buddhist Review* 8, no. 2 (Winter 1998): 21–25.

Sugandhi, Namita. "Context, Content, and Composition: Questions of Intended Meaning and the Asokan Edicts." *Asian Perspectives: The Journal of Archaeology for Asia and the Pacific* 42, no. 2 (2003): 224–246.

■ Books

Ahir, D. C. *Asoka the Great*. Delhi: B. R. Publishing, 1995.

Bhandarkar, D. R. *Aśoka*. 4th ed. Calcutta: University of Calcutta, 1969.

Embree, Ainslie T, ed. "Ashokan Edicts." In *Sources of Indian Tradition*, Vol. 1: *From the Beginning to 1800*. New York: Columbia University Press, 1988.

Falk, Harry. *Asokan Sites and Artefacts: A Source-Book with Bibliography*. Mainz, Germany: Philipp von Zabern, 2006.

Gokhale, Balkrishna G. *Asoka Maurya*. New York: Twayne Publishers, 1966.

Guruge, Ananda W. P. *Asoka, the Righteous: A Definitive Biography*. Colombo, Sri Lanka: Ministry of Cultural Affairs and Information, 1993.

Majumdar, R. C., ed. *The History and Culture of the Indian People*, Vol. 2: *The Age of Imperial Unity*. Bombay: Bharatiya Vidya Bhavan, 1989.

Mukherjee, Bratindra N. *The Character of the Maurya Empire*. Calcutta: Progressive Publishers, 2000.

Sen, Amulyachandra. *Asoka's Edicts*. Calcutta: Indian Publicity Society, 1956.

Strong, John. S. *The Legend of King Aśoka: A Study and Translation of the Aśokāvadāna*. Princeton, N.J.: Princeton University Press, 1983.

Thapar, Romila. *Aśoka and the Decline of the Mauryas*. Oxford, U.K.: Oxford University Press, 1961.

———. *Cultural Pasts: Essays in Early Indian History*. New Delhi: Oxford University Press, 2003.

———. *The Mauryas Revisited*. Calcutta: K. P. Bagchi, 1987.

—Patit Paban Mishra and Mike J. O'Neal

ROCK AND PILLAR EDICTS OF AŚOKA

Fourteen Rock Edicts

1

Beloved-of-the-Gods, King Piyadasi, has caused this Dhamma edict to be written. Here (in my domain) no living beings are to be slaughtered or offered in sacrifice. Nor should festivals be held, for Beloved-of-the-Gods, King Piyadasi, sees much to object to in such festivals, although there are some festivals that Beloved-of-the-Gods, King Piyadasi, does approve of.

Formerly, in the kitchen of Beloved-of-the-Gods, King Piyadasi, hundreds of thousands of animals were killed every day to make curry. But now with the writing of this Dhamma edict only three creatures, two peacocks and a deer are killed, and the deer not always. And in time, not even these three creatures will be killed.

2

Everywhere within Beloved-of-the-Gods, King Piyadasi's domain, and among the people beyond the borders, the Cholas, the Pandyas, the Satiyaputras, the Keralaputras, as far as Tamraparni and where the Greek king Antiochos rules, and among the kings who are neighbors of Antiochos, everywhere has Beloved-of-the-Gods, King Piyadasi, made provision for two types of medical treatment: medical treatment for humans and medical treatment for animals. Wherever medical herbs suitable for humans or animals are not available, I have had them imported and grown. Wherever medical roots or fruits are not available, I have had them imported and grown. Along roads I have had wells dug and trees planted for the benefit of humans and animals.

3

Beloved-of-the-Gods, King Piyadasi, speaks thus: Twelve years after my coronation this has been ordered.—Everywhere in my domain the Yuktas, the Rajjukas and the Pradesikas shall go on inspection tours every five years for the purpose of Dhamma instruction and also to conduct other business. Respect for mother and father is good, generosity to friends, acquaintances, relatives, Brahmans and ascetics is good, not killing living beings is good, moderation in spending and moderation in saving is good. The Council shall notify the Yuktas about the observance of these instructions in these very words.

4

In the past, for many hundreds of years, killing or harming living beings and improper behavior towards relatives, and improper behavior towards Brahmans and ascetics has increased. But now due to Beloved-of-the-Gods, King Piyadasi's Dhamma practice, the sound of the drum has been replaced by the sound of the Dhamma. The sighting of heavenly cars, auspicious elephants, bodies of fire and other divine sightings has not happened for many hundreds of years. But now because Beloved-of-the-Gods, King Piyadasi promotes restraint in the killing and harming of living beings, proper behavior towards relatives, Brahmans and ascetics, and respect for mother, father and elders, such sightings have increased.

These and many other kinds of Dhamma practice have been encouraged by Beloved-of-the-Gods, King Piyadasi, and he will continue to promote Dhamma practice. And the sons, grandsons and great-grandsons of Beloved-of-the-Gods, King Piyadasi, too will continue to promote Dhamma practice until the end of time; living by Dhamma and virtue, they will instruct in Dhamma. Truly, this is the highest work, to instruct in Dhamma. But practicing the Dhamma cannot be done by one who is devoid of virtue and therefore its promotion and growth is commendable.

This edict has been written so that it may please my successors to devote themselves to promoting these things and not allow them to decline. Beloved-of-the-Gods, King Piyadasi, has had this written twelve years after his coronation.

5

Beloved-of-the-Gods, King Piyadasi, speaks thus: To do good is difficult. One who does good first does something hard to do. I have done many good deeds, and, if my sons, grandsons and their descendants up to the end of the world act in like manner, they too will do much good. But whoever amongst them neglects this, they will do evil. Truly, it is easy to do evil.

In the past there were no Dhamma Mahamatras but such officers were appointed by me thirteen years after my coronation. Now they work among all religions for the establishment of Dhamma, for the promotion of Dhamma, and for the welfare and happiness of all who are devoted to Dhamma. They work among the Greeks, the Kambojas, the Gandharas, the Rastrikas, the Pitinikas and other peoples on the western borders. They work among soldiers, chiefs, Brahmans, householders, the poor, the aged and those devoted to Dhamma—for their welfare and happiness—so that they may be free from harassment. They (Dhamma Mahamatras) work for the proper treatment of prisoners, towards their unfettering, and if the Mahamatras think, "This one has a family to support," "That one has been bewitched," "This one is old," then they work for the release of such prisoners. They work here, in outlying towns, in the women's quarters belonging to my brothers and sisters, and among my other relatives. They are occupied everywhere. These Dhamma Mahamatras are occupied in my domain among people devoted to Dhamma to determine who is devoted to Dhamma, who is established in Dhamma, and who is generous.

This Dhamma edict has been written on stone so that it might endure long and that my descendants might act in conformity with it.

6

Beloved-of-the-Gods, King Piyadasi, speaks thus: In the past, state business was not transacted nor were reports delivered to the king at all hours. But now I have given this order, that at any time, whether I am eating, in the women's quarters, the bed chamber, the chariot, the palanquin, in the park or wherever, reporters are to be posted with instructions to report to me the affairs of the people so that I might attend to these affairs wherever I am. And whatever I orally order in connection with donations or proclamations, or when urgent business presses itself on the Mahamatras, if disagreement or debate arises in the Council, then it must be reported to me immediately. This is what I have ordered. I am never content with exerting myself or with despatching business. Truly, I consider the welfare of all to be my duty, and the root of this is exertion and the prompt despatch of business. There is no better work than promoting the welfare of all the people and whatever efforts I am making is to repay the debt I owe to all beings to assure their happiness in this life, and attain heaven in the next.

Therefore this Dhamma edict has been written to last long and that my sons, grandsons and great-grandsons might act in conformity with it for the welfare of the world. However, this is difficult to do without great exertion.

7

Beloved-of-the-Gods, King Piyadasi, desires that all religions should reside everywhere, for all of them desire self-control and purity of heart. But people have various desires and various passions, and they may practice all of what they should or only a part of it. But one who receives great gifts yet is lacking in self-control, purity of heart, gratitude and firm devotion, such a person is mean.

8

In the past kings used to go out on pleasure tours during which there was hunting and other entertainment. But ten years after Beloved-of-the-Gods had been coronated, he went on a tour to Sambodhi and thus instituted Dhamma tours. During these tours, the following things took place: visits and gifts to Brahmans and ascetics, visits and gifts of gold to the aged, visits to people in the countryside, instructing them in Dhamma, and discussing Dhamma with them as is suitable. It is this that delights Beloved-of-the-Gods, King Piyadasi, and is, as it were, another type of revenue.

9

Beloved-of-the-Gods, King Piyadasi, speaks thus: In times of sickness, for the marriage of sons and daughters, at the birth of children, before embarking on a journey, on these and other occasions, people perform various ceremonies. Women in particular perform many vulgar and worthless ceremonies. These types of ceremonies can be performed by all means, but they bear little fruit. What does bear great fruit, however, is the ceremony of the Dhamma. This involves proper behavior towards servants and employees, respect for teachers, restraint towards living beings, and generosity towards ascetics and Brahmans. These and other things constitute the ceremony of the Dhamma. Therefore a father, a son, a brother, a master, a friend, a companion, and even a neighbor should say: "This is good, this is the ceremony that should be performed until its purpose is fulfilled, this I shall do." Other ceremonies are of doubtful fruit, for they may achieve their purpose, or they may not, and even if they do, it is only in this world. But the ceremony of the Dhamma is timeless. Even if it does not achieve its purpose in this world, it produces great merit in the next, whereas if it does achieve its purpose in this world, one gets great merit both here and there through the ceremony of the Dhamma.

10

Beloved-of-the-Gods, King Piyadasi, does not consider glory and fame to be of great account unless they are achieved through having my subjects respect Dhamma and practice Dhamma, both now and in the future. For this alone does Beloved-of-the-Gods, King Piyadasi, desire glory and fame. And whatever efforts Beloved-of-the-Gods, King Piyadasi, is making, all of that is only for the welfare of the people in the next world, and that they will have little evil. And being without merit is evil. This is difficult for either a humble person or a great person to do except with great effort, and by giving up other interests. In fact, it may be even more difficult for a great person to do.

11

Beloved-of-the-Gods, King Piyadasi, speaks thus: There is no gift like the gift of the Dhamma, (no acquaintance like) acquaintance with Dhamma, (no distribution like) distribution of Dhamma, and (no kinship like) kinship through Dhamma. And it consists of this: proper behavior towards servants and employees, respect for mother and father, generosity to friends, companions, relations, Brahmans and ascetics, and not killing living beings. Therefore a father, a son, a brother, a master, a friend, a companion or a neighbor should say: "This is good, this should be done." One benefits in this world and gains great merit in the next by giving the gift of the Dhamma.

12

Beloved-of-the-Gods, King Piyadasi, honors both ascetics and the householders of all religions, and he honors them with gifts and honors of various kinds. But Beloved-of-the-Gods, King Piyadasi, does not value gifts and honors as much as he values this— that there should be growth in the essentials of all religions. Growth in essentials can be done in different ways, but all of them have as their root restraint in speech, that is, not praising one's own religion, or condemning the religion of others without good cause. And if there is cause for criticism, it should be done in a mild way. But it is better to honor other religions for this reason. By so doing, one's own religion benefits, and so do other religions, while doing otherwise harms one's own religion and the religions of others. Whoever praises his own religion, due to excessive devotion, and condemns others with the thought "Let me glorify my own religion," only harms his own religion. Therefore contact (between religions) is good. One should listen to and respect the doctrines professed by others. Beloved-of-the-Gods, King Piyadasi, desires that all should be well-learned in the good doctrines of other religions.

Those who are content with their own religion should be told this: Beloved-of-the-Gods, King Piyadasi, does not value gifts and honors as much as he values that there should be growth in the essentials of all religions. And to this end many are working—Dhamma Mahamatras, Mahamatras in charge of the women's quarters, officers in charge of outlying areas, and other such officers. And the fruit of this is that one's own religion grows and the Dhamma is illuminated also.

13

Beloved-of-the-Gods, King Piyadasi, conquered the Kalingas eight years after his coronation. One hundred and fifty thousand were deported, one hundred thousand were killed and many more died (from other causes). After the Kalingas had been conquered, Beloved-of-the-Gods came to feel a strong inclination towards the Dhamma, a love for the Dhamma and for instruction in Dhamma. Now Beloved-of-the-Gods feels deep remorse for having conquered the Kalingas.

Indeed, Beloved-of-the-Gods is deeply pained by the killing, dying and deportation that take place when an unconquered country is conquered. But Beloved-of-the-Gods is pained even more by this— that Brahmans, ascetics, and householders of different religions who live in those countries, and who are respectful to superiors, to mother and father, to elders, and who behave properly and have strong loyalty towards friends, acquaintances, companions, relatives, servants and employees—that they are injured, killed or separated from their loved ones. Even those who are not affected (by all this) suffer when they see friends, acquaintances, companions and relatives affected. These misfortunes befall all (as a result of war), and this pains Beloved-of-the-Gods.

There is no country, except among the Greeks, where these two groups, Brahmans and ascetics, are not found, and there is no country where people are not devoted to one or another religion. Therefore the killing, death or deportation of a hundredth, or even a thousandth part of those who died during the conquest of Kalinga now pains Beloved-of-the-Gods. Now Beloved-of-the-Gods thinks that even those who do wrong should be forgiven where forgiveness is possible.

Even the forest people, who live in Beloved-of-the-Gods' domain, are entreated and reasoned with to act properly. They are told that despite his remorse Beloved-of-the-Gods has the power to punish them if necessary, so that they should be ashamed of their wrong and not be killed. Truly, Beloved-of-the-Gods desires non-injury, restraint and impartiality to all beings, even where wrong has been done.

Now it is conquest by Dhamma that Beloved-of-the-Gods considers to be the best conquest. And it (conquest by Dhamma) has been won here, on the borders, even six hundred yojanas away, where the

Greek king Antiochos rules, beyond there where the four kings named Ptolemy, Antigonos, Magas and Alexander rule, likewise in the south among the Cholas, the Pandyas, and as far as Tamraparni. Here in the king's domain among the Greeks, the Kambojas, the Nabhakas, the Nabhapamkits, the Bhojas, the Pitinikas, the Andhras and the Palidas, everywhere people are following Beloved-of-the-Gods' instructions in Dhamma. Even where Beloved-of-the-Gods' envoys have not been, these people too, having heard of the practice of Dhamma and the ordinances and instructions in Dhamma given by Beloved-of-the-Gods, are following it and will continue to do so. This conquest has been won everywhere, and it gives great joy—the joy which only conquest by Dhamma can give. But even this joy is of little consequence. Beloved-of-the-Gods considers the great fruit to be experienced in the next world to be more important.

I have had this Dhamma edict written so that my sons and great-grandsons may not consider making new conquests, or that if military conquests are made, that they be done with forbearance and light punishment, or better still, that they consider making conquest by Dhamma only, for that bears fruit in this world and the next. May all their intense devotion be given to this which has a result in this world and the next.

14

Beloved-of-the-Gods, King Piyadasi, has had these Dhamma edicts written in brief, in medium length, and in extended form. Not all of them occur everywhere, for my domain is vast, but much has been written, and I will have still more written. And also there are some subjects here that have been spoken of again and again because of their sweetness, and so that the people may act in accordance with them. If some things written are incomplete, this is because of the locality, or in consideration of the object, or due to the fault of the scribe.

Kalinga Rock Edicts

1

Beloved-of-the-Gods says that the Mahamatras of Tosali who are judicial officers in the city are to be told this: I wish to see that everything I consider to be proper is carried out in the right way. And I consider instructing you to be the best way of accomplishing this. I have placed you over many thousands of people that you may win the people's affection.

All men are my children. What I desire for my own children, and I desire their welfare and happi-

ness both in this world and the next, that I desire for all men. You do not understand to what extent I desire this, and if some of you do understand, you do not understand the full extent of my desire.

You must attend to this matter. While being completely law-abiding, some people are imprisoned, treated harshly and even killed without cause so that many people suffer. Therefore your aim should be to act with impartiality. It is because of these things—envy, anger, cruelty, hate, indifference, laziness or tiredness—that such a thing does not happen. Therefore your aim should be: "May these things not be in me." And the root of this is non-anger and patience. Those who are bored with the administration of justice will not be promoted; (those who are not) will move upwards and be promoted. Whoever among you understands this should say to his colleagues: "See that you do your duty properly. Such and such are Beloved-of-the-Gods' instructions." Great fruit will result from doing your duty, while failing in it will result in gaining neither heaven nor the king's pleasure. Failure in duty on your part will not please me. But done properly, it will win you heaven and you will be discharging your debts to me.

This edict is to be listened to on Tisa day, between Tisa days, and on other suitable occasions, it should be listened to even by a single person. Acting thus, you will be doing your duty.

This edict has been written for the following purpose: that the judicial officers of the city may strive to do their duty and that the people under them might not suffer unjust imprisonment or harsh treatment. To achieve this, I will send out Mahamatras every five years who are not harsh or cruel, but who are merciful and who can ascertain if the judicial officers have understood my purpose and are acting according to my instructions. Similarly, from Ujjayini, the prince will send similar persons with the same purpose without allowing three years to elapse. Likewise from Takhasila also. When these Mahamatras go on tours of inspection each year, then without neglecting their normal duties, they will ascertain if judicial officers are acting according to the king's instructions.

2

Beloved-of-the-Gods speaks thus: This royal order is to be addressed to the Mahamatras at Samapa. I wish to see that everything I consider to be proper is carried out in the right way. And I consider instructing you to be the best way of accomplishing this. All men are my children. What I desire for my own children, and I desire their welfare and happiness both in this world and the next, that I desire for all men.

The people of the unconquered territories beyond the borders might think: "What is the king's intentions towards us?" My only intention is that they live without fear of me, that they may trust me and that I may give them happiness, not sorrow. Furthermore, they should understand that the king will forgive those who can be forgiven, and that he wishes to encourage them to practice Dhamma so that they may attain happiness in this world and the next. I am telling you this so that I may discharge the debts I owe, and that in instructing you, that you may know that my vow and my promise will not be broken. Therefore acting in this way, you should perform your duties and assure them (the people beyond the borders) that: "The king is like a father. He feels towards us as he feels towards himself. We are to him like his own children."

By instructing you and informing you of my vow and my promise I shall be applying myself in complete fullness to achieving this object. You are able indeed to inspire them with confidence and to secure their welfare and happiness in this world and the next, and by acting thus, you will attain heaven as well as discharge the debts you owe to me. And so that the Mahamatras can devote themselves at all times to inspiring the border areas with confidence and encouraging them to practice Dhamma, this edict has been written here.

This edict is to be listened to every four months on Tisa day, between Tisa days, and on other suitable occasions, it should be listened to even by a single person. Acting thus, you will be doing your duty.

Minor Rock Edicts

1

Beloved-of-the-Gods speaks thus: It is now more than two and a half years since I became a lay-disciple, but until now I have not been very zealous. But now that I have visited the Sangha for more than a year, I have become very zealous. Now the people in India who have not associated with the gods do so. This is the result of zeal and it is not just the great who can do this. Even the humble, if they are zealous, can attain heaven. And this proclamation has been made with this aim. Let both humble and great be zealous, let even those on the borders know and let zeal last long. Then this zeal will increase, it will greatly increase, it will increase up to one-and-a-half times. This message has been proclaimed two hundred and fifty-six times by the king while on tour.

2

Beloved-of-the-Gods speaks thus: Father and mother should be respected and so should elders, kindness to living beings should be made strong and the truth should be spoken. In these ways, the Dhamma should be promoted. Likewise, a teacher should be honored by his pupil and proper manners should be shown towards relations. This is an ancient rule that conduces to long life. Thus should one act. Written by the scribe Chapala.

3

Piyadasi, King of Magadha, saluting the Sangha and wishing them good health and happiness, speaks thus: You know, reverend sirs, how great my faith in the Buddha, the Dhamma and Sangha is. Whatever, reverend sirs, has been spoken by Lord Buddha, all that is well-spoken. I consider it proper, reverend sirs, to advise on how the good Dhamma should last long.

These Dhamma texts—Extracts from the Discipline, the Noble Way of Life, the Fears to Come, the Poem on the Silent Sage, the Discourse on the Pure Life, Upatisa's Questions, and the Advice to Rahula which was spoken by the Buddha concerning false speech—these Dhamma texts, reverend sirs, I desire that all the monks and nuns may constantly listen to and remember. Likewise the laymen and laywomen. I have had this written that you may know my intentions.

The Seven Pillar Edicts

1

Beloved-of-the-Gods speaks thus: This Dhamma edict was written twenty-six years after my coronation. Happiness in this world and the next is difficult to obtain without much love for the Dhamma, much self-examination, much respect, much fear (of evil), and much enthusiasm. But through my instruction this regard for Dhamma and love of Dhamma has grown day by day, and will continue to grow. And my officers of high, low and middle rank are practicing and conforming to Dhamma, and are capable of inspiring others to do the same. Mahamatras in border areas are doing the same. And these are my instructions: to protect with Dhamma, to make happiness through Dhamma and to guard with Dhamma.

2

Beloved-of-the-Gods, King Piyadasi, speaks thus: Dhamma is good, but what constitutes Dhamma? (It includes) little evil, much good, kindness, generosity, truthfulness and purity. I have given the gift of sight in various ways. To two-footed and four-footed beings, to birds and aquatic animals, I have given various things including the gift of life. And many other good deeds have been done by me.

This Dhamma edict has been written that people might follow it and it might endure for a long time. And the one who follows it properly will do something good.

3

Beloved-of-the-Gods, King Piyadasi, speaks thus: People see only their good deeds saying, "I have done this good deed." But they do not see their evil deeds saying, "I have done this evil deed" or "This is called evil." But this (tendency) is difficult to see. One should think like this: "It is these things that lead to evil, to violence, to cruelty, anger, pride and jealousy. Let me not ruin myself with these things." And further, one should think: "This leads to happiness in this world and the next."

4

Beloved-of-the-Gods speaks thus: This Dhamma edict was written twenty-six years after my coronation. My Rajjukas are working among the people, among many hundreds of thousands of people. The hearing of petitions and the administration of justice has been left to them so that they can do their duties confidently and fearlessly and so that they can work for the welfare, happiness and benefit of the people in the country. But they should remember what causes happiness and sorrow, and being themselves devoted to Dhamma, they should encourage the people in the country (to do the same), that they may attain happiness in this world and the next. These Rajjukas are eager to serve me. They also obey other officers who know my desires, who instruct the Rajjukas so that they can please me. Just as a person feels confident having entrusted his child to an expert nurse thinking: "The nurse will keep my child well," even so, the Rajjukas have been appointed by me for the welfare and happiness of the people in the country.

The hearing of petitions and the administration of justice have been left to the Rajjukas so that they can do their duties unperturbed, fearlessly and confidently. It is my desire that there should be uniformity in law and uniformity in sentencing. I even go this far, to grant a three-day stay for those in prison who have been tried and sentenced to death. During this time their relatives can make appeals to have the prisoners' lives spared. If there is none to appeal on their behalf, the prisoners can give gifts in order to make merit for the next world, or observe fasts. Indeed, it is my wish that in this way, even if a prisoner's time is limited, he can prepare for the next

world, and that people's Dhamma practice, self-control and generosity may grow.

5

Beloved-of-the-Gods, King Piyadasi, speaks thus: Twenty-six years after my coronation various animals were declared to be protected—parrots, mainas, aruna, ruddy geese, wild ducks, nandimukhas, gelatas, bats, queen ants, terrapins, boneless fish, vedareyaka, gangapuputaka, sankiya fish, tortoises, porcupines, squirrels, deer, bulls, okapinda, wild asses, wild pigeons, domestic pigeons and all four-footed creatures that are neither useful nor edible. Those nanny goats, ewes and sows which are with young or giving milk to their young are protected, and so are young ones less than six months old. Cocks are not to be caponized, husks hiding living beings are not to be burnt and forests are not to be burnt either without reason or to kill creatures. One animal is not to be fed to another. On the three Caturmasis, the three days of Tisa and during the fourteenth and fifteenth of the Uposatha, fish are protected and not to be sold. During these days animals are not to be killed in the elephant reserves or the fish reserves either. On the eighth of every fortnight, on the fourteenth and fifteenth, on Tisa, Punarvasu, the three Caturmasis and other auspicious days, bulls are not to be castrated, billy goats, rams, boars and other animals that are usually castrated are not to be. On Tisa, Punarvasu, Caturmasis and the fortnight of Caturmasis, horses and bullocks are not to be branded.

In the twenty-six years since my coronation prisoners have been given amnesty on twenty-five occasions.

6

Beloved-of-the-Gods speaks thus: Twelve years after my coronation I started to have Dhamma edicts written for the welfare and happiness of the people, and so that not transgressing them they might grow in the Dhamma. Thinking: "How can the welfare and happiness of the people be secured?" I give attention to my relatives, to those dwelling near and those dwelling far, so I can lead them to happiness and then I act accordingly. I do the same for all groups. I have honored all religions with various honors. But I consider it best to meet with people personally.

This Dhamma edict was written twenty-six years after my coronation.

7

Beloved-of-the-Gods speaks thus: In the past kings desired that the people might grow through the promotion of the Dhamma. But despite this, people did not grow through the promotion of the Dhamma. Beloved-of-the-Gods, King Piyadasi, said concerning this: "It occurs to me that in the past kings desired that the people might grow through the promotion of the Dhamma. But despite this, people did not grow through the promotion of the Dhamma. Now how can the people be encouraged to follow it? How can the people be encouraged to grow through the promotion of the Dhamma? How can I elevate them by promoting the Dhamma?" Beloved-of-the-Gods, King Piyadasi, further said concerning this: "It occurs to me that I shall have proclamations on Dhamma announced and instruction on Dhamma given. When people hear these, they will follow them, elevate themselves and grow considerably through the promotion of the Dhamma." It is for this purpose that proclamations on Dhamma have been announced and various instructions on Dhamma have been given and that officers who work among many promote and explain them in detail. The Rajjukas who work among hundreds of thousands of people have likewise been ordered: "In this way and that encourage those who are devoted to Dhamma." Beloved-of-the-Gods speaks thus: "Having this object in view, I have set up Dhamma pillars, appointed Dhamma Mahamatras, and announced Dhamma proclamations."

Beloved-of-the-Gods, King Piyadasi, says: Along roads I have had banyan trees planted so that they can give shade to animals and men, and I have had mango groves planted. At intervals of eight krosas, I have had wells dug, rest-houses built, and in various places, I have had watering-places made for the use of animals and men. But these are but minor achievements. Such things to make the people happy have been done by former kings. I have done these things for this purpose, that the people might practice the Dhamma.

Beloved-of-the-Gods, King Piyadasi, speaks thus: My Dhamma Mahamatras too are occupied with various good works among the ascetics and householders of all religions. I have ordered that they should be occupied with the affairs of the Sangha. I have also ordered that they should be occupied with the affairs of the Brahmans and the Ajivikas. I have ordered that they be occupied with the Niganthas. In fact, I have ordered that different Mahamatras be occupied with the particular affairs of all different religions. And my Dhamma Mahamatras likewise are occupied with these and other religions.

Beloved-of-the-Gods, King Piyadasi, speaks thus: These and other principal officers are occupied with the distribution of gifts, mine as well as those of the queens. In my women's quarters, they organize various charitable activities here and in the provinces. I have also ordered my sons and the sons of other queens to distribute gifts so that noble deeds of Dhamma and the practice of Dhamma may be promoted. And noble deeds of Dhamma and the practice of Dhamma consist of having kindness, generosity, truthfulness, purity, gentleness and goodness increase among the people.

Beloved-of-the-Gods, King Piyadasi, speaks thus: Whatever good deeds have been done by me, those the people accept and those they follow. Therefore they have progressed and will continue to progress by being respectful to mother and father, respectful to elders, by courtesy to the aged and proper behavior towards Brahmans and ascetics, towards the poor and distressed, and even towards servants and employees.

Beloved-of-the-Gods, King Piyadasi, speaks thus: This progress among the people through Dhamma has been done by two means, by Dhamma regulations and by persuasion. Of these, Dhamma regulation is of little effect, while persuasion has much more effect. The Dhamma regulations I have given are that various animals must be protected. And I have given many other Dhamma regulations also. But it is by persuasion that progress among the people through Dhamma has had a greater effect in respect of harmlessness to living beings and non-killing of living beings.

Concerning this, Beloved-of-the-Gods says: Wherever there are stone pillars or stone slabs, there this Dhamma edict is to be engraved so that it may long endure. It has been engraved so that it may endure as long as my sons and great-grandsons live and as long as the sun and the moon shine, and so that people may practice it as instructed. For by practicing it happiness will be attained in this world and the next.

This Dhamma edict has been written by me twenty-seven years after my coronation.

Minor Pillar Edicts

1

Twenty years after his coronation, Beloved-of-the-Gods, King Piyadasi, visited this place and worshipped because here the Buddha, the sage of the Sakyans, was born. He had a stone figure and a pillar set up and because the Lord was born here, the village of Lumbini was exempted from tax and required to pay only one eighth of the produce.

2

Beloved-of-the-Gods commands: The Mahamatras at Kosambi (are to be told: Whoever splits the Sangha) which is now united, is not to be admitted into the Sangha. Whoever, whether monk or nun, splits the Sangha is to be made to wear white clothes and to reside somewhere other than in a monastery.

Glossary

Ajivikas	members of a mendicant order in India, contemporaries of the early Buddhists
Council	the Third Buddhist Council of the third century BCE
heavenly cars	celestial horse cars, or chariots, in procession
Niganthas	members of a dharmic order present in India during the time of Aśoka
Sakyans	the tribe into which the Buddha was born
Yuktas, Rajjukas, and Pradesikas	royal inspectors

DISCOURSES ON SALT AND IRON

"Cultivate virtue in the temple and the hall, then you need only to show a bold front to the enemy and your troops will return home in victory."

Overview

During his long reign from 141 to 87 BCE, Han Wudi, the Martial Emperor of the Han Dynasty, waged an aggressive war against the Xiongnü, a pastoral nomadic people who often raided China's northern border. To finance this costly war, his government instituted state monopolies on salt, iron, and liquor production. These measures led to widespread popular dissatisfaction. In 81 BCE, to reassess these institutions' appropriateness, the Martial Emperor's successor, Emperor Zhao, convened a debate between his top government ministers and Confucian scholars who represented the voice of the people. The ministers endorsed the innovations as necessary for financing the defense of the empire; the scholars, on the other hand, complained that the reforms impoverished the people and caused them to abandon agriculture.

The *Discourses on Salt and Iron* reconstructs these debates. A provincial official named Huan Kuan wrote the text during the reign of Emperor Xuan (r. 74–49 BCE), undoubtedly to promote the Confucian governance. Despite its Confucian bias, in great detail and with a fair amount of evenhandedness, the book sets out the positions of both sides in the debate over the state monopolies. Thus, with lucid clarity, the *Discourses on Salt and Iron* exhibits the two fundamental Chinese approaches to government: the practical stance of officials interested in increasing the state's power and effectiveness versus the idealistic stance of Confucians who believed that the state's agents should concentrate on improving their moral selves and acting as exemplars to the people. For future generations, this book put forward a blueprint of how Confucian officials should govern.

Context

The early rulers of the Western Han Dynasty (206 BCE–25 CE) were adherents of a Daoist philosophy known as Huang-Lao, based on the teachings of Huangdi, known as the Yellow Emperor, and Laozi (or Lao-tzu), the traditionally recognized author of the Dao De Jing (Canon of

the Way). The Huang-Lao way of thought stressed that the best government was one that did not burden the people; as a result, it urged emperors to be frugal, limit taxes, avoid meddling in the economy, and renounce warfare as a policy instrument. To establish peace along the northern frontier with an empire led by a pastoral nomadic people known as the Xiongnü, these emperors made treaties known as the *heqin*—"harmony through kinship" agreements. In order to stop the Xiongnü from staging raids, the Chinese government provided the Xiongnü's leader, known as the *shanyu*, with a Chinese princess in marriage. By doing so, the early rulers recognized the Xiongnü state as a diplomatic equal; harmony would come from the joining of the two imperial families. The *heqin* treaties also furnished the Xiongnü with annual payments in silk, wine, and grain. These combined policies of imperial frugality, laissez-faire economics, and concessionary treaties produced an era of peace, prosperity, and overflowing imperial coffers.

Perhaps in the hope of wrenching more concessions from their affluent southern neighbors or because of the periodic freezing of their pastures, the Xiongnü often resorted to raiding China's northern frontier. Chinese policy changed dramatically during the long reign of the Martial Emperor, Han Wudi. He waged vigorous military campaigns against the Xiongnü and their client states in the Tarim Basin (in modern-day Xinjiang Uygur, in northwestern China). In pursuit of the nomads' people and animals, he sent large cavalry armies deep into the steppes, north of the Gobi Desert. After many disasters, by 101 BCE, his armies finally subdued the Tarim Basin and brought it under Chinese control. To guard these new acquisitions, the government set up walls and beacon towers all along the northern frontier. All of these victories, though, came at a huge price: The imperial coffers were empty.

The chief beneficiaries of the early Han emperors' laissez-faire economics were powerful families in the provinces, who amassed tremendous wealth and influence through both commerce and agriculture. By reclaiming land, adopting innovative agricultural techniques, and collecting the debts owed to them by their poorer neighbors, these households created huge estates that produced cash crops and other marketable agricultural goods. Private families that engaged in the production and distribution of the two most

221 BCE
- The Qin kingdom unifies China.

206 BCE
- The Han Dynasty overthrows the Qin.

141 BCE
- The reign of Han Wudi, the Martial Emperor, begins.

119 BCE
- The government institutes a monopoly on the production and distribution of salt and iron.

115 BCE
- Sang Hongyang institutes the equable marketing system to manage the transportation of goods to where they are needed.

110 BCE
- Sang Hongyang institutes the balancing standard system to regulate prices on important commodities.

101 BCE
- The Martial Emperor's armies conquer the Tarim Basin, stronghold of the nomadic Xiongnü.

98 BCE
- The government monopolizes the production and distribution of liquor.

needed commodities, salt and iron, became fabulously rich. They reinvested their profits in the purchase of land; as a result, merchant-gentry families dominated the countryside, while impoverished small landholders were legion.

To solve these problems, the Martial Emperor's administrators looked to the ideas of thinkers who were characterized as "Legalists"—they believed that the proper means of governing was the equal application of the law to everyone and the thorough use of administrative mechanisms. For these thinkers, anything that increased the state's power and limited private families' wealth was good. Their hero was Shang Yang (ca. 390–338 BCE), whose centralizing reforms laid the foundation for the state of Qin's unification of China in 221 BCE. Although Legalists condemned merchants as parasites who produced nothing, the Martial Emperor's advisers looked to the *Guanzi*, a Legalist text from the third century BCE that emphasized the importance of commerce to the state's economic viability. The *Guanzi*, meaning "Master Guan," was named after the philosopher Guan Zhong of the seventh century BCE.

Beginning in 119 BCE, through a sweeping array of reforms inspired by Legalism's teachings, the regime nationalized various aspects of the economy. One of the first measures was the establishment of state monopolies. From this point on, only the state could produce and distribute salt and iron. Later on, in 98 BCE, Sang Hongyang (152–80 BCE), the reforms' chief architect, also had the government monopolize the distribution of liquor. These monopolies directed the industries' profits to the public coffers rather than to private families and guaranteed that the government could fix these commodities' prices so that they were available to everyone.

A second set of measures was enacted to ensure that essential goods were available everywhere. Sang Hongyang established the "equable marketing" (*junshu*) institution in 115 BCE and the "balancing standard" (*pingzhun*) system in 110 BCE. The purpose of equable marketing was to redistribute the goods collected as taxes. People paid most of their taxes in grain and cloth. What kind of grain and cloth people paid depended on the staples that their region commonly produced; hence, if a person lived in the south, taxes would be paid in rice and silk, whereas in the north it might be millet and hemp. Rather than ship these bulky goods all the way to the capital, equable marketing officials were supposed to send them to places where supplies were deficient. By this means, merchants would be unable to charge exorbitant prices due to scarcity of a commodity in a particular region. The balancing standards' purpose was to fix market prices. This office would buy commodities when they were cheap and sell them at reasonable prices when they became expensive. This way the people would always have access to the goods in question at reasonable prices; consequently, the balancing standards would prevent price gouging and ensure that ordinary people had access to essential commodities in times of need. The government further enacted measures to limit the amount of wealth that merchants could accrue: They were subject to new taxes on their property and could not own agricultural land. Other measures enacted included one allowing the government to sell bureaucratic offices to or reduce the criminal sentences of men who made huge donations of grain to the government.

These reforms were successful in providing the government with much-needed revenue for frontier defense; however, their imposition created a number of hardships. To produce iron and salt and transport them, the government needed labor. To fulfill this need, as a form of taxation it conscripted workers from the people. Thus, men had less time to devote to providing sustenance for their families and earning income to pay their taxes. The debate convened by Emperor Zhao regarding the government-instituted monopolies and the associated circumstances took place in 81 BCE and was recorded sometime between 74 and 49 BCE as the *Discourses on Salt and Iron*. Both sides of debaters in the text make clear that people were abandoning their homes and fields to avoid paying taxes. There were also complaints that under the rubric of the balancing standard, government officials forced people to sell goods to the government at artificially low prices, which it then sold at much higher prices. Others criticized the fact that government-made iron products were shoddy and overpriced. Furthermore, rather than equalizing income, these measures enriched those powerful families who helped the government run the nationalized industries. These complaints had become particularly loud after the Martial Emperor's death in 87 BCE.

With the Martial Emperor's passing, Huo Guang, Emperor Xuan's father-in-law, became the de facto ruler. It seems that it was, in fact, Huo who wanted to reassess these policies and their effects on the country. It could well be that he also saw this as a means to check the influence of Sang Hongyang, the economic and political program's chief architect. In the *Discourses on Salt and Iron*, it is often Sang Hongyang himself who defends the government's policy. Oftentimes the work shows him at a loss for words in seeking to reply to his opponents' charges.

The work also reveals the ongoing struggle between two groups of educated men. The first consisted of men who were in office. They were Legalist administrators who were primarily concerned with how to practically solve the empire's problems. They believed in active government participation in the economy and an aggressive foreign policy. They valued both Legalist ideas and the Qin Dynasty's centralization of the state's power. Their opponents viewed them as careerists who never thought of remonstrating with their superiors for fear of losing their jobs. The other group consisted of Confucian scholars who by and large did not hold office and advocated far more idealistic policies. They vehemently opposed both government intervention in the economy and aggressive foreign policy. The government, they held, should instead concentrate on leading the people by virtuous example; indeed, the most loyal act a minister could perform was protesting his superior's misbehavior. These philosophers idealized the decentralized rule of the Zhou Dynasty (1040–256 BCE). Their opponents condemned them as useless men whose ideas of governance by moral transformation were completely impractical.

Time Line

87 BCE	■ The Martial Emperor's reign ends upon his death; Emperor Zhao assumes the throne, and Huo Guang becomes the de facto ruler.
81 BCE	■ Emperor Zhao calls Confucian scholars to his court to debate the government's policies' impact on the people.
80 BCE	■ Sang Hongyang dies.
74 BCE	■ The reign of Emperor Xuan begins.
74–49 BCE	■ Huan Kuan writes the *Discourses on Salt and Iron*, a record of the debates of 81 BCE.
68 BCE	■ Huo Guang, Emperor Xuan's father-in-law and China's de facto leader, dies.
49 BCE	■ The reign of Emperor Xuan ends upon his death.

About the Author

Hardly anything is known about the life of the author Huan Kuan. The historical record supplies only four facts: the place with which he was associated, his academic leanings, when he became an official, and the highest government post that he achieved. Huan Kuan was from Runan Prefecture, located in present-day Henan Province, in east-central China. During the Han Dynasty, Runan was known as being dominated by powerful families with extensive landholdings and mercantile interests. These were precisely the types of families who would have opposed the government's monopolies and antimercantile policies and favored the Confucian laissez-faire attitude.

Huan Kuan was an expert on a commentary that explains the meaning of the ancient Spring and Autumn Annals. This terse work is a year-by-year history of the seminal events that transpired in the state of Lu from 722 to 481 BCE. What made the text important was that Chinese believed that Confucius authored it. The commentary in which Huan Kuan was expert attempts to pinpoint this classic's moral and political messages. Clearly, then, Huan was a Confucian scholar who championed the importance of morality in politics.

During Emperor Xuan's reign, Huan was recommended for the position of court gentleman. This information is important because it gives us a sense of when he wrote the *Discourses on Salt and Iron*. Because he would have needed access to court records, he could have written this work only after becoming a court official. Since precisely when he wrote the book during Emperor Xuan's reign is unknown, it could be that he composed it as long as thirty years after the event. Finally, the highest position he earned was that of deputy governor of Lujiang Prefecture (just north of the Chang, or Yangtze, River in present-day Anhui Province). Hence, he was an official of some importance but not of great significance.

Explanation and Analysis of the Document

Discourses on Salt and Iron is Huan Kuan's reconstruction of the court's debates of 81 BCE. It was written eight to thirty-one years after the event. Most probably, Huan's sources were the court's own voluminous records of the discussions. By this point in time, court historians undoubtedly recorded the reigning emperor's actions and words as well as significant court debates. That the book is so long (sixty chapters) indicates that Huan must have been working with detailed and extensive records. One can see the evenhandedness of his general treatment in that both sides' views are given at formidable length. Nevertheless, since the Confucian spokesmen are often allowed the last word while the government spokesmen are often characterized as speechless, Huan surely shaped his retelling of the debates to demonstrate the superiority of the Confucian side.

The chapter provided, "The Basic Argument," is merely the first of sixty. The chapters' subjects concern a wide range of political, social, intellectual, diplomatic, and economic issues. A number of the chapters discuss specific government policies; for example, an entire chapter is devoted to the *heqin* ("harmony through kinship") treaties and another to monetary measures. Other chapters focus less specifically on policy, instead consisting of attacks on the different aspects of the legitimacy of Confucian and Legalist positions.

◆ Paragraphs a–c

The text opens by relating that in 81 BCE the emperor ordered that the chancellor, who was Tian Qianqiu, and other top officials meet with Confucian scholars, referred to as Literati, to determine the nature of the people's current complaints. Responding indirectly at first, the Confucian scholars narrate their general principle of good governance: In maintaining virtuous conduct itself, the government should aim to spread good conduct, eliminate vice, discourage commerce, and encourage simplicity.

The Confucians continue in paragraph c, now voicing major complaints about the present system. The monopolies on salt, iron, and liquor as well as the equable marketing system have in many ways negatively affected the people. To begin, the easy profits to be made from these businesses have caused people to abandon agriculture. Agriculture is necessary for the creation of wealth; if people quit agriculture, the state will become poor. In turn, owing to the easy money that comes with commerce, people who engage in it tend to become extravagant. Extravagance is marked by overspending, which will eventually cause poverty. Thus, to benefit the empire, the government should abolish the present system so that people will return to agriculture and simplicity.

◆ Paragraphs d and e

The "Lord Grand Secretary," that is, Sang Hongyang, the principal architect of the economic policies, replies that the government instituted these reforms because the frontier people were suffering as the result of the constant raiding of the Xiongnü (spelled "Hsiung Nu" in the document). To protect those citizens, the late Emperor—Han Wudi, the Martial Emperor—created a line of forts and beacon towers. Owing to their great expense, the government set up the monopolies on salt, iron, and liquor as well as the equable marketing system. In paragraph e, the lord grand secretary points out that if these financial reforms were abolished, the government would have no revenue with which to supply the armies at the frontier. There is no other way to finance provisioning them.

◆ Paragraphs f and g

Quoting the Analects (Book 16), the purported words of Confucius, the Confucians argue that the ruler should be worried not about how much wealth the people have but about whether it is distributed equally. As long as people feel that their ruler is treating them well, they will not care about precisely how much they have. Thus, the ruler should not worry about putting into place measures that will finance the troops' supplies; instead, he should be cultivating his conduct, making sure that he is a good person. If he inspires his army with his virtue, they will be victorious on the battlefield. Logistics should take a backseat to inspiration.

In paragraph g, Sang Hongyang responds by explaining why the government decided to adopt an aggressive policy toward their northern neighbors. Not wanting to unduly endanger and burden his people by forcing them to take up arms in their own defense, the emperor long endured the

Coin issued by Emperor Xuan (© The Trustees of the British Museum)

Xiongnü's outrageous behavior; however, because they were killing people along the border, he needed to act to push the Xiongnü back north of the Gobi Desert. He could only do so by making use of the revenue generated by the monopolies. It was only through the use of these institutions that the government could resolve the frontier problem.

◆ **Paragraphs h and i**

The Confucians next assert that force is not the optimal way to deal with foreign threats. The scholars frame their contention with a quotation from the Analects (Book 16) stating that if people in outlying regions are not cooperative, then the ruler must pacify them through the cultivation of civilization and virtue and through concern for their welfare. Under the present system, to the contrary, the government relies on large armies to attack the enemy and guard the border. This system forces the people to suffer, with soldiers enduring the deprivations of serving on the front and peasants enduring the hardships of being forced to supply the army. Furthermore, the monopolies and other economic measures were supposed to be merely temporary, not permanent.

In responding in paragraph i, the lord grand secretary neglects to address the proposition of subduing the Xiongnü by teaching them virtue; instead, he argues for the importance of commerce. He notes that the sage-kings of the past recognized that the circulation of goods is essential for society's welfare. Artisans are needed because they provide farmers with farm implements; merchants are needed because they furnish people with valuable objects. If not for artisans and merchants, farmers would have neither the means nor the desire to work, produce food, and amass wealth. Artisans and merchants are thereby necessary components of society who help distribute wealth. Since the state monopolies and the equable marketing system encourage artisans and merchants to engage in their professions, these measures cannot be stopped without hurting the economy. To strengthen his argument, Sang Hongyang uses a quotation from the foundational Confucian text called the Classic of Changes (I Ching), which states that the ruler should encourage commerce so that the people will work hard.

◆ **Paragraph j**

In paragraph j, the Confucians explain their condemnation of commerce and industry. They begin by paraphrasing a passage from the Analects (Book 2): It is the ruler's duty to morally transform the people through his virtue. If he does so, the people will continue to engage in agriculture; if he encourages them to manufacture or trade goods, people will abandon their farms and flock to the cities. A country in which very few people engage in agriculture can never be strong; thus, a good ruler encourages agriculture while discouraging commerce and industry. By means of imposing moral standards, he limits the people's desire for material goods. Markets still exist in his realm, but they are merely for the barter exchange of basic goods—artisans do not produce luxury goods, nor do merchants circulate them. Moreover, government policy focuses on benefiting farmers rather than artisans and merchants.

Interestingly, to bolster his point, the Confucian Huan Kuan employs a quotation said to have originated with Lao-tzu, author of the fundamental text of the Daoists, who were in direct competition with the Confucians. This use of a Daoist text underscores the fact that Daoists and Confucians shared similar economic attitudes: Both denigrated artisans and merchants, thought that peoples' desires needed to be limited, and were convinced that the government should not intervene in the economy.

◆ **Paragraph k**

In this paragraph, the lord grand secretary once again reiterates the importance of industry and commerce for the economy's health. He does so by appealing to the authority of the Legalist *Guanzi* text, with the author's name spelled "Kuan-tzǔ." Kuan-tzǔ is held to have stated that even though a country might be rich in resources, its people will be poor if there are not enough artisans and merchants. People needed goods that could be found only in other regions—this is why it was necessary to have merchants who would transport them. Many of these goods needed to be processed before they could be used—this is why it was necessary to have artisans who would turn them into finished products. The state monopolies were established to provide the people with the essential goods; the equable marketing system was created so that necessary commodities could make their way to the communities in which they were needed. To abolish these measures would be disastrous because the people would not receive the goods they required and desired.

An interesting passage here is the one that lists the various products that were being traded in Han China and their points of origin: Lacquerware and feathers came from northwestern China and modern-day Sichuan Province; leather goods, bone, and ivory came from the middle reaches of the Chang River and China's southernmost area; bamboo came from southeastern China; fish, salt, rugs, and furs came from Shandong Province and southern Manchuria; and yarn, linen, and hemp came from central China.

◆ **Paragraph l**

Using the same quotation from the *Guanzi*, the Confucians reply that the reason that a country with much fertile land might have people suffering from hunger is that the government favors commerce and industry at agriculture's expense. If no one is working in the fields, how can there be food to eat? The reason a country's mountains and seas could have rich natural resources while its people yet lacked wealth was that they squandered their wealth through extravagance. If people lived beyond their means, there could never be enough wealth to satisfy their desires; consequently, sage rulers of old encouraged frugality and simplicity. It was for this reason that Pan Geng, a Shang Dynasty ruler from the fourteenth century BCE, lived in a thatched hut; the sage-king Shun disavowed the use of gold; and the first Han Dynasty emperor, Gaozu (r. 202–195 BCE), forbad the descendants of merchants to become officials.

The Confucians further point out that, in the past, even though there were measures that discriminated against merchants, which supposedly prevented them from obtaining enormous profits, they were still able to exercise their greed and make money. If such was the case, what would happen when officials replaced merchants in controlling the industries? Certainly they, too, would be infected with greed and become corrupt. If officials were to become corrupt, it would cause the people to become unruly. Thus,

assigning the work of merchants to officials would corrupt the ruling class and lead to social instability. The Confucians clinch their argument with a quotation from an unidentified work referred to as the *Chuan*, which usually means "commentary." It states that when a ruler is enamored of obtaining wealth, his example negatively transforms each class of people, making the people become bandits.

◆ **Paragraph m**

In paragraph m, the lord grand secretary describes and defends the equable marketing and balancing standard systems. In the past, when local governments sent the goods they collected as taxes to the capital, the transportation costs were often greater than the value of the goods. By setting up transportation offices in each province, the government gained the ability to send goods directly to where they were needed and to do so in a much more timely fashion. This system is known as equable marketing. In the capital, the government had set up an office to buy essential goods when they were cheap and sell them when they were expensive. This system ensured that the people could always obtain the commodities they needed at low prices; it also ensured that merchants could not make fortunes by manipulating prices. This is the balancing standard system. Both of these measures aimed to make essential commodities accessible to all.

◆ **Paragraph n**

Allowed by Huan Kuan the last reply to conclude the chapter, the Confucians here describe the abuses of the equable marketing and balancing standard systems. They believed that the people should pay their taxes with the goods they most commonly produced—grain and ordinary cloth. They accuse government officials of demanding that citizens provide certain types of grain and cloth, which the government would buy at artificially low prices. The officials would then sell the goods back to the producers at the government's fixed price, which was much higher than the price at which they were bought; as such, the equable marketing system allowed the government to profit at the people's expense. As for the balancing standard system, officials used it to corner the market on certain goods. Because everyone had then to buy these goods from the government, their prices soared, and the officials sold the goods at an enormous profit. Likewise, private traders hoarded those monopolized goods; thus, as the government forced the rise in price of those goods, the merchants bided their time until they could sell off their stock for a tidy sum on the black market. Even though these measures were supposed to suppress the merchants, in fact, officials and merchants worked hand in hand to ensure that both parties made money at ordinary people's expense.

Audience

The primary audience for the *Discourses on Salt and Iron* was the ruler—Emperor Xuan—and his officials. The book's purpose was to convince the current emperor as well

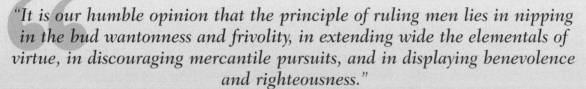
> "It is our humble opinion that the principle of ruling men lies in nipping in the bud wantonness and frivolity, in extending wide the elementals of virtue, in discouraging mercantile pursuits, and in displaying benevolence and righteousness."
>
> (Paragraph b)

> "Cultivate virtue in the temple and the hall, then you need only to show a bold front to the enemy and your troops will return home in victory. The Prince who practices benevolent administration should be matchless in the world; for him, what use is expenditure?"
>
> (Paragraph f)

> "Thus without artisans, the farmers will be deprived of the use of implements; without merchants, all prized commodities will be cut off. The former would lead to stoppage of grain production, the latter to exhaustion of wealth."
>
> (Paragraph i)

> "Hence the true King promotes rural pursuits and discourages branch industries; he checks the people's desires through the principles of propriety and righteousness and provides a market for grain in exchange for other commodities, where there is no place for merchants to circulate useless goods, and for artisans to make useless implements."
>
> (Paragraph j)

as future ones that the Confucian viewpoint was superior. It is for this reason that the text often shows the scholars' criticisms silencing the grand secretary and that, in each section, the Confucians have the last word. Nevertheless, Huan Kuan presents both sides in a relatively balanced manner, as to do otherwise would have alienated readers who were Legalist administrators. If he had made his account too one-sided, he would never have been able to convince them of Confucianism's superiority.

At the same time, Huan Kuan would have wanted to convince his fellow officials that they should recommend Confucian scholars for public office. Even though many of their arguments may seem naive to the modern reader, the Confucian spokesmen in the *Discourses on Salt and Iron*

show themselves to be men who are keenly concerned with the people's welfare and who are willing to courageously endanger their lives by criticizing the government. Such men who are more concerned with the empire's fate than with their own interests are precisely the type of men who can inspire the people and eliminate corruption.

Impact

The immediate impact of the *Discourses on Salt and Iron* was rather limited. Even though the government abandoned the liquor monopoly in response to the court debate of 81 BCE, the salt and iron monopolies continued. When the monopolies were finally discontinued at the beginning of the Eastern Han Dynasty (25–220 CE), it was due to the regime's own weakness, rather than because of Confucian objections. Nevertheless, the book undoubtedly helped strengthen Confucianism's appeal in the second half of the first century BCE. Confucians began to gain influence during the reign of Emperor Xuan's successor, Emperor Yuan (r. 48–33 BCE). Decades later, the usurper Wang Mang (r. 9–23 CE), an avowed Confucian, grabbed power, and Confucians became predominant in officialdom during the Eastern Han Dynasty. Huan Kuan's detailed account of the Confucian approach to government no doubt persuaded many officials and educated men that Confucians had comprehensive and workable means of running the empire.

The *Discourses on Salt and Iron* greatly influenced premodern Chinese intellectuals because it clearly set forth the two primary approaches to governance. The first was a practical, Legalist one that valued administrative efficiency and a strong central government. The second, the Confucian approach, prioritized the ruler's self-cultivation and moral suasion. According to this approach, since government institutions are usually subverted by greedy officials, they can never truly benefit the people; only the exemplary behavior of individual leaders can do so. While exhibiting both approaches, Huan Kuan's work underscored Confucianism's superiority; as a result, premodern Chinese officials oriented toward Confucian values could look to the *Discourses on Salt and Iron* to help solve problems of governance and find inspiration. Since Confucian government in China did not come to an end until the early twentieth century, the *Discourses on Salt and Iron* long remained an essential primer and philosophical resource for scholars and officials alike.

Further Reading

■ Articles
Kroll, J. L. "Toward a Study of the Economic Views of Sang Hung-yang." *Early China* 4 (1978–1979): 11–18.

■ Books
Hardy, Grant, and Anne Behnke Kinney. *The Establishment of the Han Empire and Imperial China.* Westport, Conn.: Greenwood Press, 2005.

Lewis, Mark Edward. *The Early Chinese Empires: Qin and Han.* Cambridge, Mass.: Harvard University Press, 2007.

Loewe, Michael. *Crisis and Conflict in Han China, 104 bc to ad 9.* London: Allen & Unwin, 1968.

Sadao, Nishijima. "The Economic and Social History of Former Han." In *The Cambridge History of China*, Vol. 1: *The Ch'in and Han Empires, 221 b.c.–a.d. 220*, eds. Denis Twitchett et al. Cambridge, U.K.: Cambridge University Press, 1986.

■ Web Sites
Kinney, Anne Behnke. "Traditions of Exemplary Women: A Bilingual Resource for the Study of Women in Early China." Institute for Advanced Technology in the Humanities, University of Virginia Web site.

   http://www2.iath.virginia.edu/xwomen/intro.html.

—Keith N. Knapp

Questions for Further Study

1. Why do you think that the early efforts of the Han emperors to establish peace on their northern border through diplomacy failed?

2. Why were salt and iron such essential commodities at the time? What parallels do you see between salt and iron in ancient China and other commodities in the modern world?

3. What similarities do you see between the debates over economic systems in ancient China and those that take place in modern industrialized nations? Consider, for example, the issues of taxation, redistribution of wealth, the government's role in creating markets, efforts by the state to impose standards of conduct, and state-run monopolies.

4. Who, in your estimation, won the debate recorded in the *Discourses on Salt and Iron*?

5. What impact did the *Discourses on Salt and Iron* have on the development of Confucianism—and, in a larger sense, on future debates regarding the role of government?

DISCOURSES ON SALT AND IRON

Chapter I. The Basic Argument

a. It so happened that in the sixth year of the *shih-yüan* era an Imperial edict directed the Chancellor and the Imperial secretaries to confer with the recommended Worthies and Literati, and to enquire of them as to the rankling grievances among the people.

b. The Literati responded as follows: It is our humble opinion that the principle of ruling men lies in nipping in the bud wantonness and frivolity, in extending wide the elementals of virtue, in discouraging mercantile pursuits, and in displaying benevolence and righteousness. Let lucre never be paraded before the eyes of the people; only then will enlightenment flourish and folkways improve.

c. But now, with the system of the salt and iron monopolies, the liquor excise, and equable marketing, established in the provinces and the demesnes, the Government has entered into financial competition with the people, dissipating primordial candor and simplicity and sanctioning propensities to selfishness and greed. As a result few among our people take up the fundamental pursuits of life, while many flock to the non-essential. Now sturdy natural qualities decay as artificiality thrives, and rural values decline when industrialism flourishes. When industrialism is cultivated, the people become frivolous; when the values of rural life are developed, the people are simple and unsophisticated. The people being unsophisticated, wealth will abound; when the people are extravagant, cold and hunger will follow. We pray that the salt, iron and liquor monopolies and the system of equable marketing be abolished so that the rural pursuits may be encouraged, people be deterred from entering the secondary occupations, and national agriculture be materially and financially benefited.

d. The Lord Grand Secretary said: When the Hsiung Nu rebelled against our authority and frequently raided and devastated the frontier settlements, to be constantly on the watch for them was a great strain upon the soldiery of the Middle Kingdom; but without measures of precaution being taken, these forays and depredations would never cease. The late Emperor, grieving at the long suffering of the denizens of the marches who live in fear of capture by the barbarians, caused consequently forts and

seried signal stations to be built, where garrisons were held ready against the nomads. When the revenue for the defence of the frontier fell short, the salt and iron monopoly was established, the liquor excise and the system of equable marketing introduced; goods were multiplied and wealth increased so as to furnish the frontier expenses.

e. Now our critics here, who demand that these measures be abolished, at home would have the hoard of the treasury entirely depleted, and abroad would deprive the border of provision for its defence; they would expose our soldiers who defend the barriers and mount the walls to all the hunger and cold of the borderland. How else do they expect to provide for them? It is not expedient to abolish these measures!

f. The Literati: Confucius observed that the ruler of a kingdom or the chief of a house is not concerned about his people being few, but about lack of equitable treatment; nor is he concerned about poverty, but over the presence of discontentment. Thus the Son of Heaven should not speak about much and little, the feudal lords should not talk about advantage and detriment, ministers about gain and loss, but they should cultivate benevolence and righteousness, to set an example to the people, and extend wide their virtuous conduct to gain the people's confidence. Then will nearby folk lovingly flock to them and distant peoples joyfully submit to their authority. Therefore the master conqueror does not fight; the expert warrior needs no soldiers; the truly great commander requires not to set his troops in battle array. Cultivate virtue in the temple and the hall; then you need only to show a bold front to the enemy and your troops will return home in victory. The Prince who practices benevolent administration should be matchless in the world; for him, what use is expenditure?

g. The Lord Grand Secretary: The Hsiung Nu, savage and wily, boldly push through the barriers and harass the Middle Kingdom, massacring the provincial population and killing the keepers of the Northern Marches. They long deserve punishment for their unruliness and lawlessness. But Your Majesty graciously took pity on the insufficiency of the multitude and did not suffer his lords and knights to be exposed in the desert plains, yet unflinchingly You cherish the purpose of raising strong armies and driving the Hsiung Nu before You to their original haunts in the north. I again assert that the proposal to do away with the salt and iron monopoly and equable marketing would grievously diminish our frontier supplies and impair our military plans. I can not consider favorably a proposal so heartlessly dismissing the frontier question.

h. The Literati: The ancients held in honor virtuous methods and discredited resort to arms. Thus Confucius said: If remoter people are not submissive, all the influences of civil culture and virtue are to be cultivated to attract them to be so; and when they have been so attracted, they must be made contented and tranquil? Now these virtuous principles are discarded and reliance put on military force; troops are raised to attack the enemy and garrisons are stationed to make ready for him. It is the long drawn-out service of our troops in the field and the ceaseless transportation for the needs of the commissariat that cause our soldiers on the marches to suffer from hunger and cold abroad, while the common people are burdened with labor at home. The establishment of the salt and iron monopoly and the institution of finance officials to supply the army needs were not permanent schemes; it is therefore desirable that they now be abolished.

i. The Lord Grand Secretary: The ancient founders of the Commonwealth made open the ways for both fundamental and branch industries and facilitated equitable distribution of goods. Markets and courts were provided to harmonize various demands; there people of all classes gathered together and all goods collected, so that farmer, merchant, and worker could each obtain what he desired; the exchange completed, everyone went back to his occupation. Facilitate exchange so that the people will be unflagging in industry says the Book of Changes. Thus without artisans, the farmers will be deprived of the use of implements; without merchants, all prized commodities will be cut off. The former would lead to stoppage of grain production, the latter to exhaustion of wealth. It is clear that the salt and iron monopoly and equable marketing are really intended for the circulation of amassed wealth and the regulation of the consumption according to the urgency of the need. It is inexpedient to abolish them.

j. The Literati: Lead the people with virtue and the people will return to honest simplicity; entice the people with gain, and they will become vicious. Vicious habits would lead them away from righteousness to follow after gain, with the result that people will swarm on the road and throng at the markets. A poor country may appear plentiful, not because it possesses abundant wealth, but because wants multiply and people become reckless, said Lao-tzǔ. Hence the true King promotes rural pursuits and discourages branch industries; he checks the people's desires through the principles of propriety and righteousness and provides a market for grain in exchange for other commodities, where there is no place for merchants to circulate useless goods, and for artisans to make useless implements. Thus merchants are for the purpose of draining stagnation and the artisans for providing tools; they should not become the principal concern of the government.

k. The Lord Grand Secretary: Kuan-tzǔ is reported to have said: A country may possess a wealth of fertile land and yet its people may be underfed—the reason lying in lack of an adequate supply of agricultural implements. It may possess rich natural resources in its mountains and seas and yet the people may be deficient in wealth—the reason being in the insufficient number of artisans and merchants. The scarlet lacquer and pennant feathers of Lung and Shu, the leather goods, bone and ivory of Ching and Yang, the cedars, lindera, and bamboo rods of Chiang-nan, the fish, salt, rugs, and furs of Yen and Ch'i, the lustrine yarn, linen, and hemp-cloth of Yen and Yü, are all necessary commodities to maintain our lives and provide for our death. But we depend upon the merchants for their distribution and on the artisans for giving them their finished forms. This is why the Sages availed them of boats and bridges to negotiate rivers and gulleys, and domesticated cattle and horses for travel over mountains and plateaux. Thus by penetrating to distant lands and exploring remote places, they were able to exchange all goods to the benefit of the people. Hence His late Majesty established officers in control of iron to meet the farmer's needs and provided equable marketing to make sufficient the people's wealth. Thus, the salt and iron monopoly and the equable marketing supported by the myriad people and looked to as the source of supply, cannot conveniently be abolished.

l. The Literati: That a country possesses a wealth of fertile land and yet its people are underfed is due to the fact that merchants and workers have prospered unduly while the fundamental occupations have been neglected. That a country possesses rich natural resources in its mountains and seas and yet its people lack capital is because the people's necessities have not been attended to, while luxuries and fancy articles have multiplied. The fountain-head of a river cannot fill a leaking cup; mountains and seas cannot overwhelm streams and valleys. This is why

P'an Kêng practised communal living, Shun hid away gold, and Kao Tsu forbade merchants and shopkeepers to be officials. Their purpose was to discourage habits of greed and fortify the spirit of extreme earnestness. Now with all the discriminations against the market people, and stoppage of the sources of profit, people still do evil. What if the ruling classes should pursue profit themselves? The Chuan says, When the princes take delight in profit, the ministers become mean; when the ministers become mean, the minor officers become greedy; when the minor officers become greedy, the people become thieves. Thus to open the way for profit is to provide a ladder to popular misdemeanor.

m. The Lord Grand Secretary: Formerly the Princes in the provinces and the demesnes sent in their respective products as tribute. The transportation was vexacious and disorganized; the goods were usually of distressingly bad quality, often failing to repay their transport costs. Therefore Transportation Officers have been provided in every province to assist in the delivery and transportation and for the speeding of the tribute from distant parts. So the system came to be known as equable marketing. A Receiving Bureau has been established at the capital to monopolize all the commodities, buying when prices are low, and selling when prices are high, with the result that the Government suffers no loss and the merchants cannot speculate for profit. This is therefore known as the balancing standard. With the balancing standard people are safeguarded from unemployment; with the equable marketing people have evenly distributed labor. Both of these measures are intended to equilibrate all goods and convenience the people, and not to open the way to profit and provide a ladder to popular misdemeanor.

n. The Literati: The Ancients in levying upon and taxing the people would look for what the latter were skilled in, and not seek for those things in which they were not adept. Thus the farmers contributed the fruits of their labor, the weaving women, their products. Now the Government leaves alone what the people have and exacts what they have not, with the result that the people sell their products at a cheap price to satisfy demands from above. Recently in some of the provinces and demesnes they ordered the people to make woven goods. The officers then caused the producers various embarassments and bargained with them. What was collected by the officers was not only the silk from Ch'i and T'ao, or cloth from Shu and Han, but also other goods manufactured by the people which were mischievously sold at a standard price. Thus the farmers suffer twice over while the weaving women are doubly taxed. We have not yet seen that your marketing is "equable". As to the second measure under discussion, the government officers swarm out to close the door, gain control of the market and corner all commodities. With commodities cornered, prices soar; with prices rising, the merchants make private deals by way of speculation. Thus the officers are lenient to the cunning capitalists, and the merchants store up goods and accumulate commodities waiting for a time of need. Nimble traders and unscrupulous officials buy in cheap to get high returns. We have not yet seen that your standard is "balanced". For it seems that in ancient times equable marketing was to bring about equitable division of labor and facilitate transportation of tribute; it was surely not for profit or to make trade in commodities.

Glossary

Book of Changes	the I Ching; a Confucian classic cited in this context to support the concept of balance in all things
branch industries	manufacturing and commerce, in contrast to the fundamental industries of farming and weaving
lindera	flowering tree of the laurel family valued for the medicinal properties of its leaves, twigs, bark, and fruit
lustrine yarn	glossy silk
Middle Kingdom	name used by the Chinese for China since 1000 BCE
Northern Marches	borderlands of the north
Son of Heaven	the Chinese sovereign, who had different titles in different historical periods

Bust of Julius Caesar sculpted in his lifetime, ca. 49–46 BCE. (AP/Wide World Photos)

LAW OF CAESAR ON MUNICIPALITIES

" [The magistrate] shall keep this list displayed daily ...
where it can be easily read from the ground level."

Overview

The text of the Law of Caesar on Municipalities comes from bronze panels known as
the Tablets of Heraclea, which were discovered in two parts in 1732 and 1735, respectively, near the town of Heraclea, a former
Greek city in southern Italy near Naples on
the Gulf of Tarentum. (Southern Italy was
once in the possession of the Greeks and was known as
Magna Graecia, or Greater Greece.) On one side are
inscriptions in Greek, dating to the third or fourth century
BCE and relating to land rights and rules of use of the areas
around two temples. On the other side, Latin inscriptions
record the Law of Caesar on Municipalities. It is unknown
whether the Latin inscriptions refer to all municipalities
gained under the Roman program of territorial expansion
or only to municipalities in the Italian peninsula or just to
the town of Heraclea itself. While the laws are representative of the new type of legislative, political, and fiscal
changes enacted by Caesar, it is not clear where these laws
applied or when exactly they were composed. It has also
been suggested that the inscriptions, which include laws
enacted in both the capital and the provinces, cannot all be
attributed to Caesar.

By the mid-first century BCE, Rome had pushed its
boundaries from the peninsula of Italy to encompass Gaul
(present-day France), almost all of modern-day Spain, parts
of northern Africa, Asia Minor (modern-day Turkey), Dalmatia, and Macedonia. The resettlement of Roman soldiers,
distribution of grain, and incorporation of new lands into the
expanding Roman world had become vital issues, and the
text of these laws seems to reflect some of the new exigencies of governing an ever-growing dominion. There was an
enormous area to be covered, each with local governments
that had become subject to Roman law. Territorial expansion
and changes in political power within Roman society led to
the formation of new laws such as those found on the
Tablets of Heraclea. Evidence in a letter from Cicero suggests that Caesar had started in 45 BCE to propose laws
regarding the composition of local senates. The Law of Caesar on Municipalities mentions these local senates, which
suggests a date of composition between 46 and 44 BCE.

Context

In part because of Julius Caesar, Rome passed from having been a republic to becoming an empire. When Caesar
was assassinated on March 15, 44 BCE, he held the title *dictator perpetuo*, or "dictator in perpetuity," and he was said to
have publicly refused the title of king. In 27 BCE Caesar's
adopted son and great-nephew, Octavian, would become
the first emperor, known as Augustus. Caesar had set the
stage for this political change by forming the First Triumvirate in 60 BCE with Marcus Licinius Crassus and Gnaeus
Pompeius Magnus, known as Pompey the Great. The First
Triumvirate was a secret political coalition that held unofficial power. It eventually divided the Senate as the result of
agrarian reforms that were heavily pushed by Caesar and his
allies. While Caesar expanded Roman territory with the
approval of much of the Senate, at the same time his pop-
ulist reforms alienated many of the Optimates in the Senate, who favored the aristocracy and supported Pompey.

After Crassus's death in 53 BCE, Pompey and Caesar
became embroiled in a power struggle. Pompey had been
declared sole consul by the Senate in 52 BCE. In 51 BCE he
ordered that Caesar, who at the time was fighting in Gaul,
must return to Rome and at the same time relinquish control of his army, in accordance with the long-standing rule
that no one was allowed to bring armies into Rome. Caesar
was reluctant to give up his army, as he feared that he would
be tried and murdered by Pompey's supporters. Instead of
complying with the law, Caesar crossed the Rubicon with
his army in 49 BCE. The resulting civil war, during which
Pompey was assassinated in Egypt in 48 BCE, enabled Caesar to consolidate his power. That year the Senate appointed Caesar dictator for the second time and consul soon
after. In 45 BCE he was appointed dictator for life.

Caesar's tactical strength on the battlefield extended to
the political arena, but only briefly. Enormously popular
with the plebeian class, he also enjoyed strong support
among the soldiers—an important base during the expan-
sionist phase of Roman history. A Roman by birth, he recognized the importance of bringing men from the provinces
into the power circles of the Senate. The extensive military
campaigns that occurred under Caesar meant that the
army expanded in size, which resulted in large numbers of

Time Line

CA. 100–102 BCE	■ Gaius Julius Caesar is born to his father of the same name, Gaius Julius Caesar, and Aurelia, daughter of Lucius Aurelius Cotta.
60 BCE	■ Caesar is elected consul; he forms the First Triumvirate with Crassus and Pompey.
52 BCE	■ Pompey is appointed sole consul.
51 BCE	■ The Gallic Wars end.
49 BCE	■ Caesar is ordered by the Senate to relinquish his command in Gaul, but he refuses to do so and, in defiance of Roman law, leads his army across the Rubicon into Italy. Pompey is appointed as dictator.
48 BCE	■ Pompey is assassinated in Egypt; Caesar is appointed dictator.
45 BCE	■ Caesar goes to Spain in pursuit of Pompey's son, Gnaeus Pompeius; Caesar defeats him and is appointed dictator for life.

soldiers who expected land and homes upon their retirement. To them, Caesar granted much of the newly conquered land as well as territories within Italy.

Roman society was hierarchical and divided into four basic classes: patricians, equestrians, plebeians, and slaves. This social hierarchy played an important role in Roman law. The patricians were old ruling families who claimed ancestry from the founders of Rome. Senators were often from this class. The equestrians gained more power during the later years of the republic. Membership in the equestrian class was based on personal wealth, and the social status of equestrians was thus more fluid than that of the nobles. Equestrians also made up the cavalry and had the right to be given a horse at public expense. The plebeians were the working class, which did not hold much political power but comprised the majority of citizens. The plebeians did have some political leverage through the office of the plebeian tribune, an elected position with responsibilities that included oversight of the plebeian council, through which laws could be brought to the Senate. There were also many slaves, some of whom were foreigners who had been captured in wars and brought back to Rome. Many of these foreigners were Greeks, who instructed their masters' sons in the language, literature, and philosophy of ancient Greece. Slaves could be freed or purchase their freedom; thus, an intermediate class of freedmen arose.

People living outside the city of Rome initially did not have Roman citizenship. As Roman territory increased, though, certain levels of Roman citizenship were extended to some residents of outlying areas, so the political palette of the Roman government began to change. In many new settlements stretching from Gaul to Asia Minor, particularly those established by Caesar, provincial authorities and former soldiers professed loyalty to Caesar. Freedmen, for example, had been able to gain the position of municipal councilors. Caesar also gave the rights of citizenship to doctors and teachers. Moreover, many immigrants came to Rome itself in search of employment and food and with the hope of eventual political enfranchisement. These developments eventually changed the scope of Roman citizenship, which came to include men from the provinces and the greater Italian peninsula.

About the Author

Gaius Julius Caesar was born on July 13, 100 BCE (a few sources give 102 or 101 BCE as the year of his birth). His family claimed illustrious beginnings as the descendants of Iulus, the son of Aeneas of Troy (who some claimed had founded Rome), and the goddess Venus. He was an expert military tactician and general and thus was instrumental in expanding the territories of Rome throughout Europe, especially in Gaul, about which he wrote the book *De bello Gallico* (*The Gallic Wars*). Caesar was also a very talented politician, who eventually commanded political power in Rome and was appointed dictator for life.

The Roman biographer and historian Suetonius described Caesar as tall, pale, and subject to the "falling sickness," by which he might have meant epilepsy. Reportedly, Caesar was fastidious about his appearance and always made sure that he was clean-shaven. He was apparently very troubled by his baldness and combed his hair forward or wore honorific laurel wreaths in order to hide it. Busts of Caesar sometimes show his receding hairline and nearly always his hair combed forward.

Caesar spent only about seven months in Rome after he defeated Pompey's sons in Spain and returned to the city in 45 BCE. He then took up extensive reforms of Roman society and government, centralizing the bureaucracy of the Roman Republic. He also consolidated his power, becoming "dictator in perpetuity." He named his adopted son, Octavian, as his first heir in his will and Marcus Junius Brutus, a member of the Roman Senate, as his second heir, if Octavian were to die first. Brutus, however, played a major conspiratorial role in Caesar's assassination in the Theatre of Pompey on March 15, 44 BCE. Caesar was stabbed twenty-three times by a group of senators led by Brutus.

Caesar's funeral was held in the Roman Forum. Mark Antony's funeral oration, as reported by the historian Appian of Alexandria, roused sympathy among Roman citizens, as did the news that Caesar had left three hundred sesterces to every Roman citizen. A riot ensued as the crowd expressed their anger at the loss of Caesar. Caesar was deified (with the sanction of the Roman Senate) in 42 BCE, and Octavian became emperor in 27 BCE.

Explanation and Analysis of the Document

Although many scholars believe that the document relates Roman law from about 44 BCE, it should be read with some degree of historical caution. As noted earlier, it is not known exactly to which municipalities it refers. By 44 BCE, Rome had expanded its boundaries from the peninsula of Italy to Gaul (modern-day France), almost all of present-day Spain, parts of northern Africa, Asia Minor (modern-day Turkey), Dalmatia, and Macedonia. There was therefore an enormous area to be covered, each with local governments that had become subject to Roman law. In some cases, local indigenous cultures with their own laws, languages, and customs had become assimilated with Romans and their culture and law.

◆ **Statutes 1–6**

The first six statutes concern census declarations for the distribution of grain to Roman inhabitants. Grain distribution was a major factor in the influx of immigrants to Rome after the civil war as well as a way for politicians to ensure favorable votes. Statute 3 stipulates that if the consul or praetor to whom one was supposed to make a declaration for receiving grain was away from Rome, the declaration must instead be made to either the urban praetor or the peregrine praetor. (These two praetors acted as judicial magistrates, the former hearing cases to which citizens were parties and the latter deciding cases between foreigners.) Statute 4 states that if no consuls or praetors were available,

Time Line

CA. 44 BCE
- Caesar promulgates the Law of Caesar on Municipalities.
- **March 15** Caesar is assassinated by members of the Senate.

27 BCE
- Caesar's adopted son and great-nephew, Octavian, becomes emperor and takes the name Augustus.

the plebeian tribune should be the locus of the declaration. The plebeian tribune had lost power under the Roman general and dictator Sulla in the first century BCE, and its inclusion here demonstrates Caesar and Pompey's restoration of the office's limited authority. Statutes 5 and 6 assume literacy among the grain distributors and those who could not receive grain. The names of these people were to be prominently posted in the Forum, a public area. Statue 6 then says that grain was not to be distributed to those whose names were listed, likely to ensure that grain goes only to the poor and not to those who do not need it. Statute 6 calls for the imposition of a heavy fine on those who broke the law by distributing grain to anyone not entitled to receive it.

◆ **Statutes 7–21**

Statutes 7 through 21 concern the use of roads and public spaces within Rome itself or within one mile of the city. The focus suggests that "law on municipalities" as applied to this text is a misnomer, since these laws refer to the capital city. It has been suggested that the inclusion of these sections is evidence that Caesar intended to turn Rome into simply another municipality, but that seems unlikely. It is more likely that existing laws from Rome were recopied in Heraclea, possibly because they were also meant to apply to that city. Sections 7 through 13 concern street maintenance. Those who owned homes that fronted a street were responsible for keeping that street in good repair and ensuring proper drainage so that the public could use it freely. The curule and plebeian aediles (essentially magistrates in charge of public buildings and festivals) were charged with the responsibility for determining jurisdiction over Rome's public streets and then coordinating maintenance, including paving and repair. If a street ran between a private building on one side and a temple or other public building on the other, it was the responsibility of the aedile in charge of that part of Rome to ensure the maintenance of the side of the street on which the temple or public building was located. Statutes 10 and 11 warn that private owners who did not keep up the streets in front of their property would have the contract for such maintenance leased out by the aedile in charge. Notice would be posted in the Forum, giving the street name and the name of the property owner. Further, property owners had to pay the contractor to do the work they had neglected. If they did not do so within thirty days, they would be fined. Statute 12, however, notes that these rules were not meant to prevent those already charged with cleaning the city's public streets to be deprived of their income or jobs. The law covers the maintenance and repair not only of streets but also alleyways, which were to be paved and their blocks inspected by the aedile in charge of that area.

Statute 14 attempts to guard against traffic congestion. It stipulates that people were prohibited from driving wagons in the city or the suburbs near apartment blocks after sunrise and before the "tenth hour of the day." The "tenth hour of the day" was probably about three or four in the afternoon, depending on the season. Romans reckoned the hours of the day from sunrise and the hours of the night from sunset. However, an exception was made for those transporting materials for building temples, public buildings, or public works. As outlined in statute 15, other exceptions to this rule were granted to vestal virgins and priests ("flamens") making their way by wagon to a sacrifice, wagons that were part of triumphal processions, and wagons necessary for games or for the procession "at the time of the games in the Circus Maximus." The Circus Maximus, located in a valley between the Aventine and Palatine hills, was essentially meant for chariot racing, but other events were also held there, including gladiatorial combats and wild animal hunts. Further exceptions were granted (in statute 16) to those who had driven donkey or ox wagons into the city at night and were either leaving empty-handed or carting out dung the next day.

Statute 17 determines that public spaces shall remain public within Rome. Except in cases where the Senate decided otherwise, private citizens were not allowed to acquire areas that have been deemed public or to erect any structures or buildings in those areas or even to modify the use of an arcade or public bar by restricting use of it to one portion of the populace. Certain areas could also be newly declared for public use in order to gain public revenue, as noted in statute 18. Statute 19 grants exceptions to those people providing games in Rome or within one mile thereof who needed to erect stages, temporary amphitheaters, or other platforms or needed to use existing public areas for staging the games.

Much of the business of Rome took place outdoors in the public areas of the markets and Forum. Thus, statute 20 contains provisions for clerks and scribes who work for magistrates in the public areas of the city. Statute 21 allows public slaves to continue to make use of and even live in areas that had been assigned to them by the censors.

◆ **Statutes 22–30**

Statutes 22 through 29 are concerned with elections and the census in "municipalities, colonies, prefectures, markets, or meeting places of Roman citizens." According to statute 22, those elected to offices outside Rome could not appoint or substitute anyone to act as decurion (member of a town council) or conscript in a local senate unless it was to replace a deceased or condemned senator. Age restrictions were imposed for candidacy. According to statute 23, no man under thirty could be a candidate or hold office in a "a municipality, a colony, or a prefecture," unless he had served in "three campaigns in the cavalry or six campaigns in the infantry of a legion … either in camp or in a province." Caesar had made his name in the army, and he must have felt that military service gave younger men maturity and developed their ability to lead off the battlefield. This is also an important clause in light of the many new provinces settled by former military men.

Auctioneers, masters of funeral ceremonies, and undertakers were altogether forbidden to hold office. Auctioneers were prohibited because of conflicts of interest. Members of the funeral trade were considered to have a low social status. They were not "gentlemen." These jobs were thought by the Romans to be unclean, thus "contaminating" the living. Statute 24 reinforces statute 23. The restrictions against men under thirty, auctioneers, masters of funeral ceremonies, and undertakers also meant that no one was allowed to announce the election of any such ineligible man, guarding against the possibility that candidates who were not fully qualified might win a place as duumvir, *quattuorvir*, or magistrate through popular acclaim or write-in votes.

Further voting and office-holding restrictions are found in statute 25. Included among those barred from voting or holding public office were thieves, fraudsters, those "condemned either by the Praetorian Law or for something that he has done or does contrary to that law," gladiators and those who trained them, those who had gone bankrupt or whose goods had been seized and auctioned off, and anyone who had been condemned in public trials either in Rome or in the municipalities. (Praetorian law was a body of legal precedents set down by the praetors.) Others prohibited from voting or holding office included those who had made false accusations, those who had been dishonorably discharged from the military, male prostitutes, actors, and brothel keepers. A fine of 50,000 sesterces was to be imposed on those who broke any of the rules listed in statutes 23–25. Although it is not mentioned in the text, women were also prohibited from holding office or voting in ancient Rome.

The law also attempts to guard against vote fixing, manipulation, or illegal elections. Statutes 26 and 27 declare that if a person was deemed ineligible as described in the law, no one aware of that ineligibility was allowed to ask the person to stand for election or to vote. No citizen could be forced to vote, either "orally or by ballot." No ineligible individual could stand for or accept the office of "duumvir, quattuorvir, or any other office" that could lead

❝ "Whenever and wherever grain is distributed to the people he [the magistrate] shall keep this list displayed daily, for the greater part of each day, where it can be easily read from the ground level."

(Statute 5)

"Each owner of property fronting on the streets of Rome or on streets within a mile of Rome, on which there is continuous settlement now or in the future, shall keep such portion of the street in repair at the discretion of that aedile who has jurisdiction in this quarter of the city."

(Statute 7)

"After January 1, in the second year following enactment of this law, no person under thirty years of age shall be a candidate for, accept, or administer the office of duumvir, quattuorvir, or any other magistracy in a municipality, a colony, or a prefecture, unless he has served three campaigns in the cavalry or six campaigns in the infantry of a legion." ❞

(Statute 23)

him to a seat in the Senate. In order to protect against public confusion about who could hold public office, politically ineligible men were not allowed to be seated with the senators or decurions at the games, gladiator combats, or public banquets. Seating at games was hierarchical; in such a large public venue, one's seat declared one's status. The phrase "with malice aforethought" appears several times in statute 26, suggesting that acting with intent had already become a legal concept.

Census taking was an important part of the Roman political system. The Roman voting system allowed for the rich to hold more votes than the poor, and thus one's economic status needed to be declared to the government. All municipalities, colonies, and prefectures had to take a census and send the results to Rome. According to statute 28, a census for an area outside the capital city had to be completed within sixty days after the chief local authority became aware that a census was being taken in Rome. Census information was to include the first and last names of all Roman citizens, the names of their parents or patrons, tribal affiliations, ages, and declarations of property owned. All of this information was to be entered into the public records of the local authority, and copies were to be sent to Rome. According to statute 29, citizens who had several residences in the municipalities, colonies, or pre-

fectures but who were registered in the census of the city of Rome did not have to be registered in the censuses for areas in which their second homes were located.

The final statue makes reference to the "municipality of Fundi," a town to the south of Rome in Volscian territory. This rather cryptic reference contributes to the uncertainty surrounding this set of laws. Some scholars believe that the tablets simply record a collection of incongruous laws that were pulled together as a matter of convenience—thus, the sudden appearance of Fundi for no apparent reason, other than perhaps the ease of creating a type of omnibus law. Others believe that the collection represents laws taken from differing sources—some applicable to Rome, others to Heraclea, and still others to Fundi, though the reason why remains unclear. It is possible that certain enactments from one portion of Rome's territories were to be imitated elsewhere. As it stands, though, scholars simply do not know.

Audience

The audience for the Tablets of Heraclea was in the first place the citizens of Heraclea, who had the right to have the laws of Rome publicly posted within their town. Use of public space was clearly regulated, and regulations about the maintenance of the roads that were used by all the inhabitants were important for all to know. Since Heraclea had been acquired by Rome, Roman law would have applied to the city. However, the tablets' inclusion of the "municipality of Fundi" has led to confusion as to who exactly the audience was, as noted earlier. Perhaps there were many such tablets distributed to many cities, and these are the only ones to have survived. The second group of laws, which dealt with voting and office holding, were addressed only to property-owning men. Women and slaves did not have the right to vote or hold office.

Impact

When Heraclea became Roman, the citizens would have had to follow Roman law. As Roman territory grew, expansion of their laws naturally followed. Imposition of Roman government included tax collection, and the appointment of new governors to rule over the cities and towns that were conquered. The Romans were often willing to adapt local customs in order to maintain order within their new territories.

Roman law is the basis for much of contemporary law in Europe and parts of Africa as well as in the Americas and Australia. Almost all areas invaded and settled by Romans or their European descendants retain aspects of Roman law. Communal use of public areas is still a primary concern in urban life. Age restrictions on holding office are still present in the electoral rules of many countries, including the United States. Traffic-congestion rules have recently been put in place in many European cities in much the same way as the wagon laws were enforced in ancient Rome. Likewise, as in ancient Rome, traffic-violation exceptions are still granted for garbage removal in most communities today.

Further Reading

■ **Articles**

Cary, M. "Notes on the Legislation of Julius Caesar." *Journal of Roman Studies* 19 (1929): 113–119.

———. "The Municipal Legislation of Julius Caesar." *Journal of Roman Studies* 27 (1937): 48–53.

■ **Books**

Kamm, Antony. *Julius Caesar: A Life*. London: Routledge, 2006.

Holland, Tom. *Rubicon: The Triumph and Tragedy of the Roman Republic*. London: Abacus, 2004.

Reid, James S. *The Municipalities of the Roman Empire*. Cambridge, U.K: Cambridge University Press, 1913.

Williamson, Callie. *The Laws of the Roman People: Public Law in the Expansion and Decline of the Roman Republic*. Ann Arbor: University of Michigan Press, 2005.

—M. Callahan

Questions for Further Study

1. The Law of Caesar on Municipalities presents problems for historians and archeologists because they cannot be certain where the laws applied and what effects they had throughout the Roman Empire. Use your imagination to explain what steps historians and archeologists might take to resolve some of these questions.

2. The Roman Empire continued to grow and was eventually vast. What problems did Rome have in administering such a large empire? How was the central government able to exert its authority in such far-flung regions?

3. Why would Roman citizenship have been valuable to people living outside the areas immediately surrounding Rome?

4. The Law of Caesar on Municipalities presents modern readers with a snapshot of life in a Roman city at that time. What would such a life have been like? What were some of the problems that city dwellers faced? How might they have been resolved?

5. Do any of the laws contained in this document strike you as particularly "modern"? In other words, do municipalities in the modern world continue to face the same issues that cities did in ancient Rome? Explain.

LAW OF CAESAR ON MUNICIPALITIES

1) If by this law it is proper for anyone to make his declaration before the consul and if he is absent from Rome when it is proper for him to make his declaration, then his agent shall declare in the same manner and on the same days before the consul all the same things that his principal properly should have declared by this law if he were in Rome.

2) If by this law it is proper for anyone to make his declaration before the consul and if he or she is a ward, then his or her guardian shall declare in like manner before the consul all the same things on the same days, just as the owner properly should have declared by this law if he or she were not a ward.

3) If the consul before whom by this law it is proper for these declarations to be made is absent from Rome, then the person required to make the declaration shall make it before the urban praetor or, in his absence, before the peregrine praetor in the same manner as one properly should declare by this law before the consul if he were in Rome at that time.

4) If none of the consuls or the praetors before whom by this law it is proper for declarations to be made are in Rome, then the required declaration shall be made before the plebeian tribune in the same manner as one properly should declare by this law before the consul or the urban praetor or the peregrine praetor if he were in Rome at that time.

5) The magistrate, before whom is made the declaration, which it is proper for anyone to make in accordance with this law, shall provide that each person's name, the things which he has declared, and the day on which he has declared them shall be entered in the public records and that all these entries shall be accurately copied on a tablet on the bulletin board in the Forum. Whenever and wherever grain is distributed to the people he shall keep this list displayed daily, for the greater part of each day, where it can be easily read from the ground level.

6) The distributor of grain to the people or whoever has charge of such distribution shall not give, order, or permit grain to be given to anyone of those persons whose names in conformity with this law have been posted by the consul, the praetor, or the plebeian tribune on the bulletin board. If anyone in contravention of this regulation gives grain to anyone of those persons so posted he shall be liable to a penalty of 50,000 sesterces payable to the State for each modius of grain so given, and anyone so minded shall be entitled to sue for this sum.

7) Each owner of property fronting on the streets of Rome or on streets within a mile of Rome, on which there is continuous settlement now or in the future, shall keep such portion of the street in repair at the discretion of that aedile who has jurisdiction in this quarter of the city by this law. The aforesaid aedile, at his discretion, shall provide that each owner of property fronting on the street shall keep in repair that portion of the street which by this law it is proper for him to maintain and he shall provide that no water shall stand there to prevent the public from convenient passage.

8) The curule and the plebeian aediles now in office and those who shall be appointed or elected or who shall enter upon this office after the passage of this law shall agree among themselves or shall cast lots, within the next five days after they have been designated to or have entered upon this office, to determine in which part of the city each shall have charge of the repair and the paving of the public streets in Rome or within one mile of Rome, and he shall have the oversight of such work. Whatever part of the city becomes the responsibility of any aedile by this law, the said aedile shall have the oversight of repairing and maintaining the streets which are in that part as is proper by this law.

9) Whatever street lies between a temple, a public building, or a public area on one side and a private building on the other, the aedile who is in charge of this region of the city shall lease the maintenance of half of the said street, where the temple or the public building or the public area is situated.

10) If anyone, who in accordance with this law properly should maintain the public street in front of his property, does not maintain it as he properly should in the judgment of the aedile concerned, the latter at his discretion shall lease the contract for its maintenance. For at least ten days before he awards the contract, he shall post in front of his tribunal in the Forum the name of the street to be maintained, the day on which the contract shall be given, and the names of the property owners on that portion of the street. To the aforesaid owners or their agents at their

homes he shall give notice of his intention to lease the contract for the aforesaid street and of the day on which the contract shall be given. He shall make this contract publicly in the Forum through the urban quaestor or whoever is in charge of the treasury. The urban quaestor or whoever is in charge of the treasury shall provide that, in the public records of money due, entry shall be made of that sum for which the contract was awarded in the name of the person or persons, before whose property the street runs, in proportion to the length and the breadth of the street in front of each property. He shall assess this amount without malicious deception, on the owner or owners, for the benefit of the person who contracts for the maintenance of the aforesaid street. If the owner on whom this assessment has been imposed, or his agent, does not pay this money or give security therefor to the contractor within the next thirty days of his notification of the assessment, he shall be obliged to pay the amount assessed and a penalty of half of the amount to the contractor. In a suit for this money the magistrate, on application, shall appoint a judex and grant an action in the same way as it is proper for a judex to be appointed and an action to be granted in a suit for the recovery of a money loan.

11) If it is proper for a contract for street maintenance to be let in accordance with this law, the aedile who properly should do so shall award the contract for the maintenance of this street through the urban quaestor or whoever is in charge of the treasury, with the proviso that the maintenance of this street shall be subject to the approval of the aedile responsible for the giving of the contract. The urban quaestor or whoever is in charge of the treasury shall provide that the amount of the contract, for which each street is so leased, shall be awarded and assigned to the contractor or to his heir, to whom it properly should be awarded in accordance with the terms of the contract.

12) It is not the intent of this law to prevent the aedile, the quattuorvirs in charge of cleaning the city streets, and the duumvirs in charge of cleaning the streets outside the city walls within a mile of Rome, whoever are appointed hereafter, from caring for the street-cleaning or from having jurisdiction in the matter as is proper by laws or plebiscites or decrees of the Senate.

13) Wherever a building abuts on an alleyway, the owner shall keep this alleyway properly paved along the whole face of the building with whole, durable, well-joined paving blocks to the satisfaction of the aedile who has jurisdiction over roads in that district in accordance with this law.

14) After January 1 next no one shall drive a wagon along the streets of Rome or along those streets in the suburbs where there is continuous housing after sunrise or before the tenth hour of the day, except whatever will be proper for the transportation and the importation of material for building temples of the immortal gods, or for public works, or for removing from the city rubbish from those buildings for whose demolition public contracts have been let. For these purposes permission shall be granted by this law to specified persons to drive wagons for the reasons stated.

15) Whenever it is proper for the vestal virgins, the king of the sacrifices, or the flamens to ride in the city for the purpose of official sacrifices of the Roman people; whatever wagons are proper for a triumphal procession when any one triumphs; whatever wagons are proper for public games within Rome or within one mile of Rome or for the procession held at the time of the games in the Circus Maximus, it is not the intent of this law to prevent the use of such wagons during the day within the city for these occasions and at these times.

16) It is not the intent of this law to prevent ox wagons or donkey wagons that have been driven into the city by night from going out empty or from carrying out dung from within the city of Rome or within one mile of the city after sunrise until the tenth hour of the day.

17) Respecting public areas and public arcades in Rome or within a mile of Rome, which are by law under the jurisdiction of the aediles or of those magistrates in charge of cleaning the streets and the public areas in Rome or within a mile of Rome, no one shall have any structure built or erected in these areas or arcades, nor shall any one acquire possession in any way of these areas or arcades, nor shall he enclose or bar off any part of them, to prevent free use and access of such areas or arcades by the people, except for such persons to whom permission has been granted by statutes or plebiscites or decrees of the Senate.

18) When the censor or any other magistrate in accordance with the terms of the contract proclaims that certain areas are to be set aside or to be used to yield public revenue or for the production of tribute, and when provision is made in the terms of the contract for those who lease the reservation and the use of such areas that they may use and enjoy them, or that these areas shall be guarded by the lessees, it is not the intent of this law to prevent these lessees from the use and the enjoyment of these areas, as

shall be allowed each one to do so without malicious intent in accordance with the terms of the contract.

19) If anyone provides games in Rome or within one mile of Rome it is not the intent of this law to prevent him from building or erecting in public places a stage or a platform or other structures that are required for such games, or from using public areas on those days on which he gives the games.

20) It is not the intent of this law to prevent clerks and copyists attending magistrates from using public areas for purposes of such attendance, wherever the magistrate commands their services.

21) If the censors assign certain areas to public slaves for dwelling or for use it is not the intent of this law to prevent such use of these areas.

22) Those persons who hold office in municipalities, colonies, prefectures, markets, or meeting places of Roman citizens, whether duumvirs, quattuorvirs, or under whatever other title they hold magisterial powers by the vote of the citizens in the aforesaid communities, shall not appoint, substitute, coopt, or have named as decurions or conscripts in the Senate anyone in the aforesaid communities, except in the place of a senator deceased, or condemned, or one who admits that he is not qualified by this law to be a senator, a decurion, or a conscript in that community.

23) After January 1, in the second year following enactment of this law, no person under thirty years of age shall be a candidate for, accept, or administer the office of duumvir, quattuorvir, or any other magistracy in a municipality, a colony, or a prefecture, unless he has served three campaigns in the cavalry or six campaigns in the infantry of a legion. These campaigns he shall have served for the greater part of each year either in camp or in a province. Two half-year campaigns may count as separate years. If anyone has exemption from military service by statutes or plebiscites or treaty, whereby he should not properly serve against his will, he is not subject to this restriction. Nor shall anyone who is an auctioneer, a master of funeral ceremonies, or an undertaker, so long as he is engaged in such a trade, be a candidate for, accept, administer, or hold the office of duumvir, quattuorvir, or any other magistracy, nor shall he be a senator or a decurion, or a conscript, nor shall he give his vote as such in a municipality, a colony, or a prefecture. If any of the above-mentioned persons acts in contravention of this law he shall be liable to a penalty of 50,000 sesterces payable to the State, and anyone so minded shall be entitled to sue for this sum.

24) If anyone holds elections in a municipality, a colony, or a prefecture after July 1 next for the elec-

tion of or the substitution for duumvirs, quattuorvirs, or any other magistrates, he shall not announce or order to be announced the election of any of the aforesaid magistrates who is under thirty years of age, unless he has served three campaigns in the cavalry or six campaigns in the infantry of a legion, during which campaigns he shall have served in camp or in a province for the greater part of each year, or for two half-years, which may count with him for separate years, if it is allowed by statutes or plebiscites, or unless he has exemption from military service by statutes or plebiscites or treaty, whereby he should not properly serve against his will. Nor shall he declare the election of anyone who is employed as auctioneer, master of funeral ceremonies, or undertaker, so long as he is employed in such a trade, as duumvir, quattuorvir, or whoever may be magistrate in that community. Nor shall he choose, substitute, or coopt such persons into the senate among the decurions or the conscripts. Nor with malice aforethought shall he call upon such persons for their vote nor shall he require them to speak or to cast their vote. If anyone does so in contravention of this law he shall be liable to a penalty of 50,000 sesterces payable to the State, and anyone so minded shall be entitled to sue for this sum.

25) No one shall be admitted among the decurions and the conscripts in the senate of any municipality, colony, prefecture, market, or meeting place of Roman citizens, nor shall anyone who comes under the following categories be permitted to express his opinion or to cast his vote in that body: anyone who is condemned for theft which he himself has committed or who compounds such theft; anyone who is condemned in an action for trusteeship, partnership, guardianship, mandate, infliction of injury or fraud; anyone who is condemned either by the Praetorian Law or for something that he has done or does contrary to that law; anyone who binds himself to fight as a gladiator; anyone who denies a debt on oath before the praetor or takes an oath that he is solvent; anyone who gives notice to sureties or creditors that he cannot pay his debt in full or who compounds with them to that effect; anyone for whom the sureties pay and settle the obligation; anyone whose possessions are seized and advertised for sale at public auction by the edict of the magistrate in charge of the administration of justice, excepting the cases of those whose property was so treated when they were wards, or of someone who was absent on public business, provided that he does not contrive fraudulently to be absent for such purpose; anyone who is con-

demned at Rome by public trial whereby it is unlawful for him to remain in Italy and who is not restored to his former status; anyone who is condemned by public trial in that municipality, colony, prefecture, market, or meeting place of which he is a citizen; anyone who is condemned of having lodged a false accusation or of having done something from collusion; anyone who is deprived of his rank in the military service because of disgrace; anyone whom a general dismisses from the army in disgrace; anyone who takes money or any other reward for bringing in the head of a Roman citizen; anyone who prostitutes his body for gain; anyone who trains gladiators or acts on the stage or keeps a brothel. If any of the aforesaid persons in contravention of this law takes his place or gives his vote among the decurions or the conscripts in the senate of the above-mentioned communities he shall be liable to a penalty of 50,000 sesterces to be paid to the State, and anyone so minded shall be entitled to sue for that sum.

26) If this law declares a person to be ineligible to serve as senator, decurion, or conscript, to speak or to cast a vote in the senate of a municipality, a colony, a prefecture, a market, or a meeting place, no one who summons the senate, the decurions, and the conscripts in the aforesaid communities shall summon with malice aforethought such an ineligible person to meet with them. He shall not ask him for an opinion there nor with malice aforethought shall bid him vote orally or by ballot. No one who has supreme authority in the aforesaid communities by the vote of their citizens shall allow with malice aforethought any ineligible person to attend the senate with the decurions or the conscripts, to be included in their number, to give his vote orally or by ballot there. He shall not accept such persons as candidates for election in any electoral assembly of the people or of the plebs. If in violation of this law such a person has been elected by the aforesaid assemblies the magistrate shall not announce the election. And no magistrate or person with authority in that community shall permit him, with malice aforethought, to witness the games or to attend public banquets with the senate, the decurions, or the conscripts.

27) Whoever by this law are not permitted to be senators, decurions, or conscripts of the aforesaid communities shall not stand as candidate for or accept the office of duumvir, quattuorvir, or any other office from which he would pass into the senate of the aforesaid communities. Nor shall such persons take their seat in the senatorial circle of decurions and conscripts to witness games or gladitorial combats or to participate in public banquets. If anyone of such persons is announced as selected in contravention of this law, he shall not become duumvir or quattuorvir or hold any magistracy or office of authority in that community. If anyone acts in contravention of this law he shall be liable to a penalty of 50,000 sesterces to be paid to the State, and anyone so minded shall be entitled to sue for this sum.

28) Whoever has the chief magistracy or the supreme authority in those municipalities, colonies, or prefectures of Roman citizens which exist in Italy at that time when the censor or some other magis-

Glossary

aediles	magistrates in charge of shrines, temples, and public games
censor	in this context, a magistrate in charge of taking the census; also responsible for public works and public buildings
conscripts	Roman senators serving their first year
curule	describing an aedile belonging to the aristocracy of ancient Roman
decurion	a member of the city senate in the Roman Empire
judex	a private individual who was appointed to hear evidence of disputes between citizens and render judgment
peregrine praetor	in Caesar's day, a magistrate who administered cases involving non-Romans
sesterces	silver or bronze coins, their value varying from period to period of history
urban praetor	a magistrate in charge of civil cases

trate takes the census at Rome shall take the census of the Roman citizens in all the aforesaid communities within sixty days after he knows that such census is being taken at Rome. He shall accept from them under oath their names, praenomens, parents or patrons, tribes, cognomens, the age of each citizen, and the statement of his property in accordance with the pattern of the census, which shall be posted at Rome by the official who is about to take the census of the people at that time. He shall enter all this on the public records of his municipality. He shall dispatch these registers to the censors at Rome by means of the envoys chosen for this purpose by the majority vote of the senate when this matter is voted. He shall provide that the census shall be completed and that the envoys shall appear before the censors at Rome and shall deliver the registers of the respective municipalities, colonies, or prefectures more than sixty days before the census at Rome is completed. This censor, or whatever other magistrate conducts the census of the people in the next five days after the arrival of the envoys, shall accept without fraudulent intent the registers of the census from

them. From these registers of the communities he shall provide that the entries shall be copied in the public records and that such records shall be filed in the same place where are filed the other public records containing the census of the people.

29) It is not the intent of this law to require a person who has residence in several municipalities, colonies, or prefectures and who is entered in the census in Rome to be registered by this law in the census of the aforesaid communities as well.

30) Whoever is or has been commissioned by a law or a plebiscite to give a charter for the municipality of Fundi or for the citizens of that municipality, whatever supplements, amendments, or corrections are made to this charter in the year immediately after the people authorize this law shall be binding on the citizens of Fundi, as it would have been if these had been incorporated by him when first he gave a charter to Fundi on the authority of the law or the plebiscite. No one shall interpose a veto or interfere in any way to invalidate the aforesaid supplements, amendments, or corrections, or to prevent them from being binding on the citizens of Fundi and obeyed by them.

DEEDS OF THE DIVINE AUGUSTUS

"At the age of nineteen ...
I raised an army by means of which I restored liberty to the republic."

Overview

After the assassination of Julius Caesar in 44 BCE, his nineteen-year-old nephew and adopted heir Octavian (later called Augustus) inherited the problems caused by inadequacies of the traditional Roman system of government that had plagued the republic for more than half a century. Like Caesar, Octavian had to engage in civil wars, first with Caesar's assassins and then with Caesar's lieutenant Mark Antony (Marcus Antonius). But Augustus succeeded where his predecessors failed in creating a new and more stable form of government: the principate. Although he always claimed justification for his actions in traditional terms, Octavian, in fact, abandoned the republican form of government (in which power was shared between a group of aristocratic families and the greater mass of citizens) in favor of forming new institutions that would support the autocratic rule of one man. As Augustus, he, not Caesar, became the first Roman emperor. The *Deeds of the Divine Augustus (Res gestae divi Augusti)* is Augustus's own testament of his achievements; it is a unique document authored by one of the most powerful and influential leaders in history. Augustus's record of his reign ever remained a touchstone in the Roman world and greatly affected the administration of the empire, which offered a model of government consulted by political leaders down to and beyond the American Revolution.

Context

Throughout the first century BCE the Roman Empire suffered a general crisis. The extent of the empire already included most of the Mediterranean basin, yet it was still governed by a political system—the republic—that originally evolved to serve a small city-state. The result was that the offices of magistrates such as the two consuls, the republic's elected heads of government, tended to grow and gain new powers that the city's constitution had never planned, leading to the creation of private armies and civil wars. As a result, the last century of the Roman Republic saw periods of dictatorship under Lucius Cornelius Sulla

and Julius Caesar, while attempts to restore stability to the government only ended in renewed chaos. The mood of the time was suggested by the poet Horace, who imagined civil war as a curse brought down on Rome when the city's mythical founder, Romulus, killed his twin brother, Remus.

On the ides of March in 44 BCE, Julius Caesar was assassinated by a conspiracy of aristocratic leaders including the generals Marcus Junius Brutus and Gaius Cassius Longinus, possibly with the complicity of his own lieutenant Mark Antony. Caesar's heir Octavian, the future Augustus, swiftly moved to protect himself and his interests. He marched on Rome with an army composed of Caesar's veterans, whom he paid with illegally seized funds that had been collected to pay for Caesar's planned invasion of Parthia. He drove Antony out of Rome as Antony had driven out the assassins. The next year Octavian and Antony's forces skirmished in northern Italy, but by the fall the two had joined forces together with Marcus Aemilius Lepidus to form the triumvirate, an extralegal body that seized dictatorial control over Rome and eventually defeated its rivals, the assassins Brutus and Cassius at Philippi, in Macedonia in 42 BCE and the last surviving republican leader, Sextus Pompey, the son of Caesar's enemy Pompey the Great, in 36 BCE. Lepidus proved to be a minor figure, and Octavian and Antony split the Roman Empire in 40 BCE, with Octavian receiving the western half, including Italy. Since the two leaders were rivals more than allies, this situation could not last and finally led to a civil war decided at the Battle of Actium in 31 BCE, resulting in Octavian's control of the entire Roman world. Octavian, who was granted the title Augustus in 27 BCE, tried various constitutional reforms to organize his rule and adopted a defensive posture at Rome's borders, expanding them only slightly, to militarily logical frontiers. In this way the last decades of his life were dedicated to consolidating power and strengthening the internal cohesion of the empire so that it could survive his death without falling into chaos.

After Augustus's death, Tiberius, his stepson and heir, read out the will in the Roman Senate, including instructions to post the *Deeds of the Divine Augustus* on bronze plaques on his mausoleum. An updated copy of the text covering Augustus's last year of life was also inscribed in the cities of the Roman province of Galatia, providing the only surviving

63 BCE

- **September 23**
Gaius Octavius
Thurinus, referred
to in English as
Octavian, is born
in Rome.

44 BCE

- **March 15**
Julius Caesar, great
uncle of Octavian,
is assassinated; the
reading of his will
reveals Octavian as
Caesar's adopted
son and heir.

43 BCE

- **August 19**
Octavian uses
loyalists from
Caesar's legions
to force the
Roman Senate
to vote him to
the consulship.

- **November 27**
Octavian, Mark
Antony, and
Marcus Aemilius
Lepidus become
triumvirs for the
regulation of the
state, effectively
obtaining shared
dictatorial powers.

42 BCE

- **October 23**
Octavian and Mark
Antony defeat the
army of Caesar's
assassins Marcus
Junius Brutus and
Gaius Cassius
Longinus at Philippi,
in Macedonia.

40 BCE

- **Autumn**
The Treaty of
Brundisium divides
the Roman
Republic between
Octavian (granted
the west) and
Antony (granted
the east), with
Lepidus given the
minor Roman
territory in Africa.

source for the text. The *Deeds of the Divine Augustus* thus presents an account of his reign viewed from its end in 14 CE. Its message, put briefly, is that Augustus "restored liberty to the republic." Yet this is not the only possible interpretation of his reign. His career of civil war, massacre (at times so outrageous that some of his enemies accused him of committing human sacrifices with the lives of Roman citizens), and self-aggrandizement looked very different as it was being conducted than it did when, at the end, he had finally achieved peace and stability. The historian Cornelius Tacitus, writing a century later in the beginning of his *Annals*, describes Augustus as having actually founded a monarchy. Another century later, the historian Dio Cassius was able to unify the different interpretations, portraying Augustus as both liberator of the people and enslaver of the republic. These repeated reevaluations show in the first place the continued importance Romans assigned to the reign of Augustus in thinking about their government. Indeed, what Augustus achieved was the establishment of a monarchy that maintained all the outward forms of a republic. The evolution of Augustus's titles and offices recorded in the *Deeds of the Divine Augustus* is not a history of his quest for power but rather a recounting of his pursuit of a form to express his power that would satisfy the people and yet not alienate the aristocratic classes whose support he also needed.

The beginning of the Roman Empire is ambiguous. There are many important events in the reign of Augustus—his first grant of imperium (executive power), his victory over Antony, his two constitutional settlements—none of which mark a precise beginning of the Roman Empire or even a definite end of the Roman Republic. The process of Augustus's political career, its length and success, created a new situation that could never have been planned or foreseen. If his whole reign is the gestation of the empire, there is no single moment when one can say it was given birth, although its enduring success was by no means clear until his successor, Tiberius, took power without opposition or political disturbance.

About the Author

Gaius Octavius Thurinus, who would be called Octavian in English, was born in Rome in 63 BCE. Adopted as the heir of the dictator Julius Caesar through Caesar's will upon his assassination in 44 BCE, Octavian took the name Gaius Julius Caesar, though historians typically append the name Octavianus to distinguish him from his adoptive father. As Roman ruler, Octavian had to enter into a series of civil wars. He proved an expert at using propaganda to present them as foreign wars, treating, for instance, his war against Mark Antony as though it were against Antony's mistress, Cleopatra VII, the queen of Egypt. Eventually, Octavian emerged as the sole ruler of Rome; Augustus was an honorific title bestowed on him in 27 BCE.

Unlike other political strongmen who gained that position in the first century BCE, Augustus was able to forge a lasting settlement between himself and the various Roman social classes, allowing for the emergence of a new political order in the form of the Roman Empire. In the early years of his long period of rule, which was marked by relative peace, he was able to experiment with several different constitutional settlements to define his power and reconcile his rivals to his supreme position. The final settlement came in July 27 BCE, when an illness forced him to consider the question of succession; the resolution was based on permanent grants of consular imperium without holding office and the tribunician power (the power to protect the people against the aristocracy).

Augustus's last decades of rule were turned toward finding a suitable heir and satisfactory borders for the empire. He favored his own descendents from the Julian line, through his daughter, Julia, but no heir from this family survived. He finally turned to his Claudian stepsons from his wife Livia's first marriage and settled upon Tiberius, allowing him to share in his titles and powers as emperor during his own lifetime to ensure the succession. In terms of the geopolitical consolidation of the empire, Augustus maintained peace with Parthia, Rome's only rival as a great power within the ancient world. Augustus also tried to establish Germany as a province but failed in gaining control of the already troubled area. In 9 CE a Roman army was ambushed and destroyed there in the Teutoburg Forest, dooming any idea of expansion in that direction. Still, by the time of his death in 14 CE, Augustus had achieved borders for the empire that would prove stable for another four centuries and had established a constitutional framework and line of succession that prevented civil war until 69 CE.

Many documents produced under the names of heads of state are actually authored by committees of secretaries and speechwriters, but the *Deeds of the Divine Augustus* is generally deemed to be Augustus's own work. The scope of his literary output is described by the ancient historian Suetonius. Augustus benefited from an excellent rhetorical education and published numerous essays on historical and philosophical topics, including a more literary autobiography whose thirteen chapters cover the years up to the mid-20s BCE. He also composed a book of epigrams and a versified drama, but this he did not consider successful enough for publication. Augustus favored a plain style meant to communicate rather than to impress with displays of literary flourishes. He would mock his minister Gaius Maecenas for his florid style, his stepson Tiberius for his archaisms, and his then-colleague Mark Antony for attempting to copy the fashionable Greek "Asiatic" style in Latin.

Explanation and Analysis of the Document

The elegant simplicity of Augustus's writing is well reflected in the *Deeds of the Divine Augustus*. The text consists of simple declarative statements of fact, not complicated explanations and justifications. Although the result builds up Augustus's image, the style is not boastful or exaggerating. The text projects Augustus's favored image of himself as the restorer of the republic and protector of the Roman people.

Time Line

36 BCE
- **September 3**
  Octavian defeats the fleet of Sextus Pompey, the last republican leader, and also absorbs the territories of Lepidus.

31 BCE
- **September 2**
  Octavian defeats Antony and Cleopatra at Actium, on the Ionian coast of Greece, becoming sole ruler of the Roman Empire.

28 BCE
- Octavian completes the construction of his family mausoleum in Rome.

27 BCE
- **January 16**
  In addition to the titles of "imperator" and "princeps," Octavian is granted the honorific name of Augustus. Over the course of the following year he works out his first constitutional settlement.

- **July 23**
  After an illness sufficiently serious to raise questions about the succession, Augustus reaches a second constitutional settlement. An early draft of the *Deeds of the Divine Augustus* is probably composed at this time.

2 BCE

- A substantially complete draft of the *Deeds of the Divine Augustus* is probably made at this time, as almost all events therein fall before or during this year.

13 CE

- **April 3** Augustus deposits his will and an updated *Deeds of the Divine Augustus* with the vestal virgins.

14 CE

- **August 19** Augustus dies while visiting his ancestral estate at Nola, in Italy; the *Deeds of the Divine Augustus* is subsequently posted on his mausoleum and published throughout the Roman Empire.

source for a period that lacks many contemporary sources comparable to the letters of Marcus Tullius Cicero (106–43 BCE) or Pliny the Younger (ca. 61–113 CE).

A comparison of the *Deeds of the Divine Augustus* to other historical sources shows that it omits as much as it reveals about Augustus's reign. Although Augustus admits to holding unconstitutional extraordinary office as a triumvir, nothing is said about the triumvirate's policy of proscription (whereby opponents, including hundreds of senators, were legally murdered), or of his resettlement of military veterans loyal to himself on land confiscated illegally from Roman citizens in Italy, or of his suppression of the consequent resistance movement by massacre. He mentions his recovery of Roman military standards lost before his time to the Parthians (at Carrhae, in Mesopotamia, in 53 BCE) but not the loss of three more standards in Germany by his legate Publius Quinctilius Varus, whose army was destroyed in one of the greatest military disasters in Roman history at Teutoburg Forest (9 CE). Augustus's enemies in civil wars, who held grants of imperium from the Roman Senate (making them official officers of the state) no different from his own, are described as a faction or as pirates or assassins. Augustus could hardly have been unaware of his shortcomings in these respects compared with the ideal he presents in the document, but perhaps one of its purposes was to offer guidance for how emperors ought to act in times to come.

Res gestae divi Augusti is provided as the document's title on the Monumentum Ancyranum, a temple to Augustus in modern-day Ankara, Turkey, and on the other inscribed copies from Phrygia. A summary of the text is attached to the end of the Monumentum Ancyranum inscription, composed certainly not by Augustus but rather probably by the provincial administration in Ancyra.

◆ **Sections 1 and 2: Threat to the Republic**
Augustus first of all portrays himself as the savior of the republic. The event being described—the 43 BCE march on Rome with an army of Caesar's veterans—may also be seen as Augustus's making sure that Mark Antony (the faction mentioned in the document) did not seize dictatorial power for himself without giving Augustus a share. Indeed, after the presence of his army in the city forced the senate to give him a grant of imperium—the executive power that enabled Roman magistrates to enforce law and carry out their duties—and then the consulship, Augustus did enter into the shared dictatorship known as the triumvirate with Antony and the relatively insignificant Lepidus. By the same token, the two battles at Philippi against Caesar's assassins in October 42 BCE more accurately constituted a civil war, and although Augustus's troops certainly participated, the victories were won under the command of Antony.

◆ **Sections 3–14: Augustus's Victories and Honors**
The most important traditional measure of a Roman politician was his war record, and Augustus dutifully supplies his. He had three triumphs (the ovation is a lesser form of the triumph), famous military parades through the

The *Deeds* does not answer charges made against Augustus by his enemies, as his earlier literary autobiography (now lost except for a few fragments) did. Rather, the later text presents an ideal vision of the state Augustus built. It is a state in which the leader rights injustice and guarantees peace, liberty, and prosperity. The document is not in any sense a full historical accounting of Augustus's reign but instead offers listings of what he did for the Roman people and the Roman state in very practical terms—and only after that of the glory he derived from those benefactions. The style of the *Deeds* grew out of the genre of the eulogium, an oration made by a son or other relative at the funeral of a great man, listing his deeds. At times these deeds were recorded as inscriptions. Augustus himself had developed this kind of writing, and in the Forum of Augustus he set up statues of many of the leading figures of Roman history together with their eulogia. But the *Deeds of the Divine Augustus* transformed this biographical approach into a personal narrative of extraordinary emotive power as well as of profound historical richness (for all that it glosses over many suspect aspects of Augustus's rule). The first-person account of Augustus's own reign is a unique historical

Gold coin, minted in Spain in 17 BCE, showing on one side a profile portrait of Augustus and, on the other side, Augustus atop a triumphal arch, driving a chariot drawn by an elephant (© The Trustees of the British Museum)

city awarded to victorious generals, and more besides that he declined out of modesty (section 4). Military victories were of service to the Roman people in that they extended the empire as well as humbled the proud foreign kings who had dared exult themselves above ordinary Romans. Augustus also tells his audience that his victories accomplished something unique in living memory and which had happened only twice in all of Roman history: They brought peace. In Rome this rarity was signaled by the closing of the doors of the temple of Janus, which Augustus achieved three times (section 13). Here Augustus had no need to fabricate. His rule brought an end to civil wars as well as to foreign wars of conquest fueled by competition between rival magistrates vying for political power.

Augustus begins in this section the meticulous numerical cataloging of his achievements, with the numbers of soldiers loyal to him in the hundreds of thousands (as noted in section 3), and the increase in the number of Roman citizens counted by his censuses in the millions (from section 8). He employs this cataloging technique throughout the *Deeds*. The use of such precise numbers certainly lends an aura of plausibility to the whole text, while their size would have been awe-inspiring to a largely innumerate Roman populace. The frequent recourse to fig-

ures may also relate to the document's genre as an inscription, a form that dealt with the realities of government—such as amounts of taxation, sizes of naval expenditures, and topics of that kind—rather than literary matters. Augustus gives dates in the usual Roman manner by citing the names of the two consuls for a given year. This was the standard practice, rather than reckoning dates from some absolute mark such as the BCE/CE divide now used.

Augustus also lists the various magistracies he held (sections 6 and 8) and, just as important, those he did not hold (section 5). He was hailed as imperator (commander) by his troops, and this is the same title that eventually became most closely associated with the Roman emperors; indeed, it is the etymological origin of the English word *emperor*. However, at that time any successful general would receive such acclamation, and the association of this title with the sole Roman ruler was not yet firmly established. The variety of titles he held indicates the difficulties Augustus faced in finding the right constitutional form to legitimize his power. After his highly irregular office as the sole surviving triumvir lapsed, Augustus held the consulship each year from 27 BCE to 23 BCE, but this soon proved unnecessary and prevented him from rewarding loyal senators with the office that he himself occupied, the highest

Red jasper portrait engraving of the head of Mark Antony, probably used as a seal

one available. After Augustus set aside his consulship (while retaining a permanent grant of imperium superior to the consuls'), he was offered the dictatorship by the senate but declined it. Although it was a traditional office, it had been used only in times of national crisis. The use of the title to keep permanent power in peacetime looked like what it was, a subterfuge—one that had made Julius Caesar unpopular enough to be assassinated.

In 23 BCE Augustus reached a new constitutional settlement, and he began to date his reign from that time. (Later historians like Dio Cassius would claim that this amounted to the restoration of the republic.) In this dispensation the mechanism of Augustus's rule became the "tribunician power" (section 10). This obscure term most likely referred to the plebeian magistrates from much earlier in the history of the republic, called tribunes, who protected the interests of the common people from the aristocratic classes; Augustus, as a patrician, could not be a tribune, so he was instead granted the powers of one. This symbolic role of protecting the common man was probably more important than the actual power of the office to veto any government action. Other titles were traditional and honorific, such as

princeps senatus (noted in section 7), which meant that he had the right to speak first in senatorial debate. Inasmuch as Roman religion was a function of the state, Augustus held all of the most important priestly offices, including that of high priest (section 7), or "pontifex maximus," once it was vacated by the death in 12 BCE of the triumvir Lepidus, who had been under house arrest since 36 BCE.

◆ **Sections 15–24: Augustus's Benefactions**

In these sections Augustus lists his outright gifts, beginning with gifts of money and food paid to the population of the city of Rome, that is, to its masses of urban poor (sections 15 and 18). He then lists the payments in cash and land that he gave to military veterans who had served under him (section 16). He mentions only after these instances where he made up a deficit in the government's budget from his private resources, which, of course, also benefited the Roman citizens in a broader collective sense. Augustus next turns to his building program (sections 19–21). He rebuilt nearly all the public buildings in Rome, including not only infrastructure such as aqueducts, bridges, and roads but also temples, theaters, and stadia for chariot racing and gladiatorial sport (sections 22 and 23). He also catalogues all of the public shows he put on, which besides the entertainment provided also entailed additional gifts of cash and food to the spectators. Last, he mentions his restoration of treasures looted by Mark Antony from temples in Asia (meaning the Ionian coast of modern-day Turkey) and his exchange of statues dedicated in his own honor into treasures devoted to the gods, marks of public piety (section 24).

If Augustus's many titles and magistracies were a search for an acceptable expression of his political power, this section begins to suggest its actual source. Roman society and government had an intricate mixture of public and official and private and unofficial power relationships. A powerful man was a patron to a vast array of clients encompassing his family, his political allies, and men with whom he had economic connections. The patron provided protection, for example, in the law courts, but also ensured the survival as well as the prosperity of his clients. In return, the clients provided political backing in the form of votes and military support. Figures like Antony, Brutus, and Augustus were the heads of large clientage networks that included all classes, from senators down to the ranks of the urban poor. In his rise to power, Augustus consolidated all of the patronage relations in Rome under his control to pave the way for his official political advancement. The gifts Augustus mentions in this document constituted his recompense for the support of the people as a whole as his clients. The unified support of the Roman people eventually made it impossible for anyone to oppose Augustus at a political level. This was why the specific political form given to Augustus's political power was a secondary consideration.

◆ Sections 25–33: Civil War and Foreign Successes

Although Augustus here omits more than he says, these sections begin with a description of his victories in civil wars. The pirates (section 25) he rather dramatically refers to were led by Sextus Pompey, the son of Pompey the Great and the last republican opponent of the triumvirs. Augustus indeed gained victory in a war waged intermittently over several years until Sextus Pompey's final defeat in 36 BCE. Far from being a pirate, however, Sextus, by the agreement of Octavian and Antony themselves, was governor of Sicily and Sardinia and consul designate. The "war in which I was victorious at Actium" was the last civil war against Antony. As described in sections 26–28, Augustus's expansion of the empire was quite modest, except for his annexation of Egypt, brought about by Queen Cleopatra's support of Antony. He attempted to organize Germany as a province, but the terrible military defeat in the Teutoburg Forest that ended his plans is not mentioned. In general, Augustus tried to find defensible borders for the empire without greatly expanding its size—in contrast, for example, to Julius Caesar, who had planned before his assassination to conquer Parthia (present-day Iraq and Iran). In fact, Augustus's greatest diplomatic success was the recovery from Parthia of the three legionary standards or eagles (section 29) that had been lost in a military disaster under the republic-era general Marcus Licinius Crassus.

◆ Sections 34–35: The Restoration of the Republic

At the end of the document, Augustus recounts his grant by the Roman Senate of the titles Augustus (January 16, 27 BCE) and "Father of my Country" (February 5, 2 BCE). He begins to address the truth of the source of his power when he says that he received "by universal consent the absolute control of affairs." He was able to relinquish the constitutional form of absolute power and allow the republic to work as it had always done precisely because he retained universal consent and no one would use the machinery of government to challenge him. Those who might have challenged him on ideological grounds, such as Cicero, had long since been proscribed. No power base among the people outside Augustus's control existed after the defeat of the republicans (Brutus, Cassius, and Sextus Pompey) and Antony. Those who survived wanted peace and the prosperity it brought, and Augustus was able to give them both. Augustus found a more politic way to present this reality: "I took precedence of all in rank, but of power I possessed no more than those who were my colleagues in any magistracy."

Audience

The first audience of the *Deeds of the Divine Augustus* was the new emperor Tiberius and the Roman Senate, who heard it read out during Augustus's funeral. But his will also instructed that the text be inscribed on bronze tablets to be affixed to the mausoleum he had built many years before in the center of Rome for himself and his family. This is one indication that the intended audience was specifically all the people of Rome. Other indications come from the text of the document, which always addresses the people of the city of Rome in the first place, listing what gifts and services Augustus had given them in particular, while mentioning the other parts of the empire only in relation to their overlordship of the provinces. Augustus's mausoleum was no ordinary private tomb. It was in the midst of a public park created by Augustus that included a grove of poplars around the place of his cremation, a gigantic sundial made from an obelisk he had captured in Egypt, and the famous Altar of Peace, which he had dedicated. This setting gave a context to people in Rome to read of Augustus's achievements as victor, builder, and benefactor. Similarly, the claims in the document of world conquest gave credence to the tomb as a site in the cult of the deified Augustus.

Although the *Deeds of the Divine Augustus* could not be as amenable to an audience of provincials as it was to the Roman citizens of the capital, within a few months of Augustus's death, Tiberius and the senate sent copies of the text to all of the provincial governors with orders that it be published. In practice, the text (or, in the east, a translation into Greek made on the spot) was probably read out at meetings of local senates or other bodies of aristocrats. But the governor of Galatia (central Turkey) decided to set up inscribed copies on marble plaques at the Temple of Augustus and Rome (Monumentum Ancyranum) in Ancyra

Bronze plow from a sunken ship that participated in the Battle of Actium in 31 BCE (© The Trustees of the British Museum)

and at least two other places in his territories, at Apollonia and Antioch, Pisidia (roughly the modern-day province of Antalya in Turkey), in both Latin and Greek versions. It is only because these copies survived into the Renaissance that the text can still be read in the modern day.

Impact

In one sense the *Deeds of the Divine Augustus* marks the end of Augustus's life and career, but it also marks an important beginning for the imperial government of Rome. In the bronze tablets of the document, Augustus created for all time a record of his own ideal image. He was a pious protector and restorer of the religion of the Roman state. He brought victory and peace to the Roman people. He was the father of the nation in the most literal sense, in that he was the patron who bestowed gifts upon the people as he would his own children. Paradoxically, his absolute rule was the guarantor of freedom for the people, as he protected the republic from any oligarchic aristocratic class that might have subverted it. As the savior of the Roman people, as master of land and sea, as the son of a veritable god and himself having been deified by the senate, Augustus established that the Roman emperor was not a mere mortal but a divine intermediary to govern the world in accord with divine will. The very terms established by Augustus would be the terms that all later emperors would use to describe themselves and which historians and orators would take as the model for emperors

considered "good," while emperors who fell short of these terms—those who failed in war, did not sacrifice their own resources for the good of the state, let religion fall into neglect, or oppressed their subjects—would be considered "bad." Thus, in the *Deeds of the Divine Augustus*, Augustus created the ideology of the Roman emperor. This imperial image not only continued through the Middle Ages in the Byzantine Empire, where emperors ruled in direct succession to Rome, but also became the basis of kingship in Western Europe. Although the document itself was lost by the end of antiquity, its ethos permeated European culture and survived until modern times.

The *Deeds of the Divine Augustus* had a very different sort of impact through its reception by modern critical scholarship. The scientific study of the past through disciplines like history and philology is not much more than a century and a half old; in fact, Augustus's record of his reign played an important role at the very beginning of modern historiography. The existence of the Monumentum Ancyranum had been known since 1555, when Ogier Ghiselin de Busbecq, serving as the Austrian ambassador to Süleyman the Magnificent of Turkey, read the most easily accessible parts of the Latin inscription and realized they belonged to the catalog of Augustus's achievements mentioned by Suetonius. But in the mid-nineteenth century an entirely new kind of historical investigation began, based on examination of the past through scientific scrutiny of all kinds of evidence, not just surviving literary texts. One part of this movement was the modern form of epigraphy, the study of inscriptions. It was reasoned that public inscriptions would give deep understanding of the workings and everyday experience of life in past eras. The text of the *Deeds of the Divine Augustus* was called the queen of inscriptions by Theodor Mommsen, the greatest scholar of that era, because it contained complete within itself an entirely new and different view of the history of one of the most crucial periods of Western culture, as it came directly from the period and was not mediated through the tendentious opinions of ancient literary writers or through a long chain of copies. By 1885 French and German expeditions had recovered the full text from Ancyra, and most of the other known copies (two small fragments have turned up since then), allowing Mommsen to publish the first full text of the document. Since then, the *Deeds of the Divine Augustus* has never lost its status as the most important document of Augustan history.

Further Reading

■ Articles

Bosworth, Brian. "Augustus, the *Res gestae* and Hellenistic Theories of Apotheosis." *Journal of Roman Studies* 89 (1999): 1–18.

Güven, Suna. "Displaying the *Res gestae* of Augustus: A Monument of Imperial Image for All." *Journal of the Society of Architectural Historians* 57 (1998): 30–45.

"At the age of nineteen, on my own initiative and at my own expense, I raised an army by means of which I restored liberty to the republic, which had been oppressed by the tyranny of a faction."

(Section 1)

"The dictatorship offered me by the people and the Roman Senate ... I did not accept."

(Section 5)

"Four times I aided the public treasury with my own money, paying out in this manner to those in charge of the treasury one hundred and fifty million sesterces."

(Section 17)

"I rebuilt in the city eighty-two temples of the gods, omitting none which at that time stood in need of repair."

(Section 20)

"I freed the sea from pirates."

(Section 25)

"The Parthians I compelled to restore to me the spoils and standards of three Roman armies and to seek as suppliants the friendship of the Roman people."

(Section 29)

"Embassies were often sent to me from the kings of India, a thing never seen before in the camp of any general of the Romans."

(Section 31)

"When I had extinguished the flames of civil war, after receiving by universal consent the absolute control of affairs, I transferred the republic from my own control to the will of the senate and the Roman people. For this service on my part I was given the title of Augustus."

(Section 34)

■ Books

Dio, Cassius. *The Roman History: The Reign of Augustus*, trans. Ian Scott-Kilvert. New York: Penguin, 1987.

Eck, Werner. *The Age of Augustus*, trans. Deborah Lucas Schneider. Oxford, U.K.: Blackwell, 2003.

Paterculus, Velleius. *Compendium of Roman History/Res gestae divi Augusti*, trans. Frederick W. Shipley. Cambridge, Mass.: Harvard University Press, 1924.

Ramage, Edwin S. *The Nature and Purpose of Augustus' "Res gestae."* Stuttgart, Germany: F. Steiner, 1987.

Suetonius. *The Twelve Caesars*, trans. Robert Graves. New York: Penguin, 2003.

Syme, Ronald. *The Roman Revolution*. Oxford, U.K.: Oxford University Press, 1952.

Yavetz, Zvi. "The *Res gestae* and Augustus' Public Image." In *Caesar Augustus: Seven Aspects*, ed. Fergus Millar and Erich Segal. Oxford, U.K.: Clarendon Press, 1984.

—Bradley A. Skeen

Questions for Further Study

1. Historians continue to read documents written in ancient Rome (and Greece) to trace the roots of modern thinking about systems of government. What would they learn about this topic from *Deeds of the Divine Augustus*?

2. What problems in Roman governance at the time led to the ascension of Augustus and thus to his record of his deeds? How did he address those problems?

3. Why can the *Deeds of the Divine Augustus* be considered one of the most important documents, if not the most important document, from this period in Roman history?

4. Other rulers of empires have used inscriptions to record their deeds. Compare this document with a similar document, such as the Divine Birth and Coronation Inscriptions of Hatshepsut. Do the documents share a purpose? How were they used to legitimize a rulership?

5. Modern politicians and world leaders want to record their deeds, or accomplishments, as a way of winning voters and defending their records; alternatively, they write books that help establish the breadth of their knowledge and hence their qualifications for office. John F. Kennedy, for example, wrote *Profiles in Courage* in anticipation of his successful run for the U.S. presidency, and President Barack Obama did the same with his book *The Audacity of Hope*. How might these and similar books (as well as articles) share a common purpose with *Deeds of Divine Augustus*? How would such documents be fundamentally different, given that they were written at different times and in different places?

DEEDS OF THE DIVINE AUGUSTUS

1. At the age of nineteen, on my own initiative and at my own expense, I raised an army by means of which I restored liberty to the republic, which had been oppressed by the tyranny of a faction. For which service the senate, with complimentary resolutions, enrolled me in its order, in the consulship of Gaius Pansa and Aulus Hirtius, giving me at the same time consular precedence in voting; it also gave me the *imperium*. As propraetor it ordered me, along with the consuls, "to see that the republic suffered no harm." In the same year, moreover, as both consuls had fallen in war, the people elected me consul and a triumvir for settling the constitution.

2. Those who slew my father I drove into exile, punishing their deed by due process of law, and afterwards when they waged war upon the republic I twice defeated them in battle.

3. Wars, both civil and foreign, I undertook throughout the world, on sea and land, and when victorious I spared all citizens who sued for pardon. The foreign nations which could with safety be pardoned I preferred to save rather than to destroy. The number of Roman citizens who bound themselves to me by military oath was about 500,000. Of these I settled in colonies or sent back into their own towns, after their term of service, something more than 300,000, and to all I assigned lands, or gave money as a reward for military service. I captured six hundred ships, over and above those which were smaller than triremes.

4. Twice I triumphed with an ovation, thrice I celebrated curule triumphs, and was saluted as imperator twenty-one times. Although the Senate decreed me additional triumphs I set them aside. When I had performed the vows which I had undertaken in each war I deposited upon the Capitol the laurels which adorned my fasces. For successful operations on land and sea, conducted either by myself or by my lieutenants under my auspices, the senate on fifty-five occasions decreed that thanks should be rendered to the immortal gods. The days on which such thanks were rendered by decree of the senate numbered 890. In my triumphs there were led before my chariot nine kings or children of kings. At the time of writing these words I had been thirteen times consul, and was in the thirty-seventh year of my tribunician power.

5. The dictatorship offered me by the people and the Roman Senate, in my absence and later when present, in the consulship of Marcus Marcellus and Lucius Arruntius I did not accept. I did not decline at a time of the greatest scarcity of grain the charge of the grain-supply, which I so administered that, within a few days, I freed the entire people, at my own expense, from the fear and danger in which they were. The consulship, either yearly or for life, then offered me I did not accept.

6. In the consulship of Marcus Vinucius and Quintus Lucretius, and afterwards in that of Publius and Gnaeus Lentulus, and a third time in that of Paullus Fablus Maximus and Quintus Tabero, when the Senate and the Roman people unanimously agreed [that I should be elected overseer of laws and morals, without a colleague and with the fullest power, I refused to accept any power offered me which was contrary to the traditions of our ancestors. Those things which at that time the senate wished me to administer I carried out by virtue of my tribunician power. And even in this office I five times received from the senate a colleague at my own request.

7. For ten years in succession I was one of the triumvirs for the re-establishment of the constitution]. To the day of writing this I have been *princeps senatus* for forty years. I have been pontifex maximus, augur, a member of the fifteen commissioners for performing sacred rites, one of the seven for sacred feasts, an arval brother, a *sodalis Titius*, a fetial priest.

8. As consul for the fifth time, by order of the people and the senate I increased the number of the patricians. Three times I revised the roll of the senate. In my sixth consulship, with Marcus Agrippa as my colleague, I made a census of the people. I performed the *lustrum* after an interval of forty-one years. In this lustration 4,063,000 Roman citizens were entered on the census roll. A second time, in the consulship of Gaius Censorinus and Gaius Asinus, I again performed the *lustrum* alone, with the consular imperium. In this *lustrum* 4,233,000 Roman citizens were entered on the census roll. A third time, with the consular imperium, and with my son Tiberius Caesar as my colleague, I performed the *lustrum* in the consulship of Sextus Pompeius and Sextus Apuleius. In this *lustrum* 4,937,000 Roman

citizens were entered on the census roll. By the passage of new laws I restored many traditions of our ancestors which were then falling into disuse, and I myself set precedents in many things for posterity to imitate.

9. The senate decreed that every fifth year vows should be undertaken for my health by the consuls and the priests. In fulfilment of these vows games were often held in my lifetime, sometimes by the four chief colleges of priests, sometimes by the consuls. In addition the entire body of citizens with one accord, both individually and by municipalities, performed continued sacrifices for my health at all the couches of the gods.

10. By decree of the senate my name was included in the Salian hymn, and it was enacted by law that my person should be sacred in perpetuity and that so long as I lived I should hold the tribunician power. I declined to be made Pontifex Maximus in succession to a colleague still living, when the people tendered me that priesthood which my father had held. Several years later I accepted that sacred office when he at last was dead who, taking advantage of a time of civil disturbance, had seized it for himself, such a multitude from all Italy assembling for my election, in the consulship of Publius Sulpicius and Gaius Valgius, as is never recorded to have been in Rome before.

11. The Senate consecrated in honour of my return an altar to Fortuna Redux at the Porta Capena, near the temple of Honour and Virtue, on which it ordered the pontiffs and the Vestal virgins to perform a yearly sacrifice on the anniversary of the day on which I returned to the city from Syria, in the consulship of Lucius Lucretius and Marcus Vinucius, and named the day, after my cognomen, the Augustalia.

12. At the same time, by decree of the senate, part of the praetors and of the tribunes of the people, together with the consul Quintus Lucretius and the leading men of the state, were sent to Campania to meet me, an honour which up to the present time has been decreed to no one except myself. When I returned from Spain and Gaul, in the consulship of Tiberius Nero and Publius Quintilius, after successful operations in those provinces, the senate voted in honour of my return the consecration of an altar to Pax Augusta in the Campus Martius, and on this altar it ordered the magistrates and priests and Vestal virgins to make annual sacrifice.

13. Janus Quirinus, which our ancestors ordered to be closed whenever there was peace, secured by victory, throughout the whole domain of the Roman people on land and sea, and which, before my birth is recorded to have been closed but twice in all since the foundation of the city, the senate ordered to be closed thrice while I was princeps.

14. My sons Gaius and Lucius Caesar, whom fortune snatched away from me in their youth, the senate and the Roman people to do me honour made consuls designate, each in his fifteenth year, providing that each should enter upon that office after a period of five years. The senate decreed that from the day on which they were introduced to the forum they should take part in the counsels of state. Moreover, the entire body of Roman knights gave each of them the title of *princeps iuventutis* and presented them with silver shields and spears.

15. To the Roman plebs I paid out three hundred sesterces per man in accordance with the will of my father, and in my own name in my fifth consulship I gave four hundred sesterces apiece from the spoils of war; a second time, moreover, in my tenth consulship I paid out of my own patrimony four hundred sesterces per man by way of bounty, and in my eleventh consulship I made twelve distributions of food from grain bought at my own expense, and in the twelfth year of my tribunician power I gave for the third time four hundred sesterces to each man. These largesses of mine reached a number of persons never less than two hundred and fifty thousand. In the eighteenth year of my tribunician power, as consul for the twelfth time, I gave to three hundred and twenty thousand of the city plebs sixty denarii apiece. In the colonies of my soldiers, as consul for the fifth time, I gave one thousand sesterces to each man from the spoils of war; about one hundred and twenty thousand men in the colonies received this triumphal largesse. When consul for the thirteenth time I gave sixty denarii apiece to the plebs who were then receiving public grain; these were a little more than two hundred thousand persons.

16. To the municipal town I paid money for the lands which I assigned to soldiers in my own fourth consulship and afterwards in the consulship of Marcus Crassus and Gnaeus Lentulus the augur. The sum which I paid for estates in Italy was about six hundred million sesterces, and the amount which I paid for lands in the provinces was about two hundred and sixty million. I was the first and only one to do this of all those who up to my time settled colonies of soldiers in Italy or in the provinces. And later, in the consulship of Tiberius Nero and Gnaeus Piso, likewise in the consulship of Gaius Antistius and Decimus Laelius, and of Gaius Calvisius and Lucius Pasienus, and of Lucius Lentulus and Mar-

cus Messalla, and of Lucius Carinius and Quintus Fabricius, I paid cash gratuities to the soldiers whom I settled in their own towns at the expiration of their service, and for this purpose I expended four hundred million sesterces as an act of grace.

17. Four times I aided the public treasury with my own money, paying out in this manner to those in charge of the treasury one hundred and fifty million sesterces. And in the consulship of Marcus Lepidus and Lucius Arruntius I contributed one hundred and seventy million sesterces out of my own patrimony to the military treasury, which was established on my advice that from it gratuities might be paid to soldiers who had seen twenty or more years of service.

18. Beginning with the year in which Gnaeus and Publius Lentulus were consuls, whenever taxes were in arrears, I furnished from my own purse and my own patrimony tickets for grain and money, sometimes to a hundred thousand persons, sometimes to many more.

19. I built the curia and the Chalcidicum adjoining it, the temple of Apollo on the Palatine with its porticoes, the temple of the deified Julius, the Lupercal, the portico at the Circus Flaminius which I allowed to be called Octavia after the name of him who had constructed an earlier one on the same site, the state box at the Circus Maximus, the temples on the capitol of Jupiter Feretrius and Jupiter Tonans, the temple of Quirinus, the temples of Minerva, of Juno the Queen, and of Jupiter Libertas, on the Aventine, the temple of the Lares at the highest point of the Sacra Via, the temple of the Di Penates on the Velia, the temple of Youth, and the temple of the Great Mother on the Palatine.

20. The Capitolium and the theatre of Pompey, both works involving great expense, I rebuilt without any inscription of my own name. I restored the channels of the aqueducts which in several places were falling into disrepair through age, and doubled the capacity of the aqueduct called the Marcia by turning a new spring into its channel. I completed the Julian Forum and the basilica which was between the temple of Castor and the temple of Saturn, works begun and far advanced by my father, and when the same basilica was destroyed by fire I began its reconstruction on an enlarged site, to be inscribed with the names of my sons, and ordered that in case I should not live to complete it, it should be completed by my heirs. In my sixth consulship in accordance with a decree of the senate, I rebuilt in the city eighty-two temples of the gods, omitting none which at that time stood in need of repair. As consul for the

seventh time I constructed the Via Flaminia from the city to Ariminum, and all the bridges except the Malvian and the Minucian.

21. On my own ground I built the temple of Mars Ultor and the Augustan Forum from the spoils of war. On ground purchased for the most part from private owners I built the theatre near the temple of Apollo which was to bear the name of my son-in-law Marcus Marcellus. From the spoils of war I consecrated offering on the Capitol, and in the temple of the divine Julius, and in the temple of Apollo, and in the temple of Vesta, and in the temple of Mars Ultor, which cost me about one hundred million sesterces. In my fifth consulship I remitted thirty-five thousand pounds weight of coronary gold contributed by the municipia and the colonies of Italy, and thereafter, whenever I was saluted as imperator, I did not accept the coronary gold, although the municipia and colonies voted it in the same kindly spirit as before.

22. Three times in my own name I gave a show of gladiators, and five times in the name of my sons or grandsons; in these shows there fought about ten thousand men. Twice in my own name I furnished for the people an exhibition of athletes gathered from all parts of the world, and a third time in the name of my grandson. Four times I gave games in my own name; as representing other magistrates twenty-three times. For the college of quindecemvirs, as master of that college and with Marcus Agrippa as my colleague, I conducted the Secular Games in the consulship of Gaius Furnius and Marcus Silanus. In my thirteenth consulship I gave, for the first time, the games of Mars, which, since that time, the consuls by decree of the senate have given in successive years in conjunction with me. In my own name, or that of my sons or grandsons, on twenty six occasions I gave to the people, in the circus, in the forum, or in the amphitheatre, hunts of African wild beasts, in which about three thousand five hundred beasts were slain.

23. I gave the people the spectacle of a naval battle beyond the Tiber, at the place where now stands the grove of the Caesars, the ground having been excavated for a length of eighteen hundred and a breadth of twelve hundred feet. In this spectacle thirty beaked ships, triremes or biremes, and a large number of smaller vessels met in conflict. In these fleets there fought about three thousand men exclusive of the rowers.

24. After my victory I replaced in the temples in all the cities of the province of Asia the ornaments which my antagonist in the war, when he despoiled the temples, had appropriated to his private use. Sil-

ver statues of me, on foot, on horseback, and in chariots were erected in the city to the number of about eighty; these I myself removed, and from the money thus obtained I placed in the temple of Apollo golden offerings in my own name and in the name of those who had paid me the honour of a statue.

25. I freed the sea from pirates. About thirty thousand slaves, captured in that war, who had run away from their masters and had taken up arms against the republic, I delivered to their masters for punishment. The whole of Italy voluntarily took oath of allegiance to me and demanded me as its leader in the war in which I was victorious at Actium. The provinces of the Spains, the Gauls, Africa, Sicily, and Sardinia took the same oath of allegiance. Those who served under my standards at that time included more than 700 senators, and among them eighty-three who had previously or have since been consuls up to the day on which these words were written, and about 170 have been priests.

26. I extended the boundaries of all the provinces which were bordered by races not yet subject to our empire. The provinces of the Gauls, the Spains, and Germany, bounded by the ocean from Gades to the mouth of the Elbe, I reduced to a state of peace. The Alps, from the region which lies nearest to the Adriatic as far as the Tuscan Sea, I brought to a state of peace without waging on any tribe an unjust war. My fleet sailed from the mouth of the Rhine eastward as far as the lands of the Cimbri to which, up to that time, no Roman had ever penetrated either by land or by sea, and the Cimbri and Charydes and Semnones and other peoples of the Germans of that same region through their envoys sought my friendship and that of the Roman people. On my order and under my auspices two armies were led, at almost the same time, into Ethiopia and into Arabia which is called the "Happy," and very large forces of the enemy of both races were cut to pieces in battle and many towns were captured. Ethiopia was penetrated as far as the town of Nabata, which is next to Meroë. In Arabia the army advanced into the territories of the Sabaei to the town of Mariba.

27. Egypt I added to the empire of the Roman people. In the case of Greater Armenia, though I might have made it a province after the assassination of its King Artaxes, I preferred, following the precedent of our fathers, to hand that kingdom over to Tigranes, the son of King Artavasdes, and grandson of King Tigranes, through Tiberius Nero who was then my stepson. And later, when the same people revolted and rebelled, and was subdued by my son

Gaius, I gave it over to King Ariobarzanes the son of Artabazus, King of the Medes, to rule, and after his death to his son Artavasdes. When he was murdered I sent into that kingdom Tigranes, who was sprung from the royal family of the Armenians. I recovered all the provinces extending eastward beyond the Adriatic Sea, and Cyrenae, which were then for the most part in possession of kings, and, at an earlier time, Sicily and Sardinia, which had been seized in the servile war.

28. I settled colonies of soldiers in Africa, Sicily, Macedonia, both Spains, Achaia, Asia, Syria, Gallia Narbonensis, Pisidia. Moreover, Italy has twenty-eight colonies founded under my auspices which have grown to be famous and populous during my lifetime.

29. From Spain, Gaul, and the Dalmatians, I recovered, after conquering the enemy, many military standards which had been lost by other generals. The Parthians I compelled to restore to me the spoils and standards of three Roman armies and to seek as suppliants the friendship of the Roman people. These standards I deposited in the inner shrine which is in the Temple of Mars Ultor.

30. The tribes of the Pannonians, to which no army of the Roman people had ever penetrated before my principate, having been subdued by Tiberius Nero who was then my stepson and my legate, I brought under the sovereignty of the Roman people, and I pushed forward the frontier of Illyricum as far as the bank of the river Danube. An army of Dacians which crossed to the south of that river was, under my auspices, defeated and crushed and afterwards my own army was led across the Danube and compelled the tribes of the Dacians to submit to the orders of the Roman people.

31. Embassies were often sent to me from the kings of India, a thing never seen before in the camp of any general of the Romans. Our friendship was sought, through ambassadors, by the Bastarnae and Seythians, and by the kings of the Sarmatians who live on either side of the river Tanais, and by the king of the Albani and of the Hiberi and of the Medes.

32. Kings of the Parthians, Tiridates, and later Phrates, the son of King Phrates, took refuge with me as suppliants; of the Medes, Artavasdes; of the Adiabeni, Artaxares; of the Britons, Dumno-bellaunus and Tim …; of the Sugambri, Maelo; of the Marcomanni and Suevi..... rus. Phrates, son of Orodes, king of the Parthian, sent all his sons and grandsons to me in Italy, not because he had been conquered in war, but rather seeking our friendship by means of his own children as pledges. And a large

number of other nations experienced the good faith of the Roman people during my principate who never before had had any interchange of embassies or of friendship with the Roman people.

33. From me the peoples of the Parthians and of the Medes received the kings for whom they asked through ambassadors, the chief men of those peoples; the Parthians Vonones, son of King Phrates, grandson of King Orades; the Medes Ariobarzanes, the son of King Artavazdes, grandson of King Ariobarzanes.

34. In my sixth and seventh consulships, when I had extinguished the flames of civil war, after receiving by universal consent the absolute control of affairs, I transferred the republic from my own control to the will of the senate and the Roman people. For this service on my part I was given the title of Augustus by decree of the senate, and the doorposts of my house were covered with laurels by public act, and a civic crown was fixed above my door, and a golden shield was placed in the Curia Julia whose inscription testified that the senate and the Roman people gave me this in recognition of my valour, my clemency, my justice, and my piety. After that time I took precedence of all in rank, but of power I possessed no more than those who were my colleagues in any magistracy.

35. While I was administering my thirteenth consulship the senate and the equestrian order and the entire Roman people gave me the title of Father of my Country, and decreed that this title should be inscribed upon the vestibule of my house and in the senate-house and in the Forum Augustum beneath the quadriga erected in my honour by decree of the senate. At the time of writing this I was in my seventy-sixth year.

Glossary

Achaia	Greece
arval brother	one of the twelve priests who made sacrifices to ensure good harvests (from the Latin *arvum*, meaning "field")
Chalcidium	committee room adjacent to the curia
coronary gold	coins of the empire made from the gold crowns worn by victorious commanders in their triumphs
fetial priest	person responsible for declaring war and offering the enemy the chance to save themselves by capitulation before hostilities began
Illyricum	province of the Roman Empire in the present-day Balkans
Jupiter Feretrius Jupiter Tonans Jupiter Libertas	epithets, or names, applied to the Roman's chief god, Jupiter
Mars Ultor	an epithet of the Roman god of war
quindecimvirs	an ancient Roman priesthood charged with keeping the sacred books that were consulted in national emergencies
Salian hymn	song sung during the procession of the Salii (dancers), an obscure and ancient Roman priesthood
sodalis Titius	priesthood dedicated to worship of the mythical Sabine king Titus revived by Augustus to worship the Roman emperors
whom fortune snatched away from me	a reference to the early deaths of the two boys

POPOL VUH

"Name now our names, praise us. We are your mother, we are your father."

Overview

The Popol Vuh is one of the most important examples of pre-Columbian literature to survive the Spanish conquest of the Americas. It is a work of epic poetry that tells the origin story of the Maya and, more specifically, the Quiché, a Mayan ethnic group that dominated the highlands of modern-day Guatemala during the postclassic period of Mayan history (925–1530 CE). The Popol Vuh begins by explaining how the world came into existence and speaks of the exploits of the Hero Twins, important figures in Mayan mythology. Finally, the book ends with the creation of humans, the foundation of the Quiché people, and their history from their migration into their homeland to the Spanish conquest.

The Popol Vuh has a long and complex history. The oldest known written copy of the work dates to about 1701–1703; however, it is much older. The modern form of the Popol Vuh took shape sometime in the 1550s when anonymous authors drew upon ancient sources to record the story. The authors spoke of an original manuscript upon which their work was based, presumably a book or documents that recorded religious and historical information written in Mayan glyphs. That source is lost to us today. The authors almost certainly also drew from oral tradition: stories, myths, and histories of the Quiché people. The story line of the Popol Vuh was well known during the classic Maya period (250–925 CE); archaeologists have identified the Hero Twins and other characters from the Popol Vuh on vases and monuments. It is likely that the sources consulted by the authors of the Popol Vuh date to this era or perhaps even earlier, to the preclassic Maya period (ca. 1800 BCE–250 CE).

After having recorded the Popol Vuh, the authors hid the manuscript from the Spanish out of fear that the conquerors would destroy it; the Spanish had destroyed countless other Mayan codices, or manuscripts. After 150 years, the work finally came to light around 1701–1703, when a Dominican monk named Francisco Ximénez somehow obtained the manuscript. Ximénez wrote out a copy and added a Spanish translation of his own alongside the Quiché. This manuscript is the earliest known copy of the Popol Vuh; no one knows what became of the original Quiché text.

Context

Around 1250 CE, a group of Toltec migrants from central Mexico entered the highlands of Guatemala and intermarried with the local Mayan people. The Quiché people came from the fusion of these two traditions. They established their capitol at Q'umarkaj and launched a series of military expeditions, conquering many other Mayan ethnic groups. They thus became the dominant people of the highlands.

On December 6, 1523, the Spanish conquistador Pedro de Alvarado set out from the recently conquered Aztec capitol of Tenochtitlán (ancient Mexico City) in the hope of discovering gold and with orders from Hernán Cortés to verify reports of rich lands and new races of people. Alvarado led 120 horsemen, 300 foot soldiers, and many native allies from the nearby cities of Cholula and Tlaxcala. As the Spanish approached Q'umarkaj, the Quiché raised an army led by the warrior Tecún Umán. The two armies met in February 1524 at the plain of Xelaju, where the Quiché were defeated.

After the Battle of Xelaju, the Quiché invited the Spanish to their capital city, ostensibly to discuss peace terms. However, the Quiché planned to trap the Spanish in the newly deserted city; they intended to remove the causeways that were the main roads into Q'umarkaj and set the city afire. The Spanish detected the trap, and Alvarado ordered his men to lay waste to the city and the Quiché themselves. After the sacking of Q'umarkaj, the Quiché nation fell. The Spanish conquest of Guatemala was lengthy, continuing until 1548. Alvarado ruled Guatemala as captain general of the region from 1527 until his death in 1541.

The Spanish conquest of Guatemala and the New World in general was not just a military one. The Spanish sought to convert native populations to Christianity and to Hispanicize their culture and way of life, thus better integrating them into the Spanish Empire through cultural transformation. The second wave of Spaniards arrived in Quiché lands soon after Alvarado's death. In the late 1540s, Mayans were gathered together into villages to be taught the catechism

CA. 1800 BCE
- The preclassic Mayan period begins, lasting until 250 CE; this is the probable era of the formation of Mayan mythology and foundational religious beliefs.

250 CE
- The classic Mayan period begins, lasting until 925; the ancient source of the Popol Vuh might date to this era.

CA. 1250 CE
- The Toltecs arrive in the Guatemalan highlands and found the Quiché ruling dynasty.

1524
- **February** Pedro de Alvarado's troops meet the Quiché army led by the warrior Tecún Umán and defeat them.

1562
- **July 12** Diego de Landa burns Mayan codices; Landa admits to burning twenty-seven books, while other sources maintain that thousands of texts went into the fire.

CA. 1554
- The Popol Vuh is redacted from its possible original source and oral traditions.

under the Spanish policy of *congregación*, or missionization. Missionization sought to change the religious beliefs of the Maya through teaching Roman Catholic doctrine. Spanish missionaries overtly and symbolically dominated Mayan religious sites by building churches nearby or on top of them and through punishing, verbally and sometimes physically, those individuals who disobeyed.

The early experiences of the Quiché with the Roman Catholic Church occurred at a crucial and turbulent time in the Yucatán Peninsula. In 1562 the Franciscan friar Diego de Landa, prelate of Yucatán, was informed that friars in the region had found caches of human skulls and figures depicting Mayan gods among missionized and, the friars presumed, Catholic Mayan Indians. Landa was outraged and ordered an Inquisition to unearth idolaters and idolatrous materials. During the Inquisition, more than 4,500 Mayans were tortured. Records show that 158 people died as a result of the torture, and many others were permanently injured. On July 12, 1562, Landa oversaw a ceremony known as an auto-da-fé (act of faith), during which more than five thousand Mayan figures were burned. Additionally, Landa burned Mayan codices. The anthropologist Inga Clendinnen records that Landa characterized the books as being nothing but "superstition and lies of the devil" (p. 70). Landa later admitted to burning twenty-seven codices; other sources claim that thousands of books were destroyed. These codices contained invaluable Mayan knowledge and records. Today, only four known Mayan codices remain. Diego de Landa was sent back to Spain to stand before the Council of the Indies, one of the ruling bodies of the Spanish American empire. The council condemned his actions as a false Inquisition. Ultimately, Landa was absolved of his crimes in 1569 and sent back to Yucatán as bishop in 1571.

It is in this context that the Popol Vuh was produced in the early 1550s. The authors were driven by two equally pressing needs: to preserve their heritage and to protect their identity. Although Diego de Landa's Inquisition had not yet begun, Mayans in the Yucatán and in the lands of the Quiché understood the need for secrecy in continuing to practice their old beliefs and customs. While colonial Spaniards might have considered many of these practices innocuous, other practices, such as human sacrifice, shocked and horrified them. Human sacrifice and the shedding of their own blood by elite Mayan individuals ("autosacrifice"), however, were integral to the Mayan religious system. There is evidence that both practices continued, largely in secret, for well over forty years after the Spanish arrived in Mayan lands.

By the early 1700s, more than 150 years later, the situation had changed considerably. Many traditional Mayan religious beliefs had merged with Catholicism in a process known as syncretism. The Quiché considered themselves to be, by and large, Catholics. Yet ancient knowledge and many traditional beliefs were still held in high esteem, and many Mayan gods were still known and spoken of, if not venerated. In this atmosphere, the Dominican Francisco Ximénez obtained and copied the 1550s document.

About the Author

There are few straightforward answers about the authors of the Popol Vuh. The authors of the 1550s manuscript chose anonymity, almost certainly to protect themselves from the anger of the Spanish. Modern historians and anthropologists have been able to speculate as to the identity of the authors based on clues within the Popol Vuh and Spanish documents preserved in the national and other archives of Guatemala and Spain.

The Popol Vuh was most likely produced in the village of Santa Cruz del Quiché. In the conclusion of the book, the authors refer to "Quiché, which is now called Santa Cruz" (Tedlock, p. 198). The text itself hints at the identities of the authors. The end of the work provides a genealogy of the Quiché, which names their great families and their rulers and their offices. The final passages of the genealogy name the minister installed in 1554 and list the current offices held. Finally, in the next-to-last passage of the work, the authors write, "And there are three Masters of Ceremonies in all. … They are the givers of birth, they are the Mothers of the Word, they are the Fathers of the Word" (Tedlock, p. 197). The passage continues to note that the three Masters of Ceremonies represent three of the noble families of the Quiché. In *The Popol Vuh: Sacred Book of the Maya*, Allen J. Christenson contends that the phrase *the Word* is used throughout the text to refer to the Popol Vuh itself. Thus, the three Masters of Ceremonies, all members of Quiché nobility, wrote the Popol Vuh. Christenson further deduces that one of the authors was named Don Cristóbal Velasco, who signed a contemporary document with the title Nim Chocoh Cavec, Master of Ceremonies for the "Cauec" (the spelling of "Cavec" in Mayan) family. We know nothing more about Velasco.

Explanation and Analysis of the Document

The Popol Vuh expresses many foundational ideas of the ancient Maya. One of the most important ideas is that the natural rhythm of the world, life, and time itself is cyclical, repeating itself endlessly in varying forms. A second theme is the struggle between order and chaos. Humans and gods alike struggle to create order from chaos, to shape the world into a form that they find pleasing. Inevitably, however, chaos disturbs this ordered plan. Ultimately, the force of chaos is the most powerful in the universe; even the gods themselves struggle against it and in the end are conquered by it, only to begin the process of creation again. In this way, the two themes overlap and interplay; the struggle between chaos and order is a never-ending cycle itself.

In the first section of the Popol Vuh, the gods create the earth out of nothingness, thus forming order out of chaos. The gods then turn their hands to the creation of humans. It is here that the excerpt from the document begins. Among the gods assembled are the Sovereign Plumed Serpent, Heart of Earth, Heart of Sky, and Hurricane. The Popol Vuh refers to them as creators, repeatedly calling

Time Line

CA. 1701
- The Dominican Friar Francisco Ximénez obtains the original 1550s document, transcribes the Quiché, and makes a side-by-side translation into Spanish.

1854
- Carl Scherzer finds Ximénez's book at the University of San Carlos in Guatemala City and commissions a copy.

1856
- Scherzer publishes the Spanish version of the Popol Vuh for the first time, and it is widely acclaimed in Europe.

1861
- The Quiché version of the Popol Vuh is published for the first time, with an accompanying French translation by Father Charles-Étienne Brasseur de Bourbourg.

1930s
- Epigraphers begin work to break the Maya code and thus decipher the Mayan glyphs.

Polychrome ceramic vase depicting a Mayan lord receiving tribute (© The Trustees of the British Museum)

them "Maker, Modeler, Bearer, Begetter," or some combination of these titles. By emphasizing the action of creation and through the repetition of the titles associated with creation, the Popol Vuh stresses the importance and significance of the struggle to bring order from chaos. Moreover, the repetition of titles in sequence, always using more than one title, is rhythmic and chantlike. The Popol Vuh's roots lie in oral history and storytelling; its use of language is deeply tied to methods of storytelling.

The excerpt from the Popol Vuh begins with the first attempt of the gods to create sentient beings who can walk and talk, reproduce and survive, and worship and make offerings. Their creation must be "a giver of praise, giver of respect." Just as important, this being must be able to be a "keeper of days." This refers to an important part of Mayan religious beliefs; *ajq'ij*, or "daykeepers," have been an important part of Mayan religion for thousands of years. Daykeepers were diviners and keepers of the Mayan calendar. The Mayan calendar was very complex and also very accurate—more accurate, in fact, than the calendar we follow today. It consisted of two calendars used for different purposes. The Haab was a solar calendar that tracked day-to-day events; the Tzolkin was a lunar calendar used for ritual purposes. These two calendars intersected to give a different day name for every day in a fifty-two-year cycle. It was the job of the daykeeper to keep track of the calendar and read the auguries associated with each day's name. Daykeepers ensured that humans kept track of ritual days and knew where they were in the cycle of the calendar and what kinds of auguries the gods had made for each day name. The daykeepers provided a vital connection between humans and the gods. They kept order in the passage of time and provided a constant reminder that time itself is cyclical, that an end is coming and a new cycle will be reborn from the death of the old cycle.

In their quest to fashion a keeper of days, the gods first create the animals: jaguars, rattlesnakes, deer, birds, and others. The gods then order the animals to worship them, commanding them to "name our names, praise us." Yet the animals cannot, and the gods conclude that their creations must be changed and brought down in the order of beings. The gods advise the animals to "just accept your service, just let your flesh be eaten. ... This must be your service." This first failure in the gods' quest to create sentient beings that are able to worship them shows us two things. First, even the gods are imperfect and subject to the forces of chaos, which destroys their carefully planned order. Second, like all origin stories, it informs us about the beliefs and worldview of its culture: Animals are created to serve humans (and more specifically, the Maya) by nourishing them with their flesh.

In their second attempt, the gods make a being of earth and mud. This attempt, too, proves to be unsatisfactory. Its body and face are malformed and soft. It is able to talk but speaks senselessly. It is crumbling and disintegrating, and even the gods cannot keep this being together; their creation breaks down before their very eyes. The gods conclude that this being was a failure. Chaos triumphs again.

Before their next attempt, the gods consult two ancient mythical daykeepers named Xpiyacoc and Xmucane. These diviners are older even than the gods themselves; the gods address them respectfully as "grandmother" and "grandfather." The gods seek advice on how to create a being that can worship them, and they are told that they should proceed with their plan to create new beings out of wood. The wood beings, or "manikins," are more successful than the gods' first two attempts. They are "human in looks and human in speech" and are able to multiply and have daughters and sons. The manikins build houses, keep domesticated animals, and cook tortillas, but they have "nothing in their hearts and nothing in their minds, no memory of their mason and builder." They do not worship the gods.

The gods, realizing that they have failed a third time, send a flood to destroy the wooden humans; they also send beings who gouge out the manikins' eyeballs and eat their flesh. All of creation turns against the manikins, the beings who neglected the gods. The domesticated animals who fed the manikins, the dogs and turkeys, tell them "now it is *you* whom *we* shall eat." Their grinding stones, tortilla griddles, and cooking pots rebuke them as well, threatening to "pound and grind [their] flesh" and "burn [them]." As the wooden humans try to flee, other creations turn on them: Houses collapse beneath them, and caves deny them refuge. And so this cycle of creation comes to an end.

This creation cycle reflects the recurring sequence of chaos and order. There may be some initial success, but ultimately chaos destroys whatever order has been imposed. Then the cycle begins again. The saga of the creation of humans is taken up again toward the middle of the Popol Vuh, when the gods fashion humans from corn, the sacred food of the Maya. This was the successful creation of humans; the birth of the Maya. Humans are created, and they finally are able to worship the gods, praise them,

The archaeologist Richard Hansen shows a limestone frieze depicting the Hero Twins, from northern Guatemala.
(AP/Wide World Photos)

give thanks, and keep their days. In the traditional Mayan worldview, today's humans are the descendants of the people of corn. Although the gods have been successful in their creation, the world and creation and humanity will end, and chaos will once again reign. And the gods will have to create order from chaos yet again.

Audience

The Quiché themselves were the initial audience of the Popol Vuh. The authors produced the document as a lasting testament and record of the origins of their people, preserving the words and beliefs of the ancestors and connecting the living population with them.

The recorded form of the Popol Vuh reflects an enormous shift in the technology and knowledge of its audience. Before Spanish contact, the Maya had been the most literate people in the Americas, and they had developed the most advanced form of writing in the Western Hemisphere. All of this changed after the collapse of the Mayan civilization and the missionization of the Maya. Knowledge of how to read the glyphs had begun to slowly fade and ultimately was lost. The authors of the Popol Vuh based the text on one or more ancient documents, which would have been

written in glyphs. Yet Francisco Ximénez records that he transcribed the document from Quiché written in the Latin alphabet. The authors made this switch partly as a reflection of the changing technologies; they also might have intended to hide the document in plain sight by disguising it in the Latin alphabet.

When Ximénez transcribed the document sometime around 1703, he had its second audience and second purpose in mind. As a Dominican, he sought not only to convert the Mayans but also to study them in order to better understand their language and culture. Monastic orders such as the Dominicans were inveterate producers of documents detailing the beliefs, customs, rituals, language, and culture of their parishioners. They produced these documents for several reasons. First, they wanted to understand the culture and beliefs of the Maya so that they could better convert them to Christianity. Second, they recorded their knowledge so that the monks who came after them could read and learn about the culture quickly upon arrival. Finally, they observed and recorded because the Spanish crown commanded it in order to better understand new and faraway subjects of the crown. Thus, for Ximénez, the Popol Vuh provided great insight into the Quiché.

Finally, the Popol Vuh has a large modern audience. Historians, epigraphers, and anthropologists value it as an

"*Name now our names, praise us. We are your mother, we are your father. Speak now.*"

(Paragraph 18)

"*The time for the planting and dawning is nearing. For this we must make a provider and nurturer. How else can we be invoked and remembered on the face of the earth? We have already made our first try at our work and design, but it turned out that they didn't keep our days, nor did they glorify us.*"

(Paragraph 28)

"*They came into being, they multiplied, they had daughters, they had sons, these manikins, woodcarvings. But there was nothing in their hearts and nothing in their minds, no memory of their mason and builder. They just went and walked wherever they wanted. Nor did they remember the Heart of Sky.*"

(Paragraph 50)

"*Such was the scattering of the human work, the human design. The people were ground down, overthrown. The mouths and faces of all of them were destroyed and crushed. And it used to be said that the monkeys in the forests today are a sign of this. They were left as a sign because wood alone was used for their flesh by the builder and the sculptor.*"

(Paragraph 71)

invaluable source about the ancient Maya. But modern Mayan peoples, Quiché among them, turn to the Popol Vuh for the same reason their forefathers in the 1550s did: to better understand their ancestors and to feel a connection with them.

Impact

Because the Popol Vuh was kept hidden by the Quiché for nearly 150 years, it is nearly impossible to truly understand and measure its impact during that era. It is certain that it did have great influence on Quiché society. Allen Christenson records that Francisco Ximénez called the Popol Vuh "the doctrine which they first imbibed with their mother's milk" and said that "all of them knew it almost by heart" (Christenson, p. 12). For the colonial Quiché, the Popol Vuh provided an alternative to the Catholic view of the universe. Both the Popol Vuh and the Bible in part function as origin stories and try to answer questions about cultural identity and divine purpose. Who are we? Where did we come from? What kind of relationship do we have with God/the gods? What place do we hold in the universe? Why were we created? The Popol Vuh furnishes very different answers to these questions than the Bible and thus helped the colonial Quiché preserve their identity.

The impact of the Popol Vuh today is much easier to explore and appreciate, though it remains largely the same: It gives us an invaluable look into the culture and beliefs of the ancient Maya. For modern epigraphers working to decipher the Mayan glyphs, the Popol Vuh may furnish suggestions of the meanings of untranslated glyphs. As knowledge of the glyphs increases, our understanding of the Popol Vuh grows, and the translation more closely approaches the authors' original intent.

For the modern Maya, the Popol Vuh offers the same thing that it did for their ancestors: answers to questions about their origins and stories about important mythical figures and gods. This knowledge was especially important for the Maya during the Guatemalan Civil War of 1960–1996. During this war, thousands of human rights violations were committed against the Mayan peoples by their government. Some two hundred thousand people died during the war, most of them Mayan. In the 1980s government death squads massacred entire villages, deeming the inhabitants poor, stupid Indians who were inferior to the city mestizo populations. Mayan peoples reacted by actively embracing their identity and culture, starting a Mayan resurgence movement. The Popol Vuh played an integral part in this movement as a foundational document of Mayan culture.

Further Reading

■ Articles

Carlsen, Robert S., and Martin Prechtel. "The Flowering of the Dead: An Interpretation of Highland Maya Culture." Man New Series 26, no. 1 (March 1991): 23–42.

Himelblau, Jack. "The Popol Vuh of the Quiché Maya of Guatemala: Text, Copyist, and Time Frame of Transcription." Hispania 72, no. 1 (March 1989): 97–122.

Houston, Stephen, et al."The Language of Classic Maya Inscriptions." Current Anthropology 41, no. 3 (June 2000): 321–356.

■ Books

Bassie-Sweet, Karen. Maya Sacred Geography and the Creator Deities. Norman: University of Oklahoma Press, 2008.

Christenson, Allen J. Popol Vuh: The Sacred Book of the Maya. Norman: University of Oklahoma Press, 2007.

Clendinnen, Inga. Ambivalent Conquests: Maya and Spaniard in Yucatan, 1517–1570. London: Cambridge University Press, 1987.

Menchu, Rigoberta. I, Rigoberta Menchu: An Indian Woman in Guatemala, ed. Elisabeth Burgos-Debray and trans. Ann Wright. London: Verso, 1984.

Tedlock, Dennis. Popol Vuh: The Definitive Edition of the Mayan Book of the Dawn of Life and the Glories of Gods and Kings. New York: Touchstone, 1996.

■ Web Sites

"Popol Wuj Online" The Ohio State University Libraries Web Site. http://library.osu.edu/sites/popolwuj/folios_eng/index.php.

"The Popol Vuh at the Newberry Library" Newberry Library Web site. http://www.newberry.org/collections/PopolVuh.html.

—Tamara Shircliff Spike

Questions for Further Study

1. What motives prompted the writing of the Popol Vuh?

2. Discuss the extent to which the Popol Vuh can be regarded as history, as mythology, and as sacred scripture.

3. The Popol Vuh consists largely of an examination of the origins of the world and of the Mayan people. In what ways are these accounts similar to—and how do they differ from—similar accounts in another religious tradition with which you might be familiar, such as the Judeo-Christian account in the biblical book of Genesis or Native American accounts contained in a variety of sources, depending on the tribe?

4. What short-term and long-term effects did Spanish conquest have on the peoples of Central America?

5. The modern world has witnessed a resurgence of interest in ancient cultural traditions, not only among the Maya but also among numerous other indigenous cultures. How does this resurgence manifest itself, and why do you think such renewed interest is taking place?

Popol Vuh

Then the mountains were separated from the water, all at once the great mountains came forth. By their genius alone, by their cutting edge alone they carried out the conception of the mountain-plain, whose face grew instant groves of cypress and pine.

And the Plumed Serpent was pleased with this:

"It was good that you came, Heart of Sky, Hurricane, and Newborn Thunderbolt, Sudden Thunderbolt. Our work, our design will turn out well," they said.

And the earth was formed first, the mountain-plain. The channels of water were separated; their branches wound their ways among the mountains. The waters were divided when the great mountains appeared.

Such was the formation of the earth when it was brought forth by the Heart of Sky, Heart of Earth, as they are called, since they were the first to think of it. The sky was set apart, and the earth was set apart in the midst of the waters.

Such was their plan when they thought, when they worried about the completion of their work.

Now they planned the animals of the mountains, all the guardians of the forests, creatures of the mountains: the deer, birds, pumas, jaguars, serpents, rattlesnakes, fer-de-lances, guardians of the bushes.

A Bearer, Begetter speaks:

"Why this pointless humming? Why should there merely be rustling beneath the trees and bushes?"

"Indeed—they had better have guardians," the others replied. As soon as they thought it and said it, deer and birds came forth.

And then they gave out homes to the deer and birds:

"You, the deer: sleep along the rivers, in the canyons. Be here in the meadows, in the thickets, in the forests, multiply yourselves. You will stand and walk on all fours," they were told.

So then they established the nests of the birds, small and great:

"You, precious birds: your nests, your houses are in the trees, in the bushes. Multiply there, scatter there, in the branches of trees, the branches of bushes," the deer and birds were told.

When this deed had been done, all of them had received a place to sleep and a place to stay. So it is that the nests of the animals are on the earth, given by the Bearer, Begetter. Now the arrangement of the deer and birds was complete.

And then the deer and birds were told by the Maker, Modeler, Bearer, Begetter:

"Talk, speak out. Don't moan, don't cry out. Please talk, each to each, within each kind, within each group," they were told—the deer, birds, puma, jaguar, serpent.

"Name now our names, praise us. We are your mother, we are your father. Speak now:

'Hurricane,
Newborn Thunderbolt, Sudden Thunderbolt,
Heart of Sky, Heart of Earth,
Maker, Modeler,
Bearer, Begetter,'

speak pray to us, keep our days," they were told. But it didn't turn out that they spoke like people: they just squawked, they just chattered, they just howled. It wasn't apparent what language they spoke; each one gave a different cry. When the Maker, Modeler heard this:

"It hasn't turned out well, they haven't spoken," they said among themselves. "It hasn't turned out that our names have been named. Since we are their mason and sculptor, this will not do," the Bearers and Begetters said among themselves. So they told them:

"You will simply have to be transformed. Since it hasn't turned out well and you haven't spoken, we have changed our word:

"What you feed on, what you eat, the places where you sleep, the places where you stay, whatever is yours will remain in the canyons, the forests. Although it turned out that our days were not kept, nor did you pray to us, there may yet be strength in the keeper of days, the giver of praise whom we have yet to make. Just accept your service, just let your flesh be eaten.

"So be it, this must be your service," they were told when they were instructed—the animals, small and great, on the face of the earth.

And then they wanted to test their timing again, they wanted to experiment again, and they wanted to prepare for the keeping of days again. They had not heard their speech among the animals; it did not come to fruition and it was not complete.

And so their flesh was brought low: they served, they were eaten, they were killed—the animals on the face of the earth.

Again there comes an experiment with the human work, the human design, by the Maker, Modeler, Bearer, Begetter:

"It must simply be tried again. The time for the planting and dawning is nearing. For this we must make a provider and nurturer. How else can we be invoked and remembered on the face of the earth? We have already made our first try at our work and design, but it turned out that they didn't keep our days, nor did they glorify us.

"So now let's try to make a giver of praise, giver of respect, provider, nurturer," they said.

So then comes the building and working with earth and mud. They made a body, but it didn't look good to them. It was just separating, just crumbling, just loosening, just softening, just disintegrating, and just dissolving. Its head wouldn't turn, either. Its face was just lopsided, its face was just twisted. It couldn't look around. It talked at first, but senselessly. It was quickly dissolving in the water.

"It won't last," the mason and sculptor said then. "It seems to be dwindling away, so let it just dwindle. It can't walk and it can't multiply, so let it be merely a thought," they said.

So then they dismantled, again they brought down their work and design. Again they talked:

"What is there for us to make that would turn out well, that would succeed in keeping our days and praying to us?" they said. Then they planned again:

"We'll just tell Xpiyacoc, Xmucane, Hunahpu Possum, Hunahpu Coyote, to try a counting of days, a counting of lots," the mason and sculptor said to themselves. Then they invoked Xpiyacoc, Xmucane.

Then comes the naming of those who are the midmost seers: the "Grandmother of Day, Grandmother of Light," as the Maker, Modeler called them. These are names of Xpiyacoc and Xmucane.

When Hurricane had spoken with the Sovereign Plumed Serpent, they invoked the daykeepers, diviners, the midmost seers:

"There is yet to find, yet to discover how we are to model a person, construct a person again, a provider, nurturer, so that we are called upon and we are recognized: our recompense is in words.

Midwife, matchmaker,
our grandmother, our grandfather,
Xpiyacoc, Xmucane,
let there be planting, let there be the dawning

of our invocation, our sustenance, our recognition
by the human work, the human design,
the human figure, the human form.
So be it, fulfill your names;
Hunahpu Possum, Hunahpu Coyote,
Bearer twice over, Begetter twice over,
Great Peccary, Great Coati,
lapidary, jeweler,
sawyer, carpenter,
plate shaper, bowl shaper,
incense maker, master craftsman,
Grandmother of Day, Grandmother of Light.

"You have been called upon because of our work, our design. Run your hands over the kernels of corn, over the seeds of the coral tree, just get it done, just let it come out whether we should carve and gouge a mouth, a face in wood," they told the daykeepers.

And then comes the borrowing, the counting of days; the hand is moved over the corn kernels, over the coral seeds, the days, the lots.

Then they spoke to them, one of them a grandmother, the other a grandfather.

This is the grandfather, this is the master of the coral seeds: Xpiyacoc is his name.

And this is the grandmother, the daykeeper, diviner who stands behind others: Xmucane is her name.

And they said, as they set out the days:

"Just let it be found, just let it be discovered,
say it, our ear is listening,
may you talk, may you speak,
just find the wood for the carving and sculpting
by the builder, sculptor.
Is this to be the provider, the nurturer
when it comes to the planting, the dawning?
You corn kernels, you coral seeds,
you days, you lots:
may you succeed, may you be accurate,"

they said to the corn kernels, coral seeds, days, lots. "Have shame, you up there, Heart of Sky: attempt no deception before the mouth and face of Sovereign Plumed Serpent," they said. Then they spoke straight to the point:

"It is well that there be your manikins, woodcarvings, talking, speaking, there on the face of the earth."

"So be it," they replied. The moment they spoke it was done: the manikins, woodcarvings, human in looks and human in speech.

This was the peopling of the face of the earth:

They came into being, they multiplied, they had daughters, they had sons, these manikins, woodcarvings. But there was nothing in their hearts and nothing in their minds, no memory of their mason and builder. They just went and walked wherever they wanted. Now they did not remember the Heart of Sky.

And so they fell, just an experiment and just a cutout for humankind. They were talking at first but their faces were dry. They were not yet developed in the legs and arms. They had no blood, no lymph. They had no sweat, no fat. Their complexions were dry, their faces were crusty. They flailed their legs and arms, their bodies were deformed.

And so they accomplished nothing before the Maker, Modeler who gave them birth, gave them heart. They became the first numerous people here on the face of the earth.

Again there comes a humiliation, destruction, and demolition. The manikins, woodcarvings were killed when the Heart of Sky devised a flood for them. A great flood was made; it came down on the heads of the manikins, woodcarvings.

The man's body was carved from the wood of the coral tree by the Maker, Modeler. And as for the woman, the Maker, Modeler needed the hearts of bulrushes for the woman's body. They were not competent, nor did they speak before the builder and sculptor who made them and brought them forth, and so they were killed, done in by a flood: There came a rain of resin from the sky.

There came the one named Gouger of Faces: he gouged out their eyeballs. There came Sudden Bloodletter: he snapped off their heads.

There came Crunching Jaguar: he ate their flesh.

There came Tearing Jaguar: he tore them open.

They were pounded down to the bones and tendons, smashed and pulverized even to the bones. Their faces were smashed because they were incompetent before their mother and their father, the Heart of Sky, named Hurricane. The earth was blackened because of this; the black rainstorm began, rain all day and rain all night. Into their houses came the animals, small and great. Their faces were crushed by things of wood and stone. Everything spoke: their water jars, their tortilla griddles, their plates, their cooking pots, their dogs, their grinding stones, each and every thing crushed their faces. Their dogs and turkeys told them:

"You caused us pain, you ate us, but now it is *you* whom *we* shall eat." And this is the grinding stone:

"We were undone because of you.

Every day, every day,
in the dark, in the dawn, forever,
r-r-rip, r-r-rip,
r-r-rub, r-r-rub,
right in our faces, because of you.

"This was the service we gave you at first, when you were still people, but today you will learn of our power. We shall pound and we shall grind your flesh," their grinding stones told them.

And this is what their dogs said, when they spoke in their turn:

"Why is it you can't seem to give us our food? We just watch and you just keep us down, and you throw us around. You keep a stick ready when you eat, just so you can hit us. We don't talk, so we've received nothing from you. How could you not have known? You *did* know that we were wasting away there, behind you.

"So, this very day you will taste the teeth in our mouths. We shall eat you," their dogs told them, and their faces were crushed.

And then their tortilla griddles and cooking pots spoke to them in turn:

"Pain! That's all you've done for us. Our mouths are sooty, our faces are sooty. By setting us on the fire all the time, you burn us. Since *we* felt no pain, *you* try it. We shall burn you," all their cooking pots said, crushing their faces.

The stones, their hearthstones were shooting out, coming right out of the fire, going for their heads, causing them pain. Now they run for it, helter-skelter.

They want to climb up on the houses, but they fall as the houses collapse.

They want to climb the trees; they're thrown off by the trees.

Glossary

Newborn Thunderbolt a god who came down from the sky along with Heart of Sky and Hurricane

Sudden Thunderbolt   the god from the sky who followed Newborn Thunderbolt

They want to get inside caves, but the caves slam shut in their faces.

Such was the scattering of the human work, the human design. The people were ground down, overthrown. The mouths and faces of all of them were destroyed and crushed. And it used to be said that the monkeys in the forests today are a sign of this. They were left as a sign because wood alone was used for their flesh by the builder and sculptor.

So this is why monkeys look like people: they are a sign of a previous human work, human design—mere manikins, mere woodcarvings.

LAWS ENDING PERSECUTION OF CHRISTIANS IN THE ROMAN EMPIRE

"We should give both to Christians and everyone the free power of following the religion which each wished."

Overview

The process by which Christianity came to occupy the commanding heights of the Roman mind was long, complex, and gradual. A crucial phase in this evolution was marked by two laws responsible for bringing to a final end the Great Persecution (303–313 CE) of the Christian Church in the Roman Empire. Persecution had already ceased in the western half of the empire in 306 CE. The Edict of Galerius, issued in the spring of 311, was intended to end persecution in the eastern half. However, persecution in the East started up again before the end of 311 under Galerius's successor. It was not until the summer of 313 that Licinius, the emperor controlling the eastern half of Roman Empire, together with Constantine, the emperor of the western half of the Roman Empire and the first Christian Roman emperor, issued the Letter of Licinius (formerly known as the Edict of Milan). It was after Constantine eliminated Licinius in 324 that pagan sacrifice was made illegal, important temples were destroyed and their treasures confiscated, and the conditions existed for the eventual creation of a distinctively Christian Roman civilization.

Context

The Roman Empire was not in general hostile toward unfamiliar religious practices, as long they did not offend by their savagery (for example, human sacrifices). A distinction was made between private approaches to fundamental questions, such as the origin of the universe and the immortality of the soul, and the civic rituals that forged a practical relationship between a community and the forces of nature on which it depended for its survival. The effectiveness of these rituals hinged on the support of the community as a whole; failure to perform them properly made the gods angry, and divine anger led to natural disasters, which affected entire communities.

From at least the early second century CE, the impulse to persecute Christians came from the cities of the empire rather than from the central imperial government. Stories circulated concerning Christians of the sort that are concocted about people already unpopular for other reasons—stories about orgies, bestiality, and baby eating. However, Christians were persecuted not for what they did but for what they failed to do. Because they believed that worship ought to be offered only to the Summus Deus (Most High God), who created the universe out of nothing, Christians opposed the performance of the sacrifices, festivals, and other rites that, by honoring the public gods, assured the security and prosperity of communities.

Persecution was generally intermittent and local, such as at Lyons, Gaul, in 177 CE or at Alexandria, Egypt, in 202–203, as recorded in Eusebius's *Church History*. At three times in Roman history, the emperors initiated action against Christians right across the empire: under the emperor Decius in 249–251, under Valerian in 257–258, and during the Great Persecution, which started under the emperor Diocletian and his three imperial colleagues, the tetrarchs, on February 23, 303, and continued in most of the western half of the empire until 306 and in most of the eastern half until 313.

Information about the Great Persecution survives in the writings of Lactantius, a Christian professor of Latin rhetoric at the imperial court at Nicomedia (modern-day İzmit) in the province of Bithynia (northwestern Asia Minor), and Eusebius, a Christian scholar. Eusebius felt the effects of the persecution on the church at Caesarea on the coast of Palestine and rewrote his *Church History* several times to keep it up to date with current events. His *Martyrs of Palestine* provides eyewitness accounts of the executions of his Christian comrades.

The mid-third century was marked by instability in the central government of the Roman Empire, caused by foreign threats on both the Rhine and the Danube frontiers and on the frontier with the Persian Empire to the east and also by frequent usurpations of imperial power. Diocletian, who became emperor on November 20, 284, restored equilibrium to the imperial administration. In 293 he divided the imperial authority among a tetrarchy of four emperors, two senior emperors with the title "augustus" (himself in the East and his colleague Maximian in the West) and two junior emperors with the title "caesar" (Constantius I in the West and Galerius in the East). The two caesars were

293

- The Roman emperor Diocletian sets up a tetrarchy (rule of four emperors), with himself and Maximian as senior emperors (augusti) and Constantius I and Maximianus Galerius as junior emperors (caesars).

303

- **February 23** Diocletian and the tetrarchs initiate the Great Persecution of the Christians.

305

- **May 1** Diocletian and Maximian abdicate and are replaced as augusti by Constantius I and Galerius; the two new caesars are Maximinus Daia in the East and Severus in the West.

306

- **July 25** Augustus Constantius I dies at York, and his troops proclaim his son Constantine I an emperor. Constantine controls Britain, Gaul, and Spain and promptly permits Christians in his territories freedom to worship.

- **October 28** Maxentius usurps power in the city of Rome and rules Italy and Latin-speaking North Africa.

seen as dependent on the two augusti. This power structure ensured that there was always a legitimate emperor responsible for each of the empire's important frontiers.

In 298 Galerius won a stunning victory against the Persians, making him a military hero and putting him in a position to exert pressure on Diocletian. Galerius (and his mother) had a particular antipathy to Christianity, so he persuaded Diocletian that the time was right for a solution to the Christian problem. Early in 303 the emperors acted. It seems that they anticipated that the resolution would be relatively simple. A pamphlet was issued "to the Christians," attempting to convince them that they should return to the worship inaugurated by their ancestors. Then, on February 23, 303, during the feast of the Roman god Terminus, the patron and protector of boundaries, orders were given that Christian property and books should be confiscated. In addition, Christian buildings were destroyed, and Christians were forbidden to gather for worship. Anyone appearing in a court of law in any capacity was required to offer incense upon an altar, and those employed in the imperial service were obliged to offer sacrifice or be dismissed. In Britain, Gaul, and Spain, the areas with the fewest Christians, persecution was relatively mild, but in the eastern half of the empire, the so-called Fourth Edict of the persecution, issued in the spring of 304, required people to sacrifice, and many who refused were martyred or imprisoned.

By spring 305 Galerius was able to persuade Diocletian as well as Maximian, the two augusti, to abdicate, leaving the caesars—Galerius in the East and Constantius I in the West—to succeed them as the new augusti. In the eastern half of the empire, Galerius continued the persecution with redoubled ferocity, but the death of the newly elevated Constantius I at York on July 25, 306, was followed by the acclamation as an emperor of his son Constantine I. Constantine promptly stopped all anti-Christian activity in his realms (Britain, Gaul, and Spain). On October 28, Maxentius, son of the former augustus Maximian, set himself up as an emperor in the city of Rome and put a stop to persecution in Italy and Latin-speaking North Africa (present-day Morocco, Algeria, Tunisia, and western Libya). In the eastern Mediterranean basin, however, persecution continued.

During the next six years, extremely complex rivalries between competing emperors developed; at one point there were seven claimants to imperial power, each backed by an army. On November 11, 308, at a conference convened by Galerius, Licinius was made an emperor, with the idea that he should eliminate the usurper Maxentius in Italy, a feat that Licinius never achieved.

It is alleged that Galerius planned to follow the example of Diocletian and abdicate after twenty years as an emperor, in 313. However, Galerius fell ill with a lingering disease. On his deathbed he issued a law that granted clemency to the Christians (and incidentally explained why he had promoted persecution in the first place). This law was published on April 30, 311 at Nicomedia in Asia Minor, the principal residence of emperors since Diocletian.

Nevertheless, the death of Galerius did not resolve the political tension. Maximinus Daia, made caesar in 305, continued to rule the East and added Asia Minor to his territories, and Licinius took over the Balkans. Persecution of Christians resumed. In the autumn of 311 Maximinus began a fresh and severe initiative against the Christians. Many Christians were tried, and church leaders were particularly singled out. Peter, patriarch of Alexandria, was killed in prison. Methodius, a learned bishop in Lycia, was martyred. Lucian of Antioch, a noted biblical scholar, was condemned by Maximinus in person. Petitions from cities in his dominions inspired Maximinus in his determination, and his responses to them echo the cities' concern for their civic rites and the practical benefits that they protected: "For who could be found so senseless or bereft of all intelligence as not to perceive that it is by the benevolent care of the gods that the earth does not refuse the seeds committed to it" (Eusebius, 1928, p. 284). Two such petitions, requesting permission to make Christians conform or harry them out of the land, survive engraved on stone.

In the meantime, Constantine launched an attack on Maxentius, the effective ruler of Italy and western North Africa. On October 28, 312, at the Battle of the Milvian Bridge, Constantine captured the city of Rome and killed Maxentius. Over the winter Constantine wrote to Maximinus "on behalf of the Christians," attributing his success to the favor of the Christian god. Maximinus brought his army westward to Asia Minor, in case of an attack from Licinius's territories in the Balkans. Also, perhaps in the interest of keeping the peace with Licinius and Constantine, Maximinus issued a law, in the form of a rescript to Sabinus, his praetorian prefect (chief minister), grudgingly permitting Christians to practice their religion while expressing the hope that they would see the error of their ways and conform to proper public worship. This may be the rescript referred to in the preamble to the Letter of Licinius.

Licinius, ruling the Balkans, found himself sandwiched between Maximinus in the East and Constantine in the West. He chose alliance with Constantine and rode in the depths of winter across the Julian Alps to Milan in northern Italy to negotiate with Constantine and, in February 313, to marry Constantine's sister. Constantine and Licinius agreed that when Licinius had defeated Maximinus, he would bring an absolute halt to Maximinus's persecution of Christians and restore their property. Licinius appears to have had no personal commitment to Christianity, though he was prepared to agree to the use of blandly monotheistic prayers in his army, no doubt as an element of his alliance with Constantine. The agreement about Christianity that Licinius and Constantine reached at Milan would be carried into effect by the Letter of Licinius, to be issued by Licinius at Nicomedia that June.

In spring 313, with his rear secure, Licinius marched eastward against Maximinus. Confronted by Licinius's army, Maximinus offered further concessions to the Christians, reiterating that they had permission to follow their religion and restoring their property to them. It was too late. Driven across Asia Minor, Maximinus took refuge at Tarsus, where he took poison. Licinius was left in possession of the entire eastern half of the Roman Empire. On June 13, 313,

Time Line

308

- **November 11**
  At a conference convened by Augustus Galerius, Licinius is made an emperor, with a view to his replacing the usurper Maxentius and then ruling Italy and North Africa.

311

- **April 30**
  Galerius's law restoring freedom of worship and property to the Christians is published in Nicomedia.

- **Spring**
  Galerius dies.

- **November**
  Persecution of the Christians resumes in Asia Minor, the Levant, and Egypt under the emperor Maximinus, supported by petitions from local cities.

312

- **October 28**
  Constantine I wins the Battle of the Milvian Bridge outside Rome, giving him sole control of Italy and Latin-speaking North Africa.

- **December**
  In response to a letter from Constantine, Maximinus issues a rescript grudgingly permitting Christians to practice their observances while praising cities keen to sustain traditional civic rites.

313

- **February**
  Licinius meets Constantine at Milan in northern Italy and marries Constantine's sister. Licinius then attacks and eliminates Maximinus, bringing an end to Maximinus's persecution of Christians in the eastern Mediterranean basin.

- **June 13**
  Licinius issues at Nicomedia an imperial letter whose terms he had agreed upon with Constantine at Milan, granting freedom of worship and restitution of property to Christians.

316–317

- Constantine I attacks Licinius for the first time.

324

- Constantine I attacks Licinius again and supplants him, becoming supreme ruler of the entire Roman Empire. Constantine subsequently makes pagan sacrifice illegal, destroys significant pagan temples, and confiscates temple treasure.

335

- **September 14**
  The Church of the Holy Sepulchre at Jerusalem, built on the site of Christ's Crucifixion and Resurrection and financed by Constantine, is consecrated.

at Nicomedia in northwestern Asia Minor, Licinius issued the Letter of Licinius (formerly and erroneously called the Edict of Milan). It granted complete freedom of worship to Christians and restored their churches and other property, granting compensation from imperial funds to those from whom the property had been confiscated.

About the Author

Imperial legislation was generally drafted by an official known as the quaestor of the sacred palace. The Edict of Galerius emanated from the court of Galerius in the Balkans. The Letter of Licinius, whose terms had been agreed between Licinius and Constantine, was drafted in the court of Licinius and published at Nicomedia in northwestern Asia Minor. Both documents survive in slightly differing forms in the Latin pamphlet *On the Deaths of the Persecutors* of the Christian courtier Lactantius and in Greek translation in the *Church History* of Eusebius of Caesarea.

Galerius became caesar in the college of four emperors (the tetrarchy), formed by the emperor Diocletian in 293. His resounding victory over the Persians in 298 enabled him to persuade Diocletian to start the Great Persecution in 303; both Lactantius and Eusebius characterize Galerius as the evil genius behind the Great Persecution. Throughout 303–311 Galerius sustained strong hostility toward Christians. In 311 he was found to be suffering from a debilitating disease, possibly cancer of the bowel, described by his Christian detractors with "singular accuracy and apparent pleasure" (Gibbon, p. 443). Among the documents he issued on his deathbed in the spring of 311 was the Edict of Galerius, a law restoring freedom of worship to Christians. By the autumn, Maximinus, who succeeded him as ruler of the eastern Mediterranean basin, had resumed persecution.

Licinius, an old comrade in arms of Galerius's, was made an emperor in November 308 in the hope that he would supplant the usurper Maxentius, who was then ruling in Italy. After the death of Galerius in 311, Licinius was left in sole control of the Balkans, including the important Danube frontier. Constantine's conquest of Maxentius in October 312 left Licinius uncomfortably placed between Constantine, now controlling everything in the West, and Maximinus, the persecuting emperor ruling the eastern Mediterranean basin. Licinius chose alliance with Constantine and in February 313 married Constantine's sister in the northern Italian city of Milan (Mediolanum). Licinius and Constantine agreed that persecution of the Christians, renewed by Maximinus in his territories in 311, should be brought to an end. This goal was achieved by the Letter of Licinius. In 316 Constantine attacked Licinius; peace was made the following year, increasing the area controlled by Constantine. In 324, partly on the pretext that Licinius was planning to persecute the Christians, Constantine attacked again, besieged Licinius in Nicomedia, and on September 19 forced him to surrender. He was put to death in spring 325.

Constantine I became an emperor on July 25, 306. His first imperial act was to stop persecution of Christians in the territories he controlled (Britain, Gaul, and Spain). In 312 he attacked his neighbor Maxentius, ruler of Italy and North Africa, killing him and capturing the city of Rome. Early in 313 Constantine married his sister to Licinius, emperor ruling in the Balkans. The alliance permitted Licinius to eliminate the persecuting emperor of the East, Maximinus, and to issue the Letter of Licinius; although the letter was issued at Nicomedia by Licinius, it arose from his negotiations at Milan with Constantine. After he overthrew Licinius, Constantine founded Constantinople as a new imperial residence, unencumbered by civic pagan religious ritual. In 325 he summoned Christian bishops to the Council of Nicaea to settle theological controversies, and at some point he made pagan sacrifice illegal. He died in 337 and was buried in the Church of the Holy Apostles in Constantinople. The *Life of Constantine*, written by Eusebius of Caesarea, contains many documents composed by the emperor himself. We know Constantine from his own words to a degree rare for a Roman emperor, and from them Constantine emerges as a Christian conviction politician.

Lactantius (ca. 250–ca. 325) was a professor of Latin rhetoric employed by the emperor Diocletian at his imperial residence at Nicomedia in northwestern Asia Minor and then, in his extreme old age, as tutor to the son of the emperor Constantine. Lactantius spent the Great Persecution writing the *Divine Institutes*, the first comprehensive exposition of Christianity in the Latin language. His pamphlet *On the Deaths of the Persecutors*, written soon after the persecution ended, is a narrative of the age of the Great Persecution and the rise of Constantine, recounted from the point of view of a well-informed, if highly partisan, political insider. It preserves both of the texts translated here in their original Latin form (though with some abbreviation).

Eusebius (ca. 260–339) was a Christian scholar from Caesarea on the coast of Palestine and after the Great Persecution became bishop of the church in that city. He wrote commentaries on the Bible and *Preparation for the Gospel*, which explains in voluminous detail how all that was best in Greco-Roman civilization found its natural fulfillment in Christianity. His brief narrative the *Martyrs of Palestine* gives a harrowing account of the suffering of his Christian comrades during the Great Persecution, including the martyrdom of his own beloved master, the scholar Pamphilus. Eusebius's *Church History*, which he rewrote several times to keep up with the events of his lifetime, remains the most important source for the history of Christianity in its first three centuries. In his old age he wrote the four-book *Life of the Emperor Constantine*, which is particularly valuable because it transcribes numerous contemporary documents. Both of the documents were translated into Greek by Eusebius for incorporation in the *Church History*.

Explanation and Analysis of the Document

These two laws were both intended to bring to an end in the eastern part of the Roman Empire the Great Persecution of Christians, which had begun in February 303 and

Time Line

337

- **May 22**
Constantine I dies and is then buried in the Church of the Holy Apostles at Constantinople.

had ended in much of the western part of the Roman Empire in 306. The first law, an edict issued on his deathbed by Galerius, the original instigator of the persecution, was of little lasting effect, as Maximinus Daia, the emperor who succeeded Galerius in Asia Minor and the Levant, resumed persecution within six months. The second law, an imperial letter issued by Licinius after he had overthrown Maximinus in 313, ended persecution and restored Christian property. This marked an important stage in the process by which Christianity came to supplant traditional public religion in the cities of the Roman Empire.

◆ Edict of Galerius

Having been the prime mover behind the Great Persecution, Galerius, as he lay dying, exercised the clemency that Roman emperors considered an important political virtue by restoring to Christians the right to practice their religion and to build places of worship. Christians had already had that right since 306 in territories that Galerius did not directly control—that is, Britain, Gaul, and Spain (controlled by Constantine) and Italy and North Africa (controlled by Maxentius); indeed, in those western territories Christians had also had restored to them the property confiscated in 303.

PREFACE The preface, giving the full titles of the emperors, is preserved only in the Greek translation of Eusebius. The titles themselves crystallize the constitutional basis for imperial authority and record the names of areas where emperors won significant military victories. It was the custom that edicts should be issued in the names of all emperors who recognized one another's legitimacy even if the motivation for a particular law came from only one of them. Here the three emperors named are Galerius, Constantine, and Licinius. It is possible that Maximinus was originally also named but was omitted by the Christian Eusebius because of his reputation as a persecutor, though Eusebius does claim that Maximinus did not publish the law in his territories, preferring to propagate its message to provincial governors by other means. In manuscripts of the *Church History* that reflect the state of the text as Eusebius had rewritten it after Constantine and Licinius had become hostile to each other, the name and titles of Licinius are also omitted.

PARAGRAPHS 1 AND 2 The surviving text opens by explaining the reasons for the Great Persecution. Few statements of the rationale for persecution survive; this one comes from the prime mover of the Great Persecution himself. Galerius was concerned not with the Christians' beliefs or practices but with their neglect of established religious practice. Earlier laws of the tetrarchs, such as their marriage edict of 295, express similar concerns in similar language. Persecution, then, was meant not to exterminate Christians but to strengthen traditional religion. This intent is apparent in various instances in which persecuting judges expressed joy upon persuading Christians to offer sacrifice to the gods.

Galerius hoped that the Great Persecution would uphold ancient laws and public *disciplina*. (The Latin word *disciplina* has a broader significance than the English word *discipline*; the Latin term refers to all those things that one might be able to learn, so it signifies something like civilization, culture, or way of life.) The emphasis on antiquity is typical of Roman conceptions of public religion. It arises not from unthinking resistance to religious change but from concern that civic religion should maintain a balance among the divine forces that were worshipped (the *pax deorum*, or peace of the gods). Experiment might unbalance such forces and make the gods angry. Popular mythology held that the Trojan War was caused by divine discord; every city was afraid of the anger of the gods, which might at any time disturb the balance of nature, producing direct and dire practical consequences for a community's security and economic survival.

Galerius thought instinctively of religion in terms of public obligations. His concern was not with the private religious opinions or practices but with the effect of Christianity on Roman public *disciplina*. For Galerius the failure of Christians to honor the gods of their ancestors amounted to their making up a set of private laws that could be observed how and when the followers wished. This behavior was something that would be attempted only by people suffering from *stultitia* (stupidity). Accusations of *stultitia* were frequently traded back and forth between Christians and pagans in the written polemic of the Great Persecution; these accusations expressed the mutual incomprehension by both Christians and pagans of each other's positions.

PARAGRAPHS 3–5 In these paragraphs Galerius affirms that many Christians were martyred and that others were put in danger. The exact number of martyrs cannot be known. Local tradition at Alexandria, one of the worst-hit Christian communities, preserved the figure of 660 martyrs, a number that may not be too far from the truth. Most surviving accounts of executions of individual Christians, the so-called Acts of the Martyrs, were written long after the persecutions and owe more to the imagination of the devout than to the facts of history; fewer than a dozen are contemporary with the Great Persecution. However, Eusebius's *Martyrs of Palestine* gives eyewitness accounts of the fate and faithful determination of many of the author's friends; further detail in his *Church History*, in the writings of Lactantius, and in other contemporary texts confirms the truth of Galerius's statement. Christians, as Galerius was reportedly warned by Diocletian, had the habit of dying gladly.

Many Christians survived in fear. Some (including Eusebius) spent time in jail but were not executed, some sought refuge in deserted places, some bribed the authorities, and some sent their friends or slaves to sacrifice for them. Many, including bishops and other clergy, simply sacrificed, and some of these even argued that sacrificing was not incompatible with being a faithful Christian. The Christian Tertullian once remarked that in time of persecution the church behaves as though it has been struck by thunder. From the pagan point of view, it may be said that to some extent persecution worked.

Whatever ulterior motives Galerius may have had for granting freedom of worship to the Christians, his stated motive was a wish to exercise *clementia*, not toleration in any modern sense, but the sort of humane and forbearing conduct toward subjects that was admired by emperors and praised by Roman philosophers, such as Seneca. The edict's effect was to revoke the three original edicts that had precipitated the persecution in 303. Christians could once more gather to worship, own property, and rebuild their churches, and they would no longer be required to sacrifice incense on an altar upon appearing in court. These freedoms were granted on the condition that Christians did nothing contrary to *disciplina*. Christians welcomed the law with enthusiasm, but the clause requiring that they do nothing contrary to *disciplina* was wide open to interpretation by provincial governors.

In the document Galerius gives no indication as to the means by which Christians were to recover property confiscated from them at the beginning of the persecution. Churches had been expressly permitted to own land and buildings, including cemeteries, and to build places of worship ever since 260, when the emperor Gallienus ended the second general persecution, started by his father, Valerian. Only one church building earlier than the rule of Constantine has been thoroughly excavated—the urban villa converted for Christian use in the early third century at Dura-Europus on the Euphrates. It is therefore difficult to say much about the places of worship that were confiscated from Christians in 303.

Laws issued by emperors regularly promised provincial governors that they would receive further instructions concerning implementation. Imperial pronouncements were in Latin; the emperor would direct governors to make them public under a governor's edict, which in Greek-speaking provinces would normally be in Greek. Laws were posted in the public places of cities; in fact, the first martyr of the Great Persecution was the Christian who tore down the persecuting edict posted at Nicomedia in February 303. Sometimes edicts were carved on stone, as were Maximinus Daia's responses to the petitions sent him in 312 by provincial cities seeking his permission to solve their Christian problem. Provincial governors held office for short periods but were able to exercise considerable initiative; hearing serious legal cases formed a large part of their duties.

In paragraph 5 Galerius indicates that he expects Christians to pray to their god for his safety. Since the second century Christians had been assuring emperors that despite their unwillingness to sacrifice incense to the emperor as a god, they were accustomed to pray to their own god for him; it is not clear whether any earlier emperor had taken such assurances seriously.

Wall painting of the martyrdom of saints during the persecution of Diocletian   (© The Trustees of the British Museum)

◆ Letter of Licinius

This document was issued by the emperor Licinius on June 13, 313, at Nicomedia in Bithynia (northwestern Asia Minor). It is an official letter to the governors of the provinces he had recently conquered from the emperor Maximinus. The copies that survive appear to be from Bithynia, preserved in the original Latin by Lactantius, and from Palestine, translated into Greek and preserved by Eusebius. There are minor variations; in particular, the Greek version has an introductory paragraph lacking in the Latin. Comparison with other imperial laws suggests that the original document was probably longer and that the paragraphs that survive are those intended to have the most practical impact.

PARAGRAPH 1 The initial paragraph is found only in the Greek translation of the text preserved in the *Church History* of Eusebius. Its convoluted language expresses the thought that each man should have the ability to make his own decisions concerning divine matters, so Christians should have the freedom to follow their way of life and worship. (The gratuitous addition "and non-Christians" found in some English translations has no manuscript authority.) This assertion about individual freedom may seem obvious to a modern sensibility, but to an ancient ear it would have sounded peculiar. Roman religion was in the first place communal and practical. It was not concerned with feelings or ideas—insofar as it aimed to give an ideological account of the gods, it did so through poetry and mythology rather than through philosophical propositions.

Civic religion ensured that the community at large received the practical and immediate benefits of prosperity and public security by performing rituals, particularly sacrifice, that secured the continuing cooperation of the forces of nature. Alongside the performance of such public obligations, Romans held a wide range of views on ultimate questions and in consequence performed a broad range of private devotions. However, they were not allowed to interfere with the fulfillment of public obligations; it would be difficult for Romans to see how civic religious responsibilities could be matters of individual choice, how, as Galerius complained was the practice of Christians, people could make up laws for themselves. The present document, then, is to be seen not as an assertion of universal religious toleration but rather as a step along the road to the Christianization of the Roman Empire. It is important because it granted leave to Christians to worship and live in their own way and implicitly permitted them not to cooperate in the public observances of their communities.

Licinius refers to an earlier rescript that had accorded freedom of worship to Christians. (A rescript is the response of an emperor to a request for a ruling, whether from one of his officials or from a private person, and it had the force of law.) It is not clear what rescript is referred to here. It may be one that survives in Eusebius's *Church History* and that was issued by Maximinus to Sabinus, his praetorian prefect, in response to the threat to him posed by Constantine and Licinius, only a short while before Licinius defeated him and drove him to suicide. The text of this rescript does indeed concede that if Christians wish to follow their own religion, they should be allowed to do so, while expressing more forcefully the hope that they would

Laws Ending Persecution of Christians in the Roman Empire   **301**

"*Such great willfulness had by some means invaded those same Christians and such great stupidity had occupied them that they would not follow those practices which their own ancestors had perhaps been the first to institute, but they have made laws for themselves which they might observe in accordance with their own will and as it seemed pleasant to them.*"

(Edict of Galerius)

"*Taking into consideration the observance of our most mild clemency and of our sempiternal custom, by which we are accustomed to indulge all men with prompt pardon, we have determined that our indulgence should be extended to these men also.*"

(Edict of Galerius)

"*We believed that, among other matters which we saw would be beneficial for many men, those which ought to be put in order first of all were those by which the reverence of divinity is sustained, so that we should give both to Christians and everyone the free power of following the religion which each wished.*"

(Letter of Licinius)

"*In this way it will come about that divine favour towards us, which we have experienced in such great things, will, as we have defined above, persist prosperously through all time on our achievements together with our public happiness.*"

(Letter of Licinius)

return to the worship of the civic gods. As Licinius's army advanced against him, Maximinus issued a further law affirming Christians' freedom to worship, allowing the building of churches, restoring Christian property, and blaming the suffering of Christians on overzealous provincial governors. It is easy to believe, therefore, that the rescript to Sabinus, issued by a defeated and dead emperor and confused by Maximinus's subsequent edict, might well have given rise to the "many and various conditions" to which Licinius refers.

PARAGRAPH 2 Licinius states clearly the circumstances that brought about the law he was about to promulgate. After Constantine had defeated Maxentius at the Battle of

the Milvian Bridge in 312 and thereby added Italy and North Africa to his territories, there were only three emperors left: Constantine in the West, Licinius in the Balkans, and Maximinus in the eastern Mediterranean basin. Licinius allied himself with Constantine, marrying Constantine's sister. Licinius was then free to assault Maximinus, who fled across Asia Minor to Tarsus. At Tarsus, Maximinus took poison, leaving Licinius in control of the eastern half of the empire.

Part of the agreement between Constantine and Licinius at Milan had been that Licinius would bring the Great Persecution to a final end. Constantine had been keen to succor the Christians ever since his accession in

306. Licinius, on the other hand, had no particular commitment to Christianity, though he was willing to have his army offer anodyne invocations to the Most High God. The letter that Licinius issued is therefore the result of an agreement between two emperors with substantially different interests. Any appearance it may have of evenhandedness cannot be separated from the probability that it is the product of compromise. The statement, however, that divine patronage was essential to prosperity and political success would likely have been endorsed by any Roman, pagan, or Christian.

PARAGRAPH 3 The statement in this paragraph that individuals should have a free choice in matters of religion has a misleadingly modern appearance. Romans had long held a broad range of philosophical views and practiced various private cults, which did not interfere with the performance of their public religious duties. Permission to practice private religion of one's choice was not the point at issue; the concern was permission to follow a religion at odds with established civic religious practices. Christians believed that only their god deserved worship. They knew that many non-Christian philosophers thought that there was only one god, but the Christians also believed that only they knew how to offer him worship. It is the favor of the Christian god, obtained through such worship, that Licinius says he wants to enjoy. Beneath the rhetoric of free private choice lies a tendency toward Christianizing public religion; by the end of the fourth century, similar rhetoric about freedom and diversity of religion was being employed by those attempting to sustain traditional public paganism.

PARAGRAPHS 4–6 We no longer have details of the stipulations that had been given to governors to implement the persecution and that Licinius here rescinds. Licinius, like Galerius before him, acknowledges the terrors that persecution aroused among Christians, though Lactantius claims that martyrs were able to endure suffering because they feared only God. Paragraphs 5 and 6 stipulate that the new liberties accorded to Christians must not interfere with the rights of others. It was not until after Constantine achieved sole supreme power in 324 that steps were taken to destroy traditional civic religion.

PARAGRAPHS 7–9 Paragraphs 7 through 9 order confiscated Christian communal property to be returned and arrangements to be made to compensate those who had acquired it during the persecution. Claimants were directed to apply to the office of the *vicarius*, a senior official who oversaw a grouping of provinces known as a *diocesis*. This provision covered all church property, not just buildings where Christians met for worship, and included Christian cemeteries, which were often the focus for the growing cult of the martyrs. Churches as corporate bodies had been allowed to own land and buildings since the law of Gallienus ending the Valerianic Persecution in 260 but had lost their property at the start of the Great Persecution in 303. Accounts of some local confiscations in North Africa at the start of the Great Persecution are preserved in a collection of documents called the Optatan Appendix, but most details of the official procedures (*forma*) have been lost.

PARAGRAPHS 10–12 This exercise of imperial *clementia* was intended to foster public peace and also to ensure divine favor for the emperors. Several surviving documents written by Constantine attribute his success to the favor of the Christian god. The Letter of Licinius, unlike the laws of the pagan Maximinus, makes no mention of divine favor for individual cities.

Audience

The Edict of Galerius is preserved in two versions, the original Latin in Lactantius's *On the Deaths of the Persecutors* and a Greek translation in Eusebius's *Church History*. It is probable that the former copy is the one that was posted at Nicomedia in Bithynia and that the latter is the one that was sent to Palestine. The document appears to have been published only in provinces directly controlled by Galerius, namely the eastern half of the empire. The Letter of Licinius is also preserved in two versions. The original Latin text in Lactantius's *On the Deaths of the Persecutors* is the copy sent to the provincial governor of Bithynia. The Greek translation incorporated in Eusebius's *Church History* presumably depends on the copy sent to the governor of Palestine. The law had practical effect in the territories that Licinius took from Maximinus Daia—Asia Minor, the Levant, and Egypt. Both laws follow common practice by requiring provincial governors to publicize them under a governor's publishing edict.

Impact

The Edict of Galerius had very limited impact. Christians had enjoyed liberty since 306 in the territories of Constantine (Britain, Gaul, and Spain) and probably also in those controlled by Maxentius (Italy and Latin-speaking Africa). The edict therefore affected only the Balkans and the eastern Mediterranean, where Christians initially welcomed it; Eusebius describes the lights burning in the churches that Eastertide. Within six months Maximinus Daia had renewed persecution in Asia Minor, the Levant, and Egypt.

The Letter of Licinius granted freedom of worship to Christians and restored their property, including churches, awarding appropriate compensation from imperial funds. Those in charge of pagan oracles that had inspired the persecutors were rounded up and tortured until they admitted that their oracles were fraudulent. However, the letter did nothing to diminish the practice of traditional civic religion; many cities remained obstinately attached to their customary practices into the fifth century. Christians, meanwhile, built churches and resumed worship. Lactantius's triumphant pamphlet *On the Deaths of the Persecutors*, glorying in the defeat and death of emperors who presumed to persecute Christians, was written between 313 and 315, soon after the Christian triumphs that it chronicles.

The Letter of Licinius was a clear expression of imperial favor for the Christians, but it did not complete the process of the Christianization of the Roman Empire. In 316 Licinius was attacked by Constantine, who took his Balkan territory. In 324 Constantine attacked again, partly on the pretext that Licinius was preparing to persecute Christians. Licinius was deposed and subsequently killed.

Between 324, when he defeated Licinius, and his death in 337, Constantine promoted Christianity extensively. One Eastertide he preached a sermon, which survives, to the Christians at his court, attributing his success to the protection of the Christian god. A new imperial residence was founded at Constantinople (modern-day Istanbul), a city whose public life was dominated not by traditional civic religion but by the emperor and the buildings and practice of Christianity. A general council, attended by some 250 bishops and by Constantine himself, was convened at Nicaea in 325 to agree upon a creed defining the essentials of Christian beliefs. Pagan sacrifice was forbidden, and several important temples were closed. The Church of the Holy Sepulchre was constructed on the site of the principal Roman temple at Jerusalem.

Despite such active imperial patronage, Christianity did not become the public religion of the Roman Empire overnight. Public religion in the Roman Empire had always been a concern primarily of individual cities. By the same token, the Christianization of the empire took place city by city, as individual communities incorporated Christianity into their communal lives, their civic calendars, and their public architecture. In some cities the process was swift: By 361 at Caesarea Mazaca, Cappadocia, in central Asia Minor (present-day Kayseri in Turkey), there was only one

temple left but numerous shrines to Christians martyrs. By contrast, in 386 at Carrhae (modern-day Haran on the Turkish-Syrian frontier), the only resident Christian was the city's unfortunate bishop. What the Letter of Licinius and Constantine's subsequent patronage of the church achieved was to ensure that the current of affairs would henceforth flow in the Christian direction.

Further Reading

■ **Articles**

Barnes, Timothy D. "Constantine and Christianity: Ancient Evidence and Modern Interpretation." *Zeitschrift für antikes Christentum* 2 (1998): 274–294.

Mitchell, S. "Maximinus and the Christians in a.d. 312: A New Latin Inscription." *Journal of Roman Studies* 78 (1988): 105–124.

■ **Books**

Barnes, Timothy D. *Constantine and Eusebius.* Cambridge, Mass.: Harvard University Press, 1981.

———. *Early Christianity and the Roman Empire.* London: Variorum Reprints, 1984.

———. *From Eusebius to Augustine: Selected Papers 1982–1993.* Aldershot, U.K.: Variorum Reprints, 1994.

Beard, Mary, et al. *Religions of Rome.* 2 vols. Cambridge, U.K.: Cambridge University Press, 1998.

Questions for Further Study

1. Religion historically has often served as the "glue" that held the social order together, uniting people in a set of common beliefs and practices. To what extent did religion serve such a purpose in the Roman Empire? How successful was it in doing so?

2. Defend or refute the following statement: Laws ending the persecution of Christians were less the result of a new tolerance for Christian belief and more the result of political infighting and rivalries within the Roman Empire.

3. Why were Christians persecuted in the Roman Empire prior to the laws ending persecution? What did authorities, particularly in the empire's cities, find offensive about Christians and Christianity?

4. Later Christians wrote documents that belonged to a genre called hagiography. This type of writing, literally, was about Christian saints, but the term also connoted the development of legends and stories designed to inspire Christians by focusing on the miracles and martyrdom of early Christian saints. To what extent did the persecution of Christians in the Roman Empire contribute to the development of hagiography and to Christian legend?

5. The Roman Empire distinguished between private religious beliefs and public religious practices. To what extent does this distinction between public and private in matters of religion continue to be debated in the modern world?

Corcoran, Simon. *The Empire of the Tetrarchs: Imperial Pronouncements and Government AD 284–324*, rev. ed. Oxford, U.K.: Clarendon Press, 2000.

De Ste. Croix, G. E. M. *Christian Persecution, Martyrdom, and Orthodoxy*, eds. Michael Whitby and Joseph Streeter. Oxford, U.K.: Oxford University Press, 2006.

Eusebius. *Eusebius, Bishop of Caesarea: The Ecclesiastical History and the Martyrs of Palestine*, trans. Hugh J. Lawlor and John E. L. Oulton. 2 vols. London: Society for the Promotion of Christian Knowledge, 1928.

———. *Life of Constantine* , trans. Averil Cameron and Stuart G. Hall. Oxford, U.K.: Oxford University Press, 1999.

Gibbon, Edward. *Decline and Fall of the Roman Empire*, vol. 1, ed. J. B. Bury. London: Methuen, 1909.

Lactantius. *Lactantius: De Mortibus Persecutorum*, ed. and trans. J. L. Creed. Oxford, U.K.: Clarendon Press, 1984.

Twomey, D. Vincent, and Mark Humphries, eds. *The Great Persecution: The Proceedings of the Fifth Patristic Conference, Maynooth, 2003*. Portland, Ore.: Four Courts Press, 2009.

—Oliver Nicholson

Laws Ending Persecution of Christians in the Roman Empire

Editor's Note: The text of the two edicts is translated from Lactantius. The paragraph numbers are those given to the text of Lactantius. Additional material present in the text surviving in Eusebius is added in square brackets thus: [...]. The more significant of Eusebius's variations are indicated in square brackets preceded by a shilling stroke thus: [/...]

Edict of Galerius

[Emperor Caesar Galerius Valerius Maximianos, Unconquered Augustus, Pontifex Maximus, Germanicus Maximus, Egyptiacus Maximus, Thebaicus Maximus, Sarmaticus Maximus five times, Persicus Maximus twice, Carpicus Maximus six times, Armenicus Maximus, Medicus Maximus, Adiabenicus Maximus, in the 20th tenure of Tribunician Power, in the 19th year as Emperor, the 8th as Consul, Father of the Fatherland, Proconsul; and Emperor Caesar Flavius Valerius Constantinus, Pious, Fortunate, Unconquered Augustus, Pontifex Maximus, Holder of Tribunician Power, in the 5th year as Emperor, Consul, Father of the Fatherland, Proconsul; and Emperor Caesar Valerius Licinianus Licinius, Pious, Fortunate, Pontifex Maximus, in the 4th tenure of Tribunician Power, in the 3rd year as Emperor, Consul, Father of the Fatherland, Proconsul, to their provincials, Greeting !]

(1) Among other measures which we are always laying down for the benefit and usefulness of the public good, we had indeed previously wished to amend all things in accordance with the ancient laws and the public *disciplina* of the Romans and to make provision that even the Christians who had abandoned the way of the life (*secta*) of their ancestors should return to their right minds.

(2) For such great willfulness had by some means invaded those same Christians and such great stupidity had occupied them that they would not follow those practices which their own ancestors had perhaps been the first to institute, but they have made laws for themselves which they might observe in accordance with their own will and as it seemed pleasant to them and they have gathered various people together in various places.

(3) At length when our command along these lines had been issued, many were subjected to danger and many also were struck down [/were afflicted by various deaths].

(4) Since many, however, persevered in their determination [/senselessness] and we saw that they did not offer to the Gods the worship and religious duty they owed them nor reverence the God of the Christians, taking into consideration the observance of our most mild clemency and of our sempiternal custom, by which we are accustomed to indulge all men with prompt pardon, we have determined that our indulgence should be extended to these men also, so that they may once more be Christians and may construct their meeting places [/houses in which they used to meet], provided they do nothing contrary to *disciplina*.

(5) We shall signify through another letter to governors what they should do. In consequence, in accordance with this our indulgence they will be [/are] obliged to pray to their God for our safety and that of the state, and for their own, so that from every side the state may be preserved unharmed and that they may be able to live free from care in their homes.

Letter of Licinius

[As we have for a long time been considering that liberty of worship is not to be denied, but that the capacity to take care of divine matters should be given to the reason and wish of each man, in accordance with his own resolution, we have urged the Christians that they should observe the faith of their way of life and worship. But considering that many and various conditions appear clearly to have been imposed upon that rescript in which this same capacity was accorded to them, it is, all things considered, possible that certain of them within a short time were repelled from this observance.]

(2) When under fortunate auspices both I Constantine Augustus and also I Licinius Augustus had come together at Milan and were holding in discussion all affairs which have to do with advantages and the public security [/usefulness], we believed that, among other matters which we saw would be benefi-

cial for many men, those which ought to be put in order first of all were those by which the reverence of divinity is sustained, so that we should give both to Christians and everyone the free power of following the religion which each wished, so that whatever there is of divinity in the heavenly place should be able to be placated and propitious to us and to all those who are established under our power.

(3) We have therefore believed [/decreed] with salutary and correct reasoning that this policy should be entered upon, that we should consider that the opportunity [/capacity] should be denied to no one who pays attention either to Christian observance or to that religion which he might feel was most suited to himself, so that the most high divinity, whose religion we obey with free minds, may be able to offer to us his accustomed favour and benevolence.

(4) Therefore it is appropriate that Your Dedicatedness should know that it has pleased us that all stipulations about the name of the Christians which were contained in documents previously given to your office should be entirely set aside, and that those things which seemed thoroughly sinister and alien to our clemency should be removed, and that now freely and in simplicity each one of those who exercise the same wish to observe the religion of the Christians may hasten to observe that same thing, setting aside any anxiety or molestation of them.

(5) We have considered these things should be fully signified to Your Solicitude so that by them you might know that we have given to these same Christians free and absolute opportunity to cultivate their religion.

(6) Since you thoroughly see that this has been granted to them by us, Your Dedicatedness understands that for others also open and free capacity for their religion or observance is granted in accordance with the peacefulness of our times, so that each should have free permission in worshipping what he has chosen. This has been done by us so that nothing should seem to be taken away by us either in respect of honour or in respect of religion.

(7) In addition we have decided that this should be decreed concerning the body corporate (*persona*) of the Christians: that if some people in an earlier time seem to have bought, either from our fisc or from anyone else, the same places where they had previously been accustomed to meet, concerning which also a certain procedure (*forma*) had before now been defined (*comprehensa*) in letters given to your office, they should restore the same places to the Christians without payment and without any request for a price, setting aside all obstruction and ambiguity.

(8) Those also who obtained them as a gift, shall similarly return the same to the Christians as fast as possible. But those who have bought or who have received as a gift, if they should seek something from our benevolence, let them make a request of the Vicarius, so that there may be relief (*consulatur*) for them from him through our clemency. All these things should be handed over to the body of the Christians immediately through your mediation and without delay.

(9) And because the same Christians are found to have had not only those places at which they were accustomed to meet, but also other property belonging by right to their body, that is to the churches, not to individual persons, you shall order all these things by the law which we have defined above to be returned to the same Christians , that is to their body corporate and to their assemblies, without any ambiguity or controversy whatsoever, observing however the above-mentioned proviso, that those who restore

Glossary

clementia	mercy
rescript	a Roman emperor's response to a legal petition
Tribunician Power	power to protect the people from the aristocrats, though by the late third century it had become a formal title indicating one of the underlying constitutional sources of imperial authority
Your Dedicatedness … Your Solicitude	Maximinus, emperor of the Eastern Roman Empire, who shared power with Licinius after the death of Galerius

the same without charge, as we have said, may hope for indemnity from our benevolence.

(10) In all these affairs you will be obliged to offer to the aforesaid body corporate of the Christians your most effective co-operation, so that our command may be completed as fast as possible, in order that through our *clementia* there may be solace for the public peace in this matter.

(11) In this way it will come about that divine favour towards us, which we have experienced in such great things, will, as we have defined above, persist prosperously through all time on our achievements together with our public happiness.

(12) In order that the principle of this ordinance and of our benevolence may be able to come to the knowledge of all, it is appropriate that you post up this document everywhere and that you bring it thoroughly to the knowledge of all, with your proclamation prefixed to it, in order that the ordinance of this our benevolence should not be hidden.

THEODOSIAN CODE

"Bloody spectacles displease Us amid public peace and domestic tranquility."

Overview

The period of history from the revival of the Roman Empire under Diocletian in the late third century until the establishment of Islam in the seventh century is known as late antiquity. This era is far better documented than earlier ages. A huge range of actual late antique documents exists (in contrast to the handful of texts, such as the letters of Cicero and Pliny the Younger and the *Res gestae divi Augusti* (*Deeds of the Divine Augustus*), that survive from the earlier empire unfiltered by the work of such literary historians as Suetonius or Tacitus). The Theodosian Code was meant as a major reform of the system of law in the Roman Empire. This was needed especially to support the faltering Western Roman Empire. It was written by the combined efforts of the legal bureaucracy of Theodosius II's court in Constantinople. The code reveals the actual operation of the Roman Empire in the communication between the center and the periphery on day-to-day matters of government and law, with more than twenty-five hundred imperial rescripts issued between 313 and 437. At the same time, the code is one of the elementary bases for the system of Roman law that is still used as the foundation for jurisprudence throughout the world outside the United States and the Commonwealth.

Context

The Theodosian Code is a document of late antiquity, a period that is characterized by the transformation of the Roman Empire. Beginning with a serious plague during the reign of Marcus Aurelius in the mid-second century, Rome was put under increasing external and internal stresses that nearly destroyed it. In 235, following a mutiny of the army that resulted in the murder of the emperor Severus Alexander, Rome suffered a succession crisis that led to civil war as rival candidates vied to become emperor. Although this situation had happened before and had been quickly resolved, the disorder now became more serious and threatened to partition the empire. At the same time, raids from Germanic tribes into the empire became an increasing

problem as the Germans themselves were put under pressure by migrations of new groups (Huns and so-called White Huns) from the East as part of a general migration out of inner Asia that would continue until the Mongol conquests of the Middle Ages. Order was eventually restored by Diocletian, although the damage done to the economy of the empire, particularly in the West, where cities began to be depopulated, could not easily be repaired.

Diocletian established the tetrarchy, a system by which the Western Roman Empire and the Eastern Roman Empire were each ruled by a senior and a junior emperor (called Augustus and Caesar), each of whom could expect to become the supreme ruler of the empire in turn. Although this system was meant to stabilize the succession, civil war again became frequent in the century after Diocletian. Constantine's granting tolerance to Christianity in 313 may also have been intended to stabilize the empire (as was his foundation of the eastern capital of Constantinople); instead, it led to virtual civil war on a city-by-city basis as the suppression of traditional religion was accomplished through devastating riots. The pressure from the Germans and other invaders (Huns now attacked the empire directly) became more intense, and in 376 a Roman army was defeated by the Visigoths deep within the empire at Adrianople (present-day Edirne). After that loss it was impossible to expel the Germans. Instead, Germanic tribes were allowed into the empire in exchange for protecting the border. This disastrous policy led to more raiding, including the sack of Rome itself by the Visigoths in 410.

In 437 the two halves of the Roman Empire were reunited briefly by the marriage alliance between the western and eastern emperors, with Valentinian III marrying the daughter of Theodosius II. By this time, however, much of the Western Roman Empire was already in the hands of independent Germanic kingdoms, the Visigoths in Spain and much of France and the Vandals in North Africa by 439. In 410 Britain had simply been abandoned as indefensible. Theodosius tried to support the Western Empire, paying tribute to the Huns to prevent them from attacking it and sending forces in the 440s for the failed attempt to reconquer North Africa. The Theodosian Code, though put in force in the East as well, was meant to reform the crumbling legal system of the West.

313
- **June**
  Constantine I consolidates his power as emperor in the West, beginning the era from which the code draws its decrees.

401
- **April 10**
  Theodosius II is born.

408
- **May 1**
  Theodosius II becomes ruler of the Eastern Roman Empire.

429
- **March 26**
  Theodosius II orders the establishment of a commission to draw up a new law code based on imperial rescripts.

435
- **December 20**
  A second editorial commission begins work to finalize the code.

437
- **March 16**
  The last law is included in the code.

- **October**
  The marriage of Theodosius II's daughter, Eudocia, to the western emperor Valentinian III reunifies the Roman Empire.

Theodosius II took a special interest in legal matters and as early as 429 had ordered the compilation of imperial rescripts from the last century. In 435, as negotiations were under way for the reunification of the two halves of the empire through the marriage of Theodosius's daughter to the western emperor Valentinian, Theodosius renewed his efforts and ordered a second commission to draw up the document that became the Theodosian Code. This document, presented by the praetorian prefect Faustus to the Roman Senate on December 25, 438, was a tremendous boon to the western administration and became one of the main foundations of medieval law. However, nothing could prevent the collapse of the Western Empire. Rome was sacked by the Vandals in 455. After this attack, the Ostrogoths were allowed to settle in Pannonia (roughly modern-day Hungary) and were put in charge of the security of Italy. In 476 the Ostrogothic king Odoacer put the child Romulus Augustulus, last Roman emperor of the Western Empire, under house arrest and declared himself king of Italy. Although the Eastern Roman, or Byzantine, Empire made occasional attempts to reconquer it, the Western Roman Empire ceased to exist. Population declined, and inhabitants abandoned the cities for the countryside. Local subsistence replaced trade as the basis of the economy.

About the Author

The composition of the Theodosian Code was a long process stretching over a century, incorporating the work of many different writers; it was based on the rescripts issued and composed by the reigning emperors between Constantine and Theodosius II and Valentinian III and their bureaucrats. The code exists because of the edict that Theodosius II gave on March 26, 429, ordering its compilation. The issuance of this order was not an isolated event, however. Whereas most emperors achieved their rank from success on the battlefield, Theodosius inherited his title when he was seven years old and managed to retain his position until adulthood. He was educated as an intellectual rather than a soldier. Like the emperors, high-ranking civil servants usually had a military background, but Theodosius increasingly tended to appoint lawyers as quaestors and praetorian prefects. These officials, in turn, insisted on having the law of the empire clarified, and Theodosius reacted to their concerns by ordering the compilation of the code.

The individual laws in the Theodosian Code consist of imperial rescripts, or documents that originated when the emperor was asked by a magistrate to clarify a point of law. A rescript is an imperial response with the full force of law. Although all rescripts were issued on the responsibility of at least one emperor, the actual wording of the rescripts was left to one of the quaestors working at the imperial court. The compilation of the code was assigned to two separate committees of quaestors and other bureaucrats, one in 429 and one in 435. According to Book I of the code, the committee of 429 included two men named Antiochus as well as Theodorus, Eudicius, Eusebius, Johannes,

Eubulus, and Apelles; the committee of 435 included Antiochus, Eubulus, Maximus, Superantius, Martyrius, Alypius, Sebastianus, Apollodorus, Theodorus, Eron, Maximinus, Epigenes, Diodorus, Procopius, Erotius, Neoterius, and others whose names are no longer known. These officials edited the rescripts and added the interpretations that are appended to many of the responses.

Explanation and Analysis

The imperial rescripts of the Theodosian Code are divided into sixteen books by subjects, each one covering such topics as the civil service (Book I), criminal law (Book IX), or church-state relations (Book XVI). Each book is further divided into several titles of closely related laws, and then each rescript is presented individually (in longer rescripts the paragraphs are numbered), preceded by the name of the emperor who issued it and followed by the date and location of its issuance. Sometimes this information is followed by an interpretation added by the bureaucratic committee members who compiled the code. The code fills more than five hundred pages. The excerpts presented here, drawn from Books I, V, VI, IX, XIV, and XV, are representative of the scope of the code.

◆ Book I

The rescripts in this section relate to the code itself. The first four establish basic legal principles: Ignorance of the law is not a defense, and the rescripts do not have retroactive force against crimes committed before the code was enacted. Another principle reflects the greatest difference between Roman law and the common law system used in the United States: Each case is decided based on the relevant laws interpreted by the guidance of the rescripts of the code; a legal decision in one case has no applicability to other cases. Thus new rulings are made not on the basis of precedent but according to governmental policy.

The remaining rescripts pertain to the history and function of the code. They give the history of the code arising in the work of the legal bureaucracy in Constantinople, describing how it derived from the work of the bureaucracy in charge of legal affairs in Constantinople. Rescript 5 is the initial order for the composition of the code based on the model of the older Hermogenian and Gregorian codes. The committee of bureaucrats assigned the work was ordered to compile all rescripts from the time period going back to Constantine, retaining even those that no longer had legal force and authorizing the committee to edit, rewrite, and interpret the rescripts for the sake of clarity. Rescript 6 is the order for the second committee to finish the work of compiling and publishing the code.

◆ Book V

Titles 9 and 10 of Book V discuss the treatment of newborns, including the practices of exposing newborn children and purchasing newborns. Poor families sometimes exposed their children—that is, abandoned them in the

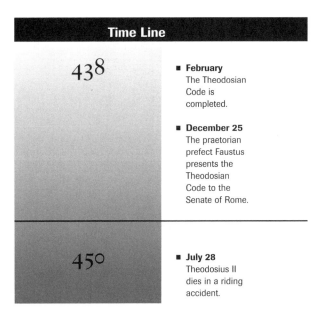

Time Line

438

■ **February**
The Theodosian Code is completed.

■ **December 25**
The praetorian prefect Faustus presents the Theodosian Code to the Senate of Rome.

450

■ **July 28**
Theodosius II dies in a riding accident.

wilderness because they could not afford to feed them. Title 9 addresses the issue of exposed children, explaining that abandoned children could be taken by other families and raised as the family's own children or as slaves. Title 10 deals specifically with purchasing newborns and the conditions under which an original owner or a father could recover a child who had been purchased. Like exposed newborns, purchased newborns could be reared as children or as slaves and were valued monetarily as slaves.

An interesting feature of the later rescript of Honorius and Theodosius I in Title 9 reveals that in the Christianizing empire, just as bishops were responsible for keeping baptismal records, a person had to register with a bishop the custody of an exposed child he had received. This practice effectively meant that the trade in infant slaves could be conducted only by Christians; if a slave owner who still practiced the traditional "pagan" religion (and therefore would not be recognized by an episcopal court) was challenged by the parent of an adult slave bought in infancy, he would have no proof to offer the court of his legal rights. This practice is one of innumerable ways in which non-Christians were disenfranchised in late antiquity as part of the imperial policy of spurring the complete conversion of the empire. Early Christians were not at all opposed to the institution of slavery (as is evident in Paul's Epistle to Philemon), for they considered servile status irrelevant to salvation.

◆ Book VI

The three rescripts (13–15) quoted from Title 2 of Book VI deal with the problem of taxing the Roman aristocracy, a class defined at its highest levels by membership in the Senate of either Rome or Constantinople. Rescript 13 states that senators must declare their land holdings or have them confiscated ("vindicated to the fisc") and that a senator's place of residence would be reported to the tax-collecting bureaucracy ("the palatine bureaus"). It is an

Portrait of Theodosius II (© Bettmann/CORBIS)

almost desperate plea that senators pay their taxes; the rescript would not have been issued if the senators usually did so. The fact that they did not led to the stipulation in the same rescript that senators pay an "alternative minimal tax" of two *folles* (large gold coins weighing a pound each, at a time when gold was worth relatively far more than it is now). Even this document concedes, however, that senators were often exempt from taxation in return for their government service.

Aristocrats constantly bartered with the central government to escape their taxes in return for their political support. Rescript 14 is typical of the rest of the rescripts of the book, establishing special circumstances for exemption from the tax on land (a glebe is a piece of land) for a small group of senators who must have lobbied for the concession. Rescript 15 declares that members of the Senate ("Council of the most August"), even if they successfully argued their poverty against the minimum tax of two *folles*, must pay seven *solidi* (just less than half of a *folles*), an amount established ten years earlier. This stipulation shows that aristocrats and their lawyers immediately began to work against any new efforts to tax their wealth. One of the increasingly severe problems faced by the Roman Empire in late antiquity was the concentration of more and more land—the main means of producing wealth in the agricultural economy of the empire—in aristocratic hands, as aristocrats were in large measure exempt from taxation. Under those circumstances, it proved impossible to meet the ever-rising defense budgets necessary to protect the empire from the barbarians pressuring it, eventually resulting in the fall of the Western Roman Empire.

◆ **Book IX**

Title 1 concerns the emperor's accusations of wrongdoings against his own officials. "Provincials" in this rescript refers to provincial governors, and "palatines" refers to bureaucrats in the central administration; "inscriptions" were written, rather than verbal, accusations. This rescript is essentially a whistle-blower law that encouraged private citizens to come forward and make accusations of corruption against government officials. People who made such accusations could receive rewards in the form of social or political advancement as well as a cash payment. Such a law was necessary for the proper running of the bureaucracy, where officials charged with purely administrative duties could easily abuse their powers if their decisions went unchecked. Therefore, the rescript itself says very little about the level of corruption, but the fact that the emperor undertook to hear such cases himself shows that corruption was considered a serious matter and that such cases must have been brought forward only rarely.

Titles 4 and 5 interpret laws relating to the person of the emperor himself. Of course, plotting to assassinate or depose an emperor would be a serious crime (high treason), but Title 4 goes much further, making it a crime merely to criticize the emperor. Even suggesting that times are bad could be construed as an insult to the emperor because he was ultimately held responsible for the condition of the empire. The Roman concept was quite different from the modern concern for freedom of speech; the person of the emperor, who was also high priest of the state religion (and in Christian times was held superior to all bishops and patriarchs, including the bishop of Rome) was considered sacred, so speaking against him was sacrilege. This rescript gave emperors absolute discretion about how they could construe any offensive remarks, even jokes. This provision was in line with the varied practice of earlier emperors. Some, such as Tiberius or Domitian, took even the slightest remark against their persons very seriously, while others, such as Trajan, refused to investigate such accusations as a sign of their respect for liberty. The language of this rescript seems self-contradictory: Although it virtually promises that the emperor will overlook such accusations, it nevertheless instructs people to turn them over to the emperor for his personal investigation.

Title 5 concerns the use of torture in the investigation of high treason. Aristocrats, who were ordinarily immune to torture, could be tortured during investigation into an accusation of treason. Witnesses, however, who tried to inform against those in authority over them would not be heard but rather would be executed themselves. The Romans believed, falsely, that judicial torture was a guarantee of the truth of testimony. Nevertheless, witnesses in criminal cases could be tortured under Roman law, unless they were of aristocratic status. This rescript makes an exception in cases involving high treason. However, it adds that slaves or freedmen who reported their masters or patrons (their former masters who maintained a degree of legal control over them), even for high treason, should not be heard but should simply be executed. A slave's betrayal of a master was seen as tantamount to a son's betrayal of his father, so such accusations were not permitted. This general law applied to any accusation made against a master or a patron, and Constantine specifically put it in force in the case of high treason. As the political situation became more chaotic and treason trials grew more common, however, later emperors rescinded this provision and allowed slaves to testify against their masters, but only in a case of treason.

Title 14 relates to ancient laws against murder. The first two rescripts clarify certain points of interpretation. The first gives the interpretation that killing a child was to be considered murder, a specification that would hardly have been needed unless exposure, which was legal, did not entail a serious risk of killing the exposed infant. By late antiquity exposure had largely become a euphemism for selling an infant into slavery, but in a case in which a child was actually exposed (abandoned in the forest or on the roadside), the likely outcome of death would not constitute murder in the eyes of the law. This rescript also rescinded the traditional right of Roman fathers to punish their children with execution, as Brutus, the hero of the early history of Rome, had done when he discovered his son in a treasonous plot, a right that had in any case long fallen into desuetude. The second rescript granted the right of self-defense against brigands, even in cases in which soldiers had taken to brigandage (another sign of the collapse of state authority in the West).

The third rescript gives a much more extended interpretation. It equates conspiracy to assassinate a government official with the actual murder. The penalty was execution together with confiscation of all the guilty party's property. (The term *fisc* refers to the state treasury.) The phrase "struck down with the sword" alludes to execution, usually by beheading, as opposed to crucifixion, the form of execution used only for members of the lowest social classes. A son of the guilty person was therefore not only disinherited but also disenfranchised. A daughter of the guilty was to inherit only from her mother's dowry, a piece of property given by a father to his daughter at the time of her marriage and controlled by her husband but legally the possession of his wife. The rest of the dowry would also be confiscated, leaving the widow of the guilty party dependent on her father or her brothers.

Title 15 discusses parricide, the murder of a parent by a child. In the Roman view, parricide went beyond mere crime and overturned the entire natural order. Accordingly, anyone guilty of such an act was to be executed by being sewn into a sack full of serpents and drowned. This method of execution was symbolic, indicating that anyone guilty of parricide had passed out of the human race and become a viper.

◆ **Book XIV**

Title 9 of this book addresses aspects of the state-run higher education system of the Roman Empire, comparable to the modern-day university system. The interest of the state in providing education was to produce well-trained civil servants. Consequently, the first rescript outlines the responsibilities of students to the government, including registering the change in their place of residence; the

rescript also provides guidelines for student behavior. One way to read this rescript is as a protection for future civil servants from their own youthful impulsiveness, which might come back to haunt them with scandal in later years.

The second rescript provided for the maintenance of the state-owned libraries that supported higher studies, and the third regulated professors employed by the state. The state paid the salaries of a certain number of professors in various subjects, not only in Rome and Constantinople but also in other cities, such Athens (especially in philosophy) and Beirut (particularly in law). The third rescript established the number of professorships the empire supported in the two capital cities and prohibited their holders from supplementing their income by taking additional private students, as the point of the state salaries was to make teaching accessible to all students. There were, however, many private teachers in the university towns, and the state-supported professors were generally promoted from their ranks.

◆ **Book XV**

Title 12 documents the efforts of the Christian emperors to outlaw the gladiatorial shows popular throughout the empire. When this proved impossible because of public demand, the emperors attempted to regulate them. The last rescript forbids senators from employing gladiators. The gladiatorial shows served an important social function. Provided by the state, they enhanced the popularity of emperors, and they were also part of the state welfare system; entry to the games was free, and free food was provided to the audiences. The Christian emperors, however, opposed the games, not only because they involved murder but also because the execution of Christians had in earlier times sometimes been part of the spectacle. Accordingly, Constantine outlawed these practices in the first rescript in Title 12. (Gladiators were generally obtained by promoters from the ranks of condemned criminals). A generation later, Constantine's son Constantius II had not only given up trying to outlaw the shows, which proved too popular to be closed, but actually had to forbid soldiers and government officials from leaving their positions to fight in the arena, drawn in—despite the loss of social status—by the enormous celebrity of gladiators. The final rescript prohibited senators from using gladiators as bodyguards, who could threaten violence for political purposes.

Audience

The Theodosian Code applied equally to everyone in the Eastern Roman Empire and the Western Roman Empire. Its principal audience was the magistrates and lawyers who had to litigate on its basis. It was also of interest to the large landowners and wealthy members of merchant guilds, who made up the bulk of litigants. The greater mass of ordinary Romans would probably have had contact with the legal system only in criminal cases, and though the code certainly addresses them, defendants in such cases (such as thievery or murder committed during a drunken brawl) would probably not have had legal representation or have been familiarized with the law by the court. The code was especially intended for circulation in the West, where the legal system was in a shambles compared with that of the East.

Although it was technically not part of the code, a rescript of Valentinian is attached to the beginning of most complete manuscripts; it is essentially an edict about the code's publication. Booksellers could make copies of the code only if they had obtained a government license to do so; if they were found to have made imperfect or falsified copies (for the purpose of interfering with justice), the penalty was a large fine or death. The code certainly was copied and distributed widely. It exists in hundreds of manuscripts, some of which survive from as early as 500 CE, and these are especially good copies in terms of both the quality of the workmanship and the accuracy of the text. No complete manuscript survives, however; it is clear that books containing the whole text were rare, and most copies consisted of only single pages intended as reference guides for rescripts on a particular subject. It is also evident that many of the individual rescripts have dropped out the text as it survives now.

Impact

The immediate impact of the Theodosian Code was to simplify and make more secure the legal system of the Roman Empire, especially that of the Western Roman Empire. The West was badly affected by the dislocations of barbarian invasions in the first half of the fifth century and required institutional support from the East. The code was part of the support Theodosius tried to provide the West, especially after the marriage of his daughter, Eudocia, to the western emperor Valentinian III in 437 briefly reunified the empire. The importance of the ideology of unification is indicated in the code by such statements (in the fifth rescript of Book I, Title 1) as "This very closely united Empire." Nevertheless, the situation was too chaotic, and little could be done to control the Germanic tribes already allowed into the empire as mercenaries or to prevent new barbarian incursions. Consequently, by 476 the Western Roman Empire had collapsed as a political entity.

What did not collapse was the concept of Roman law. The independent Germanic kingdoms in western Europe and North Africa still preserved the Roman system of administration, and the Theodosian Code flourished as a source of law. The Roman law system centered in cities competed with the common law tradition of the German rulers of Italy, Spain, France, and the other new kingdoms. By the Renaissance in the fifteenth century, Roman law had become reestablished as the sole legal system of western Europe apart from England, where common law prevailed. From there common law was spread to the countries of the Commonwealth and to the United States. In common law legal decisions are made on the basis of precedent, a ruling in a similar case made by an earlier judge. In Roman law, however, judges decided each case according to the will of the prince, that is, on the basis of government

policy. For this reason each new regime—a new emperor or king or, later, a new prime minister—could have tremendous influence in regulating legal decisions.

The Theodosian Code served several purposes within the legal systems it governed. While a separate body of laws existed, the code regulated the state's interpretation of the law. In the first place, it privileged the imperial rescripts that had been issued since the reign of Constantine in 313. These rescripts had the advantage of being more easily found than documents from earlier emperors as well as being more generally applicable to the administrative and political realities of the mid-fifth century than, for example, rescripts from the reign of Augustus three hundred years earlier would have been. These documents, with the exception of the last three years of Julian's reign (360–363), were also all issued by Christian emperors, an important consideration because many of the legal issues faced by the empire in the time of Theodosius related to church-state relations, ecclesiastical administration, the suppression of heresy, and other specifically Christian matters. Once the corpus of rescripts was established as the basis of law, the jurisprudence of actual legal cases was much simplified.

Since the code was the main basis of law (at least in the fifth century), it was no longer possible for lawyers to manipulate or delay legal proceedings by introducing some obscure or even specious imperial pronouncement that seemed to work in their favor. Even a legitimate appeal to the emperor on a matter of law that was not clearly defined in the texts available to the presiding judge could take a year or more. In addition, the emperor and his bureaucrats could not afford to spend much time on ordinary court cases. With the code, almost any matter could be settled without making a direct appeal to the emperor to obtain a new rescript. The code also specifies that future rescripts will apply only to the cases for which they are issued and will not replace the text of the code itself as a legal authority. The Theodosian Code made clearer than ever before the administrative guidance for magistrates in deciding, and for lawyers in arguing, legal cases.

Further Reading

■ Articles
Pharr, Clyde. "The Text and Interpretation of the Theodosian Code, 6, 4, 21." *American Journal of Philology* 66, no. 1 (January 1945): 50–58.

■ Books
Ammianus Marcellinus. *The Later Roman Empire (a.d. 354–378,* trans. Walter Hamilton. New York: Penguin, 1986.

Brown, Peter. *The Making of Late Antiquity*. Cambridge, Mass.: Harvard University Press, 1978.

Croke, Brian. "Mommsen's Encounter with the Code." In *The Theodosian Code*, ed. Jill Harries and Ian Wood. Ithaca, N.Y.: Cornell University Press, 1993.

"We [the Emperors] decree that ... a collection shall be made of all the constitutions that were issued by the renowned Constantine, by the sainted Emperors after him, and by Us and which rest upon the force of edicts or sacred imperial law of general force."

(Book I)

"We leave to owners and patrons no avenue of recovery if good will, the friend of compassion, has taken up children exposed in a measure to death, for no one can call his own a child whom he scorned when it was perishing."

(Book V)

"I [Constantine] Myself will hear everything; I Myself will conduct an investigation; and if the charge should be proved, I Myself will avenge Myself."

(Book IX)

"If any person should hasten the fate of a parent ..., he shall be sewed in a leather sack and, confined within its deadly closeness, he shall share the companionship of serpents."

(Book IX)

"We furthermore grant to you as prefect the authority that, if any student in the City should fail to conduct himself as the dignity of a liberal education demands, he shall be publicly flogged, immediately put on board a boat, expelled from the City and returned home."

(Book XIV)

"Bloody spectacles displease Us amid public peace and domestic tranquility. Wherefore ... We wholly forbid the existence of Gladiators."

(Book XV)

Honoré, Tony. *Law in the Crisis of the Empire, 379–455 AD: The Theodosian Dynasty and Its Quaestors*. Oxford, U.K.: Clarendon Press, 1998.

Jones, A. H. M. *The Later Roman Empire, 284–602: A Social, Economic and Administrative Survey*. Oxford, U.K.: Basil Blackwell, 1964.

Matthews, John. "The Making of the Text." In *The Theodosian Code*, ed. Jill Harries and Ian Wood. Ithaca, N.Y.: Cornell University Press, 1993.

———. *Laying Down the Law: A Study of the Theodosian Code*. New Haven, Conn.: Yale University Press, 2000.

■ **Web Sites**

The Roman Law Library Web site.
 http://web.upmf-grenoble.fr/Haiti/Cours/Ak/.

—Bradley A. Skeen

Questions for Further Study

1. The Theodosian Code was written near the end of the Roman Empire. What historical circumstances made the code necessary, at least in the eyes of its author? Why did it fail to stabilize and preserve the empire?

2. What is the distinction between common law and the type of law promulgated in the Theodosian Code? Why is the distinction important?

3. What impact did Christianity have on the development of Roman law?

4. In what specific ways did the Theodosian Code attempt to create a more civil, less violent society?

5. In modern life, people often talk about the "decline of the Roman Empire," citing it as an object lesson for modern states, including the United States. Many historians have attributed the empire's fall to softness, luxury, corruption, weakening of religious beliefs, loss of social cohesion, and similar factors. To what extent did the Theodosian Code either contribute to or attempt to resist this decline?

THEODOSIAN CODE

Book I.

◆ Title 1: Constitutions and Edicts of the Emperors

1. Emperor Constantine Augustus to the Lusitanians.

If any edicts or constitutions without the day and the year of the consulship should hereafter be discovered, they shall lack authority.

Given on the seventh day before the kalends of August at Szombathely (Savaria) in the year of the consulship of Probianus and Julianus.—July 20, 322.

INTERPRETATION : If any laws without the day and the year of the consulship should be produced, they shall not be valid.

2. The same Augustuses to Flavianus, Praetorian Prefect of Illyricum and Italy.

We do not permit any person either to be ignorant of or to pretend ignorance of the constitutions which have been carefully weighed with long deliberation by Our Serenity.

Given on the sixth day before the kalends of June at Vincentia in the year of the consulship of the Most Noble Tatianus and Symmachus.—May 27, 391.

INTERPRETATION: NO person shall be permitted to be ignorant of the laws or scornful of the statutes.

3. The same Augustuses to Aurelianus, Prefect of the City.

No constitution produces any calumny for past deeds, but all constitutions establish regulations for the future.

Given on the third day before the kalends of March at Constantinople in the year of the third consulship of Our Lord Theodosius Augustus and the consulship of the Most Noble Abundantius.—February 27, 393.

INTERPRETATION : No laws condemn the deeds which have been done at a previous time, but they establish the regulations which must be observed in the future.

4. The same Augustuses to Victorius, Proconsul of Asia.

A general regulation must be preferred to a special grant of imperial favor.

Given on the eleventh day before the kalends of September at Constantinople in the year of the third consulship of Theodosius Augustus and the consulship of the Most Noble Abundantius.—August 22, 393.

INTERPRETATION: A single person or a single case shall not nullify a law which binds all persons in common.

5. Emperors Theodosius and Valentinian Augustuses to the Senate.

We decree that, after the pattern of the Gregorian and Hermogenian Codes, a collection shall be made of all the constitutions that were issued by the renowned Constantine, by the sainted Emperors after him, and by Us and which rest upon the force of edicts or sacred imperial law of general force.

First, the titles, which are the definite designations of the matters therein shall be so divided that, when the various headings have been expressed, if one constitution should pertain to several titles, the materials shall be assembled wherever each is fitting. Second, if any diversity should cause anything to be stated in two ways, it shall be tested by the order of the readings, and not only shall the year of the consulship be considered and the time of the reign be investigated, but also the arrangement of the work itself shall show that the laws which are later are more valid. Furthermore, the very words themselves of the constitutions, in so far as they pertain to the essential matter, shall be preserved, but those words which were added not from the very necessity of sanctioning the law shall be omitted.

Although it would be simpler and more in accordance with law to omit those constitutions which were invalidated by later constitutions and to set forth only those which must be valid, let us recognize that this code and the previous ones were composed for more diligent men, to whose scholarly efforts it is granted to know those laws also which have been consigned to silence and have passed into desuetude, since they were destined to be valid for the cases of their own time only.

Moreover, from these three codes and from the treatises and responses of the jurists which are attached to each of the titles, through the services of the same men who shall arrange the third code, there shall be produced another code of Ours. This code shall permit no error, no ambiguities; it shall be called by Our name and shall show what must be followed and what must be avoided by all.

For the consummation of so great a work and for the composition of the codes—the first of which shall collect all the diversity of general constitutions, shall omit none outside itself which are now permitted to be cited in court, and shall reject only an empty copiousness of words, the other shall exclude every contradiction of the law and shall undertake the guidance of life—men must be chosen of singular trustworthiness, of the most brilliant genius. When they have presented the first code to Our Wisdom and to the public authority, they shall undertake the other, which must be worked over until it is worthy of publication. Let Your Magnificence acknowledge the men who have been selected; We have selected the Illustrious Antiochus, Ex-Quaestor and Ex-Prefect, the Illustrious Antiochus, Quaestor of the sacred imperial palace, the Respectable Theodorus, Count and Master of the Bureau of Memorials, the Respectable Eudicius and Eusebius, Masters of the Bureaus, the Respectable Johannes, Ex-Count of Our sacred imperial sanctuary, the Respectable Comazon and Eubulus, Ex-Masters of the Bureaus, and Apelles, most eloquent jurist.

We are confident that these men who have been selected by Our Eternity will employ every exceptionally learned man, in order that by their common study a reasonable plan of life may be apprehended and fallacious laws may be excluded.

Furthermore, if in the future it should be Our pleasure to promulgate any law in one part of this very closely united Empire, it shall be valid in the other part on condition that it does not rest upon doubtful trustworthiness or upon a private assertion; but from that part of the Empire in which it will be established, it shall be transmitted with the sacred imperial letters, it shall be received in the bureaus of the other part of the Empire also, and it shall be published with the due formality of edicts. For a law that has been sent must be accepted and must undoubtedly be valid, and the power to emend and to revoke shall be reserved to Our Clemency. Moreover, the laws must be mutually announced, and they must not be admitted otherwise. (Etc.)

Given on the seventh day before the kalends of April at Constantinople in the year of the consulship of Florentius and Dionysius.—March 26, 429.

6. The same Augustuses.

All the edictal and general constitutions that have been ordered to be valid or to be posted in definite provinces or districts and that have been issued by the sainted Constantine and the later emperors and by Us shall be distinguished by titles indicating their contents. Furthermore, it shall be apparent which constitutions are the most recent, not only from a computation of the year of the consulships and of the day, but also from their order of arrangement. If any of the constitutions should be divided into several headings, each heading shall be separated from the rest and shall be placed under the proper title, the words which do not pertain to the force of the sanction shall be removed from each constitution, and the law alone shall be left.

1. In order that the law may be constrained by brevity and may be lucid with clarity, We grant to those men who are about to undertake this work the power to remove superfluous words, to add necessary words, to change ambiguities, and to emend incongruities. By these methods, of course, each constitution shall stand forth illuminated.

2. The compilers of this Theodosian Code shall be Antiochus, the Most August and Most Glorious Ex-Prefect and Consular; Eubulus, the Illustrious and Magnificent Count and Our Quaestor; the Illustrious Maximus, adorned with the insignia of the dignity of Quaestor; the Respectables Superantius, Martyrius, Alypius, Sebastianus, Apollodorus, Theodorus, and Eron, Counts of the Imperial Consistory; the Respectables Maximinus, Epigenes, Diodorus, and Procopius, Counts and Masters of the Sacred Imperial Bureaus; the Respectable Erotius, Ex-Vicar, Professor of Law; the Respectable Neoterius, Ex- ...

3. If any of these men should be prevented by human fortune or detained by the care of some public affair and should thus be withdrawn from the task that has been enjoined upon him, another shall be substituted in his place in accordance with Our decision, if it should thus seem best. Thus no obstacle shall inhibit the completion of this code, which shall be valid in all cases and in all courts and shall leave no place for any new constitution that is outside itself, except those constitutions which will be promulgated after the publication of this code.

Given on the thirteenth day before the kalends of January at Constantinople in the year of the fifteenth consulship of Our Lord Theodosius Augustus and the fourth consulship of Our Lord Valentinian Augustus.—December 20, 435....

Book V.

◆ **Title 9: Exposed Children**

1. Emperor Constantine Augustus to Ablavius, Praetorian Prefect.

If any person should take up a boy or a girl child that has been cast out of its home with the knowledge and consent of its father or owner, and if he should rear this child to strength with his own sustenance, he shall have the right to keep the said child under the same status as he wished it to have when he took charge of it, that is, as his child or as a slave, whichever he should prefer. Every disturbance of suits for recovery by those persons who knowingly and voluntarily cast out from home newly born children, whether slaves or free, shall be abolished.

Given on the fifteenth day before the kalends of May at Constantinople in the year of the consulship of Bassus and Ablavius.—April 17, 331.

INTERPRETATION: If any person should take up a newly born child that has been exposed with the knowledge of its father or mother or owner and should rear it by his own effort, the child shall remain firmly in the power of the person by whom it was taken up, whether this person should wish the child whom he nurtured to be of freeborn status or a slave.

2. Emperors Honorius and Theodosius Augustuses to Melitius, Praetorian Prefect.

We leave to owners and patrons no avenue of recovery if good will, the friend of compassion, has taken up children exposed in a measure to death, for no one can call his own a child whom he scorned when it was perishing; provided only that the signature of a bishop as witness should immediately follow; and, for the sake of security, there can be absolutely no delay in obtaining this signature.

Given on the fourteenth day before the kalends of April at Ravenna in the year of the ninth consulship of Honorius Augustus and the fifth consulship of Theodosius Augustus.—March 19, 412.

INTERPRETATION: If any person through compassion should take up a child, either a boy or a girl, exposed with the knowledge of its owner or patron, such child shall remain under the ownership of the person who took it up, provided, however, that the bishop and clerics subscribe to an attestation with regard to such taking up. If a person should be proved to have cast forth a child to death, he cannot later call such child his own.

◆ **Title 10: Those Persons Who Purchase Newborn Children and Those Who Take Such Children to Rear**

1. Emperor Constantine Augustus to His Italians.
According to the statutes of former Emperors, if any person should lawfully acquire a newborn child in any manner and should suppose that he ought to rear such a child, he shall have the right to hold it in the condition of slavery; and if after a series of years any person should bring an action to restore the

child to freedom or should defend his right to it as his slave, such claimant shall provide another of the same kind or shall pay a price which can be adequate. 1. For when a person has executed a written instrument and has paid an adequate price, his possession of the slave shall be so valid that he shall have unrestricted power to sell him also for his own debt. Those persons who attempt to contravene this law shall be subject to punishment.

Given on the fifteenth day before the kalends of September at Sofia (Serdica) in the year of the eighth consulship of Constantine Augustus and the fourth consulship of Constantine Caesar.—August 18, 329; 319.

INTERPRETATION: If any person should purchase a newborn child and rear it, he shall have the right to keep and possess it. Certainly, if an owner or father should wish to recover a child that has been so reared, he shall either give to the person who reared it a slave of the same value, or the person who reared the child shall obtain the price that the child that he reared is worth....

Book VI.

◆ **Title 2: Senatorial Rank** ...

13 (8). Emperors Gratian, Valentinian, and Theodosius Augustuses to Hypatius.

If any person by Our bounty should attain the most exalted rank of Senator or if this high dignity should fall to his lot by the felicity of his birth and he should suppose that he should conceal the tax declaration of any landholding, he shall know that such landed estate will be vindicated to the fisc, whatsoever the property may be that was stealthily withdrawn from the resources that rightfully belong to the State.

1.... if any person should attain the insignia of consular, he shall not have the privilege of assuming this rank or of exercising this administration, unless by his own written statement he should declare that he acknowledges the title of Senator, that he has established his lares and his domicile or fixed residence in a province and town, and that within the various provinces he possesses nothing more than the definite amount specified in his tax declaration. When this information has been obtained by the palatine bureaus, as soon as possible the complete statement shall make readily clear what titles and how important are the ones that have increased the resources of Our immortal treasury, and to what extent.

2. But the tax declaration of two folles shall remain fixed for all Senators alike, even though per-

chance they may not have any landholding, provided that they have been advanced to the consular rank or to any very distinguished and lofty position of authority. No person shall be admitted to the insignia of authority unless he has duly affirmed his tax declaration, and from such necessity, only those shall be exempted who have been approved by the honor and their terms of service in the imperial palatine service, whence in accordance with their due, rather than by their request, they are called to the fellowship of the Senatorial order.

Given on the fourth day before the ides of January in the year of the second consulship of Merobaudes and the consulship of Saturninus.—January 10, 383.

14. (9). The same Augustuses to Clearchus, Prefect of the City.

We order that exemption from the payment of the glebal tax shall be granted to all those persons from Macedonia ... who have been added to the Most August Order of the City of Constantinople, according to the precedent of the Senators who were chosen from Thrace.

Given ... September at Constantinople in the year of the consulship of Richomer and Clearchus.—August 14–September 13, 384.

15 (10). Emperors Valentinian, Theodosius, and Arcadius Augustuses to Aurelianus, Prefect of the City.

In reply to the complaints of those persons who testify that they are not able to bear the burden of the glebal tax, It has been decreed by the Council of the Most August that seven solidi shall be paid annually for his portion by each man who is not able to fulfill the payment of the folles. By this law We confirm this decree of the aforesaid council to the extent that if the property of any man should be meager and if this tax payment is not displeasing to him, he shall have the free choice, in contemplation of the resources of his patrimony, and he shall not withdraw from his fellowship in this Most August Order; but if the tax payment seems burdensome, that is, ruinous, he shall not seek to retain the Senatorial rank.

Given on the day before the kalends of September at Constantinople in the year of the third consulship of Theodosius Augustus and the consulship of the Most Noble Abundantius.—August 31, 393....

Book IX.

◆ **Title 1: Accusations and Inscriptions** ...

4. The same Augustus [Constantine] to all Provincials.

If there is any person of any position, rank, or dignity whatever who believes that he is able to prove anything truthfully and clearly against any judge, count, or any of My retainers or palatines, in that any of these persons has committed some act which appears to have been done without integrity and justice, let him approach Me and appeal to Me unafraid and secure. I Myself will hear everything; I Myself will conduct an investigation; and if the charge should be proved, I Myself will avenge Myself. Let him speak with safety, and let him speak with a clear conscience. If he should prove the case, as I have said, I Myself will avenge Myself on that person who has deceived Me up to this time with feigned integrity. The person, moreover, who has revealed and proved the offense I will enrich with honors as well as with material rewards. Thus may the Highest Divinity always be propitious to Me and keep Me unharmed, as I hope, with the State most happy and flourishing.

Posted on the fifteenth day before the kalends of October at Nicomedia in the year of the consulship of Paulinus and Julianus.—September 17, 325....

◆ **Title 4: If Any Person Should Utter Maledictions against the Emperor**

1. Emperors Theodosius, Arcadius, and Honorius Augustuses to Rufinus, Praetorian Prefect.

If any person, insensible to decency and ignorant of propriety, should suppose that Our name should be assailed with wicked and impudent maledictions, and if, riotous with drunkenness, he should disparage Our times it is Our will that he should not be subjected to punishment or sustain any harsh or severe treatment, since, if such conduct should proceed from levity, it must be treated with contempt; if from insanity, it is most worthy of pity; if from a desire to injure, it should be pardoned. Wherefore, the case shall be referred to Our knowledge with all its details unchanged, so that We may consider the words on the basis of the character of the man and that We may decide whether the offense should be overlooked or duly prosecuted.

Given on the fifth day before the ides of August at Constantinople in the year of the third consulship of Theodosius Augustus and the consulship of the Most Noble Abundantius.—August 9, 393.

◆ **Title 5: On the Julian Law on High Treason**

1. Emperor Constantine Augustus to Maximus, Prefect of the City.

If any person should bring the charge of high treason against another, since a person convicted in a case of this kind is not protected by the privilege of any high rank from a very severe inquisition, the accuser shall know that he also must be subjected to torture if he should not be able to prove his accusation by other clear evidence. Along with the person who is discovered to be guilty of such rash criminality, that person also must be subjected to torture by whose advice and instigation he appears to have undertaken the accusation, in order that the established penalty may be exacted of all persons who are accomplices of the deed.

1. In the case of slaves also, or of freedmen who attempt to accuse their masters or patrons, respectively, or to report them to the authorities, the assertion of such atrocious audacity shall be repressed immediately at the inception of the guilty act itself, through the sentence of the judge, a hearing shall be denied such slave or freedman, and he shall be affixed to the cross.

Posted on the kalends of January in the year of the consulship of Volusianus and Annianus.—January 1, 314; 320–323....

◆ Title 14: On the Cornelian Law on Cutthroats

1. Emperors Valentinian, Valens, and Gratian Augustuses to Probus, Praetorian Prefect.

If anyone, man or woman, should commit the crime of killing an infant, such an evil deed shall constitute a capital offense.

Posted on the seventh day before the ides of February at Rome in the year of the third consulship of Gratian Augustus and the consulship of the Most Noble Equitius.—February 7, 374.

INTERPRETATION: If anyone, whether man or woman, should kill an infant, he shall be held guilty of homicide.

2. Emperors Valentinian, Theodosius, and Arcadius Augustuses to the Provincials.

We grant to all men the unrestricted right of resistance if any soldiers or private citizens should enter their fields as nocturnal ravagers or should beset frequented roads by attacks from ambush. This right is granted to everyone in order that whoever so deserves shall be subjected immediately to punishment, shall receive the death which he threatened, and shall incur that danger which he intended for another. For it is better for a man to fight back at the proper time than for him to be avenged after his death. Therefore, We entrust the right of vengeance to you, and what it is too late to punish by trial We repress by edict. Let no man spare a soldier who should be resisted with a weapon as a brigand.

Given on the kalends of July in the year of the consulship of Tatianus and Symmachus.—July 1, 391.

INTERPRETATION: Whenever anyone as a nocturnal ravager attacks either a traveler or someone's home for the purpose of committing robbery, We grant to those persons who sustain violence the right to resist even with arms, and if the one who came should be killed for his rash lawlessness, the death of the brigand himself shall be required of no one.

3. Emperors Arcadius and Honorius Augustuses to Eutychianus, Praetorian Prefect.

If any person should enter into a criminal conspiracy with soldiers or civilians, or even with barbarians, or should take or give the oaths of a conspiracy, and should plan for the death of men of Illustrious rank who participate in Our counsels and Our Consistory, or for the death of Senators, who are also part of Our body, or, finally, for the death of anyone who is in Our imperial service, he shall be struck down with the sword as one guilty of high treason, and all his goods shall be assigned to Our fisc. For the laws have willed that the intent to commit crime shall be punished with the same severity as the actual commission of crime.

His sons, indeed, to whom We have granted their lives by especial imperial leniency (for they ought to perish by the same punishment as their father's, since in them must be feared examples of paternal, that is, hereditary, crime) shall be held as persons extraneous to the inheritance and succession of their mother or grandmother, and also of all their nearest kinsmen. They shall receive nothing by the wills of extraneous persons; they shall be needy and poor perpetually; their father's infamy shall accompany them always; they shall never be admitted to any honors and to any oaths of service; finally, they shall be in such sordidness of perpetual want that death shall be to them a solace and life a punishment 1. Finally We order to be branded with infamy and to be without hope of pardon, those persons also who should ever attempt to intercede with Us for such men.

2. To their daughters, however many there may be, it is Our will that only the Falcidian portion shall come from the property of their mother, whether she dies testate or intestate, so that they shall grudgingly have the subsistence of a daughter rather than the emoluments and name of heirs completely. For the sentence ought to be lighter in the case of those persons, who, We trust, will be less daring because of the frailty of their sex.

3. Emancipation bestowed by the aforesaid criminal, whether upon sons or daughters, shall not be

valid, provided it was granted after the issuance of this law.

4. We decree to be of no force dowries, gifts, and alienations of any property whatsoever which appear to have been executed, fraudulently or legally, after the time when the aforesaid persons first thought about entering into a conspiracy or alliance.

5. Wives of the aforesaid criminals must know that they will leave to the fisc their recovered dowries, and everything that was due to the children according to law shall go to the fisc from the time when the usufruct of the wife ceases, provided that such wives are so situated that what they received from their husbands by title of gift must be reserved for their children. Even the Falcidian portion shall be assigned from these properties to the daughters only, not to the sons.

6. That which We have stipulated concerning the aforesaid children of these criminals We decree with like severity also concerning their satellites, who were their accomplices and assistants, and their children.

7. Certainly if anyone of these criminals, in the beginning of a conspiracy that has been undertaken, should be aroused by a desire for true praise and should himself betray the conspiracy, he shall be given rewards and honor by Us. But if a participant in a conspiracy should reveal the secrets of their plans, even belatedly, but while they are still unknown, he shall be considered worthy only of absolution and pardon.

Given on the day before the nones of September at Ancyra in the year of the consulship of Caesarius and Atticus.—September 4, 397.

◆ Title 15: Parricides

1. Emperor Constantine Augustus to Verinus, Vicar of Africa.

If any person should hasten the fate of a parent or a son or any person at all of such degree of kinship that killing him is included under the title of parricide, whether he has accomplished this secretly or openly, he shall not be subjected to the sword or to fire or to any other customary penalty, but he shall be sewed in a leather sack and, confined within its deadly closeness, he shall share the companionship of serpents. As the nature of the region shall determine, he shall be thrown into the neighboring sea or into a river, so that while still alive he may begin to lose the enjoyment of all the elements, that the heavens may be taken away from him while he is living and the earth, when he is dead.

Given on the sixteenth day before the kalends of December in the year of the fifth consulship of Licinius and the consulship of Crispus Caesar.— November 16, 318. Received on the day before the ides of March at Carthage in the year of the fifth consulship of Constantine Augustus and the consulship of Licinius Caesar.—March 14, 319.

INTERPRETATION: If any person should kill his father, mother, brother, sister, son, daughter, or other near kinsman, all other kinds of tortures shall be rejected, and a sack, called a *culleus,* shall be made of leather, into which he shall be cast; then serpents shall be enclosed with him, and, if there should not be a neighboring sea, he shall be thrown into whatever stream there may be, so that a person condemned to such a penalty may never obtain burial....

Book XIV.

◆ Title 9: The Pursuit of Liberal Studies in the Cities of Rome and Constantinople

1. Emperors Valentinian, Valens, and Gratian Augustuses to Olybrius, Prefect of the City.

All persons who come to the City because of their desire for learning shall first of all upon arrival present to the master of tax assessment the requisite written documents from their several provincial judges, by whom the right to come to the City must be given. These documents shall contain the name of the municipality from which each student comes, together with his birth certificate and letters of recommendation certifying to his high attainments. In the second place, immediately upon matriculation the students shall indicate the profession for which they intend to study. In the third place, the office of tax assessment shall carefully investigate the life of the students at their lodging places, to see that they actually do bestow their time on the studies which they assert that they are pursuing. These same officials of tax assessment shall warn the students that they shall severally conduct themselves in their assemblies as persons should who consider it their duty to avoid a disgraceful and scandalous reputation and bad associations, all of which We consider as the next worst thing to actual criminality. Nor shall the students attend shows too frequently nor commonly take part in unseasonable carousals. We furthermore grant to you as prefect the authority that, if any student in the City should fail to conduct himself as the dignity of a liberal education demands, he shall be publicly flogged, immediately put on board a boat, expelled from the City and returned home. Of course, permission shall be granted for all students to remain at Rome till their twentieth year, if they industriously apply themselves to the work of their profession, but if after the expiration of this time any student should neglect to return home of his own accord, by the administrative action of the prefect he shall be returned even more disgracefully to his municipality.

In order that these provisions may not perhaps be perfunctorily enforced, Your Exalted Sincerity shall admonish the office of tax assessment that for each month he shall enroll on his register the students who come, whence they come, and those who must be sent back to Africa or to the other provinces according to the periods of time. Only those students shall be excepted who are attached to the burdens of the guilds. Similar registers, moreover, shall be dispatched each year to the bureaus of Our Clemency, in order that We may learn of the merits and education of the various students and may judge whether they may ever be necessary to Us.

Given on the fourth day before the ides of March at Trier in the year of the consulship of Valentinian Augustus and the third consulship of Valens Augustus.—March 12, 370.

2. The same Augustuses to Clearchus, Prefect of the City.

We command that four Greek and three Latin copyists, skilled in writing, shall be selected for copying the manuscripts of the library and for repairing them on account of their age. To them the appropriate subsistence allowances shall be issued from the caducous supplies of the people, for the copyists themselves also appear to be from the people. For the custody of the aforesaid library, men of ignoble status shall be sought out and immediately assigned to that duty.

Given on the eighth day before the ides of May in the year of the consulship of Modestus and Arintheus.—May 8, 372.

3. Emperor Theodosius Augustus and Valentinian Caesar.

We order to be removed from the practice of vulgar ostentation all persons who usurp for themselves the name of teachers and who in their public professorships and in their private rooms are accustomed to conduct with them their students whom they have collected from all quarters. Thus if any of these teachers, after the issuance of the words of this divine imperial sanction, should perhaps again attempt to do that which We prohibit and condemn,

he shall not only undergo the brand of infamy that he deserves, but he shall know that he will also be expelled from the very city where he conducts himself thus illicitly. But by no threat of this kind do We prohibit those teachers who are accustomed to give such instruction privately within very many homes, if they prefer to keep themselves free for such students only whom they teach within the walls of private homes. If, moreover, there should be any teacher from the number of those who appear to be established within the auditorium of the Capitol, he shall know that in every way he is interdicted from teaching such studies in private homes. He shall also know that if he should be apprehended doing anything contrary to the imperial celestial statutes, he shall obtain no benefit from those privileges which are deservedly conferred upon those persons who have been commanded to teach only in the Capitol.

1. Therefore, Our auditorium shall specifically have three orators and ten grammarians, first of all among those teachers who are commended by their learning in Roman oratory. Among those professors also who are recognized as being proficient in facility of expression in Greek, there shall be five sophists in number, and likewise ten grammarians. Since it is Our desire that Our glorious youth should be instructed not only in such arts, We associate authorities of more profound knowledge and learning with the aforesaid professors. Therefore, it is Our will that to the other professors, one teacher shall be associated who shall investigate the hidden secrets of philosophy, two teachers also who shall expound the formulas of the law and statutes. Thus Your Sublimity shall provide that to each of these teachers a designated place shall be specifically assigned, in order that the students and teachers may not drown out each other, and the mingled confusion of tongues and words may not divert the ears or the minds of any from the study of letters.

Given on the third day before the kalends of March at Constantinople in the year of the eleventh consulship of Theodosius Augustus and the consulship of Valentinian.—February 27, 425....

Book XV.

◆ Title 12: Gladiators

1. Emperor Constantine Augustus to Maximus, Praetorian Prefect.

Bloody spectacles displease Us amid public peace and domestic tranquillity. Wherefore, since We wholly forbid the existence of gladiators, You shall cause those persons who, perchance, on account of some crime, customarily sustained that condition and sentence, to serve rather in the mines, so that they will assume the penalty for their crimes without shedding their blood.

Posted at Beirut on the kalends of October in the year of the consulship of Paulinus and Julianus.—October 1, 325.

2. Emperor Constantius Augustus and Julian Caesar to Orfitus, Prefect of the City.

All exhibitors of gladiatorial shows in the City of Rome shall know that it is forbidden to solicit soldiers or those endowed with any palatine rank to hire themselves out as gladiators. If any person should attempt to violate this regulation, he shall be subject to the threat of a fine of six pounds of gold. If any such soldiers should voluntarily approach a producer of gladiatorial games, the office staff of Your Sub-

limity shall send them, loaded with iron chains, to the masters of the horse and foot, or to those who govern the palatine offices, so that, pursuant to the provision of this law, the dignity of the palace may be vindicated from the detestable gladiatorial name.

Given on the sixteenth day before the kalends of November in the year of the ninth consulship of Constantius Augustus and the second consulship of Julian Caesar.—October 17, 357.

3. Emperors Arcadius and Honorius Augustuses to the People.

(After other matters.) If any persons from a gladiatorial school should appear to have passed over to the service of Senators, We decree that such persons shall be sent to the remotest solitudes.

Given and posted at Rome in the year of the consulship of Caesarius and Atticus.—April 7(?), 397; June 6, 399.

Augustuses	holders of the imperial title Augustus, a designation parallel to but not synonymous with Caesar; the religious component of the system of imperial titles
caducous supplies of the people	private property that for a variety of legal reasons went to the treasury rather than to the natural heirs
City, the	the City of Rome
desuetude	disuse
Falcidian portion	the amount that a principal heir could keep (amounting to one-fourth of an estate) if specific bequests or a badly drafted will could have caused secondary heirs' bequests to unfairly diminish the inheritance of the principal heir
masters of the horse and foot	in the late Roman Empire, high military officials
sophists	professors of rhetoric (whose work included that of the grammarian) who were frequently appointed to high-ranking posts in the government because of their reputation for competence
usufruct	right to use and have benefits of something belonging to another
Your Magnificence … Your Sublimity	respectively, forms of address for the praetorian prefect (prime minister) and for any prefect or equivalent rank of civil servant, including the praetorian prefect

Justinian in council (Digital Image © Museum Associates, Los Angeles County Museum of Art, Art Resource, NY)

CODE OF JUSTINIAN

"We order all those who follow this law to assume the name of Catholic Christians, and considering others as demented and insane."

Overview

On November 16, 534, Justinian I, the ruler of the Eastern Roman (or Byzantine) Empire, issued his *Corpus juris civilis* (The Body of the Civil Law), commonly called the Code of Justinian. It expanded on Justinian's earlier release of the Code (in 529) and was divided into three parts: the Codex, which was a compilation of the existing decrees of emperors and statesmen; the Digest (or Pandects, as they were termed in Greek), an anthology of the thoughts and decisions of the famous lawyers of antiquity; and the Institutes, a state-issued and mandated legal textbook designed to standardize legal education across the empire. A separate book of later laws, the Novels, is also considered part of the Justinian Code. With his law code, Justinian completely revolutionized the law of the Eastern Roman Empire, inherited from over a thousand years of Roman jurisprudence.

The Code of Justinian brought together all codifications and decrees put forth before it and streamlined, organized, and ultimately professionalized the vocation of the law for the vast Byzantine Empire. It removed the obsolete and Christianized the pagan, and its organization and structure provided a model during the millennia that followed, such that nearly every European legal system can trace its basic structure and form to the Code of Justinian.

Context

Justinian inherited the imperial throne from his uncle, Justin I, who had adopted him. His inheritance included not only leadership of Byzantium but also the headache of hostile borders and a populace agitated by theological controversy. As one means of dealing with these problems, the emperor planned a sweeping overhaul of the legal system. As part of a decree issued in 541, he stated that the "laws bear the same relation to practical matters as medicines have for diseases" (qtd. in Evans, p. 202). Although that pronouncement dates from after Justinian's codification of Roman law, it is clear from the sentiment that he regarded law in part as a cure for his ailing empire.

On February 13, 528, Justinian decreed that a commission of ten legal scholars be formed to update and clarify existing laws. The commission included Tribonian, who was one of Justinian's most trusted advisers and a graduate of the prestigious law school of Berytus (modern-day Beirut), and Theophilus, an esteemed legal professor at the law school of Constantinople, capital of Byzantium. Justinian hoped that the resulting code would not only be of use in the courts and legal schools of the empire but also revive respect for the rule of law.

One of the illnesses the Roman Empire had developed during its long history was legal redundancy. The legal foundation of Roman government began with the Law of the Twelve Tables, commissioned around 451 BCE. Added to these tables were countless Senate decrees from the age of the Republic, commentaries and decisions by eminent Roman jurists from the early Empire, and numerous imperial decrees issued by the emperors themselves. Two compilations of imperial edicts and rulings predated Justinian's Code. The Gregorian and Hermogenian codes, both compiled in the fourth century by independent jurists, were early attempts at collecting and simplifying the mass of imperial legislation.

Emperors preceding Justinian had recognized the problem that this jumble of conflicting juridical data presented and had tried to make various reforms. Theodosius II, who reigned over the Eastern Roman Empire from 408 to 450, and Valentinian III, who ruled the Western Roman Empire from 425 to 455, both had attempted to manage this disparate and voluminous source material by giving special weight to the opinions of five famous past jurists—Papinianus, Paulus, Ulpian, Gaius, and Modestinus. By having great legal minds fix the meaning of antiquated laws, the emperors hoped to limit enterprising attorneys' exploitation of those laws. This effort was not successful, however, and in 429 the emperors established a new commission to collect all extant laws and create a supplement for the Gregorian and Hermogenian codes. This work was drawn together in Theodosius II's own legal code, the Codex Theodosianus (Theodosian Code), promulgated in 438. Anything occurring afterward had to be consulted separately, and the code itself was never updated.

The frustration that this unorganized mass must have caused is easy to imagine, and Justinian's commission

Time Line

CA. 295
- The Codex Gregorianus and the Codex Hermogenianus are compiled; they would serve as the basis for future collections of imperial edicts culminating in the Code of Justinian.

438
- The Theodosian Code is issued by Emperor Theodosius II, compiling all imperial edicts from 306 to 337 into one code.

476
- **September 4** King Odoacer of the Ostrogoths deposes Emperor Romulus Augustulus and takes control of the Western Roman Empire.

527
- **April 1** Justinian accedes to the imperial throne.

528
- **February 13** Justinian establishes a commission to collect and codify existing laws.

529
- **April 7** The *Codex Vetus* (Old Code) is completed.

---

quickly realized the immensity of the task at hand. Within fourteen months of Justinian's establishment of a commission to tackle this mass of law, the commission had updated and revised the existing laws and compiled them into the Codex Justinianus (Code of Justinian), which was authorized on April 7, 529. This initial code, termed the Codex Vetus, or Old Code, no longer survives. Additionally, on December 15, 530, Justinian called together another commission that included Tribonian and Theophilus, who had helped with the Old Code. Their task was to sift through the ancient writings, eliminating contradictions and compiling an authoritative edition that summarized the works of thirty-nine jurists, which were collected in two thousand books. The result was the Digest, a text separated into fifty books. Tribonian and Theophilus also created a primer for use in legal studies. The Institutes was published alongside the Digest and served as the only official textbook authorized for the new system of legal education developed from Justinian's undertaking.

Finally, the Code itself needed reworking and amending. With the flurry of updating that had occurred in the five years since the commissioning of the Old Code, Justinian's legal minds felt it necessary to rework the basic code. The "new code," published on November 16, 534, collected all the imperial decrees from the time of the Emperor Hadrian (who reigned from 117 to 138) to the year of publication. Subsequent amendments to the Code were collected in a separate book, the Novels. Taken together, these four parts formed the *Corpus juris civilis*—the Code of Justinian.

About the Author

Flavius Anicius Julianus Justinianus, or Justinian I, was born in about 483 in the Roman province of Illyricum. In 518 his aged uncle, Justin I, assumed the throne of the Eastern Roman Empire, but he gradually turned authority over to his nephew. Justinian was proclaimed consul in 521 and made co-emperor in 527. When his uncle died that year, Justinian became the sole regent of the Eastern Roman Empire. During his long reign until his death in 565, he labored to restore the glories of the earlier united Roman Empire. He extended his realms through military conquest until he presided over an empire that stretched from Spain on the west to the Black Sea on the east. While he remains best known for his legal code, he is also known for his interest in the arts, particularly architecture. Two buildings that he commissioned stand out. One is the Church of Our Lady in Jerusalem, now the El-Aqsa Mosque. The other is the Church of the Holy Wisdom, generally called the Hagia Sophia, in Constantinople (now Istanbul) Turkey. The church had originally been built in the fourth century, but it was destroyed during riots and was rebuilt under Justinian's orders. Justinian and the architects he used are regarded as originating Byzantine architecture, and he undertook immense building projects that spanned the empire. In the estimation of many historians, he was the greatest of Roman emperors in the late empire.

Although Justinian is credited with giving the order to create the code that would bear his name, it was the jurists he appointed who actually compiled and edited the laws and commentaries. Among these jurists were Dorotheus, a leading figure at the prestigious law school in Berytus; Anatolius, his colleague; and Theophilus and Cratinus, both of the law school in Constantinople. The most important figure, however, was Tribonian. Tribonian was a successful lawyer in the early sixth century, renowned for his expertise. He was appointed quaestor, a powerful governmental position that gave him control of the imperial finances. Tribonian led the commissions responsible for the *Codex vetus*, the Digest, and the final codification of 534, while Dorotheus and Theophilus oversaw the creation of the Institutes.

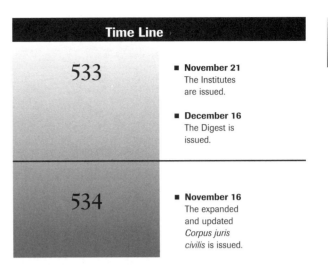

Explanation and Analysis of the Document

The complete Code of Justinian is far too lengthy to reproduce, but excerpts from the Institutes, the Digest, and the Codex are provided. The document as a whole serves to illustrate the attitudes of the day, specifically those regarding religious toleration and the status of the marginalized members of society.

◆ The Institutes

The preamble to the Institutes states that the goal of this book is to constitute the "first elements" of the science of jurisprudence, to explain principles that may have fallen into disuse but which now are to be "illuminated once more by Imperial restoration." The idea of pulling together a primer that would act as an entry point into the Roman legal system was not entirely new, as the mention (in the sixth section of the preamble) of such commentaries as the *Commentaries of Our Gaius* and other sources makes clear. Those commentaries, taken from the writings of a legal scholar and teacher, Gaius (ca. 110–180), served as the starting point for any legal education following that period, as the legal profession under the Roman Empire expanded. The fact that the commentaries are attributed not just to Gaius but to *our* Gaius shows the familiarity that the contemporary legal community had with this work. Accordingly, the "three learned men" that the preamble mentions (Tribonian, Dorotheus, and Theophilus)—all products of the elite law schools of the sixth century—would have immediately looked to Gaius for guidance in outlining the structure of the law and particularly to his practice of examining legal concepts in terms of one of three perspectives: persons, objects, or actions.

Title I of Book I begins with a definition of jurisprudence and states that it intends to explain the laws of the Roman people "most conveniently" by outlining separate subjects first and then turning to particulars. As simple as this idea sounds, the Institutes (along with the *Commentaries of Our Gaius*) were the first legal textbooks to do so. This was part of Justinian's attempt to professionalize the practice of the law.

Prior to the second century CE, Roman legal studies were informal. Typically, prospective legal students would apprentice themselves to practicing lawyers, members of the upper classes who were themselves not truly professionals as they took no pay from the practice of the law. As the legal profession became folded into the administrative elements of the government, formalized training became necessary, along with specialists to interpret the law and teach the next generation of lawyers. Thus, in the second century of the common era, teachers like Gaius began to break down the structure and logic of the law for the purposes of instruction. This led directly to the first permanent schools of law in the major cities of Beirut, Constantinople, Alexandria, and elsewhere. By 460, a lawyer practicing within the empire needed a certificate attesting to his study with a recognized teacher of the law before he would be allowed to stand before a court.

Title II expands on the division of private law (law that pertains to people) into three parts: natural law, the law of nations, and civil law. Natural law it defines as "that which nature has taught to all animals," including human beings, an idea whose roots go back to the fifth century BCE and, later, to the ideas of Aristotle and the Stoic school of Zeno. It was widely accepted that there were certain immutable principles governing human existence—for example, that each person was, by nature, free—though other laws could infringe upon those principles.

The remaining selections from Title II define civil law and the law of nations and then turn to the civil law of the Romans, both written and unwritten. Among the sources of written law listed are the Plebiscita, a term that gave us the word *plebiscite*, referring to a nonbinding referendum, but taken within the context of the document to specify the decisions of a long-defunct Roman administrative body, the Concilium Plebis, whose deliberations eventually carried the force of code. The Answers of the Jurisconsults, another source of written law, were particular legal experts' interpretations, given the authority of law by the emperor in centuries past. They were considered foundational writings on the nature of Roman law and were included in the Digest for use by lawyers.

An ivory leaf from a Byzantine diptych thought to have been associated with the accession of the Byzantine emperor Justinian (© The Trustees of the British Museum)

◆ The Digest

The first preface introduces the Digest and begins with Justinian's injunction to Tribonian to "collect and revise the whole body of Roman jurisprudence … that there may be compiled from them a summary which will take the place of all." The task put to Tribonian, therefore, was to compile, edit, and organize the thousands of opinions comprising Roman antiquity's legal heritage and publish them in one easy-to-use reference document: the Digest.

The special privilege that the Theodosian Code had given to five famous jurists of the past—Papinianus, Paulus, Ulpian, Gaius, and Modestinus—had been extended, in the intervening centuries, to dozens of ancient lawyers between the rules of the emperors Augustus (who reigned from 27 BCE to 14 CE) and Hadrian (who reigned from 117 to 138). The purpose was to give them *ius respondendi* (the right of response), which allowed their expert opinions to hold the weight of law. While the lawyers could not themselves write

legislation, their interpretations of it were deemed a suitable basis for legal argument in courts. However, over a century of writing had amassed thousands of such opinions, all holding some legal value, though some were considered weightier than others; especially the work of the five famous jurists. The Digest was to be a definitive official record of these works that would supersede all other previous records and standardize their use in the courtroom.

The selection taken from Book I, Title III, follows the model that the Digest was designed to follow: The jurists "talk to one another" in reference to a particular issue. In this case, the discussion opens with Papinianus, the most respected of the jurists quoted, who defines *statute*. Pomponius and Celsus contend that law ought to be concerned only with what often occurs and should not be created to deal with things that can "only happen in a single instance." This gradual narrowing of focus is a feature of the overall structure of the Digest, as a general proposition is put forth to be answered or expanded upon by further opinions.

In Book I, Title V, the Digest takes up the discussion of the "condition of men," specifically the institution of slavery. Gaius puts forward the general proposition that all people are either "free or slaves" and then delves into the particularities of how one might become a slave. Florentinus suggests that the law of nations that dictates slavery is "contrary to nature" and says that slavery has its origins in military conquest, when enslavement was the merciful alternative to putting captives to death. Indeed, the influx of slaves into Roman society always increased following expansion of Roman territory through conquest: Ancient authors relate that tens of thousands of people were sold into slavery as a result of the Punic Wars between Rome and the state of Carthage (264–146 BCE), and conservative estimates place the number of slaves in Roman society somewhere near two million by the end of the Roman Republic (27 BCE).

Marcianus then notes the difference between slaves made by the law of nations, that is, by conquest, and slaves made by civil law, that is, by being sold into bondage voluntarily, for nonpayment of debts, or by one's guardians. He also explains that some people are free born and others are manumitted (freed). Manumission was a common practice among ancient slaveholders, and freedmen (as they were often called), though carrying the stigma of once having been slaves, could rise to become prominent members of society.

◆ The Codex

The second preface introduces excerpted text from the Codex—the compilation of the existing decrees of emperors and statesmen. In it, Justinian states that he is directing the committee to collect into a single code the Gregorian, Hermogenian, and Theodosian compilations and those of subsequent rulers, including Justinian himself. He also instructs the committee to excise all contradictory, obsolete, or inappropriate decrees (especially those pertaining to pagan religious practices that, at the time of Justinian, were not officially tolerated), except in cases when the decree could be "considered to be susceptible of division," that is, considered capable of providing "some new principle."

"Justice is the constant and perpetual desire to give to each one that to which he is entitled."

(Institutes)

"Natural Laws that are observed without distinction by all nations and have been established by Divine Providence remain always fixed and unchangeable; but those which every State establishes for itself are often changed either by the tacit consent of the people, or by some other law subsequently enacted."

(Institutes)

"A statute is a general precept; a resolution of men learned in the law; a restraint of crimes committed either voluntarily or through ignorance; or a general obligation of the State."

(Digest)

"The principal division of the law of persons is as follows, namely, that all men are either free or slaves."

(Digest)

"We order all those who follow this law to assume the name of Catholic Christians, and considering others as demented and insane. We order that they shall bear the infamy of heresy; and when the Divine vengeance which they merit has been appeased, they shall afterwards be punished in accordance with Our resentment, which we have acquired from the judgment of Heaven."

(Codex)

Book I, Title I, deals with the Christian religion, which had become the official religion of the Roman Empire. Roughly two centuries separated the time of Justinian from the era when the official edict of toleration of Christianity was issued by the Emperor Constantine (313 CE) and the declaration was made by his successor, Theodosius I, that Christianity would become the sole tolerated religion of the Roman Empire (380 CE). Title I notes that the emperors Gratian, Valentinian, and Theodosius had declared that all

the peoples of the empire should "live under the same religion that the Divine Peter, the Apostle, gave to the Romans" and further that they should believe that the "Father, Son, and Holy Spirit" constitute a "single Deity." Those not accepting this doctrine were to be considered heretics. This not only excluded all non-Christian religions from official recognition, but marginalized those Christians who did not hold to the strictly orthodox views imposed the various ecumenical councils of the fourth, fifth, and sixth centuries. Justinian states that these unfortunates are to be "punished with Our resentment, which we have acquired from the judgment of Heaven," meaning that, in addition to whatever metaphysical repercussions would ensue from lack of acceptance of orthodox Catholic faith, unbelievers or heterodox believers would also face state discrimination.

Book VII, Title VII, expands on the punishments that might befall those who became "apostates," or willingly renounced Christianity. The punishments for apostasy included confiscation of personal property, denial of the right to make a will or to testify in court, and separation "from association" with society in general. We can take the latter to mean exclusion from participation in public life rather than imposed exile or imprisonment. Unfortunately, for those living under his reign, Justinian followed closely the spirit of these prescriptions. He outlawed "pagan" schools and banned non-Christians from teaching and he denied those who were not Christians from all representation in courts of law. Even the Neo-Platonic school of Athens was effectively suppressed. Widespread persecutions of non-Catholic sects were authorized by the emperor himself, not at the behest of any urging from the Church's leadership—an act that showcased the growing supremacy of the state over religious matters.

Audience

The primary audience of the Code of Justinian was the legal community. It was designed to serve not only lawyers representing clients but also the judges who presided over trials. The Codex and the Digest were made for easy reference and research of complex topics, so that on any topic, germane matters of law could be consulted, standard texts viewed, and a sound opinion or judgment rendered.

Justinian was very aware that history itself was also the recipient of this undertaking. He felt that the greatness of his society lay in its adroitness with the law, and he pressed his jurists to resuscitate the legal concepts of classical Rome, even if the actual laws of old were not reinstated. His devotion to the past is evidenced by the fact that the Code of Justinian was written in Latin, which, though it was his native tongue and the language of the Romans, was neither the native tongue of the local population nor the language that had begun to dominate day-to-day administration—that language was Greek. The Code of Justinian had to be translated before the provincial attorney could even understand it, a fact that led to its eventual disuse and descent into obscurity.

The average citizen of the Byzantine Empire at this time was rural, Greek-speaking, and largely unaware and unaffected by the machinery of government. Although it could be said that Justinian's measures were for his or her benefit, the decline in the central government's role in daily life left the majority of court rulings up to the traditions and practices of those who managed the locality. Often, legal matters were decided by arbiters such as bishops or other respected local figures. The expense, trouble, and precise protocol of the civil courts were avoided by most, and thus, within a hundred years after its promulgation, the Code was largely unknown by the majority of the populace.

Impact

The Code of Justinian did not have as deep an impact as might be expected. Its reliance on classical Roman terminology, its composition in a language no longer spoken by the majority of the population of the Byzantine Empire, and the tenuous and fragmentary nature of imperial rule in the empire meant that the Code was never fully put to use. Remarkably little has been written on how it affected the lawyers, lawmakers, and common people of the time. Many scholars postulate that urban centers such as Constantinople utilized the code for a time but that the hinterlands remained staunchly rooted in local customs and traditional legal practices. Future emperors made attempts to simplify the Code and make it more useful for the day-to-day concerns of Byzantine lawyers and administrators. Works such as the *Procheiron* (Manual), published in the ninth century, were issued as watered-down versions of Justinian's work and eventually supplanted it as references for imperial jurisprudence.

Yet there is a great deal of evidence to suggest that the Code exerted an immense influence on the evolution of the law in western Europe and, by extension, much of the modern world. Indeed, paradoxically, many areas that were never under the jurisdiction of the Code drew upon it the most heavily for the underpinnings of their own legal systems. The so-called renaissance of the twelfth century, an efflorescence of learning sparked by the foundation of the medieval universities in Europe, the growth of centralized government, and an expansion in trade, sparked scholars' interest in a formalized study of the law. This interest was greatly aided by the discovery of a complete text of the Digest in the 1070s. The 1070s were also when Irnerius, a professor of grammar at the University of Bologna, initiated the modern academic study of Roman law.

The Code offered a comprehensive and standardized legal framework that the burgeoning nations and empires of Europe could use as a guideline for their own legal systems. Some legal scholars hold that the Code of Justinian had a strong appeal in the twelfth through fourteenth centuries because it was universal in its tone and supported an authoritarian notion of government. For rulers attempting to consolidate their power, such as the ambitious Frederick Barbarossa, ruler of the Holy Roman Empire from 1152 to 1190, the Code legitimated law grounded in a single figure—the emperor—and offered the mantle of the tradition and glory of ancient Rome. Western Europe at that time was attracted by the notion of a universal Latin Christendom, one society united under the Christian banner, in both the temporal and spiritual spheres.

The dream of a united Christian empire was never realized, but the use and influence of the Code continued to expand. During the Renaissance, Roman law was studied as a science, even as the notion of its being the universal lynchpin holding together Christian society was fading. Nations that wished to formalize their legal systems used the Code of Justinian as a model. The seventeenth-century *gemeines Recht* (Common Law) of Germany, for example, drew heavily on the Code of Justinian as interpreted by contemporary jurists and remained in effect until 1900, nearly fifteen hundred years after Justinian's initial decree announcing its enactment.

Further Reading

■ Articles

Jolowicz, H. F. "Revivals of Roman Law." *Journal of the Warburg and Courtauld Institutes* 15, no. 1–2 (1952): 88–98.

Maas, Michael. "Roman History and Christian Ideology in Justinianic Reform Legislation." *Dumbarton Oaks Papers* 40 (1986): 17–31.

Sherman, Charles P. "The Study of Law in Roman Law Schools." *Yale Law Journal* 17, no. 7 (1908): 499–512.

■ Books

Barker, John W. *Justinian and the Later Roman Empire*. Madison, Wis.: University of Wisconsin Press, 1966.

Bury, J. B. *History of the Later Roman Empire: From the Death of Theodosius I to the Death of Justinian*, vol. 2. New York: Dover Publications, 1958.

Evans, J. A. S. *The Age of Justinian: The Circumstances of Imperial Power*. London: Routledge, 1996.

Wolff, Hans Julius. *Roman Law: An Historical Introduction*. Norman, Okla.: University of Oklahoma Press, 1951.

■ Web Sites

"Roman Law Resources." University of Glasgow Roman law Web site.
http://iuscivile.com/.

—Eric May

Questions for Further Study

1. Throughout the history of the Roman Empire, various emperors issued legal codes. Using such documents as the Twelve Tables of Roman Law, the Theodosian Code, the Law of Caesar on Municipalities, and the Code of Justinian, trace—as much as possible—the development of Roman law and its impact on the empire. Note that the Theodosian Code and the Code of Justinian were produced by the Eastern Roman Empire; the others were products of the West. Did the two sets of codes differ in any fundamental way? Explain.

2. In what specific ways did the Code of Justinian represent an advance in jurisprudence and the practice of law, not just in Rome but, ultimately, throughout much of Europe and other regions of the world?

3. Compare and contrast the Code of Justinian with the Laws Ending Persecution of Christians. Using these two documents, trace the history of Christianity in the Roman Empire.

4. Numerous documents from the first millennium demonstrate the profound influence of the state on religious affairs, and vice versa. Compare the Code of Justinian with one such document—the Capitulary of Charlemagne, for example—and explain why religion played such a large role in secular, governmental life at that time.

5. Imagine that you are a student at one of the law schools established at Beirut, Constantinople, or Alexandria. Based on what you know, how would you go about using the Code of Justinian to resolve a legal problem put to you by one of your professors?

CODE OF JUSTINIAN

The Enactments of Justinian. I. The Institutes.

♦ **Preamble.**

Of the institutes or elements of our Lord the Most Holy Emperor Justinian.

In the name of our Lord Jesus Christ....

(4) We have ordered these Institutes to be divided into the following four books, that they may constitute the first elements of the entire science of jurisprudence.

(5) In them a brief explanation has been made both of the principles which formerly obtained, as well as of those which, after having been obscured by disuse, have been illuminated once more by Imperial restoration.

(6) These Institutes collected from all those of the ancients and especially from the Commentaries of Our Gaius, embracing not only what is contained in his Institutes but also those of his work relating to daily transactions and compiled from those of many others, the three learned men aforesaid submitted to Us, and, after having read and examined them, We have accorded to them the full authority of Our Constitutions....

Book I.

Title I. Concerning Justice and Law.

Justice is the constant and perpetual desire to give to each one that to which he is entitled.

(1) Jurisprudence is the knowledge of matters divine and human, and the comprehension of what is just and what is unjust.

(2) These divisions being generally understood, and We being about to explain the laws of the Roman people, it appears that this may be most conveniently done if separate subjects are at first treated in a clear and simple manner, and afterwards with greater care and exactness; for if We, at once, in the beginning, load the still uncultivated and inexperienced mind of the student with a multitude and variety of details, We shall bring about one of two things; that is, We shall either cause him to abandon his studies, or, by means of excessive labor—and also with that distrust which very frequently discourages young men—conduct him to that point to which, if led by an easier route, he might have been brought more speedily without much exertion and without misgiving.

(3) The following are the precepts of the Law: to live honestly, not to injure another, and to give to each one that which belongs to him.

(4) There are two branches of this study, namely: public and private. Public Law is that which concerns the administration of the Roman government; Private Law relates to the interests of individuals. Thus Private Law is said to be threefold in its nature, for it is composed of precepts of Natural Law, of those of the Law of Nations, and of those of the Civil Law.

Title II. Concerning Natural Law, the Law of Nations, and the Civil Law.

Natural Law is that which nature has taught to all animals, for this law is not peculiar to the human race, but applies to all creatures which originate in the air, or the earth, and in the sea. Hence arises the union of the male and the female which we designate marriage; and hence are derived the procreation and the education of children; for we see that other animals also act as though endowed with knowledge of this law.

(1) The Civil Law and the Law of Nations are divided as follows. All peoples that are governed by laws and customs make use of the law which is partly peculiar to themselves and partly pertaining to all men; for what each people has established for itself is peculiar to that State, and is styled the Civil Law; being, as it were, the especial law of that individual commonwealth. But the law which natural reason has established among all mankind and which is equally observed among all peoples, is called the Law of Nations, as being that which all nations make use of. The Roman people also employ a law which is in part peculiar to them, and in part common to all men. We propose to set forth their distinctions in their proper places.

(2) The Civil Law derives its name from each state, as, for example, that of the Athenians; for if anyone wishes to designate the laws of Solon or of Draco as the Civil Law of Athens, he will not commit an error; for in this manner We call the law which the Roman people use the Civil Law of the Romans....

The Law of Nations, however, is common to the entire human race, for all nations have established for themselves certain regulations exacted by custom and human necessity. For wars have arisen, and captivity and slavery, which are contrary to natural law, have followed as a result, as, according to Natural Law, all men were originally born free; and from this law nearly all contracts, such as purchase, sale, hire, partnership, deposit, loan, and innumerable others have been derived.

(3) Our Law, which We make use of, is either written or unwritten, just as among the Greeks, written and unwritten laws exist. The written law consists of the Statutes, the Plebiscita, the Decrees of the Senate, the Decisions of the Emperors, the Orders of the Magistrates and the Answers of Jurisconsults....

(9) The unwritten law is that which usage has confirmed, for customs long observed and sanctioned by the consent of those who employ them, resemble law....

11) Natural Laws that are observed without distinction by all nations and have been established by Divine Providence remain always fixed and unchangeable; but those which every State establishes for itself are often changed either by the tacit consent of the people, or by some other law subsequently enacted....

The Enactments of Justinian. II. The Digest of Pandects....

♦ **First Preface. Concerning the Plan of the Digest Addressed to Tribonianus.**

The Emperor Cæsar, Flavius, Justinianus, Pious, Fortunate, Renowned, Conquerer and Triumpher, ever Augustus, to Tribonianus his Quæstor:

Greeting....

(2) ... We have hastened to attempt the most complete and thorough amendment of the entire law, to collect and revise the whole body of Roman jurisprudence, and to assemble in one book the scattered treatises of so many authors; which no one else has herebefore ventured to hope for or to expect, and it has indeed been considered by Ourselves a most difficult undertaking, nay, one that was almost impossible; but with Our hands raised to heaven, and having invoked the Divine aid. We have kept this object in Our mind, confiding in God who can grant the accomplishment of things which are almost desperate, and can Himself carry them into effect by virtue of the greatness of His power....

(4) Therefore We order you to read and revise the books relating to the Roman law drawn up by the jurists of antiquity, upon whom the most venerated princes conferred authority to write and interpret the same; so that from these all the substance may be collected, and, as far as may be possible, there shall remain no laws either similar to or inconsistent with one another, but that there may be compiled from them a summary which will take the place of all....

Book I....

Title III. Concerning Statutes, Decrees of the Senate, and Long Established Customs.

1. Papinianus, Definitions, Book I.

A statute is a general precept; a resolution of men learned in the law; a restraint of crimes committed either voluntarily or through ignorance; or a general obligation of the State.

2. Marcianus, Institutes, Book I.

The orator Demosthenes thus defined it. "A law is something which it is proper for all men to obey for many reasons, and principally because every law was devised by, and is a gift of God; the decree of learned men; the restraint of those who either voluntarily or involuntarily are guilty of crime; it is also a common obligation of the State, by whose rules all those who reside therein should regulate their lives."

Chrysius, a Stoic philosopher of the greatest erudition, began a book which he wrote as follows: "Law is the queen of all things, Divine and human. It should also be the governor, the leader, the ruler, of both the good and the bad, and, in this way, be the standard of whatever is just and unjust, as well as of those things which are civil by Nature, prescribing what should be done, and prohibiting what should not be done."

3. Pomponius on Sabinus, Book XXV.

Laws, as Theophrastus has stated, ought to be established with respect to matters which often occur, and not with reference to such as occur unexpectedly.

4. Celsus, Digest, Book V.

Laws are not established concerning matters which can only happen in a single instance....

Title V. Concerning the Condition of Men.

1. Gaius, Institutes, Book I.

All the law which We make use of relates either to persons, things, or actions....

3. Gaius, Institutes, Book I.

The principal division of the law of persons is as follows, namely, that all men are either free or slaves.

4. Florentinus, Institutes, Book IX.

Liberty is the natural power of doing whatever anyone wishes to do unless he is prevented in some way, by force or by law.

(1) Slavery is an institution of the Law of Nations by means of which anyone may subject one man to the control of another, contrary to nature.

(2) Slaves are so called for the reason that military commanders were accustomed to sell their captives, and in this manner to preserve them, instead of putting them to death.

5. Marcianus, Institutes, Book I.

One condition is common to all slaves; but of persons who are free some are born such, and others are manumitted.

(1) Slaves are brought under our ownership either by the Civil Law or by that of Nations. This is done by the Civil Law where anyone who is over twenty years of age permits himself to be sold for the sake of sharing in his own price. Slaves become our property by the Law of Nations when they are either taken from the enemy, or are born of our female slaves.

(2) Persons are born free who are born from a free mother, and it is sufficient for her to have been free at the time when her child was born, even though she may have been a slave when she conceived; and, on the other hand, if she was free when she conceived, and was a slave when she brought forth, it has been established that her child is born free, nor does it make any difference whether she conceived in a lawful marriage or through promiscuous intercourse; because the misfortune of the mother should not be a source of injury to her unborn child.

(3) Hence the following question arose, where a female slave who was pregnant, has been manumitted, and is afterwards again made a slave, or, after having been expelled from the city, should bring forth a child, whether that child should be free or a slave? It was very properly established that it was born free; and that it is sufficient for a child who is unborn that its mother should have been free during the intermediate time....

9. The Same [Papinianus], Questions, Book XXXI.

In many parts of our law the condition of women is worse than that of men....

The Codex of Justinian....

◆ **Second Preface. Concerning the Confirmation of the Code of Justinian.**

(1) But as it was necessary to reduce the vast number of the constitutions contained in the three old codes, as well in the others compiled in former times, and to clear up their obscurity by means of proper definitions, We have applied Ourselves with willing mind to the accomplishment of this work for the common good; and, after having selected men conspicuous for their legal learning and ability, as well as for their experience in business, and tireless zeal for the interests of the State, We have committed this great task to them under certain limitations, and have directed them to collect into a single code, to be designated by Our auspicious name, the constitutions of the three ancient codes, namely the Gregorian, Hermogenian, and Theodosian compilations, as well as all those subsequently promulgated by Theodosius of Divine Memory, and the other princes who have succeeded him; together with such constitutions as have been issued during Our reign; and to see that any preambles which are not confirmed by subsequent decrees, and any constitutions which are contradictory, or should be suppressed, as well as such as have been repealed by others of later date, or which are of the same character—except those which, by conferring upon them Our sanction to a certain extent, We have considered to be susceptible of division, and by such division of these ancient laws some new principle may appear to arise....

Book I.

Title I. Concerning The Most Exalted Trinity And The Catholic Faith, And Providing That No One Shall Dare To Publicly Oppose Them.

1. The Emperors Gratian, Valentinian, and Theodosius to the people of the City of Constantinople.

We desire that all peoples subject to Our benign Empire shall live under the same religion that the Divine Peter, the Apostle, gave to the Romans, and which the said religion declares was introduced by himself, and which it is well known that the Pontiff Damasus, and Peter, Bishop of Alexandria, a man of apostolic sanctity, embraced; that is to say, in accordance with the rules of apostolic discipline and the evangelical doctrine, we should believe that the Father, Son, and Holy Spirit constitute a single Deity, endowed with equal majesty, and united in the Holy Trinity.

(1) We order all those who follow this law to assume the name of Catholic Christians, and considering others as demented and insane. We order that they shall bear the infamy of heresy; and when the Divine vengeance which they merit has been appeased, they shall afterwards be punished in accordance with Our resentment, which we have acquired from the judgment of Heaven.

Dated at Thessalonica, on the third of the Kalends of March, during the Consulate of Gratian, Consul for the fifth time, and Theodosius.... /

Book VII....

Title VII. Concerning Apostates.

1. The Emperor Constantius and Julian-Cæsar to Thalassius, Prætorian Prefect.

If anyone, after renouncing the venerated Christian faith, should become a Jew, and join their sacrilegious assemblies, We order that, after the accusation has been proved, his property shall be confiscated to the Treasury.

Given at Milan, on the fifth of the Nones of July, during the Consulate of Constantius, Consul for the ninth time, and Julian-Cæsar, Consul for the second time, 357.

2. The Emperors Gratian, Valentinian, and Theodosius to Hypatius, Prætorian Prefect.

Where anyone accuses a deceased person of having violated and abandoned the Christian religion, and denounces him for having given his adherence to the sacrileges of the temples, or the rites of the Jews, and maintains that, in consequence, he has no right to make a will; he must institute proceedings within five years, as has been decided in cases brought to declare a will inofficious.

Given on the fifteenth of the Kalends of January, during the Consulate of the Emperor Gratian, Consul for the fourth time, and Merobaudus, 383.

3. The Emperors Theodosius, Valentinian, and Arcadius to Flavian, Prætorian Prefect.

Those who have betrayed the Holy Faith, and have profaned the sacred rite of baptism by heretical superstition, shall be separated from association with all other persons, and shall not have the right to testify against anyone, or to make a will (as We have already decreed), nor shall they succeed to estates or be appointed heirs.

Prince Shōtoku and attendants (Freer Gallery of Art, Smithsonian Institution, Washington, D.C.: Purchase-Parnassus Foundation, courtesy of Jane and Raphael Bernstein, Mr. and Mrs. Frank H. Pearl; Jeffrey P. Cunard; and Museum funds, F2001.1)

PRINCE SHŌTOKU'S SEVENTEEN-ARTICLE CONSTITUTION

"The sovereign is likened to heaven, and his subjects are likened to earth."

Overview

Composed in the fourth lunar month (May in the modern calendar) of the year 604, the Seventeen-Article Constitution contains a series of moral admonitions drawn from Buddhist and Confucian ideals of sage government. It is considered to be the earliest Japanese articulation of the ethical foundations of government and an indigenous political vision for a centralized, bureaucratic Japanese state. Authorship of the constitution has been generally attributed to Crown Prince Shōtoku, though there is some evidence that the text had been written by others and posthumously credited to him. Prince Shōtoku oversaw the affairs of the early Japanese state for twenty-nine years in the capacity of acting regent for his childless aunt, Empress Suiko. He has since been hailed widely as Japan's earliest native example of a wise ruler. Questions of authorship notwithstanding, the constitution is considered an accurate reflection of Shōtoku's personal erudition in the Chinese classics and dedication to the recently imported doctrine of Buddhism. While the original manuscript is no longer extant, the text of the constitution was preserved in *Nihon shōki* (*Chronicles of Japan*), an imperial history compiled in the year 720.

Context

The earliest written references to Japan as the land of Wa (also known as Wo) are found in Chinese histories such as the *Hou Han shu* (Book of the Later Han). These texts include records of tribute missions that had been sent to the Chinese court by the kings of Wa as early as the first century CE. These early Chinese texts also describe a political order within Wa that was composed of many discrete political units called *kuni*. According to Chinese historical records, by the fourth century early Yamato rule had taken the form of federations called *kuni*, which were made up of smaller clan units called *uji*. One such *kuni* federation known as the Yamataikoku, Chinese records maintain, was presided over by Queen Himiko, who sent an envoy to

China in the year 238. Chinese histories such as the *Wei chih* (Record of the Wei Dynasty), dating from the mid-third century, suggest that the rule of Queen Himiko and her successors was characterized by shamanistic practices and by a system of joint rulership in which pairs of siblings often shared administrative responsibility over the *kuni*.

Various theories exist concerning the way in which centralized state rule arose in early Japan. Most historians agree that between the third and fifth centuries the location of the rulers moved from Kyushu to the Yamato Plain, the place from which the early state would have taken its name. During the fifth century, Chinese accounts like the *Sung shu* (Book of the Sung) continued to describe how the kings of Wa had achieved political dominance through warfare and the subjugation of rival groups. Leaders were recognized with various titles under a detailed system of social ranks that established a clear political hierarchy among multiple rulers.

At the apex of this new hierarchy was the figure of the *ōkimi* (literally, "great king"). While he possessed significant power, the *ōkimi* still did not exercise centralized rule. Powerful and autonomous *uji* clans continued to exert power regionally, even as they attempted to preserve and protect their status through rendering specialized services to the *ōkimi* and pursuing marriage alliances with the *ōkimi* line. In the late fifth century, several rebellions led by local *uji* rulers against the Yamato court resulted in the deterioration of *ōkimi* authority. Consequently, there arose a need for the assistance of military clans like the Mononobe and the Ōtomo in quelling insurrections.

Throughout the sixth century, powerful *uji* clans continued to struggle with one another for regional domination and for influence over the *ōkimi*. The rise of the influential Soga clan, which had emerged from an earlier clan known as the Katsuragi, signified an important shift in the political structure during the late sixth century. The *ōkimi* gradually relinquished their reliance on military clans like the Mononobe and began to favor clans like the Soga, who were capable of assisting with administrative tasks such as levying taxes and economic oversight of state-owned rice fields. Additionally, Soga backing for the newly imported doctrine of Buddhism eventually led to direct conflict with the Mononobe and Nakatomi, clans, who were wary about

CA. 300

- Early kingship rule is established in the Yamato state; by the sixth century, this system of rule would produce the imperial line.

CA. 400

- The Chinese writing system is introduced into Japan from continental Asia.

552

- The king of the Korean kingdom of Paekche sends a Buddhist statue and manuscripts of scriptures to the Japanese *ōkimi*.

574

- Prince Shōtoku (also known as Prince Umayakado and Prince Kamitsumiya) is born.

587

- Emperor Yōmei, Prince Shōtoku's father, dies after just two years' rule; Soga forces achieve military victory over the rival Mononobe clan.

592

- Emperor Sushun, Prince Shōtoku's uncle, is assassinated on the orders of Soga Umako, who as head of the Soga clan had installed Sushun as emperor. Empress Suiko—a Soga woman and the sister of Sushun as well as the widow of Emperor Bidatsu, the daughter of Emperor Kimmei, and Prince Shōtoku's aunt—is enthroned.

the growing influence of Buddhism on the ruling classes and thus were opposed to the dissemination of the foreign religion. The Soga's military victory over the Mononobe in 587 resulted in increased Soga dominance of government positions. The conflict between the Mononobe and Soga would eventually engulf the *ōkimi* line. In 593 it resulted in the placement of a Soga woman of royal birth on the throne, Empress Suiko. This was the historical context in which Prince Shōtoku, a nephew of the new empress, was named her regent and thus stepped onto the national stage.

The reign of Empress Suiko was a watershed moment in the transition to centralized rule. During this time, there emerged the first concentrated attempts to redefine Japanese kingship and establish a ruler who could exercise supreme authority over a unified state. Chinese state structures heavily influenced the model for the new sense of Japanese kingship in the figure of the *tennō*, or emperor. However, unlike Chinese emperors, the Japanese *tennō*, was not subject to the notion of the "Mandate of Heaven" (the concept that rulership was conferred by the blessing of Heaven on a just ruler), which in China had resulted in rapid and often bloody dynastic change. Conversely, in the early Yamato state, the authority of the emperor emanated from the imperial line itself, which traced itself, albeit somewhat dubiously, directly back to the indigenous sun goddess, Amaterasu Ōmikami. Therefore, official state doctrine held that the hereditary position of emperor was derived from his or her innate divinity and was thus unassailable.

About the Author

Shōtoku appears to have been a posthumous appellation for the prince who had previously been known as Umayakado or Kamitsumiya. The second son of Emperor Yōmei, the prince was born in 574 and raised in an atmosphere rife with political intrigue. At the age of nineteen, Prince Shōtoku was named crown prince and regent for Empress Suiko shortly after her enthronement. He would remain in that position, managing the state's affairs both domestically and abroad, until his death in 622. During an administration that native histories have hailed as exemplary, Prince Shōtoku maintained key links with continental Asia. He sent an envoy to the Korean kingdom of Silla and established a variety of cultural and religious exchanges with China's Sui Dynasty. He is also credited with the creation of the twelve-rank system for court bureaucracy and the compilation of two now-lost historical chronicles, *Tennōki* (Record of the Emperors) and *Kokki* (Record of the Nation).

Key components of Prince Shōtoku's cultural legacy include his sponsorship of state-sanctioned Buddhism through authorship of an undated commentary on three Buddhist scriptures known as the *Sangyō gisho* (Annotated Commentaries on the Three Sutras) and the creation of the Seventeen-Article Constitution in 604. While historians have raised questions concerning Shōtoku's authorship of these documents, both can be reliably dated to the era of Suiko's reign, and it seems clear that Shōtoku provided key direction, if not direct authorship, for both texts. The two documents form the foundation for Shōtoku's mythos as an enlightened ruler and visionary architect of early Japanese state structures. While the *Sangyō gisho* articulates a political philosophy that draws on Buddhist religion, the Seventeen-Article Constitution is the first native-Japanese expression of a vision for moral rulership. Together, these texts have earned Shōtoku an historical reputation as the penultimate model of sage rule for the Japanese nation. While the prince never took Buddhist orders himself, there is evidence that he spent his entire life as a devout lay Buddhist and scholar of Chinese culture. Shōtoku's writings offered Japanized interpretations of Buddhist doctrine and Chinese models of statecraft, and his ideas helped establish universal rule within the Yamato state. In this respect, Shōtoku's career and literary productions provide key evidence of the importance and impacts of continental Asian culture, particularly that of China, upon the early Japanese state.

Explanation and Analysis of the Document

Prince Shōtoku's Seventeen-Article Constitution contains Confucian, Buddhist, and Taoist elements, reflecting the syncretic nature of Japanese philosophical systems during the Yamato period (ca. 300–710) and providing compelling evidence of the importance of Chinese cultural influence in Yamato state structures. The constitution outlines a three-tiered social hierarchy consisting of a morally upright ruler, ethical officials, and an obedient populace. The document primarily describes the roles of the sovereign and the officials who carry out his or her will, utilizing both Confucian and Buddhist concepts to define the proper roles and behavior of government officials. Building on diverse Chinese models, the constitution strove to place the emerging Japanese state on an equal cultural footing with Sui and Tang Dynasty China by articulating a notion of kingship that legitimated the rule of Prince Shōtoku and his successors.

◆ Article I

Shōtoku here clearly and strongly advocates the importance of "harmony" in human relations. The placement of this statement at the beginning of the document is deliberate and sets the tone for the remainder of the text. In Japanese, "harmony," or "concord," is expressed with the character *wa*, and this same concept frequently appears in the Analects of Confucius to denote propriety or decorum. It should be noted that this word for harmony is not the same "Wa" used as an early Chinese appellation for the emergent Japanese state. Those were written with a different Chinese character, meaning "dwarf." Later, the Japanese would replace that offensive character with the more flattering character employed in Article I to mean "harmony." The date of the transition in nomenclature is uncertain. In this original context, "harmony" is also tied directly to social status. The constitution suggests that harmony is achieved when men pursue "cordial" discussions that are free of "partisan feelings" and "guided by a spirit of conciliation." Only

Time Line

593	■ **May 14** On the tenth day of the fourth lunar month, Prince Shōtoku is designated crown prince and entrusted with all government administration in the name of his aunt, Empress Suiko.
594	■ Empress Suiko issues an imperial edict offering imperial support to the promotion of the "three treasures"—the Buddha, Buddhist law, and the monastic orders.
603	■ The twelve-rank court system attributed to Prince Shōtoku is put into effect.
604	■ The Seventeen-Article Constitution is issued.
620	■ Two official histories that chronicle the Yamato state and its rulers as well as local governments are compiled by Prince Shōtoku and Soga Umako. Records of these lost histories would be recorded in the eighth-century Nihon shōki.

622 ■ Prince Shōtoku dies.

628 ■ The reign of Empress Suiko ends.

645 ■ The first edicts of the Taika Reforms are issued.

702 ■ The Taihō Codes codify and expand upon the administrative systems put in place with the Taika Reforms of 645.

thus may reason prevail. This argument presupposes that human nature is innately contrary, even bigoted. Human beings must learn to supersede their latently contentious nature in the name of creating a harmonious society. Harmony depends, Shōtoku suggests, not purely on a blind obedience to a rule of law but rather upon the moral nature of the person or persons directing or governing society. If rulers and officials ("those above") earnestly seek concord, then "those below" (the polity) will follow suit.

The Analects make repeated reference to morally upright and benevolent rulership as the basis for an ordered society, stating, for example: "Ruling is straightening. If you lead along a straight way, who will dare go by a crooked one?" (Book 12, Verse 17). In Confucian thought the ideal society is one in which the rule of law is no longer necessary because the people have fully internalized the notion of right action, or *li*.

◆ **Article II**

Notably, Article II is the only section in the constitution that makes direct reference to Buddhism. This is remarkable when considered from the perspective of Prince Shōtoku's purported role as a key sponsor of Buddhism in the early Japanese state. Here, Shōtoku perceives the usefulness of the imported doctrine in government; the "three treasures consisting of Buddha, the Doctrine and the Monastic Order" provide a framework for spiritual growth and self-reflection that is also conducive to ethical governance. The admonition in Article II to "revere" these treasures with all one's heart would be one echoed by later

emperors such as Shōmu, in the early eighth century—a ruler who would adopt the appellation of "servant of the three treasures."

Article II rejects any sense of human nature as essentially corrupt or sinful and instead argues that "few men are utterly devoid of goodness." Shōtoku suggests that all sentient beings are capable of recognizing and respecting the Buddhist "three treasures" as "supreme objects of worship" and a "final refuge" from the consequences of their misdeeds. In seeking to found a centralized, universal state, Shōtoku looked toward the equally universal law of Buddhist doctrine. Empress Suiko's issuance in 594 of an imperial edict that granted official support to the promulgation of Buddhism offered additional evidence of the court's dedication to promoting the dissemination of Buddhist thought and practice. Shōtoku himself undertook many years of study of Buddhist doctrine under the tutelage of the Korean monk Eji from the kingdom of Koguryō. Numerous Buddhist temples were built in quick succession during the sixth and seventh centuries.

◆ **Article III**

Here Shōtoku comments upon the ideal relationship between ruler and subject, relating it to the cosmic relationship of heaven (the "sovereign") and earth ("subjects"). In this thoroughly naturalized hierarchy, an "imperial command" is to be obeyed with "reverence" and "diligence." Comparing the relationship between the ruler and the ruled to other natural phenomena (for example, the progression of the "four seasons" and "all that which is in nature"), Shōtoku posits that any resistance to the will of the ruler constitutes an unnatural response—one that "destroys everything" and results in "ruin." Modeled on Han Chinese notions of government, this formulation states that the relationship between the emperor (and by extension, his or her official functionaries) and state subjects (the "people") is naturally sanctioned and therefore unassailable. This new model of government was undoubtedly connected to the challenges to and decline in clan status and power during the sixth and seventh centuries.

◆ **Article IV**

The fourth article expands upon Article III's definition of the ideal ruler-subject relationship to specifically include government officials charged with the intermediate roles of carrying out the will of the imperial house. Article IV directs these "ministers" and "functionaries" to observe strict "decorum" as the "basis of governing the people." If officials are not themselves observing ethical and decorous behavior, "offenses" and insurrection will surely result. It is interesting to note that the term used in the original for "offenses" is *tsumi*, a word most often translated in Buddhist contexts as "sin." Conversely, correct behavior on the part of officials will ensure smooth administration, and the "nation will be governed well of its own." This philosophy concerning the moral righteousness of government officials can be related to the Confucian notion of the "exemplary person" (Chinese, *junzi*; Japanese, *kunshi*) whose self-cul-

A scroll showing one scene from the history of the founding of Tsukiminedera Temple, under the auspices of Prince Shōtoku (Freer Gallery of Art, Smithsonian Institution, Washington, D.C.: Purchase, F1961.23)

tivation naturally inspires reverence, peace, and stability in others. In its original content, *jun* had been a general term for a ruler. The term *junzi* (literally, "the ruler's child") came to be broadly applied to the upper classes of Chinese society, the "gentlemen." While the term had originally denoted high social status, Confucian thinkers came to define it as describing superior character and comportment based upon personal merit, rather than social class.

◆ Article V

Article V cautions officials to guard against materialism, greed, and corruption. Specific injunctions are made against accepting bribes and lending a biased ear to rich or influential constituencies. This last warning against corruption is delivered in simile form: "Thus the plaints of the rich are like a stone flung into water," causing ripples to spread far and wide, while the voices of the poor are inefficacious, "like water poured over a stone." The result of corrupt, greedy self-interest will be the denial of justice to the poor, which is clearly denounced as a "dereliction of duty." Thus, this article expresses the author's paramount concern with ethical self-improvement and rectitude for members of the ruling class. Similar injunctions against corruption are found in Chinese models, including the Analects of Confucius and writings by the Chinese Legalist scholar Han Feizi (ca. 280–233 BCE; also known as Han Fei-tzu).

◆ Article VI

Here, officials are sternly enjoined to "punish" evil and "encourage that which is good." Shōtoku's comment that "this is an excellent rule from antiquity" alludes to his formal training in the Chinese Confucian classics. He warns government officials, the intended audience of the constitution, to view "flatterers and tricksters" as direct threats to

the sovereignty of the unified state as well as to its people. "Men of this type"—that is, men who do not observe *li*, or *rei* as it was termed in Japanese—lack "loyalty to the sovereign" and "compassion for the people" and are capable of fomenting "civil disorders."

◆ Articles VII–IX

Clear delineation and separation of assigned duties are the central concerns of Article VII, which admonishes rulers to find and correctly place the "right man" in each government position. This is essentially an espousal of Chinese meritocracy, the origins of which may be traced back to Qin Dynasty reforms. Shōtoku seems to allude to that history by referring to the manner in which "sage kings of old" sought the proper "man to fill the office, not the office for the sake of the man." Article VIII simply expounds the importance of promptitude and diligence in the fulfillment of official government duties. Article IX defines "good faith" as "the foundation of righteousness," which is crucial to the success of the state. Shōtoku thus distinguishes truth as the hallmark of good government. This should be read as a reiteration of Article IV's encouragement of decorum and Article V's counsel concerning the dangers of official corruption.

◆ Articles X and XI

Article X suggests that state problems can be effectively addressed only when discussed in a harmonious environment free of acrimony and petty concerns. Shōtoku concedes that while not all persons in positions of political power are "sages," even "ordinary men" are capable of reaching a consensus in determining right from wrong. In this respect, Article X hearkens directly back to Shōtoku's unequivocal advocacy of harmony (*wa*) in Article I. Article

XI expands on the discussion of what constitutes ethical government. Here, Shōtoku instructs government functionaries to create and govern according to a "clear-cut system of rewards and punishments." Some commentators have tied this description of a minutely articulated legal code to the influence of Han Feizi, who lived during China's late Warring States period.

◆ Articles XII and XIII

Article XII is important insofar as it is perhaps the most direct statement of Shōtoku's principle of centralized rule under a hierarchy of government officials overseen by the imperial court. Article XII expressly forbids the levying of taxes by "provincial authorities" and "local nobles." Therefore, it reflects the contemporary decline of regional and local rule during Shōtoku's lifetime and foreshadows the full flowering of the imperial institution by the Nara period (710–784). Article XIII is comparable to Article VIII; it specifically cites neglect of work because of absenteeism (even when due to illness) as among the behaviors unacceptable in government officials. Shōtoku is here advocating the professionalism he envisions as important to the success of his merit-based bureaucracy.

◆ Articles XIV and XV

Like Articles IX through XI, Article XIV continues the repeated appeals for personal virtue among government officials. The plea takes the form of a request to avoid envy, particularly of the kind engendered by encounters with intellectual superiors. Shōtoku argues that envy directed toward "those who surpass us in talent" will impede the creation of a sense of community and thus a cohesive society: "If we cannot find wise men and sages, how can the country be governed?" Article XV defines the "way of a minister" as the path that upholds the "public good" over "private motives" and thus avoids the resentment that self-serving action arouses. Citing social discord and lawbreaking as the natural result of official egoism, Shōtoku again makes reference to Article I's valorization of harmony to bolster his point.

◆ Article XVI

Another important peacekeeping directive, Article XVI prohibits the arbitrary use of corvée (forced labor exacted by the government, typically for public construction projects and the like), especially at times when it would interfere with the "agricultural endeavor" of those conscripted into labor. This directive could reduce the possibility of unrest and uprisings among the governed. Like Articles V, VI, and XII, Article XVI expresses concern for the common people and an awareness of their needs. The Seventeen-Article Constitution is perhaps the earliest example of a document that clearly addresses the needs of commoners in such benevolent terms.

◆ Article XVII

The author's denunciation of one-person rule and despotism in Article XVII appears to be directly drawn from Chinese Legalist thought. Consider this excerpt from the section entitled "The Way of the Ruler" in the *Han Feizi*: "This is the way of the enlightened ruler: he causes the wise to bring forward all their schemes" (Watson, p. 17). Some commentators have hailed Article XVII's emphasis on collaborative decision making in government as the "embryonic beginning" of democratic thought in the early Japanese state.

Audience

Unlike many modern constitutions, Prince Shōtoku's Seventeen-Article Constitution did not include among its audience the subjects who would be governed under the system it describes. There is no evidence that the document was ever intended to be seen by the common people, a population that was, in an event, largely illiterate at this time in history. Rather, this document directly addressed the agents of government in seventh-century Japan: members of the imperial house, who had only recently emerged from the rule of the *ōkimi*, or "great kings." It also addressed the officials who would staff the bureaucratic structures of the new government and carry out its mandates. Thus, it can be understood as a text that delineated the fundamental moral principles and values, mostly Confucian, that the human instruments of the state were expected to uphold.

Impact

The Seventeen-Article Constitution was the first Japanese articulation of a vision for a centralized state. This was to be a state that could fully utilize the new imperial bureaucracy, which Prince Shōtoku had put into effect in 603. In addressing the definition of upright and moral behavior for the imperial rulers and other government officials who would oversee the machinery of state, Shōtoku was profoundly influenced by Chinese philosophical systems, primarily Confucianism but also Buddhism and Legalism. His reliance on Chinese models encouraged Japan's continued cultural borrowing from Sui and Tang Dynasty China.

However, the Seventeen-Article Constitution was more than a mere imitation of Chinese models. It also outlined a newly appropriated sense of Japanese sovereignty and provided a naturalized vision of the ruler-subject relationship that was not subject to the whims of the Chinese Mandate of Heaven. In this new model, the emperor was understood to be a supreme ruler imbued with authority as the earthly symbol of heaven. The far-reaching implications of this view of the imperial person for later Japanese history cannot be overstated. The location of ultimate governmental authority in the person of the emperor persisted for more than a millennium, even during long periods when de facto political power rested in the hands of aristocratic regents or military leaders outside the imperial family. As government doctrine, the text presaged the later Taika Reforms (645) and Taihō Code (702), which were similarly modeled after Chinese precedents.

"Harmony is to be cherished and opposition for opposition's sake must be avoided as a matter of principle.... If those above are harmonious and those below are cordial, their discussion will be guided by a spirit of conciliation, and reason shall naturally prevail. There will be nothing that cannot be accomplished."

(Article I)

"The three treasures, consisting of Buddha, the Doctrine, and the Monastic Order, are the final refuge of the four generated beings, and are the supreme objects of worship in all countries. Can any man in any age ever fail to respect these teachings?"

(Article II)

"The sovereign is likened to heaven, and his subjects are likened to earth."

(Article III)

"Punish that which is evil and encourage that which is good. This is an excellent rule from antiquity."

(Article VI)

"If the officials observe good faith with one another, everything can be accomplished. If they do not observe good faith, everything is bound to fail."

(Article IX)

"It takes five hundred years before we can meet a wise man, and in a thousand years it is still difficult to find one sage. If we cannot find wise men and sages, how can the country be governed?"

(Article XIV)

The prestige of Prince Shōtoku increased exponentially after his death in 622. Various legends arose about him. Some held that the prince had been a reincarnation of Eshi, an early Zen master and patriarch of Chinese Buddhism. Other persistent mythologies claimed that he had been a manifestation of the popular Buddhist figure Kannon (Avalokiteśvara). During Japan's medieval period from the twelfth

through fifteenth centuries, worship of Shōtoku as an incarnation of Kannon enjoyed tremendous popularity.

Prince Shōtoku is still held up as an icon of Japanese Buddhism. Scholarly discussion about Shōtoku—both the man and the legend—has continued to contemporary times. Recently, Shōtoku and his attendant mythology have been connected to Japanese nationalist discourse and narratives of state formation by scholars such as Ienaga Saburō and Michael Como. Perhaps Shōtoku's most lasting and readily recognized legacy is his status as an emblem of the monumental shifts in Japanese statecraft that took place during his lifetime—changes that shaped the very essence of Japan's then-emerging national identity.

Further Reading

■ Articles

Deal, William. "Hagiography and History: The Image of Prince Shōtoku." In *Religions of Japan in Practice*, ed. George J. Tanabe Jr. Princeton: Princeton University Press, 1999.

■ Books

Como, Michael. *Shōtoku: Ethnicity, Ritual, and Violence in the Japanese Buddhist Tradition*. New York: Oxford University Press, 2008.

Hall, David L., and Roger T. Ames. *Thinking through Confucius*. Albany: State University of New York Press, 1987.

Lee, Kenneth Doo Young. *The Prince and the Monk: Shōtoku Worship in Shinran's Buddhism*. Albany: State University of New York Press, 2007.

Nakamura, Hajime. *History of Japanese Thought*. London: Kegan Paul, 2002.

Tamura, Yoshiro. *Japanese Buddhism: A Cultural History*, trans. Jeffrey Hunter. Tokyo: Kosei Publishing Company, 2000.

Watson, Burton, trans. *Basic Writings of Mo Tzu, Hsuïn Tzu, and Han Fei Tzu*. New York: Columbia University Press, 1967.

Waley, Arthur, trans. *The Analects of Confucius*. New York: Macmillan, 1939.

Williams, Yoko. *Tsumi—Offence and Retribution in Early Japan*. London: RoutledgeCurzon, 2003.

—Melinda S. Varner

Questions for Further Study

1. In what ways were the political organization and social structure of early Japan similar to the feudal structure of medieval Europe? For comparison, consult the Constitutions of Clarendon and *Domesday Book*. What do these similarities tell you about the concerns of early societies?

2. The prince's constitution reflects the influence of Chinese religious beliefs. Why do you think the Japanese found these beliefs congenial for their society?

3. The history of many early societies is the history of the centralization of rule. Compare this process in early Japan with similar processes in other ancient cultures such as Greece and China.

4. Why did the Japanese come to regard the rule of their emperor as divinely given? What impact did this belief have on the social order? To what extent did this view resemble the European notion of the divine right of kings?

5. The constitution places considerable emphasis on harmony and concord—an emphasis that many observers believe still plays a key role in Japanese society. Why do you think this emphasis was so important for early Japanese leaders?

PRINCE SHŌTOKU'S SEVENTEEN-ARTICLE CONSTITUTION

Summer, 4th month, 3rd day [12th year of Empress Suiko, 604 AD]. The Crown Prince personally drafted and promulgated a constitution consisting of seventeen articles, which are as follows:

I. Harmony is to be cherished, and opposition for opposition's sake must be avoided as a matter of principle. Men are often influenced by partisan feelings, except a few sagacious ones. Hence there are some who disobey their lords and fathers, or who dispute with their neighboring villages. If those above are harmonious and those below are cordial, their discussion will be guided by a spirit of conciliation, and reason shall naturally prevail. There will be nothing that cannot be accomplished.

II. With all our heart, revere the three treasures. The three treasures, consisting of Buddha, the Doctrine, and the Monastic Order, are the final refuge of the four generated beings, and are the supreme objects of worship in all countries. Can any man in any age ever fail to respect these teachings? Few men are utterly devoid of goodness, and men can be taught to follow the teachings. Unless they take refuge in the three treasures, there is no way of rectifying their misdeeds.

III. When an imperial command is given, obey it with reverence. The sovereign is likened to heaven and his subjects are likened to earth. With heaven providing the cover and earth supporting it, the four seasons proceed in orderly fashion, giving sustenance to all that which is in nature. If earth attempts to overtake the functions of heaven, it destroys everything. Therefore when the sovereign speaks, his subjects must listen: when the superior acts, the inferior must follow his examples. When an imperial command is given, carry it out with diligence. If there is no reverence shown to the imperial command, ruin will automatically result.

IV. The ministers and functionaries must act on the basis of decorum for the basis of governing the people consists of decorum. If the superiors do not behave with decorum, offenses will ensue. If the ministers behave with decorum, there will be no confusion about ranks. If the people behave with decorum, the nation will be governed well of its own.

V. Cast away your ravenous desire for food and abandon your covetousness for material possessions. If a suit is brought before you, render a clear-cut judgment.... Nowadays, those who are in the position of pronouncing judgment are motivated by making private gains and, as a rule, receive bribes. Thus the plaints of the rich are like a stone flung into water, while those of the poor are like water poured over a stone. Under these circumstances, the poor will be denied recourses to justice, which constitutes a dereliction of duty of the ministers.

VI. Punish that which is evil and encourage that which is good. This is an excellent rule from antiquity. Do not conceal the good qualities of others, and always correct that which is evil which comes to your attention. Consider those flatterers and tricksters as constituting a superb weapon for the overthrow of the state, and a sharp sword for the destruction of people. Smooth-tongued adulators love to report to their superiors the errors of their inferiors; and to their inferiors, castigate the errors of their superiors. Men of this type lack loyalty to the sovereign and have no compassion for the people. They are the ones who can cause great civil disorders.

VII. Every man must be given his clearly delineated responsibility. If a wise man is entrusted with office, the sound of praise arises. If a wicked man holds office, disturbances become frequent.... In all things, great or small, find the right man, and the country will be well governed. On all occasions, in an emergency or otherwise, seek out a wise man, which in itself is an enriching experience. In this manner, the state will be lasting and its sacerdotal functions will be free from danger. Therefore did the sage kings of old seek the man to fill the office, not the office for the sake of the man.

VIII. The ministers and functionaries must attend the court early in the morning and retire late. The business of the state must not be taken lightly. A full day is hardly enough to complete work, and if the attendance is late, emergencies cannot be met. If the officials retire early, the work cannot be completed.

IX. Good faith is the foundation of righteousness, and everything must be guided by good faith. The key to the success of the good and the failure of the bad can also be found in good faith. If the officials observe good faith with one another, everything can be accomplished. If they do not observe good faith, everything is bound to fail.

X. Discard wrath and anger from your heart and from your looks. Do not be offended when others differ with you. Everyone has his own mind, and each mind has its own leanings. Thus what is right with him is wrong with us, and what is right with us is wrong with him. We are not necessarily sages, and he is not necessarily a fool. We are all simply ordinary men, and none of us can set up a rule to determine the right from wrong.... Therefore, instead of giving way to anger as others do, let us fear our own mistakes. Even though we may have a point, let us follow the multitude and act like them.

XI. Observe clearly merit and demerit and assign reward and punishment accordingly. Nowadays, rewards are given in the absence of meritorious work, punishments without corresponding crimes. The ministers, who are in charge of public affairs, must therefore take upon themselves the task of administering a clear-cut system of rewards and punishments.

XII. Provincial authorities or local nobles are not permitted to levy exactions on the people. A country cannot have two sovereigns nor the people two masters. The people of the whole country must have the sovereign as their only master. The officials who are given certain functions are all his subjects. Being the subjects of the sovereign, these officials have no more right than others to levy exactions on the people.

XIII. All persons entrusted with office must attend equally to their functions. If absent from work due to illness or being sent on missions, and work for that period is neglected, on their return, they must perform their duties conscientiously by taking into account that which transpired before and during their absence. Do not permit lack of knowledge of the intervening period as an excuse to hinder effective performance of public affairs.

XIV. Ministers and functionaries are asked not to be envious of others. If we envy others, they in turn will envy us, and there is no limit to the evil that envy can cause us. We resent others when their intelligence is superior to ours, and we envy those who surpass us in talent. This is the reason why it takes five hundred years before we can meet a wise man, and in a thousand years it is still difficult to find one sage. If we cannot find wise men and sages, how can the country be governed?

XV. The way of a minister is to turn away from private motives and to uphold public good. Private motives breed resentment and resentful feelings cause a man to act discordantly. If he fails to act in accord with others, he sacrifices public interests for the sake of his private feelings. When resentment arises, it goes counter to the existing order and breaks the law. Therefore it is said in the first article that superiors and inferiors must act in harmony. The purport is the same.

XVI. The people may be employed in forced labor only at seasonable times. This is an excellent rule from antiquity. Employ the people in the winter months when they are at leisure. However, from spring to autumn, when they are engaged in agriculture or sericulture, do not employ them. Without their agricultural endeavor, there is no food, and without their sericulture, there is no clothing.

XVII. Major decisions must not be made by one person alone, but must be deliberated with many. On the other hand, it is not necessary to consult many people on minor questions. If important matters are not discussed fully there may always be fear of committing mistakes. A thorough discussion with many can prevent it and bring about a reasonable solution.

Glossary

attendance	in this context, ministers and functionaries who are obliged to be present in the court to perform their duties
four generated beings	a collective designation for the four classes of life-forms recognized in Buddhism, distinguished by mode of birth—live-born, born from eggs, moisture-bred, and formed by metamorphosis
levy exactions on the people	extract additional taxes from citizens, without sanction

"Aldermen ... shall be selected from ordinary subjects ... who are sincere, incorrupt and of strong disposition."

Overview

The Taika Reform was a series of edicts, issued during the Taika era (645–650), that were a major stepping-stone in the development of the Japanese political structure. Japan had been a confederation of elite families or clans, called *uji*, that did not have a very strong allegiance to the imperial family. After the defeat of one such *uji*, the Soga, the Taika Reform edicts issued by Emperor Kōtoku and Prince Nakano-Ōe, who would later reign as Emperor Tenchi, were aimed at weakening these *uji* through adopting a Chinese-style government to strengthen imperial authority by curtailing the independence of the *uji*, which controlled various regions of Japan. Although edicts were issued in 645 and later, the edict issued on New Year's Day of 646 was the first one to call for a major overhaul of the Japanese government and served as the basis for future reforms over the next sixty years, ending with the Taihō Code in 702.

Context

Beginning in the fourth century, there was a dramatic increase in contact between Japan and the Asian continent, leading to the introduction of Buddhism, Chinese-style writing, and eventually a Chinese-style government. During this period Japan was a loose confederation of *uji*, which maintained top government positions and regulated their own lands throughout Japan. One such *uji*, the Soga, increased its influence in Japan by choosing the succession of the imperial family. Soga support of the newly introduced religion of Buddhism and the clan's control of the imperial family led to conflicts with other prominent *uji*, the most important conflict being a military victory over the Mononobe *uji* in 587. This victory led to the increase of Soga power within the imperial court, placing clan members in important government positions.

The Soga *uji*, as part of its control over the imperial court, appointed Prince Shōtoku as regent in 593. Prince Shōtoku tried to end the hereditary control of top government positions by the various *uji*, especially the Soga,

which ironically placed him as imperial regent. To accomplish this goal, Prince Shōtoku and other reformers—who were influenced by Confucianism, which had been introduced from China—adopted the view that the emperor was the supreme ruler whose authority came from the gods or heaven. These reformers found this ideology appealing and adopted it because of their belief that the imperial family descended from the sun goddess Amaterasu. However, this view was different from the Chinese notion of the Mandate of Heaven, which held that the emperor was chosen by heaven and not necessarily by heredity. With the introduction of a seventeen-article constitution, Prince Shōtoku laid the foundation for a centralized government that stepped away from the confederation of *uji* and into a system that placed the Japanese under the authority of the emperor. Despite this move to take power away from the *uji*, after the death of Prince Shōtoku, the Soga continued to make decisions about who should take possession of the throne and fill other high government positions. This practice violated the sanctity of imperial succession and several of the points that Prince Shōtoku and his reforms had fought for.

In 645 those who opposed Soga control staged a coup that ended in the deaths of the leaders of the Soga *uji*, Soga Iruka and his father, Soga Emishi. Prince Nakano-Ōe, son of the reigning empress Kōgyoku, and Nakatomi Kamatari had started plotting to overthrow the Soga in 644 but waited for the right opportunity, when they could kill the Soga *uji* leadership. The moment presented itself during the summer of 645. Their reason for eliminating the Soga *uji* was to consolidate the power of the imperial family, an aim of Prince Shōtoku and his seventeen-point constitution. With Emperor Kōtoku's ascension to the throne, the reformers named the period Taika, meaning "great reform." Shortly after Emperor Kōtoku took the throne, a series of edicts was issued, ranging from the imperial family's support of Buddhism to procedures for handling corrupt officials. These edicts paved the way for future reforms that were designed to bring under imperial authority *uji*-controlled lands and recently acquired lands that had long been on the periphery.

In essence, these edicts started the process that brought all of the Japanese people under the authority of the Japan-

CA. 300	■ The imperial family establishes control of Japan.
536	■ Soga Iname becomes adviser to the throne and takes control of the Soga *uji* over the succession of the imperial throne.
552	■ Buddhism is introduced to Japan.
604	■ Prince Shōtoku issues a seventeen-article constitution, moving toward a Chinese-style government.
630	■ Formal relations are established with Tang China.
645	■ **July** Prince Nakano-Ōe and Nakatomi Kamatari lead a coup against the Soga *uji*, and Emperor Kōtoku ascends the throne. ■ **September** The first edicts are issued as part of the Taika Reform.
646	■ **New Year's Day** The edict that begins the development of the *ritsuryō* system is issued.

ese imperial family. Although several edicts were issued, the main edict that facilitated this new direction of a Chinese-style government was issued on New Year's Day of 646. The passing of this edict is seen as the beginning of the *ritsuryō* system: a set system of laws based on the Chinese style of government and Confucianism that developed in Japan. Over the next sixty years, the edict (and others produced in this period) influenced the development of the Japanese imperial government, eventually ending with the Taihō Code (issued in 702), which codified and solidified the power of the imperial family in Japan.

About the Author

It is difficult to pinpoint the exact authors who wrote this particular Taika Reform edict, but the likely authors were Japanese Confucian scholars. Emperor Kōtoku formally issued the edicts supported by Prince Nakano-Ōe and Nakatomi Kamatari and appointed the latter as inner minister. According to tradition, Emperor Kōtoku was the thirty-sixth emperor of Japan, reigning from 645 to 654. He was chosen to take the role of emperor shortly after the Soga had been overthrown and his sister, Empress Kōgyoku, had abdicated. Prince Nakano-Ōe was one of the chief architects in the overthrow of Soga control of the imperial court. He would eventually reign as Emperor Tenchi from 668 to 672, and he continued to propagate the ideas of the Taika Reform with the Ōmi Codes. Although Nakatomi Kamatari assisted in the overthrow of the Soga, it is difficult to know how much he may have contributed to the development of the edicts. Nonetheless, Nakatomi Kamatari would establish the Fujiwara family and would assume that family's name. (The Fujiwara family was influential in later periods of Japanese history, as they occupied key positions within the imperial court and dominated the succession of the imperial family as regents in the Heian period.) Emperor Kōtoku, Prince Nakano-Ōe, and Nakatomi Kamatari's contributions to the Taika Reform edicts were influenced by the reforms of Prince Shōtoku and the writings of Confucian scholars; these writings justified the Chinese style of government that placed the imperial family, rather than a loose confederation of elite families, as head of the political system.

Explanation and Analysis of the Document

On New Year's Day of 646, Emperor Kōtoku issued an edict detailing the establishment of a new political system that would place all bureaucratic positions, people, lands, and taxes under imperial administration, with the proposal of building a Chinese-style capital where the imperial administration would be located. The issuing of this edict on New Year's Day demonstrated the importance that the imperial court was trying to place on the edict, as New Year's is a special time in Japanese and East Asian society. Although it was one of several edicts issued by Emperor

Kōtoku as part of the Taika Reform, this particular edict is important in that it highlights the major trend in policies that the imperial court tried to put into place. The four sections of the edict underscore how the authors wanted to model the administration of Japan after the Chinese style of government. However, the directives in this edict were not carried out instantaneously; some took several decades to implement fully.

The earliest available source of the edict known to scholars comes from the *Nihon shoki*, translated as *Chronicles of Japan*, the compilation of which was completed in 720. Historians are not sure whether the original edict issued in 646 is in the same form as that provided in the *Nihon shoki* or whether official scholars later revised it. Nonetheless, even if it was revised, it still contains the basis of what the original authors wished to accomplish.

◆ **Section I**

This first section highlights the reorganization of imperial and *uji* lands by bringing them under the central authority of the emperor. Previously, the imperial family and the *uji* held specific lands from which they gained revenue, and these lands were labored over by those who had been appointed to them. The edict first states that the status of these people, as it had been established by previous emperors, was to be abolished and that their association with a particular piece of land was to be eliminated. Members of the imperial family, *uji*, and local notables were to give up any titles to lands that they held in order to bring all of these lands under official administration by the imperial government. This restructuring of land was aimed at diminishing their power base, which was derived from the revenue generated by farming the land. While the confiscation of *uji*-held lands made sense, the loss of land by members of the imperial family helped further to diminish any power that could possibly be wielded against the reigning emperor.

In direct relation to this reorganization, the edict states that these lands will be governed by "Daibu," or those with a higher rank appointed by the imperial administration. These officials were to manage the people, and "if they discharge their task diligently, the people will have trust in them." The concept that an official who does his task diligently will have the support of the people is based upon Confucian precepts that were introduced to Japan during this period. This idea, not seen in previous Japanese sources, demonstrates one of the principles of the new imperial administration—that officials who placed their duty to the people first would gain the people's trust and should be rewarded with higher salaries. The new imperial administration wished to adopt the policy that official income should be based on performance.

◆ **Section II**

While the first section deals with the reclaiming of lands from *uji* and members of the imperial family, the second section focuses on the creation of a centralized government headed at a newly constructed permanent capital. The first

Time Line

662	■ Prince Nakano-Ōe ascends the throne as Emperor Tenchi.
668	■ The Ōmi Codes are compiled under the order of Emperor Tenchi.
702	■ The Taihō Code is enacted, codifying all administrative and legal changes that had begun with the Taika Reform.
710	■ Nara is selected as the first permanent Chinese-style capital in Japan.

paragraph calls for the establishment of a permanent capital where the emperor would reign and appoint governors and prefects to administer the various provinces. In addition, guard posts were to be positioned on the borders of provinces, important rivers, and mountain ranges, to control movement of people and the flow of goods and to designate provincial boundaries. The "bell-tokens" that are mentioned in this section refer to tokens that identified officials who were operating under the authority of the imperial government and that allowed authorities access to post horses designated for official use. This part of the second section of the edict redesigned Japan by creating provinces with defined boundaries with the assistance of outposts.

After the discussion of the creation of a capital and provinces, the second and fourth paragraphs detail the formation of a government hierarchy in the capital and rural villages. An alderman was to be chosen from the general population to look after a ward or a township. The alderman must be "sincere, incorrupt, and of strong disposition." In the capital, four wards were to be looked after by a chief alderman, again a person of "unblemished character, strong and upright, who can discharge the duties of the time effectively." The chief alderman's responsibilities included supervising the general population within his ward and handling criminal affairs within the capital areas. Outside the capital, the provinces were to broken down

Illustration by Hokusai of the first poem in a collection called One Hundred Poets, One Poem Each. *The first poem, written by Emperor Tenchi, shows common people laboring in a tranquil autumn harvest scene.*

(Arthur M. Sackler Gallery, Smithsonian Institution, Washington, D.C.: The Anne van Biema Collection, S2004.3.212)

into one of three categories of districts, based on the number of villages in a district: greater, middle, and lesser. These districts were to be governed by a local prefect who was to be assisted by "men of ability."

This government design with the creation of a bureaucratic hierarchy and moral standards for officials was based on Chinese society. The designation of governors, chief aldermen, aldermen, and prefects to oversee the affairs of the capital and the provinces created a system whereby all Japanese lands would be administered by the emperor through a bureaucratic hierarchy; this concept of government was influenced by scholars who had traveled and studied in China. The requirement that chief aldermen, aldermen, and prefects exhibit qualities of virtue was also borrowed from the Chinese; Confucianism placed a strong emphasis on ability and virtue. Previously, government positions were filled based on familial ties and not on ability or values. The emphasis on government leaders' having these qualities was key to stepping away from the old system in which *uji* controlled many parts of Japan. This section of the edict was designed to allow the emperor to extend his control throughout all of Japan.

◆ Section III

The third section of the document focuses primarily on making the government more efficient. The first paragraph stipulates the creation of household registers, tax registers, and a system by which land was to be allocated to the local population. The idea was to take a census of the population regularly so that officials at the local level and in the capital could properly assess the collection of taxes. This system would also allow for better control of the population so that migration could be regulated and limited by keeping the peasants on the land. The edict states that households were to be organized into groups of fifty and overseen by an alderman. It would be the alderman's responsibility to supervise the daily activities of the community, including maintaining accurate census data and overseeing tax collection. As part of making a more efficient government, the third paragraph calls for the standardization of measuring field sizes. A rice field was to be measure by a unit called a *tan*, which is equivalent to 0.29 acres, with ten *tan* equaling one *chō*. This system would enable officials to project annual tax revenues and budget accordingly. It would also allow for greater control of the population at the local level

"It is said that the duty of the Daibu is to govern the people. If they discharge their task diligently, the people will have trust in them. Therefore it is for the benefit of the people that the revenue of the Daibu shall be increased."

(Section I)

"For the first time, the capital shall be placed under an administrative system."

(Section II)

"In principle, aldermen of rural villages or of city wards shall be selected from ordinary subjects belonging to the villages or city wards, who are sincere, incorrupt and of strong disposition."

(Section II)

"It is hereby decreed that household registers, tax registers, and rules for allocation and redistribution of land shall be established."

(Section III)

"Old taxes and forced labor shall be replaced by a system of commuted taxes based on [the size of] rice fields. These taxes shall consist of fine silk, coarse silk, raw silk, and floss silk, which are to be collected in accordance with what is produced in the locality."

(Section IV)

"Under the old system, one servant was supplied by every thirty households. This system shall be altered to allow every fifty households to furnish one servant to work for various officials."

(Section IV)

by aldermen, who were acting under the authority of the emperor, again limiting the power of local elites and *uji*.

◆ **Section IV**

The last section of the edict is concerned with the collection of taxes through goods or services. The collection of

goods would be based on the size of rice fields. In addition to the collection of taxes in rice, there was also a tax requirement of silk. Silk was a highly sought-after commodity used for making clothes; the collection of silk as payment of taxes was another practice adopted from China. This section also calls for the payment of taxes by households. This payment was to consist mainly of silk and salt, another highly desirable commodity, in addition to other commodities produced in the region, such as indigo. Finally, every one hundred households were responsible for supplying a medium-quality horse or a horse of superior quality per two hundred households, with each household providing military supplies. The taxation for horses and military supplies was based on the creation of a conscription army, in which the peasants were responsible for supplying their own armaments and provisions. Although the edict did not impose the conscription requirements on the Japanese population, this section implies that when needed, an army from the peasant population would be created. However, the third paragraph does mention that every fifty households were to provide an individual and supply him with provisions to work for various officials in public works projects all over Japan. This new taxation for goods and services again was designed to strengthen the emperor by increasing his revenue and furnishing manpower for an army and for public works projects.

The last paragraph of this section deals with choosing waiting women for the imperial court. These "good-looking" women were to be selected from the families of officials with the rank of vice prefect or higher. Having waiting women from elite families was not new. However, it would now be the responsibility of every one hundred households to provide for one waiting woman at the imperial court.

Audience

Although the edict was directed to all of the Japanese, its target audience was the *uji*, members of the imperial family, and local elites, because this edict was the first of the Taika Reform edicts to discuss a major overhaul and adoption of a new style of government. Its issuance on New Year's Day also reflects the importance that Emperor Kōtoku was placing on the edict as it was read first read to influential *uji* members present for the New Year's festivities at the imperial court. Later the edict was copied and proclaimed in various parts of Japan. However, the population was not immediately affected, as many points within the edict were not brought to fruition until several decades later.

Impact

The impact of the edict was anything but immediate. The lands held by *uji* were not easily given up. Instead, compromises were made so that the *uji* retained some rights to the land; therefore, the process was slow and was never fully completed. Sometimes these compromises involved an exchange of lands traditionally held by the *uji* for lands in peripheral areas. Compromises were made within the development of government bureaucracy as well. For example, district magistrates, who were under the governor of the

Questions for Further Study

1. In the twenty-first century, Japan is a single unified nation. In the seventh century, though, the nation consisted of various enclaves, with power diffused throughout numerous ruling clans. To what extent did the Taika Reform edict help consolidate these clans into a national polity?

2. What role did contact with China have in the consolidation of Japan into a more unified nation? How did Chinese Confucianism influence Japanese thinking during this period?

3. In the modern world, the words *bureaucracy* and *bureaucrat* often have negative connotations, implying excessive regulation, red tape, and government functionaries who assert their authority over citizens. The Taika Reform edict, however, calls for the establishment of a bureaucracy and a hierarchy of government officials. Why did the reigning authorities believe that imposing this system of government would be good for Japanese society?

4. In the wake of the American Revolutionary War, the United States was governed by the Articles of Confederation. Many American leaders believed that the articles were too weak, for they left too much power in the hands of the states and not enough in the hands of the central government. The result of these concerns was the Constitution. In what ways might the situation in the United States in the 1780s be regarded as similar to that of seventh-century Japan?

5. Imagine yourself as a member of an *uji* family. How do you think you would have reacted to the Taika Reform edict? Write a letter to the imperial government in which you outline your reactions to the various provisions of the edict.

provinces, could gain more power and income as they had a direct control of the land. More important, whereas the edict calls for government positions to be based on virtuous characteristics, the district magistrate position became hereditary. This autonomy allowed district magistrates to become skilled horsemen because of their great wealth; these men could be considered protosamurai.

In conjunction with these compromises, the creation of new court titles allowed influential *uji* to seize control of certain offices within the imperial court. These positions demonstrated the social prestige of certain influential *uji* and their relationship with the imperial family, thereby making some government positions hereditary or assigned to a certain family. Later in Japanese history, influential families would control these important positions and use them to manage the role and power of the emperor.

The importance of this edict of the Taika Reform is that it launched the *ritsuryō* system and became the basis for future reforms. The first of these was the Ōmi Codes, compiled by Nakatomi Kamatari and proclaimed by Prince Nakano-Ōe, reigning as Emperor Tenchi, both of whom had helped in propagating the Taika Reform edicts. The Ōmi Codes built upon the ideas of the Taika Reform by continuing to develop the *ritsuryō* system through the adoption of a complex system of ranks and offices. The codes further break down the structure of the provinces into districts and neighborhoods, mimicking a Chinese-style government; like the Taika Reform, this new system did not take effect immediately. Finally, the Taika Reform edict influenced the Taihō Code of 702, which finished the long process of adopting the ideas of the edict. One of the major points of the Taihō Code was the establishment of a permanent capital, Nara, and the division between the capital and the newly created sixty-six provinces. However, the Taihō Code stepped away from the Taika edict in that government positions were based on heredity and familial rela-tions instead of on talent and virtuous qualities. The Taika reformers and their predecessor Prince Shōtoku were largely concerned with the prevention of these hereditary titles and offices, but over the sixty-year period of the development of the *ritsuryō* system, this concession was made.

The importance of the Taika Reform edict is that it demonstrates the desire of reform leaders to create a strong central government in which the reigning emperor held all power. However, historians have noted that these reforms did not endure and that many of the ideas and concepts of the Taika Reform edict were adjusted in later codes to appease a growing new aristocracy of elites from former *uji*. Some historians have even mentioned that the momentum of the reform was lost in the first few years after the edicts were issued. Nonetheless, the Taika Reform edict led to the creation of a system in which the emperor, in theory, held all power; the edict marked a major turning point in the Japanese political structure.

Further Reading

■ Books

Asakawa, Kan'ichi. *The Early Institutional Life of Japan: A Study in the Reform of 645 a.d.*. New York: Paragon Book Reprint Corporation, 1963.

Beasley, W. G. *The Japanese Experience: A Short History of Japan*. Berkeley: University of California Press, 1999.

Hall, John Whitney. *Government and Local Power in Japan, 500 to 1700: A Study Based on Bizen Province*. Ann Arbor: University of Michigan Center for Japanese Studies, 1999.

—Thomas W. Barker

New Year's Day Taika Reform Edict

As soon as the New Year's ceremonies were over, the Emperor promulgated the following edict of reforms:

I. Let the following be abolished: the titles held by imperial princes to serfs granted by imperial decrees; the titles to lands held directly by the imperial court; and private titles to lands and workers held by ministers and functionaries of the court, by local nobles, and by village chiefs. In lieu thereof, sustenance households shall be granted to those of the rank of Daibu and upwards on a scale corresponding to their positions. Cloth and silk stuffs shall be given to the lower officials and people, varying in value.

It is said that the duty of the Daibu is to govern the people. If they discharge their task diligently, the people will have trust in them. Therefore it is for the benefit of the people that the revenue of the Daibu shall be increased.

II. For the first time, the capital shall be placed under an administrative system. In the metropolitan region, governors and prefects shall be appointed. Barriers and outposts shall be erected, and guards and post horses for transportation and communication purposes shall be provided. Furthermore bell-tokens shall be made and mountains and rivers shall be regulated.

One alderman shall be appointed for each ward in the capital, and one chief alderman for four wards. The latter shall be responsible for maintaining the household registers and investigating criminal matters. The chief alderman shall be chosen from those men belonging to the wards, of unblemished character, strong and upright, who can discharge the duties of the time effectively. In principle, aldermen of rural villages or of city wards shall be selected from ordinary subjects belonging to the villages or city wards, who are sincere, incorrupt and of strong disposition. If a right man cannot be found in a village or ward in question, a man from the adjoining village or ward may be appointed.

The metropolitan region shall include the area from the Yokogawa [River] in Nahari on the east, from [Mount] Senoyama in Kii on the south, from Kushibuchi in Akashi on the west, and from [Mount] Afusakayama in Sasanami in Omi on the north.

Districts are classified as greater, middle and lesser districts, with districts of forty villages constituting greater districts; of from four to thirty villages consti-

tuting middle districts; and of three or fewer villages constituting lesser districts. The prefects for these districts shall be chosen from local nobles, of unblemished character, strong and upright, who can discharge the duties of the time effectively. They shall be appointed as prefects and vice prefects. Men of ability and intelligence, who are skilled in writing and arithmetic, shall be appointed to assist them in the tasks of governance and book-keeping....

III. It is hereby decreed that household registers, tax registers, and rules for allocation and redistribution of land shall be established.

Each fifty households shall be constituted into a village, and in each village there shall be appointed an alderman. He shall be responsible for the maintenance of the household registers, the assigning of sowing of crops and cultivation of mulberry trees, prevention of offenses, and requisitioning of taxes and forced labor....

All rice-fields shall be measured by a unit called a *tan* which is thirty paces in length by twelve paces in breadth. Ten *tan* make one *chō*. For each tan, the tax shall be two sheaves and two bundles of rice; for each *chō*, the tax shall be twenty-two sheaves of rice.

IV. Old taxes and forced labor shall be replaced by a system of commuted taxes based on [the size of] rice fields. These taxes shall consist of fine silk, coarse silk, raw silk, and floss silk, which are to be collected in accordance with what is produced in the locality. For each *chō* of rice field, the rate shall be one rod of fine silk. For four *chō* of rice field the rate shall be one piece of fine silk which is forty feet in length by two and a half feet in width. If coarse silk is substituted, the rate shall be two rods per *chō*, and one piece of the same length and width as the fine silk for every two *chō*....

A separate household tax shall also be levied, under which each household shall pay one rod and two feet of cloth, and a surtax consisting of salt and offerings. The latter may vary in accordance with what is produced in the locality. With regard to horses for public service, one horse of medium quality shall be contributed by every one hundred households, or one horse of superior quality by every two hundred households. If the horses have to be purchased, each household shall contribute one rod and two feet of cloth toward the purchase price. With regard to weapons, each person shall contribute a sword, armor, bow and arrows, a flag, and a drum.

Under the old system, one servant was supplied by every thirty households. This system shall be altered to allow every fifty households to furnish one servant to work for various officials. These fifty households shall be responsible for providing rations for one servant, by each household contributing two rods and two feet of cloth and five *masu* of rice in lieu of service.

Waiting women in the palace shall be selected from among good-looking sisters or daughters of officials of the rank of vice prefect or above. Every one hundred households shall be responsible for providing rations for one waiting woman. The cloth and rice supplied in lieu of service shall, in every respect, follow the same rule as for servants.

Glossary

chō	an area measure roughly equivalent to one hectare (2.47 acres)
commuted taxes	taxes paid as a substitute for forced labor
household registers	records of items possessed by individual households
masu	a square box designed to hold enough rice for one person for one day

CAPITULARY OF CHARLEMAGNE

"Judges shall judge justly, according to the written law and not according to their own judgment."

Overview

Part administrative decree, part constitution of the Holy Roman Empire, and part sermon, the Capitulary of Charlemagne, issued in 802, was one of numerous such documents promulgated by the Merovingian and Carolingian dynasties in the medieval Frankish, or French, Empire. The documents were termed capitularies because they were divided into sections called *capitula*, a Latin word meaning "headings" or "chapters." The Merovingians were the earliest Frankish ruling dynasty. "Merovingian" was derived from the name of the dynasty's first (possibly legendary) king, Merovech. This dynasty was followed by the Carolingian Dynasty, founded in the eighth century by Pépin III. "Carolingian" was derived from the name Charles, referring to Charles Martel, the brilliant eighth-century general and politician—and Pépin's father—noted for leading Frankish forces to victory over invading Muslims at the Battle of Tours in 732. Although several kings wrote and published capitularies, these documents are most closely associated with Pépin's son Charlemagne ("Charles the Great," or "Carolus Magnus" in Latin), inarguably the most famous Frankish emperor in the Carolingian Dynasty and the dominant figure in Europe in the late eighth and early ninth centuries.

It would be difficult to exaggerate Charlemagne's impact on the development of western and central Europe. Known in some circles as "the father of Europe," Charlemagne ruled over Frankish territories and, through warfare and diplomacy, expanded his realm to include Germany and numerous other territories. He was crowned *imperator romanorum*, or emperor of the Romans, by Pope Leo III, thus making him the emperor of the Holy Roman Empire and a rival to the emperor of the Byzantine Empire in Constantinople. Charlemagne's success in imposing unity on Europe became a model for later European leaders, including Napoléon Bonaparte and Adolf Hitler.

Charlemagne's Capitulary of 802, issued two years after he was crowned Holy Roman Emperor and sometimes referred to as the Great Capitulary, the Programmatic Capitulary of 802 (the date is included to distinguish it from other programmatic capitularies), or the *Capitulare missorum generale*, survives in three different forms addressed to three distinct audiences throughout the empire. Indeed, all of the capitularies from Charlemagne's reign exist in varying versions, for the documents were not intended as official records of laws and proclamations. Rather they were more in the nature of communications of decrees that the emperor had issued orally and which were then passed along to administrators throughout the empire, each of whom may or may not have preserved his written copy. The chief purpose of the Capitulary of 802 was to lay out the obligations of the government and the people of the empire in light of Charlemagne's crowning as Holy Roman Emperor in 800. It instructed officials throughout the realm to execute justice, to enforce respect for the rights of the king, to supervise the administration of royal officials, to receive from the people an oath of allegiance to the king, and to oversee the activities and conduct of the clergy.

Context

The Capitulary of 802, along with dozens of other capitularies, was issued in an ongoing effort by Charlemagne to consolidate power over his domains and to introduce administrative and ecclesiastical reforms throughout the empire. The formation of that empire was the work of Charlemagne's life. The last time any sort of unity had been imposed on Europe was under the Roman Empire, but that empire collapsed in western Europe in the fifth century. The withdrawal of the Romans left behind a large number of essentially tribal peoples who vied for ascendancy, including many "pagan" tribes, such as the Huns, the Visigoths, the Angles, the Saxons, the Celts, and particularly the Franks, who occupied the region the Romans had called Gaul.

In the wake of the Roman withdrawal, various kings rose to power in a region referred to by the Latin name Francia, but these kings followed a tradition of dividing their kingdoms among their sons upon the kings' deaths. The effect was to leave the Frankish lands fragmented, for the sons often did not get along, competed for power, sponsored assassinations, and went to war with one another. Accordingly the geography of Francia continually changed,

732

■ **October 10**
Arabs are defeated at Poitiers by Charles Martel, grandfather of Charlemagne, in the Battle of Tours.

742

■ **April 2**
Pépin III's son Charlemagne is born in Aachen (Aix-la-Chapelle), though the year is disputed.

751

■ Pépin III dethrones Childeric III, the last Merovingian king, and is acknowledged by the pope as king of the Franks.

768

■ **September 24**
Pépin III dies.

■ **October 9**
Pépin III's kingdom is divided between Charles and his brother Carloman, according to Frankish custom.

771

■ **December 4**
Carloman dies, and Charlemagne becomes king of the united Franks.

800

■ **December 25**
After going to Italy to protect the pope, Charlemagne is crowned Holy Roman Emperor.

with seats of power in various cities—Reims, Paris, Orléans, and Soissons. Adding to the instability was the kings' lack of meaningful authority, with true power wielded behind the scenes by so-called mayors of the palace. Further, Francia often felt pressure from the tribes on its borders, notably the Germanic Saxons, and in the eighth century the realm faced a threat from Muslim Arab invaders, though they were turned back by Charlemagne's grandfather Charles Martel, himself a mayor of the palace who became king in everything but name.

This state of affairs prevailed under the Merovingian kings, who ruled from the fifth century until 751, when Charlemagne's father, Pépin III, deposed the last of the Merovingian monarchs, Childeric III, inaugurating the Carolingian Dynasty. Pépin, also a mayor of the palace, was able to accomplish this takeover because he had the backing of the pope, who was threatened by an Italian tribe called the Lombards. The pope welcomed Pépin's military efforts on his behalf and rewarded him by crowning him king of the Franks—an act that the pope could get away with in an age dominated by religious faith. Under Pépin, however, the practice of dividing the kingdom between or among sons continued, so after Pépin's death in 768 rule of the Frankish kingdom was apportioned between his two sons, Charles and Carloman. The two sons cooperated in launching a joint expedition against the Lombards and put down a revolt in a region called Aquitania. The issue of divided power, however, and the friction it could cause was resolved in 771 with the death of Carloman, leaving Charles as the sole ruler of the Frankish domains.

Charlemagne spent almost his entire career expanding his realms. In the east he conquered Bavaria and defeated the Slavs in Hungary. In the south he subdued much of Italy. By the turn of the century he had forged an empire that encompassed virtually all of western Europe and much of central and southern Europe. It was under Pope Leo III that he assumed the title of Holy Roman Emperor. Leo had been under virtual siege by the Romans and feared for his life. He faced considerable competition from the Byzantine Empire—the eastern portion of the old Roman Empire and the seat of the Eastern Orthodox Christian Church. In his extremity the pope invited Charlemagne, the most powerful figure in Europe, to Rome to enlist his aid. There, on December 25, 800, he crowned Charlemagne *imperator romanorum*, or emperor of the Romans. Charlemagne's contemporary biographer, Einhard, wrote in *The Life of Charlemagne* that Charlemagne did not want the title, but modern-day historians disagree, noting that in imperial decrees from 801 onward, he styled himself "Charles, most serene Augustus crowned by God, the great, peaceful emperor ruling the Roman empire." In other words, he used the pope's coronation to position himself as the embodiment of a new Roman Empire with hegemony over Europe. In an effort to assert that hegemony, to enforce Christianity, and to impose standards of rectitude over the secular and ecclesiastical administrative apparatus of his realms and over the people he ruled, he issued the decrees at the Council of Aachen that resulted in the Capitulary of 802.

Charlemagne was born on April 2, probably at Aachen (Aix-la-Chapelle). Most sources give the year as 742, but some historians have argued that he may have been born as late as 745 or even 747. His grandfather was Charles Martel, a mayor of the palace who became the virtual king of the Frankish Empire. Charlemagne's father, Pépin III, was also a mayor of the palace until Pope Stephen II acknowledged him as the king of the Franks. In this way the Merovingian Dynasty that had ruled France since the fifth century was replaced by the Carolingian Dynasty.

Little information survives about Charlemagne's early life, though it is known that after Pépin became king, Charles accompanied him on military expeditions. When Pépin died in 768, his kingdom was divided between Charles and his brother Carloman, but after Carloman died in 771, Charlemagne presided over a united Frankish Empire. Thereafter he aggressively expanded the kingdom. He launched an expedition against the Lombards in Italy and Aquitania (along the border with Spain) and then turned his attention to the Saxons on his northeastern frontier. In the east he conquered Bavaria and initiated assaults against the Asiatic Huns in Hungary. By 795 Charlemagne had conquered practically all of Christian Europe and the areas that had fallen under the Roman Empire. In 800 Pope Leo III called on Charlemagne to protect him from the people of Rome. Charlemagne answered the call, and on Christmas Day of 800 he was crowned emperor of the Holy Roman Empire. In the years that followed until his death in 814, Charlemagne labored to promote peace, learning, and efficient administration in his realms. His intention was to divide his kingdom among his three sons, but two of them died, so the kingdom passed to the remaining son, Louis the Pious.

Explanation and Analysis of the Document

The capitulary falls essentially into four parts. The first, consisting of the first paragraph of Chapter 1, announces the role of the *missi dominici*, that is, the messengers who disseminated the capitulary. Paragraphs 2 through 9 deal with the oath of fealty that people owed to the emperor. Paragraphs 10 through 40 outline particular regulations, and this section can be subdivided into two broad parts, one regarding the clergy and the other concerning the laity.

◆ Concerning the Embassy Sent Out by the Lord Emperor

The first paragraph announces the method by which Charlemagne disseminated his decrees throughout the realm: He chose from among his nobles "the most prudent and the wisest men, both archbishops as well as other bishops, and venerable abbots, and pious laymen and did send them over his whole kingdom." Their purpose was to ensure "that men should live according to law and right." Charlemagne goes on to order his subjects to follow the written

Time Line

802
- The Council of Aachen imposes a general oath of loyalty to the emperor and other obligations in the Capitulary of 802.

814
- **January 28** Charlemagne dies, leaving the throne to his son Louis the Pious.

870
- **August 8** The Treaty of Meerssen effects the split of the empire into France and Germany.

law. He enjoins the clergy, as well as nuns, to live according to their vows and to "live together in mutual charity and perfect peace." He further empowers his messengers to "administer law and justice according to the will and to the fear of God." In summary, the emperor announces his intention to rule over a just, peaceful, pious realm.

◆ Paragraphs 2–9

Paragraphs 2 through 9 all bear on the fealty that Charlemagne's subjects owed to him as emperor. Many of his subjects' obligations to him were feudal in nature, and Charlemagne is generally credited with instituting the social and economic institution of feudalism in the Frankish realms. He states that everyone in the kingdom down to the age of twelve must take an oath of fealty to the emperor. Paragraphs 3 through 9 outline the particulars of this oath. Charlemagne made Christianity the centerpiece of his empire by decreeing that each subject was "wholly to keep himself in the holy service of God according to the precept of God." The emperor asserts his feudal rights in paragraph 4 by requiring an oath that no one would use fraud or deception to take property that belonged to the emperor by "proprietary right," including slaves; in paragraph 6 he extends this prohibition to any "fief," or feudal land, the emperor owned. In paragraph 5 Charlemagne casts himself as the protector of the church, as well as of widows, orphans, and strangers, and thus insists that no one "plunder" them.

Paragraph 7 notes the emperor's rights as feudal lord to demand military service of his subjects, stipulating, too, that a subject was not to avoid such service by flattery, bribery, or

Bronze statue of Charlemagne (© Bettmann/CORBIS)

personal relationship—that is, evading military by happening to know the right person. Paragraph 8 goes on to prohibit Charlemagne's subjects from interfering with any acts or decrees of the emperor or with the collection of taxes owed to him. Paragraph 9, the last paragraph that specifies the terms of the oath of fealty, calls for justice in court proceedings, demanding that people conduct their own defenses for such legal entanglements as debt. If necessary, though, a defendant could employ someone to defend him, but legal cases were to be decided according to the dictates of justice, not on the basis of "cleverness" and certainly not through bribery, "evil adulation," or a special relationship with the person charged with deciding the case.

◆ Paragraphs 10–24

Beginning with paragraph 10, Charlemagne outlines the duties and obligations of the clergy. He issued these decrees in the context of an environment in which many people believed that the church was becoming corrupt and that it was as much a secular as a religious institution; in some ways it was. Accordingly, Charlemagne specifies that clerics were obligated to live by the dictates of canon law, or the law of the church. Paragraph 11 notes that clerics in positions of power—such as bishops, abbots, and abbesses—should not rule by tyranny but should "carefully guard the flock committed to them, with simple love, with mercy and charity, and by the example of good works." Charle-

magne then forbids the practice of abbots and abbesses living outside of their monasteries.

Paragraph 13 illustrates the extent to which the church held secular power over the emperor's subjects. Medieval monasteries served a variety of functions. Obviously they were centers for the practice of religion, but they also served as schools, hospitals, pilgrimage sites (with the revenue pilgrimages could generate), and administrative centers. Often they owned land and derived income from that land through natural resources and the labor of peasants. Running a monastery was complicated, and monasteries often hired bailiffs to assist in the administration of their holdings. Bailiffs, as well as sheriffs, who were less law-enforcement officers than civil administrators, could misuse their positions to abuse those under them and line their own pockets. The capitulary required officials, also referred to as provosts, to "do justice in every way, wholly observing the law without malice or fraud, always exercising a just judgment in all things." Paragraph 14 amplifies this decree by specifying that all abbots, abbesses, and bishops were to seek "a right judgment" and live according to the will of God, extending their protection to widows, orphans, and pilgrims.

The aim of paragraph 15 is to prevent other potential abuses. All clerics are enjoined to submit themselves to the will of their bishops. Further, all church property was to remain under the care of the church and was not to be sold or gambled away. Paragraph 16 turns to the subject of the ordination of priests. Again Charlemagne's intent was to curb corruption, for he insists that only the best-qualified men be ordained as priests and that bribery, flattery, and any kind of special "relationship" were to play no role in the selection of priests.

A key passage in the capitulary is paragraph 17. In this paragraph the emperor is firm about the behavior of clerics, who were to live in the monastery and not to wander about and who were to derive no income from secular occupations outside the monastery walls. The emperor is quite particular in proscribing drunkenness, fornication, and any sort of homosexual activity; in paragraph 19 he tries to curb what he sees as another abuse—the clergy's keeping of hunting dogs and hawks, symbols of neglect of priestly duty. Paragraph 21 outlines similar demands on the "lesser clergy," or lower-ranking priests. In paragraph 18 Charlemagne addresses convents of nuns, again requiring them to live "justly and soberly." Interestingly, Charlemagne reflects the prejudices of his age by enjoining nuns to avoid quarreling among themselves, as if to imply that women living in close quarters would inevitably turn shrewish. Paragraph 20 specifies that any nun who needed to leave the cloister walls could do so only on the advice of the bishop.

Paragraph 22 deals with the "secular clergy." The medieval church distinguished between regular clergy and secular clergy. The former were members of a religious order; they took vows of poverty, chastity, and obedience and submitted themselves to the rule of their order. The secular clergy were ordained priests who were not members of a particular religious order. They tended to live in the larger community, and thus they were subject to its temptations. Charlemagne attempts to curb these temptations and to ensure that the secular clergy adhered not only to canon law but also to standards of morality. The term *sarabaites* was originally used to refer to heretical, vagrant monks, but later it was used to signify any clergy who lived in their own homes and acknowledged no rule. Paragraphs 23 and 24 conclude the discussion of the clergy, forbidding "vain sports or worldly feastings, or songs or luxuries" and the practice of clergy admitting women in their homes.

◆ Paragraphs 25–40

In this group of paragraphs, the capitulary turns to more secular matters. With an eye perhaps on his German domains, the emperor in paragraph 25 enjoins "counts and centenars" to "see to it that justice is done in full." A *centenar* was an official in charge of a "hundred" (hence the syllable *cent*), or an area of land analogous to a county. Young men in the service of these officials should avoid consorting not only with thieves and murderers but also with wizards and witches. In paragraph 26 judges are ordered to follow the written law and not their own judgment. Standards of behavior are further established in paragraph 27, which requires hospitality to all, particularly to pilgrims. To buttress this point, the capitulary quotes from the New Testament of the Bible, specifically Matthew 18:5 and 25:35.

Paragraphs 28 through 31 deal with the issue of the emperor's relationship with his subjects. His envoys, for example, were to be received and shown cooperation during their visits throughout the realm. Judges could not exact fines from people whom the emperor had forgiven because they were destitute. Further, no one was to interfere with any person who was attempting to arrive in the presence of the emperor to solicit alms or to provide information. Finally, no one was to harass legally those persons chosen to announce the judgments of the emperor. It is unclear what "the king's bann" was specifically, but it could have referred either to the king's curse, or to public condemnation, or to a summons for military service. It could also be a variant of *bane*, referring generally to a threat to inflict woe or harm.

Paragraph 32 constitutes a short sermon against murder. The emperor appeals to his subjects to avoid murder on religious grounds, making clear that "we wish rather to punish with the greatest severity him who dares to commit the crime of murder." Interestingly, though, the emperor avoided speaking in terms of vengeance. He orders that anyone guilty of murder was to make recompense to the victim's survivors and that "the relatives of the dead man shall by no means dare to carry further their enmity on account of the evil inflicted or refuse to make peace with him who seeks it." He also notes that the guilty person was to pay "wergeld" (wergild), or a payment of reparations (from *wer*, meaning "man," and *geld*, meaning "money" or "fee"). Much of the purpose of the emperor's decree on murder and reparations was to avoid blood feuds between clans, with further violence being the result. Blood feuds had been commonplace among the Germanic tribes that were now under Charlemagne's rule.

In paragraph 33 the emperor forbids the practice of incest, citing "the case of the incest committed by Fricco in the temple." This is likely a reference to a god in Scandinavian mythology, Freyr, sometimes called by his Latinized name, Fricco or Frikko. The image of this god in the Temple of Uppsala (Sweden) was in the shape of a giant phallus. Issues surrounding incest were complicated in medieval Europe. The taboo was influenced by biblical tradition, ancient Greek and Roman law, canon law, and the pronouncements of early church fathers, such as Saint Augustine. The perceived need for people to marry outside of the kin group, and thus to expand their network of social relationships, was so pronounced that a union was often forbidden because of the most distant of blood relationships.

The final paragraphs of the capitulary deal with several miscellaneous matters. Paragraph 34 requires subjects to answer to the emperor's demands. Paragraph 35 orders subjects to honor their priests and bishops and then goes on to urge care in marriages so as to avoid incest. Paragraph 36 threatens perjurers with the loss of their right hand, a common punishment for this crime in medieval law treatises. Paragraph 37 deals with patricide (the killing of one's father) and fratricide (the killing of one's brother). These people were to be "deprived of their property" and summoned to the emperor's presence, as were those guilty of incestuous unions, noted in paragraph 38. Paragraph 39 proscribes the poaching of game on the emperor's territory, a further assertion of the emperor's feudal rights. Finally, paragraph 40 orders that the emperor's decrees be disseminated to ecclesiastical and civil officials.

Audience

The audience for the capitularies was multileveled. The content of the capitularies originated as oral decrees from the emperor. In the case of the Capitulary of 802, these dictates were issued at one of the many councils or synods Charlemagne held at the royal palace at Aachen. The decrees, however, had to be disseminated throughout the kingdom to various functionaries, including bishops, abbots, nuns, dukes, and counts, who then were responsible for carrying out the king's orders. The intermediaries Charlemagne used for this purpose were called *missi dominici*, the plural form of *missus dominicus*, a title that means "envoy of the lord." These officials, selected from the royal court, were themselves high-ranking archbishops, bishops, abbots, dukes, and counts who were assigned to various districts. The job of these officials, who generally traveled in pairs (a cleric and a layman), was to visit their assigned district four times each year, assemble the officials in the district, and explain their duties and obligations, often as contained in the capitularies. These officials would then communicate the emperor's decrees to the people in their charge. Thus the *missi dominici* were in the nature of inspectors-general. It is because the Capitulary of 802 outlines the role of the *missi* that it is sometimes referred to as the *Capitulare missorum generale*, or the Capitulary of the Missi.

"The most serene and most Christian emperor Charles, did choose from among his nobles the most prudent and the wisest men archbishops as well as other bishops, and venerable abbots, and pious laymen and did send them over his whole kingdom; and did grant through them, by means of all the following provisions, that men should live according to law and right."

(Paragraph 1)

"And he ordained that every man in his whole kingdom—ecclesiastic or layman, each according to his vow and calling—who had previously promised fealty to him as king should now make this promise to him as emperor; and that those who had hitherto not made this promise should all, down to those under 12 years of age, do likewise."

(Paragraph 2)

"That bishops, abbots and abbesses, who are placed in power over others, should strive to surpass in veneration and diligence those subject to them; that they should not oppress them with severe and tyrannous rule, but should carefully guard the flock committed to them, with simple love, with mercy and charity, and by the example of good works."

(Paragraph 11)

"Monasteries for women shall be firmly ruled, and the nuns shall by no means be permitted to wander about, but shall be kept with all diligence."

(Paragraph 18)

"That judges shall judge justly, according to the written law and not according to their own judgment."

(Paragraph 26)

"That all men shall at all times, in the service and will of God, venerate with all honour their bishops and priests."

(Paragraph 35)

Impact

Historians have had a difficult time tracing the specific impact of the capitularies, including that of 802. These documents were not like the Constitution of the United States, for instance, which has been preserved in its original form and is widely available in exactly the same form to anyone interested in it. In a sense, the capitularies were somewhat like ninth-century memos, intended to provide information but not to be enshrined as documents. While a copy of the capitulary would have been kept at the royal palace, the fate of other copies, sent out with the *missi dominici*, would have been uncertain, for it is likely that the documents were read or summarized for the benefit of the local officials charged with the responsibility of enforcing the king's dictates. In some instances the document may have been lodged in the hands of one of those local officials; in other instances it would have remained with the *missus dominicus*, ultimately to disappear. Further, because the documents were copies, they varied, particularly because it might have been necessary to alter the instructions depending on the district to which the capitulary was going. Some of the capitularies survive in books that were published in the ninth and tenth centuries. In sum, the provenance of the actual text of any capitulary is highly uncertain and varied.

What can be said with certainty is that the capitularies, including that of 802, were an important part of the apparatus of government under Charlemagne. They were the means by which he communicated his wishes—some major, some minor—to government and to ecclesiastical officials and, ultimately, to the people in their charge. The impact of the capitularies can be traced indirectly, for through them Charlemagne established a strong, vital empire. As a patron of learning, he fostered art and literature and the formation of a large number of monastic schools. Some 90 percent of the surviving works of the ancient Romans have been preserved because they were copied in Carolingian monasteries. The offices of counts, dukes, and marquesses continued to exist in Europe for centuries. Charlemagne revised the monetary system. He became the inspiration behind "the matter of France," referring to the subject matter of epic poems about his exploits, such as the *Song of Roland*. Although the empire that he forged did not survive—having been divided by the Treaty of Meerssen in 870 into France and the principalities that became Germany—Otto the Great, who assumed control of Germany, modeled his Holy Roman Empire on that of Charlemagne.

Further Reading

■ Books

Becher, Matthias. *Charlemagne*, trans. David S. Bachrach. New Haven, Conn.: Yale University Press, 2003.

Dawson, Christopher. *The Making of Europe: An Introduction to the History of European Unity*. New York: Meridian Books, 1956.

Questions for Further Study

1. The capitularies of Charlemagne underline the problems associated with communication in early empires. Lacking telephones, printing presses, computers, and postal systems, early rulers had to find ways to communicate their wishes to the far reaches of their empires. How did Charlemagne attempt to solve that problem?

2. Charlemagne was a warrior, and he spent much of his adult life engaged in military action to consolidate his empire. Yet the Capitulary of 802 makes repeated references to peace, the rule of law, "mutual charity," and the like. Do you see any inconsistency? Or would warfare have promoted Charlemagne's desire for a peaceful realm? Explain.

3. Charlemagne established a large number of rules regulating the behavior of the clergy and nuns. Why would their behavior have been a matter of great importance to a ruler in Charlemagne's position at that time?

4. Many of the provisions of the Capitulary of 802 were designed to curb abuses of various types. What were some of these abuses, and how did the capitulary attempt to stamp them out? How effective do you think these provisions would have been?

5. In the twenty-first century, the notion of one emperor "conquering" most of Europe, or any continent, seems almost unthinkable, although Adolf Hitler, the leader of Nazi Germany, had tried to do so during World War II. In the eighth and ninth centuries, however, Charlemagne's conquest of much of Europe seems to have been beneficial in Europe's development. Why? What historical circumstances enabled Charles to become "Charles the Great"?

Einhard. *The Life of Charlemagne*, trans. Samuel Epes Turner. 1880. Rpt. Ann Arbor: University of Michigan Press, 1960.

Ganshof, François Louis. *The Carolingians and the Frankish Monarchy: Studies in Carolingian History*, trans. Janet Sondheimer. Ithaca, N.Y.: Cornell University Press, 1971.

Ganz, David, trans. *Two Lives of Charlemagne: Einhard and Norker the Stammerer*. New York: Penguin, 2008.

Heer, Friedrich. *Charlemagne and His World*. New York: Macmillan, 1975.

McDonald, Lee Cameron. *Western Political Theory: From Its Origins to the Present*. New York: Harcourt, Brace & World, 1968.

Pössel, Christina. "Authors and Recipients of Carolingian Capitularies, 779–829." In *Texts and Identities in the Early Middle Ages*, eds. Richard Corradini et al. Vienna, Austria: Verlag der Oësterreichischen, Akademie der Wissenshaften, 2006.

Story, Joanna, ed. *Charlemagne: Empire and Society*. Manchester, U.K.: Manchester University Press, 2005.

Ullmann, Walter. *Medieval Political Thought*. Baltimore, Md.: Penguin, 1975.

Wilson, Derek A. *Charlemagne: Barbarian and Emperor*. London: Pimlico, 2006.

—Michael J. O'Neal

CAPITULARY OF CHARLEMAGNE

Chapter I. Concerning the Embassy Sent Out by the Lord Emperor.

The most serene and most Christian emperor Charles, did choose from among his nobles the most prudent and the wisest men, both archbishops as well as other bishops, and venerable abbots, and pious laymen and did send them over his whole kingdom; and did grant through them, by means of all the following provisions, that men should live according to law and right. He did order them, moreover, that, where anything is contained in the law that is otherwise than according to right and justice, they should inquire into this most diligently, and make it known to him: and he, God granting, hopes to better it. And let no one, through his cleverness or astuteness—as many are accustomed to do—dare to oppose the written law, or the sentence passed upon him, or to prevail against the churches of God or the poor, or widows, or minors, or any Christian man. But all should live together according to the precept of God in a just manner and under just judgment, and each one should be admonished to live in unity with the others in his occupation or calling. The monastic clergy should altogether observe in their actions a canonical mode of living, far removed from turpid gains; nuns should keep diligent guard over their lives; laymen and secular clergy should make proper use of their privileges without malicious fraud; all should live together in mutual charity and perfect peace. And let the messengers diligently investigate all cases where any man claims that injustice has been done to him by any one, according as they themselves hope to retain for themselves the grace of omnipotent God, and to preserve the fidelity promised to him. And thus, altogether and everywhere and in all cases, whether the matter concerns the holy churches of God, or the poor, or wards and widows, or the whole people, let them fully administer law and justice according to the will and to the fear of God. And if there should be any matter such that they themselves, with the counts of the province, could not better it and render justice with regard to it: without any ambiguity they shall refer it, together with their reports, to the emperor's court. Nor should anyone be kept back from the right path of justice by the adulation or the reward of any man, by the obstacle of any relationship, or by the fear of powerful persons.

2. Concerning the Fealty to Be Promised to the Lord Emperor.

And he ordained that every man in his whole kingdom—ecclesiastic or layman, each according to his vow and calling—who had previously promised fealty to him as king should now make this promise to him as emperor; and that those who had hitherto not made this promise should all, down to those under 12 years of age, do likewise. And he ordained that it should be publicly told to all—so that each one should understand it—what important things and how many things are comprehended in that oath: not alone, as many have hitherto believed, fidelity to the emperor as regards his life, or the not introducing an enemy into his kingdom for a hostile purpose, or the not consenting to the infidelity of another, or the not keeping silent about it. But all should know that the oath comprises in itself the following meaning:

3. Firstly, that every one of his own accord should strive, according to his intelligence and strength, wholly to keep himself in the holy service of God according to the precept of God and to his own promise—inasmuch as the emperor can not exhibit the necessary care and discipline to each man singly.

4. Secondly, that no one, either through perjury or through any other wile or fraud, or on account of the flattery or gift of any one, shall refuse to give back, or dare to abstract or conceal a slave of the emperor, or a district or territory or anything that belongs to his proprietary right; and that no one shall presume to conceal or abstract, through perjury or any other wile, fugitive fiscaline slaves who unjustly and fraudulently call themselves free.

5. That no one shall presume through fraud to plunder or do any injury to the holy churches of God, or to widows, orphans or strangers; for the emperor himself, after God and his saints, has been constituted their protector and defender.

6. That no one shall dare to devastate a fief of the emperor or to take possession of it.

7. That no one shall presume to neglect a summons to arms of the emperor; and that no count be so presumptuous as to dare to release out of regard for

any relationship, or on account of flattery or of any one's gift any one of those who owe military service.

8. That no one at all shall dare in any way to impede a bann or precept of the emperor, or delay or oppose or damage any undertaking of his, or in any way act contrary to his will and precepts. And that no one shall dare to interfere with his taxes and with what is due to him.

9. That no man shall make a practice of unjustly carrying on the defence of another in court, whether from any cupidity, being not a very great pleader; or in order, by the cleverness of his defence, to impede a just judgment or, his case being a weak one, by a desire of oppressing. But each man, with regard to his own case, or tax, or debt, must carry on his own defence; unless he be infirm or ignorant of pleading—for which sort of persons the "missi," or those who preside in that court, or a judge who knows the case for the defendant, shall plead before the court. Or, if necessary, such a person may be granted for the defence as shall be approved by all, and well versed in that case. This, however, shall be done altogether according to the pleasure of those who preside, or of the "missi" who are present. And all this shall be done in every way according to law, so that justice shall be in no way impeded by any gift, payment, or by any wile of evil adulation, or out of regard for any relationship. And that no man shall make any unjust agreement with another, but that all shall be prepared, with all zeal and good will to carry out justice.

For all these things here mentioned should be observed as being comprised in the oath to the emperor.

10. That bishops and priests should live according to the canons and should teach others to do likewise.

11. That bishops, abbots and abbesses, who are placed in power over others, should strive to surpass in veneration and diligence those subject to them; that they should not oppress them with severe and tyrannous rule, but should carefully guard the flock committed to them, with simple love, with mercy and charity, and by the example of good works.

12. That abbots should live where the monks are, and wholly with the monks, according to the rule; and that they should diligently teach and observe the canons; and that abbesses shall do the same.

13. That bishops, abbots and abbesses, shall have bailiffs and sheriffs and judges skilled in the law, lovers of justice, peaceful and merciful: so that, through them, more profit and gain may accrue to the holy church of God. For on no account do we wish to have harmful or greedy provosts or bailiffs in

a monastery; for, from them, the greatest blasphemies or evils may arise for us. But let them be such as the decree of the canons or of the rule bids them to be,—submissive to the will of God, and always ready to do justice in every way, wholly observing the law without malice or fraud, always exercising a just judgment in all things: such provosts, in short, as the holy rule recommends. And they shall altogether observe this, that they shall on no account … depart from the model of the canons or the rule, but shall practice humility in all things. If they presume to act otherwise they shall feel the discipline prescribed in the rule; and, if they be unwilling to amend their ways, they shall be removed from their provostship, and others who are worthy shall be chosen in their stead.

14. That bishops, abbots and abbesses, and counts shall be mutually in accord, agreeing, with all charity and unity of peace, in wielding the law and in finding a right judgment; and that they shall faithfully live according to the will of God, so that everywhere and always, through them and among them, just judgments may be carried out. The poor, widows, orphans and pilgrims shall have consolation and protection from them; so that we, through their good will, may merit, rather than punishment, the rewards of eternal life.

15. We will, moreover, and decree, that abbots and all monks shall be subject in all obedience to their bishops, as the canonical institutions require. And all churches and chapels shall remain in the protection and power of the church. And no one shall presume to divide or cast lots for the property of the church. And what is once offered [for sale?] shall go no further, but shall be sanctified and reclaimed. And if any one presume to act counter to this, he shall pay and make good our royal fine. And the monks of that province shall be admonished by the bishop; and, if they do not amend their ways, then the archbishop shall call them before the synod; and, if they do not thus better themselves, then they, together with the bishop, shall come to our presence.

16. In the matter of choosing candidates for ordination, the emperor has confirmed this now to the bishops and abbots just as he formerly conceded it to them under the Frankish law. With this restriction, however, that a bishop or abbot shall not prefer the more worthless men in a monastery to the better ones; nor endeavour, on account of relationship, or through any flattery, to advance them over the better ones; nor bring such a one before us to be ordained, when he has a better man whom he conceals and

oppresses. We absolutely will not allow this for it seems to be done out of derision and deceitfulness towards us. But let there be prepared for ordination in the monasteries men of such kind that, through them, gain and profit will accrue to us and to those who recommend them.

17. That the monks, moreover, shall live firmly and strictly according to the rule; since we know that whoever is lukewarm in carrying out His will, is displeasing to God. As John, in the Apocalypse, bears witness: "I would that thou wert cold or hot. So then, because thou art lukewarm, I will spue thee out of my mouth." They shall on no account take upon themselves secular occupations. They shall not be permitted to go outside of the monastery unless great necessity compels them; and the bishop in whose diocese they are shall take great care that they do not gain the habit of wandering round outside of the monastery. But if it be necessary for any one, as an act of obedience, to go outside, this shall be done by the advice and with the consent of the bishop; and such persons shall be sent out, provided with a certificate of character, who are not evil-minded, and about whom no evil opinion is held. As to the outlying estates or property of the monastery, the abbot by the advice and with the permission of the bishop, shall decree who shall look after them; not a monk, unless subject to another monastery. They shall in every way avoid earthly pursuit of gain, or a desire for worldly things. For avarice and concupiscence are to be avoided by all Christians in this world, but chiefly by those who have renounced the world and its desires. Let no one presume to start a quarrel or dissension either within or without the monastery. Whoever shall have presumed to do so, shall be punished by the most severe discipline of the rule, so that others shall have fear of doing likewise. Let them altogether avoid drunkenness and feasting; for it is known to all that chiefly through them one comes to be polluted by lust. For the very pernicious rumour has come to our ears that many, in the monasteries, have been taken in fornication in abomination and uncleanness. And most of all it saddens and disturbs us that it can be said without error that from those things whence the greatest hope of salvation for all Christians is believed to arise—namely, the manner of living and the chastity of the monks—the evil has arisen that some of the monks are found to be sodomites.

18. Monasteries for women shall be firmly ruled, and the nuns shall by no means be permitted to wander about, but shall be kept with all diligence. Nor shall they be permitted to quarrel or contend among themselves, or in any way to be disobedient and refractory towards their masters and abbesses. Where they live under the rule, they shall observe all things altogether according to the rule. They shall not be given to fornication, drunkenness, or cupidity; but in all ways they shall live justly and soberly. And let no man enter into their cloister or monastery, unless a priest, with testimonials, enter it for the sake of visiting the sick, or for the mass alone; and straightway thereafter he shall go out again. And let no one enroll his daughter among the congregation of the nuns without the knowledge and consideration of the bishop to whose diocese that place pertains; and let the latter himself diligently ascertain that she is desirous of remaining in the holy service of God, and there confirm the stability of her vow. Moreover, the handmaids of other men, and such women as are not willing to live according to the manner of life in the holy congregation, shall all be altogether ejected from the congregation.

19. That no bishops, abbots, priests, deacons—no one in short, belonging to the clergy—shall presume to have hunting dogs or hawks, falcons or sparrow-hawks; but each one shall keep himself wholly in his proper sphere, according to the canons, or according to the rule. Any one who presumes to do this [have hunting dogs, etc.] shall know that he loses his standing. Furthermore he shall suffer such punishment for this, that others shall fear to wrongfully do likewise.

20. That abbesses and their nuns shall, with one mind and diligently, keep themselves within their cloister walls and by no means presume to go outside of their cloister walls. But the abbesses, when they propose to send out any of the nuns, shall by no means do this without the permission and advice of their bishop. Likewise when any ordinations are to take place in the monasteries, or any persons to be received into the monasteries, this also they shall first fully talk over with their bishops. And the bishops shall announce to the archbishop what they consider the best and most advantageous course of proceeding; and with his advice they shall carry out what is to be done.

21. That priests and the other lesser clergy, whom they have to help them in their ministry, shall altogether show themselves subject to their bishops, as the canons demand. As they desire our favour and their own advancement, let them consent fully to be taught in sacred subjects by these their bishops.

22. The secular clergy, moreover, ought to lead a completely canonical life, and be educated in the

episcopal palace, or also in a monastery, with all diligence according to the discipline of the canons. They shall by no means be permitted to wander at large, but shall live altogether apart, not given to disgraceful gain, not fornicators, not thieves, not homicides, not ropers, not quarrelsome, not wrathful, not proud, not drunken; but chaste in heart and body, humble, modest, sober, merciful, peaceful; that, as sons of God they may be worthy to be promoted to sacred orders: not, like those who are called sarabaites, living in towns and villages near or adjoining the church, without master and without discipline, revelling and fornicating, and also doing other wicked deeds the consenting to which is unheard of.

23. Priests shall carefully pay heed to the clergy whom they have with them, that they live according to the canons; that they be not given to vain sports or worldly feastings, or songs or luxuries, but that they live chastely and healthfully.

24. Moreover, any priest or deacon who after this shall presume to have women in his house without permission of the canons, shall be deprived at once of his position and of his inheritance until he shall be brought into our presence.

25. That counts and centenars shall see to it that justice is done in full; and they shall have younger men in their service in whom they can securely trust, who will faithfully observe law and justice, and by no means oppress the poor; who will not, under any pretext, induced by reward or flattery, dare to conceal thieves, robbers, or murderers, adulterers, magicians and wizards or witches, or any godless men,—but will rather give them up that they may be bettered and chastised by the law: so that, God permitting, all these evils may be removed from the Christian people.

26. That judges shall judge justly, according to the written law and not according to their own judgment.

27. We decree that throughout our whole realm no one shall dare to deny hospitality to the rich, or to the poor, or to pilgrims: that is, no one shall refuse shelter and fire and water to pilgrims going through the land in God's service, or to any one travelling for the love of God and the safety of his soul. If any one shall wish to do further kindness to them, he shall know that his best reward will be from God, who said Himself: "And who so shall receive one such little child in my name, receiveth me." And again: "I was a stranger and ye took me in."

28. Concerning embassies coming from the lord emperor.—That the counts and centenars, as they desire to obtain the emperor's favour, shall provide with all care for the envoys sent, so that they may go through their districts without delay. And he altogether recommends to all to arrange all that shall be required, in such manner that there shall nowhere be delay; but they shall speed them on their way with all haste, and shall provide for them as they, our envoys, may arrange.

29. That our judges, counts, or envoys shall not have a right to extort payment of the remitted fine, on their own behalf, from those destitute persons to whom the emperor has, in his mercy, forgiven what they ought to pay by reason of his balm.

30. As to those whom the emperor wishes by Christ's favour to have peace and defence in his kingdom—that is those who, whether Christians or pagans, hasten to his presence desiring to announce something, or those who seek alms on account of indigence or hunger—let no one dare to constrain them to do him service, or take possession of them, or alienate or sell them: but where they remain of their own will, there they, under the protection of the emperor, shall have alms from his bounty. If any one shall presume to transgress this, he shall know that he shall atone for it with his life, for having so presumptuously despised the commands of the emperor.

31. And let no one presume to contrive injuries or in suits against those who announce a judgment of the emperor, or to show hostility to them in any way. Whoever shall have presumed to do this shall pay the king's bann; or, if he deserve a greater punishment, it is ordered that he be brought into the king's presence.

32. With every kind of protestation we command that men leave off and shun murders, through which many of the Christian people perish. If God forbids hatred and enmity to his followers, much more does he forbid murders. For how can any one hope to be pleasing to God who has slain His son who is nearest to Him? Or how can any one believe that Christ will be gracious to him who has slain his brother? It is a great and inevitable risk to arouse the hatred of men besides incurring that of God the Father and of Christ the ruler of Heaven. By hiding, one can escape them for a time; but, nevertheless, one falls by some chance into the hands of his enemies. And where can one flee God to whom all secrets are manifest? By what rashness can any one hope to evade His wrath? Therefore we have taken care to avoid, by every possible regulation, that the people committed to us to be ruled over perish by this evil. For he who has not feared that God will be angry with him, will by no means find us gentle and gracious; we wish rather to punish with the greatest severity him who

dares to commit the crime of murder. Lest, then, crime increase, and in order that very great discord may not arise among men,—wherever under the devil's suasion, a murder has occurred, the guilty one shall straightway hasten to make his amends, and shall, with all celerity, compound worthily with the relatives of the dead man for the evil done. And this we firmly decree under our bann, that the relatives of the dead man shall by no means dare to carry further their enmity on account of the evil inflicted, or refuse to make peace with him who seeks it; but, pledging their faith, they shall make a lasting peace, and the guilty man shall make no delay in paying the wergeld. When, moreover, through the influence of sin, this shall have happened, that any one shall have slain his brothers or his relative, he shall straightway submit himself to the penance imposed, according as his bishop decides, and without any circumvention. But by the help of God he shall strive to work out his atonement; and he shall pay the fine for the slain man according to the law, and shall fully be reconciled to his relatives. And, having pledged their faith, let no one thenceforth dare to start hostilities. And whoever shall scorn to make proper amends shall be deprived of his inheritance until we shall have rendered our judgment.

33. We altogether prohibit the crime of incest. If any one be contaminated by sinful adultery, he shall not be released without grave severity, but shall so be punished for this that others may have fear of doing the same: so that uncleanness may be altogether removed from the Christian people, and that the guilty man may fully atone by such penance as shall be imposed on him by his bishop. And that woman shall be placed in the hands of her relatives until we pass sentence. But if the man be unwilling to submit to the sentence of the bishop concerning what amends he shall make, then let him be brought before our presence, mindful of the example which was made in the case of the incest committed by Fricco in the temple.

34. That all shall be fully and well prepared whenever our order or announcement shall come. If any one then say that he be not prepared, and avoid our mandate, let him be brought to the palace; and not only he, but likewise all who presume to transgress our bann or command.

35. That all men shall at all times, in the service and will of God, venerate with all honour their bishops and priests. Let them not dare to pollute themselves and others by incestuous nuptials; let them not presume to be wedded until the bishops and

priests, together with the elders of the people, shall diligently inquire into the degree of blood-relationship between those being joined together. And then, with a benediction, let them be wedded. Let them avoid drunkenness, shun greed, commit no theft. Let strife and contentions and blasphemy whether at feasts or assemblies, be altogether avoided but let them live in charity and concord.

36. Also that, in carrying out every sentence, all shall be altogether of one mind with our envoys. And they shall not at all permit the practice of perjury, which most evil crime must be removed from Christian people. If any one henceforth shall be proved a perjurer, he shall know that he shall lose his right hand; and he shall, in addition be deprived of his inheritance until we have judged his case.

37. As to patricides or fratricides, or those who have slain their mother's or their father's brother, or any relation,—if they have been unwilling to obey and agree to the sentence of the bishops and other priests: for the safety of their souls and that they may pay a just penalty. Let our envoys and counts keep them in such custody until they are brought into our presence, that they may be safe and may not infect other people. And they shall, in the meantime, be deprived of their property.

38. And let the like be done to those who have been reprimanded and corrected for unlawful and incestuous unions, and who art not willing to obey their bishops and priests, and who presume to despise our bann.

39. Let no one in our forests dare to rob our game which we have already many times forbidden to be done. And now again we firmly decree that no one shall do this any more. Each one shall keep guard on himself as he hopes to keep the fealty sworn to us. But if any count or centenar or lower official of ours, or any one of our serving-men, shall have stolen our game, he shall without fail be brought to our presence and called to account. Any other common man who may have stolen our game, shall compound for it to the full extent of the law; and by no means shall any allowance be made for such persons in this matter. If any one knows that this evil deed has been perpetrated by another, let him not, by the fealty which he has promised and must now promise to us, dare to conceal it.

40. Lastly, then, we wish our decrees to be known, through the envoys whom we now send, by everyone in our whole realm—by ecclesiastics, viz. bishops, abbots, priests, deacons, canons, all monks and nuns;—so that they, each one in his office or calling,

may keep our bann and decree either in cases where it shall be necessary to thank those subject to them for their good will, or to lend them aid, or in cases where there may be need of applying a remedy. Likewise we wish our decrees to be known by laymen and in all places—whether they concern the protection of churches or widows, or orphans or the weak; or the plundering of them, or the fixing of the assembling of the army, or any other matters: in order that they may be obedient to our command to our will, and that each one may strive in all things to keep himself in the sacred service of God. And thus may all these things be good and to the praise of omnipotent God, and may we give thanks where they are due; but when we think that any thing needs vengeance, may we strive with all our will and all our zeal to better it,—so that, with God's aid, we may succeed in bettering it, to the eternal gain of ourselves and all our followers. Likewise we wish that all the above decrees be made known to our counts and centenars and officials.

Glossary

abstract	steal
by reason of his balm	because of the emperor's mercy
in the Apocalypse	in the Revelation of John in Christian scripture (see Revelation 3:15–16)
ropers	thought to be a person who entices people to a gambling game, especially if the game is fixed
wergeld	value of the life of the person killed; determined in accordance with the rank of the deceased

HAN YU'S "MEMORIAL ON THE BUDDHA'S BONES"

" Buddha worship is for the purpose of bringing good fortune, but it only results in more misfortune."

Overview

In 819 CE, Emperor Xianzong of the Tang Dynasty held a ceremony in which finger bones reputed to be relics of the Buddha were publicly displayed. Although their provenance is unclear, in 558 the relics were enshrined in a special underground chamber of a stupa (a dome-shaped Buddhist shrine) built at the Dharma Gate Temple in Shaanxi Province. The relics were said to have the power to protect the surrounding area and to bestow good fortune on those who venerated them. Because the imperial family was responsible for the empire's well-being, such ceremonies also underscored the power of the ruling family. During the Tang Dynasty the relics were publicly venerated by the imperial family six times. Han Yu wrote a memorial to the emperor criticizing the practice. Han Yu argued that Buddhism was a foreign religion and that its pernicious influence had led the Chinese away from their native traditions, causing a decline of Chinese culture and political order over the centuries. He urged the emperor to destroy the bones and return to traditional practices, insisting that doing so was the best way to restore order and harmony to China.

"A Memorial on the Buddha's Bones," in conjunction with Han Yu's pro-Confucian essay "The Original Tao," came to be viewed by later generations of Chinese as the polemical foundation for the Confucian revival known as Neo-Confucianism. Neo-Confucianism became the dominant social-political discourse from the twelfth through the nineteenth centuries. While Buddhism by no means disappeared from China, as Han Yu had hoped, it lost much of its political influence at the imperial courts of later dynasties, while Confucianism's influence grew.

Context

The practice of housing Buddhist relics in stupas began in India, under the reign of King Aśoka in the third century BCE. Aśoka modeled himself upon the Buddhist concept of a *cakravartin* king, one who used his temporal power to spread Buddhism. This idea appealed to him because it

legitimized his conquests. Consequently, to spread both his authority and Buddhism, Aśoka had the remains of the Buddha divided and sent to various parts of his empire, where stupas were built to house the relics. According to one account, Aśoka organized the simultaneous housing of the relics in eighty-four thousand stupas throughout his realm to emphasize the unity of his reign. The linking of political legitimation to Buddhist patronage spread through central Asia to China. The first concrete mention of Buddhism in Chinese texts is from 65 CE, during the Han Dynasty. Han ideology was Imperial Confucianism, which combined Confucian ethics, education, and ritual with notions of maintaining state power through a strong legal system. Confucian schools were established, and Confucian scholars were fast-tracked into government office.

Confucian ethics concentrated on the efforts of the virtuous individual to create social harmony. Individuals understood their roles within the family and the state hierarchies. The focus was distinctly on the present and the living. Confucius did not deny the existence of spirits and the afterlife; however, when asked by a student about ghosts and spirits, he stated, "You are not even able to serve man. How can you serve the spirits?" When the student asked about death, Confucius replied, "You do not even understand life. How can you understand death?" (Analects, 11.11). Rituals and sacrifices to the spirits, however, were integral parts of the Confucian world. They placed the individual within the cosmological network that connected the living with their ancestors and with the powerful forces of the spirit world. Confucius believed that if one could truly understand the sacrifices, then creating harmony throughout the world would be as easy as holding something in one's hand. Confucius urged his students to study history and ritual texts to learn the patterns of order and chaos revealed in China's past. Central to the whole Confucian order was the ruler. The ruler was the "pole star" around which all others rotated (Analects, 2.1). Therefore, if the ruler was able to deal properly with both humans and spirits, he would be able to bring about harmony and stability.

With the collapse of the Han Dynasty in 220, China broke into a number of kingdoms. Northern China was invaded and controlled by non-Han Turkic peoples from central Asia. Buddhism appealed to these people because it

65
- The first historically reliable mention of Buddhism in China is recorded, though the religion may have arrived earlier.

558
- The first temple buildings at the Dharma Gate Temple site are sponsored by descendents of the Northern Wei Dynasty's imperial family.

618
- Li Yuan founds the Tang Dynasty.

659
- The Tang emperor Gaozong donates cash and goods to fund the Dharma Gate Temple.

662
- Empress Dowager Wu Zetian donates silk and a multilayered reliquary of gold and silver for the Buddha's relics.

755
- An Lushan rebels.

768
- Han Yu is born.

offered a universal religion popular in western, southern, and central Asia that was not linked to Confucian traditions. A ruler with pretensions for universal kingship did not need to learn from the Chinese past to control Chinese territory. Like Aśoka, a leader could aspire to the status of a *cakravartin* king. Hence the period from the third through the sixth centuries witnessed the flourishing of Buddhism in the north and the creation of numerous Buddhist centers. Monks from other areas of Asia were recruited to translate Buddhist texts and to teach the religion. The Turkic imperial family of the Northern Wei Dynasty sponsored the construction of the Dharma Gate Temple, near modern Xi'an, to house the Buddha's finger bones. Temple records note that the stupa was often opened for rituals so that the numinous power of the relics would guarantee the fertility of the land. During the Tang Dynasty, which many consider the pinnacle of premodern China's power and influence in Asia, the Dharma Gate Temple became a site for pilgrimage to the Buddha's bones and a center for private rituals of the imperial family. The relics were publicly venerated in lavish imperially sponsored ceremonies once every thirty years for the benefit of the broader population.

Tang emperors, at least during the first half of the dynasty, could feel some justification to claims of universal kingship. Tang was undoubtedly one of the wealthiest societies in the world and drew many non-Han Chinese people into its orbit. The Tang capital, Chang'an, was known for its cosmopolitanism, with quarters for central Asian merchants and religious institutions not only for Buddhists and Daoists but also for Manichaeans and Nestorian Christians. Tang became the center of East Asian cultural diffusion. Chang'an's layout became the model for the Japanese and Korean capitals, Tang musical styles and legal codes were adopted and adapted by other East Asian societies, and numerous monks came from all over Asia both to teach and to study Buddhism in the Chinese centers established near the capital. Esoteric Buddhism, which stressed the supernatural power of Buddhist objects, relics, formulas, and rituals, became the leading form of Buddhism in Japan. Non-Han Chinese were also able to integrate themselves into Tang society and become leading figures. One of China's most famous poets, Li Po, was born in the eighth century the northern part of what is now Afghanistan, while two of the leading generals were Korean and Sogdian. The first half of the Tang demonstrated the society's openness to foreign ideas and foreign peoples who were drawn by the wealth, power, and cultural attainment of Tang. Hence it is no surprise that Tang emperors would see themselves as legitimate patrons of Buddhist relics to be used to enhance their status and to benefit their empire.

This early cosmopolitanism was thrown into chaos and disrepute when the Sogdian general An Lushan rebelled in 755. An Lushan led his troops from their quarters in northeastern China to attack the imperial capital. The emperor, Xuanzong, was forced to flee with his court, while the capital was sacked. The rebellion and its subsequent battles lasted several years. The imperial family was able to regain a modicum of control only by buying the loyalty of the remaining generals. The generals were given both military and political authority of the territories they controlled in the name of the emperor through their new offices as governors-general.

The latter half of the Tang was a period of growing decentralization. Tax revenues to the central court declined, while the governors-general kept more of the wealth produced in their home territories. Court officials decried the declining status of the central government, but there was little to be done. The northeastern provinces were a constant source of instability. At times open warfare broke out between the imperial court and the northeastern governors-general. In 815 agents of one governor-general were even able to assassinate the prime minister in the capital. Searching for the root cause of the decline of imperial power, some pointed to the presence of non-Han Chinese at all levels of the society. Uighurs and Tibetans were banned from living in the capital, resulting in the forcible removal and ultimate slaughter of Uighur residents from Chang'an's precincts.

Intellectually some leading figures, such as Han Yu, called for a thoroughgoing cultural critique. Han Yu was at the forefront of the "ancient prose" (*guwen*) movement. Arguing that literary prose had become too florid and over-burdened with allusions and imagery, Han Yu advocated returning to the direct style of the Confucian classics. In the classics he found models for clearly stating one's ideas and intentions. The movement asserted that the Confucian classics provided not only stylistic models for essayists but also intellectual models for ordering the world. As clearly stated in "A Memorial on the Buddha's Bones," Han Yu rejected Buddhism as a foreign religion that had harmed Chinese civilization.

About the Author

Han Yu was born into a relatively poor official family based in Luoyang, the second great city of Tang. His ambition was to become a high official. To achieve his goal, he pursued the cultural and literary education required of young men without good connections. This education, steeped in Confucian traditions, was the basis of the civil service examinations through which one qualified for official rank. Successful candidates needed to memorize volumes of classical texts and to train in poetry and prose styles required by the examinations' format. Han Yu immersed himself in texts and literature, so much so that he once compared himself to bookworms that lived and died in books. Han Yu passed the examinations but railed against a civil service recruiting system that valued stylistic composition over substantial policy formulation.

Once Han Yu was in office, his irascible personality led him into confrontation with other political factions at the court. Three times he was exiled for his outspoken critiques of those in power. Nevertheless, each time he was able to return to the capital and even ascend the bureaucratic ladder because of his abilities. When Han Yu wrote

Time Line

790
- An imperially sponsored ceremony is held to display the Buddha's relics, supported with incalculable donations from aristocrats, officials, and commoners.

792
- Han Yu passes the imperial civil service examinations.

819
- Emperor Xianzong oversees another viewing ceremony of the Buddha's relics.
- Han Yu writes his memorial to the emperor condemning Buddhism and is exiled by the emperor to Chaozhou in modern-day Guangdong province.

820
- Emperor Xianzong dies, and Han Yu is pardoned through a general amnesty; he returns to high office in the capital.

824
- Han Yu dies.

880
- The Dharma Gate Temple stupa is sealed.

906
- The Tang Dynasty collapses.

1084
- Han Yu is enshrined in the official Confucian Temple.

1987
- **August** Torrential rains lead to partial collapse of the Dharma Gate Temple's stupa; the underground vault is excavated and then restored.

"A Memorial on the Buddha's Bones" in 819, the court was just coming out of a successful but expensive three-year war with a rebellious governor-general in the northeast. Han Yu had played a prominent diplomatic role in that campaign and had been rewarded with high office. However, when he witnessed what he considered the excessive extravagance of the ceremony welcoming the Buddhist relics to the imperial palace and the mortification of the flesh to which some devotees were driven, he harshly criticized Emperor Xianzong. Xianzong was incensed and wanted to execute Han Yu for his temerity, but other officials persuaded the emperor to commute the sentence to immediate exile. Exile meant assuming a remote post (more than twenty-five hundred miles from the capital) with his family. Along the way Han Yu's eleven-year-old daughter died of illness.

In exile Han Yu set up a Confucian school and encouraged Confucian political practices. As part of a general amnesty after Emperor Xianzong's death in 820, Han Yu was able to return to the capital and assume high office. He retired in 824 and died shortly thereafter.

Explanation and Analysis of the Document

In 819, Han Yu wrote his memorial in response to the extravagant ceremony staged by Emperor Xianzong to receive the relics into the imperial palace. Writing such a memorial was the right of court officials, especially ones who had a national reputation, as did Han Yu. However, Han Yu's open contempt for Buddhism was viewed by the emperor as lèse-majesté, an open attack upon the emper-

or's actions. The emperor was so incensed that he exiled Han Yu. In the memorial Han Yu was reasserting the need for the Chinese to be true to their native, ancient traditions. This meant a rejection of the cosmopolitan, pan-Asian vision that had characterized the early part of the Tang Dynasty. Later generations viewed Han Yu as the instigator of a Confucian revival that would dominate Chinese intellectual life until the early twentieth century.

◆ Paragraphs 1–2

The memorial opens by recounting the historical longevity of key rulers in China's high antiquity. One aspect of the Confucian tradition was a conservative belief that Chinese civilization was generally falling away from a "golden past." Han Yu plays upon this notion in the first two paragraphs by noting that ancient rulers were said to have lived extraordinarily long lives. This longevity was seen as evidence that they lived in harmony and balance with the world around them. The rulers mentioned in the first paragraph were also the cultural heroes of the Confucian tradition. During their years of enlightened rule, civilization was created. The written system was invented, the social structure was ordered, and humans gained power over the natural world through flood control. The rulers in the second paragraph, particularly King Wen, King Wu, and King Mu of the Zhou Dynasty, solidified the civilization. Confucius proclaimed that Zhou's culture was the most developed and therefore the one he venerated and used as the template for his own social-political ideas.

◆ Paragraph 3

Han Yu clearly blames Buddhism for the breakdown of social order and the decreased longevity of emperors. Although the Han Dynasty lasted more than three hundred years, the second half, from 25 to 220, was seen as a period of decline along the lines of the decline of the Tang. Both dynasties suffered rebellion and civil war that ended periods of power and expansion and led to decentralization and a weak court. Han Yu connects this decline to Buddhism's introduction to Han China in 65 CE. Worse still, as Buddhism became more popular, the unified state collapsed into smaller competing kingdoms. Han Yu cites the practice of Emperor Wudi of Liang, who periodically "gave himself" to Buddhist institutions, forcing his court to ransom him back so that he could govern. Wudi also followed Buddhist vegetarian precepts, but by extending this practice to imperial sacrifices, he violated Chinese custom. Ancestral sacrifice was central to the Chinese cosmic view. Ancestral spirits, if provided for, served as intermediaries with the powerful forces in the spirit world. Ancestral spirits needed to be nourished through sacrifices that entailed ritualized banquets at family temples. The spirits imbibed the essence of the food, which the living then consumed. To deny the ancestors meat was a serious mistake. Han Yu points out that Wudi, though long-lived, ultimately died of starvation while fleeing an enemy. The implication is that his death was ancestral retribution, from which the Buddha could not protect Wudi.

Stones inscribed with the writings of Confucius, Temple of Confucius, Beijing (Library of Congress)

◆ **Paragraphs 4–6**

In the two subsequent paragraphs, Han Yu observes that the Tang founder, Li Yuan, once thought of eliminating Buddhism and Daoism. There was a constant tension for rulers in China with regard to these two religious traditions. On the one hand, harnessing their influence and power to imperial interests enhanced the power and legitimacy of the throne. The emperor was, after all, the ultimate authority in all affairs that affected his realm, whether temporal or spiritual. However, Buddhism and Daoism also presented challenges to imperial authority. A number of millenarian cults based in these traditions had led to massive rebellions and the downfall of previous dynasties. In addition, because of the tradition that religious institutions and religious figures (monks, nuns, and servants in the monasteries) were not subject to imperial taxation, monasteries had developed into wealthy and powerful places, often becoming major landlords and sources of loans for those in need of cash. The central government could not tap into this wealth. Occasionally efforts were

What are believed to be the remains of one of Buddha's fingers sit in a miniature gold pagoda at Taipei International Airport, on display in 2002. (AP/Wide World Photos)

made to limit or reduce the economic power of the monasteries, but Emperor Xianzong sponsored a lavish ceremony to bring the relics from the Dharma Gate Temple to the imperial palace, from which it would proceed to various monasteries with great pomp and circumstance, not to mention expense. The emperor perhaps believed that with the victory over rebellious northeastern governors-general in 817, parading the relics would both benefit the empire and demonstrate imperial wealth and power. Han Yu's view was that after the successful and expensive war, this display was a waste of imperial resources. After all, Buddhist devotion had not saved Wudi of Liang from rebellion.

◆ **Paragraphs 7–9**

Han Yu's appeal to the emperor is couched in the formal language typical of addressing the most powerful man in the empire, who had the power to arrange or disband these ceremonies but also the power to order Han Yu's execution or promotion. Formulaically, Han Yu points to his own ignorance and appeals to the emperor's intelligence. Directly criticizing the emperor was suicidal, so Han Yu reasons that the emperor must have been supporting the ceremonies not to demonstrate personal devotion to Buddhism but to appease the desires of his ignorant subjects. Thus the emperor's intentions were in line with those of traditional sage-kings, whose main concern was the welfare of the people. Howev-

er, in the eighth paragraph, Han Yu argues that the emperor's good intentions would have the opposite effect. People would believe the emperor to be a devout Buddhist and would follow suit. However, the emperor could provide massive financial support for the ceremonies, while the common people had little to give. In misguided devotion, some devotees would go so far as to mortify their flesh as tokens of their devotion and rejection of their physical bodies. While Buddhism argued that the human physical form is ultimately not real because it is not permanent and everlasting, Confucianism held that human bodies are gifts from parents and ancestors. These gifts could not be harmed without implying a rejection of the debt that the living owe their ancestors. Furthermore, the emperor's permitting the lavish donations and mortification would seriously undermine the aura of imperial authority because, as Han Yu notes later, the relics are the disgusting remains of a barbarian.

◆ **Paragraph 10**

Harking back to the Confucian view that civilization is Chinese and was created by the rulers of high antiquity, Han Yu points out that the Buddha did not know Chinese and therefore could not engage in the development of Chinese civilization, which could be promoted only through engagement with the core Confucian classics. Furthermore, while Confucianism argued that one learned to be moral as

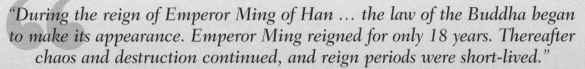

Milestone Documents

"During the reign of Emperor Ming of Han … the law of the Buddha began to make its appearance. Emperor Ming reigned for only 18 years. Thereafter chaos and destruction continued, and reign periods were short-lived."

(Paragraph 3)

"Buddha worship is for the purpose of bringing good fortune, but it only results in more misfortune. In view of this, it is evident that the Buddha is not worth worshiping."

(Paragraph 3)

"The Buddha was originally a man of the barbarians who did not speak the language of the Middle Kingdom [China] and was dressed in clothes of a different cut from ours. Neither did he cite the edifying discourses of the ancient sovereigns, nor did he don their proper attire. He was ignorant of the sense of duty between sovereign and subject, and the affections between father and son."

(Paragraph 10)

"I pray that [Your Majesty] will have the relic delivered to the government agency concerned, which will dispose of it in water or fire so as to permanently destroy its roots. If [Your Majesty] puts to rest doubts under Heaven and stops once and for all [Buddhism] from deluding posterity, all under Heaven will be aware of the achievement by you the great sage, which is hundreds of millions of times greater than that of ordinary people."

(Paragraph 12)

a child growing up in the loving authority of the household, the Buddha required monks to turn their backs on family and pursue enlightenment in the monastery. In addition, while Confucianism held that social-political harmony depended upon the obedience of the populace to moral rulers, the Buddha insisted that monastics lay outside civil authority because they had renounced the world. Han Yu further suggests that if the Buddha were alive, he would not merit the generous reception Emperor Xianzong was giving the relics. The living Buddha would instead be treated as a minor dignitary of a foreign land coming to pay homage to the emperor. The emperor would generously grant him an audience in the public hall for such ceremonies (not three days' residence in the imperial inner chambers, like the relics), provide a token gift of proper clothing (Han Yu notes at the outset of this paragraph that the Buddha did not dress properly), and then forcibly remove him from the empire to prevent his destabilizing influence. Here Han Yu endorses the proper Confucian hierarchy: The emperor is the highest authority, and the Buddha is the pilgrim. Emperor Xianzong was inappropriately reversing the order and welcoming the relics as the remains of a superior being.

◆ **Paragraphs 11–13**

Worse still, these relics were "withered and decayed bones." While the Chinese did sacrifice to ancestral spirits, the focus was not on physical relics but on a statue, a portrait, or a plaque with an ancestor's name on it. There was no traditional analogue to viewing body parts as having numinous power. Han Yu quotes another line from Confucius's Analects to underscore his point: "'Revere ghosts and spirits but keep them at a distance.'" Confucius was most concerned about the present and how concrete moral actions in the present (based in moral precedents of Chinese traditions, not in Buddhism) could create greater harmony and peace. To Han Yu's mind, the extravagant opulence of the welcoming ceremony, which in turn encouraged mortification of the flesh among the common people, was harmful. To this end he equates any numinous power in the bones with "ill-omened" spirits that rulers in antiquity sought to banish before engaging in ancestral sacrifice. True to form, Han Yu takes the moral stance that he is the only one who sees through, or at least has the courage to criticize, this display as harmful to the empire. If the emperor would simply destroy the relics, he would greatly benefit the empire and posterity; if the Buddha's power did extend through the relics, then Han Yu asks that he be punished for any wrongdoing, though he is doubtful that anything will happen to him.

Audience

Given the importance that Chinese civilization has traditionally placed on writing and history, Chinese authors wrote with an eye to audiences in the present and the future. Writing, whether personal or professional, addressed both public audiences (officials and court historians) and private audiences (friends, family, colleagues, and future readers). First and foremost, Han Yu's memorial was a public appeal to the emperor to end his sponsorship of Buddhism. Han Yu was making a statement to the emperor and his officials. The memorial was also a public document for those in the future to note. Upon submission it became part of the imperial archive and would be used by court historians when they compiled the official history of Emperor Xianzong's reign. Han Yu himself had served in the Historiography Office, drafting the official history of previous Tang emperors. He was fully aware of how memorials would be used to create official histories. The official histories were the basis of historical education throughout the empire, and one's legacy would be shaped in part by one's public documents. Becoming famous for the right reasons and leaving a good legacy repaid the debt owed to

Questions for Further Study

1. The history of Confucianism in early China was in large part a history of the intersection of politics, power, and religion. In what ways did Confucianism legitimize the power of Chinese rulers? In what ways did the influx of Buddhism challenge that power?

2. The conflict that gave rise to Han Yu's document reflected a deeper underlying conflict between progressivism and conservatism. During the Tang Dynasty, imperial China was a center of cosmopolitanism and new ideas; Han Yu called for a return to more traditional Confucian beliefs and practices. Do you see a similar conflict occurring in twenty-first-century America? If so, how does that conflict manifest itself?

3. The Confucianism that Han Yu champions placed considerable emphasis on such concepts as order versus chaos, harmony and peace, ancestor worship, family structure, ancient rituals, and social hierarchies. Why would his vision of culture, society, and organization have been attractive to the Chinese people at this time—so much so that he inaugurated the neo-Confucian movement that lasted for hundreds of years?

4. Han Yu's memorial documents a chapter in the conflict between Buddhism and Confucianism in early China. Do you see any analogues of this conflict—a conflict between two major religions—in the modern world? Why does this type of religious conflict often break out into armed conflict and violence?

5. The text states: "Searching for the root cause of the decline of imperial power [during the Tang Dynasty], some pointed to the presence of non-Han Chinese at all levels of the society. Uighurs and Tibetans were banned from living in the capital, resulting in the forcible removal and ultimate slaughter of Uighur residents from Chang'an's precincts." Can you think of other examples of nations where foreign elements were blamed for social ills? Offer an explanation for why people blame "foreigners" when things appear to be going wrong.

one's ancestors and promoted the status of one's family and clan in the present and the future.

Privately Han Yu was also a famous literary figure whose poetry and prose were published in collections during his lifetime and after his death. The memorial would be added to his collected works as a model essay and as a record of his beliefs and positions. Han Yu had an eye toward his own historical record when he wrote this piece. He knew that in posterity he would be remembered as a strongly Confucian official who had had the courage to chastise an emperor for what he considered inappropriate support for Buddhism.

Impact

Han Yu's piece had little immediate impact, other than his exile. Emperor Xianzong did not end his sponsorship of ceremonies venerating the relics. The imperial family continued to present donations to the Dharma Gate Monastery until the final years of the dynasty. However, the memorial did provide justification for Confucians who opposed Buddhism's social, political, and economic influence. In 845 the imperial court took action against many wealthy monasteries—confiscating land and wealth and returning approximately two hundred fifty thousand monks and nuns to taxable lay life. Part of the justification was that Buddhism was harming the society, as Han Yu had argued. That justification was a veneer, however, over economic motivations of a court that was increasingly unable to collect taxes and that needed cash to maintain campaigns against rebellious governors-general.

The longer-term impact was that Han Yu was credited by later Confucian scholars as the instigator of a Confucian revival. In the subsequent Song Dynasty (960–1279), when Neo-Confucianism came to dominate intellectual life, Han Yu was cited as the person who was able to recapture the ancient ideals of classical Confucianism embodied in the works of Confucius and the later philosopher Mencius. Han Yu was held up as a paragon of Confucian values: He was a successful scholar and poet, a successful official who stuck to his moral vision despite the threat of exile or worse, and a successful head of a large family.

The memorial also needs to be seen in the larger context of Han Yu's Confucian project. He promoted a style of learning that focused on classical texts. Doing so, he believed, rekindled the traditional moral values that linked private cultivation with public service: To become educated obliged one to serve in office, as Confucius had argued. Once in office, one had to employ the moral values of the classical Confucian texts. Han Yu advocated close study of the Four Books—Analects, Mencius, Doctrine of the Mean, and Great Learning—as the repository of Confucian values. These books and Han Yu's notion of reviving classical ideals became the cornerstone of the Neo-Confucian movement. Neo-Confucianism, in turn, became the ideology of the civil service examinations and the imperial bureaucracy until 1905.

Further Reading

■ **Articles**

Karetzky, Patricia Eichenbaum. "Esoteric Buddhism and the Famensi Finds." *Archives of Asian Art* 47 (1994): 78–85.

McMullen, David. "Han Yü: An Alternative Picture." *Harvard Journal of Asiatic Studies* 49, no. 2 (1989): 603–657.

■ **Books**

Bol, Peter K. *"This Culture of Ours": Intellectual Transitions in T'ang and Sung China.* Stanford, Calif.: Stanford University Press, 1992.

Confucius. *The Analects,* trans. D. C. Lau. New York: Penguin Books, 1979.

Hartman, Charles. *Han Yü and the T'ang Search for Unity.* Princeton, N.J.: Princeton University Press, 1986.

Kieschnick, John. *The Impact of Buddhism on Chinese Material Culture.* Princeton, N.J.: Princeton University Press, 2002.

Peterson, C. A. "Court and Province in Mid- and Late T'ang." In *The Cambridge History of China,* vol. 3, ed. Denis Twitchett. Cambridge: Cambridge University Press, 1989.

Wright, Arthur F. *Buddhism in Chinese History.* Stanford, Calif.: Stanford University Press, 1991.

—Robert W. Foster

HAN YU'S "MEMORIAL ON THE BUDDHA'S BONES"

Your servant says:

He humbly believes that Buddhism is a religion of the barbarians, which spread to the Middle Kingdom in Later Han [25–220 CE] times. It did not exist in antiquity. In the ancient past, the Yellow Emperor [Huang Di] reigned for 100 years, and lived 110 years; Shaohao reigned for 80 years, and lived 100 years; Zhuanxu reigned for 79 years, and lived 98 years; Di Ku reigned for 70 years, and lived 105 ·years; Di Yao reigned for 98 years, and lived 118 years; both Di Shun and Yu lived 100 years. This was a time of great tranquility under heaven. The people enjoyed peace, happiness, and longevity while there was no Buddha in the Middle Kingdom.

Thereafter King Tang of Yin too lived 100 years. Tang's grandson Taiwu reigned for 75 years while Wuding reigned for 59 years. History does not record their ages, which, judging by their reign periods, should not be shorter than 100 years. King Wen of Zhou lived 97 years, and King Wu 93 years, while King Mu reigned for 100 years. During this period the law of the Buddha did not enter the Middle Kingdom, nor did Buddha worship bring about all this.

During the reign of Emperor Ming of Han [r. 57–75 CE] the law of the Buddha began to make its appearance. Emperor Ming reigned for only 18 years. Thereafter chaos and destruction continued, and reign periods were short-lived. During and after the period of the Song [420–479], Qi [479–502], Liang [502–557], Chen [557–589], and the Yuan Wei [Northern Wei, 386–534] dynasties, as people became more devoted to Buddha worship, reign periods became particularly short. Only Wudi of Liang [r. 502–549] reigned for 48 years. During his reign on three occasions he gave up his own body for the Buddha. At the Ancestral Temple sacrifices, he stopped making animal offerings, and limited himself to one meal of vegetables and fruits every day. With Hou Jing [502–552] closing in on him, Wudi ended up dying of starvation at Taicheng. His country too was destroyed soon after. Buddha worship is for the purpose of bringing good fortune, but it only results in more misfortune. In view of this, it is evident that the Buddha is not worth worshiping.

Upon taking over the imperial mantle from the Sui, [Tang] Gaozu [Li Yuan, r. 618–626] discussed the elimination [of Buddhism]. At that time, the ministers and courtiers were not farsighted enough to comprehend the profundity of the Way of the ancient sages and the exigencies of the past and present so as to elucidate the sagely wisdom and correct that abuse. So the effort did not go any further, to your servant's constant regret.

I humble myself in front of the divine, holy, brilliant, and martial presence of Your Imperial Majesty, who is wise and sagely, and excels in literary accomplishment and the art of war. In the past thousands of years, no one can compare with [Your Majesty]. Not long after you ascended the throne you began to disallow ordinations of people as Buddhist monks and nuns or Daoist adepts. Nor did you permit the creation of Buddhist monasteries and Daoist abbeys. Once your servant believed that the wish of Gaozu would certainly be realized under Your Majesty's hand. Nowadays, even though that has not come to pass, there is no reason to encourage it [Buddhism] to flourish again.

Now I have heard that Your Majesty instructed various monks to greet the Buddhist relic at Fengxiang, mounted a loft-building to view it, and took it in both hands into the Great Within. In addition, [Your Majesty] ordered various monasteries to take turns to receive and worship the relic.

Although your servant is extremely foolish, he still knows that Your Majesty will not be deluded by the Buddha into worshiping [the relic] like this in the hope of achieving happiness and auspiciousness. This is simply a frivolous gimmick and a deceitful and exotic spectacle set up for the officials and commoners of the capital in an attempt to humor some people at a time when the harvest is good and people are happy. It cannot be true that [Your Majesty], so sagely and brilliant, believes in this sort of thing.

However, the people are inherently ignorant, susceptible to delusion, and difficult to reason with. If they should behold Your Majesty like this, they would talk about devotedly worshiping the Buddha. Everyone would say, "Even the great sage Son of Heaven is devout in his faith; who are we the ordinary people to grudge our own bodies and lives?" They would sear the tops of their heads and burn their fingers, gathering in crowds of tens or hundreds. They would doff their clothes to scatter their money, from morning till night. They would emulate one another for fear of being left behind. Old and young would all run about [doing this], abandoning their proper occupations.

If this is not henceforth banned, it [the relic] will go the rounds among various monasteries. By then, there will be people who sever their arms and cut out their flesh to make offerings [to the relic]. Corrupting our accepted mores and customs and making ourselves a laughingstock everywhere—this is no small matter.

The Buddha was originally a man of the barbarians who did not speak the language of the Middle Kingdom and was dressed in clothes of a different cut from ours. Neither did he cite the edifying discourses of the ancient sovereigns, nor did he don their proper attire. He was ignorant of the sense of duty between sovereign and subject, and the affections between father and son. If he were alive today, and were on a state mission to visit the court in the capital, and if Your Majesty would generously receive him, [Your Majesty] would merely grant him one audience in the Hall of Manifest Government [Xuanzheng dian]. After one banquet was held at the Office of Foreign Relations, and one set of attire was conferred on him, [Your Majesty] would have guards escort him out of the country so that he would not be able to delude the masses.

All the more, now that he has been dead for long, how can his withered and decayed bones and baleful and filthy remains be allowed into the forbidden palace? Confucius said, "Revere ghosts and spirits but keep them at a distance." In antiquity, when the various princes were about to hold mourning ceremonies in their states, even they would request shamans to use peach-wood charms and magic brooms to eradicate the ill-omened before they proceeded. Today for no good reason the decayed and filthy object was brought to light for Your Majesty's viewing. It was neither proceeded by shamans nor exorcised by peach-wood charms and magic brooms. No ministers have ever talked about its wrongs, and no censors have ever cited its faults. Your servant is truly mortified by this.

I pray that [Your Majesty] will have the relic delivered to the government agency concerned, which will depose of it in water or fire so as to permanently destroy its roots. If [Your Majesty] puts to rest doubts under Heaven and stops once and for all [Buddhism] from deluding posterity, all under Heaven will be aware of the achievement by you the great sage, which is hundreds of millions of times greater than that of ordinary people. Isn't that wonderful? Isn't that cause for joy?

If the Buddha should possess soul and the power to cause misfortunes, let all such calamities be visited upon your servant. Let Heaven be the witness: your servant shall never regret it.

With great gratitude and extreme sincerity, I present this memorial for Your Majesty's consideration.

Your servant in genuine fear and trepidation.

Glossary

Hou Jing	general who seized the Liang throne; he was soon deposed by a Liang prince and attempted to flee but was killed by his own partisans.
Middle Kingdom	Chinese name for China
Way of the ancient sages	in this context, the teachings on which Confucius and his followers based the ethical and philosophical system now known as Confucianism
Your Imperial Majesty	Emperor Xianzong
Your servant	Han Yu, poet and classical prose stylist who was also a member of the Chinese civil service

II AETHELSTAN, OR THE GRATELY CODE

"Everyone is to be at peace with everything

with which the king will be at peace."

Overview

The originally unnamed medieval law code that is now known as "II Aethelstan" is a tract of tenth-century Anglo-Saxon law that addresses a wide range of social concerns. These laws outline prohibitions and punishments for theft, murder, witchcraft, treachery against a person's lord, and oath breaking, as well as regulations of trade, means of ascertaining guilt, and the enforcement of the laws contained within the law code. The law code was promulgated by King Aethelstan at some point during his reign (924/925–939). Exactly when in Aethelstan's reign the law code was first produced, however, is uncertain. The law code is sometimes referred to as the "Grately Code" because, according to the epilogue included only in the twelfth-century Latin version of the document, it was originally promulgated at Grately in Hampshire, England.

Context

Records contemporary to Aethelstan's reign and throughout much of the Anglo-Saxon period in general are somewhat sketchy and incomplete. Piecing together events, especially surrounding named individuals, can be difficult, and even in the case of a king the details can be unclear. Consequently, the exact date in Aethelstan's reign when the Grately Code was composed and the circumstances behind its promulgation are uncertain. Whether the comprehensive laws in II Aethelstan were part of a general commitment to justice and social order or were the outcome of practical measures to counterbalance current circumstances is not certain. On the one hand, the broader interpretation of crime as an offence against society at large as well as against the victim is an underlying theme in Anglo-Saxon law from the reign of King Alfred (beginning in 871), Aethelstan's grandfather, through to King Canute, whose reign began almost a century later (in 1016). This approach to law contrasts significantly with the laws of the seventh century, where crime was understood primarily as an offence against the victim. Furthermore, in the 164 years between the start

of King Alfred's rule and the end of Canute's reign (in 1035), there were only three kings who did not produce law codes (or, perhaps, for whom law codes no longer survive). The reasons behind Aethelstan's promulgation of the law code at Grately and others in his name may simply be that promulgating laws is what kings are supposed to do. On the other hand, the prologue to Aethelstan's laws given at Exeter (now known as V Aethelstan) states that the new law code is being set forth because the peace pronounced at Grately was not strictly kept. As such, Aethelstan's laws can be argued to be in direct reaction to circumstances—even if they were not necessarily successful.

Despite the uncertainties surrounding Aethelstan's law codes and their promulgation, some of the background events of his reign can be sketched out. As a child, Aethelstan, son of the king of Wessex, was raised in the royal court of the kingdom of Mercia. When his father, Edward the Elder, died on July 17, 924, Aethelstan was recognized as king in Mercia, while his half-brother, Aelfweard, was recognized as king in Wessex. Aelfweard, however, died on August 2, 924. It was over a year before Aethelstan was crowned king of Wessex and of the Danes on September 4, 925. The reasons for this delay are unclear, but it has been speculated that there may have been civil war, with Wessex initially favoring Aelfweard's brother Eadwine for king.

Once Aethelstan had been crowned king, his reign was defined by expansion and conquest. At first, an alliance was made with Sihtric of York, king of Northumbria, sealed with Sihtric's marriage to one of Aethelstan's sisters in 926. This represented a major change in diplomatic relations, as previously Sihtric had refused communications with Aethelstan's father. The alliance crumbled with Sihtric's death in 927. Aethelstan then invaded Northumbria to take control of it for himself. In July 927 the Northumbrians submitted to Aethelstan, along with the Scots, the Welsh, and the Strathclyde Britons. By 931, Aethelstan was identified in charters as king of Albion, or all of Britannia, although his reign was not peaceful, and his control did not remain uncontested. In 934, Aethelstan marched his armies back into Scotland, presumably to suppress rebellion, and in 937 the Scots allied with the Norse and invaded England. Aethelstan successfully repelled the invaders, an event commemorated in the Anglo-Saxon heroic poem

CA. 895
- Aethelstan is born.

924
- **July 17**
  King Edward the Elder, father of Alfweard and Aethelstan, dies.
- **after July 17**
  Alfweard is recognized as king in Wessex, and Aethelstan is recognized as king in Mercia.
- **August 2**
  Alfweard dies.

924–939
- II Aethelstan, also known as the Grately Code, is promulgated.

925
- **September 4**
  Aethelstan is recognized and crowned as king of the Anglo-Saxons and the Danes.

CA. 926
- Wulfhelm is consecrated archbishop of Canterbury.

927
- Aethelstan acquires Northumbria and becomes king of the English.

931
- Aethelstan is identified (in charters) as king of Albion or all of Britannia.

The Battle of Brunanburh. Some two years later, on October 27, 939, Aethelstan died without an heir and was succeeded by his half-brother Edmund.

Conquest and expansion of the realm clearly underlie Aethelstan's reign. In addition to his military conquests he was a devout king, renowned as a collector of saints' relics as well as for his generous donations of relics, books, and various other treasures to monasteries and nunneries. The upholding of Christian faith and the controlling of the realm were both considered essential duties of an Anglo-Saxon king. In all, the promulgation of law, part of both the biblical and the Anglo-Saxon image of kingship, and central to the controlling of the realm, must have seemed part of the duties of Christian kingship to Aethelstan. Certainly, the influence of the church on the promulgation of the law codes, and their contents, was great. It has already been stressed that the exact point, even the year, in Aethelstan's realm when the Grately Code was first promulgated is unknown. Nevertheless, the forging and expansion of the realm and the religious faith Aethelstan displayed throughout his reign form compelling contexts to underlie the promulgation of II Aethelstan. It is impossible not to see the concerns with social cohesion and order outlined in the law codes as an integral part of that process.

About the Author

On the surface, Aethelstan may seem the most obvious candidate to have been the author of the law code. However, it is unlikely that the king actually wrote the law code or even that he composed the laws contained within it. Instead, the king should be understood as a central figure, bestowing authority on the law. As was the norm for Anglo-Saxon law, the actual laws underlying II Aethelstan were produced in a council meeting. The epilogue of the law code specifically names one other individual who was present: Wulfhelm, who served as archbishop of Canterbury from around 926 until his death on February 12, 941. In addition to Wulfhelm, the epilogue also states that there were "all the nobles and councillors whom King Aethelstan could gather together"—a significant and powerful group of advisers termed the *witan* in Old English. It is highly unlikely that the *witan* and the archbishop were present only to accept the law. Instead, their council would have contributed to the laws that were promulgated.

It should be noted that the actual law would originally have been the formal, oral declaration made in the council and upheld by oaths. The difference between law and law codes is a central point in understanding Anglo-Saxon legal culture. How much legal force the written version of the law code actually would have had is uncertain, but probably it was only a record of the meeting. Indeed, this record may not originally have been official in nature and was quite probably a personal record. Further emphasizing the distinction between the law and the written law code, the scholar Patrick Wormald goes so far as to question whether Aethelstan was even present at the council in Grately. He argues that the production of the law code may have been undertaken by others at the council, expanding earlier laws issued in the name of Aethelstan in previous council meetings into a fuller and workable document. Although it is not possible to prove, there remains a distinct possibility that Archbishop Wulfhelm himself (or scribes working for him) was originally responsible for the production of this document. Rather than the law code's being used by every administrator of the law, it may have been limited primarily to literate members of the church.

Explanation and Analysis of the Document

It is impossible to date precisely the initial promulgation of the law code II Aethelstan. The conventional dates of 924–939 given to the law code simply mean that the code was produced at some point during the reign of Aethelstan. However, II Aethelstan must be relatively earlier than most of the five other law codes attributed to Aethelstan, as most refer back to the council at Grately and the laws established there.

Although the law was originally promulgated in the early tenth century, the earliest surviving versions date to the late eleventh century or the first half of the twelfth century. The earliest surviving version written in Old English is in the manuscript "Cambridge, Corpus Christi College 383." However, this version is a fragment, and only the first fifty-four lines remain (up to clause 6). The rest has been lost since at least the sixteenth century. The other Old English version, from slightly later in the twelfth century, is in the manuscript "Rochester Cathedral Library, MS A.3.5," also known as the *Textus Roffensis*.

In addition to these two surviving Old English versions of the law code, there is also a twelfth-century Latin translation in the legal collection known as the Quadripartitus, which survives in a number of medieval manuscripts. It is in the epilogue added only to the Latin version (following on from clause 26.1) that much of the essential information regarding the context of the law code's production and promulgation is included.

◆ Compiling the Law Code

From the comprehensive scope of the law code, it is tempting to think of II Aethelstan as a complete and independent piece. After all, the law code provided regulations for a large range of social concerns. However, the law code is dependent on a broader literate and legal context. In the law code itself there are echoes of a previous document that has been incorporated into the main body of II Aethelstan. In particular, clauses 13.1 through 18 are numbered as "secondly" through "seventhly" in the law code.

It is possible that the initial part of the law code, from the prologue through to the end of clause 13, was originally intended to be the first section. The second section could have begun at the word "secondly" in clause 13.1, the third in clause 14, and so forth. As, following the title "Concerning thieves," clause 1 begins with the word *first* this argu-

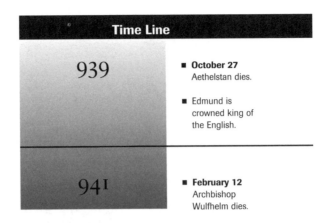

Time Line

939

■ **October 27**
Aethelstan dies.

■ Edmund is crowned king of the English.

941

■ **February 12**
Archbishop Wulfhelm dies.

ment is just plausible. However, the laws in the initial block cover a wide array of legal concerns, beginning with theft but then moving rapidly through treachery (clause 4), witchcraft and murder (clause 6), and the "ordeal" (clause 7) as well as trade and exchange (clauses 10 and 12). Conversely, the section from clauses 13 to 18 changes its numbering with each change of subject. In addition, clause 13.1, which states that all trade must take place in a town, repeats the subject of clause 12, which states that all goods with a value of more than twenty pence must be bought in a town. This evidence suggests that most likely the block from clauses 13 to 18 represents the integration of a different law code into II Aethelstan. Whether this blending occurred at the council meeting in Grately or later is impossible to tell for certain. However, given that this section is found in all three versions of the law code, it likely occurred early on and probably when the law code was first produced.

◆ II Aethelstan and the Laws of Previous Kings

In addition to the reuse of former law promulgated by Aethelstan, the law code also forms connections with the law codes of previous kings. There is sometimes a temptation to imagine that only the laws of a given king were valid during his reign and that the laws of previous kings were either amended and reissued under a new name or else abandoned. Instead, however, Anglo-Saxon law was generally cumulative, with additions and alterations being added by individual kings to the body of customary practice. In addition, direct references to previous law codes are prevalent throughout Anglo-Saxon law codes, particularly with reference to the Domboc, the law book of King Alfred the Great. In particular, clause 5 of II Aethelstan, which outlines the punishment for breaking into a church, states that the accused is "to pay according to what the law-book says." This statement refers specifically to clause 6 of the Domboc, which stipulates the extent of the fine to be paid as well as the perpetrator's physical punishment—having his or her hand cut off.

◆ Wergild

The extent of a fine was determined by the wergild of the person committing the offense. The term *wergild* literally means "man money" and was the value given to each member of society, excluding slaves. The higher a person's

Aethelstan ordering a translation of the Bible into the Saxon language (© Hulton-Deutsch Collecction/CORBIS)

social rank, the higher the wergild. Initially this was the price that had to be paid to the family if a person was killed. Throughout II Aethelstan and other Anglo-Saxon law codes, however, the use of wergild is expanded to include the price for various other infringements. References to a person's wergild appear throughout II Aethelstan as the cost and value of a sworn oath and the amount of the fine for committing criminal actions or otherwise failing to uphold the law.

◆ Concerning Thieves

Among the main concerns of II Aethelstan are the restriction of theft and the punishment of thieves. In the manuscript "Cambridge, Corpus Christi College 383," the law code was originally copied without any manner of heading or introduction. However, the heading "Concerning thieves" was added at some point in the fifty years after the manuscript was first produced. The emphasis on the prevention of theft in the law code, rather than on identifying the king in whose name the laws were published, is immediately apparent. The law code sought to prevent and to punish theft in a variety of ways. It begins by dictating that thieves were not to be spared if they were caught with the stolen goods. This directive, however, was initially tempered by allowing thieves under the age of twelve to be

spared unless, as detailed in clause 1.2, they attempted to defend themselves or to flee. The following subclauses, 1.3 to 1.5, mandated a forty-day prison sentence, coupled with oaths that the individual desist from future wrongdoing, as well as greater financial punishment equal to the full wergild for any future transgressions.

Furthermore, to ensure the punishment of the thief, in clause 1.1 the law code establishes a fine for a person who spares a thief. As this fine was equal to the person's wergild, allowing a thief to go unpunished was reprimanded at the same value as a repeat offense by a thief. However, to prevent the punishment of theft from becoming a personal vendetta, II Aethelstan also discouraged ordinary people from avenging a theft in person. Clause 6.3 awarded a hefty fine of 120 shillings to be paid to the king if a person sought revenge against a thief but failed actually to wound the thief. If the avenger wounded the victim, then the punishment was the same as for committing secret killings (which is to say murder by treacherous or dishonorable means, as opposed to open killing, where the perpetrator did not try to conceal the homicide), performing witchcraft, or committing arson, as shown in clauses 6 to 6.2. In addition to paying the 120-shilling fine, the avenger also had to pay compensation, equal to the victim's wergild, to the victim's family.

The clauses demanding that all trade occur within a town were also intended to prevent theft by limiting the opportunity for the sale of stolen goods. Limiting sales to within a town meant that trade had to be open and public. If someone traded in stolen goods, the original owners would have had more opportunity to identify their property. Conversely, any trade occurring outside a town could therefore be assumed to be in stolen goods. The injunction that all trade must occur in a town was further refined by the presence of official witnesses who were deemed to be trustworthy. Thus clause 10 declares that livestock should be exchanged only if the transaction was witnessed by either a reeve (an official administrator) or "the priest or the lord of the estate or the treasurer or other trustworthy man." The law code set a fine of thirty shillings in clause 10.1 and ordered that the goods, which were assumed to have been stolen, as they had not been traded using the official channel, be given into the ownership of the lord of the estate.

◆ **The Swearing of Oaths**

The accusation of an individual, the witnessing of transactions, and the declaration of innocence were all supported primarily by the sworn oath of the individual. Clause 6, regarding witchcraft and secret killing, punished transgressors with death if they could not deny, by oath, having killed their victims. However, the specific detail included in clause 1.1 sheds a little more light on the process of the oath in Anglo-Saxon law. The clause states that a person who spared a thief had to clear himself or herself with an oath of the same value as his or her wergild. On one hand, this clause shows the greater value attached to people of higher social standing in Anglo-Saxon culture. Those people who were of higher social status were expected to be more honest and were given more credit, and obligations, accordingly. On the other hand, putting a price to an oath shows awareness that false oaths could be sworn, and it established financial punishment accordingly.

The swearing of false oaths and the giving of false witness are specifically discussed twice in II Aethelstan. First, in clause 10.1, a fine of thirty shillings was established—although the law code does not state to whom it would be paid—and the individual's oath was never considered valid again. The second mention of false oaths occurs in clause 26, which imposed a religious injunction against the perpetrator. A person who swore a false oath was not permitted burial in consecrated ground—a severe threat in the highly Christian society of Anglo-Saxon England. If an offender undertook the penance prescribed by a confessor and procured the witness of the bishop of the diocese, the injunction against Christian burial was lifted. However, even if an offender undertook the penance, he or she still remained unable to swear oaths in the future. From the punishments outlined for giving false witness, the significance of the oath in Anglo-Saxon society speaks for itself.

◆ **The Ordeal**

The sworn oath, then, formed a central part of the legal structure and society in general and was important in the establishment of guilt and innocence. However, the recognition that false oaths could be sworn suggested that additional means were necessary to determine guilt or innocence. The main method used in Anglo-Saxon law and society was the ordeal. In most of II Aethelstan, this process is mentioned almost casually. For example, clause 14.1 refers to "[the ordeal of] hot iron." Similarly clauses 4, 5, and 6.1 mention the "three-fold ordeal," and clause 7 refers to the "simple ordeal." The sheer number of times that the term *ordeal* is used and the lack of actual details emphasize that the process must have been well established in Anglo-Saxon society. After all, if specific details were not necessary, then they were likely already well known.

Two clauses in II Aethelstan do outline specific details of the process. In particular, clause 23 describes the oath of the accused and the ordeal he or she would have undertaken in a religious framework involving fasting and attending Mass for three days preceding the ordeal, on the final day taking Communion and then swearing the oath before undergoing the ordeal itself. These religious elements suggest that it was understood to be supernatural, divine judgment that determined the outcome. The fact that these details are outlined so clearly in II Aethelstan implies that the supernatural basis of the ordeal had previously been less connected to the church, though it had probably always been Christian, rather than pre-Christian, in context.

The following clause, 23.1, adds further details to the process of the ordeal. The ordeal of water ordered the accused "to sink to one and a half ells on the rope." (An ell is the distance from one shoulder to the fingertips of the hand opposite.) The ordeal of hot iron mandated that "it is to be three days before the hand is unbound." Neither stipulation is fully informative in its own right, suggesting that the underlying principle of the ordeal was already known. Indeed, this can be seen from the laws of King Ine (688–694), included in the later Domboc of King Alfred (871–899), where clause 62 refers to a man who "is driven to the ordeal" as a way of proving his innocence (Whitelock, p. 406). However, the laws of Ine do not specifically detail how the ordeal was to be performed or judged. From the somewhat later, anonymous law code now known simply as Ordeal (first promulgated between 936 and 1000), the majority of information on the ordeal is known. For the ordeal of water, the person was bound hand and foot and submerged in water. If the person sank to the appropriate depth, he or she was declared innocent; if not, he or she was declared guilty. In the ordeal of hot iron, the accused had to hold a piece of red-hot iron in the palm of one hand and carry it for a set distance. Afterward the hand was bandaged for three days, and then the bandage was removed. If the wound was healing cleanly, the accused was declared innocent; if the wound festered, the accused was deemed guilty. The difference between the simple ordeal and the threefold ordeal was in the duration of time given to sink in the water and the weight of the heated iron and the distance it had to be carried.

To a modern audience, the ordeal may seem to be an uncertain way of determining innocence, truth, or guilt.

Silver coin of Aethelstan, 923/4–939 BCE (© The Trustees of the British Museum)

However, for Anglo-Saxon society it shows a movement away from basing guilt only on accusation to including a way of testing that guilt. Another movement in the law that can be identified is the injunction, in clause 23.2, that the ordeal was invalid if the accused had more than twelve supporters present, unless some should agree to leave. If the accused was found guilty by the ordeal, the number of available combatants would have been limited if they resorted to violence to support their case, having first failed with law. In this way and in numerous others, II Aethelstan sought to regulate and control Anglo-Saxon society.

Audience

Because the law was promulgated at a meeting attended primarily by dignitaries, these dignitaries must be considered as the initial audience. However, the law was not intended to end with them but to radiate out through them into the lands they controlled and to the people over whom they had authority. The written version of the law code would originally have been the product of one member or perhaps a few members of that audience, which is to say most likely ecclesiastics and possibly the archbishop himself. Undoubtedly, the law code is an adapted form of the oral pronouncement of the law and likewise was further changed from the time it was first written down in the meeting to the surviving copies that still exist. Nevertheless, something of the original audience can be deduced from the contents of the law code.

First, it should be observed that the law was intended to be valid throughout Aethelstan's kingdom. How much of Britain that originally included depends on how late into

Aethelstan's reign the law was promulgated. The locations mentioned in clause 14.2 of the law code—Canterbury, Rochester, London, Winchester, Lewes, Hastings, Chichester, Southampton, Wareham, Dorchester, Exeter, and Shaftesbury—would appear to imply that the audiences were located in the south of England. Whether this implies that the law code was promulgated earlier in Aethelstan's reign, before his acquisition of Northumbria in 927, is uncertain. On the surface the argument seems sound, as no northern settlements are mentioned. However, the final words, stating that the other boroughs should have one moneyer each, could equally be applied to the north. It is quite possible that Aethelstan, or whoever composed the law code, was based in the south and not familiar or concerned enough with the northern settlements to name them. A further point to consider is that clause 14.2 falls in the middle of the section discussed previously, wherein a separate set of clause numbering has been used, implying that an earlier law code was incorporated into II Aethelstan when it was being produced. In all, therefore, there is nothing in the law code that can conclusively pinpoint when in Aethelstan's reign it was promulgated and, consequently, how far his kingdom reached and to what parts of Britain the law did, or did not, apply.

In terms of social class, the contents of the law code were aimed at all strata of society. On one hand, the king is referred to repeatedly throughout the law code but by title rather than by name, implying that the law was to be valid not just under Aethelstan but under his successors also. At the other end of the social spectrum, slaves are also frequently mentioned. Numerous other occupations and social classes are cited, including "landless men," "lordless men," "moneyers," bishops, and lords.

"And we have pronounced that no goods over 20 pence are to be bought outside a town, but they are to be bought there in the witness of the town-reeve or of another trustworthy man, or, again, in the witness of the reeves in a public meeting."

(Clause 12)

"If anyone fails to attend a meeting three times, he is to pay the fine for disobedience to the king; and the meeting is to be announced seven days before it is to take place."

(Clause 20)

"And it is to be announced in the meeting that everyone is to be at peace with everything with which the king will be at peace, and to refrain from theft on pain of losing his life and all that he owns."

(Clause 20.3)

"And he who swears a false oath, and it becomes known against him, is never afterwards to be entitled to an oath, nor is he to be buried in a consecrated cemetery when he dies, unless he has the witness of the bishop in whose diocese he is that he has done penance for it as his confessor has prescribed for him."

(Clause 26)

In short, the audience of the law was the entirety of society. However, something of the people responsible for its implementation—its immediate audience—can also be seen in the law code. In clause 25 the focus of the law code turns to ensuring its enforcement, with the instruction that "if any of my reeves will not carry out this [ordinance] and is less zealous about it than we have pronounced, he is then to pay the fine for disobedience to me, and I shall find another who will." The following clause, 25.1, instructed the bishop of the diocese in question to enforce this law. Clause 25.2 expanded the attention of the law code once more to include all of society.

The main audience who needed to know the law therefore was the reeves, for it was their job to implement the law on the local and immediate level. The term *reeve* refers generally to a person with administrative duties, which were often further defined in terms of a reeve's specific authority and responsibilities. For example, there were royal reeves, bishops' reeves, town reeves, port reeves, and reeves with authority over various administrative areas, such as boroughs and shires. The final one, the shire reeve, is perhaps the best known to the modern audience, as the term is the origin of the modern word *sheriff*.

To what degree the reeves were literate is difficult to determine. At the very least some reeves must have been literate, especially those who were of higher social rank or those who were attached to ecclesiastical figures. Alternatively, it is possible that the spread of literacy was far greater and may have played a fundamental role in the administration of the kingdom and the implementation of royal decrees and the law. If such is the case, then copies of the written law code—even if their production was unofficial—may still have played a significant role in the actual administration of the law.

Impact

Although the law code covers a wide range of issues concerning Anglo-Saxon society in the early tenth century, it was not necessarily effective. The subsequent laws of Aethelstan frequently refer back to this law code. The prologue of the law code V Aethelstan, issued at a council in Exeter, is informative on this matter. In full the prologue states, "I King Aethelstan, make known that I have learnt that our peace is worse kept than I should like and than it was pronounced at Grately; and my councillors say that I have borne it too long" (Whitelock, p. 422).

In terms of immediate effect, then, it would appear that the law was, at best, ignored by a sizable proportion of the population or, at worst, completely ineffectual. However, the evidence from the surviving manuscript copies of the text allows for a different interpretation. The two surviving Old English texts of II Aethelstan and the Latin translation in the Quadripartitus manuscripts are different versions of the document. That is to say that the wording and contents are subtly varied in each. Some of this variation undoubtedly arose from subtle changes made by scribes, either accidentally or deliberately, as they copied the manuscript. Some scholars argue that the number and scope of the differences are such that each version must have been copied from a distinctly different source, and each must have diverged from the original at a much earlier point.

The implications are that numerous written copies were circulated and copied soon after the initial production of the law code. These split into the different versions that ultimately resulted in the three different texts that have survived to the modern day. The fact that so many copies and versions were produced and used suggests that the document enjoyed some popularity. On one hand, therefore, it would appear that the law had little impact on Anglo-Saxon society, and Aethelstan and his councilors were forced to reissue the law at numerous councils and gatherings. On the other hand, and perhaps because the law was not being upheld, numerous copies of the law code were produced and circulated.

Further Reading

■ Articles

Colman, Rebecca V. "Reason and Unreason in Early Medieval Law." *Journal of Interdisciplinary History* 4 (Spring 1974): 571–591.

O'Brien, Bruce R. "From Mord or to Murdrum: The Preconquest Origin and Norman Revival of the Murder Fine." *Speculum* 71, no. 2 (April 1996): 321–357.

Questions for Further Study

1. Compare this document with the Magna Carta of 1215. Aethelstan's law code predated the Norman Invasion of England by roughly a century and a half, and the other followed that invasion by roughly an equal period of time. Do the two documents, looked at side by side, help modern historians form differing pictures of pre-Norman and post-Norman England? How?

2. Compare this document with Niẓām al-Mulk's *Book of Government; or, Rules for Kings*, written about a century and a half later. How do the two documents reflect different or similar visions of government in a medieval Christian nation and in the medieval Islamic world?

3. How is the medieval English wergild similar to modern-day fines for offenses? How is it different? In medieval England, the amount of wergild was in part a function of a person's social class. Do you think that social class continues to play a part in modern-day "wergild"? If so, how?

4. A document such as the Aethelstan law code continues to be of interest because it gives modern readers a snapshot of life in a different place and at a different time. What snapshot of medieval English life do you get from reading this law code? What are the society's values and concerns? How was social order maintained?

5. In modern life, it is easy for government officials to promulgate laws and for judges, lawyers, law-enforcement officers, and others to know precisely what the law is, at least as it is written. In medieval England, though, such was not the case. How does Aethelstan's law code illustrate the problem of communicating information during the medieval period? What impact would this problem have had on the effectiveness of the law code?

Rubin, Stanley. "The *Bot*, or Composition in Anglo-Saxon Law: A Reassessment." *Journal of Legal History* 17 (April 1996): 144–154.

Wormald, Patrick. "The Uses of Literacy in Anglo-Saxon England and Its Neighbours." *Transactions of the Royal Historical Society*, 5th ser., 27 (1977): 95–114.

■ **Books**

Bartlett, Robert. *Trial by Fire and Water: The Medieval Judicial Ordeal*. Oxford, U.K.: Clarendon Press, 1986.

Griffiths, Bill. *An Introduction to Early English Law*. Norfolk, U.K.: Anglo-Saxon Books, 1995.

Ker, Neil Ripley. *Catalogue of Manuscripts Containing Anglo-Saxon*. Oxford, U.K.: Clarendon Press, 1957.

Keynes, Simon. "Royal Government and the Written Word in Late Anglo-Saxon England." In *The Uses of Literacy in Early Medieval Europe*, ed. Rosamond McKitterick. Cambridge, U.K.: Cambridge University Press, 1990.

Lapidge, Michael, et al., eds. *The Blackwell Encyclopaedia of Anglo-Saxon England*. Oxford, U.K.: Blackwell, 1998.

O'Brien, Bruce R. *God's Peace and King's Peace: The Laws of Edward the Confessor*. Philadelphia: University of Pennsylvania Press, 1999.

Oliver, Lisi. *The Beginnings of English Law*. Toronto: University of Toronto Press, 2002.

Whitelock, Dorothy, ed. *English Historical Documents, c. 500–1042*. Vol. 1. New York: Routledge, 2002.

Wormald, Patrick. *The Making of English Law: King Alfred to the Twelfth Century*. Oxford, U.K.: Blackwell, 1999.

—Thomas Gobbitt

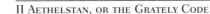

II AETHELSTAN, OR THE GRATELY CODE

Concerning thieves. First, that no thief is to be spared who is caught with the stolen goods, [if he is] over twelve years and [if the value of the goods is] over eightpence.

1.1 And if anyone does spare one, he is to pay for the thief with his wergild—and the thief is to be no nearer a settlement on that account—or to clear himself of an oath by that amount.

1.2. If, however, he [the thief] wishes to defend himself or to escape, he is not to be spared [whether younger or older than twelve].

1.3. If a thief is put into prison, he is to be in prison 40 days, and he may then be redeemed with 120 shillings; and the kindred are to stand surety for him that he will desist for ever.

1.4. And if he steals after that, they are to pay for him with his wergild, or to bring him back there.

1.5. And if anyone defends him, he is to pay for him with his wergild, whether to the king or to him to whom it rightly belongs; and everyone of those who supported him is to pay 120 shillings to the king as a fine.

2. Concerning lordless men. And we pronounced about those lordless men, from whom no justice can be obtained, that one should order their kindred to fetch back such a person to justice and to find him a lord in public meeting.

2.1. And if they then will not, or cannot, produce him on that appointed day, he is then to be a fugitive afterwards, and he who encounters him is to strike him down as a thief.

2.2. And he who harbours him after that, is to pay for him with his wergild or to clear himself by an oath of that amount.

3. Concerning the refusal of justice. The lord who refuses justice and upholds his guilty man, so that the king is appealed to, is to repay the value of the goods and 120 shillings to the king; and he who appeals to the king before he demands justice as often as he ought, is to pay the same fine as the other would have done, if he had refused him justice.

3.1. And the lord who is an accessory to a theft by his slave, and it becomes known about him, is to forfeit the slave and be liable to his wergild on the first occasion; if he does it more often, he is to be liable to pay all that he owns.

3.2. And likewise any of the king's treasurers or of our reeves, who has been an accessory of thieves who have committed theft, is to be liable to the same.

4. Concerning treachery to a lord. And we have pronounced concerning treachery to a lord, that he [who is accused] is to forfeit his life if he cannot deny it or is afterwards convicted at the three-fold ordeal.

5. And we have pronounced concerning breaking into a church; if he [who is accused] be convicted at the three-fold ordeal, he is to pay according to what the law-book says.

6. Concerning witchcraft. And we have pronounced concerning witchcrafts and sorceries and secret attempts on life, that, if anyone is killed by such, and he [who practised them] cannot deny it, he is to forfeit his life.

6.1. If, however, he wish to deny it, and is convicted at the three-fold ordeal, he is to be 120 days in prison; and his kinsmen are afterwards to take him out and to pay 120 shillings to the king, and to pay the wergild to the kinsmen [of the dead person], and to stand surety for him that he will desist from such for ever.

6.2. Concerning incendiaries. Incendiaries and those who avenge a thief are to be subject to the same penalty.

6.3. And he who wishes to avenge a thief, and yet does not wound anyone, is to pay 120 shillings to the king for the assault.

7. And we have pronounced concerning the simple ordeal, with regard to those men who have often been accused, and were convicted, and know no one to stand surety for them; they are to be brought to prison, and they are to be released as it is said here above.

8. Concerning landless men. And we have pronounced, that if any landless man took service in another shire, and afterwards returns to his kinsmen, he [any kinsman] is to harbour him [only] on condition that he brings him to justice if he commits any offence there, or he is to pay the compensation on his behalf.

9. Concerning the attaching of livestock. He who attaches livestock is to have nominated for him five men among his neighbours, and from those five get one who will swear with him that he is attaching it according to the common law. And he who wishes to

maintain his right to it, is to have 10 men nominated for him, and to get two of them and to give the oath that it was born in his possession, without the oath of the whole number. And this selected oath is to be valid [in cases where] over 20 pence [is involved].

10. Concerning exchange. And no one is to exchange any livestock without the witness of the reeve or the priest or the lord of the estate or the treasurer or other trustworthy man. If anyone does so, he is to pay 30 shillings as a fine, and the lord of the estate is to succeed to the exchanged property.

10.1. Concerning false witness. If it is then discovered that any of them gave false witness, his witness is never again to be valid; and also he is to pay 30 shillings as a fine.

11. Concerning him who should demand payment for a slain man. We have pronounced that he who should demand payment for a slain thief, is to come forward with three others, two from the paternal kindred and one from the maternal, and they are to give the oath that they knew of no theft committed by their kinsman, for which guilt he deserved to lose his life; and they are afterwards to go with twelve others and prove him liable as it was ordained before. And if the kinsmen of the dead man will not come thither on the appointed day, each who brought forward the suit is to pay 120 shillings.

12. [That one is not to buy outside a town.] And we have pronounced that no goods over 20 pence are to be bought outside a town, but they are to be bought there in the witness of the town-reeve or of another trustworthy man, or, again, in the witness of the reeves in a public meeting.

13. And we pronounce that every borough is to be repaired by a fortnight after Rogation days.

13.1. Secondly, that all buying is to be within a town.

14. Concerning moneyers. Thirdly, that there is to be one coinage over all the King's dominion, and no one is to mint money except in a town.

14.1. And if a moneyer is convicted, the hand with which he committed the crime is to be struck off, and put up on the mint. And if, however, there is an accusation, and he wishes to clear himself, he is then to go to [the ordeal of] hot iron, and redeem the hand with which he is accused of having committed the crime; and if he is convicted at the ordeal, the same is to be done as it said here above.

14.2. In Canterbury [there are to be] seven moneyers; four of the king, two of the bishop, one of the abbot; in Rochester three, two of the king, one of the bishop; in London eight; in Winchester six; in Lewes two; in Hastings one; another at Chichester; at Southampton two; at Wareham two; [at Dorchester one]; at Exeter two; at Shaftesbury two; otherwise in the other boroughs one.

15. Fourthly: that no shieldmaker is to put any sheepskin on a shield, and if he does so, he is to pay 30 shillings.

16. Fifthly: that every man is to have two mounted men for every plough.

17. Sixthly: if anyone accepts a bribe from a thief and ruins the rights of another, he is to be liable to pay his wergild.

18. Seventhly: that no one is to sell a horse across the sea, unless he wishes to give it.

19. And we have pronounced with regard to a slave, that, if he is convicted at the ordeal, the price of the goods is to be paid, and he is to be flogged three times or the price is to be paid a second time. And the fine is to be at a half-rate where slaves are concerned.

20. If anyone fails to attend a [public] meeting three times, he is to pay the fine for disobedience to the king; and the meeting is to be announced seven days before it is to take place.

20.1. If, however, he will not do justice nor pay the fine for disobedience, the leading men are to ride thither, all who belong to the borough, and take all that he owns and put him under surety.

20.2. If, however, anyone will not ride with his fellows, he is to pay the fine for disobedience to the king.

20.3. And it is to be announced in the meeting that everyone is to be at peace with everything with which the king will be at peace, and to refrain from theft on pain of losing his life and all that he owns.

20.4. And he who will not cease for these penalties-the leading men are to ride thither, all who belong to the borough, and take all that he owns. The king is to succeed to half, to half the men who are on that expedition. And they are to put him under surety.

20.5. If he knows no one to stand surety for him, they are to take him prisoner.

20.6. If he will not permit it, he is to be killed, unless he escapes.

20.7. If anyone wishes to avenge him or carry on a feud against any of them, he is to be at emnity with the king and all the king's friends.

20.8. If he escapes, and anyone harbours him, he is to be liable to pay his wergild, unless he dares to clear himself by the [amount of the] fugitive's wergild, that he did not know that he was a fugitive.

21. If anyone compounds for the ordeal, he is to compound what he can for the price of the goods, and not for the fine, unless he to whom it belongs will concede it.

22. And no one is to receive the man of another man, without the permission of him whom he served before.

22.1. If anyone does so, he is to give back the man and pay the fine for disobedience to the king.

22.2. And no one is to dismiss his man who has been accused, before he has rendered justice.

23. If anyone pledges [to undergo] the ordeal, he is then to come three days before to the priest whose duty it is to consecrate it, and live off bread and water and salt and vegetables until he shall go to it, and be present at Mass on each of those three days, and make his offering and go to communion on the day on which he shall go to the ordeal, and swear then the oath that he is guiltless of that charge according to the common law, before he goes to the ordeal.

23.1. And if it is [the ordeal of] water, he is to sink one and a half ells on the rope; if it is the ordeal of iron, it is to be three days before the hand is unbound.

23.2. And each man is to obtain [the right to pursue] his charge by a preliminary oath, as we have said before; and each of those of both parties who is present is to be fasting, according to the command of God and of the archbishop; and there are not to be on either side more men than twelve. If the accused man then is one of a larger company than twelve, the ordeal is then invalidated, unless they will leave him.

24. And he who buys livestock with a witness, and has to vouch to warranty afterwards—then he from whom he bought it is to take it back, whether he be slave or free, whichever he is.

24.1. And there is to be no trading on Sundays; if then anyone does it, he is to forfeit the goods and pay 30 shillings fine.

25. If any of my reeves will not carry out this [ordinance] and is less zealous about it than we have pronounced, he is then to pay the fine for disobedience to me, and I shall find another who will.

25.1. And the bishop in whose diocese it lies is to exact the fine for disobedience from the reeve.

25.2. He who deviates from this ordinance is to pay on the first occasion five pounds, on the second occasion his wergild, on the third occasion he is to forfeit all that he owns and the friendship of us all.

26. And he who swears a false oath, and it becomes known against him, is never afterwards to be entitled to an oath, nor is he to be buried in a consecrated cemetery when he dies, unless he has the witness of the bishop in whose diocese he is that he has done penance for it as his confessor has prescribed for him.

26.1. And his confessor is to inform the bishop within 30 days whether he was willing to submit to that penance. If he does not do so, he is to pay in accordance with what the bishop will allow him.

[All this was established at the great assembly at Grately, at which Archbishop Wulfhelm was present and all the nobles and councillors whom King Athaelstan could gather together.]

Glossary

every borough is to be repaired	a mandate for general infrastructure repair (public facilities, fences on private lands, and so on) as well as keeping tracks and waterways clear
wergild	the amount at which each person's life was valued (with the exception of slaves), in accordance with his or her rank in society, the main purpose of this valuation being to have a set monetary penalty that the family could legally demand if a person was killed and to establish the value of his or her sworn oath in courts of law

"Read widely in the classics and in history; take the past as a warning for the present."

Overview

In 918 Wang Kŏn, also known as T'aejo (meaning "Great Founder"), established the Koryŏ Dynasty, which ruled over Korea until 1392. Traditionally it has been held that while he was on his deathbed, Wang Kŏn dictated his advice for his successors, recorded in a document now known as the Ten Injunctions. These injunctions reflect his concern for maintaining a peaceful kingdom in which the people would be ruled benevolently by a virtuous monarch under the guidance of Confucian teaching with the help of the power of the Buddha. The document is important because it not only shows how T'aejo thought but also offers a window into the worldview of the early Koryŏ Dynasty.

Recently, however, the scholar Remco Breuker has called this received wisdom into question. He argues persuasively that the Ten Injunctions were actually written during the reign of King Hyŏnjong, who ruled from 1009 to 1031. If this theory is correct, then the Ten Injunctions are still important but possess a rather different meaning. Instead of being the last advice of a dying king, they represent an attempt by Hyŏnjong and his officials to strengthen the legitimacy of Hyŏnjong's troubled reign and to justify the policies they wished to pursue. For the most part, whether the Ten Injunctions were written during T'aejo's reign or Hyŏnjong's is not of concern. More important is what the document suggests about the Koryŏ Dynasty's worldview.

Context

In 676 the kingdom of Silla successfully united the southern half of the Korea Peninsula. After a period of peace and prosperity, the state, torn by struggles over succession to the throne, progressively lost control over more and more territory. In 889 a major peasant uprising against Silla erupted, soon to be followed by other rebellions, weakening the kingdom. This revolt allowed for the rise of local strongmen and, eventually, two rival states that claimed to be the successors of kingdoms that Silla had defeated during the wars of unification: Paekche and

Koguryŏ. T'aejo took control of Later Koguryŏ in 918 and renamed it Koryŏ, using a similar-sounding designation so that he could claim to be the successor of Koguryŏ while distancing himself from the previous ruler, Kungye, who had become unstable and dangerous. After fierce fighting, Koryŏ, under T'aejo, was victorious over Later Paekche. T'aejo then accepted the surrender of the last Silla king, uniting the Korea Peninsula. His dynasty would last until 1392. After a period of fruitful rule, he fell ill and died in 943. It has traditionally been held that on his deathbed he gave the Ten Injunctions as a guide to his successors so that the dynasty would continue to rule virtuously over a peaceful and happy kingdom.

If Breuker is correct in his theory that the Ten Injunctions were written during the troubled reign of King Hyŏnjong, however, then the context of their creation would be quite different. There was a dark cloud over King Hyŏnjong's rise to power. Although he was a grandson of King T'aejo, Wang Sun (Hyŏnjong being, in fact, his posthumous title) was illegitimate, born from an illicit affair. At age eighteen he was forced to enter a Buddhist monastery so that he would not threaten the power of the queen dowager and her lover, Kim Ch'iyang, who ruled through the weak and pliable king, the queen dowager's son, Mokchong—who was probably a distant cousin of Wang Sun's. When the queen dowager and Kim Ch'iyang had a child, they decided that it was necessary to remove Wang Sun completely from the scene and attempted to have him murdered. Their plot failed, and some officials, fearing the power of the queen dowager and Kim Ch'iyang and its possible effect on the health of the dynasty and the state, staged a coup. King Mokchong was overthrown and murdered as he fled the capital. Kim Ch'iyang was also killed, and the queen dowager was banished.

Wang Sun then ascended the throne, but his troubles were not over. The Khitan people, who lived north of Korea, had established the Liao Dynasty, and Koryŏ was technically its vassal. The two states were engaged in a territorial dispute, and the murder of King Mokchong became a pretext for an invasion that lasted from 1010 to 1011, forcing Wang Sun to flee the capital. Eventually the Khitan withdrew, but the country had suffered terribly. If Breuker is correct, then the injunctions were written in the after-

676

- Having defeated Koguryŏ, Paekche, and finally Tang China, the kingdom of Silla becomes master of the southern half of the Korea Peninsula.

892

- The state of Later Paekche is founded.

901

- Kungye founds the state of Later Koguryŏ.

918

- Wang Kŏn (later T'aejo), upon the urging of his fellow generals, overthrows Kungye and becomes king of Later Koguryŏ. He changes the name to Koryŏ.

935

- The last Silla king surrenders to Koryŏ.

936

- Wang Kŏn utterly defeats the kingdom of Later Paekche, uniting the Korea Peninsula.

943

- According to tradition, Wang Kŏn dictates the Ten Injunctions on his deathbed.

997

- Mokchong ascends the throne.

math of a destructive foreign invasion during the reign of a king whose succession was of questionable legitimacy. This context helps explain the concern for peace, order, and military defense found in the Ten Injunctions. In fact, it was the destruction of historical records that provided the opportunity for the writing of the Ten Injunctions. In 1013 state officials began to recompile surviving historical materials and interview elderly people in order to reconstruct as much of the historical record as possible. This allowed a window of opportunity in which the Ten Injunctions could be written and "discovered."

About the Author

There are essentially two candidates for authorship. One is T'aejo (Wang Kŏn), who, according to the Ten Injunctions, dictated the contents to Pak Surhui. However, if Breuker is correct and the Ten Injunctions were actually authored during the reign of Hyŏnjong (Wang Sun), it is likely that several officials wrote the document. During the Liao invasion, fire destroyed many important historical records housed in the capital. Several officials were given the task of collecting what remained and interviewing elderly people in order to restore as much of the lost history as they could. Breuker argues that the destruction of the historical records provided an opportunity for several high officials, loyal to Hyŏnjong and hoping to strengthen his legitimacy in the wake of the devastating Liao invasion, to write the Ten Injunctions, which they then claimed to have been the work of T'aejo. It is likely the case that the Ten Injunctions were written by Ch'oe Chean, who had "discovered" the document, and Hwang Churyang, both of whom were a part of the effort to recompile the lost history. They were probably supervised by Ch'oe Hang, a high official and respected scholar at whose house the Ten Injunctions were found, and Kim Shimŏn who was assistant supervisor of the history project. These four men were closely connected with each other and with Hyŏnjong and shared ideas that found their way into the Ten Injunctions.

After the Ten Injunctions were "rediscovered," they were published as part of the biography of a deceased official so that the government officials would become familiar with and be influenced by them. Because Hyŏnjong was quite young and because some of the officials had served previous kings, it is likely that the policies recommended by the injunctions represent not only those favored by Hyŏnjong himself but the officials' own ideas as well. By making it seem as if their own policies were really those of T'aejo, the king and his officials were able to gain support for them and strengthen Hyŏnjong's legitimacy.

Explanation and Analysis of the Document

The introductory line of the Ten Injunctions states that they were dictated to Pak Surhui in 943. However, it is likely that the injunctions were actually written in or after

1013. In either case, the introduction, though starting humbly enough, compares T'aejo to two virtuous sage-kings from Chinese history, Yao and Shun. This comparison shows the influence that Confucianism, which looked to the reigns of these kings as models to be emulated, had on Korea. The Han Dynasty (206 BCE–220 CE) was also admired in both China and Korea, and the fact that its founder rose from humble beginnings was used to justify T'aejo's own rise to power from similar origins. After stressing how T'aejo had devoted himself to the country, the document emphasizes his concern for the continuity of his dynasty, explaining why he was giving his injunctions. Thus T'aejo is portrayed as a virtuous ruler. It was important to stress his virtue in order to legitimize his coup against Kungye, his acceptance of the surrender of the last Silla king, and the continuation of his dynasty. This emphasis on the dynastic founder's virtue reflected on his successor, Hyŏnjong, and his policies, which were portrayed as T'aejo's own, making it difficult, if not impossible, to oppose them.

The edicts offer guidance on how to rule Korea morally and effectively, providing insight into the Koryŏ worldview, especially its religious understanding of the world. The admonitions found in the Ten Injunctions appealed to various religions: Buddhism, Confucianism, and Daoism, as well as native religion. Geomancy, though not a full-blown religion, has religious characteristics and was also deemed an important source of power and legitimacy and therefore plays a prominent role in the edicts. Despite the often vast differences between these belief systems, they all made up a part of the Koryŏ worldview. The Koreans of the era apparently were not bothered by these discrepancies. In fact, they seem to have embraced the edicts as sources of legitimacy and power. Because of the plurality of choices, Koreans were able, by creatively and flexibly applying these different belief systems, to find guidance to solve the problems they faced. In addition, religion, rather than being separate from the government, was a subordinate part of it, used to legitimize state authority and as a source of supernatural power. While this view on the relationship between religion and the state would continue during the Chosŏn Dynasty (1392–1910), Neo-Confucianism would stand as the sole orthodoxy, with other religions demoted to a secondary status.

The first injunction emphasizes the importance of the Buddha (though it probably refers not only to the historic Buddha, Siddhartha Gautama, but indeed to all Buddhas) in the affairs of state. Koreans believed that the Buddha could intervene powerfully in the world and assist people, either because they were virtuous and asked for help or because they (or monks on their behalf) performed certain rituals. Because of the power of the Buddha, the state actively supported the religion. However, institutionally speaking, Buddhism was not united. There were various sects that disagreed about Buddhist doctrine and competed for state support. If the Buddhist sects aligned with different factions within the government in a struggle over resources, there could be serious problems. Corruption would increase, and conflicts could even become violent. Therefore, this injunction calls for the state to make use of

Time Line

1009	■ Mokchong is murdered. Wang Sun (later Hyŏnjong), a grandson of Wang Kŏn, ascends the throne.
1010–1011	■ The Khitan (Liao Dynasty) invade Korea. Many valuable historical records are destroyed during the incursion.
1013	■ State officials begin to recompile old documents and interview elderly people in order to reconstruct the historical records destroyed during the Khitan invasions.
1018	■ Another Khitan invasion is launched. It is defeated decisively by Koryŏ forces, leading to peaceful relations between Koryŏ and Liao.
1170	■ Disgruntled military officers stage a coup, establishing a military dictatorship that would rule through the Koryŏ kings.

1258

- The last military dictator is assassinated, and the Koryŏ kings are restored to power. However, they are forced to marry princesses of the invading Mongols, and heavy Mongolian influence limits their authority.

1392

- The last Koryŏ king is overthrown, and the Chosŏn Dynasty is established.

the power of the Buddha while keeping Buddhist institutions firmly under control by preventing them from interfering in politics.

The sixth injunction also deals specifically with Buddhism as well as native religion. Two festivals, the Yŏndung (Lantern) festival, which celebrated the birthday of the historical Buddha, and the P'algwan (Eight Prohibitions) festival, in which spirits from indigenous Korean religion were worshipped, were of such importance that any attempt to modify or abolish them was forbidden. Such celebrations served in part to repay past favors granted by the spirits and the Buddha and to ask for their continued protection. In the tenth century King Sŏngjong had abolished these two festivals because he deemed them too expensive, but King Hyŏnjong reinstated them. The reinstatement of the festivals is important evidence that the Ten Injunctions were likely written during Hyŏnjong's reign and not T'aejo's, in order to justify Hyŏnjong's policies.

The second injunction also discusses Buddhism, but in the context of geomancy (feng shui in Chinese, *p'ungsu* in Korean). According to geomantic beliefs, energy that flows through the earth can affect people's lives positively or negatively. Human activity can in turn affect this energy. Thus the building of temples could help increase positive energy. However, building too many temples could cause harm. The edict points to the fall of the kingdom of Silla as proof. Therefore, there were to be no temples constructed other than those established by Tosŏn, a Buddhist monk famous for his knowledge of geomancy. It should also be pointed out that a proliferation of temples caused economic problems. When a temple was established, it was granted land, which was used to maintain it and to support the monks who prayed and meditated there. The government did not

collect taxes on such land. Therefore, the more temples there were, the less money there was in the state budget.

The importance of geomantic principles can also be seen in the fifth edict. Here the power of the topography of P'yŏngyang, which served as a secondary capital during the Koryŏ and which is the modern-day capital of the Democratic People's Republic of Korea, is credited with helping in the establishment and maintenance of the dynasty. Because of the city's importance, kings were enjoined to visit it often. P'yŏngyang was also strategically significant and central to protecting Korea from both foreign invasions and domestic upheavals. Neglect of the secondary capital could lead to serious trouble for the dynasty. In fact, Hyŏnjong often relied on powerful officials serving in P'yŏngyang for help.

A very different application of geomantic beliefs is evident in the eighth injunction. The topography of an area in southwestern Korea—which was a part of the former kingdom of Paekche —is used to explain the supposed treachery of the inhabitants of that region. That treachery, combined with their bitterness at suffering conquest by T'aejo, meant that they should be excluded from power. Similarly former slaves and those engaged in occupations that were looked down upon (such as butchers and tanners) were forbidden from entering government. Because these people were considered treacherous by nature, it was believed that they would serve the powerful rather than act virtuously. This edict shows how much Koreans were concerned with status and the belief that high status tended to equate with virtue. However, because one of T'aejo's favorite wives was from the southwest (at this time Korean men could have more than one wife), it is doubtful that the ruler would take such a negative view. In contrast, Hyŏnjong suffered poor treatment from the people from this region when he fled from the Liao invasion—further evidence that this edict was written during Hyŏnjong's reign. The prohibition against people from the southwest serving in government seems to have been largely ignored. However, the restriction against former slaves and those serving in dishonorable trades was followed with only rare exceptions.

As seen from the introduction to the Ten Injunctions, Confucianism was an important part of the Koryŏ worldview and is discussed in the third edict, which focuses on the issue of succession. The succession of kings was especially important because Korean monarchs had several wives, and there were often many possible heirs to the throne. It was believed that the ancient Chinese sage-king Yao chose Shun as his successor because his own sons were ill suited for the throne. However, choosing a successor based on merit rather than by lineage could lead to conflict, as rival claimants could put themselves forward as the most virtuous. This edict shows a kind of balance between these two principles: maintaining the throne in one family for the sake of stability while establishing a mechanism to prevent a wholly unsuitable candidate from becoming king. Koryŏ made use of Confucianism but departed from its teachings when doing so seemed necessary for practical reasons.

The seventh edict is also Confucian in nature, as seen from its emphasis on having the support of "the people"

*The worship room of an ancient temple in Korea carved out of solid granite
and featuring a thirty-foot-tall statue of the Buddha* (AP/Wide World Photos)

Modern-day Lantern Festival in honor of the Buddha's birthday, with lanterns in the shape of characters from a Buddhist legend (AP/Wide World Photos)

(that is, the commoners). The common people were expected to pay taxes and provide labor to the state, typically through military service or construction projects. If the people were taxed too heavily or were expected to perform too much labor, they would suffer and might even rebel against the state. Furthermore, according to Confucianism, a monarch was expected to be a virtuous man who ruled for the good of the people. Thus he should minimize expenses, both state and personal, in order to lighten the burden of taxation and labor on the people. Central to virtuous rule was the selection of good ministers who would serve the king. Such ministers were not to flatter but to offer constructive criticism so that the king could overcome his faults and grow in virtue. In order to have such officials and to avoid overburdening the common people, rewards and punishments must be applied carefully. Doing so actually put one in touch with the dynamic harmony of the universe, the forces of yin (represented by such things as the dark, the feminine, and the earth) and yang (represented by such things as the light, the masculine, and the sky). These forces are typically associated with Daoism. Thus the principles of government were closely linked with the principles that governed the universe.

The tenth injunction reflects the Confucian philosophy of using the past as a guide for how to act in the present. Just as Confucianism held up the ancient Chinese sage-kings as models for contemporary monarchs, so too did Confucianism look to history in order to discover the principles necessary to govern in a moral and therefore effective way. One prominent figure in Confucianism was the Duke of Zhou, who was consistently described as a virtuous and loyal man. He acted as regent for his nephew, King Cheng, to whom he wrote *Against Luxurious Ease*, giving advice to the young king on how to rule virtuously. Like the Chinese, Koreans held this work to be of great importance, and this edict calls for Koryŏ kings to post it on a wall and reflect on it often. This injunction is illustrative of the high moral standards expected of kings to enable them to govern well.

Buddhism, Confucianism, Daoism, and geomancy were all belief systems that were imported into Korea from China. At this time Song Dynasty China had an important influence on Korea, and the Khitan, who founded the Liao Dynasty (a state located in what is now Manchuria), possessed a flourishing Buddhist culture, which many Koreans admired. The proximity to these two civilizations enabled Korea to partake of their cultures as well as to spread its own. This closeness also gave Koreans a sense of their own identity as a separate people. Many Koreans felt threatened, however. How much could they borrow from other cultures while still remaining Korean? The fourth injunction tries to strike a balanced approach to this problem, recommending limited borrowing from China while asserting that because Koreans were different from the Chinese, they need not slavishly imitate their neighbors. The Khitan people, on the other hand, are presented in a very negative light, and their customs were not to be adopted. T'aejo, while at times being at odds with the Khitan, does not seem to have taken such a negative approach. On the other hand, Hyŏnjong's throne was threatened by the Khitan, and the ruler was forced to flee the capital when they invaded the country. Thus it would seem that this edict is representative of Hyŏnjong's rather than T'aejo's time.

> "The success of every great undertaking of our state depends upon the favor and protection of Buddha."
>
> (Injunction 1)

> "In the past we have always had a deep attachment for the ways of China and all of our institutions have been modeled upon those of T'ang. But our country occupies a different geographical location and our people's character is different from that of the Chinese. Hence, there is no reason to strain ourselves unreasonably to copy the Chinese way."
>
> (Injunction 4)

> "It is very difficult for the king to win over the people. For this reason, give heed to sincere criticism and banish those with slanderous tongues."
>
> (Injunction 7)

> "Since our country shares borders with savage nations, always beware of the danger of their invasions. Treat the soldiers kindly and take good care of them; lighten their burden of forced labor; inspect them every autumn; give honors and promotions to the brave."
>
> (Injunction 9)

> "In preserving a household or a state, one should always be on guard to avert mistakes. Read widely in the classics and in history; take the past as a warning for the present."
>
> (Injunction 10)

The ninth injunction is a very general admonition to avoid corruption. There is a specific concern with nepotism because selecting officials based on family connections rather than on ability could lead to the serious mishandling of government affairs. For the public good and for the security of the state, it was necessary to have virtuous and competent officials. This philosophy was especially important because Korea had hostile neighbors, especially the Khitan. Therefore, this edict calls for special attention to be paid to the military. Many soldiers were conscripts who were serving far from home. If they were not periodically given rewards or recognized for their service, their morale would be low, reducing their capability as a fighting force. Moreover, if they were treated very poorly, they might even rebel. In order to maintain the state, it was necessary to keep their happiness and welfare in mind.

Audience

Traditionally, it has been held that the injunctions were first known only to the royal family and to a select group of high officials and were then lost. This belief explains why there were no references to them before they were "rediscovered" during Hyŏnjong's reign; they were essentially a private document. However, in light of Breuker's research, it would seem that no references were made to them in the early Koryŏ because they did not exist. After their "rediscovery" and publication, they became widely known among government officials. Since they were written in order to advance Hyŏnjong's policies and support his legitimacy, the state sought to make them known as quickly as possible. In fact, they became so well known that in the early twelfth century, a government official appealed to the Ten Injunctions to argue against King Yejong's proposal to use currency like the Chinese. The Ten Injunctions continued to be important into the Chosŏn Dynasty as scholars who compiled a government history of the Koryŏ Dynasty made sure to include them. The injunctions were not above reproach, however. The famous eighteenth-century scholar Yi Ik criticized the eighth injunction, which impugned the character of people in the southwestern region of Korea because that was the place of origin of the ruling family of the Chosŏn Dynasty. Today, the Ten Injunctions are studied by schoolchildren in Korea as an important part of Korean history and culture.

Impact

The Ten Injunctions achieved their initial purpose. They helped to legitimate Hyŏnjong's rise to power and maintain him on the throne. Some immediate aims, such as the restoration of the Yŏndung and P'algwan festivals, were achieved. Likewise, the emphasis on military preparedness

in the edicts seems also to have paid off as another Khitan invasion in 1018 was soundly defeated by Koryŏ forces. Curiously, though, once they were public, the edicts could be used in unexpected ways. For instance, in the early twelfth century, when King Yejong wanted to imitate China by introducing money into circulation in Korea, officials resisted him by referring to the fourth edict to argue that they should continue to follow Korean custom in that matter.

In many ways the injunctions were contending with forces that were difficult if not impossible to contain. For instance, Hyŏnjong's successors showed less of a concern for military affairs despite the attention that the injunctions demanded be paid to them. In 1170 neglect and disrespect for the army led to a coup by powerful military officials. The resulting decades of military dictatorship reduced the kings of Korea to puppet rulers. Eventually they regained their power, but not without the help of the Mongol Yuan Dynasty. The Mongols, who first invaded the Korean Peninsula in 1231, made their own demands on Koryŏ, infringing on the authority of the kings. The injunctions dealing with Buddhism were also departed from. The continued building of Buddhist temples and consequent alienation of taxable land, despite repeated royal prohibitions, drained the state treasury. Despite restrictions to the contrary, monks were able to become involved in politics, in part as allies of the king to counterbalance the often powerful government bureaucracy. One notable example is the monk Myoch'ŏng, a favorite of King Injong. In 1135 Myoch'ŏng staged a rebellion after he failed to have the capital moved to P'yŏngyang.

Questions for Further Study

1. Historians are uncertain about when the Ten Injunctions were written. Explain how our contemporary understanding of the motivations behind the Ten Injunctions would differ depending on when the document was written. What implications does this difference have for the study of ancient history in general?

2. What influence did China and Chinese history and religion have on the development of Korea?

3. Throughout world history, similar documents have arisen out of social and political turmoil, questions about the legitimacy of a monarch or ruling family, or revolt. Locate a similar document—the New Year's Day Taika Reform Edict, the Constitutions of Clarendon, the Athenian Constitution, or the Reform Edict of Urukagina, for example—and explain how the two documents arose from comparable contexts.

4. Why do you suppose that syncretism, or the blending of native religious beliefs with those of a new religion from outside, succeeded in medieval Korea when it failed utterly in Africa—as discussed in Diplomatic Correspondence between Muhammad al-Kānāmi and Muhammad Bello?

5. While the Ten Injunctions seem to have succeeded in the short term, in the longer term they failed to produce the desired effects. Why? What factors might have motivated departure from the Ten Injunctions?

It is impossible to tell whether the injunctions had any effect on these matters. It would be reasonable to surmise that they did impose a restraining influence. Nevertheless, the forces they sought to restrain were too powerful, and the successor to Koryŏ, the Chosŏn Dynasty, sought to eliminate them. During the Chosŏn Dynasty the military was completely subordinated to civilian rule, so there were no successful military coups as there had been in Koryŏ. Monks were banned from even entering the capital, the different Buddhist sects were forcibly reduced by amalgamation into two, and much of the temple land was seized. These developments were made possible in part by the rise of a new religion, Neo-Confucianism. Many adherents to the faith heavily criticized Buddhist doctrine and practice, providing a justification for the disestablishment of Buddhism as a state religion. Neo-Confucianism then took its place, leading to massive changes in Korean family life, politics, religion, and society.

Scholarly analysis of the Ten Injunctions has changed over time. For many years the claim that T'aejo was their author was taken at face value. However, after Korea became a colony of Japan in 1910, the Japanese scholar Imanishi Ryu contended that T'aejo was not, in fact, the author of the Ten Injunctions. While he made some valid arguments, his work was marred by his attempts to use the Ten Injunctions to justify Japanese colonial rule over Korea. Korean scholars have since criticized his work and argued for T'aejo's authorship; this view has been dominant for the past several decades. In an article published in 2009, Breuker challenges this received wisdom, arguing that the Ten Injunctions were in fact written during the reign of Hyŏnjong. Because Breuker's study is so new, there has not yet been time for scholars who favor the authorship of T'aejo to respond.

Further Reading

■ Articles

Breuker, Remco. "The Emperor's Clothes? Koryŏ as an Independent Realm." *Korean Studies* 27 (2003): 48–84.

———. "Forging the Truth: Creative Deception and National Identity in Medieval Korea." *East Asian History* 35 (2009).

Vermeersch, Sem. "The Status of Monks: State Regulations Concerning Buddhist Monks in the Koryŏ Dynasty." *Buddhist Studies Review* 20, no. 2 (2003): 145–168.

■ Books

Deuchler, Martina. *The Confucian Transformation of Korea: A Study of Society and Ideology*. Cambridge, Mass.: Harvard University Press, 1992.

Duncan, John B. *The Origins of the Chosŏn Dynasty*. Seattle: University of Washington Press, 2000

Eckert, Carter J., et al. *Korea Old and New: A History*. Cambridge, Mass.: Harvard University Press, 1990.

Grayson, James Huntley. *Korea: A Religious History*, rev. ed. New York: Routledge, 2002.

Shultz, Edward J. *Generals and Scholars: Military Rule in Medieval Korea*. Honolulu: University of Hawaii Press, 2000.

Vermeersch, Sem. *The Power of the Buddhas: The Politics of Buddhism during the Koryŏ Dynasty (918–1392)*. Cambridge, Mass.: Harvard University Asia Center, 2008.

Yi, Ki-baek. *A New History of Korea*. Cambridge, Mass.: Harvard University Press, 1984.

■ Web Sites

"Goryeo." Republic of Korea Official Web site. http://korea.net/korea/kor_loca.asp?code=M04.

"Goryeo Dynasty." Asian Art Museum Web site. http://www.asianart.com/exhibitions/korea/index.html.

—Franklin D. Rausch

WANG KŎN'S TEN INJUNCTIONS

In the fourth month, summer, of T'aejo's twenty-sixth year [943], the king went to the inner court, summoned Taegwang Pak Surhui, and personally gave him the injunctions saying:

I have heard that when great Shun was cultivating at Li-shan he inherited the throne from Yao. Emperor Kao-tsu of China rose from humble origins and founded the Han. I too have risen from humble origins and received undeserved support for the throne. In summer I did not shun the heat and in winter did not avoid the cold. After toiling, body and mind, for nineteen years, I united the Three Han [Later Three Kingdoms] and have held the throne for twenty-five years. Now I am old. I only fear that my successors will give way to their passions and greed and destroy the principle of government. That would be truly worrisome. I therefore wrote these injunctions to be passed on to later ages. They should be read morning and night and forever used as a mirror for reflection.

1. The success of every great undertaking of our state depends upon the favor and protection of Buddha. Therefore, the temples of both the Meditation and Doctrinal schools should be built and monks should be sent out to those temples to minister to Buddha. Later on, if villainous courtiers attain power and come to be influenced by the entreaties of bonzes, the temples of various schools will quarrel and struggle among themselves for gain. This ought to be prevented.

2. Temples and monasteries were newly opened and built upon the sites chosen by the monk Tosŏn according to the principles of geomancy. He said: "If temples and monasteries are indiscriminately built at locations not chosen by me, the terrestrial force and energy will be sapped and damaged, hastening the decline of the dynasty." I am greatly concerned that the royal family, the aristocracy, and the courtiers all may build many temples and monasteries in the future in order to seek Buddha's blessings. In the last days of Silla many temples were capriciously built. As a result, the terrestrial force and energy were wasted and diminished, causing its demise. Vigilantly guard against this.

3. In matters of royal succession, succession by the eldest legitimate royal issue should be the rule. But Yao of ancient China let Shun succeed him because his own son was unworthy. That was indeed putting the interest of the state ahead of one's personal feelings. Therefore, if the eldest son is not worthy of the crown, let the second eldest succeed to the throne. If the second eldest, too, is unworthy, choose the brother the people consider the best qualified for the throne.

4. In the past we have always had a deep attachment for the ways of China and all of our institutions have been modeled upon those of T'ang. But our country occupies a different geographical location and our people's character is different from that of the Chinese. Hence, there is no reason to strain ourselves unreasonably to copy the Chinese way. Khitan is a nation of savage beasts, and its language and customs are also different. Its dress and institutions should never be copied.

5. I achieved the great task of founding the dynasty with the help of the elements of mountain and river of our country. The Western Capital, P'yongyang, has the elements of water in its favor and is the source of the terrestrial force of our country. It is thus the veritable center of dynastic enterprises for ten thousand generations. Therefore, make a royal visit to the Western Capital four times a year—in the second, fifth, eighth, and eleventh months—and reside there a total of more than one hundred days. By this means secure peace and prosperity.

6. I deem the two festivals of Yŏndŭng and P'algwan of great spiritual value and importance. The first is to worship Buddha. The second is to worship the spirit of Heaven, the spirits of the five sacred and other major mountains and rivers, and the dragon god. At some future time, villainous courtiers may propose the abandonment or modification of these festivals. No change should be allowed.

7. It is very difficult for the king to win over the people. For this reason, give heed to sincere criticism and banish those with slanderous tongues. If sincere criticisms are accepted, there will be virtuous and sagacious kings. Though sweet as honey, slanderous words should not be believed; then they will cease of their own accord. Make use of the people's labor with their convenience in mind; lighten the burden of corvée and taxation; learn the difficulties of agricultural production. Then it will be possible to win

the hearts of the people and to bring peace and prosperity to the land. Men of yore said that under a tempting bait a fish hangs; under a generous reward an able general wins victory; under a drawn bow a bird dare not fly; and under a virtuous and benevolent rule a loyal people serves faithfully. If you administer rewards and punishments moderately, the interplay of yin and yang will be harmonious.

8. The topographic features of the territory south of Kongju and beyond the Kongju River are all treacherous and disharmonious; its inhabitants are treacherous and disharmonious as well. For that reason, if they are allowed to participate in the affairs of state, to intermarry with the royal family aristocracy, and royal relatives, and to take the power of the state, they might imperil the state or injure the royal safety—grudging the loss of their own state [which used to be the kingdom of Paekche] and being resentful of the unification.

Those who have been slaves or engaged in dishonorable trades will surrender to the powerful in order to evade prescribed services. And some of them will surely seek to offer their services to the noble families, to the palaces, or to the temples. They then will cause confusion and disorder in government and engage in treason through crafty words and treacherous machinations. They should never be allowed into

government service, though they may no longer be slaves and outcasts.

9. The salaries and allowances for the aristocracy and the bureaucracy have been set according to the needs of the state. They should not be increased or diminished. The classics say that salaries and allowances should be determined by the merits of those who receive them and should not be wasted for private gain. If the public treasury is wasted upon those without merit or upon one's relatives or friends, not only will the people come to resent and criticize such abuses, but those who enjoy salaries undeservedly will also not be able to enjoy them for long. Since our country shares borders with savage nations, always beware of the danger of their invasions. Treat the soldiers kindly and take good care of them; lighten their burden of forced labor; inspect them every autumn; give honors and promotions to the brave.

10. In preserving a household or a state, one should always be on guard to avert mistakes. Read widely in the classics and in history; take the past as a warning for the present. The Duke of Chou was a great sage, yet he sought to admonish his nephew, King Ch'eng, with *Against Luxurious Ease (Wu-i)*. Post the contents of *Against Luxurious Ease* on the wall and reflect upon them when entering and leaving the room.

Glossary

corvée	unpaid labor exacted by a feudal lord
Meditation and Doctrinal schools	in Korean Buddhism, groups of scholars and teachers who focused on meditation and on doctrine, respectively
T'ang	the Tang Dynasty of China (618–907)

RUSSKAIA PRAVDA, OR JUSTICE OF THE RUS

"If a man kills a man [the following relatives of the murdered man may avenge him]..."

Overview

The Russkaia Pravda, or Justice of the Rus, was the secular law code of Kievan Rus, the medieval ancestor state to both modern-day Russia and Ukraine. It was written over an extended period and by several authors. The core document is attributed to Yaroslav, "the Wise," grand prince of Kiev from 1019 to 1054. Debate exists as to whether the code was first compiled during this reign or slightly earlier, when Yaroslav was ruler of the Rus city-state Novgorod—that is, when he was a provincial ruler rather than the grand prince. Additions and revisions followed, the most important of which are a supplement issued in 1072 by Yaroslav's sons and further clauses from the twelfth century attributed to Vladimir II Monomakh, grand prince of Kiev from 1113 to 1125. The Justice of the Rus remained in force through the fragmentation of the Rus lands in the eleventh and twelfth centuries and also into the subsequent period of Mongol domination over Rus lands (1237–1480). Although it was earlier supplemented or substituted in some principalities with more detailed codes, it was not replaced on a national scale until the issuance in 1497 of a new code called the Sudebnik. By then the Russian state itself had been reconstituted and expanded under the control of Moscow. Significant aspects of the Justice of the Rus passed into the new law, however.

Around 110 manuscript copies of the Justice of the Rus, in various forms, are currently known, but none is from the period of original composition. Modern scholars identify three basic redactions: the Short Version, the Expanded Version, and the Abridged Version. Attention is usually focused on the Short and Expanded Versions. (The Abridged Version is a relatively recent document that contains nothing not already in the Expanded Version.) The Short Version, of which about a dozen copies are known, includes Yaroslav's original document of eighteen brief articles as well as twenty-five articles added in 1072 by three of his sons. By contrast, around one hundred copies exist of the Expanded Version, the oldest of which dates to the late thirteenth century. This much longer document includes substantial revisions of the Short Version, undertaken in the twelfth century, as well as a new section

authorized by Vladimir II Monomakh. The Justice of the Rus continued to undergo further revision into the early Muscovite period, which began with the reign of Ivan III as grand prince of Moscow (1462–1505).

Context

The promulgation of the Justice of the Rus marked a critical step in the larger process of forming Eastern Slavic (and some Finnic) tribes into a single Rus state ruled from Kiev. (The original meaning of the term *Rus* is still debated, but it generally refers to these various tribes and their growing state.) Although some scholars argue that an organized Rus state existed from as early as the sixth century—a view based partly on trade with the wealthy Byzantine Empire and its great capital Constantinople to the south—the dominant theory argues for a founding date in the late ninth century and attributes a key role to outsiders known in Western history as the Vikings and in Russian history as the Varangians. According to a common version of this thesis, Varangians, traveling back and forth along river routes linking their Scandinavian homeland and the Byzantine Empire, began to organize and lead a growing number of raids on Constantinople, including a major attack in 860. Rus soldiers were recruited for these campaigns. Over time, Varangian princes assumed more general power over the Rus, welding them into a state.

There is considerable evidence in support of this theory from the field of linguistics, archaeological records, and the records of the Vikings themselves. Also of some use is the *Primary Chronicle*, an annalistic account of early Rus history compiled in Russia by Orthodox Christian monks during the mid-eleventh through the early twelfth centuries. This text tells how, frustrated by the persistence of their own intertribal conflicts, some Rus tribes appealed to the Varangians in 862; the document notes the wealth and promise of Rus land but also a general lack of order. Three Varangian brothers supposedly responded. Following the deaths of two, the third, named Rurik, inherited a nascent Rus state centered in the northern city of Novgorod.

Although scholars consider this story, and Rurik himself, to be only semihistorical, the Rurik Dynasty he sup-

CA. 862

- Rurik, a semilegendary Varangian ruler of Novgorod, begins the Rurik Dynasty, which will rule Russia until the death of Czar Fyodor I in 1598.

882

- Rurik's successor, Oleg, expands his domains and makes his capital at Kiev, founding Kievan Rus.

988

- Vladimir, grand prince of Kiev, establishes Orthodox Christianity as the religion of the Rus. The faith comes to the Rus from Constantinople, capital of the Byzantine Empire, with which the Rus already had longtime commercial relations.

1019

- Yaroslav, "the Wise," begins his rule as grand prince of Kiev. The first version of the Justice of the Rus is issued, probably near the start of Yaroslav's reign, with some amendments toward the end of it (1054).

1072

- Yaroslav's sons Izyaslav, Svyatoslav, and Vsevolod (each of whom ruled in Kiev for a time) significantly expand their father's law code.

posedly founded ruled Kievan Rus and Russia itself until the death of the czar Fyodor I (son of Ivan IV, "the Terrible") in 1598. There is much greater historical certainty about Rurik's immediate successor, another Varangian named Oleg. He successfully united many more Eastern Slavs, established his capital at Kiev, and is considered the true founder of Kievan Rus. His successors continued the effort to subjugate and unite more tribes under Kievan control. Eventually, the Varangians were absorbed into the surrounding populations. This mixing of Rus and Viking, along with the inclusion of Finnic and other local tribes, formed the basis of the modern-day Russian people.

The next major event in the development and consolidation of Kievan Rus came in 988, when Vladimir, grand prince of Kiev, converted to Orthodox Christianity and made it the official religion of his entire domain. The adoption of Christianity went hand in hand with ongoing efforts to forge a single, more centralized state. All of these efforts were endangered, however, by continual feuding among Rus princes, which threatened to tear the state apart completely. Following Vladimir's death in 1015, a protracted struggle ensued as several of his sons claimed power. Yaroslav, the eventual victor, had previously been prince of Novgorod. From this position he had already issued at least two local charters, serving as precedents for his Justice of the Rus.

Historians identify at least two reasons that the Justice of the Rus was promulgated. First, it helped Yaroslav secure power, gain legitimacy, and reestablish order; it can thus be seen as part of the larger princely project of state building and centralization. At the same time, in formalizing certain rules and procedures, it also defined and limited the prince's powers. Thus, many historians believe that the Justice of the Rus may have been forced upon Yaroslav by prominent Novgorodians as the price for their support of his quest to become grand prince of Kiev.

The Justice of the Rus drew on a variety of traditions and precedents. In Yaroslav's original clauses, the influence of Eastern Slavic common law is apparent, blended with rulings and clauses reflecting the interests of the prince. The additions and revisions undertaken by his sons (and others thereafter) more obviously reflect the growing needs and interests of the state and its rulers, and are thus an indication of the rise of state power at that time. The Justice of the Rus, especially later versions, also shows the influence of Byzantine law, with which the Rus would have been familiar, given a long history of commercial, military, and religious interaction.

The Justice of the Rus was not the only tradition of law in Kievan Rus. From the time of Russia's Christianization in the late tenth century, there had also existed a body of canon law. This was largely unaffected by the issuance of the Justice of the Rus. Members of the clergy, other persons employed by the church, and peasants living on church lands were subject in all matters exclusively to church law and courts. For all other persons, church law applied only in the case of family and sexual matters, such as marriage and divorce, rape, and incest. A new ecclesiastical code was also issued during Yaroslav's reign at Kiev. Thus the issuance of the Justice of the Rus created a fairly neat division of jurisdiction between secular and ecclesiastical law.

About the Author

Born around 978, Yaroslav was one of the many sons of Vladimir, grand prince of Kiev. The identity of his mother is contested, and little of his childhood is known. Yaroslav came from Varangian stock, and his life is also told in the Norse sagas (in which he is known as Jarisleif, "the Lame," because of an arrow wound). As a young man he ruled under his father's orders, first in the Rostov area and then in the important commercial city-state of Novgorod. He also founded the city of Jaroslaw, further east.

Yaroslav hoped to succeed his father as grand prince in Kiev. His brother Svyatopolk had similar ambitions. Hoping to stave off conflict, Vladimir bequeathed his throne instead to yet another son, the pious Boris. Vladimir's death in 1015 was followed nonetheless by a brutal power struggle. Boris and another brother, Gleb, were murdered—probably at the orders of Svyatopolk but perhaps by Yaroslav's supporters. Boris and Gleb were later canonized as the first saints in the Russian Orthodox Church. By 1019 Yaroslav, still also the ruler of Novgorod, had emerged victorious. It may have been at about this time that he issued the first version of the Justice of the Rus.

Despite the bloody and fratricidal start to his reign, Yaroslav is generally regarded by historians as one of Kievan Rus's finest rulers (reflected in his sobriquet, "the Wise"). This success is attributable not only to his legislation but also to successes in foreign policy, the construction under his patronage of Saint Sophia Cathedral and other religious buildings, and his promotion of book learning.

Yaroslav had seven sons from two marriages. Three from the second marriage—Izyaslav, Svyatoslav, and Vsevolod—authored the first significant expansion of their father's code. One after the other, they held the title of grand prince of Kiev nearly continuously from 1054 to 1093. Vsevolod's son Vladimir II Monomakh, who added his own statute to the Justice of the Rus, built up his base of power well to the northeast of Kiev, in the towns of Pereiaslavl, Rostov, and Suzdal. In this region he also founded the city of Vladimir, which became the de facto capital in the mid-twelfth century. Monomakh ruled in Kiev from 1113 to 1125. His reign is considered a golden age.

Explanation and Analysis of the Document

The original documents (known to scholars as the Academy copy of the Short Version and the Trinity copy of the Expanded Version) are largely unorganized. The division of both versions into numbered articles—as they appear here—was done by B. D. Grekov (1940), with translation and further editing by George Vernadsky (1947).

Time Line

1113

■ Vladimir II Monomakh, a grandson of Yaroslav, begins rule as grand prince of Kiev, a reign that ends in 1125. With his additions, the Justice of the Rus essentially assumes its final form.

◆ Short Version

ARTICLES 1–10 The first ten articles of the Short Version deal with acts of violence, starting with murder and moving toward lesser crimes. In Article 1, Yaroslav (spelled "Iaroslav" in the text) imposed order on the common-law tradition of blood revenge by designating authorized avengers for specified murder cases, and he set a man's wergild (spelled "wergeld" in the document)—the compensation for his death—at forty *grivna*. The *grivna* was the main unit of currency in Kievan Rus. It could be denominated in gold, silver, or fur. (The law does not specify which form was intended here or elsewhere. Other monetary units, most being fractions of a *grivna*, are noted in the document.) The term *izgoi*, also mentioned in Article 1, has been variously used and translated, depending on context. Generically it refers to an "outsider." Various interpretations have been offered for its use here, including an orphan, an exiled person, or someone of Ossetian or Circassian origin. The Justice of the Rus includes other references to outsiders. Article 10, for example, granted to Varangians and Kolbiags an exemption to the requirement for an eyewitness. This exemption was a concession to favored minority groups that might not easily be able to persuade a Slav to testify on their behalf. Varangians, of course, formed something of an elite class and provided most of the princes. The term *Kolbiag* has been interpreted to mean a Scandinavian (like the Varangians) or someone of Baltic or even Turkic background.

The first ten articles outline specific values for a range of common corporal offenses. Comparison of the ascribed payments reveals much about Rus social values and notions of justice. The loss of an arm required the same payment as the loss of life, for example (Article 5), perhaps because both losses meant the end of a warrior. Facial hair, which was a symbol of a man's honor, manliness, and holiness, carried four times the value of a finger (Articles 7 and 8).

Many of the articles are peculiarly specific. Article 3 treats the case of a person who "hits another with a club, or a rod, or a fist, or a bowl, or a horn"; Article 21 deals with persons who "murder the bailiff near a barn," a "horse [stable]," or a "cow [shed]" while simultaneously "stealing cows." Apparently, many of these articles were written after the fact, to deal with specific one-off cases or to justify a punishment already meted out. Some of the articles may appear naive to modern readers as well. The requirements for proof of offense in Article 2, for example, took no account of self-inflicted wounds, accidents, or other possible reasons that a man might appear before a court "smeared with blood" or "blue from bruises."

ARTICLES 11–18 These articles discuss property and commercial relations, including specific cases of a runaway slave, damage to or theft of property, and the division of business profit. The focus on business profit in particular (Article 15) speaks to the relatively advanced stage of commercial activity in Kievan Rus, compared with much of the rest of eleventh-century Europe. Business was particularly advanced in Novgorod, Yaroslav's base of power before his accession to the throne of Kiev in 1019.

ARTICLES 19–43 These articles were added in 1072 by Yaroslav's eldest sons: Izyaslav, Svyatoslav, and Vsevolod. (The first two names are rendered "Iziaslav" and "Sviatoslav" in the document text.) Among them, they ruled Kiev from 1054 to 1093. Their relations were not always harmonious. In 1073 Svyatoslav usurped his older brother's throne, holding it until his own death in 1076, at which point Izyaslav returned. He died in 1078, and the Kievan throne passed to Vsevolod.

The sons' additions are usually interpreted as evidence of the increasing power and ambition of the state (or of the princes). Indirectly the additions also reflected growing popular resentment of this power, especially in and around Kiev. More specifically, the new articles were likely a belated response to rioting in Kiev during 1068; these riots temporarily forced Izyaslav from the throne. The sons doubled to eighty *grivna* the "bloodwite" (fine, payable to the prince) for the murder of any of several classes of the prince's officials or servants (Articles 19–23). Article 21 suggests that a bailiff of the prince was indeed murdered, in the circumstances described. Articles 24–25 imposed lower fines for the murder of other lower-ranking persons in the prince's service. Article 33 is construed more broadly and seems to argue that only the state had the right to punish or to use force. Similarly it granted a level of state protection to the classes or offices listed.

Through Article 28, specific monetary values are spelled out for the murder or destruction of various classes of persons, in descending order of their importance to the prince, and on through a range of domestic animals, all of which would have constituted both income for their owners and a potential source of tax revenue for the prince. These and other articles highlight the fundamental purpose of the Justice of the Rus: establishment of a clear hierarchy of power, with the prince at the top, and a stable foundation for public order. These concerns are also apparent in Articles 34–40, which schedule fines for common, specific offenses and claims, including petty theft and boundary disputes.

Scholars believe that Articles 41 and 42 were written separately and then added in. Article 41 specifies how the fines collected from offenders were to be distributed among the prince, his officials, and the Orthodox Church. The amounts do not add up exactly, perhaps because of errors in transcription of the original documents or because of approximation. Article 42 details the types and amounts of food and other supplies that the "bloodwite collector and his assistants" could legally take from the surrounding population. These guidelines were established to satisfy or limit popular complaints against excessive seizures and levies imposed on local populations by the collector and in the prince's name. As with some of the other articles, this provision tended to promote a notion of the prince as the protector of his people. Articles 41 and 42 are also the only parts of the Short Version that refer directly to the church.

◆ **Expanded Version**

ARTICLES 1–52 The Expanded Version begins with a revised statement of Yaroslav's organized system of blood revenge. Reflecting changes earlier made by the sons, there were now two classes of officials: higher-ranking officials with a wergild of eighty *grivna* and lower-ranking officials worth forty. More precise information on the wergild of specific ranks, positions, or employments is given in Articles 11–17. Article 2 notes the cancellation of blood revenge altogether and its replacement with a system of fines ("bloodwite"). On its face, this article clearly contradicts Article 1. Certainly from the time of Izyaslav forward, the trend was toward abolishing blood revenge (which put justice partly in the hands of the aggrieved) and replacing it with fines (which put justice more squarely in the hands of the state). The inclusion here of both systems cannot easily be resolved, however, unless it is interpreted simply as a side-by-side record of the old and new pronouncements.

Articles 3–8, dealing with murder, gave the prince additional tools for collecting payments and enforcing his law, taking into account a wider variety of specific situations. The collective responsibility of any guild within whose area a murder was committed is spelled out in more detail, including instances in which the actual murderer was not found or was unknown ("dark bloodwite") or was found at some point after partial bloodwite payment had already been made on his behalf.

The Expanded Version—as far as Article 52—includes a lively admixture of clauses and rulings identical or very similar to those in the Short Version and others that were obviously altered for one reason or another. For example, the fine for cutting off a man's arm (or inflicting similar injuries) in Article 5 of the Short Version was lower than the fine imposed in Article 27 of the Expanded Version for the same offense. In addition, many new articles (especially Articles 32–46) were added to account for specific circumstances not treated in the Short Version. These articles provide a sense of the common experiences of persons of various social strata across a wide segment of Rus society.

The Expanded Version also pays increased attention to matters of trade and commerce, establishing some basic rules and procedures for legal suit (Articles 47 and 48) and for the recovery of goods stored with a third party (Article 49). Articles 50–52 concern usury, or the charging of interest. Unlike contemporary Western law and attitudes, which

A clergyman passes Mikhaylivsky Cathedral in central Kiev, Ukraine. (AP/Wide World Photos)

frowned on usury, the Justice of the Rus allowed it and attempted to regulate it. Scholars have attributed this difference to the relatively advanced stage of commerce and the backward state of agriculture in Kievan Rus, meaning that the role of money was relatively important and the influence of the merchant class quite significant. The Rus princes themselves frequently invested and transacted in money. By contrast, in western Europe at the time, because farming was more advanced and commerce less so, the economy was based more heavily on the exchange of agricultural products and the assignment of fiefs. The role of money and the influence of merchants were smaller. Of course, this situation changed rapidly thereafter, as trade and commerce greatly accelerated in western Europe during the twelfth century.

ARTICLES 53–121: THE STATUTE OF VLADIMIR, SON OF VSEVOLOD The most important and lengthy section of the Expanded Version is the Statute of Vladimir II Monomakh, organized here as Articles 53–121. Monomakh was the son of Vsevolod and a grandson of Yaroslav. Like those of Yaroslav's sons, the additions made by Vladimir II Monomakh were a response to social unrest. High interest rates charged on loans, growing indebtedness, and rising incidence of enslavement for nonpayment led to serious riots in Kiev in 1113. Moneylenders and merchants, Jews, and prosperous boyars (hereditary nobles) were targeted by an

assortment of laborers and farmers, artisans, and impoverished burghers. It was in this environment that Monomakh came to the throne of Kiev. His legislative innovations focused on regulation of interest rates and protection from debt enslavement and were designed to quell discontent and head off a possible social revolution. After Monomakh, later princes added other revisions to check or regulate the spread of slavery and the process of enslavement, along with changes and clarifications to laws concerning inheritance and family. By the middle of the twelfth century, the Extended Version had more or less achieved its final form.

Articles 53 and 53a addressed the main problems behind the riots. Various interpretations have been given for the meaning of "third-of-the-year rates" in the practice of lending money. Some scholars have attributed specific rates to the term—such as 50 percent, so that the loan principal would have been paid in full by the second payment, with the third payment adding 50 percent total interest. Other scholars have claimed that the intention behind the clause was not to set any specific interest rates in the first year but simply to limit initially agreed-upon interest payments to that one year, after which time Article 53a set a lower limit for interest paid on loans of greater duration. Taken together, these measures would have provided a certain amount of security and protection for borrowers, thus quelling unrest.

"If a man kills a man [the following relatives of the murdered man may avenge him]: the brother is to avenge his brother; the son, his father; or the father, his son; and the son of the brother [of the murdered man] or the son of his sister, [their respective uncle]. If there is no avenger, [the murderer pays] 40 grivna wergeld."

(Short Version, Article 1)

"If they kill the bailiff, deliberately, the [actual] murderer has to pay 80 grivna [as bloodwite], and the guild is not liable. And for the prince's adjutant, 80 grivna."

(Short Version, Article 19)

"And after Iaroslav his sons: Iziaslav, Sviatoslav, and Vsevolod ... met in a conference and canceled the [custom] of blood revenge, and [instead ordered] composition of [the crime] by money."

(Expanded Version, Article 2)

"After the death of [Prince] Sviatopolk, [Prince] Vladimir, son of Vsevolod, called his councilors [for a meeting] .... And they ordered that he who lends money at third-of-the-year rates be limited by the third collection of interest."

(Expanded Version, Article 53)

A related goal of Monomakh's rulings was to make it harder for a person to fall into slavery, particularly as a result personal debt or the conversion of an unfulfilled labor contract into slavery. Alternatively, in cases in which a person voluntarily arranged to be sold into slavery—perhaps to secure food, shelter, and a monetary payment—the law set a minimum price for the transaction (Articles 110 and 111). The last ten articles further attempt to regulate slavery, though certainly not to abolish it. Numerous clauses deal with the collection or payment of debts and other obligations in specified circumstances.

Under the heading "Other Enactments" (at Article 67), the Justice of the Rus returns to common themes of compensation for loss or injury. The emphasis on beehives (Articles 71–72 and 75–77) illustrates the importance of honey within Rus commerce, especially in heavily forested northern areas, where open-field agriculture was less prominent. Much information on the common affairs of life and commerce at the time can be inferred from the

expanded number of specific offenses listed under "On Peasants," "On Hunting Nets," "On Stealing Hay," and so on, and also from Articles 96 and 97 on the payment of construction workers.

Articles 88 and 89 shed some light on attitudes toward women. The punishment for killing a woman was only half that for killing a man. Further inferences on gender relations can be made through a close reading of some of Monomakh's rulings on inheritance and division of property (especially Articles 98–106). Overall, Monomakh's code seeks to impose order and a degree of fairness on a wide range of social and commercial situations and arrangements.

Audience

The Justice of the Rus was intended first and foremost for use in court. It was also a statement of political power. In both capacities it was aimed at, and would certainly have been known among, a broad range of elites, including church officials, the nobility and gentry, and prosperous merchants or townsmen. The later redactions, especially the clauses added by Monomakh, were clearly intended also for a broad, even a mass audience, especially in the capital. They were written to restore social order, to satisfy popular concerns, and to convince the ordinary urban resident that their prince would offer them protection from some of the worst abuses they might suffer from masters, landlords, creditors, and others.

Impact

Parts of the law were issued with specific goals in mind, such as to settle social unrest in and around Kiev in 1113. For the most part, these goals appear to have been met. More broadly, the Justice of the Rus furthered the development of state power, princely authority, and law and order in Kievan Rus.

The accumulation of legal articles and the specificity of many of them also led eventually to an increasingly unwieldy document, internal contradictions, vagueness, or other problems. Kievan Rus itself fragmented during the twelfth century, further undermining the effectiveness of the law. In the thirteenth century, the Rus lands were devastated and conquered by Mongol-Tatar hordes and did not regain full independence until the late fifteenth century. Even before this time, Novgorod, Pskov, and the Dvina Land—relatively unharmed by the Mongols—had issued their own legal charters.

By the late fifteenth century, however, Russia had been reborn in new guise, as the principality of Moscow rose from obscurity to near-complete domination over all of the old Rus lands. With this new political reality came the need for a new body of law. Thus in 1497 the Muscovite grand prince Ivan III issued a new Sudebnik (legal code). His grandson Czar Ivan IV ("the Terrible") issued a revised Sudebnik in 1550. Alongside innovations, elements of the Justice of the Rus were preserved in both. The new Sudebniks sought to establish laws suitable for an increasingly powerful and centralized state. Both also promoted the ongoing enserfment of the formerly free Russian peasantry. This trend would climax with the publication of Russia's next great law code, the Ulozhenie of 1649.

Further Reading

■ Articles

Dimnik, Martin. "The 'Testament' of Iaroslav 'The Wise': A Reexamination." *Canadian Slavonic Papers* 29, no. 4 (December 1987): 369–386.

Miller, David B. "The Kievan Principality in the Century before the Mongol Invasion: An Inquiry into Recent Research and Interpretation." *Harvard Ukrainian Studies* 10, nos. 1–2 (June 1986): 215–240.

■ Books

Franklin, Simon, and Jonathan Shepard. *The Emergence of Rus, 750–1200.* New York: Longman, 1996.

Questions for Further Study

1. From one point of view, the history of the world over the past millennium or more is the history of the consolidation of tribes and isolated bands of people into states. To what extent do the Justice of the Rus and the events leading to its promulgation illustrate this aspect of history?

2. Compare Justice of the Rus with another medieval document, Charlemagne's Capitulary of 802. Were there similarities in the motivations behind the two documents? How did cultural and historical factors influence each document?

3. What role did the positions of "insider" and "outsider"—that is, membership in or exclusion from the dominant ethnic group—have on the nature of law as enunciated in Justice of the Rus?

4. What role did trade and commerce play in both the legal code and the historical circumstances that gave rise to it? Why do you think trade and commerce had these effects?

5. What were the short-term and long-term impacts of Justice of the Rus? In your opinion, did this law code contribute to the evolution of modern law codes that protect the interests of individuals, or was it a code designed merely to protect the interests of the state and its rulers?

Kaiser, Daniel H. *The Laws of Rus: Tenth to Fifteenth Centuries.* Salt Lake City, Utah: Charles Schlacks, Jr., 1992.

Pushkarev, Sergei G. *Dictionary of Russian Historical Terms from the Eleventh Century to 1917.* New Haven, Conn.: Yale University Press, 1970.

Vernadsky, George, trans. *Medieval Russian Laws.* 1947. Reprint. New York: Octagon Books, 1965.

—Brian Bonhomme

Russkaia Pravda, or Justice of the Rus

A. Short Version

◆ [I. Iaroslav's Pravda]

Article 1. If a man kills a man [the following relatives of the murdered man may avenge him]: the brother is to avenge his brother; the son, his father; or the father, his son; and the son of the brother [of the murdered man] or the son of his sister, [their respective uncle]. If there is no avenger, [the murderer pays] 40 *grivna* wergeld. Be [the murdered man] a [Kievan] Russian—a palace guard, a merchant, an agent, or a sheriff—be he an *Izgoi*, or a [Novgorodian] Slav, his wergeld is 40 *grivna*.

Article 2. If [a man injures a man, and the injured man] is smeared with blood or is blue from bruises, he needs no eyewitness [to prove the offense]; if there is no mark [of injury] upon him, let him produce an eyewitness; if he cannot, the matter ends there. If he is not able to avenge, he receives 3 *grivna* for the offense and the physician receives his honorarium.

Article 3. If anyone hits another with a club, or a rod, or a fist, or a bowl, or a [drinking] horn, or the butt [of a tool or of a vessel], and [the offender] evades being hit [in his turn], he [the offender] has to pay 12 *grivna* and that ends the matter.

Article 4. If [anyone] strikes [another] with a sword without unsheathing it, or with the hilt of a sword, 12 *grivna* for the offense.

Article 5. If [anyone] cuts [another's] arm, and the arm is cut off or shrinks, 40 *grivna*.

Article 6. If [anyone cuts another's leg and] the leg is cut off, or the [injured man] becomes lame, then the latter's sons have to chastise [the offender].

Article 7. If a finger is cut off, 3 *grivna* for the offense.

Article 8. And for the mustache, 12 *grivna*; and for the beard, 12 *grivna*.

Article 9. He who unsheathes his sword, but does not strike, pays one *grivna*.

Article 10. If a man pulls a man toward himself or pushes him, 3 *grivna*, but [the offended man] has to bring two eyewitnesses; [however] in case he is a Varangian, or a Kolbiag, an oath is to be taken.

Article 11. If a slave runs away from a Varangian or a Kolbiag and [the man who conceals that slave] does not declare him for three days, and [the owner] discovers him on the third day, he [the owner] receives his slave back and 3 *grivna* for the offense.

Article 12. If anyone rides another's horse without asking the owner's permission, he has to pay 3 *grivna*.

Article 13. If anyone takes another's horse, or weapon, or clothes, and [the owner] identifies [the object] within his township, he receives it back and 3 *grivna* for the offense.

Article 14. If the owner identifies [his property outside of his town] he must not seize it outright; do not tell [the man who holds the property]: "This is mine," but tell him thus: "Come for confrontation to the place where you got it"; and if he does not come immediately he must produce two bails [to guarantee that he will come] within five days.

Article 15. If a man [engaged in business] claims his share in the balance from his partner, and the latter balks, he has to go for an investigation by [a jury of] 12 men; if [it is established] that he [the partner] maliciously refused to refund [the first man's share], the man must receive his money and 3 *grivna* for the offense.

Article 16. If anyone, having recognized his [runaway] slave [in another's possession] wants to take him, [the man who holds that slave] has to lead [the owner] to the party from whom he bought that slave, and that party has to lead [the owner] to the one [from whom he bought the slave], and [so they go eventually] even to the third party. Then tell the third party: "Give me the slave, and sue [the fourth party] for your money with [the help of] an eyewitness."

Article 17. And if a slave strikes a freeman and hides in [his master's] house, and his master is not willing to give him up, the master has to pay 12 *grivna*, and the offended freeman beats the slave whenever he finds him.

Article 18. And if anyone breaks [another's] spear, or shield, or [cuts his] clothes and wants to keep them, he must pay for them. And if he wants to return the damaged things he has to pay for the damage.

◆ [II. The Pravda of Iaroslav's Sons]

[Preamble]. The Law of the Russian land enacted when [the princes] Iziaslav, Vsevolod, Sviatoslav, [and their councilors] Kosniachko, Pereneg, Mikyfor the Kievan, Chudin, and Mikula met together.

Article 19. If they kill the bailiff, deliberately, the [actual] murderer has to pay 80 *grivna* [as bloodwite], and the guild is not liable. And for the prince's adjutant, 80 *grivna*.

Article 20. And if the bailiff is killed in a highway attack and they do not search for the murderers, that guild within the boundaries of which the body has been found has to pay the bloodwite.

Article 21. And if, while stealing cows, they murder the bailiff near a barn, or near a horse [stable] or a cow [shed], [the one who murders the bailiff] is to be killed like a dog. This also refers to [the case of the murder of] the assistant steward.

Article 22. And for the prince's steward, 80 *grivna*.

Article 23. And for the master of the stable 80 *grivna*, as constituted by Iziaslav in the case of his master of the stable whom the Dorogobuzhians killed.

Article 24. And for [the murder of] the prince's farm manager as well as of the field overseer, 12 *grivna*.

Article 25. And for the contract laborer on princely estates, 5 *grivna*.

Article 26. And for a peasant, or a herdsman, 5 *grivna*.

Article 27. And for the slave tutor or nurse, 12 *grivna*.

Article 28. And for a horse with prince's brand, 3 *grivna*, and for the peasant's horse, 2 *grivna*; for a mare, 60 *rezana*; for an ox, one *grivna*; for a cow, 40 *rezana*; and for a three-year-old [cow], 15 *kuna*; and for a yearling [heifer], a half *grivna*; and for a calf, 5 *rezana*; and for a yearling ewe, one *nogata*, and for a [yearling] ram, one *nogata*.

Article 29. And if anyone abducts another man's male or female slave, he has to pay 12 *grivna* for the offense.

Article 30. If there comes a man smeared with blood or blue from bruises he needs no witness [to prove the offense].

Article 31. And if they steal horses or oxen or [some property in the] barn, and if it was the work of one man only, he has to pay [three] *grivna* and 30 *rezana*; and if there were [as many as] 18 robbers, each pays three *grivna* and 30 *rezana*.

Article 32. And if they burn or break a prince's beehive, 3 *grivna*.

Article 33. And if they inflict pain on a peasant without the prince's order, 3 *grivna* for the offense; and for the bailiff, and for the assistant steward, and the sheriff, 12 *grivna*.

Article 34. And if anyone plows beyond the bound [of his property] or beyond a hedge, 12 *grivna* for the offense.

Article 35. And if anyone steals a boat, he has to pay 30 *rezana* for the boat and a fine of 60 *rezana*.

Article 36. And for a dove or a fowl, 9 *kuna*; and for a duck, or a goose, or a crane, or a swan, 30 *rezana*; and a fine of 60 *rezana*.

Article 37. And if they steal another man's hound or hawk, or falcon, 3 *grivna* for the offense.

Article 38. And if they kill a thief in their own yard, or at the barn, or at the stable, he is [rightly] killed; but if they hold him until daylight, they have to bring him to the prince's court; and in case [they hold him until daylight and then] kill him, and people have seen him bound [before he was killed], they have to pay for him.

Article 39. If they steal hay, 9 *kuna*; and for lumber, 9 *kuna*.

Article 40. If they steal a ewe, or a goat, or a sow, and ten people were [in the gang], each pays a fine of 60 *rezana*; and he who rescued [the ewe], receives 10 *rezana*.

Article 41. And from each [three] *grivna* [of fines collected] one *kuna* is paid to the sheriff; 15 *kuna* goes [to the church] as tithe; and the prince receives three *grivna*. And from 12 *grivna* the sheriff receives 70 *kuna*; [the church], two *grivna* as tithe; and the prince, 10 *grivna*.

Article 42. And [when the bloodwite collector and his assistants are on their journey for collecting fines, they receive provisions from the population] according to custom, as follows: the collector receives 7 buckets of malt, and a sheep or a portion [of a beef], or two *nogata* for one week; and on Wednesday, one *rezana* or [the equivalent in] curd; and on Friday, the same; and as much bread as they can eat, and millet; and two hens a day; and [they have the right] to put up 4 horses in the stable, and [the owner of the stable] has to give the horses as much [oats] as they can eat. And the bloodwite collector receives 60 *grivna*, and 10 *rezana*, and 12 *veveritsa* [of which] one *grivna* in advance. And if [the collection drive] occurs during Lent, [then the food is fish] and [he receives] 7 *rezana* for fish. Thus, they receive 15 *kuna* a week in cash, and as much food as they can eat; [but in each locality] they have to complete the collection of the bloodwite within a week. Such is Iaroslav's ordinance.

Article 43. And this is the table of payments for the builders of bridges: when they complete the bridge, they receive one *nogata* for their work and one *nogata* for lumber [for each span of the bridge]. And if they have to repair several planks of an old bridge—three, or four, or five—they are paid accordingly.

B. Expanded Version

◆ [I. The Revised Pravda of Iaroslav's Sons]

The Ordinances of Iaroslav, Son of Vladimir

Article 1. If a man kills a man [the following relatives of the murdered man may avenge him]: the brother is to avenge his brother, or the father, [his son], or the son, [his father]; or the son of the brother, or the son of the sister, [their respective uncle]. If there is no avenger the wergeld is set to the amount of 80 *grivna* in case [the murdered man] was a prince's councilor or a prince's steward; if he was a [Kievan] Russian—a palace guard, a merchant, or a boyar's steward, or a sheriff—or if he was an *Izgoi*, or a [Novgorodian] Slav, [the wergeld is] 40 *grivna*.

Article 2. And after Iaroslav his sons: Iziaslav, Sviatoslav, and Vsevolod, and their councilors: Kosniachko, Pereneg, and Nikifor met in a conference and canceled the [custom] of blood revenge, and [instead ordered] composition of [the crime] by money. And as to anything else, all that Iaroslav had decreed, his sons confirmed accordingly.

On Homicide

Article 3. If anyone kills a prince's man in a highway attack, and the [local people] do not search for the murderer, the guild within the territory where the body lies has to pay the bloodwite [which, for the prince's official, is] 80 *grivna*, and for a commoner, 40 *grivna*.

Article 4. And if a guild has to pay a "dark" bloodwite, its members [are allowed] to pay [in installments] for several years, since they pay on behalf of [an unknown] murderer.

Article 5. If the murderer appears within the guild [after the payments of the "dark" bloodwite have been already started], let him pay the balance, since they [the members of the guild] had helped him by starting payments of the "dark" bloodwite. But in any case they shall together pay 40 *grivna* [as bloodwite] in full; and as to the bot, it is only the murderer who pays it; and he pays his share of the 40 *grivna* [bloodwite].

Article 6. And if [a man] kills [a man] publicly in a brawl or at a feast he likewise shall pay his share in the guild's liabilities.

Concerning [the Man] Who Kills [Another Man] in an Attack without Provocation

Article 7. And if [a man] kills [a man] in an attack without provocation, the [members of the guild] do not pay for the murderer but surrender him with his wife and children for banishment and confiscation of his property.

Article 8. And to one who fails to assume his share in [the payments of] the "dark" bloodwite, the members of the guild give no help but he has to pay [everything] himself.

Article 9. And the customary food rations of the bloodwite collector under Iaroslav are as follows: the bloodwite collector receives 7 buckets of malt and a sheep or a portion [of a beef], or 2 *nogata* for one week; and on Wednesday one *kuna* or [the equivalent in] curd; and on Friday the same; and two hens a day; and 7 loaves of bread for a week; and 7 measures of millet; and 7 measures of peas; and 7 bricks of salt. This is to the bloodwite collector with his clerk. And oats for 4 horses. And the bloodwite collector receives 8 *grivna*, and 10 *kuna* for traveling expenses; and the sheriff receives 12 *veksha*. And the arrival [welcome] money is 1 *grivna*.

Article 10. When the bloodwite is 80 *grivna*, the collector receives 16 *grivna* and 10 *kuna* and 12 *veksha*; and the arrival [welcome] money *grivna* in advance, and 3 *grivna* head money.

Concerning the Prince's Officials

Article 11. And [the wergeld] of the prince's page, or groom, or [man] cook is 40 *grivna*.

Article 12. And for the palace steward and the stable steward, 80 *grivna*.

Article 13. And for the farm steward or the field overseer, 12 *grivna*.

Article 14. And for a contract laborer, 5 *grivna*; and as much for a boyar's contract laborer.

Concerning the Handicraftsman or Handicraftswoman

Article 15. And for the handicraftsman or a handicraftswoman, 12 *grivna*.

Article 16. And for a peasant or a slave, 5 *grivna*; and for a female slave, 6 *grivna*.

Article 17. And for the tutor, 12 *grivna*, and the same amount for the nurse, even be he or she a slave.

Concerning the Bloodwite in the Case of a Reported [Homicide]

Article 18. And if a man [not caught in the very act of committing a murder] is accused of homicide, he has to produce 7 witnesses [to prove his innocence, in order] to reject the bloodwite. And if he is a Varangian or other [alien], then [he needs two witnesses only].

Article 19. And when bones are found or a [decomposed] corpse, no bloodwite is to be imposed, since they do not know the name [of the dead man] and cannot identify him.

And if [the Defendant] Rejects the Bloodwite

Article 20. And if [the defendant] rejects the bloodwite [with the aid of witnesses], he has to pay one *grivna* of *kuna* to the clerk for the discontinuance; and the man who brought the accusation pays [to the clerk] another *grivna*; and for [the rejection of] the bloodwite, 9 [*kuna*] as proceedings costs.

Article 21. And if [the defendant] is unable to produce witnesses but [in his turn] accuses his accuser of the homicide, let them be given an ordeal by iron.

Article 22. And the same refers to all lawsuits, including theft and other accusations. If the [stolen] thing is not produced, give him [that is, the plaintiff] [ordeal by] iron even against his will [in case the amount of the damages] is over one half of a *grivna* gold. If [the amount] is less [than a half *grivna* gold] but over 2 [silver] *grivna*, [the ordeal is] by water. And if the amount is less [than 2 silver *grivna*], then let him [the plaintiff] take the oath concerning his money.

Article 23. If anyone strikes [another] with a sword without unsheathing it, or with the hilt, a 12 *grivna* fine for the offense.

Article 24. He who unsheathes his sword but does not strike, one *grivna* of *kuna*.

Article 25. If anyone hits another with a club or a bowl or a [drinking] horn or the butt [of a tool or a vessel], 12 *grivna*.

Article 26. If the man [who has been hit], will not endure it and strikes [his offender] with a sword, he is not guilty.

Article 27. If anyone cuts [another's] arm, and the arm is severed, or shrinks, or if he cuts a leg, or an eye, or the nose, then [he pays] half a bloodwite, 20 *grivna*, and the [injured] man receives 10 *grivna* for his injuries.

Article 28. If he cuts any of the fingers, a 3 *grivna* fine, and one *grivna* of *kuna* to the injured man.

If a Bloody Man Appears [to Seek Justice]

Article 29. If a man smeared with blood or blue [from bruises] comes to [the prince's] court, he needs no eyewitness [to prove the offense], and [his assailant] pays a 3 *grivna* fine; if there is no mark [of injury] upon him, he has to produce an eyewitness [to testify] word for word; and the one who started [the fight] pays 60 *kuna*. And if a man comes smeared with blood but it is subsequently proved by witnesses that it was he who started [the fight], then the beating he received serves him as remuneration.

Article 30. If anyone strikes another with a sword but does not kill him, [he pays] a 3 *grivna* [fine to the prince] and [the expenses] of the treatment of the wound to the [injured man] himself; if he kills [the man he struck, he pays] the bloodwite.

Article 31. If a man pulls a man toward himself or pushes him, or hits him in the face, or beats him with a rod, two eyewitnesses are to be brought, and

the fine is 3 *grivna*; in case he is a Varangian or a Kolbiag, then a full number of eyewitnesses should be brought and an oath is to be taken.

On Slaves

Article 32. And if a slave should conceal himself, and the owner announces it in the market place, and for three days nobody brings him in, and [the owner] should find him on the third day, he may take his slave and he [who concealed the slave] pays 3 *grivna* fine.

If Anyone Rides Another's Horse

Article 33. If anyone rides another's horse without asking [the owner's permission], three *grivna* fine.

Article 34. If anyone loses his horse, or weapons, or clothes, and announces it in the market place and later recognizes [his lost property] in his own town [at another's house], he takes it back, and [the offender] pays three *grivna* for the offense.

Article 35. If anyone recognizes [at another's] his property lost or stolen from him, such as a horse, or clothes, or cattle, do not say "It is mine," but: "Let us go for confrontation to the party where you received it" [and] settle it by confrontation. He who is guilty, assumes the responsibility for stealing; [the owner] takes his property; and if anything had been damaged, [the guilty] one must pay for it; and if the guilty one is a horse thief, he shall be surrendered to the prince for banishment; if he is a house thief, he pays three *grivna* [to the prince].

On Confrontation

Article 36. And if the investigation takes place in the same town, the plaintiff has to go to the last confrontation; if the investigation is transferred to other towns, the plaintiff has to go to the third confrontment only; and the third party pays [the original owner], for what has been found, and with it goes through the last confrontation; and the [original] plaintiff has to wait until the end of the investigation; and when the last [guilty] party is found, he pays the damages as well as the fine.

On Theft

Article 37. Similarly, if anyone buys stolen goods, be it a horse, or clothes, or cattle, he has to produce two freemen or the toll collector [to certify the fact of his buying it]; if he cannot state from whom he bought [the goods], his eyewitnesses have to swear [that he did buy the goods] and the plaintiff takes his property; and if there are losses, he [the plaintiff] may lament them; and he [who bought the stolen goods] may lament his money, since he does not know from whom he bought [the goods]. And if eventually he should recognize [the man] from whom he bought them, he receives his money from that [man], and the latter pays the damages and a fine to the prince.

If Anyone Finds His [Stolen] Slave

Article 38. If anyone finds his stolen slave and apprehends him, he must, as in the case of other property litigations, bring him along until the third confrontment; then, he must take [from the third party] some slave instead of his slave and give to him [the third party] his slave as material evidence, and he [the third party] proceeds to the last confrontation. And he [the slave] is not a beast; [in this case] the buyer cannot say, "I do not know from whom I bought him" [because the slave can talk]; and thus by the slave's word one proceeds to the end, and when the final thief is found, [the third party] returns the slave [to the original owner] and takes back his own; and he [the final thief] pays the damages and 12 *grivna* fine to the prince for the stolen slave.

More on Confrontment

Article 39. And from one's own town to a foreign land there is no confrontment; the intermediary party has to produce, in the usual way, witnesses or the toll collector, in whose presence he bought [the goods]; the plaintiff takes back [such] object [as is available] and may lament the rest which he lost; and [the intermediary party] may lament his money.

On Theft

Article 40. If they kill any thief near the barn or in any other kind of thievery, they kill him like a dog; but if they hold him until dawn, they have to bring him to the prince's court. If they kill [the thief] and some people had seen him bound, they have to pay 12 *grivna* for the offense.

Article 41. If anyone steals cattle from the stable or [things from the] barn, if he is alone, he pays 3 *grivna* and 30 *kuna*; if there are many [thieves], each pays 3 *grivna* and 30 *kuna*.

More on Theft

Article 42. If anyone steals cattle in the field, or sheep, or goats, or pigs, 60 *kuna*; if there are many [thieves], each [pays] 60 *kuna*.

Article 43. If anyone steals grain from a threshing court or from a pit, irrespective of how many [thieves] there are, each [pays] 3 *grivna* and 30 *kuna*.

Article 44. And the owner [of the stolen cattle and goods] takes back the object if there is any at hand, and receives half a *grivna* [damage refund] for each year [during which the thieves used it].

Article 45. And if there be no object at hand, and [the object stolen] was the prince's horse, [the offender] pays 3 *grivna*; and for [the commoner's] horse, 2 *grivna*.

And the Following Are the Amends for [Stolen] Cattle

Article 45a. For a mare, 7 *kuna*; for an ox, 1 *grivna*; for a cow, 40 *kuna*, for a three year old [cow], 30 *kuna*, for a second year [cow], half a *grivna*, for a heifer, 5 *kuna*; for a sow, 5 *kuna*, and for a sucking pig, 1 *nogata*; for a ewe, 5 *kuna*, for a ram, 1 *nogata*; and for a [young] stallion nobody rode on, 1 *grivna* of *kuna*, [and] for a colt, 6 *nogata*; and for milk, 6 *nogata*. These amends to be paid to the prince by the [free] peasants liable to fines.

And in Regard to Slaves Who Be Thieves, the Prince's Ordinance Is as Follows

Article 46. If slaves, be they the prince's or the boyars', or the monasteries', happen to be thieves, the prince does not fine them since they are not freemen, but they are to pay double for the offense to the plaintiff.

If Anyone Sues [Another] for Money

Article 47. If anyone sues another for money [loaned] and the latter denies the charges, he has to produce witnesses who must take an oath, and [if they do so], he receives his money back; if the loan has been overdue for many years, [the debtor] has to pay 3 *grivna* for the offense.

Article 48. If a merchant lends another merchant money for buying [some goods] or for trading, he is not required to do it in the presence of witnesses; there is no need of witnesses for him, but he takes the oath himself in case [the one who received the loan] denies the charges.

On Storage

Article 49. If anyone stores his goods at another's house, there is no need of witnesses; but if he extends claims for a large amount, he who stored the goods has to swear [as follows]: "You stored at my house such and such volume only." Because [he who accepted goods for storage] did a favor to [the owner of the goods] and kept them safe.

On Interest

Article 50. If anyone lends money at interest, or honey or grain on accruement, he has to produce witnesses; he receives interest or accruement according to the rate agreed upon.

On Monthly Interest

Article 51. As to the monthly interest, [the lender] shall collect it on short-term [loans] only; if the money has been used for a year, let him [the lender] receive the interest at the third-of-the-year rate, and the monthly rate interest is annulled.

Article 52. If there were no witnesses, and the amount of money [lent] was not over 3 *grivna*, he has to take an oath; if the amount was greater, they say to him, "It is your fault, you should have done it in the presence of witnesses."

◆ [II. Vladimir Monomach's Statute]

The Statute of Vladimir, Son of Vsevolod

Article 53. After the death of [Prince] Sviatopolk, [Prince] Vladimir, son of Vsevolod, called his councilors [for a meeting] at Berestov. [The following were present:] Ratibor, the chiliarch of Kiev; Prokopii, the chiliarch of Belgorod; Stanislav, the chiliarch of Pereiaslav; Nazhir; Miroslav; and Ivanko Chudinovich, of [Prince] Oleg's retinue. And they ordered that he who lends money at third-of-the-year rates be limited by the third collection of interest. If he has collected interest for two [third-of-the-year] terms, he receives [also] his money back; but if he has collected interest for three terms, he cannot get his money back.

Article 53a. If anyone receives yearly interest [at the rate of] 10 *kuna* for 1 *grivna*, this is not annulled.

If a Merchant Be Shipwrecked

Article 54. If a merchant with another's money in his hands is shipwrecked or loses [his goods] in war or in fire, they should not apply pressure on him, nor sell his entire property, but let him repay [the lender] in yearly installments; because his ruin is from God, and he is not guilty. If he squanders another's goods on drink or [wrecks them] in a brawl, or damages them through his foolishness, then the lenders may choose: if they so wish, they wait for their goods; if not, they sell his entire property.

On Debts

Article 55. If anyone is indebted to many creditors and there comes a merchant from another town, or a foreigner, and without knowing [of the man's indebtedness] lends him goods, and he would not pay him and [when the last lender would claim his money back] the former lenders object to his being satisfied first, they [all the lenders] shall bring the man to the market place and sell his entire property. From the proceeds, they first repay the [out of town or foreign] merchant, and the balance is divided among his home-town creditors. If the prince's money was involved, they first pay the prince, and the balance is divided among the others. And he who had [already] collected much interest, [now] receives nothing.

If an Indentured Laborer Runs Away

Article 56. If an indentured laborer runs away from his lord, he becomes the latter's slave. But if he departs openly, to sue for his money [and goes] to the prince, or to the judges, to complain of the injustice

on the part of his lord, they do not reduce him to slavery but give him justice.

More on the Indentured Laborer

Article 57. If an agricultural indentured laborer ruins a war horse, he does not pay for it. But if the lord from whom he received money intrusts to him [a work horse to work with] plow and harrow and he ruins it, he has to pay for it. But if the lord sends him away for some business of his [that is, the lord's] and [the work horse] perishes, he [the laborer] need not pay for it.

More on the Indentured Laborer

Article 58. If they steal [cattle] from [the lord's] stable, the laborer does not have to pay for it. But if [the laborer] loses cattle on the field because he failed to drive them to the yard and did not lock them where the lord ordered him, or because he worked for himself and neglected working for the lord, then he has to pay.

Article 59. If the lord offends the indentured laborer and seizes his money or his movables, he has to return all this and pay 60 *kuna* for the offense.

Article 60. If the lord transfers the indenture on the laborer [to a third person] for money, [the transaction is annulled:] the [first] lord has to return the money he accepted and pay 3 *grivna* fine.

Article 61. If the lord sells the indentured laborer into slavery, the laborer is free from all obligations for the money [he had received from the lord], and the lord pays a 12 *grivna* fine for the offense.

Article 62. If the lord beats the indentured laborer for good reason, he is without fault; but if he beats the indentured laborer foolishly, being drunk, and without any fault on the part of the indentured laborer, he has to pay for the offense to the indentured laborer the same fine as it would be for a freeman.

On Slaves

Article 63. If a full slave steals another's horse, [the owner of the slave] has to pay 2 *grivna*.

Article 64. If an indentured laborer steals [a horse] or some other [beast], his lord is responsible for him. And when they find him, the lord first pays for the horse or anything else he stole, and then [the indentured laborer] is his full slave. And if the lord does not want to pay in behalf of [his indentured laborer], he sells him, and first reimburses [the owner] for the horse, or the ox, or cattle, whatever was stolen, and keeps the balance.

And if a Slave Strikes [a Freeman]

Article 65. And if a slave strikes a freeman and hides in the house, and his lord will not surrender him, the lord pays for him a 12 *grivna* [fine]; and then whenever and wherever the injured man meets the offender, who struck him, [Prince] Iaroslav ordered to [allow him] to kill the offender, but his sons, after their father's death, ordered the matter to be settled with the alternative of payment: either to bind the slave [to a post] and beat him, or to accept 1 *grivna* for the offense to his honor.

On Witnesses

Article 66. And the slave cannot serve as a witness; however, at need, when there is no freeman, a boyar's steward [even if he is a slave] may be a witness, but no other [slave]. And in a minor litigation, at need, an indentured laborer may serve as witness.

◆ **[III. Other Enactments]**

On Beards

Article 67. If anyone tears [another's] beard, and [the offended either comes to the court] with the sign of it, or produces men [as witnesses], [the offender pays] a 12 *grivna* fine; but if there is a claim and no men [to support it], there is no fine.

On Teeth

Article 68. If they knock out anyone's tooth, and blood is visible in his mouth, or men [as witnesses] are produced, 12 *grivna* fine, and 1 *grivna* [damages] for the tooth.

[*On Theft of Game*]

Article 69. If anyone steals a beaver, 12 *grivna*.

Article 70. If there are traces on the ground or any evidence of hunting, or a net, the guild must search for the poacher or pay the fine.

If Anyone Obliterates the Sign on a Beehive [*or Any Other Marker*]

Article 71. If anyone obliterates the sign on a beehive, 12 *grivna*.

Article 72. If anyone cuts an apiary boundary [hedge], or plows through a field boundary, or bars [another's] yard boundary by paling, 12 *grivna* fine.

Article 73. If anyone cuts a landmark oak, 12 *grivna* fine.

And the Following Is the Supply Quota

Article 74. And this is the supply quota: [to the collector of fines], 12 *grivna*; to the clerk, 2 *grivna* and 20 *kuna*; and he himself and the clerk are to ride on two horses to be given oats; and as to meat, they give them a sheep or a portion of beef; and other food as much as their stomachs will hold; to the scribe, 10 *kuna*; loading [fee], 5 *kuna*; fur [fee], 2 *nogata*.

And the Following Is on Beehives

Article 75. If anyone cuts a beehive [from a tree], 3 *grivna* fine; and for the tree [on which the beehive is placed], half a *grivna*.

Article 76. If anyone carries the bees away, 3 *grivna* fine; and for honey, in case it had not been already cut out, 10 *kuna*. For [damaging] a honeyless beehive, 5 *kuna*.

Article 77. If the thief is not on hand, they pursue him on his trail. If the trail leads to a village or to a camp and they [the villagers] cannot prove that it passes [the village]; or if they would not follow the trail, or would evade it, they have to pay the damages as well as the fine. And they have to follow the trail with outside people and witnesses present. If they lose the trail on a highway, with no village in sight, or in a wilderness where there is no village nor people, they do not have to pay the fine, nor the damages.

On Peasants

Article 78. If a peasant inflicts pain on another peasant without the prince's authorization, 3 *grivna* fine, and 1 *grivna* of *kuna* [amends] for the pain. If he inflicts pain on the prince's bailiff, 12 *grivna* fine, and 1 *grivna* [amends] for the pain.

Article 79. If anyone steals a boat, 60 *kuna* fine, and the boat to be returned in kind. For a seagoing boat, 3 *grivna*; for a decked boat, 2 *grivna*; for a canoe, 20 *kuna*; for a barge, 1 *grivna*.

On Hunting Nets

Article 80. If anyone cuts a rope in the hunting net, 3 *grivna* fine, and to the owner 1 *grivna* of *kuna* [damages] for the rope.

Article 81. If anyone steals from a hunting net a hawk or a falcon, 3 *grivna* fine, and to the owner, 1 *grivna*; and for a dove, 9 *kuna*; for a fowl, 9 *kuna*; for a duck, 30 *kuna*; for a goose, 30 *kuna*; for a swan, 30 *kuna*; and for a crane, 30 *kuna*.

[*On Stealing Hay*]

Article 82. And for [stealing] hay or lumber, 9 *kuna* [fine], and to the owner according to the number of cartloads stolen, 2 *nogata* for a cartload.

On the Threshing Court

Article 83. If anyone sets fire to a threshing court, he is to be banished and his house confiscated; first, the damages are paid, and the prince takes care of the rest. The same for setting fire to anyone's homestead.

Article 84. And whoever vilely maims or slaughters [another's] horse or cattle [shall pay] 12 *grivna* fine, and, for the damages, amends to the owner.

Article 85. In all the above litigations the trial is with freemen as witnesses. If the witness is a slave, he is not to take [a direct] part in the trial; but if the plaintiff so desires, he seizes [the defendant] and says as follows: "I am seizing thee on the ground of this [man's] words, but it is I who seize thee, and not the slave." And he takes him [the defendant] to the ordeal. If he [the plaintiff] succeeds in proving his guilt, he takes back from him [the defendant] his own; if he does not succeed in accusing him, he pays him 1 *grivna* [amends] for the pain inflicted, since he seized him on the ground of a slave's words.

Article 86. And they have to pay 40 *kuna* ordeal-by-iron fee; and to the sheriff, 5 *kuna*; and to the clerk, half a *grivna*. Those are the ordeal-by-iron payments,—who receives what.

Article 87. If [the plaintiff] seizes [the defendant] for the ordeal by iron on the ground of a freeman's word; or if there is a [definite] suspicion [against the defendant]; or if [the witnesses saw the defendant] pass at night near [the spot where the crime was committed]; or [in the case of the defendant's acquittal] if perchance he is not burned [at the ordeal], he who seized him need not pay [amends] for the pain inflicted, but only the ordeal-by-iron fee.

On Women

Article 88. If anyone kills a woman he is tried in the same way as if he killed a man. If he is found guilty [he shall pay] one half of the bloodwite, 20 *grivna*.

Article 89. And there is no bloodwite for either a male or a female slave; but if a slave is killed without any fault of his, [the killer] has to pay amends for the male, as well as for the female, slave; and to the prince, 12 *grivna* fine.

If a Peasant Dies

Article 90. If a peasant dies [without male descendants] his estate goes to the prince; if there are daughters left in the house, each receives a portion [of the estate]; if they are married, they receive no portion.

On the Estates of Boyars and Members of the Princely Retinue

Article 91. In regard to the boyars and the members of the princely retinue, the estate does not go to the prince, but, if there are no sons left, the daughters inherit.

Article 92. If anyone, before dying, makes a settlement dividing his estate between his children, his will stands. If he dies without a will, the estate is divided between his children [in equal shares], except for a portion which goes [to a monastery] for prayers for the soul [of the deceased].

Article 93. If the wife survives her husband, she receives a portion [of the estate in usufruct]; and whatever her husband had given her [by a special settlement], she owns that, but she does not inherit the estate.

Article 94. [In case the deceased had been married more than once], if there are children left, those by the first wife inherit their mother's share; and whatever the deceased gave to her the children inherit from their mother's estate.

Article 95. If there is [an unmarried] sister in the house, she has no share in the estate, but her brothers marry her [off] with such dowry as they can.

The Following Is in Regard to Building Town [Walls]

Article 96. And these are the payments to the town builder: at his starting a section of the town [wall] he receives 1 *kuna*; and at completing it, 1 *nogata*; and for food and drink and for meat and for fish, 7 *kuna* a week; 7 loaves of bread; 7 measures of millet; and 7 buckets of oats for 4 horses. He continues to receive all this until he completes the wall; but as to malt, they give him 10 buckets once only.

On Bridgebuilders

Article 97. And those are the payments to the bridgebuilder. When he completes the bridge, he receives 1 *nogata* for each 10 ells. If he repairs an old bridge, irrespective of how many sections of the bridge he may have repaired, he receives 1 *kuna* for each section. And the bridgebuilder and his assistant keep two horses to be provided with 4 buckets of oats a week; and [the bridgebuilder and his assistant receive] such food as they can eat.

The Following Is on the Estate of One Deceased

Article 98. If there are children by a man's female slave left, they do not inherit and are to be set free after his death.

Article 99. If there are small children left in the house who are not able to take care of themselves, and their mother should marry, he who is their nearest relative assumes care of them as well as of all their property and the house until they be of age; and the property is to be given to him [in trust] in the presence of men. And if he succeeds in making a profit on that property, he keeps it; that is, he returns to the children the original amount, and keeps all the profit, since it was he who fed them and took care of them. Similarly in regard to the progeny of both the slaves and cattle; everything should be accounted for; if [the trustee] loses anything, he has to make amends to the children. If it is the stepfather who takes care of the children and their estate the settlement is identical.

Article 100. And the father's homestead is not subject to any division of the estate, but [is given] to the youngest son.

On the Wife Who Agrees to Manage Her Deceased Husband's Estate

Article 101. If the wife agrees to manage her deceased husband's estate and then loses the property and marries, she has to pay the children for everything.

Article 102. If the children do not want to stay on the homestead and she wants to, her will prevails and not the children's; and she remains on the homestead with what her husband had given her, or the portion [of the estate] she received [in usufruct].

Article 103. And the children cannot dispose of their mother's portion: to whom the mother gives it, he receives it; if she gives it to all of them, they divide it among themselves. If she dies without a will, he in whose home she lived and who fed her, receives her estate.

Article 104. If there are children left of the same mother by her two [successive] husbands, the children of each respective father receive his estate.

Article 105. If a stepfather spends some property of the father of his stepson [which he holds in trust] and dies, his son must return to his [half]-brother that which his father spent out of his stepfather's estate, as testified by neighbors; and he keeps what had belonged to his father.

Article 106. And as to the mother, she may give her portion to that one of her sons, whether by her first or by her second husband, who is kind to her. If all her sons are wicked, she may give her portion to her daughter who feeds her.

The Following Are the Court Fees

Article 107. And these are the court fees: from each bloodwite [the court fee is] 9 *kuna*, and the constable's fee is 9 *veksha*. And from [litigations about] the beehive lots [the court fee is] 30 *kuna*. And from all other kinds of litigation, the litigant who wins the lawsuit pays [the court fee of] 4 *kuna*, and the constable's fee, 6 *veksha*.

On the Estate of the Deceased

Article 108. If brothers contend in the prince's court concerning [their father's] estate, the clerk who divides the estate for them receives 1 *grivna* of *kuna*.

On the Fees for Administering an Oath

Article 109. And these are the oath fees: in homicide cases, 30 *kuna*; in [litigations concerning] the beehive lots, 30 *kuna* minus 3 *kuna*; the same [in litigations concerning] arable land; and at freeing a slave, 9 *kuna*.

On Slavery

Article 110. Full slavery is of three kinds: [first] if anyone buys [a man] willing [to sell himself into slavery], for not less than half a *grivna*, and produces witnesses and pays [the fee of] 1 *nogata* in the presence of the slave himself. And the second kind of slavery is this: if anyone marries a female slave without spe-

cial agreement [with her lord]; if he marries her with a special agreement, what he agreed to, stands. And this is the third kind of slavery: if anyone becomes [another's] steward or housekeeper without a special agreement; if there has been an agreement, what has been agreed upon, stands.

Article 111. And the recipient of a [money] grant is not a slave. And one cannot make a man one's slave because [he received] a grant-in-aid in grain, or [failed to furnish] additional grain [when repaying the grant]; if he fails to complete the term of work [for the grant], he has to return the grant; if he completes the term, he stands cleared.

Article 112. If a slave runs away and his owner makes due announcement, and someone else, having heard the announcement or knowing about it and understanding that the man is a fugitive slave, gives him some bread or shows him the way [to escape], he has to pay for the male slave 5 *grivna* and for the female slave 6 *grivna*.

Article 113. If anyone apprehends another's slave and informs the owner, he receives 1 *grivna* for the arrest [of the slave]; if he lets him escape, he has to pay 4 *grivna* but keeps the fifth *grivna* [as his remuneration for the attempted] arrest; in case of a female slave, [he pays] 5 *grivna* and [keeps] the sixth *grivna* for the [attempted] arrest.

Article 114. If anyone finds by himself his runaway slave in some town the mayor of which did not know about [that slave], he informs the mayor, and the latter sends a clerk with him, and they go and bind the slave, and he gives the clerk 10 *kuna* binding fee, but no remuneration for the arrest. If the slave escapes when he drives him home, that is his loss, nobody has to pay him, since the slave had not been arrested [by any authority, but on the owner's initiative].

Article 115. If anyone meets another man's slave, not knowing that he is such, and gives him information [about traveling], or keeps him in his own house, and then [that slave] leaves him, he has to swear that he did not know that that man was another's slave, and he is not required to pay [the owner].

Article 116. If a slave should receive [from anyone] money under false pretense, and the creditor lent it not knowing [that the man was a slave], the owner [of the slave] has to redeem or lose him. If the creditor lent the money knowing [that the man was a slave] he loses his money.

Article 117. If anyone authorizes his slave to trade and the latter should fall in debt, the owner redeems him but does not lose him.

Article 118. If anyone buys another man's slave without knowing it, the original owner takes the slave and the buyer receives his money back after swearing that he had bought him without knowing [who he was].

Article 119. [If a runaway slave obtains goods on credit,] the owner takes back the slave, [and assumes his debt], and also takes the goods.

Article 120. If [a slave] runs away and takes any neighbor's property or goods, his owner pays the damages.

Article 121. If a slave robs a man, the owner may redeem or surrender him, as well as those who participated with him in the robbery, but not [the slave's] wife and children unless they helped him to rob, or hid [the stolen goods]; in such a case he [the owner of the slave] surrenders them, or else he redeems them all. If freemen participated in the robbery, they are liable for the payment of the fine to the prince.

Glossary

bails	bonds, as in monetary or other assurances that a person will appear in court at a specified time
bot	a debt or responsibility
chiliarch	military commander and adviser to the prince
guild	a united community of freely associating persons (not necessarily practicing the same trade, as in later usage)
in usufruct	with rights to use and enjoy
rezana,... kuna;... nogata	monetary units; typically, 1 *nogata* equaled 1/20 of a *grivna* (the primary monetary unit), 1 *rezana* equaled 1/50 of a *grivna*, and a *kuna* could be either a marten fur or a fraction of a *grivna*, such as 1/25 or 1/50.
threshing court	here, the common area where villagers took their freshly harvested grain to thresh it (that is, to separate it from the plant materials encasing it)
veksha	monetary unit equal to 1/24 of a *nogata*

AL-MĀWARDĪ'S "ON QĀDĪS"

"The slave, having no authority over himself, cannot have authority over others."

Overview

The selection "On Qādīs" is taken from *Kitāb al-ahkām al-sultāniyya* (*Ordinances of Government*), a classic work on Islamic law that covers, among other topics, the appointment of sovereigns, military leaders, and qadis, or Islamic law judges, and their rights, responsibilities, and duties as well as issues related to wars and uprisings, taxation, and crimes and punishments. The book is one of several written in the tenth and eleventh centuries, part of the popular ethico-philosophical genre that was meant to inspire the current leadership and to educate future leaders. As such, it is part of a larger genre often referred to as Mirrors for Princes. (Note that the word *princes* is used to refer to any ruler, not literally princes.) Throughout the ancient and medieval periods, writers such as Saint Augustine, Desiderius Erasmus, and Niccolò Machiavelli wrote treatises with this end in mind. In the Middle East, Nizām al-Mulk's *Book of Government; or, Rules for Kings* (1091), written for the Seljuk ruler Malik-Shāh, is roughly contemporaneous with the *Ordinances of Government*. The preface to the *Ordinances* suggests that al-Qā'im, the Abbasid caliph (Islamic ruler) who reigned from 1031 to 1075, commissioned the work, which dates to around 1050. The author, Abū al-Hasan 'Alī ibn Muhammad al-Māwardī (called al-Māwardī or, in the Latinized form, Alboacen), was a famous Islamic jurist. "On Qādīs" lists the seven conditions required for a person to become a qadi, or Islamic jurist.

Context

Islamic jurisprudence encompasses the study and interpretation of Islamic law. Muslims may seek information regarding the rules and regulations of Islam from a number of sources. Chief among them is the Qur'an (the sacred scripture of Islam). Muslims believe that the Qur'an, from an Arabic word that means "the recitation," is the literal word of Allah. It was revealed to the prophet Muhammad by the archangel Jibrail (Gabriel) beginning in 610 until his death. The Qur'an consists of 114 suras, or chapters, and

totals just over 6,200 *ayat*, or verses. While Western translations of the Qur'an number the suras, Muslims refer to them by name, such as "The Adoration."

Also crucial to Islamic jurisprudence are the Hadith, the collected sayings and deeds of the prophet Muhammad and their interpretations. These sayings were written down by Muhammad's followers. Early on, Muhammad forbade his followers to write down his sayings because he was afraid that they might be confused with the true Qur'an. He later allowed the sayings to be recorded after it became clear that a large number of people had memorized the Qur'an. The most famous compiler of the Hadith was Muhammad ibn Ismā'il Bukhārī (810–870), who gathered some 600,000 sayings of Muhammad but was able to confirm the authenticity of only about 2,600. The Hadith form the basis of another text that is important to Islam, the Sunna, or "the Way of the Prophet," used to refer to Muhammad's life example. It should be noted that Islamic scholars dispute the relationship between the Sunna and the Hadith and the question of how much the latter influenced the former; some regard them as separate and distinct, while others consider them as essentially the same.

Muslim doctrine is studied by Islamic scholars who are called ulema. Their function is to interpret and organize Islamic teachings. In doing so, they rely on four sources, in descending order of importance: the Qur'an; the Sunna; the records of the Sahābah, or the earliest followers of Muhammad known as "companions"; and independent reasoning. While the ulema do not formulate new doctrines, they apply existing Islamic thought to new situations in modern life, such as organ donations, the buying and selling of investments, and whether loudspeakers can be used for the call to prayer. All of these documents and their interpretations help Muslims understand how they should conduct their lives with regard to worship, family relations, diet, crime, economics, and other matters.

Following the death of Muhammad, the founder of Islam, in 632 there was a dispute within the newly established Islamic empire as to who would lead the community, both politically and spiritually. The primary split was between the Sunni, who supported electing the most capable leader, and the Shia, who felt that power should be retained within the prophet's immediate family. Within

974	■ Al-Māwardī is born in Basra, Iraq.
1031–1074	■ Al-Qā'im reigns as the Abbasid caliph.
1038	■ Al-Māwardī is appointed chief qadi.
1042	■ Al-Māwardī serves as an ambassador for al-Qā'im to Toghrïl Beg, the leader of the Seljuks.
1043	■ Al-Qā'im sends al-Māwardī on another diplomatic mission to Toghrïl Beg.
1045–1058	■ Al-Māwardī writes *Ordinances of Government* for al-Qā'im.
1058	■ Al-Māwardī dies and is buried in Baghdad.

Sunni Islam, four schools of law developed; although these schools differ on matters of interpretation, all are considered equally valid. The Ḥanīfi school consists of followers of Abū Ḥanīfa (699–767). This school is likely to be followed by Muslims in such countries and regions as Bangladesh, Pakistan, India, Afghanistan, central Asia, southern Russia, the Caucasus, and parts of the Balkans, Iraq, and Turkey. The Ḥanbali school consists of followers of Aḥmad ibn Ḥanbal (d. 855), who was persecuted for his belief that the Qur'an was "uncreated," that is, that it has always existed. This branch of Sunni law is followed prominently on the Arabian Peninsula.

The Māliki school consists of followers of Mālik ibn Anas (ca. 711–795), one of the last surviving companions of the prophet Muhammad. This branch of Sunni law is

followed most prominently in Muslim Africa (with the exception of Egypt, Zanzibar, and South Africa). Finally, the Shāfi'ī school is made up of followers of Muḥammad ibn Idrīs al-Shāfi'ī (767–820). This school is most likely to be followed by Muslims in Indonesia, parts of Egypt, Malaysia, Singapore, Somalia, Jordan, Lebanon, Syria, Kerala, India, Sri Lanka, Palestine, and Yemen and by the Kurds, who live in various Kurdish regions such as those of Turkey and Iraq. Al-Shāfi'ī's chief emphasis was on the Sunna of Muhammad, as embodied in the Hadith. In addition to these four major schools, there are numerous other minor schools that are either followed by only a few Islamic scholars or have gone out of existence, primarily because of a lack of written records. Al-Māwardī was a scholar of the Shāfi'ī school.

During al-Māwardī's lifetime, the Abbasid Empire (750–1258) nominally ruled much of the Islamic world, but the authority of its caliphs was on the decline. The caliph, whose name derived from the Arabic word for "successor," was initially seen as more than the supreme political leader; he was also God's representative, the successor to the prophet Muhammad, who was known as the "messenger of God." It was his religious designation that gave the caliph his true authority. As the caliph's position eroded and his authority declined, decentralization took place, and independent states emerged on the periphery of the empire. At the same time, the empire faced the menace of invasion by the Seljuks and other Turkic tribes.

The Abbasids were the second Islamic dynasty. Like their predecessors, the Umayyads, whom they overthrew in 750, the Baghdad-based Abbasids were a Sunni dynasty. While the Umayyads had been only very distantly related to the prophet Muhammad, the Abbasids boasted a much closer connection within Muhammad's family: they were descendants of 'Abbās (566–ca. 633), who had been Muhammad's paternal uncle. Less than a century after coming to power, the Abbasid caliphs began to lose control of their vast empire as local governors and rulers started to exert autonomy. While the caliph remained the ostensible ruler, local authorities governed outlying districts. Furthermore, as the Abbasid caliphs became more settled into a life of luxury, many of them relinquished what governance duties they retained to ministers and governors. Thus, while retaining nominal authority, the Abbasid caliphs gave up actual power. In 1258 the Mongols conquered the city of Baghdad, and even nominal Abbasid rule was ended.

Despite these shortcomings, the Abbasids presided over a period that has often been referred to as the golden age of Islam, particularly after the dynasty moved its capital from Damascus, in Syria, to Baghdad, in Iraq. Under the influence of passages in the Qur'an and the Hadith that placed value on knowledge, the Muslim world became the center for the study of philosophy, science, and medicine. The Abbasids emphasized education, establishing the House of Wisdom in Baghdad. This was a library where Muslim and non-Muslim scholars gathered and translated the world's knowledge into Arabic and Persian, thus preserving numerous works of antiquity that would otherwise have disappeared. Later, many of these documents were translated into Latin, Hebrew, and Turkish. During the golden age, the Muslim world was an intellectual crossroads that gathered knowledge from Rome, India, China, North Africa, Persia, Egypt, Greece, and the Byzantine Empire.

During al-Māwardī's lifetime, the Buyids (934–1062), a Shia dynasty from Iran, controlled eastern portions of the Abbasid Empire, though the Buyids' own grip on power was threatened by Maḥmūd of Ghazna (971–1030), who was expanding a new empire in greater Iran. On the western front, another Shia dynasty, the Fatimids (909–1171), was solidifying control of North Africa from a new capital: Cairo. The Fatimids took their name from Fāṭṭimah, the daughter of Muhammad and mother of Ḥusayn ibn ʿAlī, a key figure in Shia Islam. It was within this context of weakened Abbasid power, with powerful Shia dynasties pressing the dynasty from either side, that al-Māwardī sought to legitimize the caliphate structure through his *Ordinances of Government*, both to support the Abbasids and as instruction if another group were to replace them.

About the Author

Abū al-Hasan ʿAlī ibn Muḥammad al-Māwardī, known in medieval Europe as Alboacen, was born in 974 in Basra, Iraq, the son of a seller of rosewater. He studied jurisprudence, first in Basra under Abū al-Wāḥid al-Sīmarī and then in Baghdad under ʿAbd al-ḥamīd, and ʿAbdallāh al-Bāqī. After finishing his studies, he obtained a position as a qadi. In that capacity he served various cities of the Abbasid Empire before returning to Baghdad, where he was appointed chief qadi. Al-Māwardī also served as a counselor for two Abbasid caliphs, al-Qādir, who reigned from 991 to 1031, and al-Qāʾim, and as an ambassador for al-Qāʾim. Al-Māwardī wrote prolifically on a variety of subjects, including literature, language, and religion. However, his best-known works are those on political theory, in particular, *Kitāb al-ahkām al-sultāniyya* (*Ordinances of Government*), in which he describes the necessary conditions and requirements for properly managing an empire. Additionally, he wrote *Qanūn al-wazarah* (Laws regarding Ministers), *Kitāb nasihat al-mūlk* (The Book of Sincere Advice to Rulers), and *Kitāb aadab al-dunyā wa al-dʿm* (The Ethics of Religion and of This World). He is thought to be one of the originators of the so-called doctrine of necessity, a concept in jurisprudence that says that extreme necessity can render legal something that previously had been considered illegal; this doctrine has been invoked as recently as 1985 in trials in Islamic countries.

Explanation and Analysis of the Document

Al-Māwardī favored Shāfiʿī juridical interpretations. As practical matter, this means that Islamic jurists should appeal to four sources, or *uṣṣūl al-fiqh*, in descending order: As always, the Qurʾan comes first, followed by the Sunna;

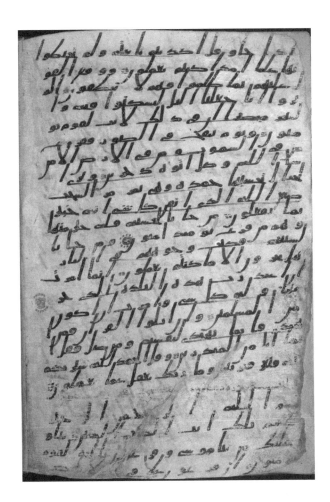

Page from a medieval Qurʾan (© British Library Board. All Rights Reserved 027733)

the *ijmā*, a word meaning "consensus"; and *qiyās*, meaning "analogy." However, in *istinbāṭ*, or "derivation of laws," this school places a great deal of emphasis on rigorous application of the principles of law, in contrast to conjecture or speculation. Private judgment is excluded in favor of legal precedent. Jurisprudence by analogy is frowned on, for it can introduce an element of private judgment and speculation. Accordingly, followers of this school are referred to as traditionalists; in contrast, followers of other schools, which do admit private judgment and jurisprudence by analogy are referred to as "people of private judgment." Although al-Māwardī emphasizes Shāfiʿī, he presents various views on many of the conditions listed as requirements for a person to be appointed a qadi. The selections of text presented here deal specifically with appointing qadis, but there are references to the appointment of other positions.

As a whole, the book presents views on a variety of other topics pertaining to Islamic public law. In addition to judges, he includes discussions about the rights, duties, and responsibilities of military commanders, governors, and other public officials. The book provides insights into a wide range of related subjects, such as how to divide the spoils of war, how to fight apostates (those who reject

Islam) and rebels, and how to address issues surrounding land reclamation and boundary disputes, taxes, and crime and punishment.

◆ Condition 1

The first condition is twofold: A qadi must be an adult, and he must be male. While al-Māwardī does not give an exact age at which adulthood is attained, in Abbasid society at that time the age would have been approximately fourteen years old, depending on the onset of puberty. That is the age at which, according to various interpretations of the prophet Muhammad's sayings, a youth is able to comprehend cause and effect and thereby becomes accountable for his own actions. A younger boy would not be responsible for his actions and therefore could not pass judgment on the actions of others. According to al-Māwardī and the Shāfiʿī school of thought, a qadi also must be male because males have been given faculties of reason and intellect superior to those of females. As support for his position on gender relations, al-Māwardī cites sura 4, verse 38 of the Qur'an: "Men have authority over women because of what God has conferred on the one in preference to the other." He interprets this verse to refer to intelligence; other interpretations suggest that the verse refers to the marital relationship or to a societal need for hierarchy.

Al-Māwardī does state that a qadi could base a ruling upon the testimony of women, which was another topic of debate among the various schools of Islamic jurisprudence. He notes that the Ḥanīfi school permits female qadis in cases in which women could provide an individual testimony; for example, a woman could be a qadi in family matters but not in financial matters. Al-Māwardī also cites Ibn Jarīr al-Tabarī (838–923), a historian who also wrote commentaries on the Qur'an. Tabarī felt that women should be allowed to serve as qadis as long as their rulings did not contradict the Qur'an or the general consensus of the Islamic community.

◆ Condition 2

According to most interpretations of Islamic law, in order to qualify for legal responsibility, an individual had to have the use of his five senses: sight, sound, touch, taste, and smell. Al-Māwardī states that as the second condition required to become a qadi, a man must possess more than that basic requirement; he must "have sufficient acumen to clarify difficulties and resolve obscure cases." Additionally, the person must be able to comprehend the difference between right and wrong and to quickly assess a situation in order to make decisions relating to it. In essence, the second condition requires a potential qadi to be free from intellectual defect.

◆ Condition 3

Personal freedom is the third requirement: A qadi could not be a slave. The rights of slaves varied according to their legal status; since Islam encouraged the eventual freedom of slaves, some owners stipulated that upon their death or after a fixed length of time, their slaves would be freed. As

al-Māwardī explains, slaves whose freedom was incomplete or those who would eventually be freed but were still slaves did not have the legal standing to provide testimony. Partial slaves likewise had no standing. (Partial slaves were the equivalent of what were known in Europe as indentured servants—servants legally bound to perform service for a specified period of time.) Once a slave had been freed, he could serve as a qadi, except in one special circumstance mentioned by al-Māwardī: Former slaves would not be able to rule in cases relating to a former master, to whom they might feel a sense of obligation or toward whom they might harbor animosity. Al-Māwardī notes that former slaves might have judicial authority because descent is not taken into account in conferring such authority—that is, slavery in one's past or one's ancestors' past was not an obstacle.

◆ Condition 4

Based on the Qur'an and according to all schools of Islamic thought, in order to be a qadi, a man had to be a Muslim. Al-Māwardī quotes the Qur'an (sura 4, verse 140), which says that God will not give unbelievers an advantage over believers. Other verses of the Qur'an list a hierarchy of other religions, with the other Abrahamic religions (Judaism and Christianity) being considered above those outside the Abrahamic tradition. Al-Māwardī notes that Abū Ḥanīfa had said that a non-Muslim might be appointed as judge of his coreligionists but the non-Muslim judge's rulings would be binding only insofar as his coreligionists accepted them.

◆ Condition 5

The fifth requirement of a person serving as a qadi is rectitude; that is, the qadi had to display a sense of justice and truth in both word and deed. Islam details various sins and forbidden actions, such as drinking alcohol, engaging in sexual relations outside of marriage, and eating forbidden foods such as pork; Muslims had to avoid such actions in order to be considered morally upstanding. Furthermore, the community had to view the individual as truthful and trustworthy. The individual had to be free of emotional bias in the cases over which he presided; he could not have a familial or business connection to either party in the case. A person who met all these requirements had the moral character necessary for a qadi.

◆ Condition 6

Al-Māwardī holds that to be a qadi, a man could not be blind or deaf, since sight and hearing were necessary in differentiating between people giving legal testimony. He notes that Māliki thought permitted a blind person to serve as a qadi because the same person would be allowed to testify. Al-Māwardī notes further that there were the same differences of opinion on whether deafness was a bar to becoming a qadi as there were regarding whether it was a bar to being an imam. (*Imam*, in this context, refers to the caliph.) He states that in both cases deafness constituted too great a handicap. He does not, however, feel that other physical disabilities should exclude a person from consideration for qadi, though he notes that "freedom from physical defects gives greater dignity to those exercising authority."

♦ **Condition 7**

Finally, a qadi had to have knowledge of Islamic law. Al-Māwardī here lists the sources of Islamic law. First is the Qur'an, Islam's sacred text. Qadis had to have a thorough education that had enabled them to develop an advanced understanding of the Qur'an's rules for proper living. Not all topics contained in the Qur'an are clear, and a qadi had to have sufficient knowledge to clarify the ambiguous portions of Islamic law. Certain verses of the Qur'an limit certain other verses; these are said to *abrogate* those other verses.

The second source of Islamic law is Sunna, customs and practices based on Muhammad's life, as recorded in the Hadith. For issues regarding daily life, not all possible scenarios are addressed in the Qur'an, and therefore Muslims look to Muhammad's life for guidance. Stories of Muhammad's life were originally transmitted orally, but during the first and second centuries of Islam, religious scholars compiled those anecdotes into structured texts. The two best known and most detailed were complied by al-Bukhārī and Muslim ibn al-Ḥajjāj (ca. 817–875). Each anecdote is preceded by a list of honorable and reliable people, reaching back to Muhammad, who passed the story down. The list typically read something like this: "Person A heard from Person B that Person C saw the Prophet Muhammad do X." This list is the anecdote's proof of authenticity.

In addition to knowing the various Hadith, it was important for a qadi to have knowledge of the Hadith-based rulings of previous leaders and judges. When issuing a ruling, judges could either follow a particular school of law or, when faced with conflicting possible rulings, could offer their own interpretation in a process of independent analysis known as *ijtihād*. However arrived at, earlier judges' interpretations comprise a third source of Islamic law. Finally, the fourth source is the qadi's personal knowledge of analogy—his ability to compare one crime and punishment with another in order to ensure fairness and equality in his rulings.

A man who has mastered these four sources would become a religious authority, or a *mujtahid*, and could become a qadi or a mufti (a scholar who interprets Islamic law and can issue pronouncements but who does not preside over legal cases). Al-Māwardī notes that if someone were appointed as a qadi but did not meet all the requirements, his appointment would be invalid and his rulings and judgments rejected. Moreover, when a qadi was wrongfully appointed, both he and the person who appointed him would be held accountable for any problems that his rulings create.

Audience

Al-Māwardī wrote the *Ordinances of Government* at the behest of the caliph al-Qā'im, so the caliph and his successors may be considered one readership. It is possible that al-Māwardī intended the work simply to further his theories among the religious and political leadership. During this

Muhammad holding the two symbols of his faith, a sword and a Qur'an (© Bettmann/CORBIS)

period of political instability and frequent changes of leadership, there was a great need for clarification of the many positions of authority. More broadly, al-Māwardī's work may have been intended as a handbook for future rulers and administrators. It was structured such that it could readily be used as a reference book: It could be read from cover to cover, or the reader could quickly locate a particular topic.

Impact

Al-Māwardī's *Ordinances of Government* was the first political study to focus on individual institutions and their functions within an Islamic state. Previous studies of Islamic law, as well as numerous later ones, organized their texts by the school of Islamic law. Al-Māwardī instead opted to structure his text by function and, within each function, to provide examples from the four Sunni schools of law. For example, the *Ordinances* has sections on the appointment of sovereigns, on amputation as a punishment for theft, and—as discussed here—on the appointment of qadis. Some later theological texts follow al-Māwardī's function-based format, but most continue to focus on the positions of one particular school of thought rather than comparing the positions of the four schools.

There is another text of the same title, written by Abū Yala Muḥammad ibn al-Ḥusayn al-Farrā (d. 1066), and there are questions as to which text was written first. However, since al-Māwardī's work provides few examples from the Ḥanbali school and Abū Yala's provides mostly Ḥanbali examples, it is reasonable to assume that Abū Yala, a Ḥanbali scholar, wrote his as a reaction to al-Mawardi's.

"*As for the child below puberty, he cannot be held accountable, nor can his utterances have effect against himself; how much less so against others. As for women, they are unsuited to positions of authority, although judicial verdicts may be based on what they say.*"

(Condition 1)

"*The slave, having no authority over himself, cannot have authority over others. Moreover, since his state of slavery makes his testimony unacceptable, all the more does it prevent his holding authority and giving valid judgments.*"

(Condition 3)

"*The fourth condition is Islam, because this is a necessary condition for the right to testify and because of the word of God, "God will not give the unbelievers the advantage over the believers." It is not lawful for an unbeliever to exercise judicial authority over Muslims or over unbelievers.*"

(Condition 4)

"*The sixth condition is soundness of sight and hearing, so that by their means he may ... distinguish between plaintiff and defendant, and differentiate between those who affirm and those who deny in such a way that the difference between truth and falsehood may be clear to him and that he may know the speaker of truth from the liar.*"

(Condition 6)

"*The sources of the rules of the Holy Law [include] ... knowledge of analogy, the method used to deduce implicit consequences from explicit and agreed principles.*"

(Condition 7)

The *Ordinances of Government* has proved to be an immensely popular and influential text, one that is still referred to in the twenty-first century. It is a key text for the modern movement called Ḥizb ut-Taḥrīr, typically translated as "Party of Liberation." This is a pan-Islamist movement founded in Jerusalem in 1953. Its goal is to unite all Islamic countries into a single political entity ruled by Islamic law. Essentially, it wants to restore the caliphate under an elected Muslim leader. In recent years this organization has been the target of controversy. Those who are suspicious of the organization accuse it of anti-Semitism and support of terrorism, despite its claimed renunciation of violence. Its supporters argue that the group is misunderstood and unfairly accused of preaching hatred and violence. Whichever point of view is correct, the group wants to return to classical Islamic processes and structures, and they find those processes and structures outlined in the *Ordinances of Government.*

Further Reading

■ Articles

Rebstock, Ulrich. "A Qadi's Errors." *Islamic Law and Society* 6, no. 1 (1999): 1–37.

■ Books

Al-Jaziri, Abd al-Rahman. *Islamic Jurisprudence according to the Four Sunni Schools.* Louisville, Ky.: Fons Vitae, 2009.

Brown, Daniel. *A New Introduction to Islam.* Malden, Mass.: Blackwell Publishing, 2004.

Calder, Norman. *Islamic Jurisprudence in the Classical Era.* Cambridge, U.K.: Cambridge University Press, 2010.

Dutton, Yasin. *Origins of Islamic Law: The Qur'an, the Muwatta' and Madinan Amal.* London: RoutledgeCurzon, 2002.

Gibb, H. A. R. "Al-Mawardi's Theory of the Khilafah." In *Studies on the Civilization of Islam,* eds. Stanford J. Shaw and William R. Polk. London: Routledge & Kegan Paul, 1962.

Hallaq, Wael B. *A History of Islamic Legal Theories: An Introduction to Sunnī uṣūl al-fiqh.* Cambridge, U.K.: Cambridge University Press, 1999.

Mikhail, Hanna. *Politics and Revelation.* Edinburgh, U.K.: Edinburgh University Press, 1995.

Motzki, Harald. *The Origins of Islamic Jurisprudence: Meccan Fiqh before the Classical Schools,* trans. Marion H. Katz. Leiden, Netherlands: Brill Academic Publishers, 2001.

Schacht, Joseph. *An Introduction to Islamic Law.* Oxford: Oxford University Press, 1964.

■ Web Sites

"Abu al-Hasan al-Mawardi." The Window: Philosophy on the Internet Web site.
> http://www.trincoll.edu/depts/phil/philo/phils/muslim/mawardi.html.

Hurvitz, Nimrod. *Competing Texts: The Relationship between al-Mawardi's and Abu Ya'la's* Al-Ahkam al-sultaniyya. Islamic Legal Studies Program Web site.
> http://www.law.harvard.edu/programs/ilsp/publications/hurvitz.pdf.

—Tia Wheeler and Michael J. O'Neal

Questions for Further Study

1. Compare Al-Māwardī's "On Qāḍīs" with other Mirrors for Princes literature, including Niccolò Machiavelli's treatise *The Prince* and Niẓām al-Mulk's *Book of Government; or, Rules for Kings.* How are the documents similar? How do they differ? How does each reflect the political realities of the time and place they were written?

2. Why do you think different schools of jurisprudence developed in Islam? What social, political, and historical factors might have accounted for differing interpretations of Islamic law?

3. In the Western tradition, jurisprudence is generally thought to be a matter entirely separate from religion. In Islam the two are closely related, almost to the extent of being one and the same. Why?

4. How did "On Qāḍīs" reflect the role and position of women in Islamic society at that time? Did it advance or diminish the position of women? Explain.

5. Why do some modern movements such as Ḥizb ut-Taḥrīr find Al-Māwardī"s work appealing after nearly a thousand years?

AL-MĀWARDĪ'S "ON QĀḌĪS"

Nobody may be appointed to the office of qāḍī who does not comply fully with the conditions required to make his appointment valid and his decisions effective. They are seven in number.

1. The first condition is that he must be a man. This condition consists of two qualities, puberty and masculinity. As for the child below puberty, he cannot be held accountable, nor can his utterances have effect against himself; how much less so against others. As for women, they are unsuited to positions of authority, although judicial verdicts may be based on what they say. Abu Hanīfa said that a woman can act as qāḍī in matters on which it would be lawful for her to testify, but she may not act as qāḍī in matters on which it would not be lawful for her to testify. Ibn Jarīr at-Tabarī, giving a divergent [shādhdh] view, allows a woman to act as qāḍī in all cases, but no account should be taken of an opinion which is refuted by both the consensus of the community and the word of God. "Men have authority over women because of what God has conferred on the one in preference to the other," meaning by this, intelligence and discernment. He does not therefore, permit women to hold authority over men,

2. The second condition is intelligence, the importance of which is universally recognized. It is not enough to have the intelligence which qualifies for legal responsibility [taklīf], that is to say, the use of the five necessary senses. He must also have discriminating judgment and great perspicacity, be far from forgetfulness and negligence, and have sufficient acumen to clarify difficulties and resolve obscure cases.

3. The third condition is freedom, since the slave, having no authority over himself, cannot have authority over others. Moreover, since his state of slavery makes his testimony unacceptable, all the more does it prevent his holding authority and giving valid judgments. The rule is the same for one whose freedom is incomplete, such as the slave whose liberation will be completed by the death of his master [mudabbar] or by contract [makātab], or the partial slave. But the state of slavery does not prevent a man from giving juridical rulings [fatwā] or from relating traditions, since neither of these involves the exercise of authority. When freed, he can act as qāḍī,

though bound by the obligations of patronage [walā'], because descent [nasab] is not taken into account in conferring judicial authority.

4. The fourth condition is Islam, because this is a necessary condition for the right to testify and because of the word of God, "God will not give the unbelievers the advantage over the believers." It is not lawful for an unbeliever to exercise judicial authority over Muslims or over unbelievers. Abū Hanīfa said that an unbeliever may be appointed to dispense justice among his coreligionists. Though it is common practice for rulers to appoint unbelievers in this way, it is an appointment as chief or head and not an appointment conferring judicial authority. His decisions bind them because they voluntarily submit to him, not because he has binding authority over them, and the Imam does not assent to his rulings in judgments rendered by him among his coreligionists. If his people do not resort to his jurisdiction, they are not compelled to do so, and they will then be subject to Islamic judicial authority.

5. The fifth condition is rectitude ['adāla], which is a requirement for any position of authority. This means that a man speaks truth, is manifestly trustworthy, virtuously refrains from forbidden things and avoids sin, is beyond suspicion, can be trusted in both approval and anger, and conducts himself as befits a man like him in both religious and worldly matters. The fulfillment of all these requirements constitutes rectitude, which qualifies him to testify and to exercise authority. If any of these qualities is lacking, he may neither testify nor exercise authority; his words shall not be heard nor his judgment executed.

6. The sixth condition is soundness of sight and hearing, so that by their means he may determine rights, distinguish between plaintiff and defendant, and differentiate between those who affirm and those who deny in such a way that the difference between truth and falsehood may be clear to him and that he may know the speaker of truth from the liar, If he is blind he is disqualified to exercise authority, but Mālik considers that a blind man may be a qāḍī just as he can bear witness. As to deafness, there are the same differences of opinion as for the Imamate. Soundness of limb is not a requirement, though it is for the Imamate. A chronic invalid may therefore sit

as qāḍī, although freedom from physical defects gives greater dignity to those exercising authority.

7. The seventh condition is that he must be learned in the rules of the Holy Law, his knowledge covering both general principles and specific applications.

The sources of the roles of the Holy Law are four:

1. Knowledge of God's book, so that he has a sound understanding of the rules contained in it, both abrogating and abrogated, both precise and equivocal, both general and specific, and both unexplained and clearly interpreted.

2. Knowledge of the authentic tradition [*Sunna*] of the Prophet of God, may God bless and save him, of his words and his deeds, how they were transmitted, by many or by few, which are genuine and which false and which refer only to a specific occasion and which are of general application.

3. Knowledge of the interpretations of the first generation of Muslims, whether unanimous or diver-

gent, conforming to the consensus or exercising independent judgment [*ijtihād*] in cases of disagreement.

4. Knowledge of analogy, the method used to deduce implicit consequences from explicit and agreed principles, so as to attain the knowledge required to settle law-suits and to distinguish true from false.

If he masters these four sources of the rules of the Holy Law, he becomes a *mujtahid* in religion, and is allowed to act as muftī or qāḍī, and may be asked to act in either capacity. But if he is deficient in them or in any part of them, he cannot be a *mujtahid* and may not act as muftī or qāḍī, and if despite this he is appointed as a judge and gives decisions, whether right or wrong, his appointment is invalid and his decisions, even if they are sound and just, are rejected, and the sin for whatever he adjudges falls both on him and on the one who appointed him as qāḍī.

Glossary

Abū Hanīfa	scholar and teacher (699–767), revered in Islam as the Great Imam
God's book	the Qur'an